Wi...
Ma...
Cre...
Ear

Eye

Face

Muzzle
Nostril
Upper lip

Mouth

Lower lip

Lower jaw
Cheek
Throatlatch
Neck
Chest

Shoulder
Knee

Cannon

Fetlock

Coronet
Heel

Hoof

**Stallion**
*(more muscular; wider neck;
thick mane and tail)*

# Horses
## of the
# World

# Horses
## of the
# World

**ÉLISE ROUSSEAU**
**Illustrated by Yann Le Bris**

Translated by Teresa Lavender Fagan

**Princeton University Press**
Princeton and Oxford

Copyright © Delachaux et Niestlé, Paris, 2014
Title of the original edition: *Tous les chevaux du monde: Près de 570 races et types décrits et illustrés*
English translation copyright © 2017 Princeton University Press.
Requests for permission to reproduce material from this work should be sent to Permissions, Princeton University Press
Published by Princeton University Press,
41 William Street, Princeton, New Jersey 08540
In the United Kingdom: Princeton University Press, 6 Oxford Street, Woodstock, Oxfordshire OX20 1TR
press.princeton.edu

Jacket images courtesy of Yann Le Bris

Library of Congress Cataloging-in-Publication Data

Names: Rousseau, Élise, 1977– | Le Bris, Yann, illustrator. | Fagan, Teresa Lavender, translator.
Title: Horses of the world / Élise Rousseau ; illustrated by Yann Le Bris ; translated by Teresa Lavender Fagan.
Other titles: Tous les chevaux du monde. English
Description: Princeton : Princeton University Press, [2017] | Title of the original edition: Tous les chevaux du monde : pres de 570 races et types decrits et illustres (Paris : Delachaux et Niestlé, 2014). | Includes bibliographical references and index.
Identifiers: LCCN 2016042566 | ISBN 9780691167206 (hardcover : alk. paper)
Subjects: LCSH: Horses—Encyclopedias.
Classification: LCC SF278 .R6813 2017 | DDC 636.1003—dc23 LC record available at https://lccn.loc.gov/2016042566

British Library Cataloging-in-Publication Data is available

This book has been composed in Meridien, Minion Pro and Myriad Pro
Printed on acid-free paper. ∞

Printed in China

For Jaouen and Titouan
For the Eliotout riders

Once upon a time there were horses
Long scattered
And the horses dipped their necks into the future
To remain living and always continue …

—Jules Supervielle, excerpt from "Chevaux sans cavaliers," in
*La Fable du monde* (1938), Editions Gallimard, 1987

It is a universal phenomenon. Equine biodiversity is in danger.
In Africa, Asia, everywhere, every day, entire sections of our living patrimony are disappearing. Instead of regretting the fate of this animal, which exists only because humans decided to make use of it, instead of wanting to limit its various uses, we must encourage its use, invent new activities for it (and us).

—Jean-Louis Gouraud, *Le Pérégrin émerveillé*, Actes Sud,
coll. "Arts équestres," 2012

# Contents

# Introduction

## Horses of the World

More than 540 breeds of horses are recognized in the world, from the best known to the most obscure, some on far-flung islands, on the steppes, or in deserts, horses whose existence we often can't even imagine—horses such as those found on Sable Island, indomitable Siberians that endure winters at −50°C; the golden-hued breeds of Central Asia that gallop like goats up the steep slopes of the Caucasus. All these marvelous animals deserve to be finally brought together in a guide whose aim is to provide a comprehensive record of horse breeds existing today, and to reveal—and sometimes seek out—the rarest and least-known breeds.

Five hundred sixty-seven breeds, types, or populations of horses, including types that are not truly breeds, will be described here. In addition, around four hundred of the breeds described are illustrated; this is an unprecedented work of documentation.

Every one of these 567 different kinds of horses exists only because one day humans decided that they would. And setting off to discover the horses of the world is also setting off to discover the people who breed them. Each horse reveals something about its breeder. Each breed tells us something about the region that created it, of its aesthetic ideal, its equestrian practices. The brio and beauty of the Andalusian tell us a lot about the Spanish people. Just as the efficiency and speed of a Quarter Horse tell us about the American people, and the purity and finesse of the Arabian speak of the Bedouins. Breeds, shaped by humans, carry within them, in the shape of their ears, in their fine or thick manes and tails, as well as in their gaits, the equestrian cultures out of which they emerged. And when a breed disappears a whole part of humanity's history is extinguished.

Globally, the great majority of the breeds in this guide are rare, with very small populations. This means they could become extinct very quickly. It would take only a war, or an epidemic, and some horse populations would fall into oblivion. Some of the breeds described here are very quietly moving toward extinction. They will perhaps have disappeared in ten years, twenty years—maybe tomorrow, for the Abaco Spanish Colonial Horse, the most threatened breed in the world, which is probably already lost. In the meantime humans will have created new breeds.

Why is this important? some might ask. A horse is only a domestic animal, not a wild species.

But that is the whole point of domestic horse biodiversity. When a breed disappears, an entire genetic section of the "horse" species disappears. The loss of equestrian culture contributes to a biological loss. Today, environmentalists, at first skeptical of the idea of protecting domestic animals, increasingly accept the idea that it is important to safeguard these breeds. Conservationists understand the usefulness of having the Camargue, the Polish Konik, the Highland Pony, and the Dülmen pastured in their native lands: these are all rustic animals adapted for life outdoors, and they have all become rare. To make the general public aware of the loss of this domestic biodiversity is sometimes the first step toward a greater awareness of global conservation problems. The domestic animal can serve as a stepping-stone to the preservation of wild nature and to an understanding of it. We don't want the gentle-eyed Konik to disappear. And in equal measure we also don't want to see extinguished the wagtail that flutters around our feet or the frog that jumps away in the field, because they are part of an entire ecosystem. With its four hooves planted solidly on the ground, the horse has always been an essential link to nature, a door that opens onto large expanses, the horse that takes care, while grazing, not to crush the nests of ground-dwelling birds, the one that allows the rider to get closer to wild animals because, when borne by a herbivore, a human is suddenly no longer a threatening predator.

On a global scale it is clear that some countries, such as Spain, are very advanced in promoting the preservation of domestic biodiversity. And this awareness is growing stronger throughout the world. After decades of standardizing and universalizing breeds of horses, people are rediscovering the importance of their local horses: those that are best adapted to their region, their climate, their practices: the horses of their ancestors, which carry within them a bit of their own history.

But the battle to save the breeds of horses that are on the path to extinction is urgent: according to the Food and Agriculture Organization (FAO) of the United Nations, each month a different domestic breed disappears (cows, goats, sheep, poultry, and so on)! And among them, how many breeds of horses?

And yet the horse, an animal that can do much more than other farm animals, will always have a considerable advantage over pigs or rabbits: because it is integral to many leisure-time activities, both athletic and recreational, it gathers around it scores of enthusiasts who are working to save it.

But if the world of the horse underwent a considerable upheaval during the first half of the twentieth century, due to the ubiquity of motor vehicles that rendered working animals and their role (for transport and other uses) much less necessary, at the beginning of the twenty-first century the equestrian milieu is undergoing a huge change on a global scale. The increasing number of women participating in equestrian sports in Western countries, the gradual evolution of the horse from a work animal into a recreational animal, even a pet: the future of breeds of horses will be affected by these transformations.

Thus the breeds used to herd livestock, threatened not long ago by a diminishing of their traditional role, are once again very sought-after since recreational horses have long been selected for their good "character," that is, their easygoing, very calm nature. Horses with their original characteristics, such as the Irish Cob, are finding new outlets thanks to recreational riding. The effects of fashion also have an impact. Some breeds, unknown twenty or so years ago, flourish when they become popular. All it takes is a champion rider to win a prestigious competition with a certain animal, or for the star of an equestrian show to use another in one of his or her acts. Tastes change. Who would believe today that the charismatic Friesian almost disappeared?

Ultimately, only a few breeds—Quarter Horse, Thoroughbred, Arabian, Shetland, and some others—are thriving.

If it is difficult to say what the equestrian world will look like tomorrow, it seems obvious that the breeds that will come out unscathed are those that are easiest to adapt for sport or recreational use, or those that possess qualities or an appearance unique enough to retain the enthusiasm of their fans.

This guide is like a snapshot of the current data on and status of equestrian breeds. Everything is changing, evolving: Which breed will be reborn from the ashes? Which one will disappear forever?

Out of this thorough research into the universe of horse breeds three facts emerge:
- A majority of breeds throughout the world are in danger, because there are so few individuals of those breeds.
- Most breeds in the world have small populations.
- There are many more gaited horses (those practicing the amble or broken amble, for instance) than we in the West could have imagined!

And we might add that most horses in the world are bay colored.

Beyond the well-known, fashionable, widespread breeds there are throughout the world scores of breeds that are unknown outside their country, sometimes outside their region.

It also appears obvious that some criteria and prejudices that are well anchored in the West have little meaning elsewhere. Must a shoulder necessarily be long and sloped? Granted, it is more agreeable for riding, but for a horse evolving on the slopes of the Himalayas a straight shoulder is more useful. Are hocks set too close a defect to be avoided? Not for a mountain horse, for which this conformation is useful. And flat hooves? They are a useful adaptation for breeds that have evolved in marshy areas! Are the amble and the tölt substandard gaits? They are so comfortable that amblers are prized in almost every country in the world! Only Europeans have eliminated these wonderful gaits in their horses. Here, again, it is only a question of culture. Is it so evident that we should eliminate aggressive, biting horses? Not for those who play *buzkashi*. Is a long back to be avoided? But it shouldn't be too short, either, for a harness horse. A shaggy mane and a disheveled tail are not distinguished? But they're very useful to protect breeds that live in extreme conditions against wind, rain, and snow. And what would Siberian horses do without their thick layer of fat? Should male horses necessarily be castrated? Surely not for peoples of North Africa who have stables full of entire horses and for whom this is the norm (mares are kept apart for reproduction); these horses offer the traveler an experience different from the more common gelding because they are more muscular, more spirited.

To set off to discover the horses of the world is to take off the blinders and open your mind. Each horse everywhere on the planet has its purpose.

The diversity of breeds and equestrian cultures is extraordinary, and it is unfortunate to think they are all one and the same.

## A rather stable global population

Whereas global populations of goats, cows, or large members of the camel family have been growing since the 1960s, the world population of horses remains fairly stable, although it is shrinking slightly. It experienced a dramatic decline during the first half of the twentieth century, feeling the full force of competition from the combustion engine. The FAO estimated the number of horses in the world to be around 58.5 million in 2011. The country with the most horses is the United States, followed by China, Mexico, Brazil, Argentina, Colombia, Mongolia, Ethiopia, Kazakhstan, and Russia. The European Union also has a large horse population (and a large diversity of breeds). In some countries, horse breeding has suffered greatly from the global economic crisis of 2008.

In the Soviet era the Russians made a few inconclusive attempts to improve the local breeds, a bit like the French who once tried, in vain, to cross the Camargue with more refined horses. These hybrids did not survive in difficult conditions. Nothing is better suited to the Camargue than a Camargue, and nothing is better adapted to Yakutia than a Yakutian. In extreme environments you can't interchange breeds, because the local breeds are the result of hundreds of years of adaptation to the land, the climate, the insects, vegetation, and so forth.

It is also important to note that although the horse is used everywhere in the world as a means of transportation, mares are also raised, especially in Asia, for their excellent milk. That milk, virtually unknown in the West, is a choice beverage for millions of people. Raising horses for their meat is also very widespread; it is a disturbing reality for a rider, but it cannot be ignored, and it has nonetheless allowed many breeds (notably draft horses) to be saved. Thus we have pointed this out when appropriate for certain breeds. For example, one of the unique characteristics of the Yakutian in Siberia is in fact its meat: sprinkled with parsley, it is very much appreciated. This cannot be denied, and the Yakutian is bred for that purpose.

The horse's place as a recreational animal is not yet ubiquitous on a global scale, even if it has developed in the past few decades due to the explosion of equestrian sports. And its very specific place, in a few Western countries, as a true pet, spoiled and pampered, remains even more limited—although this is also gaining ground. Even today, in many countries throughout the world, the horse is above all a work animal, raised for utilitarian purposes.

And yet, a Kazakh horse, leading the freest of lives on the limitless steppes, is without doubt happier, closer to its true nature, than some horses in equestrian centers, pampered, spoiled, but living the life of prisoners, locked up most of the time in stalls. A working horse's existence is not necessarily more difficult, and, in equestrian matters, every rider would have a lot to learn by encountering other cultures, other horses, other ways of riding, breeding, and learning from horses.

# How to Identify a Breed of Horse

## On the Difficulty of Identifying Horses

Many breeds look alike. A horse is still a horse: they are all members of the same species. If the differences between a Shetland, a Shire, a Thoroughbred, or an Arabian leap out, if a Marwari or a Campolina exhibit obvious physical peculiarities, if we generally easily recognize a Quarter Horse, if the trained eye sees the difference between a Sorraia and a Dülmen, it is still undeniable that sometimes it is impossible to identify certain breeds of horses outside their local context. This is notably the case with all so-called sport horses, once called "halfbreds," those large athletic, slender saddle horses, often of recent creation, the issue of countless mixes among all the other sporting breeds. This is also true of trotters.

Furthermore, breeders, especially in Western countries, love to cross and mix horses. And so their fields are teeming with "prairie cocktails." If in some countries (Iceland and Mongolia, for example), it is obvious which breed of horse is standing in front of you, if you can sometimes deduce the breed from its environment and its locality (Chincoteague in the United States, Minorca in Spain, and the Faroe Islands), it can be quite difficult, especially in some European and North American countries, to know with certainty which breed a horse belongs to, because of interbreeding that has sometimes been going on for generations.

In the equestrian world we don't talk about bastards, mongrels, and other mutts, as we do for dogs or alley cats. We more politely say that mixed breeds are "unregistered" or of "unknown origin." These crossbreds make up a large proportion of horses in the equine world.

Furthermore, there is also interbreeding among horses at the borders of the geographic zones where each breed lives.

Many Chinese horse breeds, completely unknown in the West, are thus commonly intermixed.

Finally, some breeds look alike because their similar environments caused them to evolve similarly from a physiognomic point of view. If you put a Shetland, a Yakutian, and a Faroe of the same size and color in a pen, it would not necessarily be easy to tell them apart at first glance.

The reason for this, again, is that horses are a single species, and breeds are sometimes only slight variations within that species. Although there are guides with very precise criteria to identify species of wild animals, we cannot expect to identify as easily the breeds of a single domestic species.

In addition, horses do not present a morphological diversity as marked as that of dogs, for example. Dogs can have long or flattened muzzles, protruding eyes, straight or floppy ears, very short or very long fur, and so on. Variations in horses are more subtle, less pronounced. There is size, of course, but short or tall, large or thin, a horse always has more or less the same appearance: none has floppy ears, a flattened muzzle, or the long hair of an Afghan hound.

This guide, through the text and drawings, will, however, help the user learn to recognize the many breeds of horses, and to deduce the breed from the country and the environment in which it is located. There is little chance of coming across many Skyros Ponies in South America, many Kaimanawas in Norway, or many Clydesdales in Namibia. However, there are many opportunities to come across Quarter Horses, Arabians, and Thoroughbreds just about anywhere in the world.

This guide will above all make possible an understanding of what horses around the world look like. It will also allow travelers to recognize the breeds they encounter on their journeys.

*On the steppes of Central Asia, where there is little shade due to the lack of trees, herds of horses often cool themselves in muddy pools. These horses are east of Kazakhstan.*

## A Simple, Nonjudgmental Description

Ultimately, because this is a guide intended for all horse enthusiasts and not a technical work of zoology, descriptions are based on physical characteristics that are truly identifiable to everyone, easily visible to all: head, profile, size of the eyes, ears, neck, chest, withers, back, croup, tail set, limbs, hooves, mane and tail. Thus we have chosen not to include overly technical elements in the descriptive text.

When a horse falls within average standards (such as average neck, average back length) this is not pointed out. Similarly, it sometimes happens that some information on a breed is missing, or contradictory, and thus impossible to include with certainty.

We have purposely not gone into judgmental technical zoological details of "good" or "bad" conformation, as such criteria seem much too subjective. A Mongolian rider will absolutely not have the same opinion about what is a "good and beautiful" horse as a European rider who jumps. The English Thoroughbred, considered to be the quintessential equine by many Westerners, would simply not survive the Mongolian winters, and would have neither the endurance nor the stamina sought by that equestrian people. As much as possible, then, we have tried to detach ourselves from Western criteria of judgment. For many riders the only beautiful horses are those that can jump high. But the world is wide and there are many equestrian cultures. We don't all have the same opinions on what a horse should be. What is considered a defect in one is sometimes a desirable quality in another. And this is exactly why there are so many breeds of horses.

Similarly, we always speak of sport horses to designate breeds used in Olympic competition (dressage, jumping, and eventing). These involve all the "warmblood" breeds, in which English Thoroughbred blood flows.

The label "sport" is also relative. An excellent Criollo, Maremmano, or Quarter Horse that is used to herd livestock is also a sport horse. A Kabarda that has just climbed a steep slope without stopping, as if it were nothing, is a sport horse. A Percheron that has just won a pulling competition is a sport horse. Equestrian sports are not limited to just Olympic events, however popular they may be. Horses are in large part bred to be the most effective possible in whatever they are intended to do.

## Species, Breed, or Type?

A *species* designates a group of animals capable of reproducing among themselves and producing fertile offspring. A *breed* is a division within a species; it is a term used above all for domestic animals. A *type* is a division within a breed. Thus, for example, in the domestic horse species, the Andalusian is a breed and the Chartreux is a type of purebred Andalusian. We also use the term *population* for some wild animals.

If, in our Western countries, we consider horses that are very similar to be fully separate breeds and certainly not types (the Mérens and the Castillon could, however, for example, be considered two types of an Ariégeois horse; the same is true of

the Lusitano and the Andalusian, which have been split in two), we tend to automatically assume that in distant Asian countries where there is little horse breeding, the varieties of horses there are only types of a same general breed, rather than fully distinct breeds. It is in fact sometimes extremely difficult to distinguish a type from a breed. Yesterday's type will perhaps become tomorrow's breed. A former breed might end up blending into another breed, within which it will then be only a type. All of this ultimately depends on only one thing: the subjective human point of view.

This is why, where one hesitates over whether some horses belong to different breeds or to different types of the same breed, we have as far as possible followed the advice of local specialists. Mongolian specialists thus believe that the Mongolian horse is a single breed, and that within that breed there are types. This is their point of view on their breed, and it seems to us that they are the most competent to know and to decide what is to be said on the subject. After consideration, we thus accepted their opinion, and we proceeded in this way for all countries. It seems to us that the best spokespeople for their horses are those who breed them. It is unreasonable to believe that in one's own country each variety is a different breed, while in other countries all differences arise out of the same breed.

In horse guides, for example, for a very long time only a single breed was described for the entire, huge country of China: the "Chinese Pony." What is a Chinese Pony? In truth, there are dozens of different horse breeds in China. To classify these dozens of breeds into a single and vague "Pony" is obviously extremely simplistic. For a Chinese or an Afghan, Shire and Clydesdale might also seem to be only two types of a single large British draft horse. There will always be classifications that are open to debate (Is it really a breed? Isn't it just a type?), but this is all integral to the very notion of breed. We must thus accept it and make choices while knowing that those choices will always be somewhat subjective.

The reports of the FAO (see Bibliographic Sources) have definitely been of great help and an invaluable reference throughout this research, but the best sources of information, in every country where it was possible, have been exchanges with local horse breed specialists.

## How Have Breeds Come About?

The principle behind a domestic breed, as compared to a natural species, is that at one time or another in its history it was created by humans. First, humans tamed the wild species, then crossed and selected the most docile, the strongest, or the fastest horses, depending on their intended use.

Some breeds of the Old World are indeed very old (such as the Arabian, Akhal-Teke, Exmoor, and Thessalian), others are of more recent creation (among them the Haflinger, Thoroughbred, and Quarter Horse), and others are even more recent, still in the process of evolving (for example, the American Cream Draft, Aegidienberger, and Anglo-Kabarda). But natural selection has also played a role in the creation of many breeds (such as

*Pony*  *Saddle*  *Draft*

the Yakutian, Tibetan, and Shetland), especially in extreme environments.

Today, only truly feral horses, such as the Mustang, Brumby, and Misaki, reproduce without human intervention. Humans intervene by selecting horses they want to reproduce according to criteria they hope to see develop in future generations. These criteria can be aesthetic (coat color, mane and tail), functional (gaits, size), athletic (performance), or even productive (meat, milk). Humans invent new crosses, select animals generation after generation, and thus after work and reflection create new breeds.

## Ponies or Small Horses?

The difference between a pony and a horse is simply an arbitrary question of size; it rests on no biological foundation. An Arabian less than 1.48 meters tall would be classified as a pony, and it becomes a horse if it is 1.5 meters tall. With a difference of 2 centimeters, what is the difference? Ponies and horses all belong to a single species: *Equus caballus*.

Because of this we have made the deliberate choice not to speak of "ponies," but of "small horses." First, in many countries where all the breeds of horses are small, the notion of pony doesn't exist. Also, on the global level, if we account for all breeds the norm is indeed small horses. Finally, some equestrian peoples do not choose to call their small horses "ponies" because they find the term pejorative, necessarily evoking a horse for children, almost a "sub-horse." The Camargue of Southern France is a small horse, often the size of a large pony, but it would be out of the question for those who breed the Camargue horse to call it a pony. And so we find ourselves with a number of breeds whose breeders say, "This is not a pony, but a miniature replica of a horse." Others, in order to avoid the label "pony," are ready to make their horses grow at any cost, even risking losing the character of their breed. And in fact, it is true that many small horses are otherwise morphologically closer to miniature saddle horses (like the Caspian) than a rustic Shetland. However, other small rustics (like the Fjord) suggest a smaller draft horse.

The breeds of small horses, which have often come out of extreme environments that did not enable them to develop a large build, are often rustic, compact, and have good endurance. We thus have a tendency to generalize and assume that ponies

are always more rustic than horses. But some small competition ponies are more fragile than the larger and truly rustic breeds.

Some say that ponies have a different "character"; supposedly they are more intelligent and more stubborn than large horses. But this, again, is linked more to the breed than to the size. There are breeds of horses taller than 1.48 meters on average that are also very intelligent and stubborn, while some small breeds are particularly docile.

Certain tendencies, though undeniable, are not absolute truths. And distinguishing ponies from horses, even comparing them, is a recipe for endless debate. It is a very useful distinction in the athletic domain, to adapt sport competitions to the size of the horses, but it doesn't make a lot of sense beyond that.

We have thus sometimes retained the word "pony" when it is part of the breed's name, and we might use it to designate a good mount for children, but as a general rule we have preferred to use the term "small horses" rather than "ponies," for more clarity. The concept of pony, as attractive, popular, and sweet as it may be, is too subjective; it is a cultural construct that is not universal and not a biological reality. Even if it is quite useful sometimes to be able to speak of ponies, and even if this term is part of Western sport criteria, we cannot use it generally in this guide.

The "small horse" pictogram (see *p. 23*) thus refers to all breeds measuring on average under 1.48 meters to their withers, both ponies and others!

## Different Builds: The Case of Draft Horses

Height is not the only important factor. The weight of a horse depends on its height at the withers and its morphology. Some draft horses, such as the Belgian, Shire, Percheron, and Suffolk Punch, easily weigh more than 1,100 kilograms (the record is held by a Belgian weighing 1,440 kilograms). Clydesdales, the northern draft horses, and the Ardennais can easily weigh a ton, whereas a very small Shetland (around 1 meter at the withers), even though it is hardy, will weigh around 150–180 kilograms. A miniature horse will weigh only around 40 kilograms. An adult saddle horse, depending on its size and breed, weighs around 400–500 kilograms. Some breeds have a bone structure and morphology that is larger than others: a draft horse will always be stouter than a Thoroughbred.

Draft horses can also be very tall: some horses regularly approach 2 meters, the height record being held by a Shire measuring 2.19 meters at the withers. Using a pictogram we have shown the breeds that are included in the category of "draft horse" (see *p. 23*). We've used the term "draft" instead of "heavy" horses, since the latter term is linked to the meat industry. Due to the importance of corporeal mass for these breeds, they are the only ones for which we will indicate weight. Here, too, some breeds straddle the line between saddle horse and draft horse, so we have reserved the pictogram for only truly heavy horses.

A draft horse is a large, powerful animal that, before the invention of the tractor, was crucial for agricultural work such as plowing. These horses are often very calm: they have to be docile to work for hours in the fields, and to be easily handled in spite of their power. Mechanization, the appearance of trucks and tractors, almost caused the extinction of these breeds. It was the meat industry that prevented their extinction, but it also transformed them, fattening them up so they would yield more meat. Contemporary draft horses are thus fatter than those of the past. Some breeders are now trying to return to the original standards and turn the horses into recreational breeds.

In describing horses' bodies, we speak of the *longilinea* type (types of saddle horses that are very long and light), *medioline* (more classic saddle horses of average proportions), or *breviline* (draft horses or small rustic horses that are round and stocky). These terms are not used as commonly today.

## Thoroughbreds, Halfbreds, Warmbloods, Coldbloods

These different terms mean nothing, biologically speaking. An Icelandic that has been bred with no external blood for centuries is indeed as "pure" as an English Thoroughbred, a breed that in reality is the issue of a mixture of breeds. These terms are simply general breeding terms, which are nonetheless important to know.

The term *thoroughbred* for a long time referred to only two breeds, the English Thoroughbred and the Arabian, which were considered superior to all other breeds. To deal in thoroughbreds you have to have a studbook or a closed breeding registry that shows no exposure to external blood; and the horse must also "have blood," meaning it must be highly responsive and have a great deal of finesse. Today, when we say "thoroughbred" with no other details, we in fact mean the English Thoroughbred. The Anglo-Arabian, a cross between Thoroughbred and Arabian, is itself considered a breed.

*Halfbred* designates a horse born of the cross between an Arabian horse, a Thoroughbred, or an Anglo-Arabian, or even a cross between two halfbreds. In the past in the countryside one often spoke of halfbreds, but it is a term that has fallen into disuse today. Local mares aren't really crossed with Thoroughbreds, as local breeds have since become well established. Breeders prefer to designate a breed by its own name. All these former halfbreds have in truth become actual breeds for equestrian sport (dressage, jumping): Selle Français, Belgian Sport Horse (SBS), Royal Dutch Warmblood Horse (KWPN), and so forth.

## Measuring and weighing a horse

Horses are measured up to the highest point of their withers, starting from the ground. It goes without saying that the ground must be flat and that the horse must be standing still, with its limbs parallel.

Weighing a horse is more complicated, because, as one might expect, appropriate scales are difficult to find. But there are other means to evaluate weight, the easiest being to use a special measuring tape that measures the heart girth and provides an estimate.

## Performance

**Speed.** Whereas the average horse gallops at around 20 to 30 km/hour, the English Thoroughbred is capable of going faster than 60 km/hour. But the fastest breed in the world is the Quarter Horse, which over 440 yards (around 400 meters) can reach speeds of around 70 km/hour. The record speed for a Quarter Horse has been clocked at around 88.5 km/hour.

**Endurance.** In national races, champion endurance horses can travel up to 200 km in two days, or 160 km in a single day. The best horse breeds for endurance are the Arabian and the Shagya Arabian, but others, less well known, also perform very well.

**Jumping.** The high jump record for a horse is 2.47 m. It has been held since February 5, 1949, by the horse Huaso, ridden by Captain Alberto Larraguibel Morales, and was recorded in Chile. Huaso measured 1.68 m. to his withers and was 16 years old at the time of his record. The long jump record is 8.40 m. and is held by Something, ridden by André Ferreira in Johannesburg, April 26, 1975.

## Hot-iron branding

Some breeds of horses are marked with a brand, generally on the left flank. As the horses in this book are shown from the right side, the brand isn't seen. In the beginning, branding enabled horse owners to identify their animals, especially when they lived in the open (as in Mongolia) and could mix with those of a neighbor. This is no longer always the case, especially in the West, but a brand has remained a sort of guarantee of breeding. Branding is painful for the horse: its skin is burned, and the hair no longer grows on the area where the brand is placed. The brand is usually put on the animal's flank, but sometimes on the crest or the shoulder. The practice is fairly common in Europe, as well as in South and North America. Because it causes the animal to suffer, Belgium and Holland have prohibited the practice. Others have replaced hot-iron branding with freeze branding, using liquid nitrogen, and sedating the animal. Identifying horses by implanting a microchip renders these practices increasingly obsolete.

## Characteristics unique to horses

### Large eyes
Although the giant squid has the largest eye of all animals (with a diameter of 27 cm for a specimen caught in 2007—in an animal measuring more than 8 m in length), the horse has the largest eye of all land mammals. The diameter of a horse's eyeball is 5.5 cm, compared to 2.4 cm in humans.

### Vibrissae
Around the horse's nose and eyes, and under its chin, there are long translucent hairs called vibrissae. Other animal species also have them on their muzzle: they are well known on cats, mice, or dogs, for example. These are sensorial hairs that enable the animals to sense what they don't see.

### Chestnuts and ergots
These small horny growths are vestiges of a toe that disappeared during evolution. They are located on the inner side of the leg above the knee on the foreleg and, if present, below the hock on the hind leg. Sometimes they are very small, or even absent in some breeds (as in the Curly, the Banker, and some Caspians and Mustangs).

### Curly horses
Although supple, wavy manes and tails are often observed in many breeds and are in no way unusual, horses that have truly curly manes, tails, and coats are very rare. The curly coat strictly speaking only exists in a few rare breeds: the American Curly (whose origins are unclear), but above all in Siberian horses (Bashkir, Transbaikal), the Lokai of Tadjikistan, and a few Indian Manipurs. Why do we find this prevalence of curly horses in Siberia? Curly hair, which develops in the winter (and sometimes falls out completely in the summer), enables these horses to be exceptionally resilient in the cold, and so it would seem to be a natural adaptation. It is also found in rustic breeds of ancient origin.

Finally, there are also *warmblood* or *près du sang* horses, terms used to designate breeds strongly marked by English Thoroughbred and Arabian blood, which are lively, responsive, and fast; and *coldblood* horses, to designate more rustic horses that are calm and more placid. Here, too, the terms, which in themselves don't mean very much, are becoming increasingly obsolete.

## Coats

For horse breeds, the color of the coat isn't everything. Indeed, whereas for many breeds of cattle, for example, color is a true criterion for identification, most horse breeds show a wide range of colors. It is ultimately rare for a breed to always be the same color, as are the black Friesian, the light gray Lipizzan, or even the Paint Horse, which is pinto.

Similarly, some people think that every spotted horse is an Appaloosa. And yet many breeds have a spotted coat, which in truth is a very ancient and primitive characteristic. It was once found in Spanish horses and is now found in the Knabstrup of Denmark, and it is present in many Asian and American breeds.

Horses' coats are not classified in the same way in every country: some clearly distinguish the shades in coats, whereas others don't. Advances in genetics today enable us to have a better view of coat colors.

In France, for example, coats are divided into four groups:

### Blacks
Black manes and tails, black skin, dark eyes.
- Black
- Pangaré (or mealy) black (black with light hair on the nose, flanks, stomach, inside the thighs)
  Among the blacks there are black pintos, black roans, and so on.

### Chestnuts
Tawny hair, manes, and tails. The skin can be light, but is never pink (except under white markings); the eyes are dark. The extremities are never dark. But manes and tails can be lighter.
- Chestnut (with shades: light, copper, dark)
- Liver chestnut (black skin)
- Café au lait (mane and tail and hair café au lait, light skin)
- Palomino (coat light brown, often golden, mane silver white, black or gray skin; several shades, from light to coppery)
  Within the chestnuts, there are pintos, spotted horses, and those with flaxen manes and tails.

### Bays
Black manes and tails and brown, tawny, or ashy hair. Legs, tip of the nose, and ears often black. Black skin, dark eyes.
- Bay
- Brown bay
- Burnt bay
- Light bay
- Cherry bay
- Bay dun (yellowish hair), in several shades (light to dark bay dun), sometimes with dorsal or zebra striping
- Dun (ashy hair, ashy gray to black manes and tails, black skin, dark eyes, black extremities), often with dorsal or zebra striping
  Among the bays there are pintos, spotted horses, and other variations.

### Others
These are all the coats that are neither black, bay, nor chestnut.
- White (a very rare coat, no pigment in mane, tail, or hair, which are white; skin is pink, hooves light, eyes dark).
- Cream (hair is cream, mane and tail white to grayish, pink skin; light eyes, blue, green, or light brown).
- Gray (hair, mane, and tail are white and colored, mixed; skin is black, dark eyes). This common coat lightens over the years and there are many variations, from very light gray to dark gray, speckled gray (with little tufts of tawny hair), mottled gray (little tufts of black hair), dove gray.
- Chocolate (chocolate hair, mane, and tail, dark skin and eyes).

### Blended Hair
Once the coat is established, there are "details" that enable the exact color of the horse to be determined. When there is a

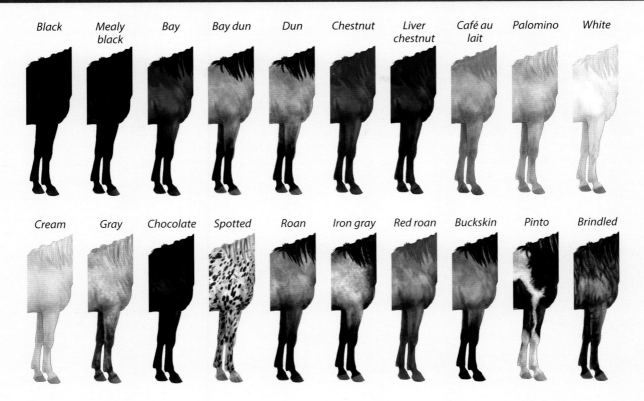

mixture of white hair, the coat is called "roan." There is black roan (blue roan or iron gray), bay roan, and chestnut roan (red roan). These coats are stable and are not to be confused with horses that are graying.

There are also coats with mixtures of black hair. The horse is then called "smoky." It can be smoky bay dun (or buckskin).

### Mottled

Mottled is used for pinto or spotted horses.

There are different varieties of pinto:

- *Tobiano* (colored head, vertical orientation of white spots, clear shape of spots, often with four stockings)
- *Overo* (head predominantly white, horizontal orientation of white markings, irregular shape of spots, mane and tail streaked with white, legs normally dark)
- *Tovero* (predominantly white coat with just a few spots)
- *Sabino* (very mixed contours of spots, irregular, often a partly white head and large white stockings that go up to the stomach)
- *Splashed white* (white head, legs, and stomach)

There are also different varieties of spotted coats:

- *Leopard* (uniform white, pink skin spotted in a clear and uniform way over the entire body)
- *Spotted* (many unequal spots over the entire body).
- *Cape* (white marking over the croup, which sometimes extends to the withers; the cape can be uniform or spotted)

### Albinism in horses

This genetic issue has been the subject of many papers but has not yet been explained satisfactorily. Classic albinism doesn't exist in horses, or only in a non-viable form (the foal dies within a few days). There are perhaps forms of partial albinism, or leucism, but they haven't been demonstrated. But the fact remains that there are still many completely white horses, with pink skin and blue or brown eyes. There is even a breed, formerly and incorrectly called "albinos" (the white Camarillo or some horses listed under American Cream and White). But these are not albinos in the strict sense, only white horses.

Various coats may give the impression that the horse is entirely white. Thus the majority of white horses that we see are in reality very light gray (such as the Lipizzan and the Camargue). Their skin is entirely or partially black, and they are dark at birth (chestnut, bay, black), becoming lighter only later and gradually, going through a whole gamut of color variations in their first months. Usually the head and the mane and tail lighten first. It can take several years for the coats of some foals to turn as completely "white" as the adults' coats, and they must sometimes wait five or six years before turning light gray. Depending on the lineages, some foals gray more or less quickly. This is not related to truly white horses, who must have pink skin.

*Whether a blaze on the forehead or stockings on the legs, white markings are very useful to identify various individuals within the same breed.*

- *Marbled* (very rare: coat covered with white hair except at the joints)
- *Striped* (extremely rare: coat with very thin white stripes of unequal size)
- *Brindled* (common in dogs or cows, but very rare in horses: coat with very thin black stripes of unequal size)

### Primitive Markings of Darker Hair

In addition, horses can have darker hair on the body, in a dorsal stripe (a band along the backbone), which is sometimes very wide in some horses (such as certain Mustangs in Sulphur Springs), or in a scapular band (a band that descends to the shoulders). If a horse has both, this forms the specific marking, the famous "St. Andrew's cross" of donkeys, that is found in some very primitive breeds such as the Polish Konik.

Often associated with the dorsal stripe, zebra striping can also be found on legs. It is often seen on Sorraias, Fjords, some Mustangs, and certain Siberian and other Asian breeds.

Some horses have a "Moor's hat" on their head, which means the head is darker than the rest of the body. This is found frequently on primitive coats such as the dun.

A unique, very rare shoulder marking is found on Przewalski's Horse, the Mongolian, the Transbaikal, and the Yakutian. In domestic breeds it marks the introduction of Przewalski blood at a moment in their history.

### Markings of Lighter Hair

When a horse has markings of lighter hair, this can create mealy coats (lighter at the tip of the nose, inner thighs, and elsewhere). These mealy coats often exist in very ancient breeds (such as the Exmoor). The lighter hair also creates dappled coats (the center lighter than the contour—we most often find dappled gray, but also very beautiful dappled bays, as, for example, in the Cleveland Bay)—or snowflake coats (small tufts of white hair, with a snowy effect). If on the contrary the little tufts of hair are black, it is called a charcoal coat.

### White Markings

Horses frequently have white markings on the head and legs that enable them to be distinguished from each other. When the marking is on the forehead it is called a *star* (which can have various shapes, such as ball, crescent, or diamond), and a *blaze* when it extends all the way down the face. The blaze can be thin, wide, scattered, or even "dipped in white paint" when it continues to the nose and mouth.

White markings on the legs are also common, and of varying size. If they are very thin and don't continue around the leg, they are called a *trace*; if they go all the way around, they are *socks* if they go above the fetlock and *stockings* if they reach close to or even past the knee or the hock. A very thin marking that goes around the leg just above the hoof is called a *coronet*.

These markings are unique to each horse. Indeed, no horse has the exact same markings as another horse, which makes this an easy criterion for identification. But some horses, even some breeds, have no markings at all.

### Other Distinctive Characteristics

The mane and tail are sometimes lighter than the coat, silvery, or mixed (white and color).

When the skin is pink dappled with black, it is called champagne.

Some horses have other specific characteristics, such as mixed eye color (one blue and one brown), and even both blue and brown in the same eye.

## How to Recognize a Stallion, a Gelding, and a Mare

For those without a lot of experience around horses, it isn't easy at first glance to tell the difference between a male and a female, because sexual dimorphism in horses is not very marked. One of the simplest ways is to locate the genitalia of the animal: those of the male horse are located under the stomach at the level of its hind legs (posterior). The genital organs of the mare, located under the tail, are not visible unless the tail is raised. The lactating mare has swollen mammaries that are sometimes visible. However, with a somewhat trained eye it is possible to differentiate the male and female by their overall build (see front endpapers). The mare has a thinner neck, and a rounder barrel if she has already given birth. She is often slightly smaller and weighs a bit less. The gelding (castrated horse) is often more muscular, with a wider neck, and a generally flatter barrel. Some breeders speak of the femininity of the mare and the virility of the male. The entire horse, or stallion (non-castrated horse), due to its hormones, develops a thick neck that is very easily recognizable,

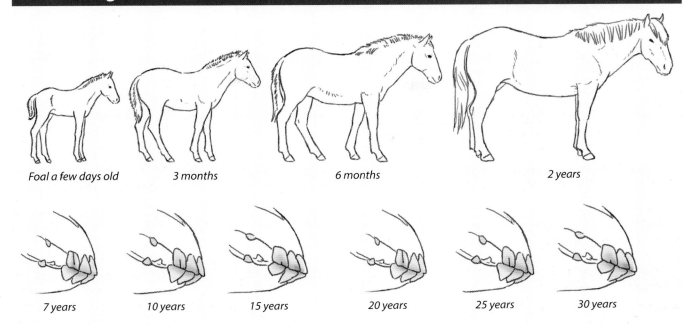

Foal a few days old   3 months   6 months   2 years

7 years   10 years   15 years   20 years   25 years   30 years

and often has a thicker and longer mane. A horse's behavior and carriage can also offer some indication of its gender.

However, sexual dimorphism in some breeds (the Andalusian, for example) is more marked than in others: in the English Thoroughbred, for example, the difference between a stallion and a mare is less clear at first glance.

As for the young horse, although all horses stop growing at around the age of six or seven, sometimes eight, some already have an adult appearance at the age of three (which sometimes causes them to be put to work too soon), whereas others keep a juvenile look longer. Before then, however, one can recognize a very young horse. It is thinner, less developed than an adult. In a period of fast growth it can have a croup that is clearly higher than the withers, or vice versa. Before age one, the hair of the mane and tail is shorter and softer to the touch (for its first months, the foal has a bristly mane and tail, as well as very soft hair, called *filling*, which it loses as it grows). The muzzle is generally still rather thin, the head a bit triangular. In very young foals the neck is still rather short and the legs very long. A precise way to know the age of a young horse is to open its mouth and look at its teeth.

## The Different Natural Gaits

The horse has three widely recognized natural gaits:
- *Walk*: a walking, symmetrical, four-beat gait, with at least two hooves always on the ground.
- *Trot*: a jumping, symmetrical, two-beat gait, with moments when all four legs are in the air. The horse moves with diagonal steps (right fore and left hind, left fore and right hind).
- *Gallop*: jumping, asymmetrical, three-beat shifting gait (the gallop can lead with the right or the left) followed by a

moment of suspension. At an extremely slow pace or a very fast one, the gallop can then be at four beats. Americans thus distinguish the *canter*, for the slow gallop, from the *gallop* when it is very fast, at four beats.

In addition to these three gaits some breeds have particularly comfortable natural supplemental gaits:
- *Amble*: a two-beat gait; the horse moves laterally, the two legs of the same side at the same time. There is a moment of suspension. Sometimes very fast, the amble, like the trot and the gallop, can be used in races. This is sometimes called the "flying amble." In American English it is called the *pace*; *slow gait* or *stepping pace* is used for a slower amble.
- *Broken four-beat ambles*
- *Tölt*: a walking, symmetrical, four-beat gait, like the walk, but with only one or two hooves on the ground. This is also called *broken amble*. The tail sways. The speed is variable, going from a walk to a gallop. In American English this is called *gait* or *singlefoot*. The *rack* is a similar gait. In Turkey this is called *rahvan* and in India *revaal*.
- *Paso*: a lateral four-beat gait, with at least two hooves always on the ground. It is divided into, from slowest to fastest, *paso fino*, *paso corto*, and *paso largo*.

The amble and the broken amble can have different names depending on the country. The *arravani* of the Greeks corresponds to the amble and the tölt. In Galicia (Spain), it is the *andadura galega*, and more exactly the *andadura dos tempos* (*andadura serrada*) for the amble, and the *andadura catro tempo* (*entrepaso* or *andadura chapeada*) for the broken amble. The American *fox trot* (of the Missouri Fox Trotter) is a sliding four-beat gait, and corresponds to the South American *trocha*.

# Gaits

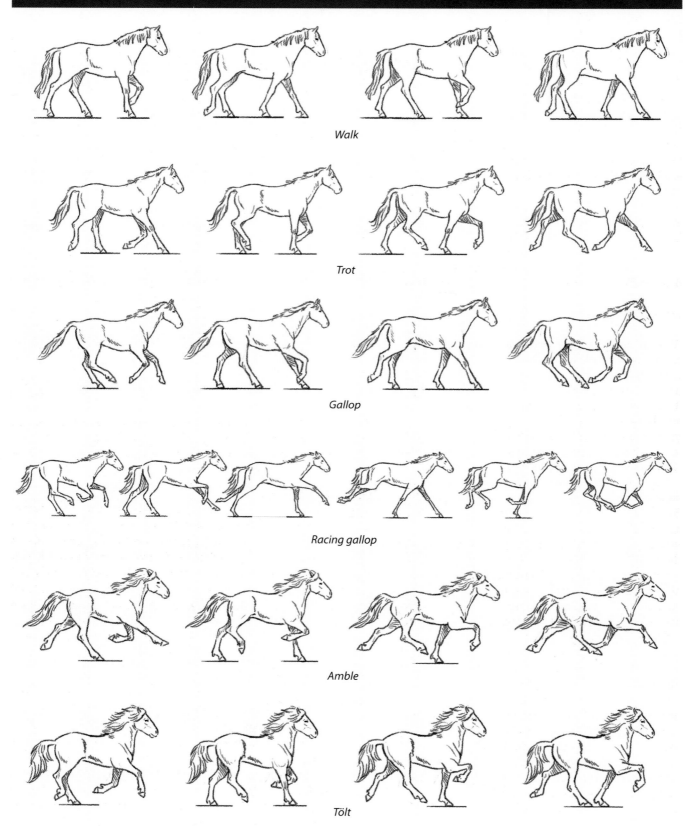

Walk

Trot

Gallop

Racing gallop

Amble

Tölt

Among the gaited horses—those with at least one additional gait—many have the amble; more rarely, some breeds have two variants of the broken amble (these are known as horses with five gaits).

Europeans have chosen to select horses with only the first three gaits (walk, trot, gallop), gradually eliminating the ambling horses that once existed on the continent. And European riders have ultimately completely forgotten that these gaits were once widespread: gaited horses therefore seem truly exceptional, almost a curiosity, whereas they exist just about everywhere else in the world, where they are appreciated for their comfort and their endurance. European breeding, by almost systematically eliminating the supplementary gaits (and quite often also spotted coats), did not follow the direction of the natural diversity of horses. However, the South and North Americans have been able to develop their extraordinary breeds with the current gaits (such as the Paso Fino and the American Saddlebred) from the former European gaited horses, notably the Jennet of Spain.

Thus one regularly finds gaited breeds, some more specialized than others in this realm, in Asia, Africa, and the Americas.

## Identity Card

When we talk about the history of horses we generally go back around sixty million years, to the underbrush of tropical forests. *Eohippus*—literally "dawn horse"—is their very distant ancestor. It was no bigger than a fox (some 30 centimeters at the withers). It was already an herbivore, but its feet didn't yet have hooves, and they looked more like those of a dog, with pads. It was found in what corresponds to Eurasia and North America today. During its evolution the horse grew bigger, going through various stages (*Orohippus, Miohippus, Parahippus, Merychippus, Pliohippus*).

The horse that we know today, of the genus *Equus*, emerged around a million years ago. Whereas *Eohippus* lived in forests, *Equus* is, on the contrary, an animal of the plains, the steppes, open spaces. It moves around in a nomadic fashion. This transposition probably occurred following changes in the climate, during which the horse became adapted to eating the grasses of the plains.

It was believed for a long time that Przewalski's Horse was the ancestor of the domestic horse, but this is probably not true. We don't really know if the domestic horse descended from the Tarpan or from a different subspecies that included the Tarpan.

**Class**: mammals

**Order**: Perissodactyles. This term comes from the Greek *perissos* ("odd") and *dactylos* ("finger"), which means that the Perissodactyles have an odd number of toes on their posterior limbs. Equines in fact have only one "finger," the hoof. The other animals of this order are the rhinoceros and the tapir.

**Family**: equines (*Equidae*). This is a small family, which includes horses, zebras, and donkeys. This family of mammals and herbivores is characterized by its single toe, the hoof. Some equines, such as the Tarpan, have disappeared recently, or a bit longer ago, such as the Hippidion, a small horse that disappeared around 10,000 years ago.

**Genus**: *Equus*.

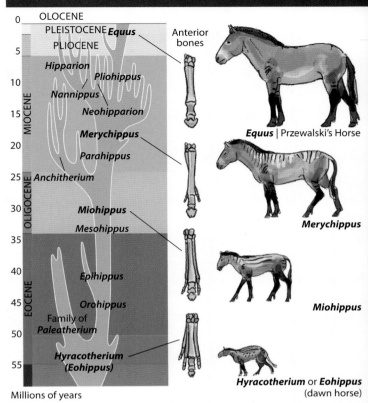

## Evolution of the Horse

Millions of years

*Equus* | Przewalski's Horse

*Merychippus*

*Miohippus*

*Hyracotherium* or *Eohippus* (dawn horse)

**Species**: *Caballus*. Today there are two species (or subspecies, depending on the theory) of horse: *Equus caballus* (or *Equus ferus caballus*), the domestic horse, and *Equus przewalskii* (or *Equus ferus przewalskii*), Przewalski's Horse.

## The Horse's Diet

Horses are herbivores: they eat exclusively grass and other plants. To graze on grasses the horse developed a solid dentition, with thick molars. But because grass contains few nutrients, horses must consume large quantities of it to meet their dietary needs. In the wild, horses spend between twelve and fifteen hours a day feeding. In a stable, horses fed on grains and hay spend a lot less time eating. This often creates behaviorial problems when domesticated horses become bored during the day once they have eaten their food. A horse can also absorb thirty to fifty liters of water a day.

## The Horse as Prey

Horses—and especially foals—are prey for large predators, such as wolves (in Mongolia), hyenas and panthers (in Namibia), pumas (in the United States), or even large wild dogs. Prehistoric man was for a long time a predator of the wild horse, which he hunted for its meat, skin, or mane and tail.

A horse has several ways of defending itself: foremost is to flee. But a horse can also kick backwards, rear up, bite, and even charge. A horse that kicks usually aims very well. It has developed good musculature and great speed in running.

## Sleeping Habits

The horse has the ability to sleep standing up, a light sleep, ready to flee at the slightest danger. Indeed, for a horse sleeping is already taking a risk: that of being attacked by a predator. Anatomically, it can lock its kneecaps and immobilize its legs so it doesn't fall down when it dozes. However, it also needs to relax completely for a half hour or an hour per day, with its legs folded against it, or completely stretched out. It is then vulnerable, but the other members of the herd are there, keeping a lookout. They don't all sleep and stretch out at the same time. A horse doesn't sleep much: around five to six hours per day. However, foals sleep more.

## A Social Animal

In the wild horses live in small herds, often made up of a stallion, a few mares, and their foals. These are profoundly social animals: union creates strength. Life in a group enables many herbivores of the plains to better protect themselves from predators. In a group there are more eyes and ears to watch the surroundings. The group also enables the individual to be less alone in the face of attacks by insects. Horses sometimes place themselves head to tail, taking advantage of the movements of the tails of their neighbor to keep flies away. Once formed, the herd is very united and its members are very close. The herd is organized around the mares and their young. Young males can be members, but only one adult male, the stallion, is connected to the mares. His role is to watch out for the herd, to protect it against predators.

## Gestation and Birth

A horse's gestation is around eleven months, or two months longer than that of humans. Mares carry only one baby at a time. Twins are extremely rare in horses, and when it happens one of the two is generally not viable. The foal is able to gallop a few hours after its birth; it is a question of survival.

## An Intelligent Animal?

The horse's form of intelligence is very different from ours. If we recognize ourselves better in a dog's way of thinking, it is because, like us, the dog thinks like a predator. The reasoning of prey and their escape reflexes tend to disconcert us. Able to learn varied and complex exercises, endowed with a great memory, the horse does possess acknowledged abilities to learn, a knowledge that lasts its entire life. Various recent scientific findings on the intelligence of the horse all suggest an animal that is much more intelligent than has long been believed.

## Communication

The horse is mostly a silent animal that communicates essentially through body language. However, its whinnying can be varied: a loud and long whinny of calling; a short whinny of greeting; the mute whinnying of a mare to her foal; the serious whinny of a courting stallion, and so on.

A horse's ears are also very expressive. Laid back, they express discontent or aggression. Laid far back, they express strong

## Absent for a long time in America

Whereas the horse's ancestors originated in America, the horse disappeared from the continent around 12,000 years ago, at the end of the Pleistocene. America was thus not always the equestrian land that we know today. The colonists reintroduced domestic horses during the conquest of the Americas in the sixteenth century. The horse is not the only creature that disappeared from North America at that time. There were also camels, mammoths, giant beavers, and other megafauna that then populated the continent. Scientists still don't know the causes for these disappearances; however, the latest studies have eliminated a meteor fall or too great pressure from hunting by humans. Some suggest a change in climate.

aggression, anger, and when you see that, it's best to be very careful because the horse may bite or kick you. By contrast, when a rider mounts his horse, it may turn its ears back toward the rider to listen to what he is saying. Pointed forward, a horse's ears mean that it is watching, listening attentively to what is in front of it. The more they are pointed, the greater the attention, expressing curiosity, even concern.

All body language in horses is important. Movements of the ears, tail, crest, mouth; movements, but also the gaze, the way it makes the other move, holding its head lowered, raising its tail, or keeping it close to its body, chewing—everything has a meaning.

## Life Expectancy

A horse may expect to live for twenty-five or thirty years. But this varies among breeds. Some, such as the Criollo, Icelandic, Black Forest Draft, Hucul, Yakutian, Arabian, and Falabella, are reputed to live for a long time, easily up to thirty years, even longer. In France, there is a Camargue called Ours (Bear) who holds the record for longevity: forty-seven years. The oldest horse in the world was Old Billy, a British horse who died at sixty-two. Longevity also depends on the horse's activity and the care it has received during its life.

## Distribution of Horses throughout the World

An animal that is closely connected to humans, the horse is found almost everywhere that humans have settled. Horses are found in the cold lands of Siberia and in the company of Bedouins in the desert, in the high Himalayan mountains, and in tropical and swampy regions.

Apart from Antarctica, there is really only one zone in the world where the horse is almost absent: Equatorial Africa, due to the very challenging breeding conditions (African horse sickness, the tsetse fly). But horses are indeed found in North Africa, Ethiopia, and South Africa.

Europe, Asia, and the Americas have the largest populations of horses.

# The Domestication of the Horse and the Main Equestrian Disciplines

Riding and harnessing horses was one of the greatest evolutions in the history of humanity. The horse revolutionized daily work, and for centuries was the primary means of transportation for people of the Old World, being forever an integral part of that history. Having become riders, people could go faster and farther, gather their herds, hunt better, improve their agriculture, but also conduct war differently.

We find horses painted in the caves of prehistoric man from 35,000 to 10,000 years ago.

It is believed that the horse was domesticated by humans around 4,000 BC, likely in Ukraine, to the north of Kazakhstan in Central Asia, according to various theories. The domestication was not really that ancient; for example, the dog was domesticated in 12,000 BC, bovines in 8,000 BC and goats around 9,500–8,500 BC. The horse was first raised for its meat, its skin, and the milk of its mares, then it was used for its power in hauling loads. It was later harnessed, then pack-saddled.

Although the horse was first used for transportation, agriculture, driving, and carrying loads, but also for meat and milk production, and although it is still used for those purposes in many places throughout the world, today we can add a great many equestrian disciplines to that list, no doubt more varied than they have ever been. We should also note that the horse is sometimes raised to produce medications for human use, often in conditions that leave a great deal to be desired.

## Work-Related Horseback Riding

The *doma vaquera* (Spanish work riding), Portuguese horseback riding, Camargue horseback riding, Italian work riding, and Western riding have all emerged from the world of ranching. They consist of tests of handling, dressage, speed, and herding, and also include many games. They are found among all peoples who raise livestock; these disciplines are not strictly formalized, for example, in South America or Asia. Western riding includes many disciplines, such as trail riding, reining, barrel racing, and cutting. The different *rodeos* (Chilean rodeo, American rodeo, and others) also came out of ranching traditions.

## Racing

- *Gallop racing*: The goal is to have the horses go as fast as possible; the first across the finish line wins the race.
- *Trotting*: This is the same thing as a gallop race, except the horse moves at a very fast racing trot. These races can be in harness (with a sulky) or under saddle.
- *Obstacle race*: Steeplechase, cross-country, or hedge race, these are speed races with obstacles.
- *Amble and tölt races*: Practiced at the highest levels by the American Standardbred (pacing races), these races take place in many countries that have gaited horses. The horses can be ridden or driven. More than a simple race, *Icelandic riding* also revolves around the particular gaits of the Icelandic horse.

- *Pulling race*: In these events, very popular in Japan, draft horses race while pulling a heavy load.
- *Ski joring*: Practiced as a race or as a simple leisure activity, ski joring consists of a person on skis being pulled over the snow by a horse. There are also harness races on snow. The horses have special shoes so they don't slip.

## Team Sports

- *Polo*: This is a team ball sport on horseback, very old, using a mallet to make goals. *Polocrosse* is a variation, using a sort of racket on a stick instead of a mallet.
- *Horseball*: This involves shooting goals in the opposite team's basket with a special ball equipped with straps that allow it to be caught and passed to team members.
- *Pony games*: These are equestrian games that are practiced individually or in a team, showing one's agility on horseback.

## Equestrian Combat Sports

Throughout the world there are also traditional equestrian games, the legacy of military training: the Turkish *cirit* consists of throwing a javelin at one's opponents; *buzkashi* involves Afghan riders knocking against each other around the carcass of a goat; there are variations of this in Central Asia and the Middle East, under different names. The Japanese have invented *yoseikan bajutsu*, a martial art on horseback, and *yabusame*, the sport of archery on horseback.

## Olympic Disciplines

- *Dressage*: The goal is to perform figures exhibiting the most perfect harmony between the rider and his or her mount.
- *Show jumping*: This is an obstacle course where most of the obstacles include bars that fall if the horse touches them.
- *Eventing*: This discipline brings together the trials of show jumping, cross-country, and dressage. The cross-country trial is an all-terrain obstacle course where the obstacles are fixed (trunks of trees, etc.).

## Traditional Riding

- *Sidesaddle*: This consists of riding with both legs on the left side with the help of a special saddle, as female riders used to do in the past.
- *Haute école*: This is the highest art of dressage, with more figures than in the Olympic discipline of dressage, notably including leaps above the ground. Depending on the exercises, the rider may be riding or on foot next to the horse.

## Spectacles and Acrobatics on Horseback

- *The circus and the show*: They combine acrobatics, haute école exercises, vaulting, and freestyle. *Cossack vaulting* is a form of vaulting that is practiced in a straight line on a galloping horse. Amazing!
- *Vaulting*: This involves performing artistic figures, alone or in a group, on the back of a horse moving in a circle.

## Shows and Exhibitions

- *Breed shows*: Especially popular in Anglo-Saxon countries, they consist of presenting horses in top form (appearance and gaits).

- *Hunter trials*: This is an obstacle course where elegance wins and where style is noted.

Horses have also always been used for various *parades*, in all countries of the world, and in *fantasias* (traditional exhibitions of horsemanship held during many North African festivals) and other entertainments.

## Outdoor Sports

- *Trekking and equestrian tourism*: This is the same thing as trekking on foot, but it is done on horseback. The TREC (Techniques de randonnée équestre de compétition), an equestrian competitive trekking program, enables a rider to compete in this discipline. The TREC is also practiced in harness.
- *Endurance*: The goal is to travel great distances while keeping the horse in good condition from start to finish.
Endurance is also practiced with horses in harness.

## Driving

This can be practiced by harnessing a single horse, a pair, or several pairs of horses to a vehicle such as a cart or carriage. This activity may be for sport or tourism. We use the terms *traditional driving* or *carriage driving* when it is practiced with old-style vehicles.

## Other Disciplines

- *Natural horsemanship*: A multifaceted discipline, it approaches the horse through its behavior, with the goal of achieving a better understanding and thus a greater harmony between the rider and his or her horse.
- *Equitherapy* uses the horse as a therapeutic mediator, and *para-equestrian horsemanship* enables people with disabilities to ride.
Also of note are *fox hunting* and *bullfighting*, controversial practices in which horses are used.

## How to use this book

### Legends

 Feral population (returned to living in the wild)

 Small horse, smaller than 1.48 m at the withers, often the equivalent of "pony" in some countries.

 Draft horse

 Gaited horse, having at least one supplemental gait (tölt, amble)

 Rare horse, fewer than 5,000 individuals in the world

 Very rare horse, fewer than 1,000 individuals in the world

The vertical line to the left of a horse corresponds to 1 meter to provide a scale of size. It visually indicates the size of the breed.

### Why drawings?

For presenting and identifying breeds, drawings offer many advantages over photos: they permit the use of different sources of documentation; the presentation of animals on a relatively similar scale to demonstrate their similarities or their differences; and a representation of the appropriate identification criteria for each breed. They make possible a visual coherence that is useful in comparing the animals.

In using this guide, the descriptive text should be read alongside the drawings in order to understand the distinctions between breeds.

The majority of breeds of horses in this guide are illustrated. Some are not, for various reasons, often due to a lack of reliable documentary resources. However, the breeds that are not pictured are no less important than those that are.

### Choice of names

For a given breed, there are often several names or several possible translations of a name. We have chosen to include the most commonly used name (which explains the occasional non-translation of some foreign names), or the one that corresponds best to the name in its language of origin, and, in all cases, to favor simplicity.

For foreign names from certain countries with different alphabets or writing systems (such as Chinese and Arabic) we have opted for transcriptions that render the pronunciation in the given language. This is useful should one go to the location and want to speak of the breed to a local rider or breeder.

Opposite: Lusitano of the Alter Real lineage being worked in long reins, Portuguese School of Equestrian Arts. Lisbon, Portugal.

# Other Equines of the World

*Although equines don't include many species, the horse still does have some cousins: donkeys and zebras. Only the donkey has been domesticated, becoming the domestic donkey (Equus asinus or Equus africanus asinus) from the now rare wild donkey of Africa (Equus africanus). There are only a thousand or so individuals of the latter species remaining in Africa, in two locales: the wild donkey of Somalia and the wild donkey of Nubia. Wild donkeys are particularly at risk, and they face the threat of extinction.*

*But certain rare and little-known donkeys also exist in Asia, such as the onager (also called onagri or wild donkey of Asia, Equus hemionus) or the kiang (or wild donkey of Tibet, Equus kiang). These equines are all threatened with extinction.*

*Similarly, there is not just one single species of zebra, but three, very different from each other in spite of a common general appearance: the mountain zebra (Equus zebra), Burchell's zebra (Equus quagga), and Grévy's zebra (Equus grevyi).*

## Wild horses, feral horses

There is only one species of wild horse in the world: *Equus ferus przewalskii*, Przewalski's Horse. The species died in the wild in 1968, having been hunted and crossed with domestic horses, but it was preserved in zoos. Thanks to programs of reintroduction, the species was released back into the wild in 1994. Other horses that are called wild, such as the American Mustang, the Australian Brumby, New Zealand's Kaimanawa, and the Namib Desert Horse of Namibia, are actually domesticated animals returned to freedom. They have adapted to life in nature, but they are not species of wild horses. Another wild horse existed on the earth until very recently: the Tarpan. The last Tarpan, which lived in the Munich zoo in Germany, died in 1887. The species has completely disappeared.

Burchell's zebra (or plains zebra), South Africa.

Opposite: Domestic donkey, Tunisia.

# TARPAN

**Scientific name**: *Equus ferus*, subspecies: *Equus ferus gmelini*

**Derivation**: Tarpan, in Turkmen, means "wild horse."

**H** Around 1.30 m.

**C** Gray dun, with a lighter coat in the winter. It had characteristic wild markings: dorsal stripe, scapular marking, zebra striping on the legs, etc.

**Description**: It greatly resembled Przewalski's Horse, but was thinner. Some scientists believe that the Tarpan and Przewalski's Horse were two closely related species; others think that they are two subspecies of the same species. There were two types of Tarpans: the Tarpan of the steppes and the forest Tarpan. These animals had a big head, long ears, small eyes, and a thick but bristly mane and tail.

**Distribution**: Once present in Europe.

**Origins and history**: The Tarpan is not a breed of horse, but a species (or subspecies) of wild horse that was described in 1770 by the naturalist Johann Fredrich Gmelin in the Ukraine and that disappeared at the end of the nineteenth century. It is the ancestor of several breeds. Some believe that the Polish Konik—notably the herd preserved in Popielno, Poland, whose members were selected for their resemblance to the Tarpan—and the Portuguese Sorraia are residual populations of Tarpans and should bear the name of their extinct ancestor. The true wild Tarpan, however, no longer exists: the horses that descend from it have all been at one time or another crossed and domesticated. Some believe that the last Tarpans described were already hybrids, but this remains hypothetical. The single and last truly wild horse still living today is Przewalski's Horse. It is nonetheless still true that the Konik and the Sorraia remain very close to the Tarpan, and for this reason deserve to be carefully protected. Before their extinction Tarpans were hunted as game, their meat was highly prized, and they were captured with a view to being domesticated. They were sometimes crossed with domestic horses to make them more resilient.

**Character and attributes**: This wild horse had an extremely ferocious nature and was difficult to train, endured captivity badly, and was combative, unlike its domesticated descendants. These horses were particularly resilient, notably to weather conditions, and they were prolific.

**Current status**: Extinct. A small population has been reconstituted.

# PRZEWALSKI'S HORSE

**Also called**: *takh* in Mongolian

**Scientific name**: *Equus przewalskii* (but its classification as a species or subspecies is a subject of debate)

**H** 1.30 m on average.

**C** It is wild bay dun, with a dorsal stripe, zebra striping on the legs, and sometimes a more or less prominent marking on the shoulder, which one finds only among the Mongolian horses, Transbaikals, and Yakutians. It is also mealy, with a lighter nose and stomach, which can give it a rather light appearance in the winter when its coat has grown out.

**Description**: Compact, it has a large head; long ears; a short, strong neck; and very solid hooves. Its tail is rather thin. Its mane grows bushy, without a forelock falling on its forehead, unlike domestic horses.

**Distribution**: Free-range herds exist in Mongolia (Hustai National Park, Gobi Desert, Khomiin Tal) and in China (Kalamely Mountain, the part of the Gobi Desert located in Dzungaria, Xinjiang). Programs of reintroduction and herds in semi-freedom exist in France (Lozère, Alpes-Maritimes), Spain, Belgium, and China. The animals have also been released onto the disaster sites of Chernobyl (Ukraine).

**Origins and history**: Przewalski's Horse is an entirely wild species discovered in 1879 by a Russian, Colonel Przewalski. It has never been domesticated. It has 66 chromosomes, whereas the domestic horse has only 64—which does not prevent them from being crossed and having fertile offspring. It became extinct in the wild in 1969, but its presence in many zoos has enabled it to be put into programs of conservation and reintroduction.

According to the latest research, Przewalski's Horse is not the ancestor of domestic horses, but it is actually very close to them; all are descendants of a common ancestor.

**Character and attributes**: This wild horse is fast, very resilient, and able to endure very extreme climate conditions. Like the zebra, it cannot be trained.

**Current status**: The species remains rare and in danger, with around 1,800 to 2,000 animals throughout the world, and a total of 383 individuals at the end of 2012 in Mongolia (269 in the Hustai National Park, 77 in the Gobi Desert, and 37 in Khomiin Tal).

### Attempts at Reconstituting the Tarpan

There have been some reasonably controversial attempts to recreate the Tarpan. One, called **Heck's horse,** was made in 1933 by the Germans Heinz Heck and Lutz Heck using a Konik Polski, Przewalski's Horse, Gotland, Dülmen, and the Icelandic Horse, all closely related to the Tarpan. Another German attempt at reconstitution, the **Liebenthaler**, has created a herd of around a hundred animals from crossings between Fjords, Koniks, and Przewalski's Horse. This horse has an abundant and bi-colored mane, black and light, sometimes with red streaks.

An attempt made in the U.S. in the 1950s, using Mustangs with primitive characteristics, including a straight mane, resulted in **Hegardt's Horse**, also called Stroebel's Horse.

Among the horses that still resemble the Tarpan, we must not forget the Hucul. The Exmoor and the Fjord also have very strong primitive characteristics.

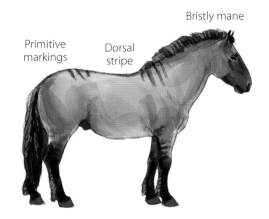

Bristly mane

Primitive markings

Dorsal stripe

A herd drinking at a water hole and rolling in the mud. Foals are slightly lighter.

Bushy mane

Large head

Lighter nose and stomach

Dorsal stripe

Some individuals have a characteristic marking on the shoulders.

Zebra striping on the legs

# Zorse (Cross between zebra and horse)

**Ⓗ** Depends on the breed of the mare that gives birth.

**Ⓒ** The zorse has many fewer stripes than the zebra, but it still has a lot, more or less depending on the individual. Its coat can be colored like that of a horse.

**Description**: Impossible to be confused with any other horse due to its strange coat, this blending of a horse and a zebra has large, round ears and the generally bristly mane of a zebra, but it can sometimes have a forelock.

**Distribution**: Mainly in the United States.

**Origins and history**: The zorse is a hybrid, the result of a cross between a domestic animal, the horse, and a wild species, the zebra—more exactly, the cross between a male zebra and a mare. The reverse (cross between a stallion and a female zebra) doesn't work: either the pregnancies don't reach term, or the foals don't reach adulthood. Like mules, zorses can be either male or female, but they remain sterile. This curious animal is of recent invention. There are few in Europe, whereas there are a larger number of them in the United States. This is why zorses are often the issue of American Quarter Horse mares. Americans also cross zebras and female donkeys (zonkey).

**Character and attributes**: Reputed to be very intelligent, from the zebra it has endurance, resilience, and speed, but also a certain wildness and wariness, and a strong personality. It is also a good jumper.

**Uses**: It is much more difficult to ride than a horse, and only equestrian experts can turn it into a mount. It is used mainly for various shows. Furthermore, a saddle doesn't stay on its back very easily, due to its build and its silky hide.

**Current status**: Although it arouses interest in the United States as a curiosity (there are more than 300 animals), its presence remains unconfirmed elsewhere in the world.

# Mule

**Ⓗ** Larger than a donkey, depending on the breed of the parents.

**Ⓒ** Often bay or mealy black, but different coats are possible.

**Description**: Larger and thinner than a donkey, more robust than a horse, the mule has a long head; prominent eye sockets; longer ears than those of its mother, but smaller than those of its father. The tail and mane (most often bristly) have more hair than the donkey's, but less than the mare.

**Distribution**: Throughout the world.

**Origins and history**: This is a sterile hybrid from the cross between a domestic donkey and a mare. Before the advent of motorized vehicles, mules were commonly used throughout the world. The hybrid from the reverse crossing—between a horse and a female donkey—is called a hinny. People didn't usually try to breed them because it has fewer useful attributes than a mule.

**Character and attributes**: It is not always known for its good temperament, even though in reality it is rather approachable and patient. It has great endurance, and a large capacity for work. It is strong, resilient, robust, and calm, with very sure footing.

**Uses**: It is traditionally an excellent pack animal, but some ride or drive it. It is increasingly popular among equestrian trekkers.

**Current status**: The mule has been in existence for a relatively long time and is highly appreciated as a work animal. The overall world population is much smaller now, except in some developing countries where it is still widespread.

Large, rounded ears.

More or less obvious stripes
over the entire body

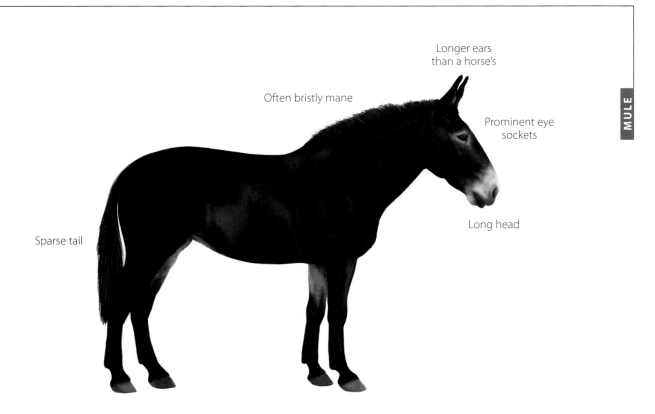

Longer ears
than a horse's

Often bristly mane

Prominent eye
sockets

Long head

Sparse tail

# Horses of Northern Europe

*One finds an extremely large number of horses on the European continent. Europe alone encompasses half the breeds on the planet! And in fact, North and South American breeds descend from European horses that were imported by European colonists. As for Northern Europe, it holds some of the most ancient breeds in the world: Icelandic horses and those from the Faroe Islands, the Shetland Pony, the Exmoor, and the Fjord, among others. But it is also in that region, and more precisely in England, that one of the most influential breeds of the past three centuries emerged: the incomparable Thoroughbred, prized for its unequaled speed. The British, pioneers in research in genetic diversity and creators of renowned domestic animal breeds since the end of the eighteenth century (cows, dogs, farm animals, and so forth), also possess aesthetically spectacular breeds of horses, among them the Hackney, Shire, and Clydesdale. In Northern Europe one finds many of the world's most popular and sought-after breeds of horses.*

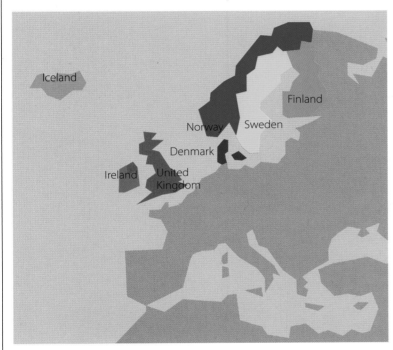

### Iceland
Icelandic

### United Kingdom
Miniature Toy Horse
Shetland Pony
Dartmoor Pony
Exmoor Pony
British Riding Pony (also Riding Pony)
New Forest Pony
Lundy Pony
Eriskay Pony
Fell Pony
Highland Pony
Dales Pony
Welsh Mountain Pony, Welsh Pony, Welsh Pony of Cob Type, Welsh Cob
British Appaloosa and British Spotted Pony
Hackney and Hackney Pony
Thoroughbred
British Warmblood
Cleveland Bay
Suffolk Punch
Clydesdale
Shire
English Hack (also Show Hack)
Gypsy Cob
Drum Horse

### Ireland
Kerry Bog Pony (also Hobby Pony, Irish Hobby)
Connemara
Irish Hunter
Irish Cob
Irish Draft

### Norway
Northlands Horse (also Northlands Pony, or Lyngen Pony, Lyngshest)
Fjord (also Vestland, West Norwegian)
Døle

### Denmark
Faroe Islands Pony (also Faroe Islands Horse)
Knabstrup
Frederiksborg
Danish Warmblood
Jutland
Danish Sport Pony
Danish Oldenburg
Danish Trotter

### Sweden
Gotland
Swedish Warmblood (also Swedish Halfbred)
North Swedish Horse
Swedish Ardennes
Swedish Riding Pony
North Swedish Trotter (also Coldblooded Trotter)

### Finland
Finnhorse (also Finnish Universal)
Finnish Warmblood

From Scotland, the Highland Pony is calm and robust.

Opposite: Young Icelandic horse, Iceland. The breed comes in a wide variety of colors.

# Iceland

Iceland has only one breed of horse, but what a breed it is! The Icelandic is one of the most amazing horses in the world, with its incredible variety of colors and its five gaits. Iceland has developed its own equestrian culture, and a specific saddle for it. The horse plays a major role in Icelandic mythology and its great sagas. Icelandic horses are also bred for their meat,

## ICELANDIC

Icelandic name: *Islenskur hestur*

**H** 1.30 m–1.45 m.

**C** All coat colors and shades are possible: pinto; palomino; black/brown dun; bay dun, etc. Along with the Mongolian horse, this breed has the widest variety of coat colors.

**Description**: It is of primitive type, with a thickset body. It has a large head with a straight profile; large eyes; small ears; short neck; unobtrusive withers; long, sloping shoulders; short back; dished croup; very resilient legs and hooves. The tail is low-set. The hair of the mane and tail is long, very abundant, and thick, often shaggy, with an abundant forelock and often a double mane. The winter coat is very thick.

**Distribution**: Iceland, quite common in Germany and almost everywhere in Northern and Western Europe. A specific variety is found in the United States.

**Origins and history**: Icelandic horses arrived on the island with colonists in the ninth century; its ancestors probably shared blood with the Fjord, Shetland, Highland, or Exmoor. The breed is particularly ancient and pure due to the ban, since 982, on importing new horses into Iceland. The horses that leave Iceland don't return. The Icelandic has thus not undergone any crossing. Today it lives in semi-freedom.

**Character and attributes**: Adapted to an extreme climate, the Icelandic is very resilient and very hardy. Many horses spend the harsh winter outdoors. It is an easy keeper. A very intelligent horse, it is calm and friendly, but independent and energetic. One of the unique characteristics of the Icelandic is its additional gaits, the tölt and the flying amble. It is one of the only gaited horses native to Europe, as European breeders have eliminated this characteristic in many breeds. Not all Icelandics possess the five gaits.

**Uses**: Because of its sure-footedness and its specific particularly comfortable gaits, it is a good, versatile horse for trekking, for endurance, and for leisure. Its good pulling ability makes it an excellent harness horse. Its intermediate size enables it to be ridden by both children and adults. In Iceland, it is still used for transportation, notably to places that are inaccessible in the winter. Maturing late, the breed isn't broken before the age of five. It is very fertile and lives a long time.

**Current status**: A horse with a strong identity, the Icelandic has been introduced successfully into many countries beginning in the twentieth century. There are currently more than 180,000 Icelandics throughout the world.

Icelandic equitation is based on the breed's specific gaits (here, the tölt).

which is traditionally eaten. Due to the ancestral ban on importing horses into Iceland, the Icelandic is the only breed that can be found on the island. Iceland also prohibits the importing of equestrian equipment, for fear that its herds might be decimated by a continental illness. Some Europeans use the term "pony" to describe this small horse, but the term "pony" isn't used in Iceland, just as it isn't in many countries of the world. There are around 80,000 horses in Iceland.

Small ears

Large head

Neck wide at the base

Often shaggy tail

Icelandic saddle

The United Kingdom is a land of horses and horse breeding, and it is no coincidence that its green pastureland feeds some of the most legendary breeds in the world. England produced the famous Thoroughbred, unequaled for speed racing, which

---

# MINIATURE TOY HORSE

**H** Under 0.90 m; around 0.50 m–0.80 m.

**C** There is a great variety in coat color, including bay dun, spotted, and pinto.

**Description:** This is the English miniature horse. It weighs only around 50 kg. It is well proportioned; it has a small head, slender legs, small hooves, and a silky mane and tail.

**Distribution:** England.

**Origins and history:** Miniature animals have long been popular in England, beginning in the sixteenth century, at first to entertain the children of the nobility. The Toy Horse has the same ancestors as the American Miniature, that is, the small Shetland, Gotland, Dartmoor, and Welsh. It is the result of a long selection for size and physical harmony. It is sometimes crossed with the Falabella.

**Character and attributes:** These small animals are intelligent, gentle, and docile, and they learn quickly. They are rustic and live a long time. Among the various miniature horses, the Toy Horse is well adapted to the European climate. It is stronger than the Falabella, although it is often smaller.

**Uses:** It is a pet that has the same specific needs of all horses: a need for space, grass, company, care, maintenance of its hooves, and so on. It is too small to carry a rider other than a very young, light child, though one must still be very careful of its back; but it is sometimes used in exhibitions or shows, with a small, very light cart, or with long reins.

**Current status:** Miniature horses are bred exclusively as pets, so they form a world slightly apart and have very devoted fans. Thus there are very few of them.

---

# SHETLAND PONY

**H** 0.86 m–1.07 m; under 0.86 m they are considered mini-Shetlands (0.68 m–0.86 m).

**C** Often chestnut, bay, black, and pinto; all coats except spotted.

**Description:** This is one of the smallest breeds in the world, with such a particular look that it can't be confused with any other breed. Its body is completely rounded. Its head is of average size; it has very small ears; large eyes; a wide forehead. The neck is short and wide at the base. It has a short back, unobtrusive withers, round barrel, and very powerful croup. The legs are short and solid. The hair of the mane and the tail is abundant, thick, and long, and the forelock is abundant. The winter coat is very thick and very long, giving it the look of a big stuffed animal. It is very popular among children.

**Distribution:** United Kingdom, and throughout the world.

**Origins and history:** As its name indicates, the breed originated in the Shetland and Orkney Islands, off the coast of Scotland. Its origins are largely unknown, but it is extremely ancient, probably the direct descendant of primitive Celtic ponies. Due to its isolation, it has not undergone crossbreeding. Its small size is the result of natural selection in a difficult environment, and of good adaptation to the cold and vegetation that offers little nutrition. Once used for agricultural work and the transportation of algae, the Shetland was also used a lot in mines. The German Classic Pony was developed from the Shetland, and there is also an American Shetland, which is thinner.

**Character and attributes:** The Shetland has a strong, lively, independent nature, and is often stubborn, which doesn't prevent it from being gentle. It has excellent endurance and is powerful for its size, capable of pulling and transporting heavy loads. Its health is good; it lives a long time and can work late in life. Of exceptional rusticity, this hardy pony has a tendency to get fat quickly, which is dangerous for its health. Often sure of itself, and not very impressionable, it is capable of standing up to large horses.

**Uses:** It is the horse par excellence for children, due to its small size. Its potential for kindness outweighs its strong nature. It can also be harnessed. It is often used in circuses or equestrian shows. Although it is almost never ridden by adults today, the inhabitants of the Shetland Islands once rode it.

**Current status:** It is one of the most popular and most widespread breeds in the world.

exists throughout the world. This essential breed has been crossed with countless other breeds in order to improve them. But we also find other famous breeds there, such as the popular Shetland Pony or the charismatic Shire. The British breed horses for sport and recreation, but they don't eat their meat, and are culturally opposed to that practice. There are around 3.5 million riders and trainers in the United Kingdom, or 6 percent of the British population, for a horse population estimated at 988,000.

Silky mane and tail

Small, proportional head

Slender legs

Herds still graze in the Shetland Islands.

Small ears

Powerful croup

Round barrel

Short, solid legs

# Dartmoor Pony

**Ⓗ** 1.14 m–1.27 m; should not exceed 1.27 m.

**Ⓒ** Bay, dark bay, black, gray, chestnut, roan. Pinto is not accepted, and it has few white markings.

**Description**: The Dartmoor Pony has a harmonious physique. It has a lovely, breed-specific little head featuring a long forelock; very small, very alert ears; a balanced and muscular neck; broad chest; slender and solid legs; and small, resilient hooves. The mane and tail are quite thick.

**Distribution**: Great Britain, but also Belgium, France, Netherlands, the United States, Australia, New Zealand.

**Origins and history**: The Dartmoor Pony, an ancient breed from southwestern England, has been regularly crossed with foreign breeds, notably the Arabian.

It has also received Fell and Welsh blood. The Dartmoor has always lived freely in the moors and bogs, which it continues in part to do today. It was once used as a pack pony and also worked in the mines.

**Character and attributes**: The Dartmoor Pony is sweet and sensitive, lives a long time, and has a hardy constitution that makes it easy to keep.

**Uses**: Its small size and easy nature make it a good saddle pony for children. Although it is capable of carrying adults, it is too small for large riders, who can, however, use it in harness. It is also a good jumper.

**Current status**: The breed almost disappeared in the middle of the twentieth century. It is still vulnerable, with only 850 horses living in semi-freedom, for a global population of fewer than 5,000.

---

# Exmoor Pony

**Ⓗ** Starting at 1.16 m; up to 1.30 m for males, and 1.27 m for mares.

**Ⓒ** Mealy bay, dark mealy bay, buckskin. No white markings. The mealy coat is often very evident and very characteristic, with a very light muzzle, stomach, and lighter hair on the inner thighs, whereas the bottom of the legs are often black. These nuances are even more visible on the long winter coat.

**Description**: This is a small, primitive horse, stocky, with a characteristic look. Its head has a wide forehead and small ears. One of its unique characteristics is its eyes, whose protruding, thick eyelids, called "toad-like," protect the cornea from rain and wind. Its legs are slender and its hooves are small. The winter coat is particularly thick to protect against harsh weather; it has a thick mane and tail. The fan-shaped tail protects against the rain.

**Distribution**: Great Britain, the United States, Canada.

**Origins and history**: The Exmoor Pony is an extremely ancient breed, a direct descendant of its primitive ancestors that hasn't undergone any crossing. Thus it is a very pure breed. It has always lived in freedom, in a difficult environment that forged the breed. A few free-range herds still exist today.

**Character and attributes**: The Exmoor Pony is intelligent and independent, with a strong personality, though it is also docile. It is solid, has good endurance, is resilient, and is a good jumper. Its health is good, and it lives a long time.

**Uses**: Although this solid little horse can carry an adult, it is above all used as a mount for children. It is very good for driving and also for endurance riding.

**Current status**: It flirted with extinction during World War II. Since then, the breed has been protected, though it remains very rare, with around 800 animals in the world.

Pony games are one of the many disciplines in which the Exmoor Pony excels.

Very small ears

Slender, resilient legs

Small hooves

Characteristically thick
eyelids, called "toad-like"

Nose, barrel, and inner
thighs clearly lighter
than the rest of the coat

Slender legs

# BRITISH RIDING PONY

Also called: Riding Pony

Acronym: RP

**H** 1.15 m–1.44 m.

**C** All coat colors except pinto; usually bay and chestnut. White markings on the head and legs are fairly frequent.

**Description**: The British Riding Pony resembles a small Thoroughbred. Its head is small, with a straight profile; small ears; and eyes spaced rather far apart. It has a long neck, prominent withers, and a rounded croup. There are two types: the Show Pony and the Show Hunter Pony.

**Distribution**: Great Britain, Australia, New Zealand.

**Origins and history**: The British Riding Pony is a recent breed, still being developed. It is the equivalent of the Hack, but smaller. The goal of breeders was to produce a Thoroughbred pony for children, and so British Riding Ponies essentially originated from small Thoroughbreds and Arabians, crossed with English ponies such as Welsh, Dartmoor, and sometimes New Forest. The French Riding Pony is a somewhat better built version of this type of sport pony.

**Character and attributes**: The British Riding Pony is nervous, energetic, and a good jumper; it is used in sporting activities in general.

**Uses**: It is better suited for experienced young riders who wish to compete or show. Larger animals can be ridden by adults.

**Current status**: The breed is doing well; it is popular in the United Kingdom and bred just about everywhere in the world.

# NEW FOREST PONY

**H** 1.20 m–1.48 m, but most are in the upper height range.

**C** All coat colors; often bay, gray, except pinto and cream with blue eyes.

**Description**: The New Forest Pony is harmonious and well proportioned. It has a nice head with a rather wide forehead and a straight profile; a rather long neck; broad chest; long back; and slender but robust legs. The mane and tail are thick.

The agility of the New Forest Pony is fully revealed in horseball matches.

**Distribution**: Great Britain, France, Europe, the United States, Canada, Australia.

**Origins and History**: The New Forest Pony is the result of much crossing among its ancestors, Celtic ponies from Great Britain, and various breeds: Arabian, Barb, Thoroughbred, Dartmoor, Exmoor, Dales, Fell, Welsh, Highland, and Hackney. New Forest Ponies have lived freely in the English region of the same name for centuries. They were found there in the eleventh century. Large herds continue to live there in the wild.

**Character and attributes**: The New Forest Pony is rustic and has a very easygoing nature: it is docile, calm, intelligent, agile, and fast. It is a good jumper.

**Uses**: It is a good little saddle horse for adults and children, often used in riding schools for its great versatility, or as a family mount. It does well in show jumping competitions, but also in dressage, eventing, polo, and driving. It is a good trekking horse, and it has done well in equitherapy.

**Current status**: The New Forest Pony's status is worrisome because in the UK the breed has recently seen a dramatic decline in its population in a very short amount of time. Only 423 foals were born in 2012, with fewer than 3,000 broodmares and 10 stallions in 2014. There are breed farms, however, elsewhere in the world.

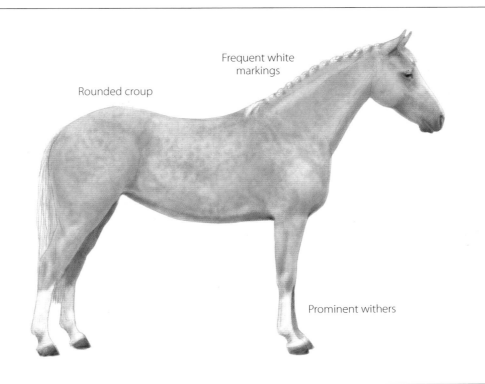

Frequent white markings

Rounded croup

Prominent withers

Refined head with wide forehead

Powerful hindquarters

Broad chest

**UNITED KINGDOM**

# LUNDY PONY

**Ⓗ** Rarely over 1.34 m.

**Ⓒ** Most often bay dun, sometimes dark bay, chestnut, palomino, roan.

**Description**: This is a small, compact breed. The head has a wide forehead and large eyes. It has a muscular neck, broad chest, solid back, and short legs. The mane and tail are thick.

**Distribution**: Lundy Island, England.

**Origins and history**: This island population has been recognized as a breed since 1928. The horses that live on Lundy Island, off the west coast of England, are the result of crossings between New Forest Pony mares and Arabian stallions, with some Welsh and Connemara blood added. They are the result of an attempt to create a new breed at the beginning of the twentieth century. They live outdoors all year long.

**Character and attributes**: The Lundy Pony has an easygoing nature. Bred in a harsh environment, it is particularly adapted to bad weather and survives on a poor diet. It has good endurance and is a good jumper.

**Uses**: Versatile, it is used in various sports, such as obstacle jumping, and is well liked among young riders.

**Current status**: The breed remains very rare.

**UNITED KINGDOM**

# ERISKAY PONY

**Ⓗ** 1.24 m–1.38 m.

**Ⓒ** Different varieties of gray; foals are born dark. Very rarely black or bay.

**Description**: The Eriskay Pony greatly resembles the Exmoor. It has a large head with a straight profile and a wide forehead, muscular neck, slightly sloping croup, and slender legs with small hooves. The winter coat is very thick and impermeable. Its thick mane and tail also offer it protection against bad weather.

**Distribution**: Eriskay Island, Scotland.

**Origins and history**: Because it is so difficult to reach the island, the Eriskay Pony is a breed that is as rare as it is pure, the descendant of ancient Celtic ponies. There is still a small number of them on Eriskay Island, off the coast of Scotland. The breed was saved from extinction in the 1970s. A few animals also live freely on Holy Island.

**Character and attributes**: The Eriskay Pony has a balanced, calm, and agreeable nature, with comfortable gaits. It is resilient and adapted to rigorous climate conditions. It is very strong for its size and has great endurance.

**Uses**: It is a good mount for children, is versatile, and can also be driven.

**Current status**: This is a very rare and threatened breed, with only 420 animals in existence. Its numbers are increasing, however, thanks to the work of protectors of the breed.

Solid back

Large eyes

Muscular neck

Thick mane and tail

Slightly sloping croup

Slender legs

Small hooves

# FELL PONY

**H** 1.32 m–1.42 m.

**C** Usually black, more rarely bay, dark bay, gray; without white markings except sometimes a white star on the forehead.

**Description**: Very similar to the Dales, the Fell looks like a smaller Friesian. It has the physique of a light draft horse. Its head, with a wide forehead, is straight and long; it narrows at the nose, and it has small ears and prominent eyes. Its neck is set high; its shoulders are long and sloping; it has a rather long back and muscular legs with bluish feathering and hooves. The mane and tail are long and thick, often wavy.

**Distribution**: England, Germany, Netherlands, the United States, Canada, New Zealand.

**Origins and history**: Resembling the Dales, the Fell also descends from ancient horses of northern England, the Pennine Pony, which disappeared a long time ago. The Fell is the result of crossing among those ponies and horses brought over by the Romans and Friesians. It also received blood from the Galloway, also an extinct breed. Fells were used for agricultural work and as pack horses, but also in mines. Herds are still bred free-range.

**Character and attributes**: The Fell is agile, intelligent, determined, easy to train, and friendly. It is known for its pleasant gaits, notably its trot, and its beautiful strides. It is robust and strong.

**Uses**: Versatile, it is suitable for adults and children for riding, driving, pack-carrying, and trekking. It is also traditionally used for herding sheep.

**Current status**: With around 8,000 horses worldwide, the breed remains small in number.

---

# HIGHLAND PONY

**H** Most often between 1.32 m and 1.48 m.

**C** Many varieties of black/brown dun and bay dun, often with zebra markings and dorsal stripes; gray, bay, dark bay, black, sometimes silver bay with silvery mane and tail, but never with white markings.

**Description**: Of average size and primarily rustic, the Highland is recognized by its thick neck, wide at the base; a massive body; strong legs; wide hooves; and feathering that goes high up on the leg with long hair inside the legs. It has a short head with small ears and a wide nose. The chest is broad, the back short, the croup powerful. The winter coat has a dense undercoat that enables it to endure harsh weather. Its mane and tail are very long and thick.

**Distribution**: Great Britain, notably Scotland; a small number in France, Belgium, the Netherlands, Germany, Poland, Australia, the United States, and Canada.

**Origins and history**: This is a very ancient Scottish breed, the descendant of primitive local horses, which received Percheron, Clydesdale, Spanish, Barb, and Arabian blood at some moment in its history. The Hebrides Islands (Rum, Skye, Uist, Barra, Harris, Mull, Islay) have herds of Highlands, slightly different types, including the Rum Island Pony. The Highland Pony was traditionally used for farm work and for stag hunting.

**Character and attributes**: The Highland Pony is known for its particularly calm and gentle nature. It is powerful and very robust, born to live outdoors. It quickly gains weight if its feed is too rich.

**Uses**: This is a good family horse, versatile and very loyal, which can carry both adults and children. It is used for riding, driving, trekking, pack-carrying, and equitherapy, and also for logging.

**Current status**: There are around 5,500 horses in existence. Although small in number, the breed is increasingly popular.

Sturdy and calm, the Highland Pony is a good horse for vaulting.

Slender nose

High-set neck

Often wavy mane and tail

Bluish-colored hooves

Long, thick mane and tail

Short, wide head

Powerful croup

Thick neck, wide at the base

Long hair on the inner legs, above the feathering

# DALES PONY

**H** 1.42 m–1.47 m.

**C** Predominantly black, sometimes bay, dark bay, gray, more rarely roan. It rarely has white markings.

**Description**: It looks like a smaller version of the Friesian, but also like the Welsh Cob. It exudes power. It has a small head and wide forehead, with small ears. Its back is long and its croup powerful. The hooves are very hard, with feathering. The thick hair of the mane and tail is slightly wavy.

**Distribution**: Great Britain; United States.

**Origins and history**: The Dales is a close cousin of the Fell, with which it shares common origins. It descends from very ancient crossings among Friesians from the Netherlands and small local horses. It was also crossed with the Welsh Cob, Norfolk Punch, and Clydesdale in the eighteenth and nineteenth centuries. It was used for a long time as a pack horse due to its ability to carry heavy loads, as well as in mines and for farm work.

**Character and attributes**: The Dales is intelligent and gentle. It is a good trotter, energetic and fast. It is very resilient and sure-footed.

**Uses**: The Dales is an excellent carriage and trekking horse, or even a pack horse. Its intermediate size and its robustness make it a particularly popular mount for both children and adults.

**Current status**: The breed was close to extinction after World War II. It remains small in number.

---

# WELSH MOUNTAIN PONY

Also called: Welsh Pony, Welsh Pony of Cob Type, Welsh Cob

**H** Section A: Welsh Mountain Pony, up to 1.22 m.
Section B: Welsh Pony, up to 1.37 m.
Section C: Welsh Pony of Cob Type, 1.37 m.
Section D: Welsh Cob, above 1.37 m.

**C** All basic colors, gray, liver chestnut, except pinto and spotted.

**Description:** The four Welsh types all have a nice head (concave, evoking the Arabian for the Welsh Mountain Pony and the Welsh Pony, but with a Spanish influence for sections C and D); large, well-spaced eyes; small ears; long neck; high-set tail; and solid legs. The thick mane and tail are often slightly wavy. The Welsh Pony of Cob Type is more robust, and the Welsh Cob is more robust and taller.

**Distribution:** Great Britain, Europe, North America. One finds Welsh herds throughout the world, because the breed has been widely exported.

**Origins and history:** Originally from Wales, the Welsh Pony breed is divided into four sections, managed in the same studbook. They are the result of crossings of Celtic ponies with Arabians. The oldest is the Welsh Mountain Pony, which looks a lot like the Arabian and has given birth to other Welsh types. The Section B Welsh Pony is a bit taller and more slender. Sections C and D have been crossed more, receiving blood from Spanish horses, and from the Yorkshire Coach horse, the Norfolk Trotter, and the Hackney. There is a Welsh K partbred registry in France for horses with at least 12.5 percent Welsh blood.

**Character and attributes:** These are excellent mounts. Welsh Ponies are rather lively and energetic, but also very gentle and intelligent. They are solid and agile, with lovely gaits, notably a wonderful trot. They are also good jumpers.

**Uses:** All Welsh types can be used as saddle horses, for competition or driving, for children and adults, depending on their size. They are also good trekking horses.

**Current status:** The Welsh Mountain Pony and the Welsh Pony are very popular among children. The rarest is the Welsh Pony of Cob Type (Section C), which was even threatened, but whose numbers have risen. The Welsh Cob is doing very well.

Slightly wavy mane and tail

Silky feathering

Head resembling an Arabian

Welsh Pony (section B)

It is more robust than the first two.

Welsh Pony of Cob Type (section C)

This is the largest and sturdiest. Solid legs with very good joints.

Welsh Cob (section D)

Small ears

Often concave face

Often slightly wavy mane and tail

High-set tail

Welsh Mountain Pony (section A)

# BRITISH APPALOOSA AND BRITISH SPOTTED PONY

**H** Over 1.47 m for the British Appaloosa; between 0.81 m and 1.47 m for the British Spotted Pony.

**C** Always spotted, with white sclera, spotted skin, and striated hooves.

**Description**: The British Spotted Pony is robust, with large eyes, small ears, and a fairly thick mane and tail. For the British Appaloosa, there are various types. The mane and tail are less abundant.

**Distribution**: England.

**Origins and history:** These two breeds, which we are listing together due to their common history and their recent separation, are often confused with the American Appaloosa, although they are indeed European and do not descend from that breed. Spotted horses have existed in Europe for centuries, notably in Spain, as can be seen in old paintings. The registry of British Spotted Ponies has existed since 1946. In 1976 the British

Spotted Horse took on the American name and became the British Appaloosa for commercial reasons. The two breeds, once managed together, were then divided. The British Appaloosa received Knabstrup blood, but also American Appaloosa blood from imported horses. The breed is still undergoing selection.

**Character and attributes**: Both breeds have a good nature and are cooperative. They are rustic.

**Uses**: They are good saddle horses and good recreational horses, one being a good mount for children, and the other better for larger riders.

**Current status**: The British Spotted Pony is fairly rare, with only 800 animals remaining. The British Appaloosa registry is being developed.

British Spotted Pony

# HACKNEY AND HACKNEY PONY

**H** 1.47 m–1.68 m for the horse; between 1.20 m and 1.47 m for the pony.

**C** Bay, dark bay, black, chestnut; frequently with white markings on the head and legs.

**Description**: This breed has a very distinctive look. It has a small head with an often lightly convex profile, wide forehead, nice ears, and a lively gaze. It has a long, slightly arched neck; short back; long croup; and a very high-set tail, which is often cropped very short. The legs are slender. The Hackney is recognized notably by its particular position when it stops, with the posterior legs extended backward, which makes it easy to identify. There are five different types of Hackney Pony.

**Distribution**: Great Britain, the United States for the two breeds; Canada, Argentina, South Africa, and Australia for the horse.

**Origins and history**: The Hackney should not be confused with the Hack. The latter is a type, whereas

the Hackney is a true, ancient breed. Although the Hackney and the Hackney Pony have been divided into two distinct breeds, we list them together, as they are registered in the same studbook. Having as ancestors the Norfolk and the Yorkshire Carriage and various trotters, it has also had an influence on several other breeds. In the beginning the Hackney was bred to provide panache and prestige to the carriages that it pulled. The Hackney Pony received Fell and Welsh blood.

**Character and attributes**: Full of vim and vigor, the Hackney is a horse for experienced riders. It is known for its spectacular, very stunning, high-stepping trot, and its way of projecting its front legs forward. It combines speed, elegance, and appearance.

**Uses**: It is a specialized breed, exhibited in horse shows and perfect for driving.

**Current status**: Competing with the automobile, the Hackney almost disappeared. The breed remains quite rare, with only 150 broodmares in the United Kingdom in 2012 and very small numbers elsewhere in the world. There are also very few Hackney Ponies.

British Appaloosa

Characteristic spotted coat

Striated hooves

Very high-set tail, carried with flair

High, arched neck

The Hackney Pony has the same wonderful trot characteristic of the Hackney Horse.

# THOROUGHBRED

**H** 1.57 m–1.73 m; on average, 1.65 m.

**C** Usually bay or dark bay, often chestnut, sometimes black or gray; some roan and palomino lineages in the United States, a few white lineages; white markings on the legs and head are frequent.

**Description**: Although selected not for its physical appearance but for its athletic performance, the Thoroughbred is a beautiful horse, tall, slender, elegant, and harmonious. It has a small, expressive head, with a straight profile; ears of average size; large, alert eyes; wide nostrils; and thin lips. It has a long, slender neck; prominent withers; a deep chest; long, sloping shoulders; a rather short or long back depending on the individual, a sloping and muscular croup, and a high-set tail. The muscular legs are long and slender. The small hooves must be hard, but they are fragile in some individuals. The skin is so fine that one can see surface veins. The coat is very soft and fine; the mane and tail are fine, silky, straight, and flat, and the mane and tail are neither thick nor very long. This description corresponds to the sprinter type. The stayer type is cleaner and finer, has a shorter back, a more horizontal croup, and a straighter shoulder. A third type of Thoroughbred, the middle distance runner, is between the other two.

**Distribution**: Thoroughbreds are found throughout the world, with large breeding farms in Great Britain, Ireland, France, Italy, the United States, Australia, New Zealand, and Japan.

**Origins and history**: This breed has been selected for its speed. Developed in the eighteenth century, its ancestors were stallions from the East, including three

There are Thoroughbred lineages in which palominos, roans, whites, and even a few pintos appear, although they are very rare.

founders—the Byerley Turk (perhaps an Akhal-Teke or a Turkoman), the Darley Arabian (Arabian from Syria), and the Godolphin Arabian (Barb or Arabian-Barb)—and English racing mares selected and improved with Eastern blood. Since its creation, it has not undergone any crossing and is bred with pure blood. Among the modern breeds, the Thoroughbred has had the greatest impact. Its creation was a turning point in global equestrian history. The breed has been used to improve a great number of other breeds. Horse racing has also definitively changed, as no horse is as fast as a Thoroughbred in speed races. It is, however, surpassed by other breeds, such as the Arabian, in endurance races.

**Character and attributes**: This is a delicate, nervous, spirited, sometimes unstable horse because it is bred for its athletic performance and not its character. It is energetic, athletic, brave, and very fast. Sensitive, it doesn't like cold and humidity, heat or insects, but in spite of this lack of rusticity it has adapted to the different climates of the world where it is bred. It needs to be well fed. It is a horse that demands time and very attentive care. It is sometimes reputed to be fragile, but its health problems are often related to intense work started at an extremely young age, when an animal has not yet stopped growing.

**Uses**: This is not a horse to entrust to beginners, due to its nervous nature and its physical power. It needs an experienced rider. It can in fact easily reach 60 km/h at a gallop, so it is best to be able to control it. Horses that no longer race must then be well trained so that there is no risk that they will take their rider off on a wild gallop. Its primary vocation is speed racing, on the flat and over hurdles, but it also excels in obstacle jumping and eventing.

**Current status**: The breed is one of the most widespread in the world, with millions of horses and more than 118,000 births every year.

At auctions, yearlings can be bought for astonishing sums.

The favored discipline of the Thoroughbred is the flat race (gallop).

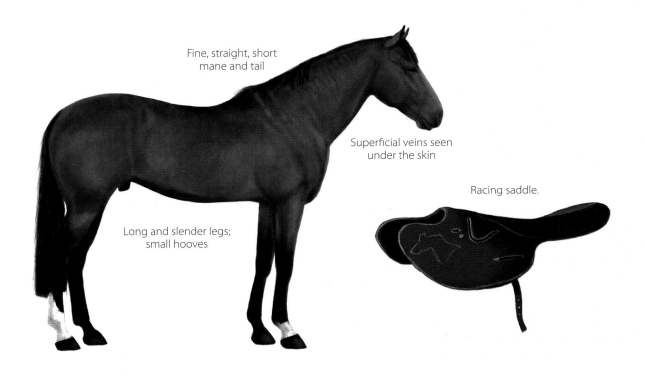

Fine, straight, short mane and tail

Superficial veins seen under the skin

Racing saddle.

Long and slender legs; small hooves

On the left, the stayer type (leaner, more slender); on the right, the sprinter type (more muscular, taller).

# BRITISH WARMBLOOD

ⓗ 1.55 m to 1.70 m.

ⓒ Mainly bay, dark bay, chestnut, black.

**Description**: Due to multiple crossings, the type is not set, and it is difficult to distinguish it from other sport horses from which it has issued. It is a large horse with long legs, an average neck, a deep chest, and prominent withers.

**Distribution**: United Kingdom.

**Origins and history**: This is a breed of very recent creation, not yet established, whose registry dates from 1977. It has a large amount of Thoroughbred blood and combines many European sport horse lines, notably those of the German Hanoverian and Trakehner, and remains open to foreign contributions and crossbreeding. Given the rise of sport disciplines such as dressage and show jumping, the British decided in turn to create a horse perfectly adapted to them. The selection criteria are very strict.

**Character and attributes**: This is a strong and athletic horse, with a good temperament.

**Uses**: This very athletic horse is used primarily for dressage competitions and show jumping.

**Current status**: It is increasingly popular.

# CLEVELAND BAY

ⓗ 1.62 m–around 1.65 m.

ⓒ Always bay, without white markings. Only a small star is acceptable. It is often dappled bay. The breed has the unique characteristic of having some gray hair blended with black.

**Description**: This is a large carriage-horse type, with a convex, rather large head; large ears; and large eyes with a sweet gaze. Its neck is long; it has unobtrusive withers, strong shoulders, and a long back. The legs are rather short, with solid, bluish hooves.

**Distribution**: Great Britain.

**Origins and history**: This horse, which originated in Cleveland (Yorkshire), has been influenced by Spanish and Eastern blood, then later by the Thoroughbred. It is one of the oldest English breeds, and its ancestors were known in the Middle Ages, under the name of Chapman. The registry was officially created in 1884. The Cleveland Bay has had an influence on many other European breeds, such as the Holstein and the Hanoverian, and has perhaps been used for crossbreeding with the Thoroughbred to produce competition horses of the hunter type.

**Character and attributes**: The Cleveland Bay is intelligent, placid, and loyal, but sometimes stubborn if not treated well. It is powerful, has endurance, and is vigorous. Its good health enables it to live longer than the average horse.

**Uses**: Versatile, it is popular for riding, driving, and even pulling royal carriages. It is also used in dressage, and for show jumping due to its jumping ability.

**Current status**: It is surprising to note that such a beautiful breed, one so emblematic of Great Britain, is threatened. The Cleveland Bay's population is very small, with only around 550 animals, but its numbers are increasing. The queen of England uses these horses regularly and is their most famous protector.

The Cleveland Bay is regularly seen pulling royal carriages, richly decked out.

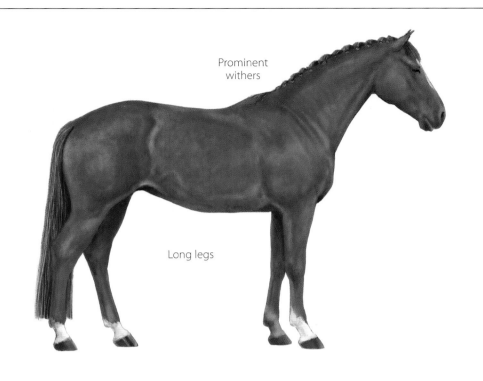

Prominent withers

Long legs

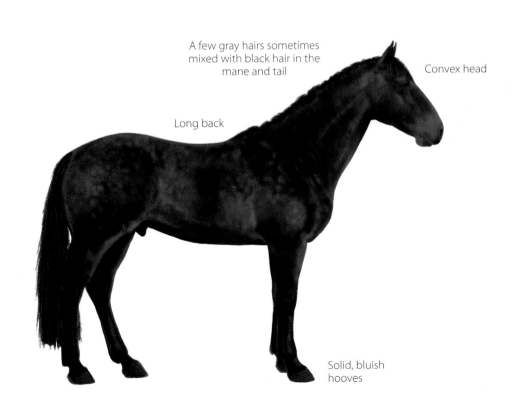

A few gray hairs sometimes mixed with black hair in the mane and tail

Convex head

Long back

Solid, bluish hooves

# Suffolk Punch

**H** 1.65 m–1.78 m.

**C** Always chestnut, with all its variants, without white markings. However, the coat can become lighter towards the bottom of the legs.

**Description**: This large, compact horse can weigh up to a ton. It has a head with a straight profile and a wide forehead; short neck, wide at the base; short back; round, muscular croup; short legs, without feathering; healthy, very hard hooves. The absence of feathering was an advantage for working in fields with damp, clay soil.

**Distribution**: England, the United States, with a small number in Australia and New Zealand and a small herd in Pakistan.

**Origins and history**: The descendant of the "great horses"—the great English chargers of the Middle Ages—and of a foundation chestnut stallion born in 1768, the Suffolk Punch is the most ancient British draft breed. It was used a lot for urban transportation and farm work. The American lineages received a small contribution of Belgian draft blood in the 1970s, and are not listed in the British registry.

**Character and attributes**: This draft horse is calm and confident, resilient and easygoing. It has good health and lives a long time. These are precocious horses, sometimes put to work at the age of two.

**Uses**: This is a powerful carriage horse.

**Current status**: In the 1970s the breed was threatened with extinction, due to competition with the tractor. Its situation is better today, as its numbers are being watched, but it remains threatened, with fewer than 2,000 animals in the world (1,200 in North America, 440–450 in Great Britain, a dozen in Australia and New Zealand).

# Clydesdale

**H** 1.62 m–1.83 m; average of 1.70 m.

**C** Most often bay, dark bay, less often black, roan, chestnut, or gray, with large markings on the legs and barrel, sometimes spotted with white. The head almost always has a large white blaze.

**Description**: This large draft horse can weigh up to a ton. Its appearance is so characteristic that it can only possibly be confused with the Shire. It has a head with a wide forehead, a straight or slightly convex profile, and large ears. It has a thick and rather long high-set neck, sloping shoulders, and a thick body with a short back and powerful hindquarters. Its legs are longer than those of other draft breeds, which gives it its height. Its wide, rather flat hooves are covered with silky feathering.

**Distribution**: Scotland, England. The breed is also bred in Ireland, the United States, Canada, Australia, and New Zealand.

**Origins and history**: The Clydesdale's origins are very old, even if the breed didn't have a studbook until 1878. Scottish mares were crossed with Flemish and Friesian stallions, then, in the nineteenth century, with Shires. The Clydesdale was once used on farms for agricultural work. It was exported to Australia, where it had an important role in that country's development.

**Character and attributes**: This is a calm and gentle horse, but also a dynamic one. It is very powerful. It is a rustic horse, easily kept. Its corpulence does not prevent it from having quick movements and lovely gaits, and the ability to move rapidly.

**Uses**: This is a carriage horse. It is sometimes used in pulling competitions. It is often used to maintain green spaces in Scotland. [And American readers are well acquainted with the famous Budweiser Clydesdales! – trans.]

**Current status**: Very threatened in the 1970s, the breed is doing better today, enjoying true popularity, but it remains small in number even though it is bred in several countries throughout the world. There are around 700 broodmares and 100 stallions in the United Kingdom.

Neck wide
at the base

Round, muscular croup

Short legs

The coat shows large
white markings

Wide head

Even Clydesdale foals exude power.

Long legs

Abundant, silky
feathering

# SHIRE

**H** Mares grow to a minimum of 1.63 m, males 1.73 m, with an average of 1.80 m. This is the tallest horse in the world, with height records of up to 2 m.

**C** Bay, dark bay, chestnut, black, gray, with large white markings on the head and legs, and often dappling.

**Description**: The Shire is a draft horse so distinctive that it is recognized immediately. Only its close cousin, the Clydesdale, resembles it. A giant in the equine world, it often weighs more than a ton. It is a harmonious and elegant draft horse with a muscular body. The head is slightly convex and elongated; it has large eyes; long ears; and a wide forehead. It sometimes has a mustache on its lip. The neck is long, the shoulders sloping, the chest wide, the back short, and the hindquarters powerful, with a rounded and sloping croup; the legs are long. The mane and tail are long. It also has thick, silky, straight feathering that goes far up the legs, and wide hooves.

**Distribution**: Great Britain, the Netherlands, France, Germany, the United States, Canada, and Australia.

**Origins and history**: This is one of the most legendary of English breeds, due to its beauty and its charisma. It is the descendant of the "great horses," the English chargers of the Middle Ages, but the breed, although old, was not really established until the nineteenth century.

**Character and attributes**: This is a particularly gentle and patient horse, an agile and powerful draft animal. It has a long life expectancy.

**Uses**: It excels in pulling carriages, but is sometimes ridden. It is today still employed by some distilleries to deliver beer, its presence always encountering great success, useful in terms of publicity.

**Current status**: Although it is the most widespread English draft horse, its numbers are still low and should be watched. There are around 3,500 Shires in Great Britain and 1,800 broodmares.

---

# ENGLISH HACK

Also called: Show Hack

**H** 1.47 m–1.60 m.

**C** Basic colors, with limited markings.

**Description**: This horse is light and elegant, necessarily refined, very noble and very beautiful, with perfect bone structure. It has a small head, long neck, prominent withers, short back, and slender legs. The Hack type is divided into three categories: Large Hack (1.52 m–1.60 m), Small Hack (1.47 m–1.52 m), and Ladies Hack (1.47 m–1.60 m).

**Distribution**: Great Britain, Ireland, the United States, Canada.

**Origins and history**: The Hack is not a breed, but a type. It still deserves to be mentioned due to its importance in Great Britain. It is the result of crossings, notably of Thoroughbred and Anglo-Arabian, sometimes with ponies. It can also be a beautiful and light post-racing Thoroughbred. It is not to be confused with the Hackney breed.

**Character and attributes**: The Hack has beautiful, high-stepping gaits and is comfortable to ride.

**Uses**: It is principally used for show competitions, in which it must be perfectly trained and present beautiful conformation and gaits.

**Current status**: It can be easily produced since it is the result of crossings among very common breeds.

---

# GYPSY COB

The Gypsy Cob is the English equivalent of the Irish Cob (see *p. 58*), a breed whose origins are little known, since it involves unregistered horses, bred within the oral traditions of Gypsies and poor English and Irish peasants. The Gypsy Cob is the result of crossings of various horses recovered by Gypsies, coming from the Shire, Clydesdale, Fell, Welsh, or Dales breeds. The Irish and Gypsy Cobs have different studbooks, which are often intermixed and are regularly the subject of debates, as these horses have only been recognized for a short amount of time. They are currently similar in their very characteristic physique, their history, and their uses. They will perhaps be more dissociated in the future, as their breeding evolves, or, on the contrary, perhaps they will be completely merged together.

Long neck

Long legs for a draft horse

Silky, very thick feathering that goes up high on the legs

One of the traditional roles of the imposing Shire is to transport beer to certain English pubs.

UNITED KINGDOM

# DRUM HORSE

**H** 1.62 m on average.

**C** It is often pinto.

**Description**: This is a large, athletic, and muscular horse. Its head has a wide forehead; it has a long neck and a broad chest. Its mane and tail and its feathering are abundant and can be straight or wavy.

**Distribution**: Great Britain, the United States.

**Origins and history**: Crossbreeding between Shires or Clydesdales and Gypsy Cobs (Irish Cobs) created the Drum Horse, which, as its name suggests, transports drums for the Queen's Guard. The breed is still being created, with breeders combining the best of the Shire, Clydesdale, and Gypsy Cob to obtain a new breed of draft horse.

**Character and attributes**: This is a very calm and very powerful horse, which has inherited the qualities of the Gypsy Cob, Shire, and Clydesdale.

**Uses**: It can be both ridden and driven.

**Current status**: There are very few of them in the world, and it is very rare to see Drum Horses, whose antecedents are also small in number.

UNITED KINGDOM

### WINDSOR GREY

Despite its lovely name, the Windsor Grey is not a breed. It is the name given to gray carriage horses that pull the carriages of the English royal family. They are selected for their appearance, their color, their height, and their nature. As for the bay-colored horses that pull the royal carriages, those are usually Cleveland Bays.

An equestrian land, Ireland has around 150,000 horses. Among them are approximately 41,000 Thoroughbreds; close to 12,000 Thoroughbred foals are born each year in Ireland, the third largest producer of the breed in the world. Ireland is also the

---

IRELAND

## Kerry Bog Pony

Also called: Hobby Pony, Irish Hobby

Ⓗ 1 m–1.20 m.

Ⓒ Most often bay, but also black, chestnut, gray, black/brown dun, bay dun. A pinto coat is accepted in the United States.

**Description**: Small and compact, the Kerry Bog Pony has a head with a straight or slightly concave profile, small ears, strong neck, muscular legs, and very solid hooves. The mane and tail are abundant. Its winter coat is very thick.

**Distribution**: Ireland, United States.

**Origins and history**: Although this breed is very old, it wasn't officially recognized until 2012. It lived in a semi-wild state in County Kerry and was used to transport peat. Recent DNA analysis shows that it is closer to the Welsh, Shetland, and Icelandic breeds than to other Irish breeds.

**Character and attributes**: The Kerry Bog Pony is intelligent, calm, easygoing, and family-friendly. It is sure-footed. It is robust and has good endurance, being adapted to a humid climate and to marshy land. It doesn't require a lot of attention.

**Uses**: In the past a draft and pack animal, today it is a gentle mount for children or, as a pack horse, a companion for trekking on foot.

**Current status**: The breed was on the brink of extinction and remains in danger. It is still little known. Thanks to conservation efforts today there are more than 380 animals..

---

IRELAND

## Connemara

Ⓗ 1.28 m–1.50 m.

Ⓒ Often gray, but also bay dun, bay, dark bay, black, chestnut, or palomino.

**Description**: The Connemara is well proportioned. It has a small head, average-size neck, and sloping shoulders. Its back is long and straight; the croup is muscular; the legs are rather short and resilient, its feet solid. Its mane and tail are abundant, and its winter coat particularly dense, enabling it to withstand extreme weather very well.

**Distribution**: Ireland, France, and just about everywhere in Europe (notably in England and Germany) and throughout the world.

**Origins and history**: These horses have always lived in the wild in Connemara, where they mixed with the Spanish Jennet (now extinct) and the Arabian. Later, the breed was improved with Thoroughbred, Hackney, Welsh, and even a bit of Clydesdale blood. The horse sense of Irish breeders enabled them to create one of the most widespread breeds in the world. In Ireland herds still live in freedom in Connemara.

**Character and attributes**: The Connemara is intelligent, adaptable, and particularly gentle. Due to its wild origins it is rustic and easygoing, and gets by with very little. It is an athlete with a great deal of energy.

**Uses**: Its size and robustness make it a mount for both children and adults. It is versatile and thus very popular in riding schools; many consider it to be ideal for both recreation and sporting competition. It is an excellent and agile competitor in show jumping, harness racing, and dressage. Being sure-footed, it is also good for trekking. Crossed with Thoroughbreds, it produces unparalleled jumpers.

**Current status**: It is an international, very popular breed.

European country with the highest density of horses per inhabitant. Horses have always been part of Ireland's traditions and folklore; they play a positive and protective role in Celtic tales and legends. The Irish are great enthusiasts of show jumping and cross-country competitions. Equestrian tourism is also well developed there, and the country offers visitors many trekking and equestrian vacation opportunities, some of which include English-language instruction.

Small ears

Sometimes slightly concave profile

Very solid hooves

**KERRY BOG PONY**

Small, delicate ears

Large eyes

Straight profile

Muscular croup

The Connemara is well known for being an excellent jumper.

**CONNEMARA**

# IRISH HUNTER

Also called: Irish Sport Horse (England); Irish Draft Sport Horse (U.S.)

Acronym: ISH

**Ⓗ** On average 1.70 m; may easily reach 1.80 m.

**Ⓒ** Often bay, dark bay, chestnut, gray, black.

**Description**: This is the Irish halfbred. It is distinguished by its height. It has a rather large head with a sometimes convex profile; long and muscular neck; very powerful back; powerful, long and sloped croup; and a low-set tail. Depending on the weight of the riders it can carry, the Irish divide them into heavy hunters (riders over 89 kg), average (from 70 to 89 kg), and light (under 70 kg).

**Distribution**: Ireland, England, and exported throughout the world.

**Origins and history**: Irish Hunters are actually not a breed, but a crossing; however, they have henceforth been recognized as separate and are interbred. In the first generation Irish Hunters are the result of crossings between a Thoroughbred and, usually, an Irish Draft mare, but in the recent past also sometimes a Cleveland Bay or a Clydesdale.

**Character and attributes**: They are intelligent, calm, and very brave; they are fast and have great endurance. It is truly a versatile horse, with a great ability for jumping and long-distance galloping.

**Uses**: Traditionally it was raised and used for hunting. It is also found in show jumping and it excels in eventing, where it wins many medals, cross-country being its specialty. Because of its easygoing nature, it is suitable for a majority of riders.

**Current status**: After the Thoroughbred it is the most widespread breed in Ireland, with more than 7,000 births every year. Hunters are known and are popular throughout the world.

Traveling the countryside and jumping natural obstacles do not frighten the Irish Hunter, which explains its excellent results in cross-country races.

# IRISH COB (IRELAND)

Also called: Gypsy Cob (England)

Other names: Tinker, Vanner, Gypsy Vanner, Gypsy Horse, Traditional Cob; the breed has several different names, which can cause confusion.

**Ⓗ** 1.40 m–1.55 m.

**Ⓒ** Often black pinto, but also various colors of pinto, or a single color with large white markings on the legs.

**Description**: This compact breed has a very characteristic look and is easy to recognize, with its roundness and hair. Its head has large, gentle eyes and a wide forehead. The neck is short, muscular, and high-set; the chest is wide, the shoulders sloping. The back is short and strong, the croup very round. The legs are strong with abundant high feathering, and the hooves are wide. The mane and tail are very abundant, long and thick, often wavy. Some animals have a mustache on their upper lip, which changes with the seasons. The winter coat is long.

**Distribution**: Ireland, England, but also Germany, France, the United States, Australia.

**Origins and history**: The breed has been recognized only very recently; the first studbook dates only from 1998. It is the result of crossings between Irish breeds: Irish Draft, Connemara, Irish Hunter, and Kerry Bog Pony. Poor Irish peasants, called "travelers," would take in horses that no one wanted anymore—for example, pintos or those that were a bit too heavy—and cross them. To that base was added Shire, Clydesdale, Friesian, and Welsh blood. These horses for a long time pulled the caravans of those nomads. A variant of the breed, the Gypsy Cob, exists in England.

**Character and attributes**: It is very peaceful and gentle, steady and loyal. This intelligent horse is also powerful and rustic. It has comfortable gaits.

**Uses**: It is a very good recreational horse for the entire family, good for children and adults. In addition to being ridden, it can be driven and also used for vaulting and in equitherapy.

**Current status**: The breed, discovered by the public, has become increasingly popular in the last few years.

A horse that is often distinguished by its height to its withers

Long, sloping croup

Powerful back

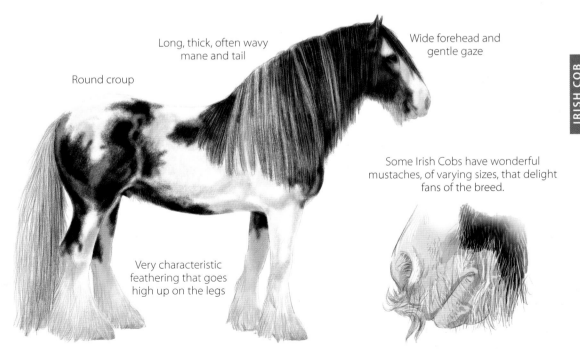

Long, thick, often wavy mane and tail

Round croup

Wide forehead and gentle gaze

Some Irish Cobs have wonderful mustaches, of varying sizes, that delight fans of the breed.

Very characteristic feathering that goes high up on the legs

# IRISH DRAFT

**H** 1.59 m–1.74 m for males; 1.55 m–1.71 m for mares.

**C** Often very light gray, or gray, bay, dark bay, chestnut, rarely black. Pinto coats are unacceptable.

**Description**: This is a fairly heavy, round, well-built horse. It weighs around 750 kg. It has a wide forehead and a straight or slightly convex profile. The neck is sometimes short, often rather thick; it has a broad and deep chest; prominent withers; wide, long back; long, sloping croup; massive legs and wide hooves. The tail is low-set. The hide is soft.

**Distribution**: Ireland.

**Origins and history**: The breed dates from the eighteenth century, when the Irish crossed their mares with Spanish and Eastern horses. It also received Thoroughbred blood. It is frequently used for crossing with Thoroughbreds to produce Irish Hunters, and that rather intensive use has contributed to a dangerous decline in their numbers.

**Character and attributes**: The Irish Draft has a calm nature. Both robust and agile, as well as energetic, it is one of the most athletic of draft horses, very capable of jumping in spite of its weight.

**Uses**: The Irish wanted to make this a versatile horse, which could be used both on the farm and for transportation or hunting. It is usually worked in harness but can also be used for dressage and eventing.

**Current status**: The Irish Draft almost became extinct due to wars, mechanization, the production of Irish Hunters, and export for slaughter. Although the breed still survives, it needs to be protected, because its numbers are low.

## Norway

In 2012 around 125,000 horses were recorded in Norway, and a good number of them were trotters. Norway has four indigenous breeds: the Fjord, Døle, Northlands, and Coldblooded Trotter, which has been bred in conjunction with Sweden (see Sweden *p. 70*). Two breeds with very low numbers are being attentively watched by Norwegian authorities: the Northlands and the Døle. The other two are doing well. Equestrian activities have been developing in Norway in the past few years, notably through the efforts of women riders.

# NORTHLANDS HORSE

Also called: Northlands Pony, or Lyngen Pony, Lyngshest

Norwegian: *nordlandshest, lyngshest*

**H** 1.25 m–1.45 m.

**C** Primarily chestnut, as well as a great variety of other coats, with the exception of bay dun and pinto.

**Description**: This is a compact horse. Its legs are robust, its hooves hard. Its profile is straight, and its ears are small. It has an abundant mane and forelock.

**Distribution**: Norway.

**Origins and history**: This is a very old breed, whose origins probably go back to the Vikings. Its ancestors certainly contributed to the development of the Icelandic, which it resembles. For a long time it was used as a farm horse by Norwegian farmers. The Lofoten Pony, now extinct, looked like it, and they are probably related. Some believe that the breed is the result of crossings between ancient Lofoten and Lyngen Ponies.

**Character and attributes**: Both calm and energetic, this horse often has a strong personality. This easy-to-keep breed has good health and lives a long time, often beyond the age of thirty.

**Uses**: This small Norwegian horse is a very good mount for the whole family, enjoyed by children and able to carry adult riders. It is used as a saddle horse, for dressage, and in harness.

**Current status**: The breed almost disappeared following World War II: there were only a few horses left. The current population is small in number, with only about 200 foals born each year, but it is becoming increasingly popular in Norway.

Sloping croup

Wide, long back

Wide forehead

Abundant mane

Robust legs

# Fjord

Sometimes called: Vestland, West Norwegian

Norwegian: *fjordhest*

**H** 1.35 m–1.50 m.

**C** Light to dark bay dun or black/brown dun, with a white-silvery mane showing a continuation of a dorsal stripe, and a blending of black in the tail. In addition to the dorsal stripe, it sometimes shows a St. Andrew's cross on its shoulders. It often has zebra striping on its legs. The muzzle is lighter, especially in the winter.

**Description**: Given its unique characteristics, the Fjord cannot be confused with any other breed of horse. It is a small, light, very round draft horse, with a very rough gait and primitive markings that evoke Przewalski's Horse. The head is small but wide, the ears spaced far apart, the gaze gentle. The neck is short and muscular, the withers unobtrusive. The back and the legs are strong, and the hooves hard. Its thick and bushy mane is almost always cut short to enable the black hair in the middle to show, accentuating and enhancing its neck and giving it an inimitable appearance. Its tail is also long and abundant. It has rather well-developed feathering.

**Distribution**: Throughout Scandinavia, Germany, France, Great Britain, the United States, and just about everywhere around the world.

**Origins and history**: This is the Norwegian horse par excellence. This very ancient breed has probably existed in its present form for thousands of years. It is very pure and the direct issue of primitive horses. The breed is sometimes crossed with the Arabian to obtain a lighter horse.

**Character and attributes**: Very gentle and cooperative, it is sometimes stubborn if its rider is not experienced. It is a very rustic and resilient horse, simple and easy to keep.

**Uses**: Its sure-footedness makes it a good trekking or pack horse. Powerful, it is also used to pull carriages. Its sweet nature and its reassuring appearance make it useful in equitherapy, and also in vaulting.

**Current status**: This very ancient European breed is popular and is found throughout the world.

# Døle

Norwegian: dølehest

**H** 1.45 m–1.60 m.

**C** Predominantly bay, dark bay, most often black, more rarely gray, buckskin, palomino.

**Description**: It has a strong head, small eyes, and a long neck. Its withers are unobtrusive; it has strong and sloping shoulders, a long back, and a wide and muscular croup. Breeders pay particular attention to the solidity of the legs, which are short and muscular. The mane and tail are long and abundant. There is a heavy type, the Gudbrandsdalen Døle, and a lighter type for trotting races, the Døle Trotter, which are often interbred.

**Distribution**: Norway.

**Origins and history**: The Døle probably has origins in common with those of the English Dales, and it has received Friesian, Thoroughbred, Arabian, Trotter, and draft horse blood. It originated in the region of Gudbrandsdalen, where it was used notably for agricultural work.

**Character and attributes**: The Døle is an energetic and powerful horse. It is also resilient and doesn't require rich food. Its trot is excellent.

**Uses**: It is still used for trotting races, and it is also a good harness horse.

**Current status**: There are more than 4,000 of the Gudbrandsdalen Døle type, and 200 to 250 foals born each year. The breed is still small in number, even if it is less threatened than it was in the mid-twentieth century.

Bristly, bi-colored mane with silvery and black hair, which must be cut into a brush

Wide forehead

Strong back

In the winter, the Fjord is covered with a very dense coat that enables it to survive in the snow and cold.

Long, powerful neck

Small eyes

Particularly solid legs

One sees many horses in Denmark, and the Danish Equestrian Federation is one of the largest athletic federations in the country. Breeding focuses mainly on saddle and sport horses. The country

DENMARK

# Faroe Islands Pony

Also called: Faroe Islands Horse

Danish: *faerøsk hest; føroysk ross* on the Faroe Islands

Ⓗ 1.14 m–1.24 m.

Ⓒ Usually bay, often black, sometimes dark bay, rarely chestnut with light mane and tail, sometimes pinto.

**Description**: The breed greatly resembles the Icelandic. It is very robust with a short neck, muscular croup, and strong legs and hooves. It has an abundant mane and tail, and the winter coat is particularly thick.

**Distribution**: Faroe Islands, Denmark.

**Origins and history**: Completely isolated, this very old breed, known for centuries, is one of the purest in the world, not having undergone multiple crossings. It is the result of horses brought to the Faroe Islands by the Scandinavians and the Celts. The breed almost disappeared due to being exported to the United Kingdom; its small size and its strength were sought-after for working in the mines.

**Character and attributes**: It has a very gentle and patient nature, though it is sometimes a bit stubborn. It is very powerful for its size, has endurance, and is sure-footed. Very resilient and very easy to keep, this pony is adapted to a windy and rainy climate, and to the many storms that lash the Faroe Islands. It has good health and lives a long time. Like the Icelandic, it can have two supplementary gaits, the tölt and sometimes the flying amble, though they are less developed than the primary gaits.

**Uses**: It is a good mount for children. It can also be harnessed, and it is a good pack horse, capable of transporting heavy loads. It can carry an adult rider.

**Current status**: It is a very rare breed, with around 63 animals in 2012. Its numbers had fallen to only 4 mares and 1 stallion. It began to be actively preserved in 1962, and the breed's numbers have been increasing.

DENMARK

# Knabstrup

Danish: *knabstrupperl*

Ⓗ 1.54 m–1.63 m.

Ⓒ Always spotted.

**Description**: This horse looks a great deal like the Frederiksborg, of which it is a lighter version, but is distinctive with its spotted coat. Because of this unique coat, it is sometimes confused with the American Appaloosa. Because the breed has been diluted, the form of the Knabstrup has been rather varied. Overall, one can say that the head of this unusual horse, with its straight or slightly convex profile, is rather big; it has large eyes; a strong, short neck; a straight back; and a slightly sloping croup. The mane and tail are thin. The hooves are striated, and the white sclera is often visible. There is a smaller variety of the breed, the Knabstrup Pony, bred for children and measuring under 1.48 m.

**Distribution**: Denmark, notably Zealand Island (Sjaelland); one also finds breeders in Norway, Sweden, Germany, Switzerland, Italy, and England, and more recently in the United States.

**Origins and history**: The breed emerged at the beginning of the nineteenth century, by crossing a Spanish mare with a spotted coat and a Frederiksborg stallion. The breed was fairly popular at the time. In the past, inbreeding, making selections that were based too strongly on the coat and not enough on the animal, almost destroyed the breed. Since 1970 breeding efforts have been made to enable it to recover its original excellence. Thoroughbred blood has thus contributed to improving the breed.

**Character and attributes**: This is an intelligent, very friendly horse, easygoing and docile. It is robust and has good endurance.

**Uses**: It is a pleasant saddle horse, good for equestrian tourism, and can also be driven. Its spectacular coat, combined with its easygoing nature and intelligence, also make it a popular circus horse.

**Current status**: Despite its unique appearance, the Knabstrup remains a rare breed.

is particularly involved in breeding trotters, but Danish Trotters emerged from imported foreign stock. Denmark has put into place a program to save three ancient breeds, the Jutland, the Frederiksborg, and the Knabstrup, which are well adapted to the local climate. In addition, in the Faroe Islands Pony Denmark has one of the oldest and purest breeds in the world.

Very thick coat to resist extreme weather

Extremely rare, the Faroe Islands Pony is perfectly adapted to harsh climate conditions.

Short and robust legs

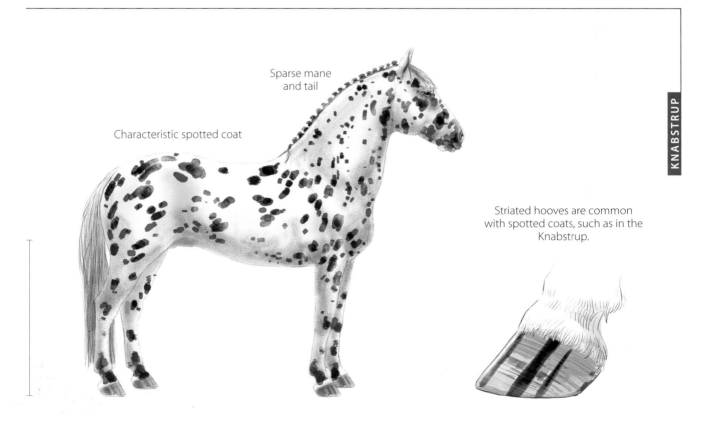

Sparse mane and tail

Characteristic spotted coat

Striated hooves are common with spotted coats, such as in the Knabstrup.

# FREDERIKSBORG

Danish: *frederiksborg*

**H** 1.55 m–1.62 m.

**C** Usually chestnut, often chestnut with light mane and tail. Light markings on the legs or head are rather common.

**Description**: Today, the Frederiksborg has the build of a good harness horse. Its head is rather wide, sometimes slightly convex. It has a strong, rather short neck; a broad chest; and powerful legs. The back is rather long, with unobtrusive withers.

**Distribution**: Mainly Denmark.

**Origins and history**: This horse is one of the oldest Danish breeds. It is the result of crossings carried out, beginning in the sixteenth century, between local mares and Spanish and Neapolitan horses. Bred at the royal stud farm of Frederiksborg, near Copenhagen, the old Frederiksborg was in the nineteenth century one of the most sought-after horses in Europe for haute école dressage, parades, and driving. The best studs were sold abroad, where they improved other breeds, such as the Lipizzan. However, the Frederiksborg, a victim of badly managed success, almost disappeared. The royal stud farm closed in 1839, but individuals continued to breed them. The current Frederiksborg is the result of horses of that old type, and above all a work of reconstitution first from Friesian and Oldenburg horses, then from the Thoroughbred and Arabian.

**Character and attributes**: With a calm nature, it is an agile horse, full of vigor, enjoyed for its high-stepping trot.

**Uses**: It is a saddle, harness, and light draft horse.

**Current status**: This native breed, well protected, is no longer threatened with extinction. The breed is maintained, but its numbers remain small, with around 2,000 horses, including 200 broodmares and 40 stallions, and a bit fewer than 100 births per year.

# DANISH WARMBLOOD

Danish: *dansk varmblod*

**H** 1.64 m–1.72 m.

**C** Usually bay, often chestnut, sometimes gray, black, dark bay. Rather discrete white markings on the head and legs are fairly common.

**Description**: This horse physically resembles other European sport horses and is difficult to distinguish from them. Its head is lovely and intelligent, its neck harmonious and muscular. It has a deep chest, sloping shoulders, solid back, and sloping croup. Danish Warmbloods are branded on the left thigh with a stylized crown over a wave.

**Distribution**: Bred in Denmark, it is exported throughout the world and bred in various countries.

**Origins and history**: This recent breed actually appeared in the middle of the twentieth century, officially in 1962, with a first studbook published in 1964. It is the result of crossings between Frederiksborg mares mixed with Thoroughbred blood and Trakehner, Anglo-Norman, Thoroughbred, Malopolski, and Wielkopolski stallions. It quickly became popular in equestrian sports, thanks to its famous champions. The Danes breed this horse with great care.

**Character and attributes**: Although very athletic, it has a cooperative and calm nature. It is energetic and powerful, supple and resilient.

**Uses**: Its best disciplines are show jumping and dressage, and it is one of the most effective horses for these competitions. It also competes successfully in eventing, and is enjoyed as a recreational horse as well.

**Current status**: This popular breed is doing very well.

Wide face

Rather long back

Broad chest

Rather long, but well-defined ears

Legs and bone structure perfect for sport activities

Very good, resilient feet

# JUTLAND

Danish: *jydske hest, jyder*

**H** 1.55 m–1.60 m for males; 1.53 m–1.58 m for mares.

**C** Most often chestnut with light mane and tail, with light feathering and often a white marking on the head. Rarely bay or black.

**Description**: The Jutland resembles the British Suffolk Punch, but also the German Schleswig, with which it has common ancestors. It is a heavy draft horse, which easily weighs 800 kg. Its body is long and wide, with massive forequarters; the neck is very thick. The hooves are wide and it has abundant feathering. The head sometimes has a slightly convex profile, and the ears are long.

**Distribution**: Denmark, notably on the Jutland peninsula.

**Origins and history**: The Jutland, the only Danish draft horse, has very ancient origins: this local breed's medieval forebears, also ridden by the Vikings, were believed to be powerful chargers. In the nineteenth century, Jutland breeding was formalized, and the breed received blood from the Frederiksborg, the Cleveland Bay, and the extinct Yorkshire Coach Horse—for its gaits—then from the Shire, Clydesdale, and Suffolk Punch, to bulk up, and finally, in the twentieth century, from the Ardennais.

**Character and attributes**: The Jutland is dynamic and docile, rustic and hardy, very powerful.

**Uses**: It is a heavy draft and harness horse.

**Current status**: The Jutland remains rare, with numbers to be watched: there are a thousand or so horses, including 250 broodmares, 25 stallions, and a hundred or so births per year.

# DANISH SPORT PONY

Danish: *dansk sport pony*

Acronym: DSP

**H** A maximum of 1.48 m.

**C** Usually gray, but also chestnut, bay, or black.

**Description**: There are three categories of Danish Sport Pony, depending on their height. It is a saddle pony with a wide forehead, rather long neck, prominent withers, a strong back, and a slightly sloping croup.

**Distribution**: Denmark.

**Origins and history**: In 1976 Danish breeders wanted to create a Danish sport pony. This recent breed is the fruit of multiple crossings. It is still developing.

**Character and attributes**: Breeding favors ponies with a good nature, obedient and calm. It is easy to ride, fast, and agile.

**Uses**: It is above all a recreational pony, for dressage and jumping competitions. It can also be driven.

**Current status**: The breed is not in danger.

# DANISH OLDENBURG

Danish: *dansk oldenborg*

**H** 1.60 m–1.70 m.

**C** Usually dark bay, often black, rarely chestnut or light gray.

**Description**: The Danish Oldenburg resembles the Oldenburg; it is a rather massive, athletic, and well-proportioned horse. There are two types: the purebred Oldenburg (*renavlet*)—the purest and closest lineage to the old type of Oldenburg—and the crossed Oldenburg (*foraedlet*), which has been refined with Thoroughbred blood.

**Distribution**: Denmark.

**Origins and history**: This breed is not native to Denmark. It is originally from Germany. As its name indicates, it is the Danish variety of the Oldenburg. Horses were imported to Denmark in the first half of the twentieth century. This Oldenburg differs from the German Oldenburg because, unlike the German horse, it has not undergone much crossing. Thus it is closer to the original Oldenburg.

**Character and attributes**: This good-natured horse is easy to handle.

**Uses**: It is a good saddle horse, notably for dressage. It is also used in show jumping and driving competitions.

**Current status**: The Danish Oldenburg remains a rare horse.

Long ears

Massive head

Short and solid legs

## DANISH TROTTER

Danish: *dansk travhest*
*See French Trotter, p. 150, and American Standardbred, p. 466.*

Denmark is a land of trotters. Indeed, eight out of the nine racecourses in Denmark are devoted to trotting races. But the selection of Danish Trotters is done essentially from a base of imported studs, mainly American Standardbreds, but also increasingly French Trotters in the past few years. This trotter is selected solely for its racing abilities. It is usually bay, chestnut, or black. It is an energetic and resilient trotter. As a breed, it is distinguished more by its association with a large and very active national breeding program than with its difference from other trotters. Danish Trotters are bred for trotting races, and often, when they retire from racing, they are used for recreational riding.

Following a steep decline in the twentieth century, related to mechanization in agriculture and forestry, the Swedish horse population has since been partially reconstituted and maintained thanks to recreation and sport, and it continues to grow. In 2012 there

---

SWEDEN

# GOTLAND

Swedish: *gotlandsruss, skogruss* (small horse of the woods)

**H** 1.15 m–1.30 m, usually between 1.23 m and 1.26 m.

**C** Bay, black, bay dun, buckskin, palomino, sometimes with a dorsal stripe, often mealy.

**Description**: This primitive pony resembles the Konik and the Hucul, with which it shares ancient origins. It also greatly resembles the Exmoor. It is a small horse, a light draft, with a small head and wide forehead; small, wide ears; and large eyes. The neck is short, the shoulders muscular and sloping, the back long; and it has rather slender legs. The mane and tail are thick.

**Distribution**: Sweden (there is still a herd living in the wild on Gotland Island), Finland, Denmark, Norway, some in the United States.

**Origins and history**: This is a very old breed; it received some Eastern blood in the nineteenth century. It was a farm horse that was also used for daily transportation.

**Character and attributes**: Intelligent, the Gotland is active and sometimes stubborn. It is an excellent trotter and a good jumper. The breed is strong, rustic, and long-lived.

**Uses**: Today the Gotland is primarily a mount for children, and is also used as a light carriage horse. It continues to be used in trotting races.

**Current status**: In the past too much exporting almost killed off the breed, but it is doing very well today and is common in Sweden.

---

SWEDEN

# SWEDISH WARMBLOOD

Also called: Swedish Halfbred

Swedish: *svensk varmblodig häst, svenskt halvblod, svenskt varmblod*

**H** 1.55 m–1.75 m.

**C** Often chestnut with markings, bay, dark bay, gray.

**Description**: This is an elegant horse; it has a slender head with a straight or convex profile, and long ears. It has prominent withers, a straight and powerful back, horizontal croup, high-set tail, and long, strong legs.

**Distribution**: Sweden, with breeding farms in Europe and the United States.

**Origins and history**: This breed was produced by crossing Swedish draft horses with many other breeds (Arabian, Spanish, Anglo-Norman, Friesian, Hanoverian, Trakhener, Thoroughbred). Once a military horse, it has become a good sport horse.

**Character and attributes**: It is a poised and intelligent horse, endowed with very lovely gaits. It is resilient in the cold.

**Uses**: It is a good horse for competition. Its best discipline is dressage, followed by eventing and show jumping. It can also be harnessed.

**Current status**: Very common in Sweden, the breed is doing well and is exported just about everywhere in the world.

were more than 362,000 horses in Sweden, including 61 percent used in equestrian disciplines and 30 percent for trotting races, followed by gallop races and logging. As almost everywhere in the world, equestrian sports have become predominantly the realm of women. The old Swedish breeds are the Swedish Ardennes, the North Swedish Horse, and the Gotland, all three of which have small populations. Sweden also breeds around thirty foreign breeds.

Wide, small ears

Small head

Rather slender legs

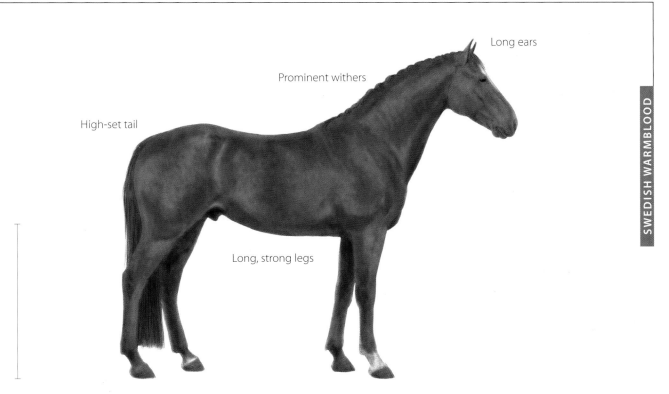

Long ears

Prominent withers

High-set tail

Long, strong legs

# North Swedish Horse

Swedish: *nordsvensk brukshäst*

**H** 1.45 m–1.60 m.

**C** Bay, dark bay, black, sometimes chestnut, often mealy.

**Description**: It resembles the Døle, with which it has common ancestors. This rather light draft horse, of average height, weighs 530–750 kg. It has a wide forehead, long ears, and small, expressive eyes. Its neck is of average size; it has a broad chest, unobtrusive withers, long and powerful back, round barrel, sloping croup, and a low-set tail. The legs are short with slight feathering and wide hooves. It has a thick mane and tail.

**Distribution**: Sweden.

**Origins and history**: It descends from horses that once lived in Scandinavia. It has been crossed with Thoroughbreds and Clydedales. The breeding of these horses is particularly controlled, and horses are carefully selected on the basis of their legs.

**Character and attributes**: This is a docile and energetic draft horse with a good trot. It is easygoing and resilient, with good health and longevity.

**Uses**: It is a good family horse, versatile and enjoyed for recreational riding. It is also used for driving and for hauling.

**Current status**: Although it is relatively unknown outside of Scandinavia, the breed has become more popular locally despite its small numbers. There are around 2,000 mares, including 550 broodmares, and 100 stallions. Around 350 foals are born each year.

# Swedish Ardennes

Swedish: *svensk ardenner*

**H** 1.55 m–1.63 m.

**C** Mainly bay or dark bay, occasionally black, chestnut, or roan.

**Description**: It greatly resembles the Ardennais, but is lighter (weighing 550–800 kg). The Ardennais has large eyes, whereas the eyes of the Swedish Ardennes are small. The Swedish Ardennes has a wide forehead; short, thick neck; broad chest; short back; round, muscular croup; and short, strong legs, with feathering.

**Distribution**: Sweden.

**Origins and history**: The Swedish Ardennes is a lineage of Ardennais and Belgians derived from horses imported from Belgium, which were then crossed with Swedish draft horses. It is bred independently of the Ardennais, and has played an important role in Sweden as a farm and draft horse.

**Character and attributes**: It is willing and easy to handle, with a good nature. It is strong and long-lived. It endures the cold climate.

**Uses**: It is still used for hauling in places accessible only to horses. It is a good harness horse.

**Current status**: The breed, with its small numbers, remains in danger, with around 4,000 horses in Sweden, including around 570 broodmares and 80 stallions.

The Swedish Ardennes is still valuable for clearing land, notably in areas that are difficult to access.

Long, powerful back

Low-set tail

Round barrel

Short, strong neck

Small eyes, unlike the French and Belgian Ardennes

Short back

Short, strong legs

# SWEDISH RIDING PONY

Swedish: *svensk ridponny*

Ⓗ Under 1.48 m.

Ⓒ All coats except cream.

**Description**: It looks like a small Thoroughbred.

**Distribution**: Sweden.

**Origins and history**: This very recent breed is still being developed, its origins dating only from the 1990s. The goal is to produce a competitive Swedish sport pony able to compete against other breeds of saddle ponies. It is the result of crossings among the Thoroughbred, Connemara, New Forest, Dartmoor, Welsh, Gotland, Anglo-Arabian, and other horses.

**Character and attributes**: It is calm, easygoing, and athletic.

**Uses**: It is a mount for young riders and excels in show jumping, dressage, and eventing.

**Current status**: The breed is currently being developed.

# NORTH SWEDISH TROTTER

Also called: Coldblooded Trotter

Swedish: *kallblodstravare*

Ⓗ 1.45 m–1.65 m.

Ⓒ Often bay, dark bay, sometimes black.

**Description**: The North Swedish Trotter has a small, wide head; broad chest; rather short back; and fairly short legs with slight feathering. The mane and tail are thick.

**Distribution**: Sweden and Norway.

**Origins and history**: The North Swedish Trotter is in fact a light variety of the North Swedish Horse, selected for its trot and registered in its own studbook since 1964. It is the only breed of trotter called "coldblood." The breeding of this native breed is shared with Norway. Trotting races on ice were once popular.

**Character and attributes**: It is an energetic and agile horse, calm and cooperative, with endurance and good health. Its trot is excellent.

**Uses**: It is essentially bred for trotting races in Scandinavian countries. After a sporting career it is often retrained for recreational riding.

**Current status**: The breed, though fairly unknown outside Scandinavia, is doing very well, trotting races being popular in Sweden and Norway. There are around 7,000 horses and 500 births per year.

Opposite: The Fjord's primitive look reminds us that this Norwegian breed is very old.

Finland has only one ancient breed of horse born on its land, the Finnhorse. The country breeds and imports a large number of horses of foreign breeds: Arabian, Anglo-Arabian, Thoroughbred, Connemara, New Forest, Gotland, Shetland, Welsh, Icelandic, and

# Finnhorse

Also called: Finnish Universal

Finnish: *suomenhevonen*

ⓗ 1.50 m–1.60 m; the "small" type measures from 1.30 m to 1.48 m.

ⓒ Mostly chestnut, sometimes bay, dark bay, more rarely black, gray; frequent white markings on the legs or head.

**Description**: It is a compact horse, with a rather square head; small ears; strong neck; rather short back; slanted croup. Its tail is set low. The mane and tail are thick. There are four types: trotter, draft, saddle, and small. Some horses can be included in several categories.

**Distribution**: Throughout Finland, a few in Germany, a small number in Sweden, a few in Austria and the Netherlands.

**Origins and history**: This native breed is very old, the result of horses living for centuries in Finland; they were crossed with different breeds, whose origin we don't know with certainty. But since 1907 and the opening of its own studbook, any outcrossing is forbidden.

**Character and attributes**: It is a docile and confident horse. Fast and with good endurance, it is a good trotter and has a pulling capacity superior to that of many other breeds. It is known for its versatility, and that is why it is sometimes called Finnish Universal. Well adapted to the Scandinavian climate, it can live for many years.

**Uses**: Once a work and farm horse, it is used today as a saddle horse (dressage, jumping, eventing), in harness, and for recreation. It is a good trekking horse. Trotting races enabled breeders to preserve the breed when motorization caused its numbers to decrease.

**Current status**: The breed, very common and the object of breeding programs, is growing. It is very popular in its country, but little known outside Finland.

# Finnish Warmblood

Finnish: *suomalainen puoliverinen*

Acronym: FBW

ⓗ 1.58 m–1.72 m.

ⓒ Most often bay, chestnut, black, sometimes roan.

**Description**: This tall horse resembles other light European warmblood breeds from which it is issued, with a long neck, prominent withers, long legs, and an athletic body.

**Distribution**: Finland.

**Origins and history**: Finland has produced a quality warmblood since 1926, the date the breeding association was established, and has defined the Finnish Warmblood since 1995. However, it is not yet really a breed, but a crossing of Swedish and European horses, 75 percent of which have been imported. The goal of the selection is to produce a high-performing horse for Olympic disciplines. The Finns consider the horse's character important and are careful not to favor animals that are too nervous or difficult.

**Character and attributes**: Energetic, agile, and easily handled, this bold horse is a good jumper and has lovely gaits.

**Uses**: It is intended for dressage, show jumping, and eventing.

**Current status**: It is doing well, and makes up 22 percent of all horses in Finland.

Fjord. However, 34 percent of its horses are Finnish breeds, 38 percent are trotters, and the rest are horses and saddle ponies. There were around 76,000 horses in the country in 2011. The number of amateur riders is continually growing, with an increasing number of riding schools. In addition to trekking, the favorite equestrian disciplines are show jumping, dressage, eventing, and harness racing, but also Western and Icelandic riding, as well as vaulting.

Thick mane

Rather squarish head

Low-set tail

FINNHORSE

# Horses of Southern Europe

*In the past Southern Europe was of great importance in the world of horses, due to two fabulous breeds: the Neapolitan, an extinct Italian breed that is being redeveloped and that influenced many other European breeds in the Renaissance; and the Andalusian, which has also been used to improve breeds since the Middle Ages. Further, Iberian horses, imported extensively by colonists to North and South America, had an essential role in the creation of American breeds.*

*However, today, with the exception of the outstanding breeds (Andalusian, Lusitano, and others), the horses of Southern Europe, in spite of their wonderful qualities, remain virtually unknown elsewhere. This is a shame, because the equine diversity of these lands is incredibly rich. The fact that they are so little-known perhaps explains why many of these breeds are so small in number, particularly in Greece.*

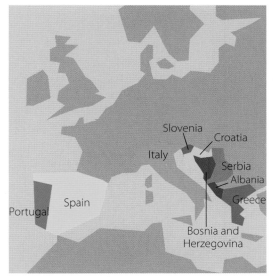

The Giara Horses live in the wild in Sardinia (Italy).

Lusitano, Alter Real lineage, Portugal.

### Portugal
Azores Pony
Garrano
Sorraia
Lusitano

### Spain
Asturian
Galician
Jaca Navarra Horse
Monchino
Losina
Basque Mountain Horse
Marismeña
Retuerta Horse
Spanish Anglo-Arab and
    Spanish Arabian
Andalusian
Menorquin
Balearic (also
    Mallorquin)
Spanish Sport Horse
Hispano-Breton
Burguete
Serrano
Catalan Pyrenees Horse
Spanish Trotter

### Italy
Giara Horse
Sarcidano Horse
Monterufoli Pony
Esperia Pony

Pentro Horse
Bardigiano
Tolfetano
Catria Horse
Neapolitan
Sanfratello
Ventasso Horse
Persano
Roman Horse of the Part
    of the Maremma That
    Is in Lazio
Murgese
Salerno (also
    Salernitano)
Siciliano
Sardinian Anglo-Arab
    (also Anglo-Arab
    Sarda)
Calabrian (also
    Calabrese)
Italian Trotter
Maremmano
Italian Heavy Draft (also
    Italian TPR Agricultural
    Horse)
Appenninico
Samolaco Horse
Italian Saddle Horse

### Slovenia
Slovenian Warmblood
Ljutomer Trotter

### Croatia
Posavac (also Croatian
    Posavac)
Croatian Coldblood
    (also Croatian
    Hladnokrvnjak)

### Bosnia and Herzegovina
Bosnian (also Bosnian
    Pony, Bosnian
    Mountain Horse)

### Serbia
Yugoslav Trotter

### Albania
Albanian (also Albanian
    Local Horse)

### Greece
Skyros Pony
Pindos Pony
Messara Pony (also Creta
    Pony)
Peneia Pony
Thessalian (also
    Thessalian Pony)
Ainos Pony (also Ainos
    Kefalonia Feral Horse)
Rhodope Pony (also
    Rhodope Horse)
Zante Horse
Andravida (also Eleia)

Opposite: The renown of the extraordinary Andalusian has traveled far beyond the Iberian Peninsula.

# Portugal

Portugal, a land of equestrian traditions, doesn't have many breeds of horses, but what breeds it does have! The famous Lusitano and its different lineages, the Alter Real, but also the very rare and amazing Sorraia, a primitive horse close to the

---

## PORTUGAL

# AZORES PONY

Portuguese: *pónei da Terceira*

**H** 1.15 m–1.30 m.

**C** Bay, dark bay, gray.

**Description**: Very nicely proportioned, the Azores Pony resembles a small Lusitano, even though they are not related. It has a head with a usually convex profile; wide forehead, tapering to the nose; rather slender legs; and small hooves. The mane and tail are silky.

**Distribution**: Azores Islands, Portugal.

**Origins and history**: This breed's origins are obscure. It might have descended from Eastern horses that were imported in the past. It has probably become smaller due to its poor diet in the Azores. In the past the breed was used for light agricultural work or to pull carriages on the islands. The breed continues to live partly in the wild.

**Character and attributes**: Intelligent, lively, and dynamic, the Azores is still very docile and easygoing.

**Uses**: Because of its small size and its good nature, it can make a good mount for children. It is also good for driving.

**Current status**: This breed is very rare. Requests for the breed to be recognized have been made. Only around 60 animals exist today.

---

## PORTUGAL

# GARRANO

Portuguese: *marrano, minho*

**H** 1.23 m–1.35 m.

**C** Bay, dark bay, black; almost never any white markings.

**Description**: The Garrano has a straight or slightly concave profile, large eyes, thick lips, a rather long neck, unobtrusive withers, a rather long back, low-set tail, round barrel, robust legs, and small hooves. The mane and tail are long and thick, sometimes wavy, and frizzy at the base of the tail. Some Garranos, showing more Arabian blood, are a bit more slender with a more concave profile.

**Distribution**: Minho and Trás-os-Montes regions, the Peneda-Gerês National Park, Portugal; Spain, a few in France.

**Origins and history**: This is a very old breed, probably the descendant of small Celtic horses, which has undergone very little crossing, except with Arabians in the nineteenth century. In the past the Garrano had an influence on many breeds, including the Andalusian. Exported to America by Spanish colonists, it is notably responsible for a Brazilian breed, the Galiceño. It is still bred in semi-freedom.

**Character and attributes**: Once tamed it is docile and intelligent, robust, very rustic, and sure-footed.

**Uses**: Traditionally used in farming or as a pack animal, it is currently used more as a saddle horse, and notably for equestrian tourism. It is suitable for driving. It is the mount for the traditional local *passo travado* races, which involve a specific gait.

**Current status**: This small native breed is still rare, but it has been protected since the 1970s. In 2012 there were around 2,000 animals. The Garrano is a prey of the Portuguese wolf, which is also protected in the Peneda-Gerês National Park.

Tarpan, and the no less rare Garrano. However, only the Lusitano is popular abroad, and the other breeds are very small in number. The country has around 70,000 horses, mainly for recreational uses. The Portuguese, great fans of work horses, have turned their own equitation into an art: Portuguese equitation, which combines dressage with cutting and herding livestock. A parade horse, bullfighting partner, or just recreational mount, the horse has a special place in Portuguese culture.

Silky mane

Head with a wide forehead that tapers to the nose

Small hooves

AZORES PONY

Often slightly concave profile

Tufts of frizzy hair at the base of the tail

Ample barrel

GARRANO

# SORRAIA

Portuguese: *sorraia*. It was sometimes called *marismeño* (horse of the marshes), a name given to another breed; to avoid confusion this term is no longer used.

**H** 1.40 m–1.50 m; on average, 1.44 m for mares, 1.48 m for males.

**C** Always black/brown dun or bay dun with zebra striping on the legs and a dorsal stripe, ears bordered with black with light hair on the inside, with darker head and legs. The hair of the mane and tail is a mixture of light and dark hair. It has a unique feature: at birth the foals seem to have zebra striping, due to a particular configuration of the hair. This striping fades as they grow. Some horses retain it slightly on the shoulders, head, and back.

**Description**: The Sorraia is easy to identify, with its characteristic coat and its build, which is lighter than that of other horses of primitive type. It has a long and straight head with a convex profile; long ears; small eyes; a thin, high-set neck; undeveloped chest; a slightly sloping croup; a rather low-set tail; and long, thin legs.

**Distribution**: The Sorraia Horse Natural Reserve in Alpiarça, Portugal.

**Origins and history**: This small horse, which still lives in semi-freedom, probably descends in a direct line from the Tarpans that once lived on the Iberian Peninsula. Its unique primitive characteristics, resembling the Tarpan's, make it a breed of great national value.

**Character and attributes**: Very agile and bold, it has an assertive nature. It is very easy to keep because of its great rusticity and simplicity.

**Uses**: Traditionally used by the Portuguese *vaqueiros* to herd livestock, for which it has natural abilities, it is also well suited for other equestrian activities, as well as for work in harness.

**Current status**: The breed is very rare and threatened; it almost became extinct. Preserved today, there are only 200 animals and a hundred or so broodmares.

# LUSITANO

Portuguese: *puro sangue lusitano*

**H** On average 1.55 m for females, 1.60 m for males.

**C** Often gray, bay, dark bay, sometimes chestnut or bay dun.

**Description**: This is an Iberian horse, with round and harmonious lines, very similar to the Andalusian. Its noble head has a convex profile, a wide forehead, and large eyes. Its neck is arched and set high. The chest is deep; the shoulders long, oblique, muscular; the back short; the croup sloping; the feet rather small; the tail low-set. The mane and tail are thick, silky, often wavy.

**Distribution**: Mainly Portugal, France, and Brazil; also Spain, Mexico, and elsewhere throughout the world.

**Origins and history**: This old breed has for a long time been registered with the Andalusian under the name *Andalou*. The Lusitano has its origins in the Barb, Garrano, and Spanish Jennet, but it has not been crossbred for a long time. In past centuries it was a highly valued war horse.

**Character and attributes**: This intelligent and outgoing horse has a peaceful and docile temperament, and is very bold. It is agile and fast. It is a very charismatic breed, with lovely gaits. It matures slowly and lives a long time.

**Uses**: The Lusitano excels in dressage, haute école, shows, bullfighting, carriage pulling, parades, and other events. But this versatile horse also excels in show jumping and horseball. An excellent sport horse, it is also a good recreational horse, and its confidence and sure-footedness make it a very good trekking horse as well.

**Current status**: With a worldwide reputation and fans, and currently very popular, the breed remains less widespread than the Andalusian. There are around 5,000 broodmares worldwide, with 2,500 in Portugal, 1,200 in Brazil, and more than 560 in France. The breed is well respected in Portugal. Victims of the economic crisis of 2012, some Portuguese breeders had to sell hundreds of horses to slaughterhouses.

Portuguese saddle

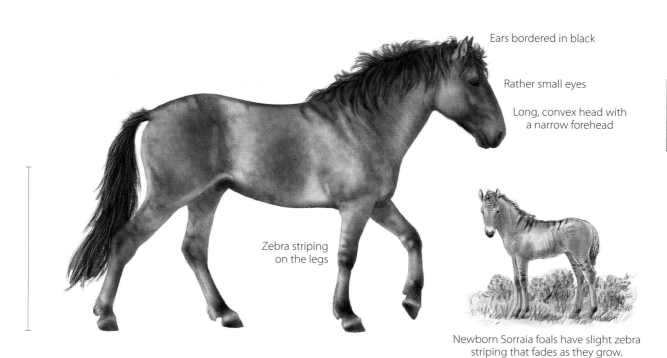

Ears bordered in black

Rather small eyes

Long, convex head with a narrow forehead

Zebra striping on the legs

Newborn Sorraia foals have slight zebra striping that fades as they grow.

Very beautiful silky, thick, often wavy mane and tail

Characteristic concave profile, often more marked than in its cousin, the Andalusian

## PORTUGAL

# ALTER REAL

Portuguese: *alter-real*

**H** 1.52 m–1.62 m.

**C** Primarily bay, dark bay.

**Description**: This Iberian-type horse has a mildly convex profile; a muscular, arched, high-set neck; short back; powerful croup; slender legs; hard and rather small hooves; and a fairly abundant, long mane and tail.

**Distribution**: Portugal.

**Origins and history**: Sometimes considered a breed or "sub-breed," the Alter Real is a lineage of the Lusitano, on the same level as the Andrade, the Veiga, or the Coudelaria Nacional Horse. It was created in 1748 for the royal stables of Lisbon. Its ancestors were Andalou horses imported from Jerez and Arabian stallions, but the animals suffered in the Napoleonic Wars. Later, various attempts were made to crossbreed with Arabian, Norman, Thoroughbred, and Hanoverian horses, but without success. It was again Andalou blood that enabled the quality of the breed to reemerge. It underwent another harsh blow when the Portuguese monarchy was abolished at the beginning of the twentieth century.

**Character and attributes**: The Alter Real is agile, intelligent, and confident. It is also a nervous and spirited horse.

**Uses:** The Alter Real excels in dressage, haute école, bullfighting, and exhibitions. It is a mount for experienced riders due to its sometimes sensitive temperament.

**Current Status**: This breed is small in numbers but, thanks to an increase in its popularity, it is not threatened.

---

# Spain

The magnificent horses of Spain have had a considerable influence on other European breeds and on breeds in North and South America, since they were the horses of the first colonists: a great many of them were exported during the centuries that

---

## SPAIN

# ASTURIAN

Spanish: *asturcón*

**H** 1.17 m–1.27 m.

**C** Brownish bay, black, without white markings.

**Description**: A small horse, the Asturian is elegant, with a straight, sometimes slightly convex head. Its neck is straight, with rather prominent withers; it has a round barrel, dished croup, and a low-set tail. It has a long mane and tail.

**Distribution**: Asturias and Galicia, Spain.

**Origins and history**: This very old breed, one of the oldest in Europe, probably descends from Celtic horses, Sorraias, and Garranos, but its origins are in fact unknown. It exists in part in the wild in Asturias. This gaited horse was once popular with European ladies, but also as a carriage horse during the Middle Ages.

**Character and attributes**: This is a rustic breed, undemanding and docile, whose distinctive characteristic is its ambling gait.

**Uses**: Once used in farming and for transportation, today it is an excellent mount for children. It can be used both for show jumping and for driving.

**Current status**: This native breed was on the brink of extinction and owes its survival to its ability to live in the wild. Even if it is still rare, it is currently watched and protected and its numbers are growing, with around 2,320 horses in 2011.

The Alter Real, with its distinct presence, is one of the best-known Lusitano lineages.

followed the discovery of America, a continent where there were no horses. A breed that no longer exists, the Spanish Jennet, the ancestor of the Andalusian and the Lusitano, had a significant influence in the global history of horse breeds. Spain has around 240,000 horses, spread evenly around the country, bred essentially for sport and recreation, since the consumption of horse meat is not very common. Spain is very active and in the forefront in the preservation of native breeds whose numbers are in decline.

Dished croup

Low-set tail

ASTURIAN

# GALICIAN

Spanish: *caballo de pura raza gallega*, formerly *caballo de monte gallego*, sometimes *gallega, galiciana, cabalo Galego de monte, faca galizana, jaca gallega*

**H** 1.20 m–1.40 m; 1.30 m on average.

**C** Bay, brownish bay, sometimes chestnut, without white markings.

**Description**: This small, primitive, and stocky horse resembles the Asturian. Its profile is straight, and it has large eyes and small, hairy ears; a powerful croup; very resilient, short, thin legs; and very hard hooves. It has a thick mane and tail, and a beard in the winter. Old mares sometimes have a mustache on their upper lip.

**Distribution**: Galicia, Spain.

**Origins and history**: This small horse, which has probably always lived partially in the wild, continues to live freely in the mountains. It is descended from Celtic and Roman horses, and is the result of much crossing. During the *Rapa das Bestas*, a traditional Spanish festival, these horses are caught, a few are sold, and their manes and tails are cut.

**Character and attributes**: Intelligent, this horse is very fearful in the wild, but calm and docile if it is domesticated. It is rustic and resilient. It is known for its ambling gait.

**Uses**: It is a good mount for children.

**Current status**: This horse is very rare, but its numbers have increased to 1,526 horses in 2011. It is now protected.

---

# JACA NAVARRA HORSE

Spanish: *jaca navarra* or *caballito de Andia de la Barranca* or *caballito de Andia de las Améscoas* or *caballo navarro* or *caballo vasco-navarro*

Basque: *nafarroako zaldiko*

**H** 1.26 m–1.36 m.

**C** Bay, without white markings.

**Description**: This small mountain horse, of light draft type, has a head with straight or slightly concave profile, small ears, a neck thick at the base, broad chest, straight back, and a developed barrel. Its skin is thin and delicate. Its mane and tail are thick. Some horses have a mustache.

**Distribution**: Navarre, Spain.

**Origins and history**: The breed's origins are a mystery; it might have come out of primitive Iberian horses. The breed was once widespread in Navarre, before it almost disappeared in the twentieth century. The Jaca Navarra is still bred in semi-freedom, without much contact with humans.

**Character and attributes**: The Jaca Navarra is gentle, strong, very rustic and easygoing, well adapted to life in the mountains. It is fertile, with good health and longevity.

**Uses**: It is primarily raised for its meat, but can be trained for recreation or as a mount for children.

**Current status**: This local breed has gradually increased in number after almost becoming extinct. With around 1,020 horses, it remains rare.

Some Jaca Navarras (like some Galicians and horses of the Catalan Pyrenees) have an unusual, more or less prominent mustache on the upper lip.

Straight profile

GALICIAN

Sometimes beard
and mustache

Thin, short, and
resilient legs

Thin, fine hide

JACA NAVARRA HORSE

Developed barrel

# MONCHINO

Spanish: *monchino, monchinu*

🄷 1.35 m–1.47 m.

🄲 Different variations of bay, black, sometimes with a white spot on the head, or socks.

**Description**: The Monchino has a large head with a straight or slightly concave profile; large eyes; small ears; thick lips; a short, strong neck; broad chest; sometimes a slightly swayed back; wide, short, sloping croup; low-set tail; slender legs; and small hooves. The barrel is large. The mane and tail are abundant, and it has a beard in the winter.

**Distribution**: Spain, especially in Cantabria, but also a few in the Basque Country, in Castile and León, and in Asturias.

**Origins and history**: This ancient breed comes from horses bred in the north of Spain, and has probably received some Celtic influence, notably from the Exmoor. It continues to be bred in semi-freedom in the mountains.

**Character and attributes**: This very rustic mountain horse remains a semi-free-range animal.

**Uses**: Once tamed, it makes a good pack or harness horse, or a good training mount for young riders, but it is most often bred for its meat.

**Current status**: This very rare breed had only 782 individuals in 2011.

# LOSINA

Spanish: *losina, caballo losino*

🄷 1.33 m on average for mares; 1.39 m for males, with a maximum of 1.47 m for both.

🄲 Black, black with reddish hues very visible in the winter. For the first two years foals have a reddish brown coat with a dark head. A white marking on the head is accepted.

**Description**: The Losina has a wide head with large eyes and small ears, a neck wide at the base, slender legs, a high-set tail, and very small hooves. Its blood vessels are visible under the fine skin of the head. The mane and tail are long and abundant.

**Distribution**: Valle de Losa, Burgos Province, Castile and León, Spain.

**Origins and history**: This is a very old native breed from Castile and León, originally a war horse. Its origins are unknown, but it is one of the oldest breeds in Europe. Some believe it is a descendant of the Arabian; others consider it to be an indigenous Iberian type, still others that it comes from Celtic horses.

**Character and attributes**: The Losina is intelligent, gentle, steady, undemanding, resilient, and has good endurance. Fertile and resistant to illness, it is easy to breed. It has the sure-footedness of all mountain horses.

**Uses**: It is a good mount for young or small riders, a good trekking horse. It can be used for light driving.

**Current status**: This very old breed is threatened, with a stable population of only about 750 horses.

The reddish hues of the Losina are particularly visible on foals.

Large head

Thick lips

Often large barrel

Small hooves

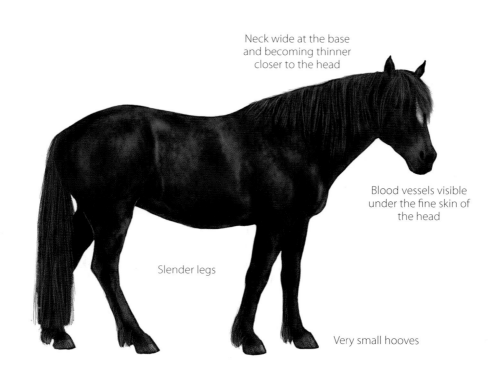

Neck wide at the base
and becoming thinner
closer to the head

Blood vessels visible
under the fine skin of
the head

Slender legs

Very small hooves

# BASQUE MOUNTAIN HORSE

Spanish: *caballo de monte del País Vasco*

Basque: *herriko mendiko zaldia*

**(H)** Around 1.40 m.

**(C)** Predominantly dark bay, mealy black.

**Description**: This horse resembles the Pottok Pony, its close cousin from the Basque Country, with which it is sometimes confused. But it is stockier and heavier. It has a head with a straight profile, short legs, a round croup, and resilient hooves. The mane and tail are thick, supple, and often wavy.

**Distribution**: Spanish Basque Country.

**Origins and history**: This mountain horse, a descendant of the ancient horses that populated the Basque Country, is bred in semi-freedom. Herds graze in the mountains in the summer and are brought in once a year.

**Character and attributes**: The Basque Mountain Horse is rustic, well adapted to the local climate.

**Uses**: Once a draft and carriage horse, it is today bred primarily for its meat. However, it is increasingly being transformed into a recreational horse.

**Current status**: This very rare native breed, which was near extinction, has seen its numbers gradually increase in the past few years, and now counts 2,100 horses.

# MARISMEÑA

Spanish: *marismeña, caballo marismeño*

**(H)** 1.40 m–1.48 m.

**(C)** Black, bay, dappled bay.

**Description**: This is a typically Iberian horse with a rather wide head and convex profile; rather short, arched neck; and low-set tail. One of its distinguishing characteristics is the development of its lower lip, which enables it to graze underwater. It has good, wide hooves and is never shod, which is typical of horses living in marshes.

**Distribution**: Doñana National Park, Andalusia, Spain.

**Origins and history**: It is believed that the Marismeña, the "horse of the marshes," is the ancestor of Iberian horses, or at least a local variety. It lives in a semi-wild state in the marshes of Guadalquivir. It has probably been crossed with horses from North Africa in the past. Once a year the wild horses are gathered to be branded and sold.

**Character and attributes**: Once tamed it is a bold and confident horse. Resilient, robust, and undemanding, it has good health and is well adapted to humid zones, able to walk long distances in difficult conditions.

**Uses**: It is a good trekking horse but is also used for *doma vaquera*.

**Current status**: The breed is rare and endangered; as of 2011, there were around 1,320 animals. It suffered from the drought and lack of food in 2012.

Thick, often wavy
mane and tail

Round croup

Short legs

Solid hooves

Low-set tail

Convex profile

Lower lip well
developed to graze on
grass covered by water

Wide hooves adapted for
life in wet environments

# RETUERTA HORSE

Spanish: *caballo de las retuertas*

**H** 1.45 m–1.55 m.

**C** Bay, dark bay, dappled bay.

**Description**: The Retuerta has a long, convex head, slender neck, slightly sloping croup, and robust legs. The skin is thick to protect against attacks by mosquitoes.

**Distribution**: The Doñana nature reserve, Andalusia, Spain. A second group was formed in 2012 in the Campanarios d'Azaba reserve, in Salamanca Province, to diminish the risk of extinction linked to epizootic disease.

**Origins and history**: The breed is currently being recognized, and scientists are delighted to be studying it. This very old breed lives in the wild in swamps, isolated from other equine populations. According to genetic analyses, it is one of the oldest European breeds.

**Character and attributes**: Very wild, very cautious, rebellious, it is not easily broken. It is very rustic and very resilient in hot conditions. It is particularly resistant to illness, and is able to survive in an environment that many other breeds could not tolerate.

**Uses**: Although it was once used as a work horse on ranches or for agricultural work, today it lives in the wild. Because of its wild nature, it can only be handled by very experienced professionals.

**Current status**: The breed is extremely rare and in danger of extinction, with only a hundred or so horses, but the population is stable. It is protected in order to avoid genetic contamination through crossings with Marismeñas or Andalusians.

# SPANISH ANGLO-ARAB AND SPANISH ARABIAN

Spanish: *hispano-arabe, tres sangres, cruzado*

**H** 1.55 m–1.58 m.

**C** Bay, light gray, chestnut.

**Description**: This is an ever elegant horse, of noble, light gait. It has a head with a straight or slightly convex profile, prominent withers, long and solid legs, and a slightly sloping croup.

**Distribution**: Spain, primarily in Andalusia; Portugal, but also a few in Great Britain and Australia.

**Origins and history**: The Spanish Arabian is the result of crossings between Iberian horses and Arabians. The Spanish Anglo-Arab is the result of crossings among three breeds—Andalusian, Thoroughbred, and Arabian or Anglo-Arab—which explains why it is sometimes called *tres sangres* ("three bloods") or *cruzado*. The Spanish crossbreed with Andalusians, the Portuguese with Lusitanos, and each country has its own studbook. The Portuguese also produce an Arab-Lusitano crossbred.

**Character and attributes**: It has a remarkable temperament. It is particularly agile, very brave, responsive, and spirited, all the while maintaining great calm.

**Uses**: This athletic and confident horse is used for the *doma vaquera*, bullfighting on horseback, dressage, and show jumping. It is also the horse with which young bulls are trained to fight. But it is also used for endurance racing or trekking.

**Current status**: The Spanish Arabian is a protected breed, with only around 7,280 horses in 2011. Its numbers are increasing.

The Spanish Anglo-Arab, sturdy and responsive, is used for *doma vaquera*.

Thin neck

Long, convex
head

*Doma vaquera*
saddle

The Spanish influence
is often seen in the way
the head is carried

Prominent
withers

Long, solid legs

**Spanish Arabian**

# ANDALUSIAN

Spanish: *pura raza española*

Acronym: PRE

Old name: *andalou*

**(H)** 1.60 m on average (1.50 m minimum for mares, 1.52 m for males).

**(C)** Often gray, sometimes bay, more rarely black, chestnut, roan. Many are born dark gray and lighten with age. All coats are possible.

**Description**: The Andalusian is a very beautiful horse of baroque style, with rounded lines. It has a noble and proud look, a compact and elegant body. The face is straight or slightly convex. Its gaze is expressive; its ears are nicely shaped. The neck is slightly arched and muscular. The shoulders are long, sloping, and muscular. The croup is round, powerful, slightly sloping. The mane and tail are supple, silky, and very thick. The hair of the hide is fine and short. It has pronounced sexual dimorphism; mares are clearly more slender than males, especially in the neck.

**Distribution**: Native to Andalusia, Spain, it is bred almost everywhere in the world, throughout all of Europe and America. It is a founder of many breeds, notably in North and South America, after it was introduced by the conquistadors.

**Origins and history**: Andalusians are the result of crossbreeding first between native Iberian horses and

In Spain, broodmares, which live outdoors, often have their manes and part of their tails cut, out of tradition and for ease of care.

Germanic horses in the fifth century following the invasion of the Vandals, then between Barb, Arabian, and Syrian horses imported by the Moors when they invaded Spain in 711. Spanish horses (whose ancestors were Spanish Jennets) were very highly regarded beginning in the Middle Ages, notably as war horses, and they have improved many other breeds.

A slightly more rustic variety, with a very pure lineage, the Carthusian (*cartujano*) has been bred and preserved by monks since 1476. It is most often gray. Like the Moyle in the United States, it sometimes has two small protuberances on its forehead.

In the United States Andalusians and Arabians are crossed to produce the Aralusian, corresponding to the Spanish Arabian. Crossed with the Friesian, the Andalusian gives the Warlander (in the United States) or the Ispazon (in Europe), and with the Quarter Horse, the Azteca (Mexico).

**Character and attributes**: This is a dynamic, balanced, intelligent, and agile horse. It is known for its good nature, its courage, its calm, and its ability to learn and to adapt. Its gaits are wonderful, light, and high-stepping. It has great endurance.

**Uses**: Quite versatile, it can excel both in very high-level disciplines, and is a pleasant recreational horse. It is traditionally used in haute école, exhibitions and the circus, bullfighting, *doma vaquera*, dressage, and driving, but it is also a good trekking horse. It can also compete in show jumping.

**Current status**: Because the Andalusian is one of the most beautiful horses in the world, the breed remains very popular. The global population is at more than 170,000 horses, and it is bred in more than sixty countries.

Because of its great stage presence, the Andalusian is also an incomparable exhibition horse.

Spanish saddle

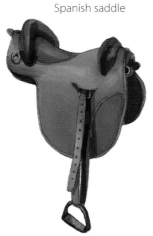

Andalusian stallions are known for their charisma and their lush mane and forelock.

Powerful and curved neck

Round and muscular croup

Silky and very thick mane and tail

Well-formed ears

Low-set tail

Large, expressive eyes

Profile often slightly convex

Deep chest

Slender and solid legs

Esteemed in many disciplines, this horse with light gaits is accomplished in dressage and in haute école.

The Carthusian is an ancient lineage of Andalusian. Some of them sometimes have two little bumps on the forehead, like the Moyle (p. 460) or the Datong (p. 344).

# MENORQUIN

Spanish: *menorquina, menorquino*

**H** Around 1.60 m, but as tall as 1.80 m, with a minimum of 1.54 m for males and 1.51 m for mares.

**C** Black, without white markings.

**Description**: This is a thin and light Iberian horse, with a noble gait; slender, elongated, slightly convex head; small ears; thick and muscular neck; rather long and straight back; slightly sloping croup; long and slender legs; and small and solid hooves. The mane and tail are thick and long.

**Distribution**: Most of these horses are in the Baleares, on the island of Minorca, in Spain; a few are also in Italy and France.

**Origins and history**: The origins of this island horse are unknown, but it is clear that it has received some Spanish, Barb, and Arabian blood. It is an ancient breed, whose breeding truly began in the sixteenth century under the reign of King Jaime II of Minorca, who wanted an excellent war horse. Versatile, it was used in both agricultural work and in parades during island festivals.

**Character and attributes**: The Menorquin is agile, fast, very calm and poised, with lovely light and comfortable gaits. It is rustic.

**Uses**: It is suitable for parades, dressage, haute école, exhibitions, and notably the tourist attraction of *jaleo*, the festival of dancing horses. It is a good trekking horse, but it can also perform in show jumping and can be harnessed. The local dressage discipline is called *doma menorquina*.

**Current status**: This native breed is rare but growing, and has become increasingly popular among riders in the know. In 2012 there were around 3,500 horses in the world, with more than 650 broodmares and an average of 250 births per year.

During popular festivals Baleares riders make their richly decorated Menorquins dance before a clamoring crowd.

# BALEARIC

Also called: Mallorquin

Spanish: *mallorquina*

**H** 1.62 m on average.

**C** Always black. It can have a white marking on the forehead, but nowhere else.

**Description**: This small, thin, and willowy horse is often confused with the Menorquin, which it greatly resembles, even though it is smaller. It has a long head with a convex profile; small ears; a short, arched, not very wide neck; broad chest; straight back; long croup; muscular legs; and low-set tail. The mane and tail are long and abundant.

**Distribution**: Island of Majorca, in the Baleares, in Spain; a few individuals in France, England, Switzerland, and Hungary.

**Origins and history**: Originating in Majorca (Baleares), the Balearic is a horse whose origins are not well known, though it is probably the descendant of ancient Celtic horses and a Catalan breed that is now extinct.

**Character and attributes**: It is calm, docile, strong, rustic, and easygoing.

**Uses**: It is essentially a saddle horse, and can also be harnessed.

**Current status**: This native breed is extremely rare, with only slightly more than 320 animals recorded in 2011.

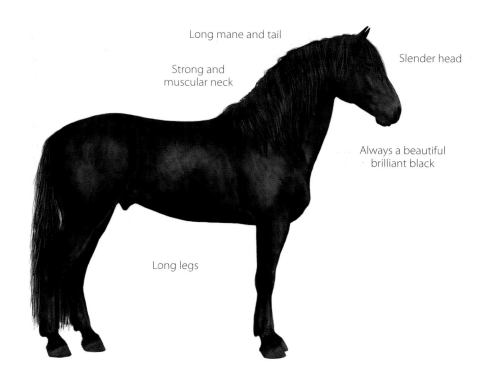

Long mane and tail

Slender head

Strong and
muscular neck

Always a beautiful
brilliant black

Long legs

Short, arched neck

Long head with
slightly convex
profile

Low-set tail

Broad chest

Muscular legs

# SPANISH SPORT HORSE

Spanish: *caballo de deporte español*

Acronym: CDE

**H** Often over 1.60 m.

**C** Bay, dark bay, chestnut, black, gray.

**Description**: This is a European sport horse, without a standard, which can scarcely be distinguished from other breeds of this type. All these breeds have been too greatly interbred, in the goal of obtaining horses with excellent sport results, for them to be truly differentiated.

**Distribution**: Spain.

**Origins and history**: This very recent Spanish breed, which has not been officially established, represents the crossbreeding on Spanish territory of many European sport horses, and responds to a strong demand by Spanish riders. For the time being it is more a registry than a breed in the strict sense. The breed is selected for sport results in show jumping, dressage, and other disciplines. A Spanish Sport Horse is the result either of two Spanish Sport Horse parents, or of a crossing among many different breeds.

**Character and attributes**: This is an athletic and energetic horse.

**Uses**: It is intended above all for show jumping, but also for dressage and eventing.

**Current status**: The Spanish Sport Horse population has stabilized and is decreasing slightly after a period of great expansion (more than 11,300 horses in 2011).

# HISPANO-BRETON

Spanish: *hispano-bretón*

**H** 1.45 m–1.54 m.

**C** Chestnut, chestnut with light mane and tail, dark bay, black.

**Description**: It weighs around 700 kg. It has a head with a straight profile, muscular and round body, broad chest, straight back, and solid legs. The hooves are hard. The mane and tail are abundant.

**Distribution**: Spain, especially in Castile and León and Aragon.

**Origins and history**: This breed was created at the beginning of the twentieth century to respond to the need for powerful horses for agricultural work, by crossing Breton Drafts with native Spanish mares who would provide better adaptation to the Spanish climate. The breed was only officially recognized in 1997.

**Character and attributes**: Calm and powerful, it is content with poor pastureland and is easy to keep.

**Uses**: It is suitable for work in harness, and for various agricultural work. It is principally raised today for its meat. Crossed with a donkey, the mares produce good mules. It is being increasingly used as a recreational horse.

**Current status**: The breed is rare but growing, with only around 5,500 horses.

Athletic physique

Long legs

Thick mane
and tail

Wide croup

Broad chest

## SPAIN

# BURGUETE

Spanish: *burguete, burguete navarra*

**H** 1.48 m for mares, 1.55 for males.

**C** Bay, chestnut, with all variations.

**Description**: This heavy horse has a head with a straight, sometimes slightly convex profile and wide forehead; strong neck; broad chest; and a wide, long, and double croup. The mane and tail are long and abundant, and it has feathering on the legs.
**Distribution**: Navarre, Spain.

**Origins and history**: The Burguete is the result of crossings between indigenous breeds of Jaca Navarra and French stallions (Postier Breton, Percheron, Ardennais, Comtois). It is bred in semi-freedom in the mountain pastureland of the Pyrenees.
**Character and attributes**: Resilient and maturing early, the Burguete has conserved the rusticity of the Jaca Navarra.
**Uses**: Originally intended for agricultural work, this horse is now bred mainly for its meat. Mares were once crossed with donkeys to produce mules. It is suitable for work in harness.
**Current status**: This native horse is rare, with 4,814 individuals, including 2,991 broodmares, in 2011, and the population is protected to prevent extinction.

## SPAIN

# SERRANO

Spanish: *cavallo serrano*

**H** Around 1.30 m–1.40 m.

**C** Bay, dark bay, black.

**Description**: The Serrano is small, with a long and straight head.
**Distribution**: The Community of Madrid, notably the Sierra de Guadarrama, Spain.
**Origins and history**: This small, ancient population is not recognized. They are the descendants of horses that were used locally for agricultural work. The Serrano is threatened by crossbreeding with foreign breeds.
**Character and attributes**: Robust, resilient, simple, well adapted to the sometimes harsh local climate, it is a mountain horse with a very docile nature.
**Uses**: Once used for agricultural work, it is today raised for its meat and for recreation. It can make a good trekking horse.
**Current status**: In 2012 the Madrid Assembly declared this horse a historical and cultural national treasure, which is good for the breed, as it will benefit from a conservation program. There are only 7 pureblood stallions and 29 mares left.

## SPAIN

# CATALAN PYRENEES HORSE

Spanish: *cavall pirinenc català* (CPC)

**H** 1.45 m–1.60 m.

**C** Bay, chestnut, notably chestnut with light mane and tail, black, a few roans; white markings on the legs and head must be discreet.

**Description**: This draft horse weighs between 650 and 750 kg on average. Its head is sometimes large, with an often slightly convex profile; it has a strong and muscular neck; broad chest and back; voluminous barrel; and powerful and round croup. The mane and tail are abundant. Old horses often have mustaches.
**Distribution**: Catalan Pyrenees, Spain.
**Origins and history**: This breed was recognized in 2012 in Spain. It is the result of crossings between the ancient Catalan horse and the Breton, Comtois, and Ardennais. These horses were once erroneously considered to be Hispano-Bretons. It is bred in semi-freedom, grazing in the mountains.
**Character and attributes**: The Catalan Pyrenees Horse is very rustic, simple, and fertile; it is easy to breed due to the reproductive capabilities of the mares. It is calm but full of vigor.
**Uses**: It is essentially bred for the meat of its foals, but also for tourism and recreation. It is used for harness work such as hauling debris.
**Current status**: With more than 5,000 animals (in 2010, 4,555 mares and 492 stallions) and official recognition, the breed is doing fine for a draft horse and should be able to develop even further.

Long, double croup

Feathering on legs

# SPANISH TROTTER

Spanish: *trotador español, trotador mallorquín*

**Ⓗ** 1.60 m–1.70 m.

**Ⓒ** Bay, dark bay, black, sometimes with white markings on the head and legs.

**Description**: It has the physique of a trotter, with a muscular croup and strong legs.

**Distribution**: Mainly on the Balearic Islands; most of the population is found on Majorca, followed by Minorca and Ibiza, Spain.

**Origins and history**: The breeding of this trotter began with the importing of French trotters at the end of the nineteenth century. It is a mix of French, American, and Orlov Trotters, and of Balearic (Mallorquin) and Menorquin horses.

**Character and attributes**: It has the characteristics of trotters: docile and cooperative, strong, energetic, and confident.

**Uses**: The inhabitants of the Balearic Islands are great fans of trotting races, for which they breed this horse. Because of its good nature, it can also be used for recreational riding.

**Current status**: Spain counted more than 9,300 Spanish Trotters in 2011.

Italy has a large number of horse breeds of quite varied types, more than most other European countries, as well as the rest of the world. Italian horsemanship was greatly renowned during the

---

ITALY

# Giara Horse

Italian: *cavallino della Giara*

**H** 1.25 m–1.35 m for males; 1.15 m–1.30 m for mares.

**C** Brown bay, black, bay, dark chestnut.

**Description**: The Giara is small and stocky, with a large, boxy head; small ears; a short but strong neck; unobtrusive withers; a rather narrow chest; slender legs; hard hooves; and a low-set tail. The mane and tail are thick.

**Distribution**: Sardinia, on the high plateau of Giara, Italy.

**Origins and history**: This small horse has lived in a semi-wild state on the island of Sardinia since at least antiquity. Its origins, very ancient, are obscure. It might have been imported to the island by the Phoenicians. Giaras were once used for agricultural work during the harvest. Crossed with the Arabian, it creates the Giarab, which is more of a sport horse.

**Character and attributes**: This is a wild animal, therefore fearful and very lively. It is rustic, agile, and sure-footed.

**Uses**: Giaras can be trained, notably as mounts for children, but this does not happen much today. Integrated into their local environment, they are above all a tourist attraction at the national park where they live.

**Current status**: The breed remains very rare, since there were only around 700 animals alive in 2012. Its numbers are, however, increasing slightly.

---

ITALY

# Sarcidano Horse

Italian: *cavallo del Sarcidano*

**H** 1.25 m–1.45 m for males; 1.15 m–1.35 m for mares.

**C** Most often bay or black, sometimes gray.

**Description**: The Sarcidano has a wide head with a straight profile, large eyes, a muscular neck, short and muscular croup, and short and strong legs. The mane and tail are abundant.

**Distribution**: Sardinia, Italy.

**Origins and history**: This is a very ancient Sardinian breed that still lives in a semi-wild state and whose origins are unknown. It might share ancestors with the Andalusian. The unique genetic legacy of this island breed, isolated from other Italian breeds, is of great interest to scientists.

**Character and attributes**: The Sarcidano is lively and responsive. It is also rustic, undemanding, and sure-footed.

**Uses**: Once tamed, it can adapt to various sporting or recreational uses.

**Current status**: This horse, which is of great national historical value, is in danger, with just slightly more than a hundred horses recorded in 2011.

Renaissance. Italian breeds, though very interesting, don't have the reputation abroad that they deserve. The Neapolitan horse, which disappeared but is in the process of being reconstituted, did once have a considerable influence throughout all of Europe. Italy has more than 420,000 horses. The racing industry is well developed there. Riding is also popular in Italy. There are around 2.5 million people who ride regularly.

Thick mane and tail

Low-set tail

Large, squarish head

Slender legs

The very rare Giara still lives in the semi-wild in Sardinia.

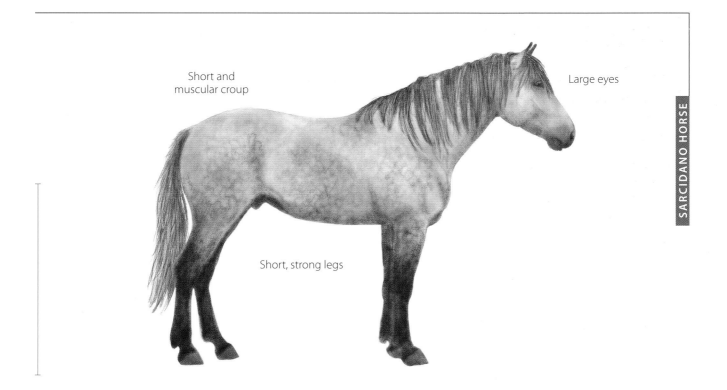

Short and muscular croup

Large eyes

Short, strong legs

# MONTERUFOLI PONY

Italian: *cavallino di Monterufoli*

**H** 1.32 m on average for males; 1.30 m for mares.

**C** Almost always black or dark bay, with no, or very discreet, white markings.

**Description**: The Monterufoli Pony resembles a small Maremmano. It has a rather long head, a muscular neck, and a wide and slightly sloping croup. The mane and tail are thick.

**Distribution**: Region of Monterufoli, in the province of Pisa, Italy.

**Origins and history**: The Monterufoli breed is descended from the small horses that lived in the wild in Monterufoli. It was crossed at the beginning of the twentieth century with the Maremmano, Tolfetano, and Eastern horses, in order to improve them. Once tamed, Monterufolis were used as pack horses and for transportation by the inhabitants of the region. They are still bred in semi-freedom.

**Character and attributes**: It can be rather spirited, but still remains very docile. It is rustic and simple.

**Uses**: It is a good mount for children, and can compete in show jumping or in dressage; it is also used for pulling carts and light carriages.

**Current status**: This small native breed was on the brink of extinction and remains very rare, with only around 240 individuals in 2011, but its numbers are increasing thanks to conservation efforts carried out on its behalf.

# ESPERIA PONY

Italian: *pony di Esperia*

**H** 1.38 m on average for males; 1.32 m for mares.

**C** Usually black, sometimes with discreet white markings.

**Description**: It has a short head with a straight profile, prominent withers, and strong legs. The mane and tail are abundant.

**Distribution**: Province of Frosinone, Italy.

**Origins and history**: This breed has ancient origins. It received Arabian blood at the beginning of the nineteenth century. Its name comes from one of its breeders, the Baron Ambrogio Roselli di Esperia. The Esperia was once used as a pack horse and for agricultural work. It is still bred in semi-freedom. The breed has been officially recognized since 1962.

**Character and attributes**: The Esperia is lively but listens to its rider; it is resilient and undemanding, well adapted to harsh living conditions.

**Uses**: This breed is used as a lesson horse in riding schools, due to its size, which is suitable for young riders, and its aptitude for equestrian sports, including show jumping.

**Current status**: This native breed remains in danger, with small numbers—only around 800 individuals in 2012. Breeders regularly report wolf attacks on the foals in herds raised in the wild.

Muscular neck

Thick mane
and tail

Rather long head

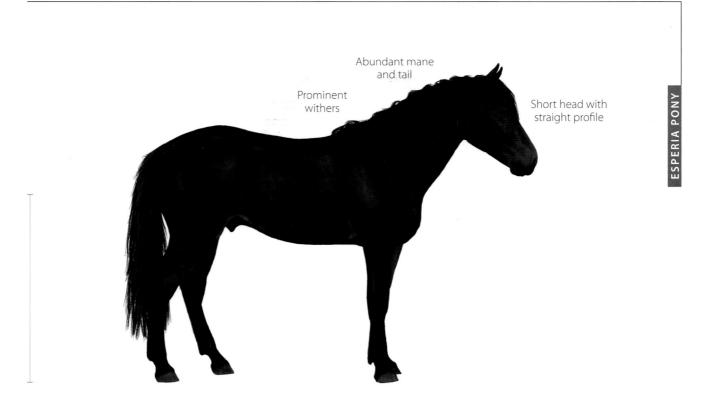

Abundant mane
and tail

Prominent
withers

Short head with
straight profile

# PENTRO HORSE

Italian: *cavallo del Pentro*

**H** On average 1.37 m for males; 1.33 m for mares.

**C** Bay or black, very few white markings.

**Description**: The Pentro Horse has a head with a straight or slightly convex profile, large eyes, a muscular neck, slightly prominent withers, a broad chest, and a muscular and slightly sloping croup. The mane and tail are long and thick.

**Distribution**: Molise region, Italy.

**Origins and history**: The breed probably originally descended from Barb horses, but it has above all been forged by the sometimes harsh mountainous environment in which it lives. It was used for farm work and carrying loads. It is still bred in semi-freedom. The breed was only recognized in 2005.

**Character and attributes**: It has both a nervous and a docile character, and is content with meager food.

**Uses**: It is a work horse that is also used in various equestrian sports. It is valued for equestrian tourism. It is also bred for its meat.

**Current status**: This native breed is being watched, as its numbers are small, even if they are growing, with around 600 horses in 2012.

Rustic and not too big, the Pentro is a good trekking horse.

# BARDIGIANO

Italian: *bardigiano*

**H** 1.39 m–1.49 for males; 1.35–1.47 for mares.

**C** Often black, but also bay and dark bay, sometimes roan, with very few white markings.

**Description**: This small, compact horse resembles the Mérens or Dales. It has a small head with a wide forehead, small ears, a powerful neck wide at the base, unobtrusive withers, a broad chest and back, muscular croup, low-set tail, and wide hooves. The hair of the mane and tail is abundant.

**Distribution**: Italy. Some in Germany and Hungary; a few in Switzerland and Belgium.

**Origins and history**: This mountain horse, the ancestral mount of Italian knights, might have very ancient Belgian ancestors. It was only recognized in 1977. A Bardigiano-Arabian was created by crossbreeding with an Arabian, to obtain a more athletic horse.

**Character and attributes**: This is a robust and energetic but also docile horse. It is undemanding and rustic. Accustomed to living in the mountains, it is sure-footed.

**Uses**: It is used as a saddle or harness horse, or for equestrian tourism. It was for a long time used to produce mules. It is also employed in equitherapy.

**Current status**: This native horse suffered greatly from the two world wars and saw its numbers decrease in the middle of the twentieth century, but since the 1970s efforts to save it have borne fruit. The breed is now well stabilized, with more than 3,550 animals counted.

Prominent withers

Large eyes

Wide back

Neck wide at the base

Wide hooves

# TOLFETANO

Italian: *tolfetano*

ⓗ 1.45 m–1.55 m; 1.50 m on average for males, 1.47 m for mares.

ⓒ Mainly bay, dark bay, but also black, chestnut, gray, with very few white markings.

**Description**: The Tolfetano has a head with a straight or slightly convex profile; rather short, wide, and muscular neck; a somewhat narrow chest; short shoulders; a wide and sloping croup; and rather short legs. The mane and tail are thick.

**Distribution**: Central Italy.

**Origins and history**: The Tolfetano derives its name from the village of Tolfa. This very ancient breed has existed since the Etruscan era. It probably has had Berber and French influences. It is the Italian equestrian work horse of the most ancient type, not having undergone various crossings intended to improve it, as the Maremmano has.

**Character and attributes**: Lively, generous, and adaptable, the Tolfetano is a robust, agile, and sure-footed horse. Naturally selected for a sometimes harsh environment, the breed is simple and resilient.

**Uses**: Traditionally used for livestock herding by the *butteri*—Italian cowboys—it is also a good, versatile recreational horse. It is employed as a lesson horse in riding schools. It is also suitable for light harness work, and is bred for its meat, as well.

**Current status**: This native breed is still small in number, with only slightly more than 1,280 individuals in 2012.

The butteri are Italian cowboys. They ride Tolfetanos or Maremmanos.

# CATRIA HORSE

Italian: *cavallo catria, cavallo del Catria*

ⓗ 1.45 m–1.60 m for males, 1.40 m–1.55 m for mares.

ⓒ Bay, sometimes black; few markings.

**Description**: The Catria Horse has a head with a straight profile; broad chest; wide and short back; very muscular, dished croup; and wide, solid hooves.

**Distribution**: The Appennines, Italy.

**Origins and history**: The origins of the Catria Horse remain obscure, but it was crossed a lot with Maremmanos and Freiburgs and with draft breeds such as the Breton or the Italian Draft. The breed was traditionally used on farms, for various light work. It is generally bred in semi-freedom until it is broken.

**Character and attributes**: It is confident, undemanding, rustic, with the sure-footedness of mountain horses.

**Uses**: The Catria Horse is suitable for riding, light harness work, trekking, or even as a pack horse. It is also used to produce mules, and is bred for its meat.

**Current status**: This native breed with small numbers remains endangered, with only around 400 individuals in 2012.

Rather short, wide, and muscular neck

Somewhat narrow chest

Fairly short legs

Short, wide back

Head with straight profile

Wide, solid hooves

# NEAPOLITAN

Italian: *napoletano*

**Ⓗ** Minimum of 1.50 m.

**Ⓒ** Bay, black, liver chestnut, gray.

**Description**: This is a baroque-type horse. It has a boxy head with a straight profile that becomes convex near the nose; a wide forehead; large eyes; small ears; a long, muscular, arched neck; prominent withers; long, sloping, muscular shoulders; a broad chest; a very wide, round croup; and muscular legs. The mane and tail are long and thick.

**Distribution**: Campania, Italy.

**Origins and history**: During the Renaissance this was one of the most sought-after of Italian breeds, enjoying great popularity throughout Europe; the Neapolitan has been used to improve many other breeds, such as the Lipizzan and the Hanoverian.

The breed is, however, extinct. But following reconstitution efforts begun in the 1980s, it is slowly reemerging among Italian breeds now that it has been officially recognized. An enthusiast has in fact discovered a strain of Serbian Lipizzans that have a lot of Neapolitan blood, which has enabled him to create a small breeding group.

**Character and attributes**: The Neapolitan is spirited and outgoing, with very elegant gaits.

**Uses**: It is an excellent horse for dressage and haute école. It can also be harnessed.

**Current status**: In the process of being reconstituted, its numbers are still extremely small; there were only 30 in 2011.

# SANFRATELLO

Italian: *sanfratellano*

**Ⓗ** 1.52 m on average for males, 1.50 m for mares.

**Ⓒ** Black, bay, dark bay.

**Description**: The Sanfratello has a head with a straight profile; a long, muscular neck; a broad chest; short, sloping shoulders; and a wide, round croup. Its mane and tail are thick.

**Distribution**: Sicily, Italy.

**Origins and history**: The origins of this horse are rather obscure, but it has been crossed with Eastern horses, notably Barb, Spanish horses, Neapolitans, and English halfbreds. It has also received Nonius blood. It is bred in semi-freedom until it is broken.

**Character and attributes**: This is a willing, adaptable, simple, and resilient horse with endurance and sure-footedness. Due to its life in semi-freedom, it has adapted to the sometimes challenging climate and environmental conditions in Sicily.

**Uses**: It is essentially used for sporting activities such as show jumping, but also for trekking where its sure-footedness is an asset. It is also good for pulling carts and light carriages.

**Current status**: A native breed, its numbers are still small but are growing because the Sanfratello is beloved by Sicilians. There are around 1,100 horses.

Long, muscular, arched neck

Very wide, round croup

Broad chest

Wide, round croup

Broad chest

# VENTASSO HORSE

Italian: *cavallo del Ventasso*

**Ⓗ** 1.52 m–1.64 m for males; 1.50 m–1.62 m for mares.

**Ⓒ** Most often bay and gray, sometimes chestnut and black.

**Description**: The Ventasso Horse has a head with a straight profile, muscular neck, prominent withers, a broad chest, and a powerful croup.

**Distribution**: Emilia-Romagna, Italy.

**Origins and history**: The Ventasso Horse, which has ancient origins, received Lipizzan and English Thoroughbred blood in the 1960s, but also Selle Français and Anglo-Arab blood. The Lipizzan stallion was introduced primarily to soften the breed's character, which was very nervous. The Ventasso was once a military horse. To promote the breed, mounted guards at the Appennino Tosco-Emiliano National Park ride these horses.

**Character and attributes**: It is balanced, though lively and rather nervous. It has endurance and is powerful, rustic, and undemanding.

**Uses**: It is a versatile saddle horse, good for sport or recreation.

**Current status**: This native breed is extremely rare and its numbers are very small, with only 189 individuals in 2011. The population is increasing slightly thanks to the conservation efforts that have been put in place to save it.

---

# PERSANO

Italian: *persano*

**Ⓗ** Minimum of 1.50 m, often 1.55 m–1.65 m.

**Ⓒ** Bay, chestnut, gray, black.

**Description**: The Persano has a head with a wide, slightly concave forehead that becomes convex lower on the face; large eyes; small ears; a long, muscular, slightly arched neck; prominent withers; a short back; rather thin legs; and a sloping croup. The mane and tail are thick.

**Distribution**: Campania, Italy.

**Origins and history**: The Persano, whose breeding began at the end of the eighteenth century with King Charles III, is the result of crossings of Arabian, Syrian Arabian, Persian, Andalusian, Mecklenburg, and Thoroughbred horses. It was once a military horse, but was also used for hunting, being popular for its robustness. Very similar to the Salernitano, it is overseen by the same association.

**Character and attributes**: Docile, gentle, and willing, it is an athletic and robust horse.

**Uses**: It is a good saddle horse that excels in eventing, dressage, and show jumping.

**Current status**: This once prestigious horse is now extremely rare, and almost became extinct after World War II. Today the breed counts only around 80 horses (2012).

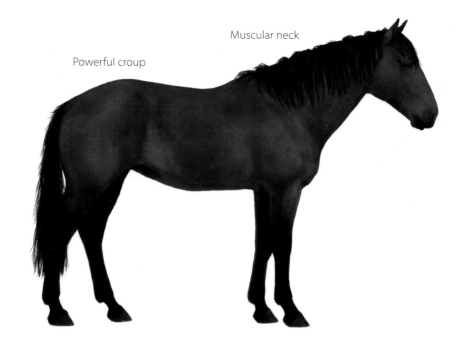

Powerful croup

Muscular neck

Thick mane
and tail

A slightly concave
profile, but convex
close to the nose

# ROMAN HORSE OF THE PART OF THE MAREMMA THAT IS IN LAZIO

Italian: *caballo romano della Maremma Laziale* or *romano maremma lazial* or *branconero*

**Ⓗ** 1.55 m–1.65 m for males, 1.50 m–1.62 m for mares.

**Ⓒ** Most often bay and all its variations; black; gray. Limited white markings are authorized.

**Description**: It has a long head; a muscular neck, wide at the base; a broad chest; a short and straight back; a wide and sloping croup; strong legs; and wide hooves. The mane and tail are long and thick.

**Distribution**: Maremma in Lazio, Italy.

**Origins and history**: This ancient breed, whose origins go back to Roman and Etruscan horses, was used by Italian shepherds and cowherds. It differs from the Maremmano, a similar breed that is also used for herding livestock. A herd still lives in freedom.

**Character and attributes**: The Roman Horse of Maremma in Lazio is docile and willing, agile and fast, with energetic gaits. It is resilient and adapted to a swampy environment.

**Uses**: It is a work horse, but it can also be used in various equestrian sports.

**Current status**: The breed was only recognized in 2010, and its numbers are small (800).

# MURGESE

Italian: *murgese*

**Ⓗ** 1.55 m–1.68 m for males; 1.50 m–1.62 m for mares.

**Ⓒ** Almost always black, sometimes dark bay. Some individuals are a beautiful metallic gray with a black head. There are no white markings.

**Description**: It has the build of a light draft horse, with a convex profile; a wide forehead; large eyes; a powerful neck, wide at the base; broad chest; straight back; wide croup; and low-set tail. The mane and tail are long and abundant.

**Distribution**: Puglia region, Italy, but the breed is also present in other European countries, including France, Germany, Belgium, Great Britain, and Switzerland.

**Origins and history**: It is descended from Eastern horses, notably Barbs, but also Spanish horses. It is also a descendant of the Neapolitan and has received some Thoroughbred blood. Once very sought-after as a military horse, it saw its numbers fall in the twentieth century.

**Character and attributes**: The rustic Murgese is easy to keep. It is sure-footed, energetic, but very docile and calm, with good endurance.

**Uses**: It is a good horse for dressage, but also for light harness work and trekking. Crossed with a donkey, the breed produces good mules.

**Current status**: This native breed remains rare, but is reemerging after almost disappearing. There are around 3,000 horses. Its beautiful black coat, physique, and good nature should enable it to grow again in popularity.

The well-balanced Murgese makes a good horse for dressage.

Neck wide at
the base

Long head

Strong legs

Characteristic
convex profile

Usually the coat is black, but
sometimes it is black roan with a black
head that is magnificently satiny

Broad chest

# SALERNO

Also called: Salernitano

Italian: *salernitano*

Ⓗ 1.63 m–1.73 m; 1.58 m minimum for males, 1.50 m for mares.

Ⓒ Generally bay, chestnut, black, sometimes gray, usually with white markings on the head and legs.

**Description**: This large horse resembles the Thoroughbred, with which it has been crossed. It has an elegant and slender head, a wide forehead and long neck, prominent withers, sloping shoulders, a powerful and long croup, and very long and solid legs. The mane and tail are thick.

**Distribution**: Salerno, Italy.

**Origins and history**: The Salerno is an ancient breed that resulted from crossings between Neapolitan, Spanish, Eastern, and Thoroughbred horses. It was appreciated as a military horse and for a long time was considered to be one of the best Italian saddle horses.

**Character and attributes**: Energetic and spirited, it is a very good jumper. It is particularly resilient in hot temperatures.

**Uses**: It is above all a sport horse, notably for show jumping and eventing. It is also used by the mounted police. A lively animal, it is best for experienced riders.

**Current status**: This once very popular horse now has an extremely small population, with only a few dozen horses, which makes it one of the rarest of Italian breeds.

# SICILIANO

Italian: *siciliano*

Ⓗ 1.55 m–1.60 m for males, 1.53 m–1.58 m for mares.

Ⓒ Bay, black, chestnut, gray.

**Description**: The population is not truly homogeneous. It has a light head with a straight profile, small ears, a powerful neck, prominent withers, and long, thin legs.

**Distribution**: Sicily, Italy.

**Origins and history**: The Siciliano is a very ancient breed, the result of crossings between native Sicilian horses, which have been present for a long time on the island, and Eastern horses imported over time. The Eastern blood is very noticeable. Every Siciliano must be born in Sicily to be considered a legitimate Siciliano. Breeders have established the importance of the lineage of foals in their plans for the breed.

**Character and attributes**: The Siciliano is nervous and lively, but docile at the same time. It is a vigorous and powerful horse.

**Uses**: Used under saddle and in light harness, it can also compete in show jumping. It is also used in equestrian tourism. It is one of the mounts of the *carabinieri* regiments.

**Current status**: This native breed remains rare and threatened, although its currently dynamic breeding program has given it new life over the past twenty years.

Long croup

Slender head

Long and solid legs

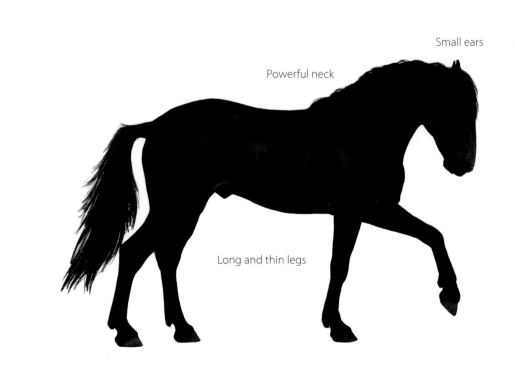

Small ears

Powerful neck

Long and thin legs

# SARDINIAN ANGLO-ARAB

Also called: Anglo-Arab Sarda

Italian: *anglo-arabo sardo*

**H** There are three different sizes possible. Small: 1.53 m–1.58 m; average: 1.58 m–1.65 m; large: taller than 1.65 m.

**C** Chestnut and bay above all; sometimes gray or black.

**Description**: The Sardinian Anglo-Arab has a head with a straight profile, small ears, and large eyes. It has a slender and elongated neck, prominent withers, a broad chest, straight back, and solid legs. The tail is set high.

**Distribution**: Sardinia, Italy.

**Origins and history**: The Sardinian Anglo-Arab is the result of crossings between native horses and Arabians, then Iberian horses, and with Thoroughbreds and French Anglo-Arabs. It was once used as a military horse before making the transition to a sport horse.

**Character and attributes**: The breed is lively but has a good nature; it is manageable and fast, has endurance, and is a good jumper.

**Uses**: This is a very good horse for show jumping and eventing; it is also used for gallop racing or steeplechase. It is also employed by the mounted police.

**Current status**: Although this native horse is well adapted for equestrian sports, its breeding has encountered some difficulties owing to the recent economic crisis, with fewer than 500 births per year in the past few years.

# CALABRIAN

Also called: Calabrese

Italian: *calabrese*

**H** 1.60 m–1.65 m.

**C** Often bay, dark bay, chestnut; sometimes black, gray.

**Description**: This good-sized horse resembles the Salerno. It has a slender and sometimes slightly convex head, a long neck, rather prominent withers, a straight and rather long back, a high-set tail, and wide hooves.

**Distribution**: Italy.

**Origins and history**: Originally from Calabria, the Calabrian is an ancient breed whose Arabian ancestors were crossed with Andalusians. A contribution of Thoroughbred blood in the twentieth century enabled it to become taller. It also received Salerno blood. In the nineteenth century the Calabrian was a popular mount in Italy.

**Character and attributes**: This fast horse has great endurance. Although lively and energetic, it is still docile.

**Uses**: It is used as a saddle horse, notably for show jumping, its best discipline, but also for equestrian tourism. It is often used in riding schools.

**Current status**: Once very popular, the breed has become less well known, but is still appreciated by connoisseurs.

Long, slender neck

Straight profile

Straight back

Broad chest

Long neck

High-set tail

Slender head, sometimes convex

Wide hooves

# ITALIAN TROTTER

Italian: *trottatore italiano*

**H** 1.60 m–1.65 m.

**C** Often bay, dark bay; more rarely black, chestnut.

**Description**: The Italian Trotter has a slender head with a straight profile; small ears; thin, solid legs; and a powerful croup.

**Distribution**: Italy.

**Origins and history**: Breeding of the Italian Trotter, a rather recent breed, began in the second half of the nineteenth century; then, beginning in the 1940s, it was crossbred selectively with Russian and American trotters, Thoroughbreds, French Trotters, and Hackneys. It is one of the fastest trotters, capable of competing with French and American trotters, and has produced great champions, such as the famous Varenne.

**Character and attributes**: The Italian Trotter is a rather lively horse, sometimes nervous, and above all very fast—and an exceptional trotter.

**Uses**: It is bred essentially for trotting races both in harness and under saddle. Once it is trained to adapt to life after racing, it can be used as a recreational horse, but its lively temperament makes it best suited for experienced riders.

**Current status**: For the moment the breed is doing very well, even if the horse racing industry in Italy has encountered some difficulties in recent years. It remains little known outside of Italy.

# MAREMMANO

Italian: *maremmano*

**H** 1.60 m–1.72 m.

**C** Most often bay, dark bay, black; sometimes mealy.

**Description**: The Maremmano has a long head that is often convex, a neck strong at the base, prominent withers, a broad chest, particularly solid legs, a sloping croup, and hard hooves.

**Distribution**: Tuscany, Italy.

**Origins and history**: The Maremmano is the work horse of the *butteri*—cowboys—of Maremma, in Tuscany. It is likely the result of crossings between native mares of Etruscan origin and Barbs, then later between Norfolk Trotters and Neapolitans. It has more recently received Thoroughbred blood. Young Maremmanos are often bred in semi-freedom before they are broken. Through new crossings with Thoroughbreds, breeders obtain the Maremmano Megliorato ("improved"), a more athletic but less rustic horse.

**Character and attributes**: This brave and energetic worker is robust and has great endurance. Although assertive and sometimes lively, it has the excellent nature, cooperative and calm, of livestock-herding horses, as well as the easy handling and responsiveness typical of this type of horse. Furthermore, it is a good jumper. In addition, it is hardy and well adapted to difficult climate conditions.

**Uses**: As is often true with livestock-herding breeds, the Maremmano is very versatile. Beyond its vocation as a livestock horse, it is used for riding, light harness work, trekking, and mounted police work. There is an equestrian culture that revolves around this horse and the *butteri*.

**Current status**: Although it is very popular in its country, the breed remains rather rare, with only around 2,500 individuals.

The traditional *scafarda* (Italian stock) saddle. It is one of the saddles used by the *butteri* riders (see Tolfetano, *p. 108*).

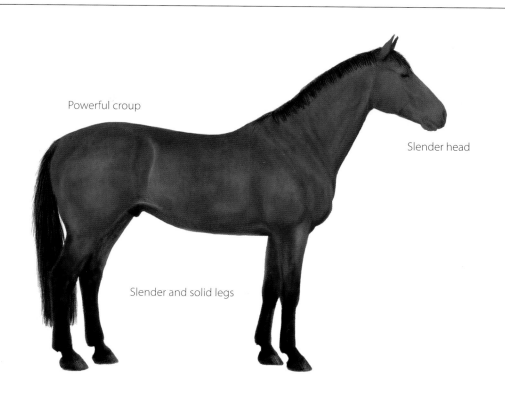

Powerful croup

Slender head

Slender and solid legs

Sloping croup

Long head

Solid legs that
enable it to move
easily over all terrains

# ITALIAN HEAVY DRAFT

Also called: Italian TPR Agricultural Horse

Italian: *tiro pesante rapido* or *caballo agricolo italieno da tiro pesante rapido (CAITPR)*

**H** 1.52 m–1.60 m for males; 1.48 m–1.58 m for mares.

**C** Chestnut, often with lighter mane and tail; sometimes bay, chestnut roan; often with white markings on the legs or head.

**Description**: It resembles the Breton, with which it has been crossed a lot. It weighs around 700–900 kg. It has a rather small head with a wide forehead; short neck, powerful and wide at the base; short back; often double croup; and short and solid legs, with feathering.

**Distribution**: Italy.

**Origins and history**: This draft horse is the result of crossings between native mares and Arabian, Hackney, and Thoroughbred horses, then with Breton, Belgian, Boulonnais, and Ardennais, and finally, after World War I, again with the Breton.

**Character and attributes**: It is an active and vigorous draft horse, sometimes nervous, but still docile. It is rustic. As its Italian name indicates, it is a draft horse endowed with speed, notably when it trots. It matures quickly.

**Uses**: This breed is still primarily bred for meat. It is also used as a coach horse and for hauling.

**Current status**: For a draft horse, it is doing fairly well, with around 6,300 horses in 2011.

Once appreciated as a farm horse, the Italian Draft remains an excellent partner for farms using equine pulling power.

# APPENNINICO

Italian: *appenninico*

**H** 1.50 m–1.60 m for males; 1.40 m–1.50 m for mares.

**C** Bay and chestnut, sometimes with white markings on the head and legs.

**Description**: This is a light draft horse, which weighs around 550–600 kg and greatly resembles the Freiburg. It has a head with a straight profile; broad chest; wide back; long, wide, sloping croup; and wide, solid hooves.

**Distribution**: Upper Tuscany, Emilia-Romagna, Italy.

**Origins and history**: The breed was recognized recently, in 2010. It is the issue of light draft horses that lived in this region. It received Freiburg blood to avoid problems of inbreeding.

**Character and attributes**: It is intelligent, dynamic, docile, powerful, resilient, and hardy. It is very well adapted to its mountainous environment, and is easy to breed.

**Uses**: It is a good harness horse, and is used for equestrian tourism.

**Current status**: Its recent recognition will enable this breed, whose numbers are small, to be consolidated. Around 2,300 individuals were counted in 2011.

# SAMOLACO HORSE

Italian: *samolaco, chiavennese*

**H** Probably around 1.50 m.

**C** Chestnut, often with light mane and tail; bay.

**Description**: It has a light head, broad chest, and round croup. The mane and tail are thick.

**Distribution**: Lombardy, Italy.

**Origins and history**: This breed is not recognized and hasn't been studied much. It is probably of Spanish origin, the issue of horses abandoned by soldiers in the seventeenth century then crossed with native horses. Haflinger blood has recently been introduced into the breed, giving the so-called Samolaco-Avelignese strain. It was once a work horse.

**Character and attributes**: It is known to be undemanding, rustic, and resilient. Used to living in the mountains, it is sure-footed.

**Uses**: There are far too few remaining today, but this horse could be used for equestrian tourism.

**Current status**: This very little known horse is endangered, perhaps already extinct, with only a few animals left. There were only twelve purebred horses left in 1995.

Often double croup

Rather small head
for a draft horse

# ITALIAN SADDLE HORSE

Italian: *italiano da sella, sella italiano*

**H** 1.60 m–1.70 m, a minimum of 1.56 m.

**C** Most often bay, dark bay, black, chestnut.

**Description**: As is often true of sport breeds, which result from much crossbreeding, the Italian Saddle Horse's build is not much different from that of other breeds. It has a balanced physique, robust and muscular; a long neck; wide and powerful back; and long and slender legs.

**Distribution**: Italy, exported elsewhere in Europe.

**Origins and history**: This very recent breed was created from Italian breeds, notably the Sardinian Anglo-Arab, crossed with European sport breeds and Thoroughbreds. The idea was to combine the reliability of Italian breeds with the athletic prowess of the Thoroughbred. The breed is still evolving.

**Character and attributes**: With a lively, nervous, willful, and sensitive temperament, the Italian Saddle Horse is an athletic, powerful, fast, and reliable horse.

**Uses**: This sport horse excels in show jumping, dressage, eventing, and endurance events.

**Current status**: The breed, sought-after for sporting competition in Italy, is doing very well.

# AVELIGNESE

Italian: *avelignese*
*See Haflinger, Austria, p. 204.*

Avelignese is the Italian name of the Haflinger, but the Italian lineage is a bit more massive and taller. The town of Avelengo (whence Avelignese) has the German name of Hafling (whence Haflinger). This town, on the border between Italy and Austria, was Austrian until 1918. The brand, an edelweiss flower, is the same in Italy and Austria. The Italian brand has HI in the center, and the Austrian or Southern Tyrol brand has H.

# DELTA HORSE

A population of Camargue horses is bred in semi-freedom in the Po River delta, where they were introduced in the 1970s. They are known in Italy by the name of Delta Horse, but they are direct descendants of Camargues. Camargues have been perfectly acclimated to similarly humid zones close to the marshes of the Camargue.

In Slovenia horses have been bred above all for farm and forest work, and draft horses have long been in the majority. The arrival of tractors caused the equine population to decline dramatically, but it has been growing in the past thirty years thanks

---

SLOVENIA

# SLOVENIAN WARMBLOOD

Slovenian: *slovenski toplokrvni konj*

🔘 1.60 m–1.70 m for males; 1.70 m for mares.

🔘 Often bay, black, chestnut, gray; all colors are possible.

**Description**: This willowy horse, the result of recent crossings, has the typical build of a sport horse and resembles its cousins. It has a head with a straight profile; large eyes; a long, muscular neck; wide, long, and straight croup; and thin, solid legs.

**Distribution**: Slovenia.

**Origins and history**: This very recent breed was created some twenty years ago from German and Austrian horses (Holstein, Oldenburg, Hanoverian). Faced with the growing popularity of equestrian sports and recreation, Slovenes decided to have

their own competitive saddle horse, which led to the establishment of this breed.

**Character and attributes**: Lively and with a good nature, it is robust and has energetic gaits.

**Uses**: It is perfectly suited for dressage or show jumping, but also for recreational riding.

**Current status**: The breed is still local, with small numbers, and is in the process of development and consolidation. Breeding is dynamic in Slovenia. This sport horse is still little known outside the country. In 2009 there were 795 animals, including 250 broodmares. The breed is not endangered, since it has just been created and its numbers will probably increase.

---

SLOVENIA

# LJUTOMER TROTTER

Slovenian: *ljutomerski kasač*

🔘 1.55 m–1.65 m for males; 1.50 m–1.65 m for mares.

🔘 Mainly bay, dark bay; sometimes chestnut, with white markings.

**Description**: See the Yugoslav Trotter *(p. 128)*, the result of the same sort of crosses. It has a neck that is often long and quite muscular; a long body; and a long, wide, and muscular croup.

**Distribution**: Slovenia.

**Origins and history**: It has been bred since the end of the nineteenth century with a foundation of very

fast Eastern horses, and has undergone the same types of crossings as the Yugoslav Trotter, i.e., with Anglo-Arabs and American Standardbreds. Breeding race horses was important for the aristocracy of the time, but for a long time this horse was also bred for farm work.

**Character and attributes**: The Ljutomer Trotter is fast, robust, lively, and good-natured.

**Uses**: In addition to being a race horse, this trotter was once used a lot as a draft horse. It continues to compete at the Ljutomer racecourse. It also makes a good recreational horse.

**Current status**: There were only around 250 of these local trotters in 2012, and 118 mares and 6 stallions in 2010. But Slovenian breeders aim to develop this breed considerably.

to sporting and recreational equine activities. There are more than 20,000 horses in Slovenia. In terms of breeding, the majority of broodmares is made up of the Croatian Coldblood, locally called the Slovenian Draft, a breed shared with Croatia (see Croatia, p. 126), followed by trotters. Among the foreign breeds bred in Slovenia, the Haflinger and the Posavac are the best represented. Slovenes are also breeders of Lipizzans, a breed they share with Austria.

Long, muscular neck

Wide, long, straight croup

Thin, solid legs

SLOVENIAN WARMBLOOD

The number of horses in Croatia has declined, going from 190,000 in the 1970s to only 10,000 in 2001. It fell by 65 percent during the war in the former Yugoslavia. But the equine population has only increased since then, and there are now more than

---

# POSAVAC

Also called: Croatian Posavac

Croatian: *posavac*

**H** 1.43 m on average for mares; 1.50 m for males.

**C** Mainly bay, dark bay, sometimes black, gray; few markings.

**Description**: This compact draft horse weighs between 500 kg and 650 kg. It has a long head with large eyes; small, well-spaced ears; a short and powerful neck; wide croup; low-set tail; and the wide, flat hooves typical of horses raised in swampy zones. The mane and tail are abundant.

**Distribution**: Croatia and Slovenia.

**Origins and history**: This is a very ancient Balkan breed, rarely crossed. However, it has received Arabian, Spanish, and Italian blood, from the Nonius and the Lipizzan. Its strength comes from human selection and from living in a region with rich pastureland.

**Character and attributes**: It has a good, calm nature. It is powerful, resilient, and long-lived; it has good endurance and good health. It is well adapted to the swampy areas in the flood zones where it grazes. Posavacs generally receive additional feed (hay) during the winter.

**Uses**: This is primarily a work horse, intended for farm work, clearing, and transportation, but it is also increasingly used for recreation and equestrian tourism. It is a good horse for equitherapy.

**Current status**: The Posavac is still rare, but has been officially protected since 1993 by the state and by impassioned breeders. The breed's numbers have been growing since then, from only 550 horses in 1995 to more than 4,500 in 2011.

---

# CROATIAN COLDBLOOD

Also called: Croatian Hladnokrvnjak

Croatian: *hrvatski hladnokrvnjak, domaci hladnokrvan*

**H** Around 1.60 m for mares; 1.65 m for males.

**C** Mainly bay, dark bay, sometimes black, more rarely chestnut or bay dun.

**Description**: The breed is rather heterogeneous. It is a tall, heavy horse, which weighs on average 625–750 kg. It has a head of average size, with a wide forehead and a straight or slightly convex profile; a long and powerful neck; a broad chest; unobtrusive withers; a strong and rather long back; a wide and sloping croup; solid, short legs; and wide hooves. The mane and tail are long, thick, and wavy. The mane is often double. It has light feathering on the legs.

**Distribution**: Croatia and Slovenia.

**Origins and history**: The breed was created, starting in the first half of the nineteenth century, by crossing native mares with breeds of foreign draft horses such as the Ardennais, Percheron, Belgian, and Hungarian Coldblood.

**Character and attributes**: It is a robust horse, undemanding and fertile. It is an easy keeper.

**Uses**: This breed is raised to produce meat. It is a good draft horse.

**Current status**: It is currently the most widespread breed in Croatia, with a growing population and more than 5,500 individuals. Even if the numbers are modest, local breeding is dynamic. It is also very present in Slovenia, with a thousand mares and 150 stallions.

17,000 horses. Around seventeen different breeds are registered in Croatia. The dominant breed is the Croatian Coldblood, followed by the Posavac. The Lipizzan is also bred there. Sport and recreation breeds are regularly imported, but their breeding remains underdeveloped. Horses are in fact mainly raised to produce meat. The Murakoz, shared with Hungary, is considered primarily Hungarian, and is believed to be endangered in Croatia, where its numbers are very small.

Low-set tail

Small, wide-spaced ears

Wide, flat hooves well adapted for wet pastureland.

POSAVAC

The war in the former Yugoslavia had a considerable impact on equine populations, which diminished by 49 percent. The Bosnian horse conservation program was seriously affected. Before 1992 Bosnia

BOSNIA AND HERZEGOVINA

# BOSNIAN

Also called: Bosnian Pony, Bosnian Mountain Horse

Bosnian: *bosanski brdski konj*

(H) 1.30 m–1.48 m.

(C) Most often bay, dark bay, less often black, gray.

**Description**: It resembles the Konik, the Hucul, and the Albanian. A small, compact horse, it has a head with a straight profile, small ears, and large eyes; a strong and muscular neck; broad chest; rather long back; sloping croup; low-set tail; and rather small hooves. The mane and tail are thick. The Glasinacki type has been influenced more with Arabian blood, and is heavier than the Podveleski type.

**Distribution**: Bosnia and Herzegovina, a few in Montenegro, Serbia, Macedonia, Croatia, and Slovenia. Germany also appreciates and raises the breed.

**Origins and history**: This horse of ancient and primitive origin has in the past received contributions of Eastern blood, probably Mongolian, too. It has been the object of rigorous selection since the beginning of the twentieth century. Crossed with the Arabian, it produces a very popular local riding horse.

**Character and attributes**: The Bosnian is intelligent, with a strong but friendly and calm nature. It is a resilient, sure-footed, and undemanding mountain horse with good endurance and is well adapted to its environment.

**Uses**: Even today it is used as a draft and pack horse as well as for riding. It is used primarily to transport heating wood. It is a popular trekking horse. It is also used to produce mules.

**Current status**: The breed is common in Bosnia, with more than 10,000 horses, but is not well-known outside its borders.

In Serbia one finds Thoroughbreds, Arabians, Lipizzans, and a few Nonius and Bosnian Mountain Horses, as well as, more specifically, the Yugoslav Trotter. Due to the mechanization of transport and agricultural work, but also because of the war, the number of Serbian horses has dropped. Riding for recreation and equestrian tourism are gradually developing alongside the traditional racing industry. Horses are also raised for their meat.

SERBIA

# YUGOSLAV TROTTER

Serbian: *jugoslovenski kasac*

(H) On average 1.67 m for males; 1.65 m for mares.

(C) Most often bay, with white markings on the head and legs.

**Description**: This tall horse has a muscular body, long legs, and a powerful croup.

**Distribution**: Serbia.

**Origins and history**: This breed is not indigenous to Serbia, since it is the result of crossings between Anglo-Arabs and American Standardbreds, with the goal of producing a good horse for trotting races. But it was created and bred in Serbia, where its numbers are now declining. A trotter from equivalent crossings, the Ljutomer Trotter, is found in Slovenia.

**Character and attributes**: This athletic horse is bred for its fast trot.

**Uses**: It is used for trotting races that are primarily held in Belgrade.

**Current status**: The breed has become very rare, with a population estimated at between 500 and 700 individuals in 2012.

and Herzegovina had 99,803 horses. In 2002 there were only 31,779. Seventy percent of these horses are Bosnian; the remaining 30 percent are crosses between Bosnians and Lipizzans or draft horses. The Bosnian hasn't suffered from the competition of imported foreign breeds.

Low-set tail

Broad chest

Small, hard hooves

## Albania

Around 70 percent of the horse population in Albania is made up of native Albanian horses. The rest are the result of crossings of these Albanians with Haflingers, Nonius, and Sardinian Anglo-Arabs, but these crosses are decreasing due to a lack of Thoroughbred stallions. One finds Albanian horses mainly in hilly and mountainous regions. They are still used there for agricultural work. The horse is used above all as a work animal, as sport and recreational riding is still not very well developed in Albania.

### ALBANIA

# ALBANIAN

Also called: Albanian Local Horse

Albanian: *myzequea* for the plains type

**H** 1.24 m–1.43 m.

**C** Often black or bay, brownish bay, chestnut, gray.

**Description**: This small, stocky horse resembles the Hucul. In the past there were two types—a mountain type, which was smaller, and a taller plains type—which were mixed. It has a head with a straight profile, small ears, sloping croup, a low-set tail, and hard hooves.

**Distribution**: Albania, mainly in its mountainous terrain.

**Origins and History**: Breeds of horses from the Balkans are all of very ancient origin, probably having received Mongolian, Turkoman, and Arabian blood at some point in their history.

**Character and attributes**: The Albanian has a good nature; it is agile and resilient, and has good endurance. It is powerful despite its small size. It has good health. It is a sure-footed mountain horse. Many have a comfortable natural amble.

**Uses**: It is a good pack horse, used for farm work and for equestrian tourism. Its good pulling ability allows it to be harnessed for different tasks. The Albanian is also frequently used to produce mules, by crossing with a breed of local donkey.

**Current status**: The breed is very widespread in its country and remains stable, with several thousand horses.

Although horses have long been an integral part of Greek mythology, from Pegasus and Bucephalus, the Trojan Horse, Centaurs, and Amazons, the number of Greek breeds of horses has been dramatically reduced

# Skyros Pony

Greek: *Skyros, helliniko alogaki*

**H** 0.90 m–1.10 m.

**C** Bay, dark bay, generally mealy, gray, bay dun, buckskin, with primitive markings.

**Description**: This is one of the smallest breeds in the world. This very small horse resembles the British Exmoor, but also other primitive Turkish or Chinese breeds. It has a small head with a wide forehead and a slightly convex face, and very small ears. It has a short neck; narrow chest; a short, straight back; undeveloped hindquarters; a sloping croup; low-set tail; slender legs; and hard, black hooves. The mane and tail are long and abundant.

**Distribution**: Island of Skyros, Greece; a few in Scotland.

**Origins and history**: This very ancient breed, dating from antiquity, is characterized by its small size, the result of adaptation to living on an island in harsh conditions. Very isolated, the breed clearly has not received blood from external sources, which makes it a very pure breed. Skyros Ponies live most of the time outdoors.

**Character and attributes**: The Skyros Pony is intelligent, and has a particularly calm and easygoing temperament. It is strong, very resilient, rustic, and hardy. It tolerates very high heat.

**Uses**: Because of its small size and its very good nature, it makes an ideal mount for children. It can also be used as a pack horse, for pulling carts or light carriages, or even in equitherapy. Skyros Ponies have also been used to produce mules.

**Current status**: Despite its excellent temperament and its size, which make it an ideal mount for pony clubs, sometimes even better than the popular Shetland, the Skyros is in great danger of extinction. There were only 210 of them in 2011. Now protected, the breed is gaining ground.

# Pindos Pony

Greek: *pindos*

**H** 1.15 m–1.25 m.

**C** Gray and light gray, bay, dark bay, black, roan.

**Description**: In general the Pindos Pony is not very muscular, which doesn't prevent it from being very resilient. It has a long and slender head with a straight profile; small eyes; a wide forehead; a rather long, thin neck; prominent withers; a straight back; dished croup; high-set tail; slender but strong legs; and small, solid hooves. The mane and tail are thick.

**Distribution**: Thessaly, Epirus, Greece.

**Origins and history**: The Pindos Pony is the best known of all Greek horses. It is an ancient breed with uncertain origins, probably crossed in the past with Eastern horses that gave it a certain balance. It is bred in mountain regions.

**Character and attributes**: It is an agile, sure-footed, and resilient mountain climber that has good endurance and a strong personality, which can quickly turn stubborn if a handler is inexperienced. It lives a long time and is able to work well into advanced years. It is very hardy.

**Uses**: This is a versatile horse. Its small size makes it a mount for young riders, though it is robust enough to carry an adult. It is also a good draft or pack horse, and is often used to produce mules.

**Current status**: Although the Pindos is rare, it is one of the Greek breeds that is doing the best, with 3,198 horses in 2011, and its numbers are growing.

with the mechanization of farming, and most Greek breeds are in danger of extinction. Currently, there are around 30,000 horses in Greece (2011), most being the result of various crosses. Breeds that originated in Greece are rather small in number. Traditionally used for farm work, they are today converted to riding and equestrian tourism. Some island breeds are very ancient. Various herds of wild horses also live in Greece.

Abundant mane and tail

Very small ears

Low-set tail

Slender legs

Prominent withers

Small eyes

High-set tail

Slender but very solid legs

# MESSARA PONY

Also called: Creta Pony

Greek: *messara*

🅗 1.25 m–1.45 m; on average 1.40 m for males, and 1.34 m for mares.

🅒 Bay, dark bay, black, with specific shades of gray-brown, sometimes with primitive markings; almost no white markings.

**Description**: It is rather slender, with Arabian characteristics. It has a small, rather long head; a slender neck; narrow chest; thin legs; and small hooves. The mane and tail are long and abundant, but the tail is generally cut short.

**Distribution**: Predominantly Crete.

**Origins and history**: Present on the island for centuries, the Messara as it is known today is the result of crossings that occurred in the seventeenth century between Arabian stallions and mares from the local mountains.

**Character and attributes**: It is intelligent, generally gentle, sometimes lively. It has good endurance and is robust and resilient. It has very comfortable gaits, and is known for its supplemental fourth natural gait, a broken amble, locally called *arravani*, which makes it very pleasant to ride. It is sure-footed.

**Uses**: The Messara is increasingly used for recreational riding and equestrian tourism.

**Current status**: Very rare, the breed is protected; there were only slightly more than 250 individuals in 2012. Its numbers are increasing slightly.

---

# PENEIA PONY

Greek: *pineia*

🅗 1.25 m–1.40 m; generally 1.42 m for males, and 1.36 m for mares.

🅒 Chestnut, black, gray, dark bay, roan, sometimes with white markings on the head and legs.

**Description**: The Peneia Pony has a large, boxy head with a convex profile; thick neck; unobtrusive withers; a broad chest; short back; slanted, muscular croup; low-set tail; slender but solid legs; and small, resilient hooves. The mane and tail are abundant.

**Distribution**: The Peneia Valley in the Peloponnesus, Greece.

**Origins and history**: This local horse has probably received Arabian blood. It is a very ancient breed, dating from Greek antiquity.

**Character and attributes**: The Peneia Pony sometimes has a nervous temperament. It has good endurance and is strong, sure-footed, and well adapted to mountain terrain. It is also a good jumper. Like the Messara, it has a supplementary natural gait, a broken amble called *arravani*, which is very comfortable for the rider. It is a very rustic and hardy horse.

**Uses**: It is generally used for riding, as a pack horse, and for light work in harness.

**Current status**: With only slightly more than a hundred animals, the Peneia Pony is in great danger of extinction, even if its numbers have been stable for the past few years.

---

# THESSALIAN

Also called: Thessalian Pony

Greek: *thessalia*

🅗 1.35 m for mares; 1.42 m for males.

🅒 Bay, dark bay, chestnut, gray.

**Description**: The Thessalian has a large head with a straight profile, large eyes, and long ears; a neck wide at the base; a straight back; muscular, sloping croup; rather thin but solid legs; and black hooves. The mane and tail are abundant.

**Distribution**: Thessaly, Greece.

**Origins and history**: This very ancient breed, once quite renowned, was crossed after World War II with Arabian, Anglo-Arab, and Lipizzan stallions with the goal of making it bigger. Legend has it that Bucephalus, the horse of Alexander the Great, was a Thessalian. It was the horse of the Greek and Roman cavalries.

**Character and attributes**: These intelligent horses are generally very close to their riders. They are patient and calm. Possessing great endurance, they tolerate hot and humid climates.

**Uses**: It is a good trekking horse and pack horse and is used for farm work and recreation in general. It is also used to produce mules.

**Current status**: Long thought to be extinct, there are still a few of them left. Today the breed is on the brink of extinction. There were slightly more than 580 in 2011.

Slender neck

The Messara's comfortable gait and its sure-footedness enable long-distance trekking through the Greek garigue.

Narrow chest

Squarish head

Slender but solid legs

Small hooves

Neck wide at the base

Large head

# AINOS PONY

Also called: Ainos Kefalonia Feral Horse

Greek: *ainos*

🐴 1.15 m–1.25 m.

🎨 Bay, brownish bay, mealy bay, roan.

**Description**: A small horse, the Ainos has a small head with a straight profile, prominent withers, narrow chest, muscular croup, and small, hard, black hooves. The mane and tail are thick.

**Distribution**: In the forests of Mount Ainos, on the island of Cephalonia, Greece.

**Origins and history**: This small, wild horse is the issue of ancient Greek Pindos horses that escaped and returned to the wild. It is really more a wild population than a true breed; however, the living conditions on the island have created a particular type of horse, selecting the most resilient individuals and those most able to live in the mountains.

**Character and attributes**: Often hunted, the Ainos has become fearful and difficult to approach in the wild. It is a small, very sure-footed mountain horse with great endurance and great rusticity.

**Current status**: The Ainos is in great danger of extinction. There is only a small population of horses (25, including only 7 mares in 2010), which an association is attempting to have recognized and to preserve. The future of this breed is very uncertain.

# RHODOPE PONY

Also called: Rhodope Horse

Greek: *thráki, rodopi*

🐴 1.25 m–1.45 m, an average of 1.35 m.

🎨 Bay, gray, roan, a few bay dun, with white markings on the head and legs.

**Description**: The Rhodope has a thin and compact body, solid legs, and hard black hooves. The mane and tail are abundant, but the mane is often cut into a rounded brush cut, giving it the look of an ancient horse.

**Distribution**: Rhodope Mountains, Thrace, Greece.

**Origins and history**: The breed is being studied but is not yet officially recognized.

**Character and attributes**: This good-natured horse is well adapted to rough terrain.

**Uses**: It is used for transportation in mountain terrain, for trekking, and for the production of mules.

**Current status**: This little-known breed is very rare, with probably fewer than a thousand horses.

# ZANTE HORSE

Greek: *zakynthos*

🐴 1.45 m–1.55 m.

🎨 The main color is black, even if other coat colors sometimes appear.

**Description**: This little horse has a harmonious physique, but no standard has yet been established. Some consider it one of the most beautiful of all Greek horses.

**Distribution**: Zante Island, Greece.

**Origins and history**: This pretty horse is the result of crossings between local Andravida mares with Anglo-Arab stallions at the beginning of the twentieth century. The breed is being studied but is not yet officially recognized. It is bred by a few Greek families on Zante Island.

**Character and attributes**: The Zante has a good nature and proud gaits.

**Uses**: It is used for transport, equestrian tourism, and carriage driving.

**Current status**: This native horse, very rare, is not recognized, and therefore not protected.

# ANDRAVIDA

Also called: Eleia

Greek: *eilia, eleia, andravida, orinis ilias, pedini eleia*

**Ⓗ** 1.50 m–1.60 m.

**Ⓒ** Bay, dark bay, chestnut, black, roan, sometimes very light gray, with white markings on the head and legs.

**Description**: This is the tallest of the Greek horses. Some individuals resemble the Nonius, but the breed has preserved its ancient form. The head is wide, with big ears. The chest is broad, the croup developed, the legs rather slender but sturdy. Crossed with Thoroughbreds, it produces good jumpers.

**Distribution**: Eleia, in Greece.

**Origins and history**: This breed is the result of crossings between local mares and Anglo-Norman and Nonius stallions at the beginning of the twentieth century. The fertile plains of Andravida have enabled these horses to develop well. It was once a military horse. Negligent crossings have been detrimental to the breed, leading to its disappearance.

**Character and attributes**: Intelligent and strong, it is a good jumper.

**Uses**: It is used for riding, driving, and light draft work, as well as for recreational sports.

**Current status**: Considered extinct, the breed is in the process of being reconstituted, with only 35 purebred individuals in 2010. Crossbreds, numbering 75 in 2010, are the result of the introduction of a Selle Français nicknamed Pegasus.

## POPULATIONS OF GREEK WILD AND ISLAND HORSES

In addition to the breeds described above, there are also populations of horses living in semi-freedom, without owners. There are more than 200 near the Achelous River delta in southwestern Greece and in the Epirus region, near the Kalama River delta; around 200 in the mountain region of the city of Amfilochia in western Greece, and around 400 in the Axios and Haliacmon River delta, in the Evros River delta, and in the Rhodope Mountains near the city of Drama. They are often Pindos returned to the wild. Administrators watch over the local populations, aware that they could be a tourist attraction.

The wild horses of Axios (90 in 2010) are black, dark bay, bay, and gray.

One also finds small wild populations similar to the Ainos on other islands. Notably on the island of Lesvos there is a little-known horse by the name of *midili* or Mytilene Pony (see Turkey, where the breed is raised). And on the islands of Leipsoi, Samothrace, and Sifnos other small populations have been found. On the island of Rhodes for a long time there has been a small population of horses (the Rhodes Small Horse), not recognized but studied, probably similar to the Skyros, which is almost extinct today (3 stallions and 8 mares in 2007), measuring 0.80 m–1.15 m and with either a bay or chestnut coat.

## ARRAVANI HORSE

Also of note is the controversial Arravani horse, located in western Macedonia, which is, as its Greek name indicates, a gaited horse. Indeed, horses of the Messara and Peneia breeds have supplemental natural gaits, an amble and a broken amble, called *arravani*. According to the Greeks, there is only one local farm breeding gaited horses of Greek origin, under the name "Arravani Horse"; it will probably end up producing a distinct type. Horses have been exported to Austria and Germany. There is no studbook in Greece. These horses measure between 1.30 m and 1.50 m, and are generally black, light gray, dark bay, or sometimes chestnut. They have a small head with large eyes, a strong neck that is wide at the base, a sloping croup, and a high-set tail. The hair of the mane and tail is sometimes wavy. They are calm and have great endurance. There are around 300 of them.

# Horses of Western Europe

Western Europe, with its excellent German, French, and Dutch sport horses, has some of the most competitive breeds in the Olympic disciplines of dressage, show jumping, and eventing, and the French Trotter is a fearsome competitor in trotting races. In addition to competition horses, Western Europe also has breeds that are very popular and exported throughout the world (among them the Haflinger, Friesian, and Percheron), and many breeds of draft horses, whose numbers are small, but which are well protected. As elsewhere in Europe, but even more clearly in this region, which has been marked by strong military and agricultural traditions, horses of Western Europe generally are of more basic coloring (bay and chestnut, because they are less visible), and there are very few gaited horses, although the Germans have recently created the Aegidienberger.

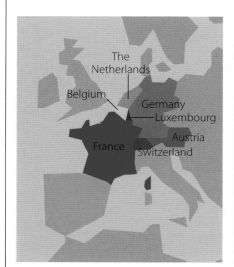

Of Slovenian and Austrian origin, the Lipizzan is a well-known, yet rare breed.

### France
Pottok
Landais Pony
French Riding Pony
Corsican
Camargue
Castillon
Mérens Horse
Auvergne
Barraquand
Henson
French Anglo-Arab
French Chaser
French Trotter

Opposite: In France, one can often come across Comtois grazing freely in the mountains, in Franche-Comté or in Auvergne.

Selle Français
French Cob
Boulonnais
Comtois
Breton
Poitevin
French Ardennais
Auxois
Trait du Nord
Percheron
Megève

### Belgium
Belgian Riding Pony
Belgian Warmblood
Belgian Halfblood (also Belgian Sport Horse)
Flemish Horse
Belgian
Belgian Trotter

### Luxembourg
Luxembourg Warmblood

### The Netherlands
Gelderland
Groningen (also Groninger Horse)
Dutch Warmblood (also KWPN Riding Horse)
Friesian
Dutch Heavy Draft
Dutch Tuigpaard (also Dutch Carriage Horse, KWPN Harness Horse)

### Germany
German Classic Pony
Dülmen Pony
Lewitzer
German Riding Pony
Aegidienberger

Hanoverian
East Friesian (also East Friesian Warmblood)
Saxon-Thuringian Heavy Warmblood
Zweibrücker
Bavarian Warmblood
Mecklenburger
Rhenish Warmblood (also Rhinelander)
Trakehner
Brandenburg
Württemberg
Holstein
Westphalian (also Westphalian Warmblood)
Oldenburg
Black Forest Chestnut

Pfalz-Ardenner
Schleswig
Rhineland Heavy Draft (also Rhenish German Coldblood)
Lehmkuhlener
Arenberg-Nordkirchen
Small German Riding Horse
Senne (also Senner Horse)
Beberbeck Horse
Sachsen-Anhaltiner Warmblood (also Sachsen Warmblood)
Hessen
German Trotter
Saxon-Turinga Coldblood
South German

Coldblood
Hanoverian Coldblood of Schleswig Origin

### Switzerland
Freiberg
Swiss Warmblood and Einsiedler

### Austria
Haflinger
Lipizzan
Austrian Warmblood
Noriker

Like almost everywhere else in the world, the popularity of equestrian sports is causing the number of horses in France to rise: there are now around 900,000 in the country. Many foreign breeds are bred in France. Based on the number of licensed

# POTTOK

French: *pottok/pottock, basque*

Ⓗ 1.15 m–1.47 m.

Ⓒ Black, bay, chestnut, or pinto.

**Description**: The Pottok has a light build. It has a unique head with a hollow at the level of the eyes (a concave forehead) and a bump at the bottom of the face (convex), a short neck, long back, sloping croup, and low-set tail. Its hooves are small, with very hard horn. The hair of the mane and tail is straight with reddish hues. Today Pottoks are divided into the slightly smaller "mountain" Pottoks (which live outdoors nine months of the year) and the "prairie" Pottok, raised from birth or from weaning around people; the latter is a bit bigger because it is well fed. There is also an original type, which has not been crossed, and which resembles the original wild type, of which there are only a very few individuals left. The studbook has a book A (purebred) and a book B (Pottok crosses).

**Distribution**: France, in the Pyrenees, and notably in the Basque Country. This border breed is also found in Spain.

**Origins and history**: This Basque word is pronounced "pottiok." The Pottok is a very ancient breed and one of the symbols of the Basque Country. It is possible to run into these horses in the mountains living in semi-freedom, following their ancestral mode of breeding. Always maintained as a pure breed, over the centuries the Pottok has undergone a few crossings with the Arabian, but it has maintained its unique characteristics. It almost disappeared in the 1970s, but was recognized in 1972, which enabled the breed to be protected. It originated in the mountains of Ursuya, Baigoura, Artzamendi, and Larrun.

**Character and attributes**: This is an excellent, small mountain horse, notably because of its endurance. It has a sociable and attentive nature.

**Uses**: It is a good training pony for children. Versatile, it can compete in dressage, driving, or eventing.

**Current status**: The Pottok's progress has been truly significant over the last thirty years. Between 1,500 and 2,000 Pottoks have been counted, a large portion of which live in the mountains of the Basque Country. But there are only around 20 pure Pottoks of the original type in France (and 220 in Spain, where the Basque government has protected them since 1988).

# LANDAIS PONY

French: *landais, poney barthais, poney des Barthes, cheval landais des Barthes*

Ⓗ 1.18 m–1.48 m.

Ⓒ Bay, black, chestnut, or chocolate, with white markings authorized.

**Description**: Well proportioned, it has a slender head, small ears, and a short back. The mane and tail are thick.

**Distribution**: France, in the region of Pau and the department of Landes.

**Origins and history**: The Landais Pony is a breed forged by the marshy prairies and forests of the Landes around the River Adour. It was crossed with Arabian and Barb horses in the eighth century, then later with Spanish, English, and Breton horses. After World War II its numbers were so low that breeders reintroduced

Arabian and Welsh blood to avoid too much inbreeding, which would have imperiled the breed. Those crosses helped to make the Landais a very good sport pony. The breed has never been very widespread. At the beginning of the nineteenth century there were around 2,000 horses. By 1945 there were only 150 left. The studbook was established in 1967.

**Character and attributes**: It has a calm nature. It is an excellent trotter and a good jumper. Rustic, it lives outdoors throughout the year.

**Uses**: It is a very good sport mount for children, and stands out in dressage, jumping, and eventing. Its versatility enables it to adapt well to various disciplines.

**Current status**: There are around 100 mares and 20 stallions of this breed. The Landais is one of the most threatened horse breeds, and its preservation should be a priority. The Conservatoire des races d'Aquitaine (an animal preservation organization in Aquitaine) maintains a herd of the original type on its pastureland.

horses (more than 700,000), France has the second largest equestrian organization in the world. The chief sectors are racing and equestrian activities. The mounted police are making a small comeback in French cities. France is one of the countries that has been able to preserve its breeds of draft horses, first through the meat industry, but increasingly by converting these horses into recreational mounts. Although the breeds are rare, these horses are protected through conservation programs.

Short neck

Sloping croup

Hollow in the forehead at eye level, and a bump at the bottom of the face

The coat of the original type is dark and of a single color.

Small hooves

POTTOK

Short back

Small ears

Slender head

The Landais Pony is well adapted to wet conditions.

LANDAIS PONY

# FRENCH RIDING PONY

French: *poney français de selle*

**H** 1.25 m–1.48 m.

**C** Often bay, dark bay, chestnut, gray; all colors are possible.

**Description**: This very young breed does not have a homogeneous physique, but is a miniature version of a sport saddle horse. It resembles other European saddle ponies, although it is perhaps a bit more rustic. It has a broad chest, prominent withers, and a solid back.

**Distribution**: France, especially Normandy, Mayenne, and Brittany; it is increasingly exported.

**Origins and history**: This recent breed has been developed to offer young riders a small, competitive mount. It is the result of multiple crossings among Pottok, Landais, Connemara, Welsh, New Forest, Dartmoor, and small Arabian horses.

**Character and attributes**: Docile and energetic. Breeders select for its good nature, which is suitable for young riders.

**Uses**: The French Riding Pony excels in dressage, show jumping, and eventing. It is also good in harness and for recreational riding in general. It is frequently found in riding schools as a lesson horse for beginning riders. The largest can also be ridden by adults.

**Current status**: With more than a thousand French Riding Ponies, the breed is still small in number, although it has been aggressively developed.

---

# CORSICAN

French: *corse*

It is sometimes also called *u paganacciu*, "the rebel," by Corsicans.

**H** 1.30 m–1.50 m.

**C** Almost always bay, sometimes black, usually without white markings.

**Description**: It has a rather light build; a somewhat short head with a straight or mildly convex profile; slightly prominent withers; a short, wide neck; rather short back; sloping croup; and small, hard hooves.

**Distribution**: France, the island of Corsica. A small population still lives in the wild in the mountains of Tenda.

**Origins and history**: The Corsican has been present on Corsica for centuries. It underwent multiple crossings in the past, notably with Barb, Arabian, and Spanish horses. It was used as a means of transportation, as a pack horse, or for light farm work. The breed has been protected since 1989, starting with a group of five stallions and some thirty mares. The breed was recognized only in 2012.

**Character and attributes**: This is an energetic horse, generally calm, but it can show a lot of spirit. It is a mountain horse, sure-footed, particularly resilient, and very well adapted to the hard land of Corisca. It matures late.

**Uses**: It is used a lot in trekking, as it is very accustomed to moving in a mountain environment. It can also compete in endurance races, or make a good polo pony.

**Current status**: At the beginning of the nineteenth century there were more than 10,000 Corsicans. Since then, its numbers have steadily decreased. In 2013 there were slightly more than 180 Corsican horses.

Prominent
withers

Broad chest

Short, wide
neck

Sloping
croup

Rather short back

Small, hard hooves

# CAMARGUE

French: *camargue*

**H** 1.35 m–1.50 m.

**C** Very light gray—people speak of the "white" horses of Camargue. As they get older, the coats of certain animals have a tendency to become speckled. Foals are born dark and lighten within a few years (the age differs depending on the lineages).

Camargue "cowboys" herd raço di biou cattle.

**Description**: The Camargue has a big, boxy head with a straight profile and short ears; slightly prominent withers; muscular shoulders; slightly sloping croup; low-set tail; strong legs; and wide, very resilient hooves. The hooves of horses raised on marshy land are more spread out than those of other horses. Its mane and tail are abundant, and it sometimes has a double mane.

**Distribution**: Present above all in the south of France (Gard, Bouches-du-Rhône, Var, Vaucluse, Hérault, Aude). It is also bred in Sweden.

**Origins and history**: This is the horse of the *gardians* (cowboys) of the Camargue. Its presence was mentioned in antiquity; it is one of the most ancient breeds in the world. But its origins remain rather obscure; some think that centuries ago it received contributions of Eastern blood. It is above all a horse forged by its environment. It is one of the only breeds that can endure the climate conditions of the Camargue, where it lives in semi-freedom: swamps, mosquitoes, a very hot summer, and glacial winter winds. The breed was recognized in 1978. It was endangered in the 1960s.

**Character and attributes**: The Camargue has a calm but energetic and very responsive nature. Breeders attach great importance to the character of these horses. The Camargue is rustic, hardy, endowed with good health, and lives an exceptionally long time. Mares are very fertile.

**Uses**: Its best discipline is working cattle, because it has the famous "cow sense." But it is a very versatile horse, good for recreation, teaching, trekking, dressage, driving, and other activities. When trained, it can compete in endurance races.

**Current status**: The Camargue has always been a local breed, with rather small numbers. In 2009 there were 1,070 mares and 157 active stallions; 284 breeders were counted in 2011.

# CASTILLON

French: *castillon, castillonnais, cheval du Biros, saint-gironnais, ariégeois de Castillon*

**H** 1.35 m–1.55 m; 1.45 m on average.

**C** Dark bay to mealy black. It has a tapered nose, with markings on its flanks.

**Description**: The Castillon has a long head with a straight or slightly concave profile, wide forehead, slightly prominent withers, wide back, very round croup, and wide hooves with black horn. The mane and tail are abundant and rough, sometimes wavy.

**Distribution**: France, mainly in the Midi-Pyrénées region, in Ariège.

**Origins and history**: People sometimes think that the Castillon is only a bay variety of Mérens. Although it is not as well known as the Mérens, it is indeed a separate breed, officially recognized since 1996. It is a mountain horse of ancient origins, once used for transportation, farming, or the army. In the past it received Eastern and Iberian blood. It almost disappeared in the 1980s, when a few enthusiasts saved the breed from extinction with some fifty mares.

**Character and attributes**: Its easy nature, hardiness, rusticity, and spirit make it a very versatile mount.

**Uses**: It is a very good mountain horse, used for trekking, driving, and recreation in general. It is as good as a mule in the mountains.

**Current status**: Although the Castillon breed has never been large in number, it was always well established in its country before it almost disappeared in the twentieth century. Even today it is not well known, and there are very few of them. Whereas the Mérens has become popular among French riders, for whom it is the mountain horse par excellence, the Castillon is still not recognized. At the end of 2011 the breed had 491 registered horses, 283 mares, 127 broodmares, and 13 approved stallions; 27 births and 54 pregnancies were recorded.

Low-set tail

Large,
squarish head

Hard, wide hooves

Camargue work saddle.

Abundant, bushy,
sometimes wavy tail
and mane

Wide forehead

Wide hooves

# MÉRENS HORSE

French: *mérens*; in the past, *poney noir de l'Arège* or *trait ariégeois, ariégeois*

**H** 1.45 m–1.55 m.

**C** Always solid black, without white markings.

**Description**: The breed is very homogeneous, because it was isolated in the mountains for a long time. Compact and round, it has a head with a straight profile, wide forehead, short and hairy ears, a rather broad chest, an often double croup, a low-set tail, and wide hooves. It has a beard. The mane and tail are thick, coarse, and often kinky and wavy. Some breeders have selected more sporty traits; others prefer to preserve the rustic characteristics of the breed.

**Distribution**: France, mainly in Ariège, in the Pyrenees and the Midi-Pyrénées region, but also on the island of Réunion, where there is a large population. It is exported abroad, primarily to Italy, the Netherlands, Switzerland, and Belgium.

**Origins and history**: The Mérens is a very ancient breed that has always lived in the wild in the Pyrenees, in Ariège. Like many horse breeds, it was on the brink of extinction in the 1970s: there were only four stallions and some forty mares. It owes its survival to the development of recreational riding. Its attractive physique, with its expressive head and black coat, has contributed to its expansion. Its studbook was established in 1947. In 1991 there were only around 400 horses left. Today, it is no longer rare to see a Mérens outside the Pyrenees region.

**Character and attributes**: The Mérens has a good nature and is an excellent mountain horse; it has good endurance and is sure-footed. Rustic, it is particularly resistant to the cold.

**Uses**: It was used a lot as a pack horse or for light farm work. It is an ideal companion for trekkers. It is a reassuring, very calm recreational mount. It is also a good carriage horse. Versatile, it has proven itself in various disciplines, such as amateur dressage, endurance, and TREC.

**Current status**: Although the breed is still small in number, the Mérens is now no longer endangered. There are 500 births per year, some hundred stallions, and more than a thousand mares.

Mérens mares in the mountain pastures sometimes wear bells to make them easier to locate.

# AUVERGNE

French: *Auvergne, cheval d'Auvergne*

**H** 1.43 m–1.57 m.

**C** Various bays, sometimes mealy black, with the smallest possible number of white markings on the head and legs. The legs are very black.

**Description**: This light draft horse has a small head, with a straight or slightly concave profile; small ears; short, wide back; and a double croup. The mane and tail are abundant and sometimes slightly wavy.

**Distribution**: France, in the Massif Central region.

**Origins and history**: The Auvergne region has rightly protected its horse, this hardy bay animal which is one of the rarest of French horses. Like all work horses used for light farm work, it suffered a great deal during the twentieth century from the growth of motorization. The origins of the Auvergne are obscure. Some believe it might have received Eastern blood in the thirteenth century. But according to breeders it is above all a horse forged by its mountainous environment. It was on the brink of extinction.

**Character and attributes**: This very gentle and docile horse has all the qualities of a good recreational mount thanks to its rusticity and easygoing nature. It is a sure-footed mountain horse.

**Uses**: Versatile, the Auvergne is suited for driving as well as for trekking. It is also a good lesson horse in riding schools. It is a good mount for both young riders and adults.

**Current status**: Breeders are attempting to maintain and stabilize the breed rather than to develop it. Though its numbers are growing every year, they still remain very low. In 2011 around 350 horses were counted, but before that the numbers had dropped much lower, to fewer than 100 horses. The breed owes its survival to a handful of enthusiasts. Following an excellent breeding push and more than twenty years of protection, it should soon be officially recognized.

Coarse, often wavy
mane and tail

Low-set tail

Wide hooves

Sometimes slightly wavy
mane and tail

Double crop

Short, wide back

# BARRAQUAND

French: *barraquand, cheval du Vercors, cheval de Barraquand*

**H** 1.45 m–1.55 m.

**C** Always bay, without markings.

**Description**: The Barraquand resembles the Auvergne, as the two breeds were crossed in the past. It has a rather small head; a double, sloping croup; and a high-set tail. The mane and tail are thick, and the mane is often double.

**Distribution**: France, in the Vercors (Isère, Drôme) region.

**Origins and history**: The Barraquand was a small, rustic, local mountain horse, whose popularity reached its peak at the end of the nineteenth century and the beginning of the twentieth century when Jules Barraquand created a small farm to breed them, which was fairly successful in this region of France. The breed is so linked to this breeder that it usually bears his name. But this peasant breed was almost extinct after World War II, until Barraquand's grandson relaunched it in the 1990s. Considered extinct, it has finally picked up from a few individual horses. Some think that it is not a breed but a type, very close to the Auvergne.

**Character and attributes**: These resilient horses spend the entire year outdoors, and they have the sure-footedness of mountain horses. Resilient, agile, and versatile, the Barraquand is known for being easy to train, but also for its uncomplicated nature. It is an easygoing horse, and breeders select for horses with the most balanced temperament possible.

**Uses**: This ancient mountain and light farming horse can make a very good recreational horse, for trekking, and for work in harness.

**Current status**: The breed isn't recognized, so it remains small in number. The market for recreational horses is growing, so it might develop in the future. There are currently around 150 horses and a dozen breeders. It is one of the rarest of French breeds.

# HENSON

French: *henson*

**H** 1.50 m–1.60 m.

**C** Various shades of bay dun with an obligatory dorsal stripe and eyes ringed in black, sometimes zebra striping on the legs, without white markings. The mane and tail are black or bi-colored.

**Description**: Since the breed is still young, it is not always homogeneous. It has a slender head, with a straight or slightly concave profile; short ears; a rather short, wide neck; broad chest; and a short, wide back. The mane is sometimes cut short.

**Distribution**: Mainly in the Somme, France; some in Belgium.

**Origins and history**: This recent breed, whose breeding began only in the 1970s in the Bay of the Somme, is the result of crossings among Fjord and Selle Français horses or Anglo-Arabs, resulting in 25–50 percent Fjord blood; in the next generation the offspring are bred to each other. The goal was to create a pleasant outdoor horse with an attractive coat for recreation. It is raised in semi-freedom in the swampy zones of the Bay of the Somme.

**Character and attributes**: The Henson is calm, rustic, easy to handle, and fast.

**Uses**: This horse is mainly intended for recreation and outdoor riding. It is also well suited for horseball and as a carriage horse.

**Current status**: The breed is small in number, with around 1,200 horses, because it is just beginning to be bred. Thus it isn't endangered; its numbers are growing. The breed was officially recognized in 2003.

Often double mane

Sloping
double croup

High-set tail

Rather short and
wide neck

Often bi-colored
mane and tail

Slender head

# FRENCH ANGLO-ARAB

French: *anglo-arabe*; in the distant past it was called *tarbais*

Acronym: AA

**H** 1.58 m–1.65 m.

**C** Often chestnut and bay, sometimes gray. It frequently has white markings on the legs and head.

**Description**: This light horse resembles the Arabian. It has a small head with a straight or slightly concave profile, wide forehead, small ears, and large eyes. Its neck is long and a bit curved, its chest broad. It has prominent withers; long shoulders; a straight, short back; long croup; long, slender legs; small hooves with resilient horn; and a high-set tail. The skin and hair of the coat are fine; the mane and tail are fine and silky.

**Distribution**: France, Great Britain, and just about everywhere in the world. Other Anglo-Arabs are also bred in Poland (see Malopolski, *p. 218*), in Bulgaria (see East Bulgarian, *p. 246*), and in Hungary (see Gidran, *p. 234*). The Sardinian Anglo-Arab of Italy and the Spanish Anglo-Arab are also similar breeds.

**Origins and history**: As its name suggests, this breed is the result of crossings between the English Thoroughbred and the Arabian. It cannot have less than 25 percent Arabian blood. This crossing produces a more resilient horse that has more endurance than the English Thoroughbred and is larger and more powerful than the Arabian. The studbook has existed since 1833. The French were not the only ones to think of this crossing, but they have bred this horse rigorously. Anglo-Arabs, which have become a separate breed in France, are also bred to each other. The Anglo-Arab has been used to improve other breeds.

**Character and attributes**: This is an intelligent, confident, lively horse with a strong temperament. It is fast, athletic, has good endurance, and is is a very good jumper, energetic and agile. The horse, which is selected according to sport criteria, has sometimes been criticized for being nervous, but this is no longer true today. It requires attentive care.

**Uses**: It is a high-performing horse in eventing, show jumping, and dressage, in which it has excellent results. The breed is suitable for experienced riders. It is also used as a hunter and in steeplechasing.

**Current status**: In France, the breeding is less active than it once was, with slightly fewer than 1,000 births a year.

# FRENCH CHASER

French: *AQPS (autre que pur-sang)*

**H** 1.60 m–1.70 m.

**C** most often bay, chestnut.

**Description**: This is a tall, athletic horse, which calls to mind a robust Thoroughbred. It has a head with a straight profile; long neck; long, slender legs; and small, sometimes fragile hooves due to its Thoroughbred lineage.

**Distribution**: France.

**Origins and history**: Hiding behind the somewhat strange French name and acronym is a breed that has been recognized in France quite recently, since 2005. It is the perfect example of a register type that ends up becoming a completely separate breed. The French Chaser is the result of Thoroughbred crossed with other breeds, notably the Selle Français and the Anglo-Arab, with the goal of creating good racehorses and good steeplechase jumpers.

**Character and attributes**: The breed is a bit slower than a Thoroughbred, with which it cannot compete on flat race courses, but it jumps very well, is more resilient, and has better endurance, which makes it a fearsome adversary in steeplechases. It requires careful maintenance and supplemental feed, especially in the winter.

**Uses**: Basically bred for steeplechase racing, the breed is suitable for other sport disciplines. After a career on racetracks, these horses can be trained to compete in show jumping.

**Current status**: Now recognized, the breed is doing rather well, with more than 1,100 births a year.

Steeplechase races require speed, endurance, and good jumping abilities.

Long, horizontal croup

High-set tail

Fine skin and hide, silky to the touch

Long, slender legs

Straight profile

Long legs

# FRENCH TROTTER

French: *trotteur français*

Acronym: TF

🄗 1.60 m–1.70 m.

🄒 Most often chestnut, often bay or dark bay, rarely roan or bay dun, never gray.

**Description**: Selected for sport performance, it doesn't have a standard look, but nevertheless has a recognizable appearance and is generally taller and more robust than other trotting breeds. It is a tall, athletic, and compact horse. It has a straight or slightly convex head; a wide forehead; long ears; prominent withers; a short back; wide, muscular, sloping croup; long and powerful legs; and hard hooves. It has fine skin.

**Distribution**: France, mainly Normandy and the northwest; Italy, Scandinavia, United States, Canada.

**Origins and history**: The breed originated in the nineteenth century and is the result of coach-type Anglo-Normans crossed with Orlov, Norfolk, and Thoroughbred horses. In the 1970s it was also crossed with the American Standardbred.

**Character and attributes**: This incredible trotter, fast and with great endurance, has a good nature and is calm and confident, since breeders eliminate difficult horses from their breeding programs.

**Uses**: This is one of the best trotters in the world, in harness or saddle races. It is indeed capable of rivaling American trotters on racetracks while being the best over long distances. When retrained to gallop correctly, it can make a pleasant recreational horse due to its easy temperament. It does well in show jumping competitions. The breed is well represented in riding schools, since it can be acquired for an attractive price after retiring from racing. Because of its good endurance it can also be converted into a fox hunting horse.

**Current status**: This breed is very widespread and is doing quite well, with more than 11,000 births per year in France.

Belgian Trotter (see *p. 166*), a bit more slender than the French Trotter. This is a harness race.

# SELLE FRANÇAIS

French: *selle français*

Acronym: SF

🄗 1.65 m–1.70 m, up to 1.80 m.

🄒 Often bay, dark bay, chestnut, more rarely gray, with frequent white markings on the head and legs.

**Description**: This athletic horse usually has a head with a straight or convex profile and a wide forehead; long ears; powerful neck; prominent withers; long, sloping shoulders; straight back; long, slightly sloping croup; and muscular legs.

**Distribution**: France, and a few throughout the world, notably in the United Kingdom, the United States, and South America.

**Origins and history**: This is a former military horse converted into a great sport horse. It is the descendant of French halfbreds, notably the Anglo-Norman, which were regrouped in 1958 under the name Selle Français and bred to each other.

**Character and attributes**: Selection has for a long time focused on sporting abilities and not behavior; the latter is variable and depends on the lineages. But breeders are now selecting for this criterion. The breed is generally calm and intelligent. It is a strong, robust, and energetic horse.

**Uses**: The Selle Français is a very renowned sport horse, with excellent results in show jumping competitions and eventing, for which it is considered one of the best breeds in the world. It is also suitable for dressage, and it is often used in riding schools as a lesson horse.

**Current status**: This is one of the most widespread breeds in France and is doing very well (in 2008, there were more than 7,500 births, 11,000 broodmares, and 500 stallions).

The Selle Français is outstanding in show jumping competitions.

Trotting race under saddle.

Long ears

Powerful sloping croup

Fine skin

Long legs

Prominent withers

Long, slightly sloping croup

# FRENCH COB

French: *cob normand*

**H** 1.60 m–1.70 m.

**C** Bay, chestnut, mealy black, more rarely gray or chestnut roan. It often has white markings.

**Description**: This is a light, rather tall draft horse, weighing between 550 kg and 800 kg. It has a head with a straight or convex profile; small ears; a thick neck; prominent withers; wide, sloping shoulders; a short back; double, muscular, sloping croup; short, muscular legs; and wide hooves. The mane is sometimes cut short.

**Distribution**: It is found mainly in western France. It originates in Normandy.

**Origins and history**: The French Cob is the descendant of the ancient Norman Coach Horse. In its veins flows Thoroughbred and Norfolk Trotter blood. The breed truly developed in the twentieth century, with a studbook created in 1950. Unlike other draft horses, it has not been made heavier and bred for its meat, because, when crossed with the English Thoroughbred, it has been used to produce another breed, the Selle Français. Thus it has preserved its original morphology and is the lightest of all nine French draft horse breeds.

**Character and attributes**: Versatile and energetic, it is an elegant horse. It has wonderful gaits. It is a precocious horse that can be put to work rather young. Rustic, it can live outside all year long.

**Uses**: It is very popular for harness racing, in which it has excellent results, but it is also saddled for recreational riding. It offers a good compromise between heavy draft horses and saddle horses.

**Current status**: Following a decrease in its numbers up to the 1990s, the population of French Cobs seems stabilized now; 457 births were noted in 2008. The number of mares has been estimated at 800. In 2012, some 60 stallions were active. This horse is known and enjoyed in Normandy, but is still relatively unknown in the rest of France.

# BOULONNAIS

French: *boulonnais*

**H** 1.50 m–1.70 m.

**C** Most often gray (very light to darker), sometimes black or chestnut. Foals are born dark and become gray as they grow. Other coat colors are not accepted.

**Description**: It is said that the Boulonnais is the Thoroughbred of draft horses. It weighs from 600 kg to a ton. Its rather short head has a very purebred aspect, with a straight profile and very alert eyes. It has sloping shoulders; a long, slanted croup; and a rather high-set tail. Its skin is particularly fine and delicate for a draft horse. The mane is often double.

**Distribution**: France, mainly in Pas-de-Calais, the North, Somme, Seine-Maritime et l'Oise; Belgium, Luxembourg, the Netherlands, and Germany; a few in Brazil and Denmark.

**Origins and history**: The Boulonnais is a very ancient breed of draft horse. Among other influences, in the fourteenth and seventeenth centuries it received Spanish blood that contributed to its well-proportioned physique. For a draft horse, it is also rather lively. As its name indicates, it is originally from the Boulonnais region. There were once two types of Boulonnais: the light "fishmonger" model, and a taller model. It was famous for hauling fish from Boulogne-sur-Mer to Paris. It was a thriving and widespread breed until the twentieth century, when its numbers

The Arabo-Boulonnais makes an excellent carriage horse.

fell with the increase in cars and tractors. The breed was in a very precarious situation in the 1970s and 1980s, due to too much inbreeding. Like many draft breeds, breeding for the meat industry has made the breed considerably heavier. It was crossed with the Arabian, producing the Arabo-Boulonnais, an excellent, competitive harness racing horse.

**Character and attributes**: Although calm, the Boulonnais is more energetic and livelier than most other draft horses. It has great endurance and a sustained trot. This resilient horse lives outside throughout the year. It is precocious and matures rapidly.

**Uses**: It can excel in harness competition and is suitable for recreational activities under saddle as well. As an energetic and powerful horse, it is best for experienced riders. It is still bred a lot for its meat.

**Current status**: This horse population went from more than 600,000 at the beginning of the twentieth century to almost zero seventy years later. Today, the Boulonnais's numbers have stabilized. In 2009, 50 Boulonnais stallions were active, and there were 421 pregnant mares.

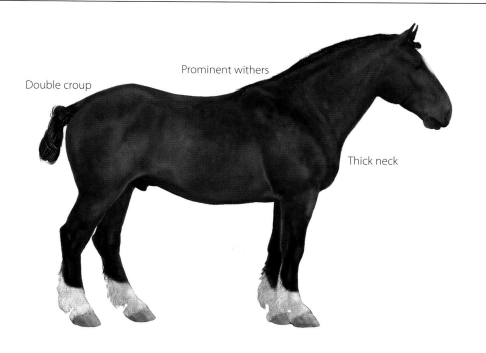

Double croup

Prominent withers

Thick neck

Often double mane

Long, sloping croup

Fine and
soft hide

# COMTOIS

French: *comtois*

**H** 1.50 m–1.65 m.

**C** Dark or coppery chestnut with light mane and tail; bay with light mane and tail, the issue of a silver bay gene, which sometimes produces a silvery mane and tail; the lower legs are dark; rarely chocolate with light mane and tail, very rarely bay; few white markings.

**Description**: This compact draft horse generally weighs from 650 kg to 800 kg. It has a large, boxy head with small ears and a wide forehead; short, muscular neck; broad chest; prominent withers; wide, sloping shoulders; wide croup; and a low-set tail. The mane and tail are abundant and often wavy. It has light feathering on the legs.

**Distribution**: France, especially in mountain zones, but also Spain, Belgium, Holland, and Germany.

**Origins and history**: This ancient breed is the result of native mares first crossed with Germanic stallions, then later with other draft breeds, including the Ardennais.

**Character and attributes**: The Comtois is gentle, rustic, and long-lived. It has good endurance.

**Uses**: Its primary use is for agricultural work and hauling, but it is suitable for carriage driving, equestrian tourism, and recreational riding. It is often bred for its meat and sometimes for its milk.

**Current status**: The Comtois, originally from Franche-Comté, is the most common draft breed in France. Its numbers are increasing every year. It primarily ends up at the slaughterhouse. There are 3,724 breeders. In 2008, 4,632 foals were registered, in 2009, 8,811 mares were impregnated and 937 stallions were active.

# BRETON

French: *breton*

**H** 1.58 m on average.

**C** Most often chestnut, chestnut with light mane and tail, chestnut roan, more rarely roan or bay, very rarely black.

**Description**: This very powerful horse weighs around 750 kg. It has a boxy head with a straight or sometimes concave profile; wide forehead; wide neck; broad chest; long, slanted shoulders; a short, wide back; powerful, slightly sloping croup; and short, strong legs. There are two types of Breton: the lighter Postier Breton and the Bretron Draft, which is heavier. Registered foals are branded with a cross on top of a splayed, upturned "V" on the left side of the neck, the symbol of Brittany.

**Distribution**: France, mainly in Brittany, but also in Southern Europe, North Africa, South America, and Japan.

**Origins and history**: This is an ancient breed, well known in the Middle Ages, but which existed well before that. The Postier Breton has received Norfolk and Hackney blood, whereas the Breton Draft has been crossed with Percheron, Boulonnais, and Ardennais. The Breton itself has been used to improve many draft breeds. An ancient type of Breton, the Corlay Horse, very refined with Arabian and Thoroughbred blood, has influenced the French Chaser.

**Character and attributes**: This docile draft horse is very strong, confident, and energetic, with good endurance. It is a precocious horse.

**Uses**: It is an excellent carriage horse and can be used for farm work; it is also used for equestrian tourism. It is often bred for its meat.

**Current status**: It is one of the rare draft breeds that is doing well. In 2011 around 15,000 Bretons were counted in France, including 711 stallions and 5,780 broodmares. It is bred in many countries.

The power of the Breton is on display in conformation competitions.

Prominent withers

Large, squarish head

Low-set tail

The bay coat carrying the silver gene is common in the Comtois. It differs from the chestnut with light mane and tail (see the Breton below) in its dark legs and the more silvery tone to its coat.

Powerful, slightly sloping croup

Thick neck

Wide forehead

Short, strong legs

# POITEVIN

French: *poitevin, trait poitevin, mulassier poitevin, poitevin mulassier, trait mulassier*

Ⓗ Between 1.55 m and 1.65 m for mares; 1.65 m–1.70 m for males.

Ⓒ Varied and unusual coats, such as gray with black head and dorsal stripe, bay dun, black/brown dun, mealy black, chestnut roan, and others. All colors are accepted, except pinto.

**Description**: It weighs around 750 kg. It has a long head with a convex profile; long ears; rather long neck; broad chest; prominent withers; long, sloping shoulders; a long back; wide, sloping croup; powerful legs; and wide hooves. The mane, tail, and feathering are very long and abundant. The hair is often wavy, and is sometimes curly at the knees and the hocks.

**Distribution**: France, in the West Atlantic region: Poitou-Charentes, Pays de la Loire. There is a breeding farm in the United States, and also one in Sweden.

**Origins and history**: The Poitevin was created from crossings between local mares and Dutch and Flemish stallions during the sixteenth century. It is known as the producer of the famous Poitevin mules, the result of crossings between Poitevin mares and male donkeys from Poitou. The breed's numbers began to decline at the beginning of the twentieth century, as the demand for mules diminished. Its numbers were at the lowest levels in the 1990s. This horse grows slowly; it is bony, and thus of little interest to the meat industry. It has thus remained lighter than other draft horses, which is lucky for the breed, as it has remained quite beautiful.

**Character and attributes**: This is an extremely gentle horse, very calm and intelligent; it reassures beginners or fearful riders. Because of its origins, it is rustic and adapts well to humid prairies.

**Uses**: It can be ridden or used in harness. It is a good horse for equitherapy. Recreational riding may save the breed.

**Current status**: In the past the Poitevin was the leader in the mule industry, and at the beginning of the twentieth century 18,000–20,000 mules were produced and exported annually from around 50,000 mares. To avoid inbreeding, since 1998 the Poitevin has followed a mating plan and for the time being is not producing as many mules, the priority being to revive the population of mares. In 2011 there were 222 mares, 33 active stallions, 84 births for Poitevin drafts and 32 births for Poitevin mules. The Poitevin remains one of the rarest and least known of all French draft horses.

# FRENCH ARDENNAIS

French: *Ardennais, trait ardennais*

Ⓗ 1.60 m–1.62 m on average.

Ⓒ Often bay or roan, sometimes chestnut, chestnut roan, or iron gray.

**Description**: This is a compact, muscular horse that weighs between 700 kg and a ton. It has a long head with a straight or concave profile, small ears, broad chest, muscular shoulders, rather short back, short legs, and often a double croup. Its hooves are wide, with abundant feathering. The mane and tail are thick.

**Distribution**: It is found mainly in northeastern France. The breed is also bred with separate studbooks in Belgium, Luxembourg, and Sweden.

**Origins and history**: The French Ardennais is one of the most ancient of draft horses, known since antiquity. It probably received the influence of Eastern horses in the Middle Ages. It was originally a light draft horse. Among its historical attributes, it is said that under Napoleon it was more resilient than other horses in the Russian campaign, notably due to its ability to endure the cold and its natural hardiness. In the nineteenth century it received both Belgian and Percheron blood, which made it bigger and more powerful. Its numbers fell with the advent of motorization, and in the 1970s it began to be bred for its meat, which saved the breed. The goal of breeding became to produce foals that fattened quickly and horses that were as heavy as possible, which further modified the breed's appearance. It gave rise to three other breeds, the Auxois, the Trait du Nord, and more recently the Aratel. It has been used to improve many draft breeds.

**Character and attributes**: It is docile and powerful, has great endurance, and is resilient. Very rustic, it can live outdoors all year long.

**Uses**: In the past twenty years, with the rise in recreational riding and equestrian tourism, new outlets have opened for this horse. The Ardennais is once again selected for sport criteria. It is a very docile carriage horse that can still be used for farm work. It is also used for logging and for maintaining green spaces.

**Current status**: The breed is increasing again. It is the fourth most numerous breed of French draft horse, following the Comtois, the Breton, and the Percheron. There are 240 stallions, 1,500 mares, and 524 breeders. Around 800 foals are born every year.

Long, wavy
mane and tail

Wide, sloping croup

Long ears

Long head with
convex profile

The Poitevin mule is particularly
tall and strong.

Wide hooves

Often double croup

Wide hooves with
abundant feathering

Belgian Aratel

# AUXOIS

French: *auxois*

**H** 1.60 m–1.70 m.

**C** Mainly bay and roan, sometimes chestnut or chestnut roan.

**Description**: This is a tall, massive draft horse, which weighs from 750 kg to 1,100 kg. It looks a lot like the French Ardennais, but is taller. The head is short, with a wide forehead and small ears. It has a short, muscular neck; prominent withers; broad chest; sloping shoulders; wide, short back; muscular croup; and a low-set tail. It has strong legs, with light feathering.

**Distribution**: France; it is mainly bred in the Burgundy region.

**Origins and history**: This farm horse is the result of crossings between Ardennais and Trait du Nord stallions and local Burgundian mares. Some crossbreeding with Percheron and Boulonnais stallions also took place in the nineteenth century. In the past it was sometimes considered a variety of Ardennais. This breed was not really known before the beginning of the twentieth century. It originates in the Côte-d'Or, Yonne, Saône, Loire, and Nièvre regions of France. The Auxois almost disappeared in the 1970s. Converted into a meat-producing horse, it is losing its athletic qualities and is gaining weight, becoming a "heavy horse;" but the breed is now protected. However, other breeds have proven better for producing meat, and the Auxois's numbers are declining. There is some improvement, however, as it is beginning to be used for recreational riding.

**Character and attributes**: This is a docile and strong horse. Rustic, it can live outdoors throughout the year.

**Uses**: This horse is being increasingly bred for recreational riding, which has enabled it to recover a more sport horse type. It is currently used in harness, for work in vineyards and for logging, and even for milk production.

**Current status**: There have never been a great many Auxois, and this is why it almost became extinct. It has some of the smallest numbers of all French breeds. In 2008 only 111 births occurred. In 2009, 22 stallions were active, for 270 mares, and there were 131 breeders.

# TRAIT DU NORD

French: *trait du nord*. In the past it was called *ardennais du Nord* or *trait ardennais du Nord*

**H** 1.60 m–1.79 m.

**C** Mainly bay, roan, sometimes chestnut, chestnut roan, iron gray, or black.

**Description**: The Trait du Nord is taller and stouter than the Ardennais. It is a muscular, well-built horse that weighs from 800 kg to a ton. It has a small head with an often concave profile, small eyes, short ears, a powerful neck, short back, and broad chest. The mane and tail are fine, but thick.

**Distribution**: France, in the Oise, Aisne, Somme, North, and Pas-de-Calais regions.

**Origins and history**: Although the breed's ancestors existed long ago, the Trait du Nord is a relatively recent breed, created around 1880 from an Ardennais and a Belgian draft. It also received some Boulonnais blood. A first breed association was established in 1903, but World War I wiped out the first efforts at selection. A genealogical chart was opened in 1919 to jump-start the breed, and it was hugely successful until the 1960s. The Trait du Nord was then commonly exported abroad, as far as the United States. It was a farm horse par excellence, laboring in the farmlands of northern France. With motorization, the breed's numbers declined and it was directed toward the meat industry, but this did not help to preserve it.

**Character and attributes**: Very powerful and energetic, it is very attentive to humans. It is a particularly docile horse.

**Uses**: It excels in harness and is used for clearing forests, marshes, and other areas.

**Current status**: Today its numbers are among the lowest of all French horse breeds. The numbers have stabilized, but births are very slowly decreasing. In 2011, 180 mares were impregnated; 37 stallions were active.

Prominent withers

Short head with a
wide forehead

Low-set tail

Fine mane
and tail

Small eyes

Short back

Broad chest

# PERCHERON

French: *percheron*

**H** 1.55 m–1.85 m.

**C** Only black and gray in France. The American Percheron is most often black, and is rarely roan, chestnut, or bay.

**Description**: The Percheron is a tall, muscular horse that weighs between 500 kg and 1,200 kg. Its head has a straight or concave profile, a wide forehead, rather long ears, and very wide nostrils. It has prominent withers; long, sloping shoulders; a straight back; a long, ample, and often double croup; and a high-set tail. The mane and tail are thick. There are two types: the Percheron Draft, tall, heavy and powerful, with a more sloping croup, and the lighter Diligencier Percheron, whose croup is less slanted. It is branded on the neck with a sort of S with a vertical half-slash.

**Distribution**: France, Great Britain, the United States, Canada, Japan, Germany, Argentina, and Australia.

**Origins and history**: This ancient French breed was developed in the Perche region, known for its rich grasslands, through crossings between Eastern horses taken during battles or the Crusades and local mares. It absorbed ancient local breeds: Nivernais, Maine Draft Horse, Augeron, and others. The breed was once hugely popular, considered one of the best draft horses in the world, and was exported widely.

**Character and attributes**: This very powerful horse is docile, alert, and intelligent. Rustic and endowed with great longevity, it is an easy keeper.

**Uses**: The slaughterhouse is no longer its primary destination, and this horse is often used for recreational riding. It excels in pulling competitions. The Percheron Draft Horse is well suited to clearing land and farm work, and the Diligencier is better suited for sport driving and recreational riding.

**Current status**: Although it is not the best represented draft horse in France (the Comtois and the Breton are ahead of it), it is certainly the best known abroad. It once had a very large population. There are 1,211 breeders. In 2008, 1,297 pregnancies took place in France. In 2009, there were more than 20,000 Percherons throughout the world.

Since the ban on tail docking, braiding the Percheron's tail is a way of highlighting the croup.

# MEGÈVE

French: *cheval de Megève*

**H** 1.55 m–1.60 m.

**C** Mainly bay, sometimes chestnut, with a few white markings.

**Description**: This light, compact draft horse weighs around 600 kg. It has a broad chest, a powerful croup, and strong legs.

**Distribution**: Haute-Savoie, France.

**Origins and history**: The Megève is the product of attempts made in the 1990s to reconstitute an old local breed that once existed in Haute-Savoie, and which had essentially disappeared. It is the result of crossings between Comtois mares and Freiberger stallions, a crossing that has led to a type of horse very similar to the original Megève.

**Character and attributes**: Due to its Comtois and Freiberger origins, it is has a good temperament and is calm. It has great endurance and is easy to keep.

**Uses**: It is suited both for work in harness and for equestrian tourism. It is used in ski areas for various purposes.

**Current status**: There are around 150 of them, and some 50 breeders, but the breed is not officially recognized. Due to the recent economic crisis, breeding has stagnated a bit in 2013.

Long, ample, often double croup

High-set tail

Rather long ears

Belgium, known for its famous Belgian horse, one of the greatest breeds of draft horses in the world, is also a nation of riders. It has around 290,000 horses. Belgium shares the breeding of the Ardennais draft horse with France (see France, *p. 156*), and the

---

# BELGIAN RIDING PONY

Dutch: *Belgische Rijpony*

Acronym: BRP or PSBI

**H** 1.32 m–1.49 m; there is also a small type, from 1.10 m to 1.32 m.

**C** Mainly chestnut, bay, dark bay, gray, palomino.

**Description**: It greatly resembles other European sport saddle ponies and, like them, has the athletic and well-proportioned physique of a perfect miniature saddle horse: a slender head with a straight profile; a rather long neck; broad chest; prominent withers; and slender legs.

**Distribution**: Belgium.

**Origins and history**: This recent breed has been bred since 1973 from crossings with various sport ponies, with the idea of producing a good competitive small mount for young Belgian riders.

**Character and attributes**: The Belgian Riding Pony is gentle and energetic, and is a good jumper.

**Uses**: It is particularly suitable for show jumping or dressage, but can also be used for various other disciplines, both in harness and under saddle.

**Current status**: Breeding is in full swing, responding fully to current equestrian sporting tastes.

---

# BELGIAN WARMBLOOD

Dutch: *Belgisch Warmbloed Paard*

Acronym: BWP

**H** 1.65 m–1.70 m.

**C** All coats are possible, often with white markings on the head and legs.

**Description**: This compact horse has the muscular physique of a sport horse. It has a head with a straight profile, a rather short neck, broad chest, sloping croup, high-set tail, and rather short and strong legs.

**Distribution**: The Flemish region in northern Belgium.

**Origins and history**: This is a very recent breed, dating from the 1960s, the result of crossings between local light draft mares and Gelderland, Selle Français, Hanoverian, and other English, German, and Irish sport horses. The aim is to obtain an excellent sport horse through rigorous selection.

**Character and attributes**: The Belgian Warmblood is calm, willing, energetic, and athletic, and has good endurance.

**Uses**: It is a horse intended above all for show jumping at the highest levels, and which is also suited very well to dressage and eventing.

**Current status**: Because of its impressive competition results, the breed is very successful and is doing well.

Belgian state supports their breeding. Two recent Belgian breeds, the Belgian Halfblood and the Belgian Warmblood, are the result of frequent crossings among foreign breeds such as the Oldenburg, Holstein, and Selle Français. Belgium also has breeding farms for many foreign breeds, which make up a large part of its equine population.

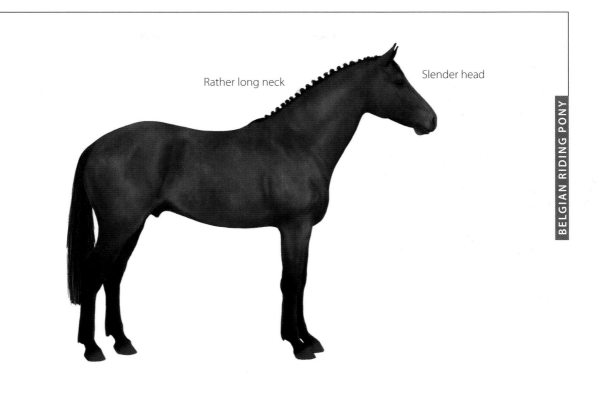

Rather long neck

Slender head

Rather short neck

Sloping croup

# BELGIAN HALFBLOOD

Also called: Belgian Sport Horse

Dutch: *Belgisch Sportpaard*

Acronym: sBs

ⓗ 1.58 m–1.80 m.

ⓒ Mainly bay, chestnut, roan, black, gray.

**Description**: This athletic horse has a large head with a convex profile, small eyes, large ears, long neck, and slender but solid legs.

**Distribution**: Belgium, United States.

**Origins and history**: This recent breed, which dates from the beginning of the twentieth century, was first a military horse. It is the result of many crossings, notably between Belgian draft, Thoroughbred, Selle Français, and German halfbloods. The Belgian Halfblood is traditionally bred in the Wallonia region, and is not to be confused with the similar Belgian Warmblood, raised in the north of Belgium, even if the two breeds have a Belgian Halfblood as a common ancestor. The Belgian Sport Horse is subjected to rigorous selection.

**Character and attributes**: The Belgian Sport Horse is gentle, willing, and is a good jumper.

**Uses**: The breed is principally intended for show jumping and dressage, as well as for eventing.

**Current status**: It is enjoyed by riders for its athletic abilities and is doing very well.

# FLEMISH HORSE

Dutch: *Vlaams Paard*

It should not be confused with the *vlaamperd*, also called Flemish Horse, a rare breed that was developed in South Africa. Although the names are almost the same, they are not the same breed.

ⓗ 1.65 m–1.75 m.

ⓒ Generally chestnut with light mane and tail.

**Description**: This is a tall, powerful horse. It has a powerful neck, a broad chest, a muscular croup, and rather slender legs for a draft horse.

**Distribution**: The Flemish region of Belgium, the Netherlands, with a few in France and Germany, the United States, and Canada.

**Origins and history**: This ancient breed, which has been used to improve a number of other draft breeds, was until recently considered to be extinct. But horses were exported in large numbers to North America in the past, and Amish communities preserved the breed as it was until it was rediscovered. Thanks to the horses preserved by the Amish the breed has been able to continue. It has been rehabilitated and reconstituted since 1993. The Flemish Horse was once used for farm work.

**Character and attributes**: The Flemish Horse is docile, reliable, and robust. It has endurance and is flexible.

**Uses**: This powerful horse is a good harness horse.

**Current status**: The breed remains very rare, with around 300 horses in existence.

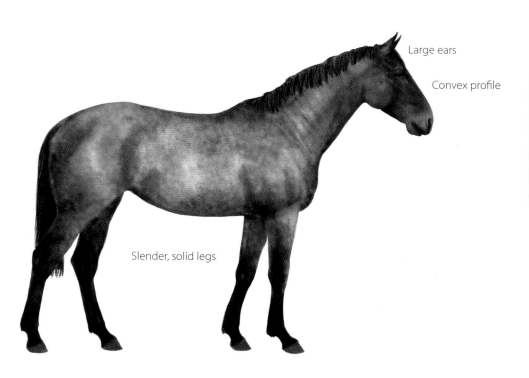

Large ears

Convex profile

Slender, solid legs

Powerful neck

Muscular croup

Broad chest

Slender legs for a
draft horse

# BELGIAN

French: *belge, brabançon, brabant, cheval de trait belge, trait lourd belge*

**H** 1.63 m–1.73 m.

**C** Roan with black mane and tail and legs, chestnut roan, iron gray, chestnut, sometimes bay, dark bay.

**Description**: This tall, very massive, and very muscular draft horse easily surpasses a ton. It has a rather small and boxy head; small eyes; small ears; a wide, short, and powerful neck; broad chest; very muscular shoulders; a wide, short back; very wide double croup; short, strong legs; and big, flat hooves. American Belgians can be taller and are often chestnut.

**Distribution**: Belgium, United States, Australia; there are breeding farms in Europe and throughout the world.

**Origins and history**: The Belgian draft horse, a very ancient breed, is the descendant of strong medieval chargers that carried armored knights, notably the horses of Flanders: Ardennais, Brabançon, and Flemish. There were once three types: the Gros de la Dendre lineage; the Gris de Nivelles or Hainaut lineage, and the Colosse de Méhaigne lineage. In mixing, they produced the Belgian Draft horse. Americans, great admirers of the breed, opened their own studbook of American Belgians in 1887 (the Belgian studbook had existed since 1855).

In the past the breed contributed to the creation or the improvement of other draft horses, such as the Suffolk Punch and Clydesdale. Its power made it the preferred farm horse before the appearance of tractors. By refusing to cross their breed the Belgians succeeded in preserving its specific qualities.

**Character and attributes**: It is probably the most powerful of all draft horses. Indeed, it is extremely strong. But it is a docile horse, calm and very cooperative. It lives a long time.

**Uses**: It is a powerful harness horse, used also in pulling competitions.

**Current status**: In Belgium it is considered a national treasure, and its breeding is supported by the state. Although rather rare, it is one of the draft breeds that is still doing relatively well, with a thousand births per year.

The enormous Belgian draft horse can be ridden, but this is not its most common use.

## BELGIAN TROTTER

Dutch: *Belgische Draver*

**Description**: See French Trotter (*p. 150*). It can be a bit more slender and smaller than the French horse.

**Distribution**: Belgium.

**Origins and history**: This very close cousin of the French Trotter, a breed from which it is descended, is a type of trotter that has received some Norfolk and American Standardbred blood. Trotting races, usually in harness, are very popular in Belgium, and the French Trotter is also common there.

## ZANGERSHEIDE

The Zangersheide is not a breed but a Belgian registry of show jumping horses. It should still be included here because it could potentially become a breed. The stud farm in Zangersheide in fact selects horses based on their performance in show jumping. The registry was started in 1993, and the horses admitted from this selection have the suffix Z. It is still open to all breeds, which are mixed, the selection bearing on sport results. Included in the registry one finds, among others, the Hanoverian, Holstein, and Selle Français.

Very wide, very powerful neck

Very wide, muscular croup

Big hooves

The Grand Duchy of Luxembourg is a small country, but its Luxembourg Federation of Equestrian Sports and its hundred or so riding clubs demonstrate its true interest in horses and riding. The development

## LUXEMBOURG

### LUXEMBOURG WARMBLOOD

Acronym: SL

🄗 1.62 m–1.70 m.

🄒 Often bay, dark bay, gray; all coats are accepted, except pinto.

**Description**: This is a saddle horse that resembles other European halfblood saddle horses. It is very muscular and has solid legs.
**Distribution**: Luxembourg.
**Origins and history**: This recent breed is the issue of some thirty stallions, mostly Thoroughbreds.

The offspring of these stallions, too light for farm work, were sold as riding and carriage horses. Following the Belgian revolution of 1830 the stud farm stopped its activities and the stallions were transferred to Brussels. It was only in 1958 that the purebred studbook was established. Between 1958 and 1970 Hanoverian mares were imported and served as a foundation for the Luxembourg Warmblood; they were often crossed with Holstein stallions. Selection is rigorous.
**Character and attributes**: This intelligent, good-natured horse is a good jumper.
**Uses**: The Luxembourg Warmblood is well suited for show jumping and dressage.
**Current status**: There are between 150 and 200 foals of this recent breed born each year.

Horse breeding in the Netherlands involves almost exclusively the recreation and equestrian sports sectors. There are around 500,000 horses. A country that exports horses, notably the Dutch Warmblood

## THE NETHERLANDS

### GELDERLAND

Dutch: *Gelderlander Paard, Gelders Paard*

🄗 1.55 m–1.63 m.

🄒 Often chestnut, sometimes gray, black, or bay, often with white markings on the legs or head.

**Description**: It is similar to the Groningen Horse, but is lighter. It has a straight or slightly convex profile, large eyes, arched neck, long back, horizontal croup, and a high-set tail held in a way that is characteristic of the breed.
**Distribution**: Gelderland Province, Netherlands.
**Origins and history**: The Gelderland is the result of much crossbreeding between local mares and Andalusian, Neapolitan, Friesian, Thoroughbred, Anglo-Norman, Hackney, Oldenburg, Arabian, and

even Orlov horses. It was for a long time a carriage and military horse.
**Character and attributes**: This is a docile and energetic horse. It is supple and powerful, with high-stepping gaits, and is a good jumper. It has good health and lives a long time.
**Uses**: It is used in harness racing, but also in dressage and in show jumping. It is also a good horse for equestrian tourism.
**Current status**: Surprisingly, this breed has lost its former popularity and is declining; its numbers are currently rather low. It is considered to be endangered, with some dozen stallions and around 500 mares, but is being preserved to avoid its blending with the Dutch Warmblood.

of a new breed, the Luxembourg Warmblood, has helped introduce Luxembourg into the competitive world of equestrian sports.

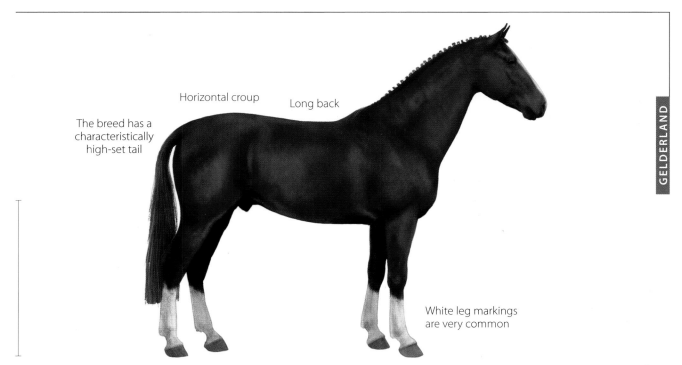

Prominent withers

Long, very muscular neck

Solid legs

(KWPN), the Netherlands also breeds many foreign breeds, particularly the Shetland, Haflinger, Icelandic, Konik, and Fjord. Among its indigenous breeds, the Netherlands has the famous Friesian, the large black horse that has recently been very much in fashion thanks to its unique physique. Experienced riders, the Dutch are serious competitors in Olympic and other international competitions.

Horizontal croup

Long back

The breed has a characteristically high-set tail

White leg markings are very common

# GRONINGEN

Also called: Groninger Horse

Dutch: *Groninger Paard*

**H** 1.55 m–1.70 m.

**C** Often black, brownish bay, less often bay, chestnut; frequent white markings on the head and legs.

**Description**: It resembles the Gelderland but is more powerful, and also resembles the Frederiksborg. It is a massive horse, with a straight or convex profile; rather long ears; short, high-set neck; broad chest; long back; wide croup; strong, rather short legs; wide feet; and a very high-set tail.

**Distribution**: Province of Groningen in the Netherlands.

**Origins and history**: The breed is the issue of East Friesian, Arabian, and Oldenburg horses, but almost became extinct in the 1970s. A contribution of Oldenburg blood enabled it to be relaunched. The Groningen contributed to the creation of the Dutch Warmblood, a breed with which it almost completely blended.

**Character and attributes**: The Groningen is very docile and cooperative. It has endurance and is easygoing, with cadenced gaits. It has good health.

**Uses**: Although driving is its primary use, this versatile horse is also suitable for riding, notably for dressage and equestrian tourism. Its dependable nature enables it to be ridden by many different riders.

**Current status**: After a dramatic fall in its numbers, the breed remains rare, although its breeding has become more active. There are only around 20 stallions and 400 mares.

# DUTCH WARMBLOOD

Also called: KWPN Riding Horse

Dutch: *Koninklijk Warmbloed Paard Nederland*

Acronym: KWPN

**H** 1.58 m–1.78 m.

**C** Bay, dark bay, chestnut, sometimes black or gray, rarely pinto; all coats are possible.

**Description**: The Dutch Warmblood has a head with a straight profile; rather long and muscular neck; prominent withers; sloping shoulders; short, straight back; long, muscular legs; and a high-set tail. There are three types—for harness (see Tuigpaard, *p. 174*), dressage, and show jumping—to which is added the Gelderland, which is also included in the KWPN registry (see Gelderland, *p. 168*).

**Distribution**: The Netherlands. Exported throughout the world, notably to France, Germany, and the United States.

**Origins and history**: This recent breed (the studbook dates from 1958) is the result of crossings between Dutch saddle breeds, the Groningen, the Gelderland, and the Thoroughbred. Then Oldenburg, Hanoverian, and Selle Français blood was added. The goal was to obtain a good show jumping and dressage horse, and, in fact, a very athletic horse has been the result. It has quickly become very popular.

**Character and attributes**: It has a calm, docile, and cooperative nature, and is intelligent. It is very athletic and powerful, with lovely gaits. It requires attentive care.

**Uses**: Its best disciplines are dressage, show jumping, and eventing, in which it excels at the highest levels. It is also suitable for driving. Although it is a very athletic horse, its good nature makes it accessible to a greater number of riders than other breeds of this type.

**Current status**: The breed is popular and widespread due to its very good results in competition, with more than 10,000 foals registered each year.

A high-stepping trot, characteristic of the Tuigpaard.

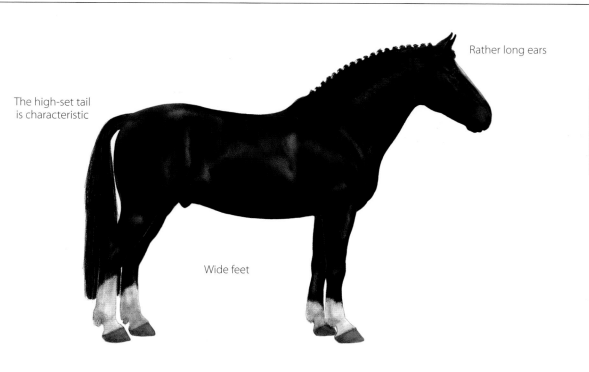

Rather long ears

The high-set tail
is characteristic

Wide feet

High-set neck

Prominent
withers

Short back

High-set tail

Long, muscular legs

Large hooves

# FRIESIAN

Dutch: *Fries Paard*

**H** 1.55 m–1.70 m.

**C** Always black, without white markings (only a small star on the forehead is accepted).

**Description:** This horse has a very characteristic appearance with a proud bearing, which makes it easily recognizable. It has a long head with a straight profile; a powerful, high-set neck; broad chest; long, sloping shoulders; straight, short back; sloping croup; and long feathering on the legs. The mane and tail are long, silky, very thick, and wavy.

**Distribution:** Netherlands and throughout the world.

**Origins and history:** This is a very ancient native horse with primitive origins. It later received Arabian and Andalusian blood. It was ridden by knights in the Middle Ages, then was a carriage horse with a renowned trot. It has contributed to the creation of many breeds: Hackney, Shire, Oldenburg, Fell, Dales, and Døle. It almost disappeared at the beginning of the twentieth century, and a contribution of Oldenburg blood enabled the breed to be relaunched.

**Character and attributes:** This very good trotter is docile, gentle, very calm, and yet energetic with wonderful gaits. Resilient, it is easy to keep.

**Uses:** Versatile, it is suitable for riding as well as for driving. A good horse for dressage, it is also enjoyed in equine exhibitions and in haute école.

**Current status:** A once-endangered breed, the Friesian is currently enjoying great popularity and is doing very well, with around 60,000 horses throughout the world.

The Friesian has light gaits.

### FRIESIAN CROSSBREDS

The Friesian is also used for crossbreeding. Crossing it with an Andalusian or a Lusitano gives the Ispazon in France, and the Warlander in the United States. As for the Arabo-Friesian, it is a Friesian with 10–20 percent Arabian blood, which creates a slightly more slender, more athletic horse, and above all one with more endurance. These crossbred Friesians will perhaps become separate breeds in time and with selection.

Characteristic
high-set neck

Long head

Long, silky, and
wavy mane and tail

Broad chest

Long feathering

Arabo-Friesian

Ispazon or Warlander (Andalusian x Friesian)

# DUTCH HEAVY DRAFT

Dutch: *Nederlands Trekpaard*

**H** 1.60 m–1.75 m.

**C** Chestnut, chestnut with light mane and tail, bay, light bay, gray, sometimes black, roan.

**Description**: This very heavy and muscular horse resembles the Belgian, with which it has common origins. It easily reaches 750–1,000 kg. It has a rather small head with a straight profile and small ears. It has a short neck; broad chest; short croup; low-set tail; strong, short legs; and large hooves with feathering.

**Distribution**: Netherlands, notably Zeeland.

**Origins and history**: Its history is linked to that of the Belgian, because there were many exchanges between the two countries, and a lot of crossing with Zeeland mares, a native breed that was used by knights in the Middle Ages. It also received Ardennais blood. The breed was established at the beginning of the twentieth century.

**Character and attributes**: This is a very placid, calm, yet energetic horse, intelligent and sometimes a bit stubborn. It is very strong and resilient, and agile in spite of its weight.

**Uses**: It is above all a work horse that is suited for being harnessed and for farm work.

**Current status**: In decline with 50 stallions and 1,100 mares (2002), the breed remains very vulnerable although it is quite popular in the Netherlands.

When it trots, the Dutch Heavy Draft demonstrates all its power.

# DUTCH TUIGPAARD

Also called: Dutch Carriage Horse, KWPB Harness Horse

Dutch: *Tuigpaard*

**H** 1.60 m on average.

**C** Often chestnut, less often black, bay, brownish bay, more rarely gray, roan, often with white markings.

**Description**: The Tuigpaard has a rather large head with a straight profile; long ears; small eyes; a high-set neck; rather long back; short, horizontal croup; high-set tail; and large hooves.

**Distribution**: Netherlands, North America.

**Origins and history**: The Tuigpaard, a name that in Dutch means "harness horse," is a type of Dutch Warmblood (see *p. 170*). Its different physical appearance means that it will perhaps ultimately become a separate breed; it is actually already considered as such. It also has Groninger and Gelderland ancestors. It has received Hackney, then American Saddlebred blood. It is rather different, both in its physique and in its use, from the KWPN show jumper. The Tuigpaard is selected for its athletic abilities in harness.

**Character and attributes**: This is a lively, sometimes nervous horse with a proud gait and a characteristic, very high-stepping trot. The gaits are truly natural because special shoes are not authorized.

**Uses**: It is above all used for showing in harness but also for combined driving events.

**Current status**: There are around 40 stallions and 2,000 broodmares, and the breed seems to be gaining in popularity.

Short croup

Rather small head
with small ears

Strong, short legs

With more than a million horses in 2010, Germany is the European country with the most horses, even more than England and France. It also has more than a million and a half regular riders; with the strength of those numbers, the German National Equestrian

# GERMAN CLASSIC PONY

German: *deutsches Classic Pony* or *Classic Pony*

**H** A maximum of 1.12 m.

**C** Often chestnut with light mane and tail, palomino, bay dun, but many other colors are possible.

**Description**: This is a very sporty version of the Shetland Pony, from which it is issued, and it is considered more elegant. It has a small head with small ears; a round, muscular croup; high-set tail; and thin legs. The forelock is thick, and the mane and tail are abundant.

**Distribution**: Germany.

**Origins and history**: Beginning in 1965 this recent breed has been selected from the American-type Shetland Pony, so as to achieve a taller and more sport horse type. It is clearly quite different from the traditional Shetland. In 2001 Germany obtained official recognition for a separate breed following international disagreement among Shetland breeders. Germany breeds the horses following its own criteria.

**Character and attributes**: The German Classic Pony is intelligent, cooperative, and gentle. It is robust and hardy.

**Uses**: It is a perfect mount for children, both for sport and for recreation. It can pull small, light carts.

**Current status**: The breed's numbers in Germany are still small, with only 200 broodmares and some forty stallions.

# DÜLMEN PONY

German: *Dülmener*

**H** 1.25 m–1.35 m.

**C** Most often black/brown dun, buckskin, sometimes black, dark bay or liver chestnut, often with a dorsal stripe and zebra striping on the legs.

**Description**: This compact pony has a primitive appearance. It has a head with a straight or slightly concave profile; wide forehead; small ears; short neck; unobtrusive withers; powerful back; sloping croup; and small, hard hooves. The mane and tail are thick.

**Distribution**: The Wildpferdebahn Merfelder Bruch nature reserve in Westphalia, Germany.

**Origins and history**: Its existence was mentioned for the first time in 1316, which shows that the breed is very old. The lords of Merfeld, the Dukes of

Croy, have always allowed wild herds of Dülmens to graze on their land. The breed nevertheless almost disappeared in the nineteenth century, before recovering. It received contributions of English and Polish (Konik) blood. It continues to live freely; each year at the end of May young males are pulled from the herd and sold.

**Character and attributes**: Full of good will once broken, the Dülmen is an intelligent mount. Because of its free-range life and natural selection, it is undemanding, robust, and very rustic; it has endurance and is adapted to cold winters. It lives a long time.

**Uses**: It is a recreational horse and is also suitable for driving. Its size makes it a good mount for young riders.

**Current status**: Although protected, the breed's numbers are still small, with only around 300 animals.

Federation is a powerful organization. Germany is known for the great quality of its sport horses, which are highly esteemed throughout the world. German riders and horses excel in Olympic sports and are often on podiums, notably for dressage competitions.

Not only does Germany have many indigenous breeds, it also breeds many foreign horses. Alongside its most flourishing breeds, it also has several breeds whose numbers are quite small.

Small ears

Abundant mane and tail hair

GERMAN CLASSIC PONY

Short neck

Sloping croup

Small, very black hooves

DÜLMEN PONY

# LEWITZER

German: *Lewitzer*

**H** 1.30 m–1.48 m, with three size categories.

**C** Always pinto, mainly tobiano, with often light hooves, and often blue or light-colored eyes.

**Description**: The Lewitzer has a head with a straight or slightly concave profile; large eyes; prominent withers; and a wide back and croup.

**Distribution**: Western Mecklenburg Pomerania, Germany.

**Origins and history**: This recent breed was created in the 1970s in East Germany. It is the result of crossings between Fjord, Shetland, Arabian, Trakehner, and Thoroughbred horses. The goal of these various crossings was to obtain a good sport mount for children, with an easy nature and an attractive color.

**Character and attributes**: The Lewitzer is popular for its good nature. It is also robust and a good jumper. Broodmares are fertile.

**Uses**: The Lewitzer is a versatile breed that is suitable for both saddle and harness. Athletic, it can compete in eventing or show jumping. It is also found in endurance races.

**Current status**: This recent breed is small in number. It is scarcely known outside of Germany, but its qualities make it increasingly popular in its own country.

# GERMAN RIDING PONY

German: *deutsches Reitpony*

**H** A maximum of 1.38 m–1.48 m.

**C** Mainly chestnut, bay, black, gray.

**Description**: The German Riding Pony resembles a miniature saddle horse. It has a small head with large eyes and small ears; large nostrils; a long neck; long, slightly sloping croup; somewhat high-set tail; and slender legs.

**Distribution**: Germany.

**Origins and history**: Having begun in the 1960s this recent breed is the result of crossings among Welsh B, Connemara, New Forest, Arabian, Anglo-Arab, and Thoroughbred horses, then later with Trakehners, Hanoverians, and Holsteins, with the goal of producing an excellent sport horse for young riders.

**Character and attributes**: Lively, confident, attentive, and powerful.

**Uses**: The German Riding Pony is at its best with young riders who are already at an advanced level; it is not the ideal mount for beginners since it is somewhat nervous. Bred for competition, it can compete notably in dressage and show jumping, its best disciplines. It is also suitable for light adult riders.

**Current status**: The breed is quite successful in Germany, where it is widespread and popular (in 2008 there were 6,155 mares and 706 stallions).

Light eyes

Often light hooves

Long neck

Small head

Slender legs

# AEGIDIENBERGER

German: *Aegidienberger*

**H** 1.43 m–1.52 m.

**C** All colors, few markings.

**Description**: The Aegidienberger is compact, with a strong head; short, high-set neck; unobtrusive withers; and slightly sloping croup. The hair of the mane and tail is abundant.

**Distribution**: Germany.

**Origins and history**: This recent breed was created in the 1970s. It is the result of crossings among the Icelandic and Peruvian Paso, two breeds renowned for their supplemental natural gaits. The goal was to produce a new breed of rustic gaited horse that was taller than the Icelandic.

**Character and attributes**: This is a cooperative and intelligent breed, docile, energetic, very robust, with great endurance, whose unique characteristic is its natural predisposition for the tölt and the amble, which makes it comfortable to ride, especially over long distances. The Aegidienberger is better adapted to hot temperatures than the Icelandic.

**Uses**: This versatile riding horse is suitable for young and adult riders alike; it is a good family horse and a good trekking horse. It can also be driven.

**Current status**: The breed was recognized in 1994. Its numbers are still fairly low, with around 600 horses.

The Aegidienberger was selected for its supplementary gaits (tölt).

# HANOVERIAN

German: *Hannoveraner*

**H** 1.55 m–1.75 m; on average 1.63 m.

**C** Mainly bay, chestnut, sometimes black, gray, and other basic colors, often with white markings on the head, and stockings.

**Description**: This powerful horse has a balanced physique: a head with a straight, sometimes convex profile; long, muscular neck; deep chest; good, sloping shoulders; straight, long back; rather long, muscular croup; a high-set tail; and excellent legs and hooves.

**Distribution**: Originally from Lower Saxony and Hanover in Germany, the breed has conquered all of Europe and America, and is bred just about everywhere in the world.

**Origins and history**: The Hanoverian's military origins date from the seventeenth century. It is a breed that has been crossed a lot. The horse was improved in the eighteenth century through multiple crossings with the English Thoroughbred. In the twentieth century it also received Trakehner and Arabian blood, with the goal of making it more versatile. It was once a carriage horse before becoming one of the most sought-after sport horses in the world. The Hanoverian has contributed to improving the Oldenburg. The Celle stud farm in Lower Saxony, founded in 1735, is devoted to the breed.

**Character and attributes**: It is an energetic, balanced, intelligent horse with great endurance. Breeders also select horses for their character, removing from reproduction animals whose nature is not sufficiently balanced.

**Uses**: It is one of the best sport horses in the world, used for dressage, show jumping, eventing, and other disciplines. In international competitions it is always found at awards ceremonies. It is a versatile horse whose best individuals can demand astronomical sums.

**Current status**: Very popular, this great athletic breed is doing very well.

The Hanoverian excels in dressage.

Short, high-set neck

Slightly sloping croup

Rather long, muscular croup

Long, straight back

Prominent withers

High-set tail

Long, muscular neck

# East Friesian

Also called: East Friesian Warmblood

German: *Ostfriesan, Alt-Oldenburger, oldenburger Karossier*

ⓗ 1.58 m–1.65 m.

ⓒ Bay, dark bay, black, more frequently light gray, chestnut, with rather rarely white markings on the legs or head.

**Description**: Despite its name, the breed does not resemble the Friesian of the Netherlands, but rather the Oldenburg, to which it is very close. The East Friesian is more massive than the Oldenburg, with a more convex profile. It also has large eyes; a long, high-set neck; rather prominent withers; a rather long back; slightly sloping croup; and long, muscular legs.

**Distribution**: East Frisia, Germany.

**Origins and history**: The East Friesian greatly resembles its close cousin, the Oldenburg, with which it has common origins. It was in fact the division of Germany following World War II that split up the breeding stock.

**Character and attributes**: The East Friesian is a very good saddle horse, docile and calm but energetic. Like the majority of sport breeds, it needs attentive care, such as shelter and additional food.

**Uses**: This is a competition horse that is suited for show jumping, but which excels in harness competitions.

**Current status**: The breed almost disappeared when the Oldenburg was modernized with contributions of Thoroughbred and Trakehner blood, but was saved at the end of the 1970s. It is very rare, with only around 160 broodmares and some 20 stallions.

# Saxon-Thuringian Heavy Warmblood

German: *sächsisch-thüringisches schweres Warmblut*

ⓗ 1.58 m–1.68 m.

ⓒ Dark bay, black, few white markings.

**Description**: This is a powerful and rather massive horse, with a head with a straight profile; a long, muscular neck; prominent withers; a long back; and a muscular, slightly sloping croup.

**Distribution**: Saxony, Thuringia, Germany.

**Origins and history**: This rather ancient German breed has origins in common with the East Friesian. It was basically a harness horse, used in farm work, but also a military mount.

**Character and attributes**: It is known for its good nature: it is easygoing, reliable, and confident at the same time. It is a powerful horse.

**Uses**: The breed is suitable for riding, but it stands out particularly in harness, notably in competitions, where it is very successful. Its gentle nature makes it a pleasant recreational and family horse.

**Current status**: This native horse remains rare and little known, with around 80 stallions and more than a thousand mares (1,415 in 2008). It was on the brink of extinction in the 1960s and remains watched as an endangered breed. Its breeding is carefully managed to avoid problems related to inbreeding.

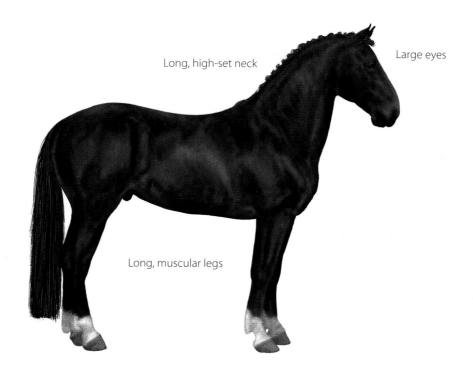

Long, high-set neck

Large eyes

Long, muscular legs

Prominent withers

Long back

# ZWEIBRÜCKER

German: *Zweibrücker, zweibrücker Warmblut*

**H** 1.58 m–1.68 m.

**C** Often chestnut, bay, gray, black, but also a few palominos, bay duns, pintos.

**Description**: This tall horse has a head with a straight profile; large eyes; a long, slender, rather high-set neck; straight back; muscular croup; and strong legs. It is branded on the left thigh, in reference to its name and its original city, with two bridges beneath a crown.

**Distribution**: Southwestern Germany, North America.

**Origins and history**: The breed, quite old and founded by Duke Christian IV (1722–1775), is the result of crossings among halfblood mares and Arabian stallions, then other breeds, notably Hanoverians, Trakehners, Holsteins, Oldenburgs, and Westphalians. Its breeding suffered from wars in the past.

**Character and attributes**: The Zweibrücker is a balanced and reliable horse. It is powerful and a good jumper.

**Uses**: This saddle horse is bred with a view to competition in dressage, show jumping, and eventing, but also in harness.

**Current status**: Competing with the other famous breeds of German sport horses, the Zweibrücker remains local, with only a bit more than 1,200 horses, and is less known abroad. Its lineages with multicolored coats, always unusual in sport horses, will perhaps enable it to be developed more in the future.

# BAVARIAN WARMBLOOD

German: *bayerisches Warmblut*

**H** 1.58 m–1.75 m.

**C** Often chestnut and bay, sometimes black or light gray.

**Description**: It resembles the Hanoverian. It has a head with a straight profile and large eyes; prominent withers; long, sloping shoulders; slightly sloping croup; and strong legs. It is branded with a B on its thigh.

**Distribution**: Bavaria, Germany; Great Britain.

**Origins and history**: Originally a draft and war horse, the Bavarian Warmblood has been refined through crossings with Thoroughbred, Cleveland Bay, Norman, and then Oldenburg horses. The breed from which it issued, the Rottaler, has been completely blended into the Bavarian Warmblood. Selection is also based on character, eliminating difficult horses from the breeding stock.

**Character and attributes**: The Bavarian Warmblood has an easy nature; it is confident, powerful, and solid. It is a good jumper.

**Uses**: This sport horse is suited both to dressage and show jumping, as well as to eventing.

**Current status**: Enjoyed for its physical qualities and its good temperament, the breed is doing well, with a few thousand horses, around 3,500 of which are broodmares and 125 stallions. There are still a few horses with the look of the earlier Rottaler.

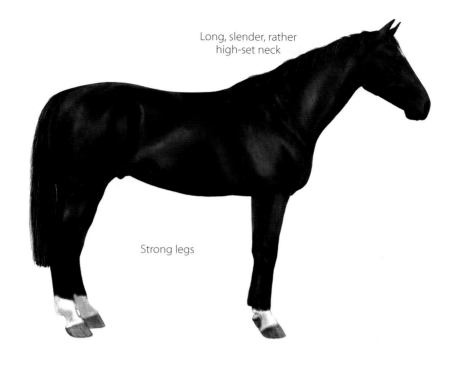

Long, slender, rather high-set neck

Strong legs

Prominent withers

Large eyes

Strong legs

# MECKLENBURGER

German: *Mecklenburger*

**H** 1.60 m–1.70 m.

**C** Most often bay, dark bay, black, gray, chestnut.

**Description**: The Mecklenburger resembles the Hanoverian, but is shorter and more compact, with a more slender head. It has a straight profile; a muscular, rather long neck; broad chest; prominent withers; straight back; and a long, slanted croup. It has a brand in the shape of an M with a crown on top.

**Distribution**: Mecklenburg–Western Pomerania, Germany.

**Origins and history**: The Mecklenburger breed was founded in 1812, and was originally a carriage and military horse. It received Arabian and Thoroughbred blood, as well as that of the Anglo-Arab. Later it was influenced by the Hanoverian and Trakehner.
The current goal of breeding is to have a good saddle horse with athletic qualities.

**Character and attributes**: This dynamic horse is lively and docile, bold and confident. It has endurance and is robust.

**Uses**: A versatile saddle horse, it especially stands out in dressage and show jumping; it is also a good harness horse.

**Current status**: The breed remains rather local, with around 1,500 mares and 90 stallions, but it is being actively bred.

# RHENISH WARMBLOOD

Also called: Rhinelander

German: *rheinisches Warmblut*

**H** 1.60 m–1.70 m.

**C** Mainly bay, dark bay, chestnut, black, gray.

**Description**: The Rhenish Warmblood has a classic saddle horse physique, with a head with straight profile; a long, slender neck; prominent withers; a muscular, slightly sloping croup, low-set tail; and long, slender legs.

**Distribution**: Rhineland, Germany.

**Origins and history**: The Rhenish Warmblood is a recent breed; its breeding began only after World War II, in a region that up until then was more focused on breeding draft horses. With the goal of producing a good athletic saddle horse, it received Hanoverian, Holstein, Trakehner, and Thoroughbred blood.

**Character and attributes**: The Rhenish Warmblood is reliable and confident, with an athletic physique. It has lovely gaits and is a good jumper.

**Uses**: A good, versatile saddle horse, it stands out particularly in show jumping competitions, and is also perfectly suited to dressage. It is also a good carriage horse.

**Current status**: The breed remains local, but is doing well, because it is responding to the needs of contemporary equestrians.

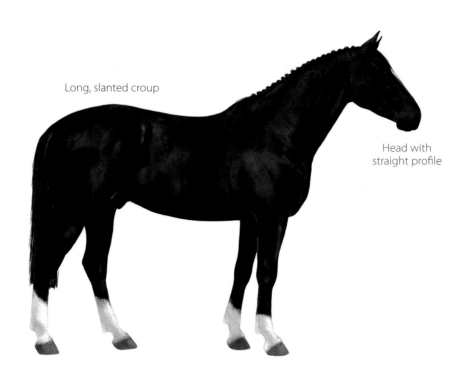

Long, slanted croup

Head with
straight profile

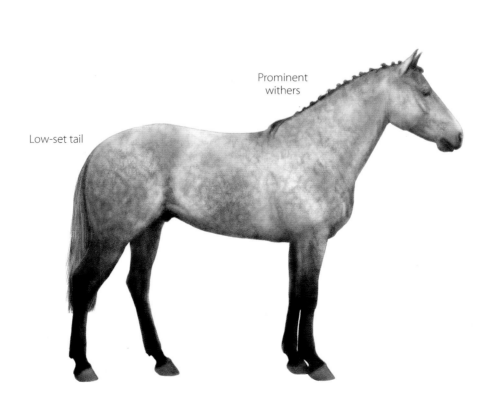

Prominent
withers

Low-set tail

# TRAKEHNER

German: *Trakehner*

**H** 1.60 m–1.70 m.

**C** Bay, dark bay, black, chestnut, more rarely gray.

**Description**: Well built and slender at the same time, the Trakehner has a straight head with a wide forehead, becoming more slender toward the nose; rather long, slender ears; a long neck; broad chest; prominent withers; long, sloping shoulders; solid back; slightly sloping croup; high-set tail; thin but solid legs; and resilient feet. The hair of the mane and tail is fine and thin.

**Distribution**: Germany, Poland, Russia, United States, and a few in the rest of the world.

**Origins and history**: This ancient breed of saddle horse is the result of crossings between local mares and Eastern horses, then later with Arabians and Thoroughbreds. In 1732 a royal stud farm was created in the region of Trakehnen to develop the breed, which was for a long time a military horse. The breeding encountered problems during the wars, with some thrilling evacuations, notably during World War II. The breed then lost a lot of horses, but was saved each time.

**Character and attributes**: This is currently one of the best sport horses. It is intelligent, energetic, calm, and pleasant. Very athletic, it is fast, resilient, has endurance, and is very versatile, with very lovely gaits. It requires attentive care.

**Uses**: It excels in dressage, eventing, and endurance, and also competes in show jumping and in light harness.

**Current status**: The breeding of the Trakehner is lucrative, and riders think very highly of this horse.

The Trakehner is endowed with mass and suppleness.

# BRANDENBURG

German: *Brandenburger*

**H** 1.62 m–1.70 m.

**C** Often chestnut, bay, black.

**Description**: It greatly resembles the Hanoverian. It is a tall horse with a muscular neck; very prominent withers; and a powerful, muscular, slightly sloping croup. The tail is set high. It is branded with an arrow shooting to the left, around which a snake is curled.

**Distribution**: Brandenburg, in Eastern Germany.

**Origins and history**: Originally a renowned military horse, the Brandenburg over time has undergone competition with the Hanoverian. It is the issue of ancient saddle horses—mentioned in the fifteenth century—crossed with Thoroughbred and English halfblood, Eastern, Trakehner, and Hanoverian horses. It has been known in its current form since the 1960s.

**Character and attributes**: The Brandenburg is a lively and sensitive horse, but calm and balanced. It is very agile when ridden.

**Uses**: This saddle horse is suited in particular to dressage, show jumping, and eventing.

**Current status**: The breed remains local, with small numbers (around 1,600 broodmares and 70 stallions in the 2010s). The breed suffered notably during World War II.

Thinnish mane
and tail

Head becomes more
slender near the nose

No feathering

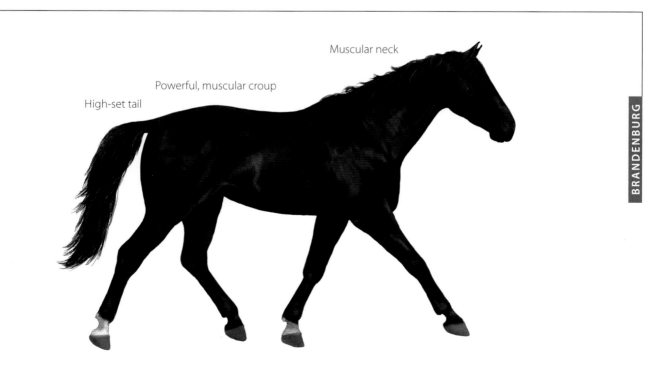

Muscular neck

Powerful, muscular croup

High-set tail

# WÜRTTEMBERG

German: *Baden-Württemberger, württemberger Warmblut*

🔴 1.60 m–1.75 for the modern type; 1.55 m–1.65 m for the ancient type.

🟢 Mainly chestnut, liver chestnut, bay, dark bay, more rarely black, sometimes with white markings.

**Description**: It has a head with a straight profile and large eyes; broad chest; long, straight back; slanted croup; and solid legs. There are two types: ancient (Alt-Württemberg), which is more compact, resembling a cob, and more rare; and a more slender modern type, which is the most common.

**Distribution**: Baden-Württemberg, Germany.

**Origins and history**: The origins of this rather old breed go back to the sixteenth century. It is the result of crossings among local mares and many other breeds, including the Arabian, Barb, and Andalusian, then the Anglo-Norman, Suffolk, Trakehner, and Holstein. It was once a military horse and was also used for farm work. The older type of the breed, called Alt-Württemberg (literally, "old Würtemberg"), still exists but is endangered, even though it provides excellent mounts.

**Character and attributes**: The Württemberg is a horse with a calm, docile, and gentle nature. It has endurance and is resilient.

**Uses**: It is a saddle horse whose best disciplines are dressage and show jumping, and combined driving competitions.

**Current status**: Although the modern type of Württemberg is common, the old type is rarer, with only around sixty broodmares.

The old type, Alt-Württemberg, is more solidly built.

# HOLSTEIN

German: *Holsteiner*

🔴 1.65 m–1.75 m.

🟢 Mainly bay, sometimes black, liver chestnut or gray; almost no white markings.

**Description**: This is a beautiful, well-built, and powerful horse. It has a long head with a straight profile; rather long ears; large eyes; a muscular neck; prominent withers; a deep chest; long, sloping shoulders; a powerful, straight, long back; powerful, slightly sloping croup; solid, muscular legs with powerful hocks and forelegs rather spread apart; and big hooves.

**Distribution**: Germany, United States, Denmark, and scattered throughout the rest of the world.

**Origins and history**: The Holstein has been bred since the thirteenth century, producing powerful horses issued from crossings of rustic local horses living in the marshes with Arabian and Andalusian, then later with Neapolitan and Yorkshire Carriage (two breeds that are now extinct). They were exported to England and France in great numbers. It was at that time a war and farm horse. In the twentieth century it was refined with Trakehner, Thoroughbred, and Selle Français blood.

**Character and attributes**: The Holstein is a versatile horse that has numerous assets: intelligent, docile, and cooperative, it adapts easily to many situations. It is fast and energetic, has endurance, is very athletic, and is a great jumper. It is also overall more rustic than other sport breeds, even if it needs to be sheltered during bad weather.

**Uses**: This competition horse excels in harness racing, show jumping, and dressage. Versatile, it is very good at eventing.

**Current status**: The breed, a popular sport horse, is doing very well.

Long, straight back

Large eyes

Prominent
withers

Elongated head with
rather large ears

Forelegs spaced
rather far apart

Large hooves

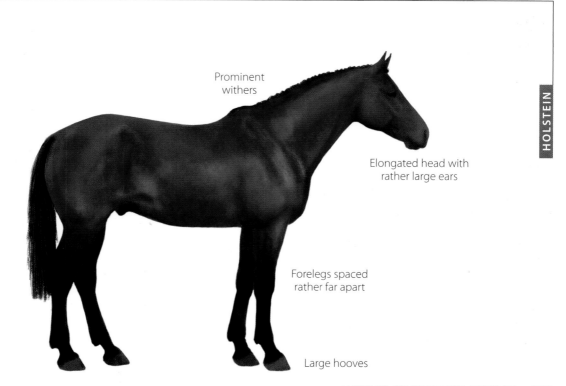

# WESTPHALIAN

Also called: Westphalian Warmblood

German: *Westfalen*

🄷 1.65 m–1.72 m.

🄲 Usually chestnut, bay, gray, black, with white markings on the legs and head.

**Description**: This large, athletic horse greatly resembles the Hanoverian, with which it has been crossed a great deal. The type still remains rather variable. It generally has a head with a straight profile; a long, muscular neck; prominent withers; a broad chest; short back; muscular, sloping croup; long, solid legs; and large hooves. It is sometimes branded with a W.

**Distribution**: Germany, Europe, United States.

**Origins and history**: The Westphalian is the result of crossings between local mares and Oldenburg, Anglo-Norman, Hanoverian, then Thoroughbred and Trakehner horses. It was once a military horse, before being bred to compete at the highest levels in Olympic disciplines. The breed can still receive contributions of outside blood.

**Character and attributes**: This calm, good-natured horse is confident and versatile. It is an excellent jumper.

**Uses**: The Westphalian excels in dressage and show jumping, where it is often in the winner's circle. It is also used for light harness racing and eventing.

**Current status**: This horse corresponds perfectly to the demands of current equestrians, and the breed is one of the most popular in Germany, where its breeding is very dynamic. It is known and appreciated throughout the world.

# OLDENBURG

German: *Oldenburger*

🄷 1.65 m–1.79 m.

🄲 Bay, dark bay, black, gray, chestnut.

**Description**: The Oldenburg, a well-built horse, has a head with a straight, rarely convex profile; long ears; long, muscular, high-set neck; broad chest; long, sloping shoulders; straight, strong, rather long back; slightly sloping, powerful croup; high-set tail; and thin but very strong legs. It is branded with an O with a crown on top.

**Distribution**: Germany, and elsewhere throughout the world.

**Origins and history**: The breed originated in the sixteenth century, when horses of the Friesian type were bred in the Oldenburg region in Germany. They then received Andalusian, Eastern, Neapolitan, Barb, Thoroughbred, Cleveland Bay, and Hanoverian blood. The East Friesian corresponds to the old type of the Oldenburg, before it became a sport horse through supplemental contributions of Thoroughbred, Anglo-Arab, Trakehner, and Hanoverian blood.

**Character and attributes**: A gentle, cooperative horse, it is powerful and energetic. It lives a long time.

**Uses**: The Oldenburg is perfectly suited to all sporting disciplines, and notably excels in dressage and show jumping competitions. Due to its origins as a carriage horse, it is also very good in harness.

**Current status**: The Oldenburg is doing very well throughout the world, where it meets with great success, with more than 8,400 broodmares and more than 5,000 foals born each year.

For comparison, the old type, the East Friesian (*p. 182*) is heavier, with a more convex profile.

Broad chest

Long, solid legs

High-set neck

Slightly
sloping croup

Rather long
back

# BLACK FOREST CHESTNUT

German: *schwarzwälder Fuchs, schwarzwälder Kaltblut*

○ 1.48 m–1.56 m for mares; up to 1.60 m for males.

○ Always chestnut (typical when it is very dark, almost black) with very light, cream or almost white, mane and tail.

**Description**: This superb draft horse, which weighs in the 500–600 kg range, is recognizable by the typical color of its coat. It has a small, narrow head with large eyes; small ears; a wide forehead that becomes thinner near the nose; a long, muscular neck; unobtrusive withers; a broad chest; powerful shoulders; a long croup; and small hooves. The mane and tail are abundant, and the forelock long.

**Distribution**: Germany, notably the region of Baden-Württemberg, and Canada.

**Origins and history**: This ancient breed, essentially forged by the environment of the Black Forest, and with the introduction of Noriker and Breton blood, was traditionally used for farm work and hauling.

**Character and attributes**: This is an active and energetic, very gentle draft horse. It is agile, powerful, and sure-footed. It is fertile, has good health and good endurance, and lives a long life.

**Uses**: Its intermediate size makes it suitable for the entire family. It is also harnessed and used for forest work, or in equitherapy, or for horse shows.

**Current status**: The breed, which was on the brink of extinction, is still small in number, with hardly more than a thousand mares and 80 stallions, but the numbers are growing because the Black Forest Chestnut is increasingly popular as a recreational horse, notably due to its good nature and its unique look.

Snow doesn't bother the Black Forest Chestnut, here hitched to a sleigh.

# PFALZ-ARDENNER

German: *Pfalz-Ardenner, Pfalz-Ardenner Kaltblut*

○ 1.52 m–1.62 m.

○ Bay, chestnut, black, light gray, roan.

**Description**: It resembles the Ardennais, but is lighter. It has a rather small head with a wide forehead; small ears; broad chest; and a long, muscular croup.

**Distribution**: Rhineland-Palatinate, Germany.

**Origins and history**: The breeding of the Pfalz-Ardenner began in 1900 with the crossbreeding of Ardennais, Comtois, and Belgian horses with local mares. Like all draft breeds it suffered from mechanization. The breed has such small numbers that, to save it, crossings are currently still authorized among horses issued from certain breeds (Ardennais, Breton, Comtois, Swedish Ardennais) if they correspond perfectly to selection criteria.

**Character and attributes**: The Pfalz-Ardenner is gentle, calm, energetic, and confident.

**Uses**: It is a good carriage horse and is also enjoyed for recreational riding.

**Current status**: This native breed is very rare; it was on the brink of extinction in the 1970s. Its numbers are still very small: only some twenty broodmares, and fewer than a dozen stallions. The conservation efforts undertaken to save it should nevertheless enable it to be relaunched in the coming years.

Long forelock

Characteristic very light mane and tail, inherited from the Haflinger influence

Small, slender head

Long, muscular croup

Wide forehead

# SCHLESWIG

German: *Schleswiger*

**H** 1.56 m–1.62 m; on average 1.58 m for males and 1.56 m for mares.

**C** Chestnut or chocolate with light mane and tail, frequent white markings on the head and legs, more rarely bay and gray.

**Description**: The Schleswig weighs in the 700–800 kg range and is less massive than other draft horses. It has a rather short head with a straight profile; a wide forehead; long ears; a short, muscular neck; unobtrusive withers; a muscular, slightly sloping croup; a high-set tail; rather short, muscular legs; and big hooves. It is branded on the right thigh with VSP in an oval.

**Distribution**: Schleswig-Holstein, Germany.

**Origins and history**: It is the result of various crossings (notably Suffolk Punch, and recently Breton and Boulonnais), and among its most important ancestors is the Jutland, which it greatly resembles.

**Character and attributes**: This is a docile, energetic, and rather lively horse. Fairly undemanding, it is easy to keep.

**Uses**: It has lost its vocation as a farm horse, but continues to be used as a carriage horse.

**Current status**: Once widespread, this breed's numbers are now very small, around 210 mares and 30 stallions. It is endangered, although it is protected.

---

# RHINELAND HEAVY DRAFT

Also called: Rhenish German Coldblood

German: *rhenisches Kaltblut, rheinisch-westfälisches Kaltblut*

**H** 1.58 m–1.70 m.

**C** Often roan with black mane and tail and legs, or roan with blond mane and tail, sometimes chestnut with light mane and tail, or bay.

**Description**: It resembles the Belgian. It is a large, massive horse weighing around 750–1,000 kg. It has a large head with a straight profile; a rather short, wide, very muscular neck; very broad chest; short, wide back; wide, muscular, rather sloped croup; round barrel; and wide hooves with feathering. One of the characteristics of the breed is its double mane, which falls on either side of the neck, with a thick forelock.

**Distribution**: Rhineland, Germany.

**Origins and history**: This breed is the result of different crossings in the nineteenth century between Ardennais, Belgian, and Percheron, and, less frequently, with Shire, Suffolk, or Clydesdale. It was a horse for transportation and farm work.

**Character and attributes**: The Rhineland Heavy Draft is very powerful, strong, and resilient. It is a calm and cooperative horse.

**Uses**: Its pulling abilities make it a very good carriage horse.

**Current status**: Once thriving, the breed has become rare, with only slightly more than 1,500 horses (2008: 1,342 mares and 186 stallions).

The type called "Westphalian Draft" is similar to the old Rhineland Heavy Draft.

High-set tail

Slightly convex
profile

Large hooves

The mane is always double

Very broad
chest

Wide hooves

## GERMANY

# LEHMKUHLENER

German: *Lehmkuhlener*

◐ 1.25 m–1.40 m; 1.35 m on average.

◓ Bay, dark bay, black; it often has a dorsal stripe and primitive markings.

**Description**: The Lehmkuhlener is compact; it has a head with a straight profile; a broad chest; and a powerful, sloping croup. Its mane and tail are thick, and particularly long in stallions, as sexual dimorphism is very clear in this breed.

**Distribution**: Mainly in the Schleswig-Holstein region, Germany.

**Origins and history**: It has existed since 1913, and is the result of crossings between native mares, notably Dülmens, and an English stallion, probably a Dartmoor.

**Character and attributes**: Robust and hardy, it lives a long life, has good health, and is fertile. It is a good jumper.

**Uses**: Versatile, the Lehmkuhlener is suited to both saddle and harness.

**Current status**: Its breeding was discontinued in the 1950s. There are only around twenty members of this very rare breed.

## GERMANY

# ARENBERG-NORDKIRCHEN

German: *Arenberg-Nordkirchener*

◐ 1.32 m–1.40 m.

◓ Often bay, dark bay, sometimes chestnut, black/brown dun, sometimes with primitive markings.

**Description**: This small horse has a head with a straight profile, a rather high-set neck, prominent withers, and small hooves.

**Distribution**: Westphalia, Germany.

**Origins and history**: The breed, which dates from the beginning of the twentieth century, is the result of crossings between the Panje (an extinct breed similar to the Konik), Dülmen, and Welsh B.

**Character and attributes**: It is intelligent, lively, energetic, and robust, with good health.

**Uses**: The Arenberg-Nordkirchen is a mount for young riders, notably for show jumping.

**Current status**: Its numbers have always been low, and the breed has suffered from the sale of its primary stud farm. It was already believed to be extinct, but there are still around 20 horses left. It is greatly endangered.

## GERMANY

# SMALL GERMAN RIDING HORSE

German: *kleines deutsches Reitpferd*

◐ 1.49 m–1.58 m.

◓ All colors are possible.

**Description**: It has the classic physique of a saddle horse.

**Distribution**: Germany

**Origins and history**: This very recent breed was created in 1995. It is the issue of many breeds of sport pony as well as Arabian, Anglo-Arab, Thoroughbred, Trakehners, and other horses. The idea is to obtain a small, intermediate saddle horse, between the ponies and the large German sport horses.

**Character and attributes**: It is a peaceful and easygoing horse. It is robust.

**Uses**: It is suitable for recreation and for sport competition for young riders and for those who want a sport horse of average size.

**Current status**: The breed is still rare, but it is still being developed. There are around 200 of these horses.

## SENNE

Also called: Senner Horse

German: *Senner, Senne*

**H** 1.58 m–1.65 m.

**C** Gray, sometimes bay, but all colors are possible.

**Description**: It has a head with a straight or often concave profile, long neck, slightly slanted croup, and slender legs.
**Distribution**: Westphalia, Germany.

**Origins and history**: This ancient German breed was first crossed with Andalusians, a foundation to which were added mixtures of Thoroughbred, Arabian, and Anglo-Arab. The Senne was once a military horse.
**Character and attributes**: It has a good nature and good endurance.
**Uses**: It is a saddle horse suited to various English-style disciplines, notably eventing and show jumping competitions.
**Current status**: Very rare and endangered, the breed almost disappeared during World War II. Around 40 animals still remain, including 5 stallions and some 20 mares.

## BEBERBECK HORSE

GERMANY

German: *Beberbeck*

**H** Over 1.60 m.

**C** Bay, dark bay, or chestnut.

**Description**: It resembles a heavier Thoroughbred.
**Distribution**: Northwestern Germany.
**Origins and history**: Having begun in the 1720s, the Beberbeck Horse is the result of crossings between local mares and Arabian stallions, with a later contribution of Thoroughbred blood. It was a military horse.

**Character and attributes**: The Beberbeck Horse is cooperative, very gentle, patient, and brave. It has good endurance.
**Uses**: It is essentially a sport horse and can also be harnessed.
**Current status**: Its principal stud farm closed in 1929 and the horses were dispersed. The breed is very rare, limited to its original region, and has a tendency to blend into other breeds of German sport horses. It is probably going to become extinct soon.

## SACHSEN-ANHALTINER WARMBLOOD

GERMANY

Also called: Sachsen Warmblood

German: *Sachsen-anhaltiner Warmblut*

**H** 1.57 m–1.70 m.

**C** Mainly chestnut, bay, dark bay, gray, black.

**Description**: It resembles other German saddle horses. It has a head with a straight or slightly concave profile; a slender, muscular neck; and a broad chest. The horses are branded with a crown sitting atop a wheel.

**Distribution**: Saxony-Anhalt, Germany.
**Origins and history**: This saddle horse, which originated in the 1920s, is the result of crossings between local mares and first Thoroughbred, then Hanoverian, Trakehner, and Oldenburg stallions.
**Character and attributes**: It is a balanced and energetic horse.
**Uses**: This saddle horse stands out in dressage and show jumping competitions. It is also suited to eventing and harness competitions.
**Current status**: The population is at around 1,680 horses, but the breed is beginning to be known for its success in sport competitions and is becoming more popular. Its numbers should soon begin to increase.

# HESSEN

German: *Hessen*

ⓗ 1.60 m–1.70 m.

ⓒ Bay, chestnut, black, light gray, pinto.

**Description**: This is a sport horse that resembles the Hanoverian, with which it has blended.
**Distribution**: Holstein, Germany.
**Origins and history**: The breed was combined with the Hanoverian in 2009.
**Character and attributes**: Intelligent and easygoing, very robust, endowed with good health, it is an agile horse with pleasant gaits.

**Uses**: It is a very good show jumping horse and is also used in dressage and eventing.
**Current status**: The lineages are at present found in the Hanoverian.

# GERMAN TROTTER

German: *deutscher Traber*

ⓗ 1.50 m–1.75 m.

ⓒ Often dark bay, black.

**Description**: It greatly resembles the French Trotter. It has prominent withers; a thin, muscular croup; and long, slender, solid legs.
**Distribution**: West Germany.
**Origins and history**: The German Trotter is the result of crossings between the Orlov Trotter, the American Standardbred, and the French Trotter.

**Character and attributes**: It has good endurance and is energetic and endowed with long strides characteristic of trotters.
**Uses**: It is intended for trotting races, which are popular in Germany.
**Current status**: The breed is doing well.

# SAXON-TURINGA COLDBLOOD

German: *sächsisch-thüringischen Kaltblut*

ⓗ 1.58 m–1.65 m; an average of 1.62 m.

ⓒ Black, chestnut, bay, sometimes roan.

**Description**: This massive horse has a head with a straight profile, a strong neck, and a muscular croup. The mane and tail are thick.
**Distribution**: Saxony-Thuringia, Germany.

**Origins and history**: Draft horses have been bred for a long time in this region. This draft horse was originally a work horse on farms and in forests.
**Character and attributes**: The Saxon-Turinga Coldblood is a calm, easy, and cooperative horse. Like all draft horses, it is powerful.
**Uses**: It is above all a pulling horse.
**Current status**: The breed's numbers are very small. It is being watched so that it won't become extinct.

# SOUTH GERMAN COLDBLOOD

German: *süddeutsches Kaltblut*

**H** 1.60 m–1.64 m.

**C** Often chestnut with light mane and tail, bay, dark bay, black, gray.

**Description**: The South German Coldblood remains very similar to the Noriker, though is a bit smaller. It has a large head; strong, short neck; wide back; and powerful croup.

**Distribution**: Bavaria and Baden-Württemberg, Germany, and North America.

**Origins and history**: The breed is the direct issue of lineages of Norikers present in South Germany known as Oberlanders, which were crossed with Holstein, Oldenburg, Clydesdale, Cleveland Bay, and Norman horses. In the past, this draft horse was mainly a farm and military horse.

**Character and attributes**: The South German Coldblood is reliable, calm, very powerful, agile, and resilient. It is faster than a Noriker.

**Uses**: The breed is suited for farm and forest work in harness, and it also makes a good vaulting horse.

**Current status**: This breed's modest population comprises slightly more than 2,300 horses in Germany and around 100 in North America.

# HANOVERIAN COLDBLOOD OF SCHLESWIG ORIGIN

German: *hannoversches Kaltblut schleswiger Ursprungs*

**H** 1.57 m–1.65 m for mares; 1.60 m–1.70 m for males.

**C** Usually chestnut with light mane and tail.

**Description**: It is a big, powerful horse.

**Distribution**: Germany.

**Origins and history**: Using the Schleswig, there is currently an attempt to create a new breed: the Hanoverian Coldblood of Schleswig Origin. This involves crossings among English Thoroughbred mares and Schleswig stallions. The breed can still receive Boulonnais, Breton, Noriker, Suffolk Punch, or French Cob blood.

**Character and attributes**: The Hanoverian Coldblood of Schleswig Origin is calm and cooperative.

**Uses**: It is above all a good carriage horse.

**Current status**: This breed's numbers are small, but we can't call it endangered since it is in the process of being created. There are around 30 of these horses.

# LIEBENTHALER

*For the small herd of Liebenthalers, see Tarpan, p. 26.*

With around 85,000 horses, Switzerland breeds more than thirty imported breeds in its territory to respond to the ever-growing demand for recreational horses. The local horse breeds disappeared from Switzerland

# FREIBERG

Swiss German: *Freiberger*

**(H)** 1.50 m–1.60 m.

**(C)** Most often bay, sometimes chestnut, rarely light gray or black.

**Description**: This light draft horse is compact, with pleasant curves. It has a small head with large eyes; short ears, with sometimes an obvious Arabian influence; a short, strong neck; broad chest; long, sloping shoulders; a short back; rather short, solid legs; and hard hooves.

**Distribution**: Franches-Montagnes and Jura, Switzerland. Italy, France, Germany, Belgium.

**Origins and history**: The Freiberg is the result of crossings, notably between English Thoroughbred, Anglo-Norman, Ardennais, and Arabian stallions with local mares of the Swiss Jura. It was first a farm and military horse, before becoming a popular recreational mount.

**Character and attributes**: This calm horse, known for its good nature, is intelligent, energetic, powerful, agile, and sure-footed. It is rustic, has endurance, and is undemanding and easy to keep.

**Uses**: This former farm horse makes a good saddle horse. It is versatile, suitable for the entire family, and enjoyed for recreational activities. It is also a good carriage horse, including for driving competitions, and with its sure-footedness it is used for trekking in the mountains. And with its very calm temperament, it is also used in equitherapy and for vaulting.

**Current status**: The breed remains very popular and widespread in its country: there are more than 30,000 Freiberg horses in the world, 25,000 of which are in Switzerland.

# SWISS WARMBLOOD AND EINSIEDLER

Swiss German: *schweizer Warmblut, CH-Warmblut*

**(H)** Up to 1.68 m.

**(C)** Predominantly chestnut, often bay, more rarely black, all basic colors, sometimes even roan or palomino.

**Description**: This Swiss halfblood has a head with a straight or convex profile; a muscular neck; prominent withers; a straight, powerful back; long, solid legs; and good hooves.

**Distribution**: Switzerland.

**Origins and history**: The Swiss Warmblood as it is today was developed after World War II. But the indigenous horses from which the breed in part emerged, Einsiedlers, are of very ancient origin for a saddle horse, since they were bred by monks of the Einsiedeln abbey beginning in the tenth century. In addition to the Einsiedeln strain, many other light horses also existed at the end of the nineteenth century in several regions of the country. Later, the breed was crossed notably with the Yorkshire Coach Horse, the Anglo-Norman, and the Holstein. Breeding is very rigorous, with a selection for sport performance. It is a renowned former military horse.

**Character and attributes**: It is an intelligent, calm, and docile horse. It has endurance and is versatile, with robust health. It is a good trotter.

**Uses**: It stands out in show jumping competitions and in dressage. It can also be harnessed.

**Current status**: In 2012 there were 687 Swiss Warmbloods born in Switzerland, a bit fewer than in 2011 (744) and 2010 (788). As for the old strain, the Einsiedler, the breed practically disappeared during the twentieth century, and some think it has disappeared, even though there are small numbers of them and they are being selected. It still needs to be recognized.

### EINSIEDLER

Called *cavalla della Madonna* in Italy, the Einsiedler was the saddle horse bred in the abbey of Einsiedeln, and corresponds to the ancient lineages of Swiss halfbloods. There hasn't been a studbook for the Einsiedler since 1945. Historically, it should be noted that only horses born at the Einsiedeln abbey (fewer than a dozen per year) were considered to be Einsiedlers. Today, a foundation is seeking to preserve the traces of this horse by recording all horses that have an original maternal affiliation with the abbey. Currently, only a half-dozen foals are born each year from such mares. The Einsiedler stock counts one hundred or so horses, with a few animals in France and Canada.

during the twentieth century, with the exception of the Freiberg, which is still doing well and remains the best-represented horse in Switzerland, and the Swiss Warmblood, whose numbers are small.

Short back

Small head with large eyes

The Freiberg excels in harness races.

Prominent withers

Muscular neck

Long, solid legs

With a dynamic equestrian culture, the number of horses in Austria is increasing, with more than 80,000 horses spread over the entire country. They are essentially used for recreation, as Austrians eat very little horse meat. Austria is known especially for

---

### AUSTRIA

# HAFLINGER

German: *Haflinger*

**H** 1.35 m–1.55 m.

**C** Always chestnut with light mane and tail, in all possible hues, often mealy (nose, stomach, inner legs lighter); white markings on the head are common, but rare on the legs.

**Description**: The breed is easily recognizable, with its average height, its well-proportioned and athletic physique, and its characteristic coat. The Haflinger has a small, refined head, with an often slightly concave profile, in which Arabian influence is seen; large eyes; small ears; wide forehead; broad chest; prominent withers; sloping shoulders; and a short, muscular croup. The mane and tail are supple, thick and long, sometimes slightly wavy, and it has an abundant forelock.

**Distribution**: Austria and Italy, Germany, Switzerland, United Kingdom, United States, and elsewhere throughout the world.

**Origins and history**: All Haflingers descend from the

same stallion, Folie, born in 1874, the fruit of a cross between a local mare and an Arabian halfblood. The breed has been refined to correspond to a model better adapted to recreation and to the saddle. A crossing that occurred with the Arabian, called Haflo-Arab or Arabo-Haflinger, results in a more athletic, but also livelier horse.

**Character and attributes**: It is intelligent, calm, gentle, friendly, and easy to work with. Solid, with endurance, and rustic, it has supple gaits and lives a long time. Originally a mountain horse, the breed remains very sure-footed.

**Uses**: It is a breed for the whole family, and perfect for recreation. Versatile, it can be used for a variety of disciplines, from dressage to trekking, from show jumping to Western riding. Its pulling ability makes it a good carriage horse. Its gentleness makes it a good mount for children, but since it is strong, it can also be ridden by adults.

**Current status**: The breed, as lovely as it is gentle, is extremely popular in Europe and throughout the world, with a population estimated at more than 250,000 horses.

---

### AUSTRIA

# LIPIZZAN

German: *Lipizzaner*

**H** 1.48 m–1.65 m.

**C** Usually very light gray after the age of six, foals are born dark and lighten very gradually for several years.

**Description**: This baroque horse resembles the Andalusian. Its head is long, with an often convex profile. It has large eyes; small ears; a powerful, high-set neck; unobtrusive withers; muscular, sloping shoulders; a long back; short, straight croup; and muscular legs. The hair of the mane and tail is thick, long, and silky.

**Distribution**: Austria, Slovenia, Hungary, Romania, Croatia, Serbia, Czech Republic, Slovakia, Italy, France, United States, and elsewhere.

**Origins and history**: These are the famous white horses of the renowned Spanish Riding School of Vienna. This breed goes back to the sixteenth century. It originated in Slovenia and Austria (the Lipizza stud farm, today in Slovenia, at the time belonged to Austria). Andalusian horses were crossed with horses that were the result of crossings between Kladruby, Neapolitan, Frederiksburg, and Arabian horses.

**Character and attributes**: The Lipizzan has a very good nature; is intelligent, docile, and gentle but at the same time energetic and agile; and has lovely gaits. It has great longevity. Maturing late, it can work to an advanced age if it is well cared for in its youth.

**Uses**: It excels in all disciplines of dressage—haute école, circus, exhibition—and also makes a good carriage horse.

**Current status**: Although found in many countries throughout the world, this superb breed remains surprisingly rare, with only around 3,500 horses.

its Lipizzans and the famous Spanish Riding School of Vienna, one of the temples of the haute école, where these magnificent light gray horses elegantly display their talents and those of their trainers.

The Italian Avelignese is slightly heavier.

Supple, silky mane and tail

Short, muscular croup

Nice, small head

The Haflinger is popular for skijoring.

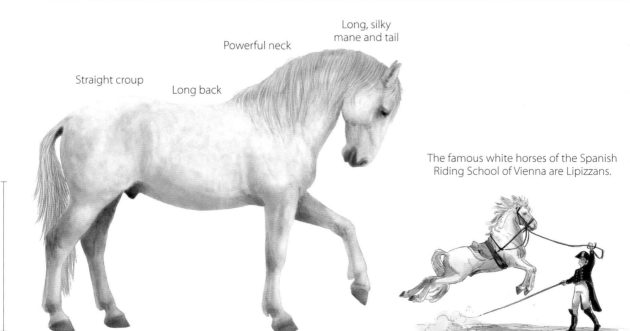

Long, silky mane and tail

Powerful neck

Straight croup

Long back

The famous white horses of the Spanish Riding School of Vienna are Lipizzans.

# AUSTRIAN WARMBLOOD

German: *österreichisches Warmblut*

🐴 1.64 m–1.68 m on average, a minimum of 1.58 m.

🎨 Most often bay, dark bay, chestnut, black, gray.

**Description**: The type remains quite variable, while being faithful to the classic morphology of sport horses: that is, it has an athletic body, a long neck, and long legs. It is branded with an A on the left thigh.

**Distribution**: Austria.

**Origins and history**: In the 1960s crossings of Austrian halfbloods, the issue of local mares and Nonius, Shagya Arabian, Gidran, and Furioso stallions, with German horses (Hanoverian, Oldenburg, Holstein) made possible the creation of a show jumping and dressage horse.

**Character and attributes**: Breeders select horses for their good character and their easy handling. This breed is also robust.

**Uses**: Though it distinguishes itself in dressage or show jumping, it is also bred for recreational riding.

**Current status**: With around 2,500 mares and 80 stallions, the breed is doing rather well in its country, where its breeding is robust. It is, however, not very widespread outside Austria, despite its remarkable sport results.

# NORIKER

German: *Noriker*

🐴 1. 58 m–1.73 m.

🎨 This is the only draft horse to have spectacular spotted coats. It is often also liver chestnut with light mane and tail, but can also be black, bay, or roan, with original variations. A few rare horses have an astonishing brindled coat.

**Description**: This is a draft horse with rounded curves and a purebred look. It weighs in the 600–800 kg range. Its head is big, with a straight or convex profile. It has a short, arched neck; broad chest; long back; round, muscular croup; short, strong legs; and a low-set tail. The hair of the mane and tail is thick and often wavy.

**Distribution**: Austria, southern Germany, Italy, United States.

**Origins and history**: This ancient breed of Austrian draft horse is one of the oldest in Europe, with origins that go back to the eighth century. It has had an influence on many other breeds. The Noriker has itself received Neapolitan and Andalusian blood. The breed was traditionally divided into five lineages: Pinzgauer-Noriker (often with a spotted coat), Carinthian, Steier, Tyrol, and Bavarian Oberlander (lighter; see South German Coldblood, *p. 201*). It was used a lot in farm work. The Abtenauer, once a breed but which has since been absorbed into the Noriker, is a small Noriker whose foals have the unique characteristic of being born with slightly curly hair.

**Character and attributes**: This is an agile and fast draft horse. It is also docile and calm. This rustic and powerful mountain draft horse is also sure-footed.

**Uses**: It makes a good draft horse for logging, but it is also enjoyed as a family horse.

**Current status**: The breed remains popular locally, and it is one of the European draft horses that is doing best, even though its numbers fell dramatically in the 1970s. Today there are more than 10,000 horses. In addition to its other assets, its unique coat assures it a promising future.

Long neck

Long legs

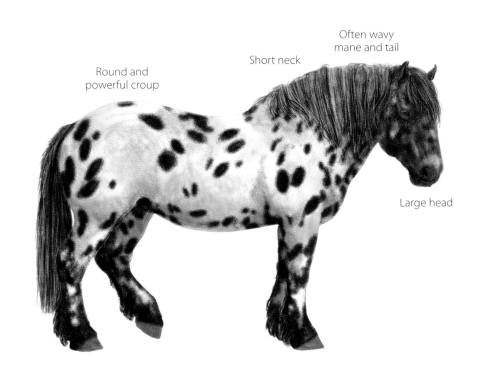

Often wavy
mane and tail

Short neck

Round and
powerful croup

Large head

# Horses of Eastern Europe and Russia

The following breeds span a large territory, starting in Eastern Europe and ending at the edges of Siberia. This includes the former USSR, which is important due to the exchanges that took place for decades among these various countries. These regions of the world, like Southern Europe, have an extraordinary diversity of horse breeds, which are still little known outside their borders. Russia, in particular, is a rich equestrian land, and although more curious riders may have heard of the best-known breeds (like the Orlov and the Don), these horses are still not bred elsewhere in the world. These breeds do, however, have quite interesting specific characteristics, notably their ability to endure very cold temperatures.

## Estonia
Estonian Native (also Estonian Native Horse, Klepper Native)
Toric (also Tori)
Estonian Heavy Draught (also Estonian Draft, Esto-Arden)

## Latvia
Latvian

## Lithuania
Žemaitukas (also Zhemaichu, Little Samogitian)
Large Žemaitukai (also Žemaitukai [Modern Type], Large-Type Žemaitukai)
Lithuanian Heavy Draft

## Poland
Konik (also Polish Konik)
Hucul (also Carpathian Pony)
Malopolski
Silesian
Wielkopolski
Polish Draft
Panje
Polish Coldblood

## Belarus
Polesian Horse (also Polesskaya Local Horse)
Byelorussian Harness Horse (also White Russian Carriage Horse)

## Czech Republic
Kinsky Horse
Kladruby (also Old Kladruby Horse)
Czech Warmblood
Bohemian-Moravian Belgian Horse (also Bohemian-Moravian Belgik, Czech-Moravian Belgik, Czech Coldblood)
Czechoslovakian Small Riding Pony (also Czech Riding Pony)
Silesian Noriker

## Slovakia
Slovak Sport Pony
Slovak Warmblood

## Hungary
Nonius
Shagya Arabian
Gidran
Kisber Felver (also Kisber Halfbred)
Leutstettener
Furioso
Hungarian Sport Horse (also Hungarian Warmblood, Mezőhegyes Sport Horse, Halfbred of Mezőhegyes)
Hungarian Coldblood (also Hungarian Draft Horse)
Murakoz (also Mura Horse)

## Romania
Danube Delta Horse (also Letea Forest Horse)
Romanian Pony
Romanian Trotter
Romanian Saddle Horse (also Romanian Sport Horse, Romanian Warmblood)
Bucovina Horse
Romanian Draft Horse (also Romanian Traction Horse)

## Bulgaria
Danubian
East Bulgarian (also Bulgarian Sport Horse)
Pleven

## Moldova
Local Moldovan

## Ukraine
Ukrainian Riding Horse (also Ukrainian Saddle Horse)
Novoalexandrovsk Cart Horse

## Georgia
Megruli Horse (also Megrel, Mingrelian)
Tushin (also Tushuri Horse, Tusheti Horse, Tushetian)
Javakheti Harness Horse

## Russia
Altai
Transbaikal
Yakutian
Bashkir
Tersk
Vyatka
Kabarda
Anglo-Kabarda
Don (also Russian Don)
Russian Trotter
Orlov Trotter
Budyonny
Orlov-Rostopchin (also Russian Saddle Horse, Russian Riding Horse)
Russian Heavy Draft (also Russian Draft)
Vladimir
Soviet Heavy Draft
Tuva
Dagestan Pony
Priob
Buryat
Pechora
Narym
Minusin
Kalmyk
Chernomor (also Black Sea Horse)
Chumysh Horse
Tavda
Megezh
Upper Yenisei Horse
Mezen
New Altai
Kuznetsk
Voronezh Coach Horse (also Voronezh Draft)

Opposite: Csikós rider in traditional costume and a Nonius horse, Hungary.

The number of horses in Estonia fell dramatically during the twentieth century, going from more than 229,000 in 1927 to fewer than 5,500 today. As elsewhere in the world, mechanization has played a role in this drop, but it isn't due to that alone. Estonia has, in fact, undergone a true agricultural crisis, as the forest expanded throughout the entire Soviet era,

---

ESTONIA

# ESTONIAN NATIVE

Also called: Estonian Native Horse, Klepper Native

Estonian: *eesti hobune*

🐴 1.35 m–1.55 m; on average, 1.44 m–1.45 m for males, 1.42 m–1.45 m for mares.

🎨 Mainly bay, black, chestnut, gray, but also black/brown grayish dun, bay dun, buckskin. They often have a dorsal stripe.

Young Estonian Native horse at work.

**Description**: The Estonian Native has a rather small head with a wide forehead and a generally straight profile; short, muscular, thick neck; broad chest; unobtrusive withers; short, wide back; very round croup; short legs; and hard hooves. The hair of the mane and tail is thick and abundant.

**Distribution**: Estonia, notably on the islands (Saaremaa) and the west coast; a few in Sweden.

**Origins and history**: This ancient breed, the issue of local horses, has escaped much crossing, although it perhaps received some Arabian blood in the past, but in an insignificant quantity. The studbook has existed since 1921. The breed has itself influenced other breeds in this region, notably the Toric.

**Character and attributes**: The Estonian Native has a pleasant temperament and is lively and energetic, while remaining calm and focused. It is a robust horse with good endurance, endowed with good health and long life. It is easygoing, well adapted to the Estonian climate, and easy to keep.

**Uses**: It is suitable for riding, notably for equestrian tourism, for draft work, and in harness. This horse is good for both young and adult riders.

**Current status**: The breed is considered endangered, with currently approximately 390 broodmares and 1,000 males.

---

ESTONIA

# TORIC

Also called: Tori

Estonian: *tori hobune*

🐴 1.58 m–1.66 m; 1.62 m for males, 1.59 m for mares.

🎨 Often chestnut, dark chestnut, sometimes bay, dark bay, black, rarely palomino.

**Description**: This horse, of light draft type and with a vigorous constitution, has a head with a wide forehead; strong neck of average length; broad chest; long, wide back; muscular croup; well developed, sloping, short legs; and wide hooves. The hair of the mane and tail is thick.

**Distribution**: Estonia, Ukraine.

**Origins and history**: The breed has been bred since 1862. It is the result of crossings among Estonian Natives and Hackneys, to which were added some Breton Draft, which made the breed more compact, and then more recently some Hanoverian to increase its speed even more. The goal is to have a good horse for transportation and farm work.

**Character and attributes**: The Toric is a docile, yet lively and powerful horse with dynamic gaits. It is reputed to learn easily and to be easy to break. It has endurance and is well adapted to the local climate; it is fertile, with rather good health and longevity.

**Uses**: This horse, first intended for use in harness, can also be used for riding, notably for recreation and equestrian tourism.

**Current status**: This native breed is very rare and endangered, with only around 200 purebred horses remaining.

and it is now one of the European countries with the fewest horses per inhabitant. Nevertheless, although small, the horse population in Estonia is growing, due to an increase in recreational riding. The three native horse breeds are, however, endangered, even though they are being actively preserved. Estonia also has a population of trotters. Given the global development of equestrian sports, the situation in Estonia should certainly improve in the years to come.

Short, muscular, wide neck

Round, muscular croup

Wide forehead

Short, solid legs

**ESTONIAN NATIVE**

Strong neck

Short legs

**TORIC**

## ESTONIA

# ESTONIAN HEAVY DRAUGHT

Also called: Estonian Draft, Esto-Arden

Estonian: *eesti raskeveohobune*

**H** 1.48 m–1.64 m for males, 1.66 m–1.60 m for mares.

**C** Bay, chestnut, black.

**Description**: The Estonian Heavy Draught weighs in the 650–700 kg range. It has a long head with a wide forehead; a short, muscular neck; a short, wide back; and hooves with sometimes slightly crumbly horn.

**Distribution**: Mainly in Ida-Viru and Lääne-Viru counties in Estonia.

**Origins and history**: The breed was developed from Estonian Natives crossed with the Swedish Ardennais, with the goal of producing a good farm and silviculture horse. It was recognized in 1953.

**Character and attributes**: The Estonian Heavy Draught is calm, endowed with good health, and well adapted to the northern climate of Estonia.

**Uses**: This farm and forest work horse is also suited to recreational use, notably in equestrian tourism or, due to its calm nature, to reassure beginning riders.

**Current status**: The breed is endangered, on the brink of extinction, with fewer than a hundred broodmares and around 200 males, although it is growing slightly. There are about 20 births per year.

# Latvia

In Latvia, horses have a particular place in folklore and popular songs. They are used today in several ways: still for draft work, but above all, and

## LATVIA

# LATVIAN

Latvian: *latvijas zirgs*

**H** 1.62 m on average for stallions; 1.58 m for mares, but males can often exceed 1.70 m and mares 1.60 m.

**C** Bay, dark bay, sometimes chestnut, more rarely gray.

**Description**: This large, well-built, muscular horse has a rather massive head with a straight profile; large eyes and small ears; a long, powerful neck; broad chest; straight back; long, slightly sloping croup; and rather short legs. The hair is very thick, notably in the forelock. There are three types: a saddle type, the most widespread; a harness type; and a heavy type, which is becoming rare.

**Distribution**: Latvia, Ukraine.

**Origins and history**: It was originally a draft horse. Its ancestors were primitive native horses, and it is probably related to the North Swedish and the Gudbrandsdalen Døle. The breed was refined through crossings with German horses (Oldenburg, Hanoverian, Holstein), Arabians, and Thoroughbreds.

**Character and attributes**: This is a docile, very calm, and powerful horse. It is very fertile and lives a long time.

**Uses**: Versatile, it can be ridden and harnessed, and can be used for recreation in general. The saddle type does well in dressage, show jumping, and eventing.

**Current status**: The breed is popular in Latvia, with 4,924 horses recorded in 2005, including 1,570 mares and 109 stallions, but it remains local and unknown abroad. It is suffering from competition with an increasing demand for horses of foreign breeds.

Draft-type Latvian.

# ESTONIAN SPORT HORSE

Estonian: *eesti sporthobuse*

Acronym: ESH

Of note in Estonia is a very recent attempt to create a new breed of sport horse from European saddle breeds. On April 26, 2000, a society was created, promoted by the minister of agriculture, to undertake the breeding of distinctly Estonian sport horses. It was to make up for the lack of a sport breed in the country.

increasingly, for recreation and sport. The most widespread breed is still the Latvian, a native breed, but demand for even more athletic horses, like the Holstein and the Hanoverian, continues to grow. This Baltic country has around 30,000 horses.

Long, powerful neck

Thick forelock

Rather large head

LATVIAN

# Lithuania

The three native Lithuanian breeds, the Žemaitukas, the Large Žemaitukai, and the Lithuanian, are all in danger of extinction because of their low numbers, but Lithuania is aware of the importance of

# ŽEMAITUKAS

Also called: Zhemaichu, Little Samogitian

Lithuanian: *žemaitukas* (plural *žemaitukai*)

**H** 1.28 m–1.42 m.

**C** Most often bay, from light bay to dark bay, black, buckskin, black/brown dun. It often has a dorsal stripe.

**Description**: This small, ancient-type horse has a rather compact body. It has a head with a straight profile; wide forehead; large eyes; small ears; a rather short, muscular neck; short, straight back; very sloping croup; low-set tail; short, thin, but solid legs; and hard hooves.

**Distribution**: Lithuania.

**Origins and history**: The Žemaitukas is the most ancient of all Lithuanian breeds, and one of the most ancient in Europe—it was already known in the sixth and seventh centuries, and in the thirteenth and fourteenth centuries it was reputed to be excellent in combat. It probably descends from primitive Eastern horses of Mongolian type, and probably has received Arabian blood.

**Character and attributes**: This is an intelligent, agile, vigorous, energetic, sometimes lively horse, and a very cooperative one. It has endurance and is extremely resilient in difficult climate conditions. Its hardiness enables it to find nutrition in plants that other horses won't eat. It is easy to keep.

**Uses**: Versatile, it is a saddle (notably show jumping) as well as a harness horse, traditionally used for farming and transport. Capable of covering long distances in a day, it is well suited for trekking.

**Current status**: Although its bloodline deserves to be protected on an international scale, the Žemaitukas has been rapidly declining since the 1990s. The lowest point was reached in 1994 when there were only 30 horses left. The efforts made to preserve the breed brought the numbers up to over 100 horses in 2003, but the breed remains endangered, with fewer than 400 horses in 2011, and fewer than forty births per year. Lithuanian breeders count on its versatility to help develop the breed.

# LARGE ŽEMAITUKAI

Also called: Žemaitukai (Modern Type), Large-Type Žemaitukai

Lithuanian: *stambieji žemaitukas*

Once called Eastern Lithuanian Driving Horse

**H** 1.52 m on average for males; 1.49 m for mares.

**C** Bay, dark bay, black, bay dun, black/brown dun, often with a dorsal stripe.

**Description**: It is more powerful and larger than the Žemaitukas.

**Distribution**: Lithuania.

**Origins and history**: The breed's numbers increased at the end of the nineteenth century because the traditional Žemaitukas was no longer powerful enough for farm work. The breed was then crossed with trotters such as the Orlov in northeastern Lithuania, while in the southeast they were crossed with the North Swedish. Then the animals were crossed among themselves, and a stronger, more imposing horse than the Žemaitukas emerged. The two breeds were officially differentiated in 1946, and in 1985 the new breed took the name of Large Žemaitukai.

**Character and attributes**: This horse has a good temperament, is cooperative and resilient, has endurance, and is uncomplicated, well adapted to harsh climates, and easy to keep.

**Uses**: It is used as a saddle horse, for equestrian tourism, in harness, and for farm work.

**Current status**: This breed, whose numbers have continued to decrease since the 1990s, is nearing extinction, with only 150 horses and fewer than forty births per year.

preserving this genetic legacy. German (Trakehner) and Russian breeds are also bred in Lithuania. Only 10 percent of the horse population are saddle horses intended for sport or tourism; the rest are work horses or horses raised for their meat, but things are evolving more toward recreational horses. Lithuania had around 65,000 horses in 2013.

Low-set tail

Often a dorsal stripe

Thinnish but solid legs

Muscular neck

Large eyes

Straight profile

More massive than the Žemaitukas.

# LITHUANIAN HEAVY DRAFT

Lithuanian: *lietuvos sunkieji arkliai*

**H** 1.55 m–1.66 m; on average 1.60 m for males, 1.57 m for mares.

**C** Mainly chestnut and bay, sometimes black, gray, roan.

**Description**: The Lithuanian Heavy Draft is very similar to the draft-type Latvian. This massive horse, which weighs in the 645–700 kg range, has a wide head with a straight profile; long ears; a short, powerful neck; broad chest; straight back; round croup; short, strong legs; and wide hooves. The hair of the mane and tail is abundant.

**Distribution**: Lithuania.

**Origins and history**: The breed was developed at the end of the nineteenth century and was recognized in 1963. Local mares of Žemaitukas type were crossed with Belgian, Percheron, and Ardennais stallions, then, after the war, with draft horses from the Netherlands and Swedish Ardennais. These crossed horses were better adapted to the local climate than imported horses.

**Character and attributes**: It is a calm and powerful horse, resilient in a sometimes harsh climate, with a long life and good fertility.

**Uses**: Once used for its strength as a work horse, it is now increasingly exported abroad for its meat. Mares produce a lot of milk.

**Current status**: The breed was once popular, but its numbers continue to decline rapidly, with a dramatic disappearance of certain lineages. It is close to extinction, with only a few hundred horses left (probably fewer than 700).

# Poland

In 2000 there were 549,700 horses in Poland, with 98 percent belonging to individuals. But those numbers have fallen in the past ten years, dropping to 264,000 horses in 2010. The number of horses

# KONIK

Also called: Polish Konik

Polish: *konik polski*

*Konik polski* means "small Polish horse." Outside of Poland it is sometimes called a "Tarpan," even though the breed is domesticated, whereas the Tarpan is a wild animal.

**H** 1.30 m–1.40 m.

**C** Black/brown dun with a very dark head and a black band around the eyes, ears rimmed with black with sometimes dark bands, a dorsal stripe that sometimes descends into a faint St. Andrew's cross and is sometimes doubled on the shoulders, dark legs with zebra striping, bicolored mane and tail, rarely a little white tuft on the forehead, and rarely other coats. The coat becomes very thick in the winter.

**Description**: This stocky horse resembles the Hucul, but is more massive. It has a large, wide head, with a slightly concave face, and a convex nose in the males, whereas the females more often have a straight profile; small ears; a short, muscular, high-set neck; broad chest; unobtrusive withers; a short, wide back; a powerful, short, sloping croup; rather low-set tail; short, solid legs; and small, hard hooves. The mane and tail are abundant, but rather short and bushy.

**Distribution**: Poland, Netherlands, France, Germany, Baltic countries, United Kingdom (often in natural reserves).

**Origins and history**: Polish Koniks are the direct issue of the Tarpan, whose look and unique coat they have inherited. Along with the Portuguese Sorraia, this horse has remained closest to its wild ancestor. It was perhaps crossed in the past with Arabians. Koniks were once hunted as game. A large number of Koniks are still bred in conditions close to a wild environment.

**Character and attributes**: The Konik is active, very intelligent, gentle and docile, but sometimes independent and assertive. It is very strong for its size, has good endurance, and is very rustic, hardy, resilient, and well adapted to a harsh climate. It is also very fertile and lives a long time. It has firm gaits.

**Uses**: Once used for farm work, it is also suited for riding and driving. It makes a good trekking horse: despite its small size, the breed is very strong and can be ridden by adults as well as children. Its gentleness makes it well suited to equitherapy.

**Current status**: This breed, cherished in its native land, is still small in number. In Poland there are 430 mares and 140 stallions, and around 3,500 Koniks around the world, a large number of which are in the Netherlands (2,000); there are 500 in France. The breed is making progress.

Wide head

Short, powerful legs

in Poland is decreasing. This country raises a lot of horses for meat, notably for Italy. Although equine activities are very popular, the percentage of sport horses remains weak; however, the number of horses used for recreation is clearly on the rise, notably for equestrian tourism. New equestrian disciplines are appearing in Poland, as is equitherapy.

Polish Koniks are enjoyed in natural reserves.

Short and muscular neck

Ears ringed with black

Marking above the eyes

Large head

# HUCUL

Also called: Carpathian Pony

Polish: *hucuł*

**H** 1.32 m–1.45 m.

**C** Often bay dun, buckskin, bay, dark bay, sometimes gray, pinto; often has a dorsal stripe that continues to the shoulders as a St. Andrew's cross; and zebra striping on the legs.

**Description**: The Hucul is similar to the Konik. It has a compact body; slightly convex head; small eyes and ears; a short, muscular neck; straight shoulders; a rather wide back; short, strong legs; a low-set tail; and solid hooves. The hair of the mane and tail is thick.

**Distribution**: Throughout the Carpathian Mountains, Poland, Hungary, Romania, Slovakia, Austria, Czech Republic, Ukraine; a few in Great Britain and France.

**Origins and history**: This is one of the oldest breeds in Poland. Like the Polish Konik, it resembles the Tarpan, but has undergone more crossings. Its ancient origins probably go back to the primitive local horses crossed in the Middle Ages with Mongolian horses, and later with Arabians. It is a relatively pure breed, its mountain life having preserved it from much outcrossing.

**Character and attributes**: The Hucul is known for its very gentle temperament, its great patience, its docility, and its cooperative nature. This intelligent mountain horse is sure-footed and has good endurance. It is rustic, very hardy, and very easy to keep, and it lives a long time.

**Uses**: It is a good pack and harness horse, but can also be ridden, and is good for trekking. It is also used in equitherapy.

**Current status**: This breed, popular in Eastern Europe, is fairly small in number, with only 800 broodmares and more than a thousand horses throughout the world.

# MALOPOLSKI

Polish: *koń małopolski*

**H** 1.50 m–1.65 m. The breed has been tending to grow in the past 20 years, up to 1.76 m.

**C** Mainly chestnut or bay, sometimes gray, black, roan.

**Description**: The Malopolski has the morphology of an Anglo-Arab, with a small head and slightly concave profile; a wide forehead reminiscent of the Arabian; small ears; long neck; prominent withers; a rather broad chest; sloping shoulders; long back; slightly sloping croup; a high-set tail; and long, slender legs. The mane and tail are rather long, soft and silky. There are four types: the Sadecki, the Darbowsko-Tarnowski, the Lubelski, and the Kielecki.

**Distribution**: Poland.

**Origins and history**: This rather recent Anglo-Arab, in addition to Arabian, Thoroughbred and Anglo-Arab blood, has been influenced by Shagya Arabian, Furioso, Gidran, and local mares. The goal was to create a good, light saddle horse with endurance.

**Character and attributes**: This horse is both energetic and lively, poised and cooperative. For a sport horse, it is easy and robust, endowed with good health.

**Uses**: A good jumper, the Malopolski is a popular saddle horse for show jumping or eventing, and it stands out in cross-country. It is suitable for experienced riders, for whom it can be a good recreational horse.

**Current status**: The breed is popular in Poland, but its numbers are decreasing.

The Malopolski is a naturally good jumper, and the breed excels in cross-country races.

Short, strong
neck

Low-set tail

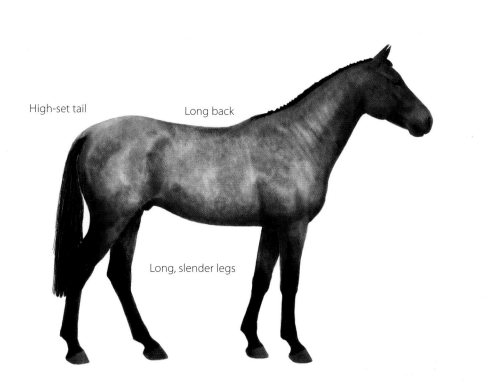

High-set tail

Long back

Long, slender legs

# SILESIAN

Polish: *śląski*

**H** 1.58 m–1.70 m.

**C** Often black, and also bay, dark bay, gray.

**Description**: There is an ancient type of this horse, massive, with a strong head and a slightly sloping or straight croup; and a modern type, lighter, with a more delicate head and a more sloping croup. Both types have a long, muscular neck, a broad chest, and solid legs.

**Distribution**: Silesia, in southwestern Poland.

**Origins and history**: The breed was created at the end of the nineteenth century by crossing halfblood local mares with Oldenburg and East Friesian horses. It was a good carriage horse. After World War II it received Thoroughbred blood. Today, it is sometimes again crossed with Thoroughbreds to obtain good horses for dressage and show jumping.

**Character and attributes**: The Silesian is powerful, gentle, confident, and endowed with lovely gaits. It is resilient and has good health.

**Uses**: It is a good carriage horse, and notably performs well in harness races. It is a pleasant recreational horse that is very well suited to equestrian tourism.

**Current status**: With probably fewer than 3,000 horses, around 1,600 of which were broodmares and 220 stallions in 2011, the breed is popular in Poland, but remains rare and little known elsewhere.

# WIELKOPOLSKI

Polish: *koń wielkopolski*—"big Polish horse"

**H** 1.57 m–1.68 m, but often taller.

**C** Bay, dark bay, black, gray, chestnut, very few markings.

**Description**: This saddle horse has a small head with a straight profile; long neck; prominent withers; broad chest; long shoulders; a straight, rather long back; a slightly sloping, muscular croup; long, muscular legs; and good hooves. The hair of the mane and tail is fine.

**Distribution**: Poland.

**Origins and history**: This recent breed, developed only after World War II, descends from native horses (the ancient Poznan and Mazury breeds), themselves issued in large part from the Trakehner, then crossed with Arabian, Anglo-Arab, and Thoroughbred with the goal of producing a good saddle horse.

**Character and attributes**: This is an intelligent and calm horse, athletic, with lovely gaits. It is a good jumper.

**Uses**: It is suitable for both riding and driving, and excels especially in show jumping. It can also compete in dressage.

**Current status**: Thanks to its results in sport competitions, the breed is popular in Poland and is increasingly sought-after, but it is relatively unknown abroad.

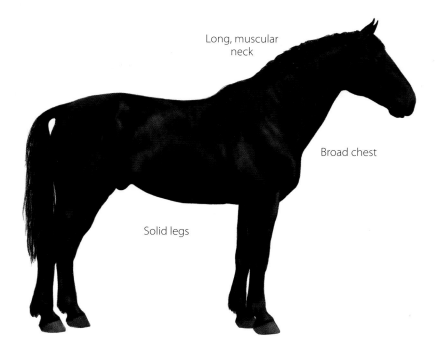

Long, muscular neck

Broad chest

Solid legs

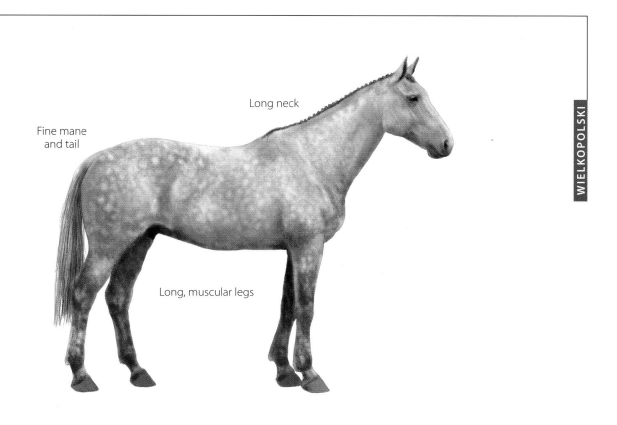

Long neck

Fine mane and tail

Long, muscular legs

# Polish Draft

Polish: *polski koń zimnokrwisty*

**H** 1.45 m–1.58 m.

**C** Chestnut, often with light mane and tail, bay or roan, sometimes black.

**Description**: This heavy, massive draft horse, which weighs in the 500–800 kg range, resembles the Ardennais. It usually has a straight profile; muscular neck; a wide, long back; powerful croup; and small hooves. There are several types of Polish Draft. One of the best known is the Sokolsky, which is found in northeastern Poland, often with a chestnut coat with light mane and tail. There is also the Kopczyk Podlasky (light draft), the Lidzbarsky, the Lowicz, the Sztumski, and the Garwolin.

**Distribution**: Poland.

**Origins and history**: The Polish Draft is the result of many crossings carried out in the nineteenth century between various native draft horses and Muraköz, Ardennais, Breton, Boulonnais, and Belgian horses. The goal was to create a good horse for farm work.

**Character and attributes**: This is a docile horse with endurance and resilience, able to tolerate the harsh climate. It grows quickly.

**Uses**: Once a good farm horse, it is now raised principally for its meat.

**Current status**: After declining in number, the breed seems to have stabilized and remains very common for a draft horse, with active breeding.

# Panje

Polish: *panjeskaya*

**H** 1.32 m–1.48 m.

**C** All common colors, often dark gray, sometimes with primitive markings such as a dorsal stripe and zebra striping on the legs.

**Description**: In part issued from the Konik, the Panje generally has its compact and robust look but is less primitive, and the breed is not homogeneous.

**Distribution**: Poland, Ukraine, Russia.

**Origins and history**: When the Poles decided to save the Polish Konik, the horses that had undergone too much crossing were put aside, and they became the Panje. Thus it is a Konik that received Arabian, Trotter, and Belgian blood. It is more of a type than a breed.

**Character and attributes**: It has kept the hardiness and rusticity of the Konik. It is fertile and very easy to keep.

**Uses**: It is used as a saddle horse, to pull carts, or for any light farm work.

**Current status**: This type of horse is rather common, but demand for it is decreasing.

Powerful croup

Small hooves

POLAND

# POLISH COLDBLOOD

Polish: *polski koń szlachetny półkrwi*

**H** 1.60 m–1.70 m.

**C** All solid coat colors are most common.

**Description**: The morphology of this generally tall, elongated, and muscular horse varies depending upon the crossings that produced the individual. It has a head with a straight profile; solid legs; and a powerful croup. There is a type for show jumping, tall, energetic, and with particularly robust legs; a type for dressage, well balanced and intelligent; and a type for eventing, powerful and with good endurance.

**Distribution**: Poland.

**Origins and history**: This type of horse developed after the war and is becoming a popular breed whose breeding will be increasingly shaped by its good results in competition. This horse is the result of various crossings among Polish breeds such as the Wielkopolski and the Malopolski, and horses of foreign breeds, notably German (Hanoverian, among others), French, and Dutch.

**Character and attributes**: It is calm, confident, and energetic.

**Uses**: This sport horse excels notably in dressage and show jumping. It is also suitable for eventing and harness racing.

**Current status**: The Polish Coldblood is one of the most popular breeds in Poland and is doing fairly well, even if it is unknown in other parts of the world.

The horses of Belarus are essentially Belarusian Drafts (75.3 percent), Russian Drafts (10 percent), and Russian Trotters (4 percent). One also finds Trakehners, Torics, and Latvian and Lithuanian

BELARUS

# POLESIAN HORSE

Also called: Polesskaya Local Horse

Belarusian: *polesskaya* (literally, "horse of the forest")

**H** 1.30 m–1.40 m; on average 1.42 m–1.44 m for males, 1.38 m–1.40 m for mares.

**C** Often bay, chestnut, black, also buckskin, black/brown dun, gray. It frequently has dorsal stripes and zebra striping on the legs.

**Description**: This small, compact horse resembles the Konik. It has a head with a straight profile; a rather broad chest; unobtrusive withers; a long, strong, straight back; strong legs; and hard hooves. There are two types, one heavier than the other.

**Distribution**: Pinsk Marsh, the forest and marshy zone of Polesia near the Pripyat and Horyn rivers, and Pina, in Belarus and Ukraine.

**Origins and history**: This ancient breed, which for a long time remained pure, is certainly very similar to the Tarpan, and was crossed, notably during the Soviet era, with several breeds such as the Arabian, Orlov, Russian and Soviet Draft Horse. But these crossings did not have a strong impact, since the crossed horses, less resilient than the Polesians, did not tolerate the breed's harsh living conditions. Indeed, the Polesian evolved in marshy and forest regions, in very dense, inaccessible forests, with poor vegetation.

**Character and attributes**: It has an excellent nature and lots of endurance. It also has good longevity and fertility. Forged by a challenging environment, the breed is robust and uncomplicated, and needs little maintenance. It is well adapted to humid environments. Mares provide a lot of milk.

**Uses**: It is suitable for young riders, for equestrian tourism, and for light farm work.

**Current status**: The breed almost disappeared during the twentieth century, having suffered greatly from World War II, and it is still endangered. It is often absorbed in the breeding of the Byelorussian Harness Horse. The last numbers recorded were in 1991, with 200 stallions, 600 mares, and around 2,000 horses, but they have declined. In 2010 only 10 stallions and 96 mares of pure type were identified. The breed is little known, including in its own country.

BELARUS

# BYELORUSSIAN HARNESS HORSE

Also called: White Russian Carriage Horse (Belarus is sometimes called White Russia)

Belarusian: *belorusskaya uprazhnaya*

**H** 1.50 m–1.60 m; on average 1.55 m–1.61 m for males, 1.48 m–1.56 m for mares.

**C** Bay, light bay, chestnut, palomino, bay dun, buckskin, roan, pinto, with white markings on the head and legs.

**Description**: This stocky horse, whose size is in between the heavy draft and a light draft, weighs around 500–600 kg. It has a rather small head with a wide forehead and a straight profile; a muscular neck; broad chest; unobtrusive withers; and a short, wide croup. The hair of the mane and tail is very thick, sometimes slightly wavy. There are six lineages, each having its own characteristics, and two basic types, one more massive than the other.

**Distribution**: Belarus, Russia.

**Origins and history**: The breed was formed at the beginning of the mid-twentieth century through crossings among native mares (notably Polesians) and Døle, Belgian, Breton, and Ardennais, as well as Russian draft horse breeds. It was bred in western Belarus, where pastureland is richer. It was officially recognized in 2000.

**Character and attributes**: The Byelorussian Harness Horse is gentle, docile, and energetic, sensitive and very cooperative. A particularly powerful draft horse with good speed, it also has excellent endurance. The Belarusians are proud to say that it has the most pulling strength per body weight of all breeds of draft horses in the world. It lives a long time and is extremely fertile, as mares can give birth at an advanced age. They also give a lot of milk (nine liters of milk per day on average).

**Uses**: This draft horse can be ridden; it can even jump obstacles. It is of course suited for harness, for forest and farm work, and it is well adapted for work in swampy terrain. It is also bred for its meat and for the milk intended for koumiss. It is also a good equitherapy horse.

**Current status**: The lovely colors of this draft horse's coat and its well-proportioned physique may contribute to ensuring it a future in recreational riding. Even though its numbers, once very high, have fallen, the breed remains quite widespread and popular, with more than a thousand broodmares. It is increasingly exported to Russia.

Drafts, as well as other breeds. The Polesian Horse is a rare and little-known breed, often not recorded, even if various enthusiasts have mobilized in Belarus in the past few years to save this little forest horse. In 2003, the country had 200,000 horses. They are raised as draft horses, for riding, but also for milk (to produce koumiss) and meat.

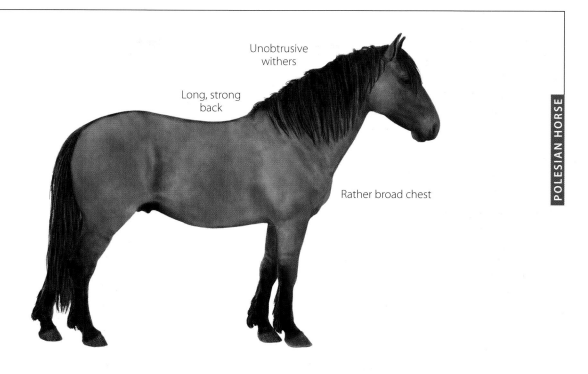

Unobtrusive withers

Long, strong back

Rather broad chest

POLESIAN HORSE

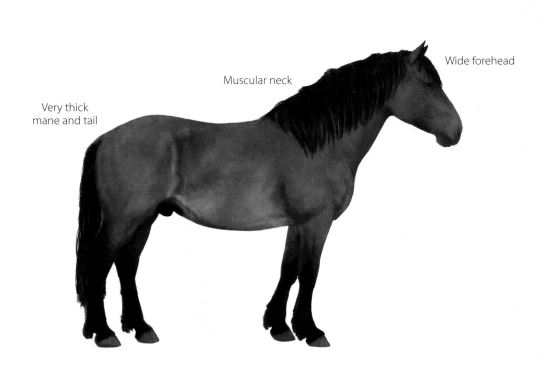

Wide forehead

Muscular neck

Very thick mane and tail

BYELORUSSIAN HARNESS HORSE

Horse breeding is on the rise again in the Czech Republic, under the impetus of societal changes and active breeders. This expansion has caused the number of horses to go from fewer than 30,000 in the 1990s to more than 74,000 in 2010. Many of

# KINSKY HORSE

Also called: Equus Kinsky

Czech: *kůň Kinský*

**H** 1.57 m–1.73 m.

**C** Bay dun, palomino, with strong golden highlights. The light coat is specific to the breed. More rarely bay, chestnut, very rarely black.

**Description**: The Kinsky has the light build of a racehorse. It has a head with a straight profile, a long neck, long legs, and a slightly sloping croup. The hide is silky; the hair of the mane and tail is fine.

**Distribution**: The region of Bohemia, in the Czech Republic; a few in England and the United States.

**Origins and history**: Once quite popular, this now very rare racehorse was created during the nineteenth century by Count Kinsky from light-colored Thoroughbreds and halfbloods.

**Character and attributes**: This is an athletic sport horse known for its good nature. It is an excellent galloper and good jumper, with endurance.

**Uses**: This racehorse (both on the flat and in steeplechases) is also excellent for various Olympic equestrian disciplines. It is also sought-after for fox hunting. Its easy temperament makes this athlete a good lesson horse in riding schools.

**Current status**: Once popular and widespread, the breed has become very rare and almost forgotten. It has now stabilized, with fewer than a thousand horses. The Czech Republic considers it a national treasure. Because of its beautiful coat and its sporting and behavioral qualities, it is reasonable to believe that the breed will recover.

# KLADRUBY

Also called: Old Kladruby Horse

Czech: *Kladrubský kůň, Starokladrubský kůň*

**H** 1.62 m–1.75 m, frequently reaches 1.80 m.

**C** Most often light gray, sometimes black. The light lineage is the most common.

**Description**: In its light form this baroque horse can be confused with the Lipizzan. It is a tall horse that exudes power. Its long head has a convex profile, wide forehead, and large eyes. It has a muscular, arched neck; broad chest; long back; wide, round, and powerful croup; strong legs; and wide hooves. The hair of the tail is abundant.

**Distribution**: Czech Republic, Eastern Europe, a few in the United States.

**Origins and history**: The Kladruby has ancient Spanish and Neapolitan origins, through crossings with local horses. It has been bred for more than 400 years in the Czech Republic, primarily to be used as a carriage horse. It is the oldest Czech breed. It played a role in the creation of the Lipizzan.

Kladruby foals are born dark and become gray as they grow older.

**Character and attributes**: This is a calm, docile, and gentle horse. Solid, it is fertile and lives a long time. It has lovely gaits.

**Uses**: This breed was conceived as a harness horse, but it is also suited for recreational riding, and even for haute école and exhibitions. It is also a good family horse.

**Current status**: The Kladruby was designated a national cultural treasure in 1995, but its numbers are still low, with a bit more than 1,500 horses, including 500 broodmares.

them are Czech Warmbloods, the most widespread breed in the country (28 percent of all horses) or Thoroughbreds. Recreational riding is in full development. Many horses of foreign breeds are also imported. The Czech Republic has succeeded in preserving two breeds of draft horse. The Noriker (see Austria, *p. 206*) is also well represented. In the Czech Republic there are 180 Hucul broodmares and 19 stallions (see Poland, *p. 218*).

KINSKY HORSE

Fine and silky mane and tail

Characteristic metallic highlights

Long legs

KLADRUBY

Muscular, arched neck

Large eyes

Characteristic long, convex head

# CZECH WARMBLOOD

Czech: *Ceský teplokrevník*

🅗 1.65 m–1.75 m.

🅒 Mainly bay, often chestnut, sometimes gray, rarely black, a few bay dun.

**Description**: This tall and solid halfblood is very similar to the Slovak Saddle Horse. It has a powerful and rather long neck; long, sloping shoulders; a wide back and croup; and solid, muscular legs. The hair of the mane and tail is very thick. There can be a very light or a bit heavier type.

**Distribution**: Czech Republic.

**Origins and history**: The Czech Warmblood has actually been bred with care since the 1960s, and is the result of different crossings among local halfbloods and notably Oldenburg, Hanoverian, Furioso, and Thoroughbred horses. It is selected for its sport qualities. The Kinsky Horse, discussed above, is related to the Czech Warmblood, although it represents a racing type with a stronger Thoroughbred influence.

**Character and attributes**: It has a good nature, is a good jumper, and has fluid gaits. It is a robust and powerful horse, with a good life expectancy.

**Uses**: This is a saddle horse particularly well suited for show jumping competitions, but also for dressage and other recreational activities.

**Current status**: This is the most widespread breed in the Czech Republic, with more than 20,000 horses and 1,165 foals born in 2011. It is beginning to be known outside the country.

# BOHEMIAN-MORAVIAN BELGIAN HORSE

Also called: Bohemian-Moravian Belgik, Czech-Moravian Belgik, Czech Coldblood

Czech: *Ceskomoravský belgický kůň, Ceskomoravský belgik*

Acronym: CMB

🅗 1.52 m–1.60 m.

🅒 Most often chestnut and chestnut with light mane and tail, sometimes bay, more rarely roan or black.

**Description**: This muscular and massive horse weighs in the 600–800 kg range. It has a small head with a straight profile; a short, high-set neck; unobtrusive withers; a broad chest; long back; wide, sloping croup; short, muscular legs; and hard hooves. The mane and tail are thick.

**Distribution**: Regions of Bohemia and Moravia, in the Czech Republic.

**Origins and history**: This draft horse was created from imported Belgians in the 1880s–1930s. The importing has stopped since then; from the outset the breed has been bred to produce a powerful draft horse.

**Character and attributes**: This strong horse has a calm and gentle nature.

**Uses**: It is used above all for forest and farm work, but is also bred for its meat. It is popular in equitherapy due to its calm temperament.

**Current status**: This local draft horse, once widespread, has a population of around 1,500 broodmares and 800 stallions.

Thick mane
and tail

Wide back
and croup

Solid legs

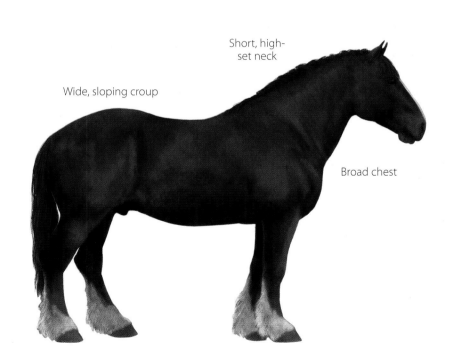

Short, high-
set neck

Wide, sloping croup

Broad chest

# CZECHOSLOVAKIAN SMALL RIDING PONY

Also called: Czech Riding Pony

Czech: *Ceský športovní pony*

**H** 1.11 m–1.48 m.

**C** Often chestnut, bay, black, gray.

**Description**: This is a light sport pony.
**Distribution**: Czech Republic.

**Origins and history**: This pony is a very recent breed, developed only since the 1980s from Arabian, Hanoverian, Slovak, and Hucul mares crossed with Welsh stallions. The goal is to obtain a good small sport mount for children and adolescents.
**Character and attributes**: Lively, but docile and calm, intelligent and confident, it is robust and rather easygoing.
**Uses**: A versatile recreational mount for young riders, it is suited for show jumping competitions.
**Current status**: As this very recent breed is being developed, its numbers are small, but it is gaining ground.

# Slovakia

The number of horses in Slovakia has decreased significantly in the past fifty years, but it has recently started to rise and is developing very quickly due to the great passion in Slovakia for equestrian sports. In 2003 there were only 6,500 horses in the country,

# SLOVAK SPORT PONY

Slovak: *slovenský sportový pony*

**H** 1.40 m–1.48 m; 1.43 m on average.

**C** Gray, bay, black/brown dun.

**Description**: This is a smallish saddle horse. It has a head with a straight or slightly concave profile, small ears, pronounced withers, a slightly sloping croup, slender legs, and small hooves.
**Distribution**: Regions of Banská Bystrica and Nitra, Slovakia.
**Origins and history**: This is a recent breed, which has existed for only around thirty years, conceived for equestrian sports and the recreational activities of young riders from around eight to sixteen years old. The breeding program was started in 1980. The breed is the result of crossings between Slovakian Warmblood, Arabian, Thoroughbred, Welsh Pony, and German Saddle Pony horses.

**Character and attributes**: The Slovak Sport Pony is known to be calm and to have a good nature. It is resilient and has light gaits.
**Uses**: This is a small mount adapted for recreational riding or competition, and is also suitable for driving. It is perfect for teaching young riders, and it is also used in equitherapy due to its gentle nature.
**Current status**: This native breed, which is being developed, is still small in number.

# SILESIAN NORIKER

Czech: *Slezsky norik*

Acronym: SN

**H** 1.65 m on average for mares, 1.66 m for males.

**C** Chestnut, notably with light mane and tail, bay, very rarely black.

**Description**: This is a powerful draft horse, with a wide head, slightly prominent withers, and a powerful croup.

**Distribution**: Czech Republic.

**Origins and history**: As its name indicates, the Silesian Noriker has origins in the Noriker and the Silesian. Norikers were imported from Austria and Bavaria around one hundred years ago, and crossed with mares of Silesian origin.

**Character and attributes**: This is a gentle and energetic horse, powerful and agile. It lives a long time.

**Uses**: It is a draft horse, traditionally used for work in forests and on farms. It is also raised for its meat.

**Current status**: There were only around 250 horses registered in 1991. With around 595 broodmares and 320 stallions in 2009, and a thousand animals, the population is still small in number. It should be watched carefully, and its breeding program already aims to avoid problems of inbreeding.

but in 2011 the equine population had doubled, to more than 14,600 animals. It is a country where the equestrian economic potential is very strong because it is starting from a very low level. Horses are bred most often for sport competition, but there are also many draft horses. The country breeds the Hucul (see Poland, *p. 218*) and the Murakoz draft horse (see Hungary, *p. 240*), as well as other foreign breeds.

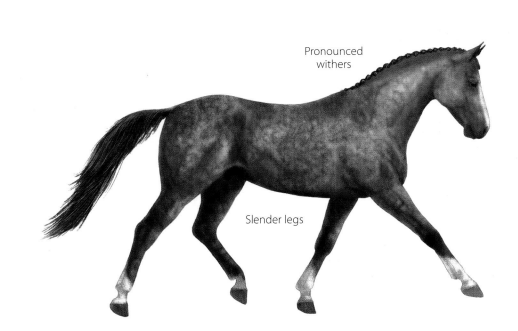

Pronounced withers

Slender legs

SLOVAK SPORT PONY

# SLOVAK WARMBLOOD

Slovakian: *slovenský teplokrvník*

🅗 1.70 m–1.80 m.

🅒 Brownish bay, dappled gray, more rarely chestnut.

**Description**: Very similar to the Czech Warmblood, this tall horse doesn't have a very fixed standard. It has a head with a straight or slightly concave profile; a slender neck; wide, straight back; and muscular legs.

**Distribution**: Czech Republic, Slovakia.

**Origins and history**: This is a breed that is very close historically to the Czech Warmblood, developed from local horses, but which has received more Gidran, Furioso, Nonius, Trakehner, and Hanoverian blood.

The goal of the breeding is to produce good horses for Olympic sports.

**Character and attributes**: The Slovak Warmblood is powerful, athletic, lively, and energetic. It is sometimes stubborn. It has good health.

**Uses**: This is a riding and carriage horse. It is used for instruction in riding schools.

**Current status**: The breed is small in number.

# Hungary

Hungary is traditionally a land of horse breeding thanks to its vast pastureland. The stud farm of Mezőhegyes was one of the largest in the world. The number of horses clearly declined in the twentieth century, going from more than two and a half million to around 80,000, but, strong in its unique saddle

# NONIUS

Hungarian: *nóniusz*

🅗 1.55 m–1.65 m. There are two types, a taller one in Mezőhegyes, and a smaller in Puszta.

🅒 Most often black, mealy black, less often bay, few white markings.

**Description**: The breed is very homogeneous. It is characterized by a long head with an often slightly convex profile; a wide forehead; long ears; a strong, long, high-set neck; long back; short, muscular croup; solid legs; and resilient hooves.

**Distribution**: Hungary, Romania, Czech Republic.

**Origins and history**: The Nonius is the issue of an Anglo-Norman stallion by the name of Nonius Senior, taken from France in 1813 during the Napoleonic Wars, crossed with local mares, Arabian, Andalusian, Lipizzan, and Kladruby, then later with Thoroughbred horses. The Nonius was for a long time a military horse. It is often crossed with Thoroughbreds to produce competitive horses for dressage and show jumping.

**Character and attributes**: The Nonius is very docile, easygoing but also energetic, with lovely gaits. It is very resilient, has endurance, and lives a long time.

**Uses**: In the past it was used for farm work and as a carriage horse; today it is a riding horse and also excels in harness racing. Its easygoing nature makes it a good recreational horse.

**Current status**: The Nonius is a very important breed in Hungary, but it almost disappeared during World War II. It is still not very common and is unknown outside Hungary, with only slightly more than 500 broodmares and 80 stallions in 2013.

A Hungarian csikós rider performing the spectacular Hungarian post with Nonius horses.

Rather slender
neck

Straight profile

Muscular legs

breeds, the country remains competitive. In Hungary, 50,000 horses are used for work or tourism, 20,000 are sport horses, and around 6,000–8,000 are sold for their meat, though the demand is clearly decreasing.

The breeds with small numbers supported by the government are the Gidran, Hucul (see Poland, *p. 218*), Kisber Felver, Lipizzan (see Austria, *p. 204*), Furioso, Nonius, and Shagya Arabian.

Long ears

High-set neck

Convex profile

Long back

Long head

# SHAGYA ARABIAN

Hungarian: *shagya arab*

**H** 1.54 m–1.62 m.

**C** Generally gray, most often satiny gray, sometimes bay, more rarely chestnut or black.

**Description**: It resembles the Arabian of Siglavi type, but this model is better built and taller. It has a head that is very Arabian, slender, with a concave profile; large eyes; small ears; a slender, arched neck; sloping shoulders; long, muscular legs; a high-set tail; and small feet. The mane and tail are straight and silky. It is often branded with a six-pointed sun and a number.

**Distribution**: Hungary, Germany, France, Poland, Austria, Czech Republic, Slovakia, Yugoslavia, Russia, with a few in the United States.

**Origins and history**: The foundation sire of the breed was a tall gray Arabian stallion from Syria by the name of Shagya, who was crossed with local and Eastern mares. The breed received Lipizzan and English Thoroughbred blood. The Shagya Arabian was for a long time a renowned military horse.

**Character and attributes**: This is a gentle, brave, and intelligent horse. It is lively, energetic, fast, and athletic. It has endurance and is resilient.

**Uses**: This saddle horse is one of the best breeds for endurance races. It also competes in eventing and is well suited for driving. It can make a very good trekking horse.

**Current status**: Even though it has become well-known and is enjoyed for its great qualities, and is very beloved in its country, the breed is still rare; there are around 4,000 horses throughout the world.

The Shagya Arabian is one of the best horses for endurance races.

# GIDRAN

Hungarian: *gidrán*

**H** 1.55 m–1.68 m.

**C** Almost always chestnut in Hungary, sometimes bay and light gray in Romania.

**Description**: Physically, this is an Anglo-Arab. It has a small head with a straight profile; large eyes; small ears; wide forehead; long neck; broad chest; prominent withers; a long, straight back; a rather short croup; and a high-set tail.

**Distribution**: Hungary, Poland, Romania, Bulgaria.

**Origins and history**: The breed emerged in the nineteenth century, from a stallion called Gidran II, the issue of an Arabian crossed with an Andalusian mare, and a Thoroughbred. Thus it is a Hungarian variety of the Anglo-Arab. It is considered to be a national treasure in its country.

**Character and attributes**: The Gidran is a bold, lively horse, truly spirited, whose energy is sometimes difficult to channel. It is an athlete that can adapt to harsh climates.

**Uses**: The Gidran is a good horse for show jumping and dressage, not recommended for beginners, but well suited to experienced riders. It is also suitable for harness racing.

**Current status**: The breed is popular in Eastern Europe, but it suffered during the two world wars. The Romanians recovered most of the stock as booty during World War I and today continue to breed these horses, whose breeding stock they send back to Hungary. Its numbers remain very small, with only 102 broodmares in 2009.

Arched neck,
with silky mane

The Arabian tail
is high-set

Long legs

Wide forehead

Large eyes

High-set tail

# KISBER FELVER

Also called: Kisber Halfbred

Hungarian: *kisbéri-félvér*

**H** 1.55 m–1.70 m; 1.63 m on average for males, 1.61 m for mares.

**C** Generally bay, dark bay or chestnut, rarely black or gray.

**Description**: The Kisber Felver, a type of halfblood, is more massive and solid than a Thoroughbred. It has a slender head with a straight profile; large eyes; small ears; a long, curved, rather high-set neck; prominent withers; a wide, very round, muscular croup; and thin legs. The hair of the mane and tail is fine.

**Distribution**: Eastern and western Hungary; also found in the United States.

**Origins and history**: Begun in 1853, the breed is the result of crossings between Thoroughbred stallions and local mares, and, since the 1950s, with the addition of Trakehner and also Furioso, Anglo-Arab, Selle Français, Arabian, and other blood.

**Character and attributes**: Lively, known for its good nature, the Kisber Felver is intelligent and confident, has endurance, and is endowed with lovely gaits. It is a robust, rustic sport horse.

**Uses**: This is a good, very versatile saddle horse, which stands out notably in show jumping and dressage.

**Current status**: This native breed suffered a lot during the two world wars; 150 horses were taken as spoils of war by the Americans during World War II. It is still little known, but is increasing slightly in number, and the situation could improve thanks to its good record in equine sports. There are more than a thousand mares and 124 stallions in Hungary.

# LEUTSTETTENER

Hungarian: *leutstettener*

Former name: Sarvar, Sarvarer

**H** 1.56 m–1.58 m.

**C** Mainly bay, dark bay, sometimes black, rarely with slight white markings on the head and legs.

**Description**: The Leutstettener has a head with a straight profile, long ears, a long neck, prominent withers, and slender legs.

**Distribution**: Hungary; a few in Bavaria, Germany.

**Origins and history**: The Leutstettener is also bred and found in Germany, but it originated in western Hungary. The breed was created at the beginning of the nineteenth century from mares crossed with Nonius and Furioso stallions, and later with English Thoroughbreds to obtain a good cavalry horse. It was bred at the stud farm of Sárvár. In 1945 the arrival of the Russians threatened the breed, and some horses were secretly transferred to Leutstetten, Germany, and it was then that its name was changed. Horses were finally able to return to Hungary in 1980.

**Character and attributes**: This is a sensitive horse with a good nature. It has good endurance.

**Uses**: This saddle horse is suited for various disciplines; it is particularly good in cross-country and harness racing.

**Current status**: The breed is extremely rare, since only around fifty horses survive. It is urgent that those horses be consolidated to save the breed.

Fine mane
and tail

Wide, round croup

Slender, lean head

Long ears

Straight profile

Slender legs

# FURIOSO

Hungarian: *furioso*, sometimes *mezőhegysi félvér*

Former name: Furioso North Star

**H** 1.60 m–1.65 m, easily as tall as 1.70 m.

**C** Mainly bay, dark bay, sometimes black, sometimes with light and limited white markings.

**Description**: It resembles a Thoroughbred, but is better built. It has a head with a straight profile; a rather long, muscular neck; broad chest; prominent withers; sloping shoulders; straight back; long legs; and a high-set tail.

**Distribution**: Hungary, Poland, Austria, Romania, Czech Republic.

**Origins and history**: Originally, the Furioso and the North Star were two separate lineages named after their Thoroughbred foundation sires. They were crossed with mares of different origins, some of them Nonius or Arabian. In 1885 the two lineages were united. The Hungarians declared the Furioso a national treasure in 2004 and are working actively to preserve this rare breed.

**Character and attributes**: The Furioso is active, docile, intelligent, and sensitive. It is also resilient.

**Uses**: This saddle horse is often used in dressage, show jumping competitions, and eventing. It sometimes competes in steeplechases. It is also suitable for harness racing.

**Current status**: The breed is rather popular in Eastern Europe and is gaining popularity in the West, although the numbers are still low, with only around 500 broodmares and 80 stallions.

The Furioso makes a good show jumper.

# HUNGARIAN SPORT HORSE

Also called: Hungarian Warmblood, Mezőhegyes Sport Horse, Halfbred of Mezőhegyes

Hungarian: *Magyar sportló, mezőhegyesi sportló*

**H** 1.65 m–1.70 m.

**C** Most often bay, but all colors are possible.

**Description**: This recent breed is still rather variable, but overall it is homogeneous. It is a light horse, with a refined head; straight profile; wide forehead; a long, curved neck; prominent withers; and a round, muscular croup.

**Distribution**: Hungary.

**Origins and history**: This breed, Hungary's newest, was created in the 1960s with the goal of producing a good show jumping and dressage horse. It became official in 1990. It is the issue of local Nonius, Furioso, Kisber, and Gidran mares, crossed with Thoroughbred, Holstein, Hanoverian, and Selle Français stallions. The selection is made on rigorous sport criteria.

**Character and attributes**: Intelligent, lively, active, docile, the Hungarian Sport Horse is a good jumper and has elegant gaits.

**Uses**: It is bred for show jumping competitions, dressage, eventing. It can also be driven.

**Current status**: Although it is native and in the process of being developed, the breed is doing very well and it is still growing, notably due to its success in international competitions. There are 1,700 broodmares and 200 stallions, and a few thousand other horses.

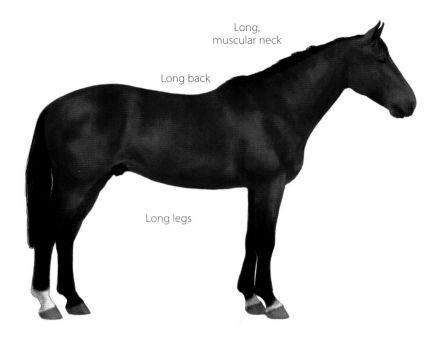

Long,
muscular neck

Long back

Long legs

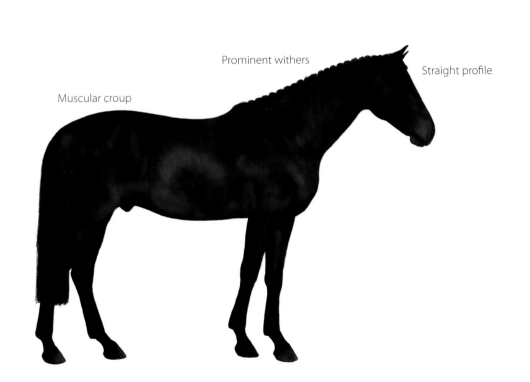

Prominent withers

Straight profile

Muscular croup

# HUNGARIAN COLDBLOOD

Also called: Hungarian Draft Horse

Hungarian: *Magyar hidegvérü*

ⓗ 1.50 m–1.65 m.

ⓒ Bay, black, often light chestnut with light mane and tail. Sometimes gray, rarely roan or buckskin.

**Description**: This massive, sturdy draft horse has a powerful neck, broad chest, a wide back and croup, and large hooves. The hair of the mane and tail is long and thick; it often has a double mane.

**Distribution**: Hungary.

**Origins and history**: The breed is not the issue of local horses, but of different draft breeds brought to Hungary in the eighteenth and nineteenth centuries. Crossings among the Noriker, Murakoz, Belgian, Ardennais, and Percheron created this heavy draft horse.

**Character and attributes**: The Hungarian Coldblood is a calm, docile, and intelligent horse. Robust, it has good longevity and is easy to keep.

**Uses**: Traditionally used for farm work, clearing land, and as a harness horse, it is also bred for its meat, primarily for export, because Hungarians eat very little horse meat. Its patience makes it a good horse for equitherapy, or simply for the family.

**Current status**: This native breed remains rare, with only 650 mares and 260 stallions. The numbers are carefully watched to keep them from dropping any further.

# MURAKOZ

Also called: Mura Horse

Hungarian: *muraközi*; Croatian: *medjimurski*

ⓗ 1.55 m–1.65 m.

ⓒ Chestnut, often with a light mane and tail and light legs; bay, sometimes black or light gray.

**Description**: The Murakoz is a compact and round draft horse, weighing between 650 kg and 800 kg. It has a long, wide head with a straight profile; large eyes; a short neck; unobtrusive withers; broad chest; a very sloping, double croup; low-set tail; short legs; and large hooves. The hair of the mane and tail is abundant, and there is feathering on the legs.

**Distribution**: Southern Hungary, Medimurje county, Croatia; Poland.

**Origins and history**: This recent draft breed was created from local horses (the ancient Mur Island horse) and crossings with the Noriker, Percheron, Ardennais, Flemish, Belgian, and Norfolk, but also with the Hungarian Halfbred and the Arabian. It owes its name to the Mura River. Blood from the Freiburg will be added to limit problems of inbreeding; two Swiss stallions were exported to Hungary in January 2012 for this purpose.

**Character and attributes**: This horse is docile, powerful, and fast for a draft horse. It is easy to keep and enjoys good health.

**Uses**: This is an excellent horse for carriage driving and for clearing land. Once a farm horse valued for its work, it is now raised for its meat.

**Current status**: It was once one of the most popular and widespread draft horses in the world, making up as much as 20 percent of the horse population in Hungary. But its numbers dropped enormously, and are still dropping. World War II had a very negative impact on the numbers, with many Murakoz killed. In 2013 there were fewer than fifty-five remaining, including only three stallions.

Powerful neck

Thick mane
and tail

Wide back

Large hooves

Large eyes

Very wide, very
sloping croup

Large head

Short legs

There are many horses in Romania, but their numbers are declining: there were fewer than 500,000 in 2013. Horses are being increasingly used as recreational animals, but their numbers are declining overall, notably following a Romanian

# DANUBE DELTA HORSE

Also called: Letea Forest Horse

Romanian: *cal sălbatic de la Letea, cal sălbatic din Delta Dunarii*

**H** Around 1.35 m–1.40 m.

**C** Bay, black, sometimes mealy, a few chestnuts and dark grays; rarely white markings.

**Description**: This small horse has a head with a straight profile, sloping croup, low-set tail, slender legs, and small hooves.

**Distribution**: The Danube Delta, Letea Forest, Romania.

**Origins and history**: This is not a true breed, but a population that has been returned to the wild. It has been the subject of lively debates following the slaughtering that occurred in 2002. Some of the horses are carriers of equine infectious anemia, which means the population cannot be exported.

The horses threaten the ecological balance of the natural area, notably by consuming the bark of trees during harsh winters. From recent research, these animals are believed to be linked in part to the Hucul, and probably were influenced by horses from the steppes of Central Asia. They are also descended from horses abandoned at the end of the Ceausescu era. Some of these horses belong to the local population.

**Character and attributes**: This horse is perfectly adapted to its local environment, resilient in cold temperatures, and uncomplicated. Living in the wild, the animals are fearful and are difficult to approach.

**Uses**: Some individuals are domesticated. They are sometimes captured for their meat.

**Current status**: Although rare, the population is rather well developed for horses living in the wild, with around 4,000 animals. But the regular attempts to cull this horse population threaten it greatly, even if the authorities appear to be seeking solutions to regulate it, notably by placing the animals in an independent reserve.

# ROMANIAN PONY

Romanian: *poneiul romanesc*

**H** 1.10 m–1.20 m.

**C** Bay, dark bay, black, bay dun.

**Description**: The Romanian Pony is compact and stocky, with a very thick mane and tail.

**Distribution**: Romania.

**Origins and history**: The Romanian Pony has been developed recently, since 1989, from crossings between Shetland stallions and Hucul mares. But the breed hasn't been very successful, as the Hucul has already been established as a small mount. It is notably bred in the stud farm of Lucina.

**Character and attributes**: Lively but easy to handle, it combines the great rusticity of the Hucul and the Shetland.

**Uses**: It is a mount for any young rider, and is also used in equitherapy.

**Current status**: The breed, fairly unknown, is currently being developed.

law of 2008 forbidding the use of carriages on main roads to limit the number of road accidents, and the mechanization of farming. Romania has seen some of its breeds die out in the twentieth century, and only small numbers remain of other native breeds.

Romania shares the breeding of the Hucul (see Poland, *p. 218*). In addition to its native breeds, Romania has other breeds from Eastern Europe: Gidran, Furioso, Nonius, Shagya Arabian, and Lipizzan.

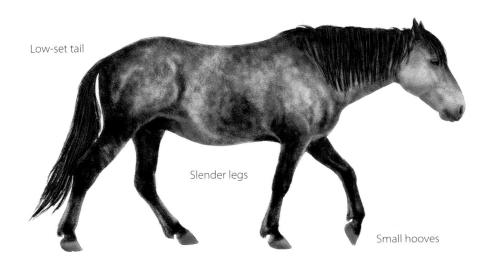

Low-set tail

Slender legs

Small hooves

# ROMANIAN TROTTER

Romanian: *trapas romanesc*

**H** 1.55 m–1.57 m on average.

**C** Most often bay, sometimes black.

**Description**: It has the typical morphology of trotters: a head with a straight profile; a muscular neck; prominent withers; a long, strong back; a long, wide, muscular croup; and solid hooves.

**Distribution**: Romania.

**Origins and history**: The Romanian Trotter is the result of crossings, starting in 1887 and continuing throughout the twentieth century, between the American Standardbred (80 percent of the breed's blood); Orlov, French, and Russian Trotters; Nonius; and Furioso. Selection continues to improve its speed in racing. It has played an important role in the creation of the Romanian Draft Horse.

**Character and attributes**: It is lively and docile at the same time, has endurance, and is resilient, a very fast trotter.

**Uses**: It is mainly used for trotting races, although it is less competitive than its French and American counterparts. Due to its good trotter nature, it is also suitable for recreational riding.

**Current status**: This Romanian breed is very small in number.

## ROMANIA

# ROMANIAN SADDLE HORSE

Also called: Romanian Sport Horse, Romanian Warmblood

Romanian: *cal de sport romanesc*

🅗 1.62 m–1.72 m.

🅒 Mainly bay, also chestnut, black, very occasionally roan, gray, often with white markings on the head and legs.

**Description**: A classic, tall saddle horse, it has a small, slender head with a rather concave profile; small ears; a muscular neck; rather broad chest; short back; muscular croup; long, solid legs; and hard hooves.

**Distribution**: Romania.

**Origins and history**: The breed was developed from the middle of the twentieth century, starting in the 1960s, with crossings of Thoroughbred, Arabian, Gidran, Furioso, Trotter, and Anglo-Arab, and follows rigorous selection with a view to sport results.

**Character and attributes**: The Romanian Saddle Horse is intelligent and lively, and at the same time docile and easy. It is robust and a good jumper.

**Uses**: This is a sport horse bred for dressage, show jumping, and eventing competitions. It can also be used in harness.

**Current status**: The breed is being developed, but it is beginning to be known due to its success in competition.

---

## ROMANIA

# BUCOVINA HORSE

Romanian: *Bucovina*

🅗 1.46 m on average for mares; 1.48 m for males.

🅒 Often roan.

**Description**: It is lighter than the Romanian Draft Horse, closer to a light draft horse.

**Distribution**: The Bucovina region, Romania.

**Origins and history**: This breed is formed from the Romanian Draft Horse, the Hucul (very common in Bucovina), and the Ardennais.

**Character and attributes**: The Bucovina is a calm draft horse, which inherited its robustness from the Hucul.

**Uses**: The Bucovina is used especially in forest work and for transportation.

**Current status**: This local breed is very rare, and not widely known.

---

## ROMANIA

# ROMANIAN DRAFT HORSE

Also called: Romanian Traction Horse

Romanian: *semigreu romanesc*

🅗 1.51 m–1.58 m.

🅒 Bay, roan.

**Description**: The Romanian Draft Horse resembles the Ardennais, from which it is descended. There are two types. One is taller and more massive, formed from Romanian Trotter and Furioso crossed with Ardennais, and weighs in the 580–600 kg range. The other, smaller and weighing around 510 kg, was created from Ardennais stallions and Lipizzan and local mares. Both types have more than 68 percent Ardennais blood. It has a straight or slightly convex profile, wide forehead, long ears, a broad chest, double croup, and strong legs. The hair of the mane and tail is thick and wavy.

**Distribution**: Romania.

**Origins and history**: This is a relatively recent draft horse, whose formation dates from the 1960s. The goal was to obtain a farm horse with endurance that was well adapted to the climate of Romania.

**Character and attributes**: Lively and energetic, but docile and gentle.

**Uses**: This powerful draft horse is still bred for transportation and for farm and forest work, as well as for its meat.

**Current status**: This local breed has seen its numbers decline.

Opposite: In the Caucasus on the border with Russia, in northern Georgia, this small horse is traveling without stopping from Kazbegi (or Stephantsminda), at an altitude of 1,740 meters, to a 3,000-meter mountain pass in the Mount Kazbek range. This effort in the rocky slopes seems to be business as usual for this lean, thin, sure-footed horse.

In Bulgaria, horses are sometimes still used for transportation and farm work, and local breeds continue to be very important. They also have a role in sports and tourism. Sport breeding is still being developed, as Bulgarian breeders are often hindered by the high prices of European studs, but it survives thanks to the East Bulgarian Sport Horse.

---

BULGARIA

# DANUBIAN

Bulgarian: *dunavski kon*

🅗 1.60 m–1.63 m on average for males, 1.58 m–1.61 m for mares.

🅒 Black, dark bay, sometimes dark chestnut.

**Description**: Tall, rather massive, and compact, the Danubian has a long head with a straight profile; rather small eyes; a powerful neck; a long, straight back; strong legs; a wide, slightly sloping croup; and a rather high-set tail. The hair of the mane and tail is long.

**Distribution**: Western and northwestern Bulgaria.

**Origins and history**: Created at the beginning of the twentieth century, the breed is the result of crossings of non-native breeds, notably Nonius and Don stallions with Gidran Arabian mares. Crossed with the Thoroughbred, the Danubian produces very good show jumping horses.

**Character and attributes**: The Danubian is energetic, strong, and powerful.

**Uses**: This recreational horse is mainly intended for harness work, but makes a good saddle horse.

**Current status**: It is popular in its country, even though its numbers remain very low, with only around 750 horses, including 33 stallions and 103 pure broodmares in 2011. But the population is slowly growing.

The Danubian is a rather sturdy horse (here, working with a long tether).

---

BULGARIA

# EAST BULGARIAN

Also called: Bulgarian Sport Horse

Bulgarian: *istotchnobolgarskiï kon*

🅗 1.62 m–1.66 m.

🅒 Chestnut, black, sometimes bay or dark bay, more rarely gray.

**Description**: The East Bulgarian is a type of rather compact Anglo-Arab. It has a head with a straight profile; a long neck; prominent withers; a broad chest; a rather long, straight back; a muscular croup; and resilient legs.

**Distribution**: Bulgaria.

**Origins and history**: This recent breed, dating from the end of the nineteenth century, is bred on the stud farms of Kabiuk and Bozhurishte. It was obtained by crossbreeding local halfbloods with Thoroughbred, Arabian, and Anglo-Arab horses, with the goal of obtaining a good military horse. In the 1980s selection aimed for a more sporty horse, with the addition of Hanoverian, Holstein, Trakehner, and Selle Français blood.

**Character and attributes**: Both calm and energetic, this intelligent horse has endurance and is versatile. It is rather rustic for a horse of this type, and thus well adapted to the Bulgarian climate (cold winters, easily reaching −20°C, and very warm summers, often over 35°C). It is a good galloper.

**Uses**: Both a recreational and competition horse, it is suited for dressage, show jumping, eventing, and endurance and harness racing. It is sometimes used in obstacle and steeplechase races.

**Current status**: The breed is popular in Bulgaria and is doing well. It is the most commonly used breed in equestrian sports.

Among the horses that are bred in addition to native breeds, of note is the Karakachan, a mountain draft breed that is also bred in Turkey (see Turkey, p. 284). The Bulgarians also breed foreign horses, mainly Arabians, Thoroughbreds, Shagya Arabians, Trakehners, Hanoverians, Shetlands, and Haflingers. The horse is very important to Bulgarians, from a cultural and religious point of view. There are more than 140,000 horses in Bulgaria, and the numbers are increasing.

Wide croup

Rather high-set tail

Elongated head with straight profile

DANUBIAN

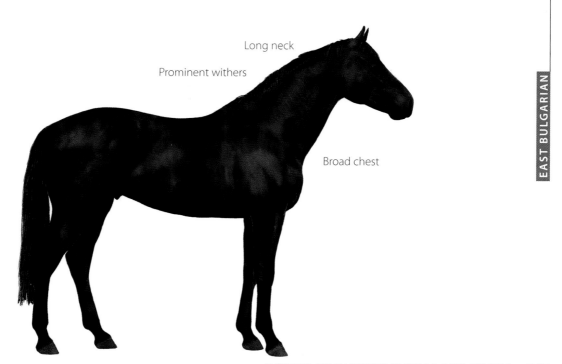

Long neck

Prominent withers

Broad chest

EAST BULGARIAN

# PLEVEN

Bulgarian: *plevenski kon*

**H** 1.63 m–1.67 m for males, 1.60 m–1.65 m for mares.

**C** Always chestnut, often light chestnut with gold highlights; few white markings.

**Description**: This light horse, of Anglo-Arab type, has a very typical Arabian head, a long, muscular neck; straight, rather long back; short, slightly sloping croup; high-set tail; slender legs; and hard hooves.

**Distribution**: Bulgaria.

**Origins and history**: Created at the beginning of the twentieth century, the breed is the result of many crossings among local halfblood mares, and Thoroughbred, Arabian, Russian Anglo-Arab, Gidran Arabian, and Shagya Arabian stallions. The goal was to obtain a good military horse that could also be used for farm work.

**Character and attributes**: The Pleven is an intelligent horse, bold, very lively and spirited. It has good gaits and is a good jumper. This sport horse requires attentive care. It lives a long time, which enables it to work for many years.

**Uses**: This versatile saddle horse excels notably in show jumping and dressage.

**Current status**: The number of Plevens has sharply decreased. There is still a small local population, and although the breed is popular in its country, it is endangered, with 11 stallions and 34 broodmares in 2011.

# Moldova

In addition to its local horses, Moldova breeds Soviet Draft Horses. Its equine stock is increasing. The horse is still used as a work animal, harnessed to various carts and carrying all sorts of things, but it is also raised for its meat. One also finds racehorses. There are around 76,000 horses in Moldova.

# LOCAL MOLDOVAN

Moldovan: *moldoveneascá localá*

**H** 1.45 m on average for males; 1.40 m for mares.

**C** Bay, black, chestnut, gray.

**Description**: The type is not completely homogeneous. It is a small horse with slender legs.

**Distribution**: Moldova.

**Origins and history**: This native horse is the result of a blend of breeds, notably Russian Trotter, Orlov, and Don. It is probably not a separate breed, but a type of horse that one finds just about everywhere in Moldova. It continues to be used as a work animal in its home country.

**Character and attributes**: Moldovan horses are resilient and bold; they have endurance and are well adapted to the local climate and environment.

**Uses**: It is used as a saddle horse, in harness, and for farm work. It is also used for equestrian tourism and is raised for its meat.

**Current status**: There are probably tens of thousands of these horses.

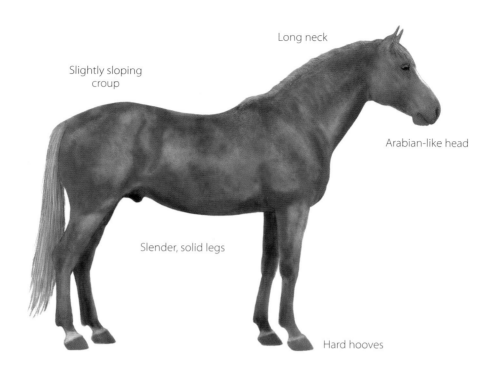

Long neck

Slightly sloping
croup

Arabian-like head

Slender, solid legs

Hard hooves

Rather sloping
croup

Fairly straight
profile

Slender legs

Seventeen breeds of horses are bred in Ukraine. In addition to the two Ukrainian breeds, the Ukrainian Riding Horse and the Novoalexandrovsk Cart Horse, there are Russian and German breeds, but also the complex crossings among Nonius, Furioso, and Gidran mares with Thoroughbred, Hanoverian, Hungarian, and Trakehner stallions. The blood of the Orlov-Rostopchin (a possibly extinct breed that is being reconstituted in Russia) still flows in its veins. The Bespechny lineage is the closest to the Orlov-Rostopchin.

UKRAINE

# Ukrainian Riding Horse

Also called: Ukrainian Saddle Horse

Ukrainian: *ukrainskaya verkhova*

**H** 1.63 m for mares; 1.68 m for males.

**C** Often chestnut, bay, dark bay, chestnut, sometimes black.

**Description**: The massive Ukrainian Riding Horse has a rather large head with a straight profile; a long neck; prominent withers; a broad chest; rather long back; long, sloping croup; high-set tail; and strong legs. The hair of the mane and tail is thin and sparse.

**Distribution**: Ukraine, a few in Poland, Russia, Belarus.

**Origins and history**: This recent breed, dating from the middle of the twentieth century, is the result of

**Character and attributes**: Calm and easygoing, it is powerful and has endurance, is a good jumper, and has elegant gaits. It is precocious and quite fertile.

**Uses**: This is a saddle horse that excels in dressage, show jumping, and eventing. It is also suitable for harness racing. Although it is quite athletic, its good nature also makes it a pleasant recreational horse.

**Current status**: This breed is still developing and is small in number, with probably no more than 2,000 horses, but it is increasingly popular and sought after in Ukraine's neighboring countries.

UKRAINE

# Novoalexandrovsk Cart Horse

Ukrainian: *novoalexandrivska vahovozna*

**H** 1.51 m on average for mares, 1.56 m for males.

**C** Often chestnut with light mane and tail.

**Description**: This horse has a solid, muscular body, thick neck, broad chest, and powerful croup. The hair of the mane and tail is thick, and sometimes wavy.

**Distribution**: Mainly in Crimea, Ukraine.

**Origins and history**: This breed is the Ukrainian version of the Russian Draft Horse. It is the result of crossings that took place at the end of the nineteenth century among local mares and stallions imported mainly from Belgium—Belgian and Ardennais, as well as a few Percheron—and founded on the Russian Draft type from the stud farm of Novoalexandrovsk.

**Character and attributes**: This is an energetic, vigorous, and balanced horse. It is very fertile and has a long life span. It can work late in life.

**Uses**: It is essentially a draft and carriage horse. The mares provide a lot of milk.

**Current status**: The breed's situation is critical, with fewer than 349 horses recorded in 2011.

American Standardbred. Ukraine's horse population is large but declining: 701,200 were counted in 2001, 675,000 in 2007. Horses are mainly bred for work and sport, a bit for meat and milk. Ukrainian riders are fearsome competitors, notably in show jumping competitions.

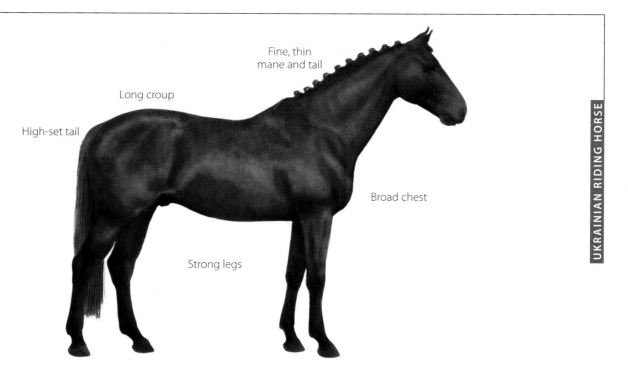

Fine, thin mane and tail

Long croup

High-set tail

Broad chest

Strong legs

**UKRAINIAN RIDING HORSE**

Thick, sometimes wavy mane and tail

Very muscular croup

Broad chest

**NOVOALEXANDROVSK CART HORSE**

You have to see one of the little Georgian horses, loaded with cargo, climb up and down the rocky, steep slopes of the Caucasus to understand what "sure-footed" means. The Georgians bred athletic, thin, energetic, fast horses with endurance for their

---

GEORGIA

# MEGRULI HORSE

Also called: Megrel, Mingrelian

Georgian: *megruli*

**H** 1.32 m for males; 1.29 m for mares.

**C** Bay, dark bay, black; the nose, around the eyes, and legs have a red, or sometimes gray, coloring, without white markings.

**Description**: This is the smallest horse of the Caucasus, with a compact and lean morphology. It has a head with a straight, rather wide profile; fairly small eyes; small ears; a rather wide neck; slightly prominent withers; a straight back; long, strong legs; and hard hooves.

**Distribution**: Mainly the coasts of the Black Sea, but found throughout western Georgia.

**Origins and history**: A very ancient breed of the Caucasus, it is the direct descendant of an extinct breed, the Kolkhuri, raised on the coasts of the Black Sea from perhaps the second or third century. Georgian breeders have tried to increase its size by crossing it with the Kabarda, but without much success, and the horses remained small while losing many of their distinctive qualities.

**Character and attributes**: The Megruli Horse is calm, strong, agile, and sure-footed; it has endurance and is a good pack horse. It is a good mountain horse, reputed in its country to be a good worker, very well adapted to the sometimes difficult local climate conditions, and at ease in the mountains as well as in a wet environment. It matures late.

**Uses**: It is traditionally used for farm work, as a pack horse (in spite of its small size, it can carry loads of 100–130 kg), and in harness.

**Current status**: This native breed is small in number and is considered endangered.

---

GEORGIA

# TUSHIN

Also called: Tushuri Horse, Tusheti Horse, Tushetian

Georgian: *tushuri*

**H** 1.36 m on average for males, 1.34 m for mares.

**C** Mainly dark bay, sometimes gray, chestnut, black, a few rare individuals are pinto or spotted.

**Description**: The Tushin is a small, robust horse, with a light head with a straight profile; short neck; slightly prominent withers; a short, straight back; slightly sloping croup; broad chest; slender legs; and small, black, hard hooves. The hair of the mane and tail is thick. Now raised in better conditions, its situation is improving.

**Distribution**: Tushuri, and mainly eastern Georgia.

**Origins and history**: This small mountain horse is the descendant of ancient native horses, bred in the first through the third centuries AD, that received contributions of Eastern blood (Arabian, Persian, Turkoman); it is one of the most ancient breeds in the Caucasus. It was a military horse, and it is still the horse of nomadic shepherds in these mountain regions with steep slopes, as it can be ridden in areas without roads.

**Character and attributes**: The Tushin is patient, calm, and gentle. Endowed with an excellent sense of direction and very good balance, as well as great endurance, it is bold but careful and very sure-footed. It is at ease in the high mountains on steep slopes. Simple, robust, and easy to keep, it is resilient in the variable climate. It matures late and lives a long time. Some can amble.

**Uses**: This is a saddle horse, popular in equestrian tourism. It is also a work horse for sheep herding. The mares are good milk producers.

**Current status**: This native breed is rare, with slightly more than 1,000 animals, and considered to be endangered in its country, even if the breeding program remains stable.

cavalry. Riding was very important for this people; to be a good rider was essential. Between Europe and Asia, this hilly country is, however, witnessing a decline in the numbers of the local horse breeds. All three breeds are endangered, and very little has been done to save them. Equestrian tourism is beginning to develop in Georgia, and the small mountain breeds, true all-terrain horses, could benefit from this. Georgia also shares with Russia a breed with exceptional qualities, the Kabarda (see Russia, *p. 260*).

**MEGRULI HORSE**

Small ears

Small eyes

Strong legs

**TUSHIN**

Georgian breeds are particularly at home in the mountains.

Short neck

Slender legs

Small, resilient hooves

# Javakheti Harness Horse

Georgian: *javakheti*

🅗 1.46 m on average for males, 1.41 m for mares.

🅒 Mainly dark, dark bay, dark gray, black, often with white markings.

**Description**: This is a small saddle horse with a solid constitution, a head with a rather straight profile, slightly prominent withers, a rather long back, slightly sloping croup, rather low-set tail, and slender legs. There are three types, which vary depending on their weight.

**Distribution**: The volcanic plateau of Javakheti (high Armenian plateau), in southern Georgia.

**Origins and history**: This horse has been bred on the pastureland of the plateau of Javakheti since the nineteenth century (1841–1845), by crossing local mares from Crimea and the Don region with Russian Draft stallions. Later, beginning in 1938, mares were crossed with Ardennais, Belgian, and Percheron horses.

**Character and attributes**: The Javakheti Harness Horse is intelligent and obedient; it has endurance and a vigorous temperament, and is capable of enduring harsh working conditions. It is a good trotter. It is resilient and well adapted to the harsh climate conditions of Georgia, and to the long, cold winters. It is easy to keep.

**Uses**: It is suitable for riding and is also used as a pack horse. It is also often crossed with donkeys to produce mules.

**Current status**: This local horse remains fairly unknown, including in its own country. The exact numbers of this breed are not known. It is considered rare.

# Russia

Russia has always been a great equestrian country. It had as many as 38 million horses at the beginning of the twentieth century, though now there are only around 1,300,000. Nevertheless, it remains the nation with the greatest number of horses. Recreational riding has become very popular there. Though during the Soviet era horses belonged to

# Altai

Russian: *altaïskaya*

🅗 1.30 m–1.45 m; 1.37 m on average for mares, 1.40 m for males.

🅒 Chestnut, light gray, black, regularly spotted, often with primitive markings (dorsal stripe, zebra striping on the legs).

**Description**: The Altai has a large head with a straight or slightly concave profile; small eyes; short neck; broad chest; long back; muscular, sloping croup; short, solid legs; and hard hooves. The hair of the mane and tail is thick.

**Distribution**: The Altai Mountains, Russia, Mongolia, eastern Kazakhstan.

**Origins and history**: This small horse from the Altai Mountains is very ancient and its origins are unknown, but it is physically and geographically very close to the Mongolian horse. It is the horse of the nomadic populations of the Altai. Breeding is done in the semi-wild, and the breed benefits from the good pastureland in this region. Crossed with heavy draft horses, it produces the New Altai.

**Character and attributes**: It has good endurance, is resilient and confident, and tolerates the very cold winters and poor food. It has the sure-footedness of mountain horses.

**Uses**: This is essentially a pack horse, due to its ability to carry heavy loads up steep paths. It is also suited for equestrian tourism.

**Current status**: In 2003 the Altai population was at 3,190.

Rather low-set tail

Rather straight profile

Slender legs

the state, today owning one's own horse is again a symbol of wealth and good taste. Due to the great political and economic changes Russia has undergone in the past twenty years, many Russian breeds are threatened with extinction. Some forty breeds of horses are bred in Russia. In addition to the numerous Russian breeds, one also finds breeding farms for the Akhal-Teke, which is of great benefit to the breed. Russia also produces English Thoroughbreds, Arabians, Hanoverians, and other breeds.

Long back

Large head

Short legs

# TRANSBAIKAL

Russian: *zabaykalskaya, zabaikal*

**H** 1.35 m–1.40 m.

**C** Quite variable: gray, bay, chestnut, spotted, pinto, bay dun, black/brown dun, buckskin, often with a dorsal stripe and zebra stripes on the legs. Like Przewalski's Horse, the Yakutian, and the Mongolian, it sometimes has primitive markings on the shoulder, which some local breeders call a "butterfly wing."

**Description**: It resembles the Buryat. It is compact with a large head and wide forehead; straight profile; a short, thick neck; broad chest; unobtrusive withers; very muscular croup; short legs; and hard hooves. In the winter it regularly has a very thick and very curly coat. The mane and tail are thick.

**Distribution**: Transbaikalia, in Siberia, Russia.

**Origins and history**: This ancient Siberian breed, traditionally bred by the nomads of the steppes, is situated between Yakutia and Mongolia. Similar to the Buryat, with which it is sometimes confused, the Transbaikal has uncertain origins, perhaps Turko-Mongolian, but its primitive shoulder marking without doubt connects it to the Yakutian and the Mongolian.

**Character and attributes**: The Transbaikal is very friendly, intelligent, hardy, rustic, and resistant to illness; it has great endurance. It endures extreme temperatures (up to −50°C). It is very fertile to an advanced age and lives a long time. It can amble, but also has a gait called *tropata*, which resembles the "running walk" of the American Tennessee Walker.

**Uses**: This horse is good for recreation and for trekking. It makes a good mount for young riders.

**Current status**: It remains little known and rare in a pure state (perhaps fewer than 300 individuals), and has suffered from crossings aiming to improve it. But its amazing, unique qualities are making it increasingly popular.

# YAKUTIAN

Russian: *yakutskaya*

**H** 1.37 m–1.40 m; 1.37 m on average for mares, 1.39 m on average for males.

**C** Gray, bay, black/bay dun, roan, with a tendency to lighten. The eyes are sometimes of different colors. Often a withers stripe, and zebra striping on the legs. Those with a black/brown dun coat sometimes have a dark patch on the shoulder, a primitive and rare marking in horses, which is also found on the Mongolian horse, the Transbaikal, and Przewalski's Horse.

**Description**: Very primitive, the Yakutian is recognized by its round, massive, compact physique, and its incredible winter coat, which is very long and dense, and which can reach 29 centimeters in length on top of a thick undercoat. It resembles a large Shetland. It has a large, rather short head; convex profile; small nostrils; a short neck; low withers; straight shoulders; a short, wide back; a sloping, even dished croup; rather short, very solid legs; and small, hard hooves. The hair of the mane and tail is long and very thick. Its skin is thick, and it has a good layer of fat. Like the Mongolian, it has the rare characteristic of having almost no chestnuts. There are three types, which vary depending on their weight; the main one is called Kolyma or Verkhoyansk.

**Distribution**: Russia, Siberia, north of the Arctic Circle.

**Origins and history**: This very ancient Siberian breed probably descends from primitive ponies from the tundra and from Mongolian horses. It lives in the wild, getting along on its own. The Yakutian plays a very important role in the local economy. There is a Yakutian draft, the Megezh (see *p. 275*).

**Character and attributes**: The Yakutian is known to be intelligent; it is also powerful and has great endurance. Adapted to extreme climate conditions that no other breed could tolerate (long winters, temperatures reaching −70°C), there is no other horse in the world better adapted to the cold. But it also endures very hot summers. Very hardy, it digs in the snow for food. It lives an exceptionally long time, which enables it to work and to reproduce late in life.

**Uses**: It is used for riding and as a pack or draft horse. Mares are milked to make koumiss. The hide is used to make felt, and the leather is also used. It is essentially raised for its meat, which, served with parsley, is considered a delicacy in Russia due to its high fat content.

**Current status**: Although it is little known outside of Russia, the Yakutian is one of the most widespread breeds in Russia and is considered a precious gift by the local population.

The Yakutian Horse is the breed best adapted to the most extreme cold.

The Transbaikal is one of the rare horses (with the Yakutian, below) to regularly show a primitive marking on the shoulder, probably the legacy of distant crossings with Przewalski's Horse.

Large head and wide forehead

Often curly hair, very thick in the winter

Very thick mane and tail

Short neck

Big, rather short head

A thick layer of fat

Small nostrils

Regular presence of a primitive marking on the shoulder

Rather short, very solid legs

In Siberia, the Yakutian is a versatile horse.

# BASHKIR

Russian: *bashkirskaya*

**H** 1.38 m–1.42 m on average for mares, 1.42 m–1.45 m for males.

**C** Chestnut, bay, black/brown dun, buckskin, roan, some spotted; often with a dorsal stripe.

**Description**: This astonishing horse has the very rare characteristic of being curly. Indeed, its thick hair becomes very long and curly in the winter, whereas the summer coat is straight, and the hair of the mane and tail is thick and very wavy. This unusual trait is probably a natural adaptation that enables it to be better protected from the cold. It has a stocky body; rather wide head; small ears; small nostrils; a short, thick neck; long, wide back; low-set tail; rather short legs; and small hooves. There are two types: the Bashkir of the mountains, which is smaller, and the Bashkir of the steppes, which is heavier.

**Distribution**: Southern Urals, Bashkiria, Russia.

**Origins and history**: The origins of this very ancient horse are not known; it is thought to have come from primitive local horses that lived on the steppes. The Americans also have a curly breed, the Curly, whose origins are also unknown, but which was for a long time called the Curly Bashkir due to an erroneous belief that the two breeds were related.

**Character and attributes**: The Bashkir is docile, calm, and cooperative. It is agile and fast. With great endurance and very robust, it is extremely resilient in the cold, able to feed itself even in the snow.

**Uses**: It is suitable for both saddle and harness, and as a pack horse. It excels in trekking and in endurance races. In the past the hair was collected to make yarn to weave garments. The mares produce a lot of milk, which is used to make koumiss, a fermented beverage. The Bashkir is also raised for its meat. Because of its special hair, the breed has the unique advantage of being able to be ridden by people who are allergic to horses.

**Current status**: Although little known in the rest of the world, the breed is doing very well and is one of the most numerous in Russia. In the past it was even more widespread.

# TERSK

Russian: *terskaya*

**H** 1.43 m–1.50 m.

**C** Most often light gray with unique silvery highlights, more rarely bay or chestnut.

**Description**: Its conformation is close to that of the Arabian. It has a small head with Arabian influence; large eyes; rather long ears; a high-set neck; prominent withers; a broad chest; straight back; short croup; high-set tail; slender, but very solid legs; and resilient hooves. The hair of the mane and tail is fine, silky, and sparse. The skin is thin and the hair of the hide is fine.

**Distribution**: Russia, in the North Caucasus.

**Origins and history**: Of recent origin, this light saddle horse was developed in the first quarter of the twentieth century. It is the issue of the Strelet Arabian, a now-extinct breed, that was crossed with Kabarda, Don, Shagya Arabian, and Arabian horses.

**Character and attributes**: The Tersk is intelligent, very gentle, and fast; it has good endurance and lovely gaits. It is well adapted to the Russian climate and lives a long time.

**Uses**: This very athletic horse is well suited to show jumping, dressage, eventing, and endurance races. It participates in certain galloping races. Its unique silvery coat makes it popular in circuses.

**Current status**: This breed, although exceptional both for its unique physical appearance and for its sport abilities, remains surprisingly very rare, with fewer than a thousand animals and slightly more than a hundred mares.

Tersks competing in a gallop race.

Small ears

Curly hide

Curly mane and tail

The nostrils are small, to protect against the cold

Small hooves

High-set neck

Concave profile with Arabian influence

Silky and sparse mane and tail

Slender but very solid legs

# VYATKA

Russian: *vyatskaya*

**H** 1.46 m on average for mares; 1.48 m for males.

**C** Bay, chestnut, black/brown dun, buckskin, roan, with a dorsal stripe and dark extremities, or slight zebra striping on the legs.

**Description**: The Vyatka is robust and rather massive; it is a primitive-type breed with with a wide forehead and a slightly concave profile; a short, thick neck; wide back; sloping croup; rather short, solid legs; and small hooves. The hair of the mane and tail is thick, and the winter coat is particularly thick.

**Distribution**: Kirov, Udmurtia, Russia.

**Origins and history**: The Vyatka, a small horse living in the boreal forests, has obscure origins. It surely descends from primitive native horses, and it is similar to the Estonian Klepper and the Polish Konik. It was a sleigh horse popular with the local population. It continues to be used for transportation, notably in periods of great snowfall.

**Character and attributes**: The Vyatka is lively, energetic, and confident, and has good endurance. Very hardy, it tolerates very harsh climate conditions and is well adapted to moving around in the snow. It is resistant to attacks by insects and is fertile.

**Uses**: It is suitable for both saddle and light harness. It often pulls troikas. Its size makes it a good mount for young riders.

**Current status**: This native breed is endangered, with no more than 300 animals, including only 150 mares. But fans of the breed are mobilizing to save it.

# KABARDA

Also called: Kabardin

Russian: *kabardinskaya*

**H** 1.52 m–1.58 m on average for males, 1.53 m for mares.

**C** Often cherry bay, dark bay, black, sometimes gray, rarely liver chestnut; without white markings.

**Description**: This is a tall mountain horse. It has a long, slender head with a straight profile, more convex near the nose; small eyes; long ears whose tips are turned inward; a narrow forehead; long, high-set neck; broad chest; sloping shoulders; unobtrusive withers; straight back; sloping croup; high-set tail; thin, solid legs (sometimes slightly curved in the back, which is not a defect in a mountain breed); and very hard hooves. It has thin skin, fine hair, and an often wavy mane and tail. There are three types: the basic Kabarda, the Eastern-type Kabarda, and the massive type. When bred in Germany or in the richer regions of Russia, the breed tends to increase in size.

**Distribution**: The mountains of the Caucasus, in southern Russia, the republic of Kabardino-Balkaria, Stavropol Krai, Georgia; a few in Germany.

**Origins and history**: This ancient breed, probably the issue of horses from Mongolia and from the local steppes, has received Karabakh, Turkoman, and Arabian blood, which then produced the Kabarda, once a popular war horse. It is raised free-range. The riders of the Caucasus were noted for respecting their mounts. They never beat a horse, and they rode without spurs, carrying only a simple leather crop to encourage their animals, in order to preserve a good rapport between horse and rider.

**Character and attributes**: Known for its great endurance and extreme sure-footedness, the Kabarda is agile, very energetic, fast, bold, very calm, and known for its intelligence. It is an excellent mountain horse, probably the best in the world, renowned for its sense of direction and its natural balance in hilly terrain. It is a very adaptable and resilient breed, hardy, and able to work in quite variable climate conditions. It is very fertile and has good health and longevity.

**Uses**: This versatile saddle horse is also used for light harness work and as a pack horse. It excels in endurance competitions. Mares are used to provide milk.

**Current status**: Very popular in Georgia and throughout the Caucasus, this exceptional breed is not well known elsewhere in the world. Its numbers have fallen due to a high demand for its meat, making the Kabarda a breed with only a few thousand animals recorded, few of which are of the pure type. There are 400 in Germany. This uncommon horse will hopefully eventually become known and appreciated for its extraordinary qualities.

As a pack horse, the Kabarda is an invaluable companion in the mountains.

Short, thick neck

Head with a slightly
concave profile

Small hooves

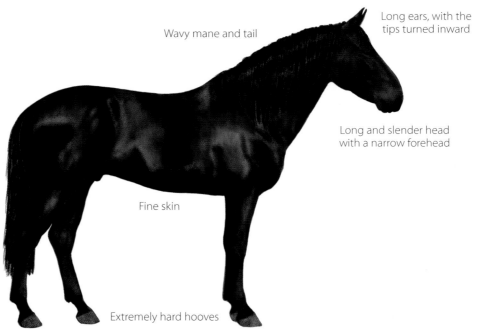

Wavy mane and tail

Long ears, with the
tips turned inward

Long and slender head
with a narrow forehead

Fine skin

Extremely hard hooves

# KARACHAI

The Karachai (*kaeachaevskaya*) is a breed very
similar to the Kabarda, found in the North Caucasus,
developed from excellent Kabarda individuals. It is, in
fact, simply a more massive type of Kabarda, with a
longer body.

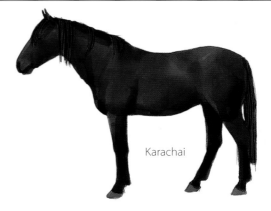

Karachai

# ANGLO-KABARDA

Russian: *anglo-kabardinskaya*

**Ⓗ** 1.52 m–1.64 m.

**Ⓒ** Mainly bay, dark bay, sometimes black, with a few white markings on the head and legs.

**Description**: The Anglo-Kabarda is taller than the Kabarda, with a longer neck, a shorter back, and long legs.

**Distribution**: Caucasus, Russia, Georgia.

**Origins and history**: This recent breed is the fruit of crosses among the Kabarda (and the Karachai) and the Thoroughbred starting in the 1920s. The excellent Kabarda thus combines its assets with those of the Thoroughbred, which creates a very athletic horse, one well adapted to the sometimes very cold climate of the Caucasus and to a mountain environment, which the Thoroughbred can't tolerate. An Anglo-Kabarda must have at least 25 percent Thoroughbred blood.

**Character and attributes**: The Anglo-Kabarda is both a spirited and energetic horse and a docile one. It is agile, but also faster than the Kabarda; however, it is less rustic. Although resilient in the cold, it is also needier and can require additional food in the winter. It inherited its extreme sure-footedness from the Kabarda.

**Uses**: This is a saddle horse that excels in the Olympic disciplines: dressage, show jumping, and eventing. It is also a good steeplechase horse. It is most suitable for experienced riders.

**Current status**: The breed is doing well.

# DON

Also called: Russian Don

Russian: *donskaya*

**Ⓗ** 1.55 m–1.65 m.

**Ⓒ** Mainly chestnut with golden metallic highlights, but also bay, black, gray.

**Description**: The Don has a head with a straight or slightly convex profile; large eyes; small ears; a broad chest; long back; long, slightly inclined croup; long, very solid legs; and wide, hard hooves.

**Distribution**: Widespread in the North Caucasus, southern Siberia, Russia, Ukraine, Kyrgyzstan, and Kazakhstan.

**Origins and history**: This old Russian breed was created from the seventeenth to the nineteenth centuries on the steppes of southern Russia from local horses and Turkoman, Karabakh, Kabarda, and Persian Arabian horses. It was the horse of the Cossacks. It made a name for itself during the Napoleonic Wars by outlasting the French horses that couldn't endure the Russian winter. In the twentieth century, breeding was intensified, with contributions of Orlov and Thoroughbred blood. The Don continues to be raised partially free-range.

**Character and attributes**: This is an independent, bold, and vigorous horse with good endurance. It is rustic and simple and of great resilience in the very cold winters, during which it can manage alone in the snow.

**Uses**: This saddle horse does well in eventing and in show jumping competitions. It is also good for teaching riding, for recreation, and for equestrian tourism. It is also suited to light harness work. It is an excellent endurance horse.

**Current status**: This is one of the most widespread breeds in Russia. It is doing well, after being on the brink of extinction after World War I.

Although a sport horse, the Don is resilient and does well in the cold.

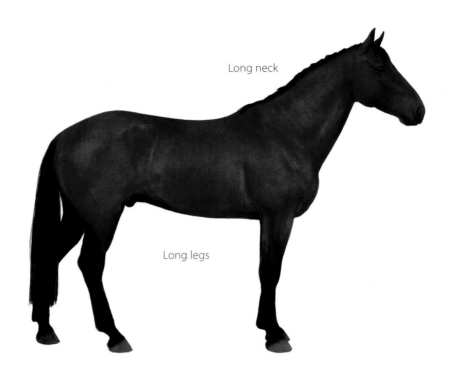

Long neck

Long legs

Slightly sloping croup

Broad chest

Long, very solid legs

# RUSSIAN TROTTER

Russian: *russkaya rysistaya*

Ⓗ 1.55 m–1.65 m.

Ⓒ Black, chestnut, bay, dark bay, gray.

**Description**: This trotter has a head with a straight or slightly convex profile; a long neck; a broad chest; long shoulders; a long back; long, slender legs; and a high croup.

**Distribution**: Primarily northwest Russia and western Siberia, Ukraine.

**Origins and history**: The breed was developed in the nineteenth century and especially in the mid-twentieth century by crossing Orlovs with American Standardbreds to create a Russian breed capable of competing with American trotters. It continues to be regularly crossed with the Standardbred to improve its sporting performance. Faster than the Orlov, but with less endurance, the Russian Trotter still can't win over American and European trotters.

**Character and attributes**: Energetic and fast, it has the good nature of trotters.

**Uses**: It is essentially bred for trotting races, and is also suited to light harness work. Its agreeable nature enables it to be used as or converted to a recreational horse.

**Current status**: The Russian Trotter is a very widespread breed in Russia, and is doing well.

# ORLOV TROTTER

Russian: *orlovskaya rysistaya*

Ⓗ 1.53 m–1.72 m.

Ⓒ Most often dappled gray, also black and bay, rarely chestnut.

**Description**: This powerful horse has a small head with a straight profile; wide forehead; large eyes; small ears; a long, high-set neck; a broad chest; straight shoulders; a long back; long, solid legs; a muscular croup; a high-set tail; and large hooves. The hair of the mane and tail is thick.

**Distribution**: Russia, Ukraine.

**Origins and history**: The breed was developed in Russia in the late eighteenth century by Count Alexei Orlov. Orlovs emerged as the result of crossing various European mares with Arabian stallions.

**Character and attributes**: This excellent trotter is docile and energetic. It is fast and has endurance. Endowed with a long life, it is well adapted to the Russian climate. The mares are very fertile.

**Uses**: Though trotting races specific to the breed continue to be held, the Orlov Trotter is now used more for light carriage driving and as a saddle horse. It is popular for pulling troikas.

**Current status**: The Orlov Trotter is one of the most important breeds in Russia, once very widespread, with tens of thousands of horses. But the numbers have decreased significantly, with only around 800 broodmares remaining, making the breed's status worrisome. It is known outside of Russia.

Harnessed to a troika, the Orlov Trotter works easily in the snow.

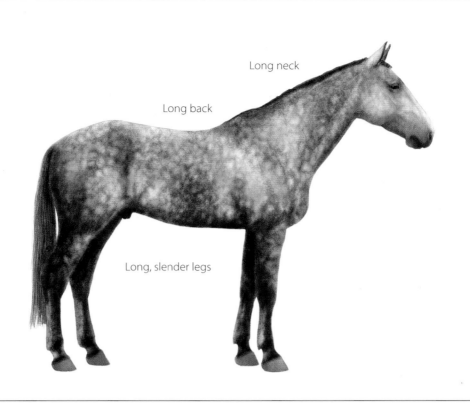

Long neck

Long back

Long, slender legs

High-set tail

Long back

Small head with a wide forehead

Large hooves

# BUDYONNY

Russian: *boudenovskaya*

**H** 1.62 m on average for mares; 1.65 m for males.

**C** Most often chestnut with golden highlights, but also bay, dark bay, gray and black.

**Description**: The Thoroughbred influence is very noticeable in this big Russian halfblood, but it has a more solid constitution. It has a head with a straight profile; large eyes; small ears; a long neck; prominent withers; a short back; long croup; low-set tail; long, slender legs; and small hooves.

**Distribution**: Mainly southern Russia, Ukraine.

**Origins and history**: The breed is recent, created in the Rostov region in the first part of the twentieth century by Marshal Budyonny. It was recognized in 1948. Don and Chernomor mares were crossed with Thoroughbred stallions, then later with Arabians. Contributions of Kazakh and Kyrgyz blood were attempted, without encouraging results. The original goal was to produce a very good military horse.

**Character and attributes**: The Budyonny is intelligent, patient, and easygoing, athletic, vigorous, and fast, and it has endurance. It is a good galloper and a good jumper. Thanks to its Russian origins, it has the advantage of being resilient enough to live outdoors.

**Uses**: This is a good saddle and sport horse; it is suitable for steeplechase, cross-country, show jumping, and dressage.

**Current status**: Thanks to its success in equine sports, the Budyonny has taken hold in Russia. The breed is doing very well.

The Budyonny is a versatile sport horse.

# ORLOV-ROSTOPCHIN

Also called: Russian Saddle Horse, Russian Riding Horse

Russian: *russkaya verkhovaya*

**H** 1.63 m–1.70 m.

**C** Always black, or dark bay, without white markings.

**Description**: It has a head with a straight or slightly concave profile; a wide forehead; long neck; very pronounced withers; sloping shoulders; a straight back; and resilient hooves. The hair of the mane and tail is silky, and the tail is often wavy.

**Distribution**: Russia.

**Origins and history**: The breed was created from a lineage of Orlov Trotters and another breed called Rostopchin, itself the issue of crossings of Russian breeds. It was used a lot by the military. The Orlov-Rostopchin has sometimes been declared extinct, due to the losses it suffered during the two world wars and the Russian Revolution. Using the last Orlov-Rostopchins, Arabian, Thoroughbred, and Akhal-Teke blood was added to save the breed, which resulted in the Ukrainian Riding Horse (see Ukraine, *p. 250*). From the Ukrainian Riding Horse, reconstitution was accomplished through the addition of Trakehner, Thoroughbred, Akhal-Teke, and Orlov Trotter blood, and a careful selection of subjects close to the Orlov-Rostopchin. The Russians now prefer to call it the Russian Saddle Horse.

**Character and attributes**: It is a very intelligent horse, lively, energetic, confident. It has endurance and is endowed with lovely gaits.

**Uses**: It is a good saddle horse in general. It stands out particularly in dressage but can also compete in show jumping and eventing.

**Current status**: After almost disappearing, the breed is in the process of being reconstituted. Its success in equine sports offers the hope that its numbers will soon begin to increase.

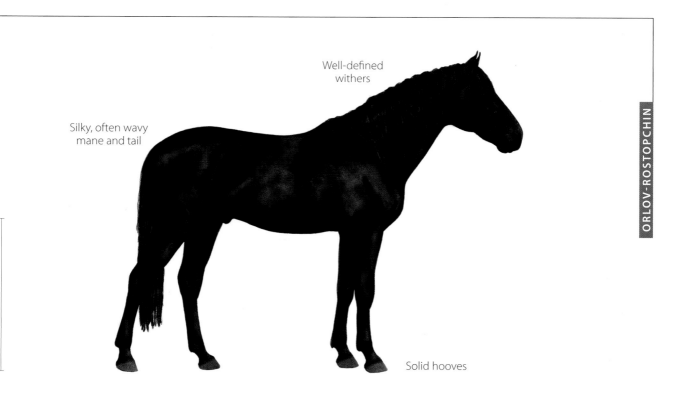

Long neck

Long, slender legs

Small hooves

Well-defined
withers

Silky, often wavy
mane and tail

Solid hooves

# RUSSIAN HEAVY DRAFT

Also called: Russian Draft

Russian: *russkaya tyazhelovoznaya*

🅗 1.50 m on average for mares; 1.53 m for males.

🅒 Often chestnut, sometimes bay, dark bay, roan.

**Description**: This compact draft horse weighs in the 580 kg–700 kg range. It resembles the Ardennais. It has a head with small ears; a muscular neck; unobtrusive withers; a broad chest; muscular croup; short, powerful legs; and small hooves. The hair of the mane and tail is thick. It has light feathering on the legs.

**Distribution**: Russia, Ukraine, Belarus.

**Origins and history**: Developed at the beginning of the twentieth century, this breed is the result of crossings of local mares with Belgian, Percheron, Ardennais, and Orlov Trotter stallions. The goal was to produce a good farm horse.

**Character and attributes**: It is very calm, resilient, but also agile and energetic. Very powerful, it is known for its ability to pull. It has good longevity and is very fertile. It has lovely trotting gaits inherited from the Orlov Trotter. It grows quickly and tolerates very cold temperatures.

**Uses**: It is essentially a farm and carriage horse. The mares are also used for their milk to produce fermented milk (koumiss). It is also raised for its meat.

**Current status**: Popular in Russia, this draft breed is doing very well.

The Russian Heavy Draft is perfectly acclimated to harsh Russian winters.

# VLADIMIR

Russian: *vladimirskaya tyazhelovoznaya*

🅗 1.55 m–1.65 m.

🅒 Often bay, dark bay, sometimes chestnut, black, with frequent white markings on the head and legs.

**Description**: This tall, heavy draft horse weights around 700 kg, and its British influence is very visible. This muscular horse has a long head with a slightly convex profile; a long, high-set neck; long croup; long legs; and large hooves, with feathering.

**Distribution**: Russia.

**Origins and history**: The Vladimir was created at the beginning of the twentieth century, the issue of a mixing of local horses with Shires and Clydesdales, but also with Cleveland Bay, Suffolk Punch, Ardennais, and Percheron horses. The breed was recognized in 1946. Its numbers fell with the mechanization of Russian farming.

**Character and attributes**: The Vladimir is powerful with great endurance. It is calm, but its personality is more assertive than is usually the case with draft horses. It is fast for its weight. It is precocious and fertile, well adapted to its local environment.

**Uses**: It is a carriage horse (notably for the troika) and is used in farm work. It can also be ridden.

**Current status**: This native draft horse is endangered, with only 650 animals and fewer than 200 broodmares.

Unobtrusive
withers

Small ears

Short, muscular legs
enabling good traction

RUSSIAN HEAVY DRAFT

Long neck
carried high

Long head with a
convex profile

Feathering on
the legs

VLADIMIR

# Soviet Heavy Draft

Russian: *sovetskaya tyazhelovoznaya*

**H** 1.60 m–1.70 m.

**C** Most often chestnut, bay, dark bay, roan, very rarely black.

**Description**: It is sometimes erroneously confused with the Russian Draft. It is more massive than the Russian Draft, and weighs between 700 kg and 1,000 kg. It has a head with a straight or slightly convex profile; small eyes; long ears; a short, muscular neck; straight shoulders; a wide back; a muscular, very sloping croup; solid legs; and wide hooves.

**Distribution**: Russia.

**Origins and history**: The breed began to appear at the end of the nineteenth century, from the crossing of local mares with Percheron, Belgian, and Suffolk stallions, and was recognized in 1952. This horse participated in intensive farm work in the Soviet era.

**Character and attributes**: It is very calm, very powerful and rustic. It works hard and is precocious, but is less rustic than other draft horses.

**Uses**: This is a draft and harness horse. The mares are very good milk producers, and it is also raised for its meat.

**Current status**: The breed, once quite popular, has lost a huge number of animals.

# Tuva

Russian: *tuvinskaya*

**H** 1.27 m–1.29 m on average.

**C** Bay, dark bay, black, chestnut, and gray.

**Description**: The Tuva resembles the Mongolian, with a long body and a very thick mane and tail.

**Distribution**: The republic of Tuva, in the extreme south of Siberia, Russia.

**Origins and history**: This Siberian breed has Mongolian origins, as the republic of Tuva is on the Mongolian border.

**Character and attributes**: This is an extremely robust horse, with excellent endurance.

**Uses**: It is bred to be ridden (the Tuvans are riders and, like their Mongolian neighbors, learn to ride at a very young age), but also for its meat and the milk of the mares.

**Current status**: This native horse is still little known outside its home territory. Pureblood animals are probably rare, as the breed suffered from too many crossings with the Don and the Budyonny. The overall number of horses in the republic of Tuva is growing.

Muscular croup

Long ears

Small eyes

Wide hooves

# DAGESTAN PONY

Russian: *dagestan*

**H** 1.30 m–1.36 m.

**C** Bay, chestnut.

**Description**: This is a small, sturdy mountain pony. It comes in several varieties: the Kumyk (*kumylskaya*), a more massive variety of the Dagestan; the Avar (*avarskaya*), a smaller variety; and the Lezgian (*lezginskaya*), a variety from southern Dagestan.

**Distribution**: North Caucasus, Russia, Georgia.

**Origins and history**: It is the horse of the local populations of Dagestan, who still live primarily from farming and raising sheep.

**Character and attributes**: It has endurance, is resilient, and has the sure-footedness of mountain horses. It can tolerate the harsh local climate.

**Uses**: These horses are used for riding, as pack horses, or for milk production.

**Current status**: The breed has been rare for a long time (fewer than 500 animals in 1995), and might be extinct today.

# PRIOB

Russian: *priobskaya*

**Ⓗ** 1.30 m–1.40 m; 1.32 m on average for mares, 1.36 m for males.

**Ⓒ** Often bay, black/brown dun, with a dorsal stripe and zebra striping on the legs.

**Description**: It resembles the Narym and the Yakutian, as it is also small and compact. It has a head with a convex profile; a short, thick neck; broad chest; long, straight back; sloping croup; and short legs. The hair of the mane and tail is thick. It has thick skin and during the summer puts on thick layers of fat in preparation for the winter.

**Distribution**: Khanty-Mansi, western Siberia, Russia.
**Origins and history**: The Priob was used a lot in the past by the local population for transporting fish and other merchandise, and for various work in the fields. It was crossed with Russian trotters and draft horses, but those crossings were not satisfactory.
**Character and attributes**: The Priob has good endurance and is very resilient in harsh climate and environmental conditions (cold winters, swampy pastureland in the summer, a great many insects). It lives a long time and is fertile. It is able to work late in life.
**Uses**: It was originally a draft and pack horse, used for forest work, and it continues to play this role in places that are difficult to reach in motorized vehicles.
**Current status**: This rare Siberian breed is very small in number.

---

# BURYAT

Russian: *buryatskaya, byryatskaya*

**Ⓗ** 1.32 m–1.38 m.

**Ⓒ** Gray, bay, chestnut, often with a dorsal stripe and zebra striping on the legs.

**Description**: A small, massive horse, the Buryat resembles the Transbaikal. It has a heavy head with a straight profile and a wide forehead; a short, muscular neck; and short legs. The winter coat is very dense, and the hair of the mane and tail is thick.

**Distribution**: Republic of Buryat, Russia.
**Origins and history**: This ancient Siberian breed most likely descends from Chinese and Mongolian horses crossed by the Russians with heavier breeds.
**Character and attributes**: The Buryat has endurance, is resilient, and is able to work in difficult conditions. It is adapted to a very cold climate (up to −50°C) and is happy with meager food. It is very fertile until late in life. It can amble.
**Uses**: Traditionally used for farm work and transport, it is also ridden, and is raised for its meat and milk.
**Current status**: This small local horse remains rare and little known, even in Russia.

---

# PECHORA

Russian: *pechorskaya*

**Ⓗ** 1.36 m for mares; 1.44 m for males.

**Ⓒ** Bay, dark bay, black.

**Description**: The Pechora is compact. It has a large head with a straight profile;, broad chest, sloping shoulders, a straight back, a very sloping croup, and strong legs. The hair of the mane and tail is thick. The winter coat is very dense.
**Distribution**: Pechora region, Komi Republic, near the Arctic Circle, Russia.

**Origins and history**: The Pechora is the issue of local breeds from the Urals, Siberia, and Estonia. It was developed in a region with abundant pastureland. Due to its great resistance to the cold, the breed was once very useful to the local population, and still is today.
**Character and attributes**: The Pechora has endurance and is hearty, very robust, and very resilient in the harsh climate. It is capable of working in the snow in glacial temperatures. It is very resistant to insects.
**Uses**: It is used for riding, transport, and farm work due to its good pulling ability.
**Current status**: This native breed is rare.

## RUSSIA

# NARYM

Russian: *narymskaya*

**H** 1.38 m on average.

**C** Mainly bay and chestnut.

**Description**: The breed is similar to the Priob (see above); the Narym is simply a bit more massive and taller. It has a large head; a short, thick neck; broad chest; strong legs; and hard hooves. The hair of the mane and tail is thick.

**Distribution**: Northern Siberia, Russia.

**Origins and history**: This Siberian breed is a cousin of the Priob. The Narym is often crossed with draft horses and trotters to increase its height.

**Character and attributes**: It has endurance and is well adapted to the rigorous climate conditions of northern Siberia.

**Uses**: Once used a lot for transport and farm work, it is also raised for its meat.

**Current status**: This native breed is rare and endangered.

## RUSSIA

# MINUSIN

Russian: *minusinsk, minusinskaya*

**H** 1.44 m–1.45 m on average.

**C** Bay, gray, roan, black/brown dun.

**Description**: It has a head with a convex profile, a thick neck, and solid legs.

**Distribution**: Minusinsk Basin, Russia.

**Origins and history**: This horse of the steppes in the Minusinsk Basin was developed in good breeding conditions (rich pastureland) and has been improved with Don, Thoroughbred, and Budyonny blood.

**Character and attributes**: It is robust and very well adapted to local conditions (hot summers, rainy winters).

**Uses**: It is traditionally used for transport, riding, and farm work.

**Current status**: This rare local breed is sometimes considered extinct due to its being overcrossed with breeds meant to improve it.

## RUSSIA

# KALMYK

Russian: *kalmutskaya, kalmyskaya*

**H** 1.44 m–1.52 m.

**C** Mainly bay, chestnut.

**Description**: It resembles the Kyrgyz, but is bigger. The winter coat is very dense.

**Distribution**: Russia, in the regions of Astrakhan and Volgograd.

**Origins and history**: A horse of the steppes, the Kalmyk has its origins in the Mongolian horse, crossed with local Russian breeds in southern Russia.

The Kalmyks, descendants of the Mongolians, are a nomadic, horse-breeding people. They provided horses for the cavalry.

**Character and attributes**: The Kalmyk is simple, has endurance, and is resilient to the cold. Many Kalmyks have the amble as a supplementary gait.

**Uses**: This is a saddle horse capable of working in very rigorous climate conditions.

**Current status**: This local breed is very small in number, with around 3,700 animals (2003).

# CHERNOMOR

Also called: Black Sea Horse

Russian: *chernomorskaya*

● 1.52 m–1.54 m on average.

● Dark bay, black, a few chestnuts with golden highlights.

**Description**: This very muscular horse looks like the Don.

**Distribution**: Russia, regions of Krasnodar and Rostov.

**Origins and history**: The Chernomor dates from the end of the eighteenth century. It is a mixture of Russian breeds. It is the issue of ancient breeds that have disappeared—the Nogai, the ancient Kuban—and of local mountain horses, Don, Kabarda, and Eastern horses that the Kazakhs brought with them, but also of Thoroughbreds and Orlov Trotters.

**Character and attributes**: It is calm and has endurance.

**Uses**: It is above all a saddle horse.

**Current status**: The breed has very few horses, or is considered to be extinct. A few animals may still exist, but it is likely that they have disappeared.

---

# CHUMYSH HORSE

Russian: *chumyshskaya*

● 1.53 m on average.

● Often bay, black, or gray.

**Description**: The Chumysh Horse is a breed similar to the Kuznetsk and the Voronezh. It has a wide head, often with a convex profile; a wide, sloping croup; and long legs.

**Distribution**: Northeast of the Altai Mountains, in Russia.

**Origins and history**: The Chumysh Horse is the issue of crossings that took place in the nineteenth century between local horses and the Orlov Trotter, the Kuznetsk, and breeds of draft horses. These horses were used for herding livestock, but also as military horses, notably during World War II.

**Character and attributes**: It lives a long time. The mares are good milk producers and have many foals. The breed is well adapted to the very cold climate.

**Uses**: It is a saddle horse that is also suitable for light harness work.

**Current status**: This local breed is very rare, with probably fewer than 500 horses.

---

# TAVDA

Russian: *tadvinskaya*

● 1.37 m on average.

● Black/brown dun, bay, dark bay, often with a dorsal stripe and zebra striping on the legs.

**Description**: The Tavda has a broad chest, a very muscular croup, and strong legs. The hair of the mane and tail is long and thick, sometimes wavy.

**Distribution**: Northeast Sverdlovsk and western Tyumen regions, Russia.

**Origins and history**: The breed was forged by its natural environment and the rigorous climate of the regions where it lives.

**Character and attributes**: The Tavda is resistant to harsh winters and to attacks by insects.

**Uses**: This is a draft breed, used in harness and for transport.

**Current status**: Taller draft horses have been preferred to the Tavda, and it remains a local breed with small numbers.

## RUSSIA

# MEGEZH

Russian: *megezhekskoy*

**H** 1.42 m–1.53 m on average.

**C** Bay, chestnut, gray, roan, black/brown dun, buckskin.

**Description**: This is the draft horse of Yakutia. It is taller and thicker than the Yakutian, weighing between 520 kg and 600 kg.

**Distribution**: Russia, the Yakutia region.

**Origins and history**: In 2011 a new breed of Siberian horse, the Megezh, was made official and considered separate from the Yakutian. The Megezh is the result of crossings carried out in the last forty years between the Yakutian and the Kuznetsk, as well as other draft horses (including the Russian Draft) and the Orlov Trotter. The creation of this new breed is not connected to equestrian sports, but is intended to develop a Yakutian horse able to produce more meat.

**Character and attributes**: The Megezh has great endurance and is powerful, but a bit less well adapted to the Siberian climate than the Yakutian. The mares are very fertile.

**Uses**: This draft horse is raised essentially to produce meat or milk. It can of course, however, be ridden and harnessed.

**Current status**: The breed is rare because it is still being developed, but its numbers are increasing.

---

## RUSSIA

# UPPER YENISEI HORSE

Russian: *verkhne-eniseiskaya*

**H** 1.45 m–1.52 m.

**C** Bay, dark bay, chestnut, black gray.

**Description**: It resembles the Kuznetsk and the Chumysh.

**Distribution**: The Tuva Republic, Russia.

**Origins and history**: This local breed has been developed from the Tuva, the latter having been crossed with the Kuznetsk, Mongolian, Russian Draft, and Russian Trotter.

**Character and attributes**: Powerful, with great endurance, and undemanding, it is very resilient in the climate conditions of the region.

**Uses**: This is a horse traditionally used for transportation and farm work.

**Current status**: This local horse is little known elsewhere.

---

## RUSSIA

# MEZEN

Russian: *mezenko*

**H** 1.48 m–1.51 m for mares; 1.51 m–1.58 m for males.

**C** Chestnut, bay, dark bay, black, gray.

**Description**: It resembles the Pechora, but is more massive. It has a head with a wide forehead and small ears; a very muscular neck; broad chest; straight, long back; and resilient hooves. Its winter coat and undercoat are very thick.

**Distribution**: Russia, northeast of the region of Arkhangelsk and Komi.

**Origins and history**: This Siberian breed is the issue of multiple crossings, notably with Estonian, Danish, and German breeds and the Ardennais. But it is the harsh climate conditions, along with rich pastureland, that have contributed to its selection for close to two hundred years. This horse is notable for having once been used to transport fish from Arkhangelsk to Moscow and St. Petersburg.

**Character and attributes**: The Mezen has a balanced and energetic nature, and has great endurance. It is a simple horse that easily stores fat, is very resilient to the cold and insects, and is very well adapted to the Siberian climate, to the humidity and the tundra. It is very fertile and endowed with good health.

**Uses**: It is traditionally used for farm or forest work, but it is also very well suited for riding and driving. It remains a means of transportation during the long, harsh winters (notably hitched to a sleigh), and it is a good horse for equestrian tourism.

**Current status**: This once respected breed is now small in number, with probably only fewer than 4,000 individuals. After the breed began to decline, the Russians decided to revive it and have been actively breeding it.

## RUSSIA

# NEW ALTAI

Russian: *novoaltaiskaya*

**H** 1.50 m–1.56 m.

**C** Often bay, chestnut.

**Description**: This is a muscular horse weighing up to 670 kg. It has a strong head; a broad chest; a muscular, strong back; strong legs; and good hooves.
**Distribution**: Altai Mountains, Russia.
**Origins and history**: A new breed, the New Altai has been in the process of development for the last thirty years, by crossing the Altai with heavy horses

(Lithuanian, Soviet, and Russian Drafts). The goal is to conserve the rusticity of the Altai while producing a more massive horse for meat, one that can be raised in harsh climate conditions. Because it is so easy to raise, it is contributing greatly to the economy of the region.
**Character and attributes**: Powerful, it has inherited the robustness and good health of the Altai. Simple, it can endure the winter conditions without additional food, finding food in the snow.
**Uses**: It can be ridden, notably in equestrian tourism, and harnessed, but it is above all bred for its meat. The mares are good milk producers for making koumiss.
**Current status**: This local breed is still recent. The New Altai population is around 2,000 individuals.

## RUSSIA

# KUZNETSK

Russian: *kuznetskaya*

**H** 1.50 m–1.60 m; on average 1.52 m.

**C** Mainly bay, sometimes black.

**Description**: This is a relatively light draft horse. It has a big head, long ears, a very muscular neck, prominent withers, a long back, and a wide and sloping croup.
**Distribution**: Russia, notably western Siberia.
**Origins and history**: This Siberian breed was created in the eighteenth century and was developed during the nineteenth century, with crossings among local

horses and Mongolians, Belgians, Orlov Trotters, American Standardbreds, and Anglo-Normans. This was the horse of the Russian peasants who colonized Siberia. It was once used to transport goods and was prized for its resilience. The breed was also recruited by the Russian army, notably during the two world wars.
**Character and attributes**: The Kuznetsk is a horse with great endurance, very resilient in the Siberian climate, endowed with good health, longevity, and fertility. It can work late in life.
**Uses**: Initially a farm horse, it can be retrained for recreational riding.
**Current status**: The breed was decimated during World War II. It remains very rare and little known, even in Russia.

## RUSSIA

# VORONEZH COACH HORSE

Also called: Voronezh Draft

Russian: *voronezhskaya upryazhnaya*

**H** 1.62 m.

**C** Bay, roan, pinto, black.

**Description**: The British influence can still be seen in this light draft-type horse weighing around 550 kg. It has a wide forehead, a long croup, and a thick mane and tail. The breed is traditionally divided into three types, from the lightest to the heaviest.
**Distribution**: Oblast of Voronezh, Russia.

**Origins and history**: The Voronezh descends from a breed once renowned but now extinct, the Bityug, a big, heavy draft horse that disappeared as a result of over-crossing. The Bityug had been crossed with the Clydesdale and Orlov Trotter during the twentieth century with the goal of improving it, with more or less success, because some crossings caused it to lose its rusticity.
**Character and attributes**: This is an intelligent, calm, and confident horse, robust, simple, and with good endurance.
**Uses**: It is suitable for both riding and harness work.
**Current status**: Sometimes considered extinct, but a few individuals remain, which are all the more important since they still carry Bityug blood.

Opposite: The head of a Kabarda, perhaps the best mountain horse in the world.

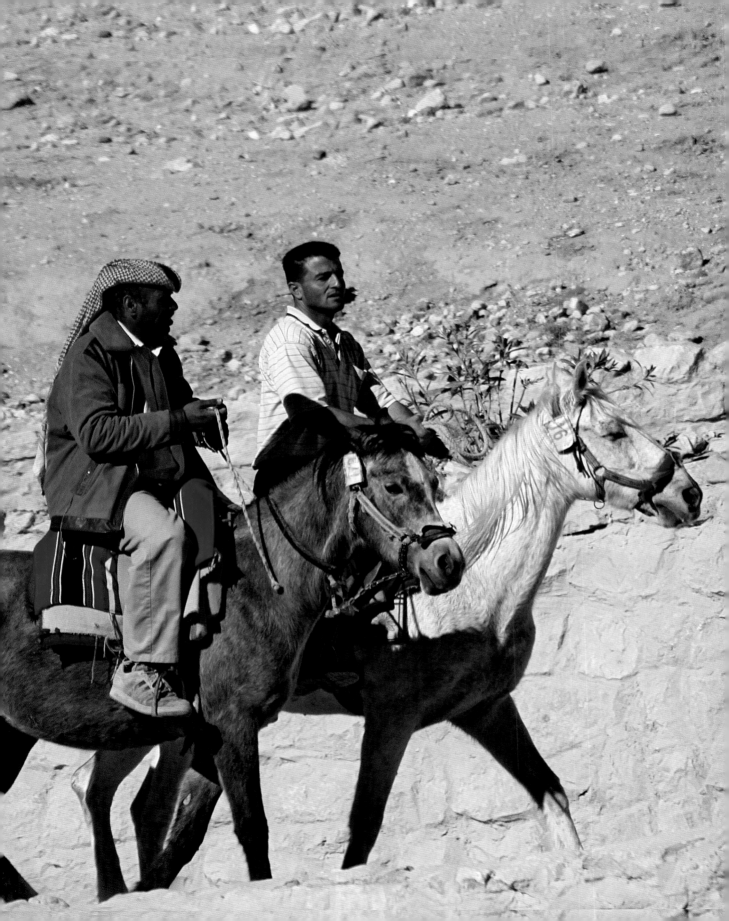

# Horses of the Middle East

*This region of the world, recognized as one of the cradles of human civilization, is also one of the most important places in the universe for horse breeds. In fact, it was on these desert lands, a very long time ago, that the small, hard hooves of one of the most legendary horse breeds appeared. The Arabian, a wonderful horse that has influenced and continues to influence a considerable number of other breeds throughout the world, was born here. It is considered to be one of the most beautiful, most ancient, and purest of breeds, endowed with many assets, and is an extraordinary improver. A wonderful horse, forever popular, it has a tendency to eclipse the other breeds of the Middle East. But the presence in Iran of the very rare and very ancient Caspian Miniature Horse, rediscovered only a few decades ago, is additional proof of the extraordinary equestrian wealth of this part of the world. Finally, and this is less well known, one also finds a number of horse breeds in Turkey.*

An Arabian stallion, with the slender and chiseled head of the Saqlawi lineage.

**Turkey**
Mytilene Pony
Anadolu (also Native Turkish Pony, Anatolian Native)
Çukurova
Rahvan (also West Black Sea Rahvan Horse)
Canik
Karakachan (also Karakacan)

Malakan
Hinis
Uzunyayla
Gemlik

**Syria**
Syrian

**Israel**

**Saudi Arabia**
Arab (also Arabian)

**Azerbaijan**
Guba
Karabakh

Deliboz
Shirvan

**Iran**
Caspian (also Caspian Miniature Horse)
Kurdi
Turkoman
Persian Arab
Tchenaran
Dareshuri

Opposite: Horsemen riding with bitless bridles, Jordan.

At the crossroads between Europe and Asia, Turkey has an interesting geographic position, but also a great variety of terrains (mountains, plains, plateaus), which is expressed in its different breeds of horses. Very little known outside their country of origin, rarely described or only vaguely assembled under the generic term "Turkish," they are, however, sometimes

---

**TURKEY**

# MYTILENE PONY

Turkish: *Ege midillisi, Ayvacik midillisi*

**H** 1.16 m–1.20 m.

**C** Mainly chestnut, also bay, sometimes gray.

**Description**: A small, stocky animal, the Mytilene has a wide forehead; a short, strong neck; a broad chest; short, strong legs; a short, round croup; and hard, wide hooves.

**Distribution**: The coasts of the Aegean Sea, Canakkale Province, northwestern Anatolia, Turkey.

**Origins and history**: This very ancient breed is originally from the island of Lesbos, where it was selected for centuries from the smallest Anadolu ponies. Its small size was notably useful and sought after for olive-picking.

**Character and attributes**: It is very docile, resilient, and undemanding, with endurance, and it has a supplementary gait, called *rahvan* in Turkish, similar to the tölt of the Icelandic horses.

**Uses**: This is a good pack horse, more docile and faster than a mule, and would make a good mount for children if it weren't so rare.

**Current status**: Endangered, this local horse had no more than 300 individuals in 2010.

---

**TURKEY**

# ANADOLU

Also called: Native Turkish Pony, Anatolian Native

Turkish: *Anadolu ati, Anadolu yerli*

**H** 1.23 m–1.35 m.

**C** Common colors, frequently with primitive markings.

**Description**: The Anadolu is a stocky horse with a small head with a variable profile (sometimes straight, sometimes concave, sometimes convex); long ears; a short, strong neck; narrow chest; sloping croup; and hard hooves. Within the breed there is a more powerful harness type, called Araba.

**Distribution**: Anatolia, Turkey.

**Origins and history**: Though little known, this breed is ancient: it is thought to be around a thousand years old. It is the result of crossings of breeds found near Turkey, such as the Turkoman, Arabian, Persian Arab, Kabarda, Karabakh, Akhal-Teke, Deliboz, and Mongolian. Crossed with the Arabian, it produces good horses for *cirit*, Turkey's traditional equestrian game (see *p. 289*).

**Character and attributes**: The Anadolu is resilient and robust. It has good endurance and is rather fast and very undemanding.

**Uses**: The breed is generally used for transportation, farm work, and as a pack and harness horse.

**Current status**: Although popular in Turkey and once widespread, this native breed has seen its numbers decrease significantly, and needs to be watched.

Crossed with the Arabian, the Anadolu makes a bold *cirit* horse, the Turkish equestrian team sport.

quite ancient. In addition to its native breeds, Turkey raises the English Thoroughbred, the Arabian, and, to a lesser degree, the Haflinger and the Nonius, among others. There were 180,000 horses recorded in 2009. They are mainly used in harness, as draft horses for farming or for recreation. A note: the Karacabey breed, sometimes described in various books, has unfortunately been extinct since the 1980s.

Very round croup

Short neck

Wide forehead

Short legs

MYTILENE PONY

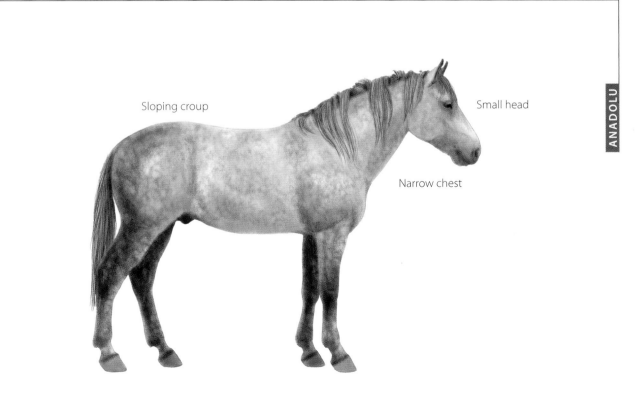

Sloping croup

Small head

Narrow chest

ANADOLU

# ÇUKUROVA

Turkish: *Çukurova*

**H** 1.37 m.

**C** Common colors.

**Description**: The Çukurova is lighter and taller than the Anadolu; it has a long head with a straight or convex profile; long ears; a long neck; narrow chest; long, sloping shoulders; and a long, sloping croup. There is a saddle type (closer to the Arabian) and a harness type (the most common).

**Distribution**: Mainly in south-central Turkey, in the provinces of Adana and Osmaniye, the plains of Çukurova.

**Origins and history**: This breed emerged from a breeding program begun in 1894 by the Ottomans. A first attempt to revive the program failed due to World War I, then it was relaunched successfully in 1935. The Çukurova is the result of crossings between the Uzunyayla, Arabian, and Anadolu.

**Character and attributes**: The Çukurova is fast and spirited.

**Uses**: It is used as a saddle and harness horse.

**Current status**: This native breed is rare.

# RAHVAN

Also called: West Black Sea Rahvan Horse

Turkish: *Rahvan, Bati Karadeniz Rahvan ati*

**H** 1.39 m.

**C** Quite variable, all common colors.

**Description**: It has a head with a straight profile; a wide forehead; large eyes; a short, muscular neck; broad chest; short back; strong legs; and solid hooves.

**Distribution**: Black Sea region, north-central Turkey.

**Origins and history**: This little-known breed is, however, very ancient, probably eight hundred years old. It is the result of crossings between Anadolus and Caniks.

**Character and attributes**: It is docile and agile and has good endurance. Thanks to its unique gait, the equivalent of the Icelandic tölt, called *rahvan* in Turkish, this horse is very comfortable to ride.

**Uses**: *Rahvan* gait races were once, and still occasionally are, held in Turkey. Today this breed makes a pleasant recreational and trekking horse.

**Current status**: The breed is not common, but its status isn't known.

Ambling races remain popular locally.

Long and sloping croup

Long ears

Long head

Narrow chest

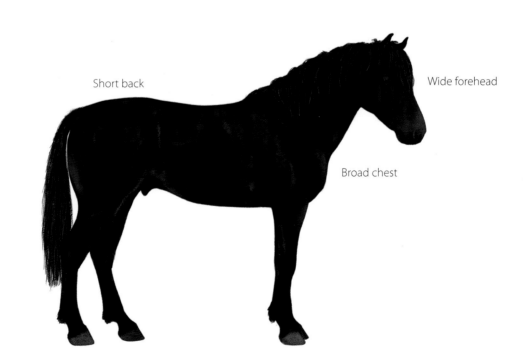

Short back

Wide forehead

Broad chest

# CANIK

Turkish: *Canik*

**H** 1.32 m–1.45 m.

**C** Mainly bay, common colors.

**Description**: The Canik is very similar to the Anadolu, but is taller. It has a head with a straight profile, a wide forehead, large eyes, a slightly sloping croup, and strong legs. The hair of the mane and tail is thick and sometimes wavy.

**Distribution**: Northeastern Turkey, near the Black Sea.

**Origins and history**: This ancient Turkish breed has received the influence of cavalry horses from the Caucasus. Some Caniks are bred to create a variety of Anadolu.

**Character and attributes**: The Canik is not always known to be good-natured; it can be nervous, but it is an energetic and fast horse, and a sure-footed one. It has a supplementary gait.

**Uses**: It is above all a saddle horse, best for an experienced rider due to its temperament.

**Current status**: Rather rare, this native breed should be watched.

---

# KARAKACHAN

Also called: Karakacan

Turkish: *Karakaçan*

Bulgarian: *Karakachanski kon*

**H** 1.44 m–1.55 m.

**C** Mainly bay, sometimes chestnut and black.

**Description**: This light draft horse has a long head with a slightly convex profile; a wide forehead; small eyes; a short, muscular neck; sloping shoulders; prominent withers; a broad chest; short, wide back; long, slightly sloping croup; short, solid legs; and hard hooves.

**Distribution**: Turkey (especially Anatolia); it is also found in Bulgaria (the Balkan and Rhodope mountains).

**Origins and history**: An ancient breed, the Karakachan is the result of crossings between Trakya Horses and horses brought to Turkey from France, Hungary, Romania, Bulgaria, and elsewhere.

**Character and attributes**: The Karakachan is very strong and active.

**Uses**: It is used as a saddle or harness horse, and for transportation. It is well suited for equestrian tourism.

**Current status**: The breed has suffered from being over-crossed and pure individuals are rare. Fortunately, its numbers are growing in Bulgaria, with 2,500 animals in 2013.

Sometimes wavy
mane and tail

Large eyes

Strong legs

Long, slightly
sloping croup

Slightly convex
profile

Long head

# MALAKAN

Turkish: *Malakan*

**H** 1.35 m–1.42 m.

**C** Mainly bay, then gray, sometimes chestnut, sometimes black, occasionally bay dun.

**Description**: The Malakan is a massive horse, with a short, muscular neck; a broad chest; a wide back and croup; large barrel; and strong legs.

**Distribution**: Northeastern Turkey (Kars and Ardahan provinces).

**Origins and history**: This horse, the only draft breed in Turkey, was developed in the nineteenth century. The Malakan has Shire, Clydesdale, Percheron, Ardennais, Orlov, and Anadolu ancestors. It has received Haflinger blood, as well.

**Character and attributes**: With an easy and calm nature, the Malakan is very strong and has great endurance, and it tolerates cold temperatures very well.

**Uses**: This horse is intended for pulling and is traditionally used for harness and farm work.

**Current status**: Once common, this native horse, like other draft horses, has suffered from the advent of mechanization. It is now considered endangered.

 TURKEY

# HINIS

Turkish: *Hinis ati, Hinis'n kolu kisasi*

**H** 1.35 m–1.38 m.

**C** Mainly bay, but all common colors are possible.

**Description**: The Hinis has a typically Arabian head, with a wide forehead; wide-spaced eyes; small ears; a short, wide neck; a particularly broad chest; very short forelegs; and hard, black hooves. The tail has abundant hair and is set high.

**Distribution**: Province of Erzurum, northeastern Anatolia, on the border of the Caucasus, Turkey.

**Origins and history**: The Hinis is the result of Arabian, Turkish, or Iraqi horses crossed with the Anadolu at the end of the nineteenth century. In Turkish, the breed's name means "horse with short front legs."

**Character and attributes**: This is a bold, very agile, fast horse with good endurance and an excellent ability to recover after effort.

**Uses**: It is above all a saddle horse, suitable notably for the Turkish game of *cirit*, for which it was once used a lot and in which it has now been replaced by horses with more Arabian blood.

**Current status**: According to the FAO and Turkish authorities, the Hinis became extinct within the past fifty years. Others believe the breed is not extinct; a few individuals remain and they should urgently be protected from extinction.

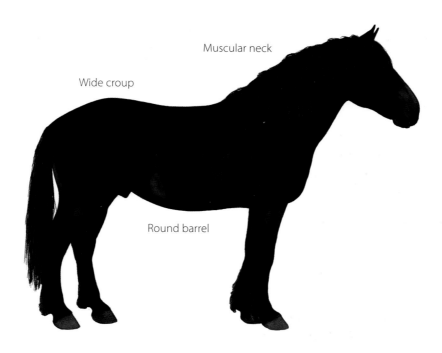

Muscular neck

Wide croup

Round barrel

**Current status**: Very rare, not officially recognized; it is possible that this breed is on the brink of extinction, or is already extinct.

# UZUNYAYLA

Turkish: *Uzunyayla, Çerkes, Çerkez ati*

Ⓗ 1.40 m–1.55 m.

Ⓒ Generally bay, also black and gray.

**Description**: The Uzunyayla has a wide head with a concave profile; small eyes; prominent withers; a long back; a short, sloping croup; and strong legs. It has a thick hide and long, thick mane and tail.

**Distribution**: Provinces of Sivas and Kayseri, east-central Turkey.

**Origins and history**: Developed in the middle of the nineteenth century, the Uzunyayla is probably the result of Kabardas imported to Turkey, and later (1930) crossed with Anadolu and Nonius horses.

**Character and attributes**: The Uzunyayla is reputed to be very intelligent and friendly with its rider. It has good endurance.

**Uses**: It is suitable for both riding and driving and is used as a pack horse.

## TURKEY

# GEMLIK

We should also point out a recent sport horse breed, the Gemlik, developed at the Gemlik Military Veterinary School and Education Center, in the Marmara region in Turkey. The Gemlik was born in the 1970s from a rigorous selection starting in 1941 with a foundation of Nonius, Karacabey, and Turkish Arabian blood, to which in 1962 were added Karacabey/Nonius and Karacabey. The breed has only been registered since 2002. It is essentially bred for competition, notably show jumping. The breed is in the process of development, and thus is still small in number.

## TURKEY

### THE ALACA, A PINTO HORSE TO BE STUDIED

A population of pinto horses (*alaca*) in northeastern Turkey, small and particularly placid, seem distinct from other Turkish breeds and might have come from American breeds (Paint, Pinto). This population still remains to be studied.

# Syria

When one travels through Syria, that magnificent country now ravaged by war, one encounters very few horses, but much more often donkeys or camels. There is only one native breed, the Syrian. Syria

## SYRIA

# SYRIAN

**ⓗ** 1.48 m–1.58 m.
**ⓒ** Chestnut, light bay, gray.

**Description**: The Syrian is a more rustic and slightly taller Arabian horse, a desert horse whose selection has not been as rigorous as that of the Arabian. While being of Arabian type, the head is not as slender, and the overall appearance is more muted. The hide and the mane and tail are fine and silky.

**Distribution**: Syria.
**Origins and history**: This is an Arabian-type horse, a traditional mount of Syrian Bedouins, and it can still be found among them.
**Character and attributes**: The Syrian is an energetic, resilient, undemanding horse with good endurance and longevity. It is well adapted to life in semi-desert environments.
**Uses**: It is raised for sport, notably for speed or endurance races, or as a simple saddle horse.
**Current status**: Given the political situation in Syria, it is difficult to know how the breed is doing, but probably not very well.

# Israel

We should point out that there is a population of indigenous horses in Israel (the Israeli Horse), the result of many crossings (Thoroughbred, Fjord, Quarter Horse, Waler, and others), with a strong foundation of Arabian. Measuring 1.42 m–1.52 m, mainly gray, but also bay and chestnut, the Israeli has a somewhat variable morphology, with a fairly long head, a rather narrow chest, and a short back. It is an energetic saddle horse, manageable and docile, resistant to illness and well adapted to the heat. Its breeding is not organized.

## HAS THE TRAKYA COMPLETELY DISAPPEARED?

The Trakya (also known as the Rumelian Pony) is considered to be extinct by the FAO. The breed is, however, mentioned in reports dating some dozen years ago. If the extinction is recent, one is led to believe that there might still exist animals with similar characteristics, especially since a population of not yet recognized Thracian horses is being studied in Greece. The Trakya is the result of ancient crossings among Anadolus and native horses from Thrace. A bit taller than the Anadolu (1.40 m–1.45 m), it has a short neck, narrow chest, and strong legs. It is powerful, has endurance, is undemanding, and is suitable as a saddle, harness, or pack horse. It is originally from Thrace in Turkey.

## CIRIT

This is not a breed, but a prized type of horse bred for the traditional Turkish equestrian sport of *cirit* (sometimes called *jeered*), played by two teams of 6, 8, or 12 players, in which the riders must touch each other with light javelins, protected by a rubber tip to avoid injury (this sport was once dangerous, and remains fairly risky). These horses are the result of crossings among Arabian, Karabair, and Anadolu horses. They are good sport horses, agile and responsive. Some consider this type of horse to be a breed.

does, of course, breed Arabians, whose stallions were greatly prized and exported at the beginning of the nineteenth century, notably to Great Britain and France. Given the current political situation, it is difficult to know the status of the equine livestock, which must, like the Syrian population, be suffering enormously from the war. A few years ago it was possible to encounter a Bedouin with his horse.

Bedouins have a very strong connection with their horses.

Fine mane and tail

Large eyes

SYRIAN

Saudi Arabia is the land of the Arabian breed, which is now found almost everywhere in the world. It might seem surprising that one of the best breeds of horse that has ever existed was born in such desert lands. But it is indeed there, among the Bedouins who have bred it with care and intelligence, that this resilient, fast horse with great endurance was forged. Saudi Arabia continues to take great care in the breeding of its horses.

# ARAB

Also called: Arabian

Arabic: 'arabia

A poetic name for it is "one who drinks the wind."

Ⓗ 1.45 m–1.56 m.

Ⓒ Mainly gray, light gray, often chestnut, but also bay, brownish bay, and black, roan. Pinto is not accepted.

**Description**: This very refined horse, very pure and quite unique, is instantly recognizable. It is not very tall. It has a small, slender head with a straight or sometimes concave profile, sometimes very noticeable in some individuals; wide, sometimes slightly rounded forehead; slender nose with large nostrils; large, protruding, expressive eyes; small ears (sometimes long in mares); a light, arched neck; a broad chest; well-defined withers; slightly sloping shoulders; a short back and flanks (some individuals have the unique characteristic of having only 5 lumbar vertebrae and 17 pairs of ribs instead of 6 and 18 for other breeds); a very slim barrel; a horizontal croup; a short, very high-set tail carried with flair; long, slender, solid legs; and small, hard hooves. Its skin is very fine and one can see the veins; it has fine and silky hair, but a long and sufficiently thick mane and tail. The thinness of the skin sometimes makes it sensitive during grooming. There are three original strains: the Koheilan (or Kuhaylan), compact and powerful; the Saqlawi (or Siglavi), light and slender; and the Muniqi (or Maneghi, or Miniqi), a racing type, taller, less refined, out of which several maternal lineages (including the Koheilan, Hamdani, Muniqi, Saqlawi, Dahman, Abbeyan, and Hadban) have issued, as well as various types. The pure lineages are called "Asil," the others "Arabian horse."

**Distribution**: The Arabian Peninsula (Saudi Arabia, Yemen, Oman, United Arab Emirates, Qatar), North Africa, Egypt, Iran, Syria, and elsewhere around the world.

**Origins and history**: This is one of the most ancient breeds in the world, existing probably for three thousand years and prized for its beauty and great sporting abilities. The Arabian was for a long time a war horse. It has had an extraordinary influence on a great number of horse breeds, and has been the most used "improver" in the world. For centuries Arabs have practiced a rigorous selection for this horse, which was cherished by the prophet Muhammad and which they venerate, forbidding crossings with other breeds. Mares were particularly sought after as mounts.

**Character and attributes**: The Arabian is intelligent, sensitive, lively but docile, and bold. It is easily handled, can carry heavy loads, has exceptional endurance, and is fast. It is undemanding, and lives a long time. An animal forged by the desert, it can withstand high temperatures. It has light gaits.

**Uses**: This is the endurance horse par excellence, but it is versatile and suited to many equestrian disciplines, both for recreation and competition, as well as to light harness work. There are speed races especially conceived for the Arabian. It is also a show animal; its particular beauty fascinates many people, and it is also used in circuses. Arabian blood is often used to improve other breeds.

**Current status**: The breed is doing very well because it remains one of the most popular and sought after in the world, with animals selling for enormous sums. All the same, the purebred lineages must be carefully watched.

### A SMALL NUMBER OF ARABIANS IN YEMEN

We don't know the exact number of horses in Yemen, but in 2003 Yemeni specialists estimated that the equine population was decreasing, with probably fewer than 2,000 horses (approximately 1,337 animals). The minister of agriculture of the Republic of Yemen records six lineages of Arabians (Abbeyan, Dahman, Jofi or al-Jawf, Abu'urquob or Omarqub, Saqlawi, Chuwayman or Shweimaa). The Arabians of Yemen are rather tall (around 1.52 m). Currently these horses are above all used for work, and occasionally for recreation.

To gallop on a richly decorated purebred Arabian is still a sign of prestige.

The Arabian has a wide forehead, large eyes, and flaring nostrils.

The bulging forehead is particularly noticeable in young foals; it becomes less pronounced as they grow.

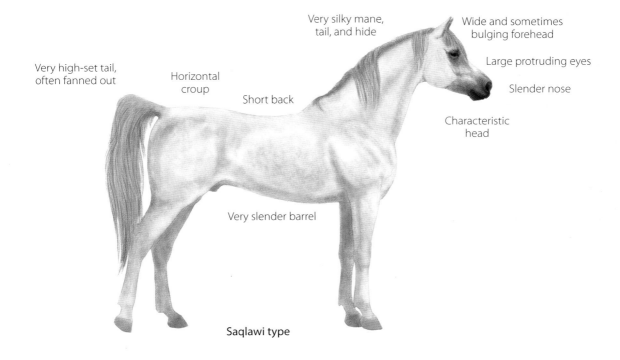

Very silky mane, tail, and hide

Wide and sometimes bulging forehead

Large protruding eyes

Slender nose

Very high-set tail, often fanned out

Horizontal croup

Short back

Characteristic head

Very slender barrel

**Saqlawi type**

**Saqlawi type,**
the most slender

**Koheilan type,**
more compact

**Muniqi type,**
taller, for racing

The history of the horse in Azerbaijan goes back several thousand years, since this country is in the cradle where the species was domesticated. Archeological digs have found bones of horses in locations of human

---

## AZERBAIJAN

# GUBA

Azeri: *Quba yor asi*

Ⓗ 1.36 m on average.

Ⓒ Mainly bay, sometimes gray, black, chestnut, buckskin, bay dun.

**Description**: The Guba is smaller than the other breeds in Azerbaijan, rather slender, but of robust constitution. It has a head with a straight profile; large eyes; a rather long neck; prominent withers; slender, short, solid legs; and a low-set tail.

**Distribution**: The breed is spread over the mountains of the Greater Caucasus, in Azerbaijan, notably in the Guba-Haçmaz, Abseron, and Shamakhi districts.

**Origins and history**: The Guba was probably influenced by the Persian and the Karabakh, and later improved with Tersk and Arabian blood. Today it receives Karabakh and Deliboz blood.

**Character and attributes**: The Guba is very resilient; it has great endurance, good longevity, and fertility. It has the sure-footedness of a mountain horse. Many individuals are natural amblers. It is well adapted to its environment and is not very demanding.

**Uses**: In spite of its small size, it is used under saddle, in harness, and as a pack horse.

**Current status**: This horse, widespread in the nineteenth century, has seen its numbers fall, but can still be found in its native land.

---

## AZERBAIJAN

# KARABAKH

Azeri: *Qaraba*

Ⓗ 1.38 m–1.40 m, can reach 1.54 m.

Ⓒ Most often chestnut, bay dun, golden buckskin with dorsal striping and very dark legs, bay, gray, with characteristic golden or silver metallic highlights.

**Description**: This well-proportioned horse has a small, slender head with a straight profile; large, expressive eyes; a wide forehead that becomes more slender at the nose; a powerful neck; broad chest; long, slender, solid legs; wide, muscular croup; low-set tail; slender, short legs; and resilient hooves. It has thin skin and a soft, shiny hide, with fine, silky, fairly thin mane and tail. There are two types, one more massive than the other.

**Distribution**: The mountains of Upper Karabakh, in Azerbaijan; a small number in Iran; a few in the United Kingdom.

**Origins and history**: The Karabakh, the oldest saddle and mountain horse in Azerbaijan, is the issue of a very ancient breed. It was influenced from the middle of the eighteenth century by the Arabian, Persian, and Akhal-Teke, from which it inherited its coat with golden highlights. It has itself influenced other breeds, including the Don (Russia) and the Kabarda (Russia, Georgia), and was used as a stud horse in Iran, Iraq, and

Egypt.

**Character and attributes**: The Karabakh is an energetic horse, fast and agile, though still calm. It is also resilient and rustic, and has good endurance. It has comfortable gaits and the very sure-footedness of mountain breeds.

**Uses**: This is a good saddle and pack horse, used for trekking but also for dressage or speed and endurance racing. Considered excellent, the breed is also used to improve other breeds.

**Current status**: Although once very admired and widespread, the breed has practically disappeared, having suffered notably from the Armenian-Azerbaijani border conflict (the Nagorno-Karabakh War). It is still very threatened and rare, in spite of serious conservation efforts, with slightly more than 130 individuals remaining. There are a few in Iran (around 200 in 2004).

The Karabakh is full of energy.

occupation as early as the fifth millennium BC. The Azerbaijan horse is divided into three types: breeds from the Lesser Caucasus, the Karabakh and the Deliboz (the best known breeds in the country), which are of average height; horses of the Greater Caucasus (the Guba), which are smaller; and a heavier type of plains horse, the Shirvan. In 2012 it was estimated that the total number of horses was around 75,000.

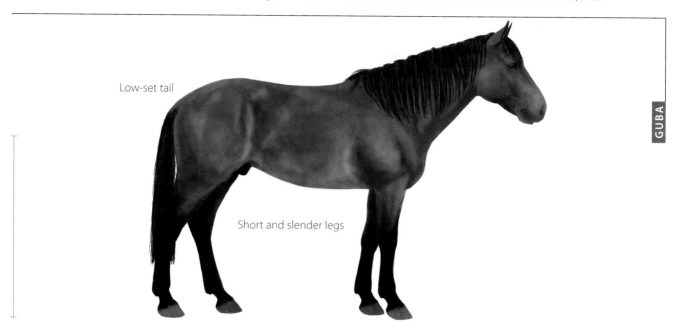

Low-set tail

Short and slender legs

GUBA

Fine and silky coat

Slender head

Broad chest

KARABAKH

# DELIBOZ

Azeri: *Dilbaz*

**H** 1.35 m–1.40 m for mares; 1.37 m–1.52 m for males.

**C** Usually gray, bay, dark bay, black, often mealy, sometimes buckskin, bay dun, often with light hooves.

**Description**: It is taller than the Karabakh, which it resembles. It has a short head with a wide forehead and slender nose; a rather thick, compact neck; broad chest; massive body; and long croup. An unusual feature is a peculiar lengthwise fold on the tongue that gives the impression that the tongue is forked.
**Distribution**: Notably the Ganja-Kazakh and Shaki-Zagataia Regions in Azerbaijan.
**Origins and history**: A descendant of the ancient native horses of Azerbaijan, and notably of the Karabakh, the Deliboz was developed at the end of the eighteenth century through crossings between the Persian Arab and the Turkoman (now extinct). It received influence from the Tersk and Arabian breeds in the middle of the twentieth century.
**Character and attributes**: Its character is not always reliable; it is sometimes nervous, but good individuals are simply very energetic. It is an agile horse, has good endurance, and can carry a large load. It has good health and fertility, and is resilient for life in the mountains. Some individuals are natural amblers.
**Uses**: It is suitable for saddle and light harness.
**Current status**: This native horse has sometimes been listed as extinct; it is actually quite rare.

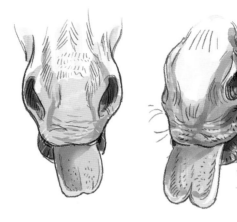

On the left, a tongue of a typical horse; on the right, the tongue of the Deliboz. In the Deliboz, the lengthwise fold in the middle of the tongue is a bit more evident (this sometimes occurs in other breeds too).

# SHIRVAN

Azeri: *irvan*

**H** 1.40 m on average.

**C** Mainly bay, dark bay, and chestnut.

**Description**: Of robust constitution, it is more massive than most mountain breeds.
**Distribution**: Widespread on the plains of Kur-Araz, Azerbaijan. It is found mainly in the districts of Agdash, Goychay, Kurdamir, and Ucar in Shirvan.
**Origins and history**: Locally this breed is considered a hybrid type of Karabakh. The breeding conditions on the farming plains of Kur-Araz are better than in the mountains, and enable the breed to grow bigger.
**Character and attributes**: The Shirvan is well adapted to rustic living conditions.
**Uses**: Because of its strength, it is suitable for work in harness and as a draft horse.
**Current status**: Popular at the beginning of the twentieth century, its numbers have been declining.

Long croup

Wide forehead

Broad chest

There were 155,000 horses in Iran in 2004. In addition to the Arabian, which is quite widespread throughout the Middle East and one of whose most ancient lineages can be found in Iran, this country

---

IRAN

# CASPIAN

Also called: Caspian Miniature Horse

Persian: *mouleki*

**H** 1.17 m on average; from 0.96 m–1.20 m.

**C** Chestnut, bay or gray, more rarely bay dun, black, generally without white markings, often with shiny highlights in the summer.

**Description**: Sometimes very small, the Caspian looks like a miniature Arabian. It has a small Arabian head, with a straight or slightly concave profile; large, prominent, almond-shaped eyes; very small ears; a broad, bulging forehead; a slender nose with large nostrils; arched neck; prominent withers; sloping shoulders; long, slightly sloping croup; high-set tail; slender, resilient legs; and small, oval-shaped hooves with extremely resilient horn. The skin is fine; the hair of the mane and tail is smooth, thick, silky, and long.
**Distribution**: Northern Iran, United Kingdom, United States, Australia, New Zealand.

**Origins and history**: For centuries it was believed that the breed was extinct, until it was rediscovered in 1965. This is one of the most ancient of breeds, perhaps even older than the Arabian; some believe that the Caspian is an ancestor of the Arabian. It could be the direct issue of a primitive Eastern ancestor. An American woman rediscovered this small breed in the Elbrus mountain range, on the coast of the Caspian Sea, and had a few of the horses exported.
**Character and attributes**: It is very intelligent, sensitive, and lively, but docile, easy to handle, with light gaits. It is an excellent jumper.
**Uses**: Once a farm and pack horse, it is an ideal saddle horse for children; its easy nature makes it a good horse for teaching beginners, and its sporting abilities are the delight of more advanced riders.
**Current status**: Although rare, the breed is protected and has been able to develop in the last few decades. Its beauty and attributes ensure its breeding, and the Caspian is no longer threatened with extinction. In 2004 there were 700 throughout the world, with 500 in Iran.

---

IRAN

# KURDI

Persian: *kurdi*

Known in Turkey as *Do u Anadolu* (Anadolu of the East)
**H** 1.40 m–1.50 m.

**C** Light gray, chestnut, bay, rarely black; all colors are possible.

**Description**: This elegant and solid horse is the Eastern type, similar to the Persian Arab: it has a straight head with a wide forehead, large eyes, a sloping croup, and hard hooves. There are four types of Kurdi: Jaf, Afshari, Sanjabi, and Kalhor.
**Distribution**: Mainly Iran, the mountainous region of Kurdistan (northwestern Iran, southeastern Turkey, northeastern Iraq, northern Syria).
**Origins and history**: The Kurdi, which derives its name from the Iranian Kurds, has received blood from the Persian Arab and Turkish horses.

**Character and attributes**: The Kurdi is a lively and very resilient horse, with good endurance. It is perfectly adapted to life in the desert and mountain regions of Iran.
**Uses**: It is essentially a saddle horse; versatile, it is also used as a pack horse and for farm work.
**Current status**: In 2004 there were 2,700 Kurdis in Iran. It is becoming increasingly rare in Turkey.

has its own breeds, some very ancient, others more recent. Its equestrian heritage deserves to be studied more closely. Starting in antiquity, Persia was well known for its breeding of native horses. The very small Caspian, rediscovered in 1965 and considered to be one of the most ancient horse breeds, is one of its jewels. The Karabakh (see Azerbaijan, *p. 292*) is also present in small numbers.

CASPIAN

Silky hide, mane, and tail

Bulging forehead

High-set tail

This very ancient breed has proven to be excellent in show jumping.

Small, extremely resilient hooves

KURDI

Sloping croup

Arabian-type head

# TURKOMAN

Persian: *turkemin*

ⓗ Around 1.53 m.

ⓒ Bay, dark bay, gray, black, chestnut.

**Description**: The Turkoman has a long head with a straight profile; long ears; large eyes; wide forehead; slender nose; a light, sometimes "stag-like" neck; sloping shoulders; a straight back; long, sloping croup; slender barrel; very slender, long, solid legs; and small hooves. It has thin skin, thin hide; the mane and tail are fine, silky, and not very thick.

**Distribution**: Iran (everywhere, but especially in the northeast, Aqqala and Gombad-e-kavus regions); Turkmenistan.

**Origins and history**: The ancient Turkoman, which has influenced many other horse breeds, is extinct, but there are still horses called by this name in Iran. The Iomud and the Akhal-Teke are sometimes also called Turkoman horses, the name designating a type of Eastern horse different from the Arabian. Like them, the modern Turkoman descends from those ancient Turkoman horses. But the latter has sometimes been crossed with English Thoroughbreds in order to increase its speed, and so one sometimes speaks of the "Turkoman Thoroughbred." Herds have been returned to the wild.

**Character and attributes**: It is intelligent, lively, has great endurance, and is fast. It is an excellent galloper.

**Uses**: The Turkoman is a saddle horse, prized especially for speed racing, which is very popular in Iran, in Gonbad-e Kavus.

**Current status**: It is very rare, with around 400 horses in 2004, having sometimes undergone too much crossbreeding with the English Thoroughbred.

# PERSIAN ARAB

Persian: *tazi*

ⓗ Around 1.50 m.

ⓒ Bay, chestnut, or gray, rarely black.

**Description**: This is a tall Arabian (see Arab, *p. 290*).

**Distribution**: Mainly in southwest Iran.

**Origins and history**: This is a very ancient lineage of Arabians (believed to go back 2,000 years), rather tall for a desert horse.

**Character and attributes**: It has the lively temperament of the Arabian, as well as its speed and adaptability to living conditions in the desert.

**Uses**: It is primarily a saddle horse.

**Current status**: It is not very common, with only a thousand horses remaining.

# TCHENARAN

Persian: *tchenârâni*

ⓗ Around 1.50 m.

ⓒ All colors are possible.

**Description**: This is a Persian halfblood, very elegant, which looks like the Persian Arabian, but with a sloping croup.

**Distribution**: Iran.

**Origins and history**: Bred for more than three hundred years, but perhaps even older, this breed is the result of crossings among Persian Arab stallions and Turkoman mares. The idea was to create a very fast race horse with good endurance.

**Character and attributes**: The Tchenaran is energetic, resilient, and robust, has great endurance, and is well adapted to life in desert environments.

**Uses**: It is essentially a saddle horse.

**Current status**: The breed has become very rare.

Long ears

Fine skin

Long head

Very slender legs

Small hooves

IRAN

# DARESHURI

Persian: *dareh shuri*

**Ⓗ** Around 1.50 m–1.55 m.

**Ⓒ** Chestnut, bay, light gray, rarely black; often white markings on the legs.

**Description**: This elegant horse is a type of Persian Arab, with an Arabian-type head; a light, thin body; slender legs; a high-set tail; hard hooves; and a fine and silky mane, tail, and hide.
**Distribution**: Southern Iran, Shiraz region.
**Origins and history**: This horse was developed from the Persian Arab.
**Character and attributes**: It is lively, fast, resilient, with very good endurance.
**Uses**: It is a saddle horse.
**Current status**: Very rare; there were only 400 horses in 2003.

IRAN

## OTHER IRANIAN BREEDS

For Iran, we should also point out the Pahlavan, a breed started and bred by the shah in the 1950s, created from mixes of Persian Arab, Thoroughbred, and horses from the Iranian plateau, of Kurdi or Dareshuri type, with the goal of creating a good sport horse, specifically for show jumping. This Persian Arabian halfblood, slightly taller than other native horses (1.52 m–1.60 m), is hardly mentioned in Iran anymore, and the animals have perhaps been absorbed into other breeds. As for the Taleshi, this is a breed of around 4,500 horses (in 2004) scattered over the Iranian plateau and about which we don't know very much. The Yabu is a type of horse present in both Afghanistan and Iran. The name designates a horse of little value, less refined than the other breeds raised in Iran. Much research on native breeds in Iran still remains to be done.

# Horses of Central Asia

*Another cradle of the equestrian world: Central Asia, where one finds two of the most legendary breeds in the world, the small, indomitable Mongolian horses and the amazing Akhal-Teke with its golden hues. Also in Central Asia, and more specifically in Mongolia, one finds Przewalski's Horse, living in the wild since being reintroduced into its original environment after disappearing from it years ago. These countries of mountains and vast steppes are excellent for breeding horses in the semi-wild. The plains of Kazakhstan and Mongolia are thus scattered with herds of horses grazing, surviving alone, and enduring sometimes extreme climate conditions. Thus it is no coincidence that the breeds of Central Asia are known for their great endurance and robustness.*

**Turkmenistan**
Yamud (also Yomood)
Akhal-Teke
**Uzbekistan**
Karabair
**Kyrgyzstan**
Kyrgyz (also Local
  Kyrgyz)
New Kyrgyz
**Tajikistan**
Lokai
Tajik (also Tajik Riding
  Horse)

**Afghanistan**
Afghan
**Kazakhstan**
Kazakh
Kushum (also West
  Kazakh Saddle-
  Draft)
Kustanai
Mugalzhar
**Mongolia**
Mongolian
New Mongolian

A Mongolian rider going to round up his herd.

*Opposite: In Mongolia, the horse is still an indispensable ally for herding livestock.*

In 2004 Turkmenistan had an equine population estimated at slightly fewer than 30,000 horses, quite far behind the thriving numbers of its Kazakh and Mongolian neighbors. But the horses of Turkmenistan

TURKMENISTAN

# YAMUD

Also called: Yomood

Russian: *iomudskaya*

**H** 1.49 m on average for mares; 1.52 m for males.

**C** Most often gray, but also chestnut or golden bay, sometimes black.

**Description**: Resembling the Akhal-Teke, the Yamud is less slender. It has a large head with a straight or sometimes convex profile; large eyes; a rather long neck; sloping shoulders; prominent withers; a slim barrel; long, slender legs; fine hair; and a fine, sparse mane and tail.

**Distribution**: Mainly in the Daşoguz Province, Turkmenistan; Iran.

**Origins and history**: Like the Akhal-Teke, the Yamud descends from ancient Turkoman horses and probably received Arabian blood in the past. It is still bred in arid zones.

**Character and attributes**: This is a fast and energetic horse, with great endurance; it is an excellent jumper. It is very resilient in both cold and hot climates, easy to keep, undemanding, and long-lived.

**Uses**: It excels in endurance racing, but is also suited to other sports.

**Current status**: The Yamud is the most widespread breed in Turkmenistan, even if it is little known elsewhere. It has nevertheless seen its numbers decline in the past few decades, which has caused the authorities to pay attention to the rigorous breeding of purebred animals.

TURKMENISTAN

# AKHAL-TEKE

Russian: *akhal-tekinskaya*

**H** 1.57 m for mares; 1.58 m for males.

**C** Buckskin or golden bay dun with black points, bay, gray, chestnut, black. It is known for its characteristic and particularly striking golden or silver metallic shimmer, a quality rare among other horses. White markings are frequent on the legs and head.

**Description**: Extremely elegant and sleek, the Akhal-Teke can be recognized at first sight. Its head is slender and long, with a wide forehead; it has large, almond-shaped eyes; long ears; a straight profile; and wide nostrils. It has a long, very slender, very high-set neck; prominent withers; a somewhat narrow chest; sloping shoulders; a slim barrel; slender, very long legs; a sloping croup; low-set tail; and hard hooves. Its skin is extremely fine. In its country it is often protected by thick blankets which contribute to keeping its hair very short. It has a sparse mane and tail, and the hair is very fine. It is sometimes said that the Akhal-Teke is to horses what the greyhound is to dogs. One of its varieties is called *goklan*.

**Distribution**: Turkmenistan, Russia, Kazakhstan, Kirghizstan, Uzbekistan, Iran, a few in Europe (England, France, Germany, Austria).

**Origins and history**: This breed, among the most ancient, a descendant of the ancient Turkoman horses, was once a fearsome war horse admired for its speed and endurance. It is the object of curious traditions in its country (protein-rich feed, protected with felt blankets). The breed has influenced many saddle breeds, notably the Thoroughbred.

**Character and attributes**: This exceptional horse probably has the best endurance of any breed in the world. Its uncommon resilience enables it to tolerate the most diverse climates, from extreme heat to extreme cold. This resilience and hardiness, to which is added great longevity, are rare in such a sport and competitive breed. It is very fast, has light gaits, and is a good jumper. Its nature is delicate and sensitive, and it is best for experienced riders. It is said that it is a one-rider horse.

**Uses**: This racehorse excels in endurance races, where it has held various records throughout history, because its running works with its breathing. But it is also suitable for show jumping, dressage, and eventing.

**Current status**: An animal venerated in Turkmenistan and increasingly admired abroad, the Akhal-Teke, though it remains a rare breed, is no longer endangered.

are very pampered saddle and sport animals, and thus considered a luxury. One of its breeds, the Akhal-Teke, has acquired an international reputation and probably remains to this day one of the most prodigious of horses. It represents about 8 percent of all horses in Turkmenistan (around 2,300). The rest of the animals are essentially Yamuds, a much more common horse in this country, but little known elsewhere.

Fine, sparse mane and tail

Large eyes

Slim barrel

YAMUD

Yamud in traditional decoration.

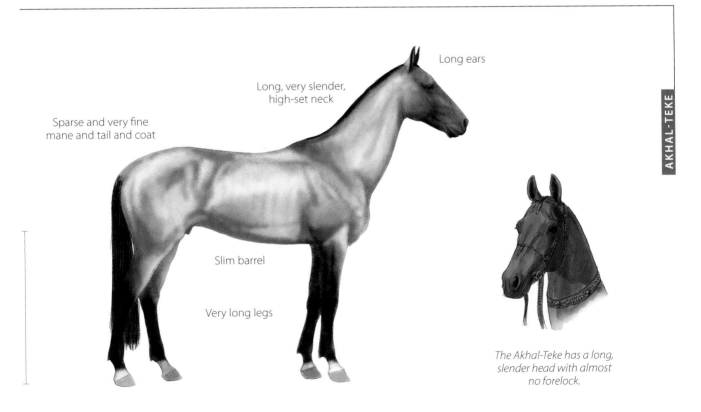

Long ears

Long, very slender, high-set neck

Sparse and very fine mane and tail and coat

AKHAL-TEKE

Slim barrel

Very long legs

*The Akhal-Teke has a long, slender head with almost no forelock.*

# Uzbekistan

Only one breed of horse originates in Uzbekistan, the Karabair. In 2003 there were slightly more than 145,000 horses in the country, mostly Karabairs. The Uzbek nomads continue to use horses, notably for milk and meat, and *kokpar* (equivalent of the Afghani *buzkashi*) is still a popular equestrian sport for which the Karabair's endurance is greatly appreciated.

UZBEKISTAN

## KARABAIR

Not to be confused with the Karabakh.

Uzbek: *karabair*

Russian: *karabairskaya*

Ⓗ 1.49 m on average for mares; 1.52 m for males.

Ⓒ Often gray, chestnut or bay, more rarely dark bay and black, sometimes spotted or bay dun.

**Description**: This is a thin horse with a straight or convex profile; a thin, muscular neck; prominent withers; a short back; round croup; slender legs; and a high-set tail. There are more or less heavy types.

**Distribution**: Uzbekistan. Also present in Kazakhstan and Tajikistan (notably in the north, in the Sughd Region and the Fergana Valley), but they are also found in Afghanistan and India.

**Origins and history**: This very ancient Central Asian breed is the result of crossings among desert horses (Arabian, Turkoman, Persian) and horses of the Mongolian steppes (Mongolians, Kazakhs), and probably Kyrgyz and the extinct breed Argamak.

**Character and attributes**: It is docile, simple, and robust.

**Uses**: This is a good horse for sport or in harness. The mares are good milk producers (for koumiss). It is also raised for its meat.

**Current status**: The breed is doing fine in its country.

# Kyrgyzstan

In Kyrgyzstan, where horses have always been intimately connected to the life of nomadic horse breeders, the horse population is growing, with around 380,000 animals, after a drop in its numbers during the Soviet era. Horses are primarily raised

KYRGYZSTAN

## KYRGYZ

Also called: Local Kyrgyz

Russian: *kirgizskaya*

Ⓗ 1.37 m–1.49 m at most; often an average of 1.45 m.

Ⓒ Variable. Mainly bay, chestnut, sometimes gray, black, bay dun, roan, chestnut roan.

**Description**: The Kyrgyz has a rather short head with a straight or slightly convex profile; small ears; wide, muscular neck; short, straight shoulders; short back; solid legs; sloping, wide croup; low-set tail; small, very hard hooves. The hair of the mane and tail is thick and abundant, the winter coat is very dense.

**Distribution**: Kyrgyzstan, with a large population in China, a few in Kazakhstan and Tajikistan.

**Origins and history**: The breed is believed to come from native horses crossed with Mongolians. This is the horse of the nomads of Kyrgyzstan. It continues to be bred free-range throughout the year.

**Character and attributes**: The Kyrgyz has a good nature, is fast, resilient, with great endurance, hardy, undemanding, with good health and longevity. It is still a very good breed on hilly terrain because it has the sure-footedness of the mountain horse. It can amble.

**Uses**: It is used as a saddle or pack horse.

**Current status**: Sometimes thought to be extinct, it is not considered as such in its country. The breed simply suffered greatly during the Soviet era and from the attempts to improve it with crossbreeding that resulted in the New Kyrgyz. But people remain attached to this rustic breed that is connected to their history, and it is also frequently found in China. Under the efforts of local agents and a French journalist, the breed has benefitted from increased attention.

Thin neck

Slender legs

Steep mountain paths don't frighten the Karabair.

for their meat and milk, the latter of which is used to make koumiss. In 2002, 285,000 horses were New Kyrgyz, 78,000 Kyrgyz, 6,500 Orlov and Russian Trotter, and 1,200 Thoroughbred and other crossbreeds. Riding as a recreational activity is being developed, as is equestrian tourism. The Kyrgyz people respect horses and develop a strong bond with their animals.

Low-set tail

Wide neck

Eagle hunting on horseback

Small hooves

# New Kyrgyz

Also called: Nova-Kyrgyz

Russian: *novokirgizskaya*

**(H)** 1.51 m on average for mares; 1.55 m for males.

**(C)** Mainly bay, dark bay, chestnut, sometimes gray.

**Description**: This small, rather muscular horse resembles the Don. It has a small head with a straight profile, a long neck, long back, dished croup, and slender, short legs.

**Distribution**: Kyrgyzstan, a few in Kazakhstan.

**Origins and history**: The New Kyrgyz, as its name indicates, is a transformed Kyrgyz. The traditional native breed, thought too small by the Russians, was in fact crossed in the 1930s with Turkoman and Kabarda, and above all with Thoroughbred, Anglo-Don, and Don; it now has no more than 25 percent Kyrgyz blood. The idea was to create a taller and more powerful animal, while preserving the Kyrgyz's rusticity. It lives outdoors in a herd, on the steppes and in the mountains.

**Character and attributes**: The New Kyrgyz is an active horse with good endurance, robust and hardy. A mountain horse, it is very sure-footed. It is less rustic than the Kyrgyz.

**Uses**: It is bred for riding and driving; it is used as a pack horse and for endurance racing, but also for its meat and milk, notably to make the fermented drink koumiss.

**Current status**: The breed is doing very well in its country, with more than 200,000 horses.

# Tajikistan

In 2002 Tajikistan had a population of 71,300 horses. Horses are appreciated there, used for transportation, pulling (carriage driving and working the land), recreation, or sport competitions. Three breeds are raised in Tajikistan: the Lokai in the south, the Karabair in the north (see Uzbekistan, *p. 304*); and the Tajik, a more recent breed.

# Lokai

Tajik: *lakayskiy*

Russian: *lokaiskaya*

**(H)** 1.45 m–1.47 m on average for mares; 1.50 m–1.62 m for males.

**(C)** Most often gray, bay, and chestnut, with beautiful golden highlights.

**Description**: This rather short saddle horse, with a slender physique, has a head with a straight, sometimes convex profile; small ears; a rather long neck; short back; long, sloping, quite muscular croup; rather low-set tail; resilient legs; and very hard hooves. The hair of the mane and tail is sparse. Of note is a characteristic that is both rare in other breeds and very interesting: Lokais often have a wavy coat, and one of the Lokai lineages has visibly curly hair. There are different types of Lokai.

**Distribution**: Central and southern Tajikistan, Khatlon Region.

**Origins and history**: The Lokai was created three hundred years ago by Uzbek Lokai tribes from local horses (of Mongolian and Yamud types) to which was added Turkoman, Arabian, and Karabair blood. It is raised partially free-range.

**Character and attributes**: The Lokai has great endurance, is fast, agile, easy to handle, lively, but docile; it can also be a good jumper. In addition, it is well adapted to the mountains and to a hot climate. It is often said that it is a one-rider horse.

**Uses**: This versatile horse is used for transportation, pulling, as a pack horse, but also for sport and games (of the *buzkashi* type, called *kôkpar* in this region of the world; see Afghanistan, *p. 308*). The mares produce a lot of milk, and the horse is also raised for its meat.

**Current status**: Although the breed is doing well in its country of origin, it is a shame that its attributes are not more widely known throughout the world.

Long neck

Long back

Small head

Slender legs

Sparse mane
and tail

Very hard hooves

The Lokai is one of the very rare
breeds that can have a curly
coat and a curly mane and tail.

# TAJIK

Also called: Tajik Riding Horse

Russian: *tadzhikskaya*

**H** 1.43 m–1.54 m.

**C** Chestnut, bay, gray, with many white markings on the head and legs.

**Description**: This halfblood Tajik is taller and lighter than the Lokai, with a longer neck, sloping shoulders, and broad chest; but it has inherited the Lokai's thick winter coat.

**Distribution**: Tajikistan.

**Origins and history**: Based on the Lokai breed, a new breed of Tajik horse has been created within the past fifty years with English Thoroughbred and Arabian blood.

**Character and attributes**: The Tajik is energetic, a sport horse adapted to variations in continental climates.

**Uses**: The goal of the breeding is to create a good saddle horse, a good *kòkpar* player, a more athletic horse than the traditional Lokai.

**Current status**: The breed is being developed.

# Afghanistan

In the universe of horses Afghanistan is known for its team equestrian game, which is also a combat sport, *buzkashi*, a game that is also practiced in other Central Asian countries under different names (such as *kòkpar* in Kazakhstan). Legend has it that this game goes back to Attila's warriors, who used it in their training. Riders must fight to get the prize of a decapitated goat. All manner of fighting is permitted, which makes the game brutal for riders and horses alike. The nomadic

# AFGHAN

Also called: Tooraq, Samand, Qazal, Buzkashi, Yargha, Kohband, Dawand

Afghan Persian: *tooraq, samand, qazal, buzkashi, yargha, kohband, dawand*

**H** 1.20 m–1.50 m.

**C** The Tooraq is black or brownish-bay. The Samand has black legs, mane, and tail. The Qazal is chestnut, light gray, or palomino. White markings on the head and legs are frequent in Afghan horses.

**Description**: These are light horses of average to rather small height. Some show Arabian influence. They have a head with a wide forehead and slender nose; slender, solid legs; and hard hooves.

**Distribution**: Afghanistan. The Kohband is found is the mountainous regions of the north. The Buzkashi is also present in Pakistan. Breeding is concentrated above all in the northern provinces.

**Origins and history**: Under the name "Afghan horse," there are in fact seven breeds of horses (or seven types, according to the authors, "type" probably being more appropriate here) among which the Afghans make a very clear distinction: the Tooraq, the Samand, the Qazal, the Buzkashi, the Yargha, the Kohband, and the Dawand. Due to a lack of information we are describing them all together here, and Afghans themselves admit to a lack of knowledge concerning these breeds and their performance. The Tooraq is well known. The Buzkashi, which Afghans consider to be one of the best horses in the world, might have originated in Tajikistan and been imported after the revolution of October 7, 1919. These horses are very prized, and they can be sold for large sums locally. The Dawand, a sport horse, is the fastest of all: it is thus used for sport competition and racing. There is active horse trading between Afghanistan and Pakistan. Other types are sometimes cited, among them the Herati, Mazari, Qatgani, Waziri, and Yabu.

**Character and attributes**: These horses all have in common easy handling, speed, resiliency, and endurance. The Buzkashis, very highly regarded, are powerful, robust, fast, and agile.

**Uses**: These horses are used mainly for transportation, as pack horses, and for farm work, but also for sport, notably *buzkashi*. Good Buzkashis command a high price and are trained intensively for several years (aggressive and combative horses are thus selected). These Afghan horses would no doubt make excellent polo ponies.

**Current status**: We don't know very much about the status of these native horses because of the current political situation, but given the Afghans' passion for *buzkashi*, good horses will certainly continue to be conserved as much as possible.

Taller than the Lokai due to the addition of foreign blood, the Tajik is suited for sport and for very long rides.

peoples of Afghanistan also still need horses (as well as donkeys and mules) for transportation and as pack animals. Horse breeding, among many other things, has been upset in the past few years by the war and the political situation, but horses are still used in the hilly regions. Horses are an important status symbol for Afghans. The Afghan horse population is estimated to be around 360,000. According to Afghans, there are seven breeds (or types), which still need to be studied.

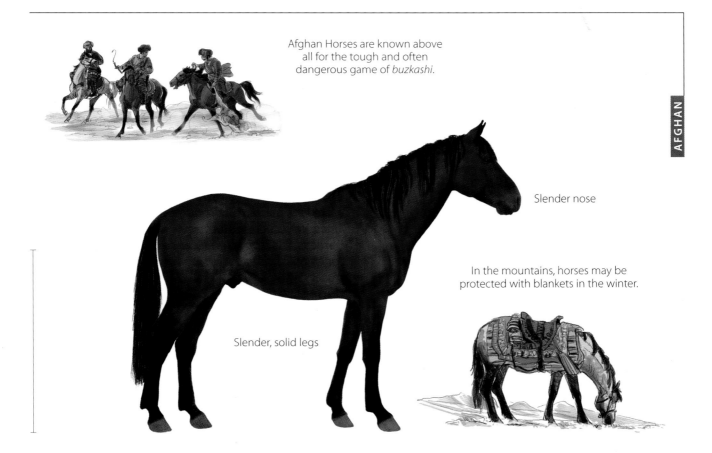

Afghan Horses are known above all for the tough and often dangerous game of *buzkashi*.

Slender nose

In the mountains, horses may be protected with blankets in the winter.

Slender, solid legs

The horses of Kazakhstan are still fairly unknown in the West, although this land of vast steppes contains herds of horses as far as the eye can see. In 2003 their population was estimated at more than 1,216,000;

---

# KAZAKH

Russian: *kazakhskayai*

**ⓗ** 1.40 m for the Jabe type; 1.36 m–1.40 m for the Adaev type.

**ⓒ** Bay, dark bay, liver chestnut, chestnut with light mane and tail, buckskin, bay dun; more rarely gray, pinto, often with primitive markings.

**Description**: The Kazakh resembles a more slender Mongolian horse. There are two types. The Jabe-type Kazakh is robust and stocky, with a large head; wide forehead; small ears; a short, thick neck; broad chest; straight shoulders; straight back; and a rather short croup. This type most resembles Mongolian horses. The Adaev-type Kazakh has been crossed more and is lighter and smaller, has a light head, is longer and more slender, has a rather high-set neck, and more prominent withers. Common to both types is a head with a straight or slightly convex profile, short back, sloping croup, and an extremely dense winter coat, particularly the Jabe.

**Distribution**: Central Aktobe Region, Kazakhstan, south of Aktobe; for the Jabe: China.

**Origins and history**: This is the ancient horse of nomadic tribes. It has origins in the Mongolian horse. The Jabe type has been influenced more by the Don, and the Adaev by Karabair, Yamud, and Akhal-Teke horses. It is raised outdoors on the steppes of Kazakhstan.

**Character and attributes**: The Kazakh is confident, has great endurance, and is very resilient in the cold, able to endure extreme temperatures and get along alone in very difficult conditions. It is simple, sure-footed, and very fertile. The Adaev type is less resilient than the Jabe. Some horses, notably the Adaev, can amble.

**Uses**: It is used for transportation, working with livestock, and local endurance racing. The mares, good milk producers, are used to produce koumiss. Jabes become fat quickly, which enables them to endure the winter, and their meat is eaten locally. Unlike the Jabe, the Adaev is not a good meat producer.

**Current status**: Although little known in the rest of the world, the breed is very widespread in its country and is doing very well.

---

# KUSHUM

Also called: West Kazakh Saddle-Draft

Russian: *kushumskaya*

**ⓗ** 1.54 m on average for mares; 1.60 m for males.

**ⓒ** Bay, dark bay, chestnut.

**Description**: This is a rather tall horse, fairly compact, with a wide head with a generally straight profile, broad chest, solid legs, and a very muscular croup.

**Distribution**: Aktobe region, western Kazakhstan; Russia.

**Origins and history**: This recent breed was developed in the middle of the twentieth century (1930s–1950s) from crossings among local Kazakh mares and Thoroughbred, Orlov, Russian Trotter, and, later, Don stallions. The hybrids produced good saddle horses, resilient and capable of living outside all year long. The goal at the time was to obtain good cavalry horses for the Red Army.

**Character and attributes**: These horses have great endurance; they are robust, fertile, and healthy. The mares are good milk producers.

**Uses**: Versatile, the Kushum is suitable for saddle or harness. It is a good endurance horse. It is also raised for its milk and meat, which is considered of high quality.

**Current status**: This resilient and versatile breed is doing well, with a population estimated at 12,000–14,000 in 2011.

today it is around 1,600,000 animals and it continues to grow. The Kazakhs, originally a nomadic riding people, breed horses for riding and as pack animals, but also for meat and milk, for they're great consumers of koumiss. Horses are of great importance in this country.

Short, thick neck

Wide forehead

Big head

Jabe

Adaev

Wide head

Solid legs

# KUSTANAI

Russian: *Kustanaiskaya*

🄷 1.60 m on average for mares; 1.63 m for males.

🄲 Mainly bay, dark bay, chestnut, less often black, gray, roan, sometimes with golden highlights.

**Description**: The Kustanai is a saddle version of the Kazakh, combining the assets of a halfblood with those of a steppe horse. It has a small head with a straight profile; long neck; prominent withers; broad chest; long, sloping shoulders; wide back; sloping, very muscular croup; muscular legs; and hard hooves.

**Distribution**: Kostanay Region, northwestern Kazakhstan.

**Origins and history**: The Kustanai is the result of crossings undertaken at the end of the nineteenth century between Kazakh mares and Thoroughbred, Don, Strelet Arabian (now extinct), Kalmyk, and Russian Saddle Horse (Orlov-Rastopchin) stallions.

**Character and attributes**: It is intelligent and rather lively and fast, has excellent endurance, and is resilient, fertile, and long-lived.

**Uses**: It is essentially a saddle horse suited to equestrian sports, trekking, or carriage pulling. It is also used in breeding to improve other breeds.

**Current status**: Widespread in the 1980s, this horse remains very local and has small numbers. It is the least widespread of all the Kazakh breeds.

A rider crossing a river, getting ready to go into slightly deeper water. The Kustanai is an all-terrain horse!

# MUGALZHAR

Russian: *mugalzharskaya*

🄷 1.45 m on average.

🄲 Bay, chestnut, buckskin, bay dun.

**Description**: The Mugalzhar is a type of light draft horse, rather massive, with a fairly thick neck and well-rounded barrel. The hair of the mane and tail is very thick.

**Distribution**: Aktobe Region, Kazakhstan.

**Origins and history**: This very recent breed was created through crossings among native mares and Kazakh stallions of the Jube type. This is one of the rare horse breeds that has been created from the start with the primary goal of obtaining a good yield of meat and milk.

**Character and attributes**: This is a fertile, rustic breed that is easy to raise.

**Uses**: These horses are notably bred for their meat and milk, as the mares are good milk producers.

**Current status**: This recent breed is developing and is popular among local breeders due to its good productivity.

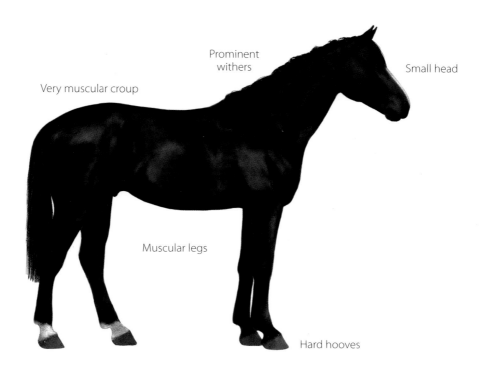

Very muscular croup

Prominent
withers

Small head

Muscular legs

Hard hooves

Mongolia is one of the most legendary equestrian lands on the planet. In 2011 there were 2.93 million horses, and the number is increasing. The Mongols, whose population is approximately 2.8 million, thus possess around one horse per inhabitant, which is the highest density of horses in the world. The Mongols, a riding people, are enthralled with horses. Even today, the Mongolian horse is bred with three main goals: transportation, the production of milk (drunk

---

# MONGOLIAN

Mongolian: *Mongol aduu*

**H** 1.23 m–1.42 m (1.26 m on average for mares; 1.31 m for males).

**C** As with the Icelandic, all colors are possible, and one finds surprising varieties. 60 percent of the horses are bay and chestnut, but also black, black/brown dun, bay dun, palomino, café au lait, cream, spotted, or pinto. Many chestnut and bay horses have golden highlights. Often carriers of the dun gene, they often have dorsal stripes and zebra striping on the legs. A particular characteristic of note: like Yakutians and Transbaikals and Przewalski's Horse, some individuals have a dark marking on their shoulder.

**Description**: This is a compact horse that has a large head with a straight profile; small ears and eyes; a rather short, thick neck; unobtrusive withers; muscular shoulders; a straight, short back; a long, sloping croup; very solid legs; a rather high-set tail; and extremely hard hooves, which are never shod. The hair of the mane and tail is thick. The winter coat is particularly dense and enables the horse to withstand extreme temperatures. The horses have small brands on the left thigh, with various designs depending on the owner.

**Distribution**: Mongolia, China (Inner-Mongolia).

**Origins and history**: The Mongolian horse is one of the most ancient horse breeds in the world, perhaps the most ancient, and has had a considerable influence in Asia, due especially to the many invasions of other countries by Mongolian riders. Almost all breeds of Asian horses have at one point or another received Mongolian influence. The Tibetan horse, in particular, greatly resembles the Mongolian, as does the Chinese Mongolian. But its influence has gone far beyond Asia, and is found as far away as Europe.

The Mongolian horse, which Mongols consider to be a single breed, is divided into four types: Tes, Galshar, Darkhad, and Jargalant. The Galshar is bred especially for racing. It is the result of selective breeding that went on for about a hundred years in the steppes, which has enhanced its abilities in long-distance racing. This is not the most widespread type.

The Darkhad is adapted to life at high altitudes (more than 2,300–2,500 m above sea level) and to life in the taiga. It is particularly well adapted to extreme living conditions (winters at −50°C, snow cover of 50–60 cm). It has very well developed lungs and solid legs. It is essentially used for transportation. The Darkhad mares produce more milk than other Mongolian types. The Jargalant occupies a region in central Mongolia. This type is characteristically taller. It has in fact received a little blood from the Russian Budyonny, which was imported into this region in the 1960s and 1970s.

Also noteworthy is that Inner Mongolia (China) has a very large population of Mongolian horses. This is where one finds the Ujumqin, a more refined type of Mongolian horse, raised on rich pastureland and popular in China.

**Character and attributes**: This horse has an assertive character, but is serene due to its way of life outdoors. It is energetic, easy to handle, fast and agile, docile once it is trained. Though small, it is very strong, powerful when harnessed, and a good saddle horse. It is known for its extreme, uncommon endurance, which once was the glory of the Mongolian cavalry,

A Mongolian saddle, richly decorated with various motifs, has the special characteristic of being made of wood with wide leather sides. Its very high seat distributes the weight of the rider well and doesn't interfere with the horse's movement. The saddle blanket is made of felt. Flat stirrups are the most common.

fermented by the name of *airag*, another name for koumiss), and meat. But they are also bred for riding, hunting, and racing (very important in Mongolia). Horses exist everywhere in the country: in desert regions, in the mountains (herds are present at more than 3,500 meters), and of course, everywhere on the steppes. They are found just outside of cities, and one can also come across them in Ulan Bator. In addition, Mongolia has a herd of Przewalski's Horses (more than 360), which were reintroduced into the wild there (see *p. 26*).

(see *p. 26*)

Mongols are great consumers of horse milk, to which they attribute many virtues. Mares only produce milk in the presence of their foals. This is the Darkhad type.

During endurance races (such as the Naadam), small female riders are active participants. Some horses bear a dark marking on their shoulder, most likely the sign of mixing with Przewalski's Horse. This is the Galshar type.

MONGOLIAN

Long croup

Rather short neck

Large head

Geldings generally have the mane cut, with a handful of long hair left at the withers. Most mares' hair is left long. The mane of the stallion—a very respected animal—is never cut. It is supposed to protect him from wolves while he is watching over his herd.

Very hard hooves

Nomads use a device called an uurga to catch horses and other livestock, with the help of a horse trained to herd. In western Mongolia, a lasso of rope and leather is used more often.

a true "weapon of war" under Genghis Khan. Some of them can amble. It is one of the most resilient breeds in the world, capable of enduring temperatures from 30°C and up to 40°C in the summer, and easily −30°C and as low as −50°C in the winter. Hardy and very robust, it gets by on food that provides little nutrition. It is extremely fertile.

**Uses**: It is essentially a horse used for riding (for work, endurance racing—notably during the annual Naadam festival—and transportation), or for milking because Mongols adore their milk (notably in the form of koumiss, called *airag* in Mongolian). It is also a good pack horse and is used for light draft or farm work. Its meat is also eaten.

**Current status**: With a population estimated at 2.9 million animals, the Mongolian is one of the most numerous breeds in the world.

Mongolian riders often ride bareback. They use knotted halters, reminiscent of American or "natural" halters, or those of the Blackfeet Indians. This horse is of the Jargalant type.

MONGOLIA

# New Mongolian

**(H)** Around 1.50 m.

**(C)** Mainly bay, chestnut, but all coat colors are possible.

**Description**: The New Mongolian is taller and more refined than the Mongolian horse. The result of crossings, the breed is not yet really established.

**Distribution**: Mongolia.

**Origins and history**: The recent New Mongolian Horse is the result of crossbreeding with Don, Budyonny, Thoroughbred, Arabian, or Akhal-Teke. Businessmen tried to create this breed for racing, but it remains rather rare. One encounters these horses near Ulan Bator.

**Character and attributes**: These horses are larger and faster than the Mongolian over short distances, but they can't rival it over long distances. Above all, they are not as resilient in the Mongolian climate, and do not have the Mongolian's highly developed survival instinct. They cannot work as hard, and need much more care and food. In that they resemble humans more than the Mongolian horse.

**Uses**: They are intended for racing.

**Current status**: This breeding project is still fairly limited and the horses command a high price in Mongolia.

Opposite: A shepherd in eastern Kazakhstan watches over his goats.

316

# Horses of the Indian Subcontinent

*The Indian Subcontinent, whose flamboyant equestrian culture seems mysterious to the rest of the world, is renowned for a very ancient game, much loved by the English, a royal sport still practiced by the elite— polo. It is also there that one discovers the amazing breeds of horses with ears that curve inward, a typical characteristic peculiar to horses from this region of the world: the Indian Marwari and Kathiawari and the Pakistani Baluchi. Who else but the warriors of India could have created these extravagant horses with two crescent moons on top of their heads? When the Hindus make them dance, prancing and tossing their heads, it is a fascinating sight. During the colonial period, the British brought the Thoroughbred and gallop races to this region.*

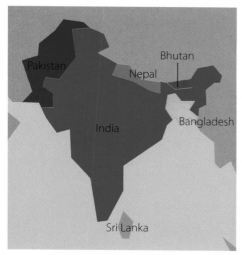

**Pakistan**
Baluchi
Sindhi
Siaen
Morna
Hirzai (also Heerzai)
Unmol
Kajlan
**India**
Spitii
Bhutia
Manipuri
Kathiawari
Marwari
Zaniskari (also
  Zanskari)

Deccani
Indian Half-Bred
**Sri Lanka**
Sri Lankan Pony
**Nepal**
Jumli Horse
Tarai Pony
**Bhutan**
Jata
Merak
Yuta
**Bangladesh**
Bangladesh Native
  Horse

Horse dancing during a festival, India.

Opposite: With its ears curved inward, the Indian Marwari is one of the most spectacular of breeds (Dundlod, Rajasthan, India).

In Pakistan horses, symbols of power, are linked to a long tradition of riding and remain very popular. They are now used more in harness, but sport and recreational riding are being developed, and polo

---

PAKISTAN

# BALUCHI

Urdu: *baluchi*

🇭 1.40 m on average.

🇨 Bay, dark bay, chestnut, gray, white, also black.

**Description**: A light horse, the Baluchi has a slender head with a rather straight profile, with ears that curve inward, like the Marwari and the Kathiawari, breeds that it resembles. It has a long neck, prominent withers, slender legs, and solid hooves. The hair of the mane and tail is fine and thin.

**Distribution**: Balochistan, Sind, Pakistan.

**Origins and history**: The Baluchi is believed to be of Barb descent.

**Character and attributes**: The Baluchi Horse is intelligent, fast, and undemanding. It has endurance and is a good mountain horse.

**Uses**: Versatile, it is ridden and driven, for work or recreation.

**Current status**: The breed has become very rare, notably from too much outcrossing. In its non-pure form, there are, however, around 16,000 animals.

Pakistanis are big fans of shows in which a beautiful horse "dances." These horses are trained to execute difficult figures in rhythm.

---

PAKISTAN

# SINDHI

Also called: Makra

Urdu: *makrana*

🇭 Around 1.50 m.

🇨 Brownish bay, black, bay dun, often with large stockings.

**Description**: This light horse, a close cousin of the Kathiawari and Marwari, but smaller, has slightly curved ears, but much farther apart than those of its cousins. It also has a head with a convex profile.

**Distribution**: Sind region (southeast Pakistan) and Kutch district, in Gujarat (western India).

**Origins and history**: The Sindhi (or Makra) probably descends from Arabian horses, with possible Turkish and Baluchi influences. Genetic testing was done at the beginning of 2013 to differentiate it from Kathiawari and Marwari horses.

**Character and attributes**: The Sindhi is intelligent, lively, and reliable, and it has good endurance. It has an amble as an additional gait, and it is considered very comfortable to ride.

**Uses**: An athlete, it is used for races. It is also traditionally used for various farm work.

**Current status**: The breed is very rare and on the brink of extinction. Indians are trying to protect it and to have it officially recognized. A hundred or so horses have been identified in India.

The Sindhi is used for ambling races.

is still very popular. Whereas donkeys and mules are increasing in the country, the horse population (currently around 320,000 individuals) is declining, although the price of gas might curb the decline.

Pakistanis do not eat horse meat. To produce mules, Pakistanis also breed Percheron and Suffolk horses. One encounters Arabians and, close to the border, Afghan horses. Like Indians, Pakistanis love dancing horses.

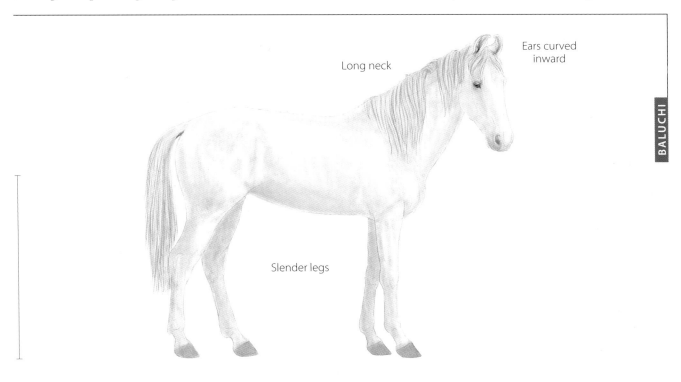

Long neck

Ears curved inward

Slender legs

BALUCHI

Curved ears, but spaced farther apart than the Marwari's

Convex profile

SINDHI

# SIAEN

Urdu: *siaen*

**H** 1.40 m–1.45 m.

**C** Bay, chestnut, black.

**Description**: Smaller than the Morna, which it resembles, the Siaen has a head with a convex profile, large eyes, and a broad chest.

**Distribution**: Faisalabad and Okara (Punjab Province), Pakistan.

**Origins and history**: It may have descended from the Saqlawi type of Arabian. Acording to recent genetic analyses, it is closely related to the Morna.

**Character and attributes**: Like the Morna, it is a sport horse.

**Uses**: It is used as a saddle horse.

**Current status**: It seems to be rather rare.

# MORNA

Urdu: *morna*

**H** 1.40 m–1.50 m.

**C** Bay, chestnut, black.

**Description**: The Morna has a compact body; a small, elongated head; slightly curved ears; a lovely arched neck; broad chest; long, slender legs; and a long, silky mane and tail.

**Distribution**: Faisalabad and Okara (Punjab Province), on the banks of the Ravi River, Pakistan.

**Origins and history**: The breed is believed to be descended from the Arabian and is very close to the Siaen.

**Character and attributes**: It is athletic.

**Uses**: It is a saddle horse.

**Current status**: It is probably very rare.

# HIRZAI

Also called: Heerzai

Urdu: *hirzai*

**H** Around 1.52 m.

**C** Essentially gray, white.

**Description**: This light horse resembles the Baluchi. It has a lovely head with a wide forehead, muscular neck, very sloping shoulders, and a short back.

**Distribution**: Balochistan, Pakistan.

**Origins and history**: The Hirzai was created from an Arabian stallion that arrived in Pakistan during the first Anglo-Afghan war (1839–1842) and was crossed with native mares.

**Character and attributes**: It is resilient and has good endurance.

**Uses**: It is a saddle horse.

**Current status**: Very rare, the breed is considered endangered.

## PAKISTAN

# UNMOL

Urdu: *unmol*

**H** Around 1.53 m.

**C** Mainly light gray, gray, and bay.

**Description**: Elegant and strong, it has a compact body, slightly curved ears, and a long mane and tail.
**Distribution**: Punjab, eastern Pakistan and northwest India.

**Origins and history**: The name of this horse literally means "inestimable." It might have Turkoman origins.
**Character and attributes**: The Unmol is a sport horse.
**Uses**: It is above all a saddle horse.
**Current status**: An essentially extinct breed, having undergone too much outcrossing, there are almost no pure animals remaining; the last ones are found in the Sargodha Division (Punjab).

## PAKISTAN

# KAJLAN

Urdu: *kajlan*

**H** 1.45 m–1.56 m.

**C** All coat colors except pinto.

**Description**: The Kajlan is known for its beautiful, very black eyes. It is of Arabian type.
**Distribution**: Chiniot and Pindi Bhattian, Jhang and Hafizabad Districts, Punjab, Pakistan.

**Origins and history**: It is most probably of Arabian origin.
**Character and attributes**: The Kajlan is a sport horse. It is a good ambler and is popular for this supplemental gait.
**Uses**: It is used above all as a saddle horse, because its comfortable gait enables its rider to go for miles without tiring.
**Current status**: There were about 2,000 horses in 2011.

## PAKISTAN

### OTHER HORSES IN PAKISTAN

In addition to those breeds, there are other varieties: the Kakka Biralanwala, a sport horse that is found in the Punjab, and the Topra, a horse found in the Shorkot region, in the Jhang District.

The Waziri, also found in Afghanistan, is found in northwest Pakistan (Khyber Pakhtunkhwa Province) and is a rather small and light type. It is a good mountain horse that is also used locally for polo. There's little information available on it.

Pakistanis also breed Thoroughbreds throughout the country under the name of Pakistani Thoroughbreds or Pak Thoroughbreds.

Pakistanis are fans of horses, and Pakistani breeds, which are relatively unknown, deserve to be studied in greater depth in their own country.

In 2003 India had 790,000 horses. Some traditional Indian breeds have declined significantly, almost becoming extinct, for lack of breeding and following a reduction in their use. They are still endangered. All

## INDIA

# SPITII

Hindi: *spiti*

**H** 1.24 m on average.

**C** Often gray, dark gray, black, sometimes chestnut or bay, occasionally palomino, pinto. Often carries the dun gene; it frequently has primitive markings.

**Description**: The Spitii is similar to the Bhutia and the Tibetan. It has a rather large head with a straight but sometimes concave profile; small eyes; small ears; a short neck; sloping shoulders; a short back; slightly sloping croup; short, strong, rather hairy legs; and resilient hooves. The hair of the mane and tail is long, thick, and dense. The Chummarti is a light animal very similar to the Spitii.

**Distribution**: Northern Himalayas, notably the Spiti and Kangra valleys in the Himachal Pradesh region, northwestern Punjab, Ladakh, India.

**Origins and history**: It is raised outdoors on the high plateaus of the Himalayas. It is a very ancient breed, created from indigenous horses and having probably received Tibetan and Arabian blood.

**Character and attributes**: Rather docile, it is not known for always being good-natured, and it can be rather nervous. It is, however, resilient, undemanding,

and very sure-footed. Made for life in the mountains, it is not adapted to tropical climates, but endures extreme temperatures (from −30°C to 30°C). Like the Icelandic, it has comfortable supplemental gaits.

**Uses**: This horse is used for transportation and as a pack horse.

**Current status**: Less useful since the arrival of motorized vehicles, the breed is in steep decline, with probably fewer than 1,000 individuals in 2012. As for the Chummarti, it has essentially disappeared.

The Spitii is a resilient mountain pack horse.

## INDIA

# BHUTIA

Hindi: *buthia*

Dzongkha: *buthia*

**H** 1.27 m on average.

**C** Mostly bay, gray, light gray, iron gray, less often chestnut.

**Description**: This is a compact animal that greatly resembles the Spitii, but is a bit taller, and the Tibetan, though is a bit more slender. It has a wide head with a straight profile; short, thick neck; straight shoulders; and short, strong legs. The hair of the mane and tail is long, thick, and bushy. One finds varieties of this breed in Nepal (Chyanta, Tattu). It is the equivalent of the Bhutanese Boeta (which means a horse of Tibetan origin).

**Distribution**: Sikkim, Darjeeling, Arunachal Pradesh, India. Nepal and the districts of Bumthang, Trashiyangtse, Gasa, Thimphu, in northern Bhutan.

**Origins and history**: This Himalayan breed is similar to the Spitii and the Tibetan.

**Character and attributes**: Though it is better known for its intelligence than its good character, it is nevertheless resilient, has good endurance, and is undemanding. It is above all perfectly adapted to the harsh living conditions in the high mountains. In spite of its small size, it is a good, very sure-footed pack horse.

**Uses**: It is essentially used as a mount or as a pack horse, and is a popular mountain horse.

**Current status**: In decline, the breed is endangered in India. In Bhutan, the closing of the border with Tibet has not helped the breed to propagate. There are few pure individuals left in Bhutan.

draft and pack animals have suffered, as elsewhere in the world, from the advent of mechanization, and conservation efforts must still be undertaken to save them. The famous dancing horses can be found in India. Featuring the Marwari, one of their horses with curved ears, decorated with jewels, the dance is an exotic equestrian spectacle.

Slightly sloping croup

Rather large head

Short, strong legs

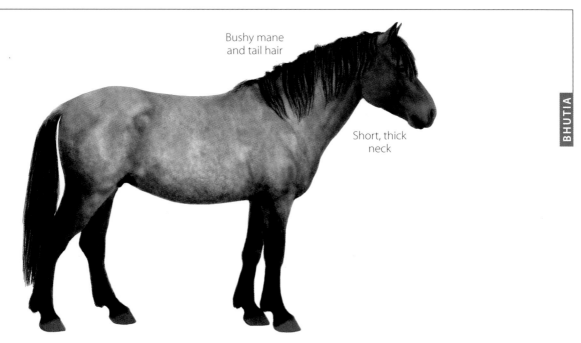

Bushy mane and tail hair

Short, thick neck

# MANIPURI

Hindi: *manipuri*

**H** 1.29 m on average.

**C** Often bay, also dark bay, gray, chestnut, more rarely pinto, black, cream, or carrying the dun gene.

**Description**: Elegant, very muscular, the Manipuri has a light head with a straight or concave profile; almond-shaped, slightly protruding eyes; small ears; sloping, muscular shoulders; a short, straight back; muscular, slightly sloping croup; and robust legs. Its solid hooves are generally not shod. The hair of the mane and tail is thick. The skin is thick with a hard hide, and there are a few animals with curly hair known by the name of *tukhoi*.

**Distribution**: Manipur, Assam, in northeastern India.

**Origins and history**: The origins of this very ancient Indian breed are uncertain. Contrary to what was believed for a long time, the Manipuri probably doesn't have connections with the Arabian, but might be a descendant of the wild Asian horse. It was a war horse, but also used in games, for polo.

**Character and attributes**: An energetic mount, the Manipuri is intelligent, fast, and sure-footed; it has good endurance. It is well suited to mountain regions.

**Uses**: This good mount has been particularly popular for a long time as a polo pony. It is also used in racing.

**Current status**: Somewhat forgotten in the West today, it remains well-known in Asia thanks to polo. It has nevertheless undergone a steep decline and has suffered from exporting abroad (it was a prized polo pony for the British). There are slightly more than 2,300 remaining.

---

# KATHIAWARI

Hindi: *kathiawari*

**H** 1.50 m on average, sometimes taller.

**C** Variety of coat colors, except black. Often bay, dark bay, all variations of gray, chestnut, bay dun, more rarely cream and pinto. It often carries the dun gene with different shades (bay dun, buckskin, black/brown dun).

**Description**: This horse greatly resembles the Marwari. Extremely elegant, it also evokes the Akhal-Teke. The shape of the ears is characteristic: they are shaped like a lyre, or, as the Indians say, a "scorpion sting." As in the Marwari, they are curved inward and their tips touch together. They have the most curved ears in the world. The Kathiawari has a small, slender, high-set head with a concave profile; slender nose; large forehead; large, protruding eyes; a long, slender neck; prominent withers; sloping shoulders; a long, straight back; slanting croup; high-set tail; long, slender, resilient legs; and small, very solid feet. The skin is fine, and the coat fine and silky.

**Distribution**: The Kathiawar peninsula, in western India.

**Origins and history**: Its origins are the same as those of the Marwari, its close cousin: these two breeds are the result of crossings among small native horses and Arabians. It was once a military horse.

**Character and attributes**: Lively and often endowed with a strong personality, reputed to be very intelligent, it also has great endurance, is fast, robust, and undemanding, and tolerates heat very well. It has a comfortable supplemental natural gait, a form of broken amble, called *revaal* in Hindi.

**Uses**: It is a saddle and pack horse, and also used for light harness or polo. It is the horse of the Indian mounted police. This lively horse requires an experienced rider.

**Current status**: The Kathiawari remains rare. Unknown abroad, the breed is very popular in India. With its small numbers, it should be watched. It has undergone a lot of outcrossing, and in 2012 there were only around forty pure individuals remaining.

The characteristic position of the ears touching at the tips

Almond-shaped eyes

Some Manipuris have a
curly coat.

Lyre-shaped
ears

High-set head

Fine hide

Long, slender legs

## INDIA

# MARWARI

Hindi: *marwari*

ⓗ 1.52 m–1.60 m, sometimes taller.

ⓒ All coats are possible, but most are bay and dark bay, sometimes with a metallic sheen, less often chestnut and gray, more occasionally pinto, palomino. There are white horses, not standard, that are used for religious purposes.

**Description**: Very elegant, the Marwari resembles the Kathiawari, though it is a bit taller and longer, and brings to mind the Akhal-Teke. Whereas the ears of the Kathiawari must always touch, those of the Marwari, also typically curved inward like crescent moons, do not always do so. It has a very expressive head; large, protruding eyes; a generally straight profile; high-set neck; rather narrow chest; prominent withers; a short back; long, muscular croup; long, slender, solid legs; and small, resilient hooves (no need to shoe). The hide is fine and silky, and the hair of the mane and tail is not very long.

**Distribution**: Marwar, northwestern India, a few in Sri Lanka. A sampling still lives in Europe (England), and there are a few in the United States. Indians rarely export it, and it is unusual to see it outside the country.

**Origins and history**: This ancient breed has rather obscure origins—the same as the Kathiawari—with a foundation of indigenous, Arabian blood, probably Turkoman, and perhaps Mongolian. It was a well-respected military horse, the mount of the Rathore kings.

**Character and attributes**: Bold and lively, it is known to be intelligent and very faithful to its rider. With good endurance, it is fast and hardy; it has light gaits and, like the Kathiawari, has a broken amble, the *revaal*.

**Uses**: This is a saddle horse for experienced riders, excelling in dressage, haute école, equestrian exhibitions (notably the dancing horses), and endurance. It is also a horse for the mounted police.

**Current status**: The extraordinary Marwari was on the brink of extinction but has since been protected; there are around 500 horses.

Richly adorned, moving to the rhythm of a drum, the Marwari performs the very popular equine dance.

## INDIA

# ZANISKARI

Also called: Zanskari

Hindi: *zanskari, zanaskari*

ⓗ On average 1.26 m.

ⓒ Mainly gray, sometimes black or bay, brownish bay, more rarely chestnut with coppery highlights.

**Description**: It resembles the Spitii. Compact, it has a wide head with protruding eyes and a straight or convex profile. It has shiny, fine, long hair, a thick hide, and a very long, thick mane and tail, which sometimes touches the ground.

**Distribution**: Northern Himalayas, northern India: Zanskar, Ladakh, Jammu and Kashmir State.

**Origins and history**: Not much is really known, but the breed probably has Tibetan origins.

**Character and attributes**: Very robust and resilient in the most glacial and arid valleys of the Himalayas, it is considered to have good endurance and to be a good worker, and very sure-footed.

**Uses**: Mainly used as a saddle and pack horse, it also makes a good polo pony. With competition from motorized vehicles, its role as a pack horse is now limited to areas that are difficult to access.

**Current status**: This small horse is endangered. Its breeding is badly organized, it is the victim of too much crossbreeding, and its numbers are in decline, with only a few hundred horses left. A conservation program is in the works.

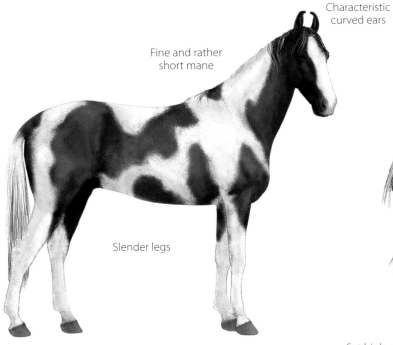

Fine and rather
short mane

Characteristic
curved ears

Slender legs

Set high, and with silky hair, the Marwari's head is slender and expressive. The tips of the ears are slightly more wide-set than those of the Kathiawari.

# DECCANI

Hindi: *deccani*

The existence of this breed is mentioned, but Indians have very little information about it. A small horse, originating in the Bombay region in India, it is very rare and the breed has probably essentially disappeared.

## INDIAN HORSES WITH CURVED EARS

Some Indian work horses have Kathiawari or Marwari blood, which contributes to their good endurance. They are recognized by their curved ears. But not every horse that has curved ears is necessarily of pure blood.

# INDIAN HALF-BRED

**H** 1.50 m–1.63 m.

**C** Bay, chestnut, and other basic colors.

**Description**: The Indian Half-Bred sometimes inherits crescent-shaped ears, which are less noticeable than in the Marwari or the Kathiawari, and has characteristics of the Half-Bred: long neck, prominent withers, sloping shoulders, a rather broad chest, muscular croup, long legs, and a silky hide.

**Distribution**: India.

**Origins and history**: In India, there is a lot of crossbreeding among Marwaris and Kathiawaris, either with native horses or with Thoroughbreds. Slightly curved ears therefore don't necessarily indicate a purebred. Halfbreds are notably obtained by crossing those two breeds with English Thoroughbreds and Australian Walers (which were imported in large numbers into India at the beginning of the twentieth century), and with a bit of Arabian, with the goal of creating a good military horse.

**Character and attributes**: The Indian Half-Bred has endurance, is energetic and docile, and is a rustic sport horse.

**Uses**: It is well suited to equestrian sports and makes a good military horse.

**Current status**: Still relatively new, and not always well known in India, this type of horse may not be very widespread, though it is not considered truly rare.

# Sri Lanka

In Sri Lanka there are only a small number of horses, and they are widely dispersed, since it is not a horse-breeding country. For the most part, the horses are not very tall. Of note is a small population of wild

# SRI LANKAN PONY

**H** 1.25 m for mares; 1.30 m for males.

**C** Often chestnut, liver chestnut, sometimes bay.

**Description**: Often quite thin due to droughts, with protruding ribs and prominent barrel, it doesn't often appear in the best light. It has a rather large head with a straight profile; a short, sloping croup; and thin legs.

**Distribution**: The island of Delft and the Puttalam District, in northwestern Sri Lanka.

**Origins and history**: A theory holds that its origins can be found in Europe. It might have been imported at the end of the nineteenth century to Delft Island by Portuguese colonists. It was then raised by the Dutch and the British. The population, which was returned to the wild, then became smaller, and was displaced as far as Puttalam. These horses still live in the wild and sometimes suffer from a lack of food, and they are then seen slurping algae on beaches.

**Character and attributes**: It is resilient.

**Uses**: They are sometimes caught and used for work and for riding.

**Current status**: Endangered and in decline, notably due to overgrazing and lack of water, there are no more than 600 remaining, 400 of which are on Delft Island. Pakistani authorities are considering developing tourism around these wild horses, making it possible to save the breed.

## HIMALAYAN HYBRIDS

The small horses of the Himalayan Mountains are the result of much crossing among Spitiis, Tibetans, and Bhutias. One finds these crossbreeds in Bhutan and India (the regions of Sikkim and Darjeeling). Such crossbreeding is sometimes described in English by the term "Indian Country Bred." These are essentially pack horses, well adapted to life in the high mountains, simple, with endurance, resembling the breeds from which they come in their small size; large head; short neck; unobtrusive withers; broad chest; straight shoulders; short, strong legs; and so forth.

horses on the island of Delft (widely known as Neduntheevu or Neduntivu), which is gaining more attention. Sri Lanka has also obtained a few Marwaris in the past ten years or so, which are useful given the rise in equestrian tourism in the country and the interest traveling riders have in discovering horses with an exotic appearance.

Rather large head

Short and sloping croup

Thin legs

SRI LANKAN PONY

Nepal breeds more bovines (including yaks) than horses. The size of the Nepalese horse population is not really known. The only breed that is known is the Jumli Horse, although, according to the Nepalese,

---

### NEPAL

# Jumli Horse

Nepalese: *jumli*

**H** From 1.25 m–1.42 m for mares; from 1.22 m–1.44 m for males.

**C** Mainly bay, a few gray and dark bay.

**Description**: The Jumli Horse resembles the Bhutia. It is a small, solid animal with a wide forehead; almond-shaped eyes; a horizontal-set neck; straight back; extremely sloping croup; low-set tail; small hooves; and a dense, thick mane and tail.

**Distribution**: Essentially in the Jumla district, Nepal, and the Uttarakhand region in India.

**Origins and history**: This is the best-known indigenous breed.

**Character and attributes**: The Jumli is resilient, has endurance, and is very well adapted to hilly and mountain regions. It is very sure-footed, even in snow. It has good health and is undemanding and easy to raise.

**Uses**: The Jumli is a good pack horse, still used for transportation in difficult-to-reach areas. It has also been used for tourism, to accompany trekkers. The mares are used to produce excellent mules.

**Current status**: Essentially the all-purpose horse of the Nepalese, mechanization made it less useful, and the population is in decline.

---

In Bhutan the horse population was at more than 25,000 in the 2010s, and it is in decline due to the construction of roads and the extensive production of mules. The country counts four native breeds and an imported breed, the Haflinger (in small numbers and for crossbreeding, the breed clearly not being resilient or sure-footed enough for local conditions).

---

### BHUTAN

# Jata

Dzongkha: *jata*

**H** Probably under 1.25 m.

**C** All common colors likely.

**Description**: This is probably a small mountain breed, solid and compact.

**Distribution**: Southern Bhutan.

**Origins and history**: The Jata is of Indian origin. Bhutanese specialists themselves lack information on this horse, but a study has been proposed to find out more about them.

**Character and attributes**: The Jata is sure-footed and well adapted to the local environment.

**Uses**: It is mainly used as a pack horse or to produce mules.

**Current status**: The breed is in decline, in competition with mules.

there are others that could be identified and classified. In Nepal one also finds the Bhutia and the Tibetan. Equestrian tourism is being developed here. The horse remains a useful means of transportation in mountain zones that are difficult to access by motorized vehicles.

## NEPAL

# TARAI PONY

Nepalese: *tarai*

(H) 1.15 m on average.

(C) Often bay, sometimes light gray, a few chestnut; primitive markings possible.

**Description**: This small horse has a rustic look.
**Distribution**: Terai Region, southern Nepal.
**Origins and history**: This is a region of swampy prairies, close to India, and the Tarai Pony is the type of horse that comes out of this environment. Not much is known about it.
**Character and attributes**: The Tarai is adapted to the subtropical climate and to life in the swamplands.
**Uses**: Unlike the Jumli, which is a mountain horse, the Tarai is a plains animal.
**Current status**: Unknown.

## NEPAL

### TATTU, CHYANTA, TANGHAN: NEPALESE VARIETIES OF THE BHUTIA

We should mention the presence in Nepal of the Tattu, the smallest variety of Bhutia, measuring 1.04 m, which lives in the high mountains and is used mainly as a pack horse. The Chyanta is a small variety of the Bhutia, measuring around 1.28 m more massive than the Tattu. The Tanghan is a larger variety of Bhutia, measuring around 1.36 m.

One also finds Tibetan and Indian horses (notably the Spitii). The Bhutia (*boeta* for the Bhutanese) is a breed shared with India (see India, *p. 324*). Horses are often raised outdoors. Their role remains essential to Bhutan, a land of high mountains, for transportation in zones that aren't accessible to motorized vehicles, which is still the case for many villages. Horses are raised mainly as pack and draft animals, not for riding. They are sometimes sheltered and fed in the winter.

## BHUTAN

# MERAK

Dzongkha: *merak saktenpata;* also called *yuta trashigang* by local populations

(H) 1.29 m on average.

(C) Variable.

**Description**: It greatly resembles the Yuta. It is an animal with solid legs and often the close-set hocks characteristic of mountain horses.

**Distribution**: Trashigang region, far eastern Bhutan.
**Origins and history**: Connected to the history of the Yuta, it is one of the native horses whose origins we don't know, but which seems always to have been there.
**Character and attributes**: Like the Yuta, it is sure-footed and well adapted to the mountains.
**Uses**: It is essentially a pack horse, carrying loads of 40–60 kg. It is also used to produce mules.
**Current status**: The breed remains quite local.

# YUTA

Dzongkha: *yuta*

**H** 1.23 m on average.

**C** Variable. Often bay, chestnut, black, gray, light gray.

**Description**: It has a narrow chest; a straight back; short, very strong legs that tend to have the close-set hocks characteristic of mountain horses; a short, sloping, dished croup; low-set tail; and hard, solid hooves. The hair of the mane and tail is thick and abundant.

**Distribution**: Throughout Bhutan, especially in the central regions.

**Origins and history**: This is a purely native horse of Bhutan that one encounters frequently since it is very popular among the local population.

**Character and attributes**: The Yuta is efficient and bold in difficult terrain, endowed with sure-footedness. Well adapted to life in high mountains, it is undemanding and easy to keep.

**Uses**: It is essentially a pack horse popular among the Bhutanese, carrying loads of 40–80 kg. Mares are also used to produce mules.

**Current status**: This is the dominant breed in Bhutan; it suffers less from competition with mules.

High-mountain horses are very sure-footed. Yutas never get vertigo.

# Bangladesh

Horses are present in all regions of Bangladesh, although the equine population is very limited. It is believed that the breeds of native horses, long present and close to the small horses of Southeast Asia, have received blood from Arabian and Persian horses, which arrived from western India. They were traditionally used for pulling and farm work, which has since evolved, except in some regions. Foreign breeds are used by the police and the army.

# BANGLADESH NATIVE HORSE

Bengali: *Bangladesh*

**H** 1.20 m–1.30 m on average.

**C** Bay, light gray, chestnut, sometimes cream.

**Description**: It resembles other small horses of Southeast Asia, being rather slender, with a head with straight profile, narrow chest, sloping croup, and a low-set tail. Another breed or type that is sometimes cited, the Rajshahi Pony, is smaller (1.13 m for males; 1.09 m for mares, probably taller), mainly bay, also light gray, primarily present in the districts of Rajshahi, Jessore, Tungi, Mymensingh, Sylhet, and Dhaka, in western Bengal, Bangladesh.

**Distribution**: Bangladesh.

**Origins and history**: This is not really a distinct breed, but a type of horse that is found in Bangladesh. Resembling the small horses of Southeast Asia, it has received blood from Arabian and Persian horses, which arrived from western India.

**Character and attributes**: These animals tolerate the humid climate, monsoons, and high temperatures.

**Uses**: This is a versatile horse: it can be used as a pack horse, in harness, for transportation, and for light farm work. It also participates in races, with very young riders riding bareback, at certain events that bring together dozens of riders. The horses' manes are then sometimes dyed and images are painted on their bodies.

**Current status**: The population is in decline.

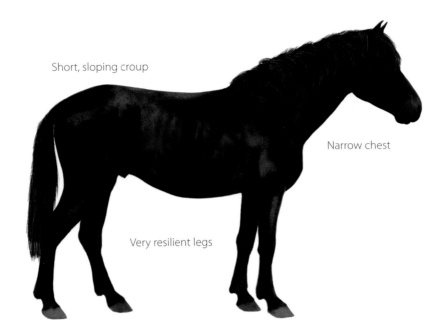

Short, sloping croup

Narrow chest

Very resilient legs

# Horses of the Far East and Southeast Asia

*The equestrian realm of Asia, although immeasurably vast, is almost completely unknown to Westerners. In old documents, or in certain guides to China, one simply finds mention of the "Chinese pony." This, of course, doesn't mean much: China is huge, and there are dozens of perfectly identifiable breeds. The density of the horse population there is still very high. The breeds of horses in the Far East and continental Southeast Asia are strongly influenced by the Mongolian horse. These animals, small and robust, do not always correspond to Western equestrian criteria. However, in the Himalayas, a beautiful European Warmblood or an American Quarter Horse would be quite lost, whereas a rustic Himalayan would be completely at ease. When animals must live in extreme conditions, the criteria change.*

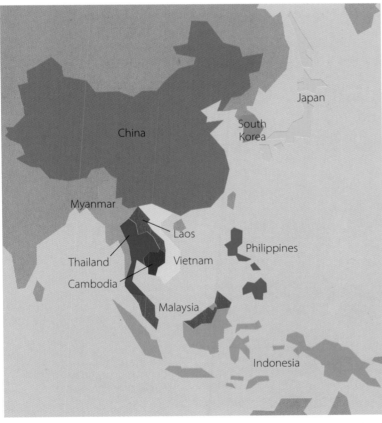

**China**
Baise
Yunnan
Guizhou
Jianchang
Tibetan (also Southern Barbarian Pony, Southern Native)
Balikun
Datong
Chakouyi
Erlunchun (also Erlunchun Hunting Horse)
Yanqi
Hequ
Sanhe
Buohai
Yili
Jilin (also Jilin Harness Horse)
Guanzhong
Ningqiang
Wenshan
Lichuan
Yongning (also Yongning Tibetan Horse)
Zhongdian
Jinjiang
Lijiang (also New Lijiang)
Ganzi (also Tibetan-Sikang Pony)
Yushu
Cadamu
Agaba Dark Horse (also Sengseng Dark Horse)
Xiangfen
Yiwu (also New Barkol)
Xini
Sandan
Xilingol
Zhangbei
Keerqin
Jinzhou
Heilongkiang
Heihe
Tieling Draft (also Tieling Harness Horse)
Henan Light Draft

**Myanmar**
Shan (also Burmese)
Myanmar

**Thailand**
Thai (also Siamese Pony)

**Laos**
Laotian

**Vietnam**
Annamese Pony (also Vietnamese Horse, Color Horse)
Vietnamese Hmong Horse

**Cambodia**
Cambodian

**South Korea**
Jeju

**Japan**
Noma
Tokara
Yonaguni
Miyako
Misaki
Dosanko
Kiso
Ban'ei
Taishuh

**Philippines**
Baguio (also Tagaytay)

**Malaysia**
Bajau
Kuda Padi (also Paddy Horse)

**Indonesia**
Timor
Sumba and Sumbawa
Batak
Sandalwood
Lombok
Sulawesi (also Macassar)
Flores
Java
Bali
Sumbar
Minahasa
Indonesian Racing Horse

Opposite: The very rare Misaki, small feral horses from Cap Toi (on the island of Kyushu, Japan), are classified as national natural treasures.

China is a huge territory with a lot of horses. There were 11 million in 1982 and still 6.77 million in 2011. Some Chinese breeds exceed in numbers the total number of horses in some countries; some are on the brink of extinction. The Mongolian horse has

---

# BAISE

Chinese: *baise*

**Ⓗ** 1.09 m for mares; 1.14 m for males; an average of 0.97 m for the smallest type.

**Ⓒ** Mainly bay, a few gray, chestnut, black, roan.

**Description**: Extremely small, the Baise has a rather short head with a straight profile; wide jaws; large eyes; small ears; a thick, short neck, set horizontally; unobtrusive withers; a sloping croup; short, strong legs; often straight or close-set hocks; and small, hard hooves. There are two types, the Tushan, which is of average size, and the smaller Shishan.

**Distribution**: The Guangxi Zhuang Autonomous Region (Tianlin, Longlin, Xilin, Jingxi, Debau, Lingyun, Leye, Youjiang counties, under Baise city) in southwestern China.

**Origins and history**: The Baise has obscure origins. It is one of the most ancient of Chinese breeds.

**Character and attributes**: It is docile and undemanding, useful in mountain regions.

**Uses**: Small but robust, the Baise is used as both a pack and saddle horse and also in harness; it has good pulling abilities. It is also raised for its meat.

**Current status**: This is a common breed in China. There were 200,000 horses in 1980, and there were still around 201,500 at the end of 2005.

At the end of 2008 only 1,578 Shishan remained. It needs to be better protected. The smallest variety of the Baise and also one of the smallest breeds in the world, the Shishan (also called *baiseshishan*, *debao*, or **guoxia**) measures on average 0.97 m (the range is from around 0.86 m to 1 m) and can be an excellent mount for children. It is about the same size as the Shetland Pony but much more lightly built. Despite its very small size, it is particularly robust. Sometimes it is considered a breed separate from the Baise, or as one of its types.

---

# YUNNAN

Chinese: *yunnan*

**Ⓗ** 1.04 m–1.19 m on average.

**Ⓒ** Mainly bay and chestnut, sometimes black, gray, more rarely light gray.

**Description**: A small, solid, and compact horse, it has a slender head with a wide, slightly concave forehead; big eyes; small ears; a short, thick neck; unobtrusive withers; a short back; rounded croup; robust legs; and hard hooves.

**Distribution**: West and east of Yunnan Province, notably Heqing County, in southwestern China.

**Origins and history**: Of ancient origin, it is one of the smallest Chinese breeds. It resembles the Mongolian less than do other Chinese breeds, and has perhaps not been influenced by it.

**Character and attributes**: The Yunnan is docile and simple.

**Uses**: It is a pack horse that can also be trained as a children's mount and for pulling small carriages.

**Current status**: In 1980 there were 710,000 Yunnans, but only 1,520 at the end of 2009.

greatly influenced Chinese breeds, but the Kazakh has also played an important role. Something unique to China is the presence of very small, long-lived rustic breeds. In addition to the forty or so native breeds and those being developed, China also has the Thoroughbred, Orlov, Don, Kabarda, Soviet Draft, Ardennais, Akhal-Teke, and others. The equestrian domain is in full expansion in China.

Sloping croup

Short and thick neck

Small, hard hooves

BAISE

Rounded croup

Wide, slightly concave forehead

YUNNAN

## Tengchong, Dali, and Wumeng: Three Breeds Related to the Yunnan

The Chinese have horses that are related to the Yunnan. The Tengchong, which is also found in western Yunnan Province, has larger numbers; there were 12,135 individuals at the end of 2005. The Tengchong is a bit taller than the Yunnan: 1.13 m for mares and 1.25 m for males. It has a large head with a straight or slightly convex profile; a thin, short neck; broad chest; sloping croup; robust legs; and thick mane and tail. It is often bay, chestnut, sometimes black, gray, rarely light gray or pinto. It has endurance and is adapted to very hot and humid temperatures.

---

# Guizhou

Chinese: *guizhou, qian, kweichow*

**(H)** 1.12 m for mares; 1.16 m for males.

**(C)** Mainly bay and chestnut, less often gray, black; sometimes carries the dun gene.

**Description**: A small, compact, and stocky horse, the Guizhou has a head with a straight profile; large eyes; small ears; large nostrils; broad chest; straight, short shoulders; a sloping croup; robust legs; and hard hooves. Pack horses have a more horizontal neck than those used for riding or for draft. The mane and tail are thick.

**Distribution**: Western and central Guizhou Province, southern China.

**Origins and history**: Forged by its mountainous environment, the breed was once used extensively for farm work.

**Character and attributes**: The Chinese consider the Guizhou an excellent small native mountain breed. These are patient and gentle horses.

**Uses**: It is used as a saddle and draft horse. Because it is small and willing, it is perfect for teaching children to ride.

**Current status**: The breed is doing very well. There were 502,400 horses in 1983, and an estimated 825,000 at the end of 2005.

---

# Jianchang

Chinese: *jianchang, chuan*

**(H)** 1.14 m for mares; 1.17 m for males.

**(C)** Bay, chestnut, black.

**Description**: Rustic and compact, it is a small horse. It has a rather large head with a straight profile, large eyes, small ears, neck sometimes set horizontally, a narrow chest, slightly sloping croup, thin but robust legs, very hard hooves, and a low-set tail.

**Distribution**: Sichuan Province, west-central China.

**Origins and history**: This very ancient breed was once extremely popular.

**Character and attributes**: The Jianchang has an easygoing nature, it is undemanding, resilient, and sure-footed and is well adapted to the mountains and to steep slopes.

**Uses**: It is used as a saddle or pack horse, or even as a light carriage horse.

**Current status**: From an initial estimate of 70,000 horses in 1980, its population surpassed 239,970 individuals in 2005.

They also have the Dali, also called Dian, and once called Yuedanju, which belongs to the group of Yunnan horses. It is found in western Yunnan Province, and 15,800 individuals were recorded in 2008. It is a delicate animal with a head with a straight profile, small eyes, and a broad chest. It is usually bay or chestnut, sometimes gray or black. It measures 1.18 m for mares, 1.21 m for males.

Finally, there is the Wumeng, which is also related to the Yunnan. It is found at altitudes of 1,200–3,000 m in the mountains between Yunnan and Guizhou provinces. At the end of 2005 its population was at 127,300 horses. There is a heavy and a light type. It measures 1.20 m on average for mares and 1.26 m for males, has a straight profile and small eyes and ears, and is generally bay or chestnut.

Sloping croup

Straight profile

Short, straight shoulders

GUIZHOU

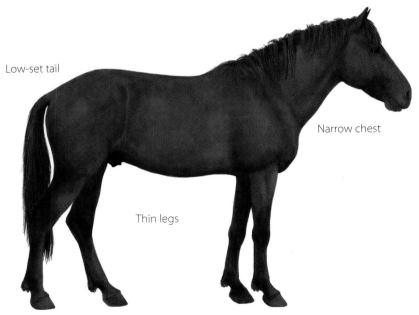

Low-set tail

Narrow chest

Thin legs

JIANCHANG

# Tibetan

Also called: Southern Barbarian Pony, Southern Native

Chinese: *xizang ma*

**H** 1.27 m on average for mares; 1.29 m for males.

**C** Mainly bay, chestnut, gray, bay dun with a dorsal stripe.

**Description**: The Tibetan resembles the Bhutia (see *p. 324*) but is lighter. Compact, it has a small head with a straight profile; large eyes; small ears; a square muzzle; a thick, rather short neck; unobtrusive withers; a broad chest; straight shoulders; and robust legs with close-set hocks. Other breeds are sometimes listed as types of Tibetan: the mountain type (*Ganzi*), the plateau type (*Yushu*), and the valley type (*Zhongdian*). But the Chinese consider them all different breeds.

**Distribution**: Mainly east and west of the Tibet autonomous region, Qinghai Province, China.

**Origins and history**: This very ancient breed has probably been influenced by Mongolian and Chinese horses.

**Character and attributes**: The Tibetan is very strong for its size and has great endurance, is agile, and is very sure-footed in the mountains. It is very well adapted to extremely cold temperatures at high altitudes (more than 3,000 m), and to conditions in which there is little oxygen. It has a predisposition for the amble.

**Uses**: It is used for transportation and as a pack horse in the high mountains, and for trekking.

**Current status**: The breed is very widespread, with around 410,000 horses at the end of 2007.

The khampas of Tibet have long been known as agile riders.

# Balikun

Chinese: *balikun, barkol*

**H** 1.31 m on average for mares; 1.32 m for males.

**C** Bay, chestnut, sometimes gray, pinto.

**Description**: The Balikun has a compact body and a large, wide head with a straight or slightly convex profile; large eyes; small ears; a short, thick neck; broad chest; straight shoulders; a short back; short, sloping croup; short, strong legs; and hard hooves. The hair of the mane and tail is thick, sometimes wavy, and the coat is very thick in the winter.

**Distribution**: Barköl Kazakh Autonomous County, Yiwu County, Hami Prefecture, Xinjiang autonomous region, China.

**Origins and history**: The breed is the result of more than two centuries' worth of crossings between native horses and Altai, Mongolian, and Kazakh horses.

**Character and attributes**: This bold mountain horse has a gentle temperament and can tolerate very low temperatures.

**Uses**: Used as a pack horse, or as a saddle or carriage horse, it is also raised for its meat and milk.

**Current status**: This is a native breed. In 1985 there were 15,000 horses, and only 5,800 at the end of 2006.

Thick neck

Small head,
square muzzle

Close-set hocks

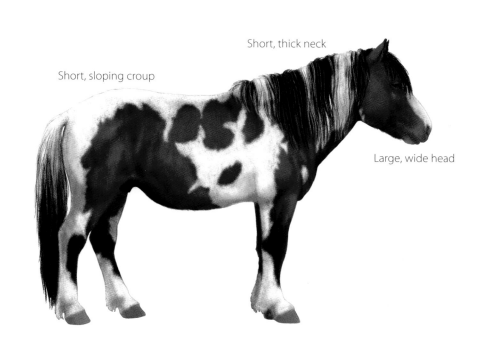

Short, thick neck

Short, sloping croup

Large, wide head

# DATONG

Chinese: *datong*, once called *haomen*

**H** 1.30 m for mares; 1.35 m for males.

**C** Mainly bay, also black, chestnut, sometimes gray.

**Description**: Though small, this is a very muscular horse. It has a rather large head with a straight profile; large eyes; a wide forehead; straight shoulders; a broad chest; long legs; and a short, slightly sloping croup. There is a light type and a heavier one. Occasionally, some individuals have the surprising and rare characteristic of having two small growths on the forehead, above the eyes (like the American Moyle; see *p. 460*).

**Distribution**: North of the Qinghai-Tibet Plateau, notably the basin of the Datong River, the Haibei Tibetan Autonomous Prefecture, Qinghai Province, China.

**Origins and history**: This is a very ancient Chinese breed—perhaps a descendant of the Dragon Horse, an extinct royal Chinese breed, which has small bumps on the forehead. It probably has Kazakh blood as well. It resembles the Chakouyi.

**Character and attributes**: The Datong is gentle and very strong, has excellent endurance, and is fertile. One finds amblers among them, which are popular with riders. It is well adapted to life at high altitudes, at more than 3,500 m, but it is a bit less rustic than the Hequ.

**Uses**: It is suitable for riding and for farm work. It is also raised for its meat.

**Current status**: In 1980 there were 60,000 horses, but by 2005 there were only 23,024 of this native horse.

# CHAKOUYI

Chinese: *chakouyi*

**H** 1.31 m on average for mares; 1.35 m for males.

**C** Mainly bay; a few black and gray, often with a white star on the forehead.

**Description**: This solid horse has a head with a straight profile; large eyes; a rather slender neck; broad chest; short, robust legs; and small, hard hooves.

**Distribution**: Tianzhu Tibetan Autonomous County, Yongdeng and Gulang counties, Gansu Province, China.

**Origins and history**: This is an ancient breed, sometimes considered a type derived from the Datong. This horse was found on the Silk Road, as its amble was a less tiring gait for travelers.

**Character and attributes**: Well adapted to cold and resistant to illness and insects, it is lively, has endurance, and is comfortable to ride due to a supplemental gait, a natural amble.

**Uses**: As a saddle horse, it is popular for its comfortable ride; it is also used in harness.

**Current status**: In 1980 there were 24,000 horses; in 2006 there were 9,855.

The Chakouyi, popular for its amble, is considered an excellent racehorse.

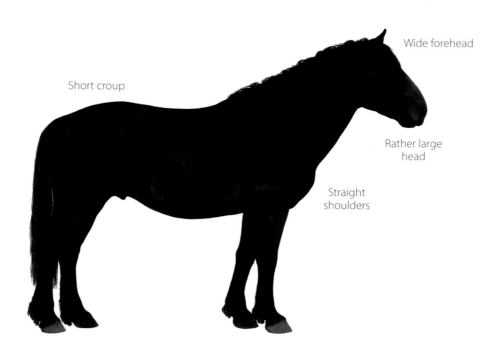

Wide forehead

Short croup

Rather large
head

Straight
shoulders

Slender neck

Short legs

# ERLUNCHUN

Also called: Erlunchun Hunting Horse

Chinese: *elenchus*

**H** 1.29 m on average for mares; 1.37 m for males.

**C** Mainly gray, also bay.

**Description**: Compact and strong, it has a rather large head with a straight profile; a wide forehead; large eyes; small ears; a muscular neck set horizontally; broad chest; sloping, muscular shoulders; short, robust legs with close-set hocks; and wide, hard hooves. The winter coat and the mane and tail are very thick and long.

**Distribution**: Oroqen Autonomous Banner, Greater Khingan and Lesser Khingan mountain ranges, Heilongjiang Province and Inner Mongolia Autonomous Region, China.

**Origins and history**: This breed was developed in the middle of the seventeenth century by the Oroqen, by crossing Chinese Mongolian horses, Helongjiang, and Soulun (now extinct).

**Character and attributes**: The Erlunchun is sensitive, has endurance, and is a good pack horse, very easygoing and capable of working hard, of adapting to life in the snow and to fighting predators (wolves, among others) thanks to a strong survival instinct. Very resistant to cold, it can withstand temperatures as low as −50°C and also drought. Agile and sure-footed on slopes, it is a very good mountain horse.

**Uses**: It is primarily a saddle horse, and is known to be an excellent hunting horse, for which it was traditionally used.

**Current status**: The Erlunchun is endangered: for a long time there were fewer than 1,000 animals, and at the end of 2006 only 312 horses remained. This breed, which has so many assets, urgently needs to be protected. The decline in its numbers is related to the lifestyle changes of the Oroqen people.

The Erlunchun is a faithful ally of Oroqen hunters, just like their dogs.

# YANQI

Chinese: *yanqi*

**H** 1.35 m for mares; 1.39 m for males.

**C** Most often bay, chestnut, black, sometimes gray.

**Description**: Similar to the Mongolian Horse, the Yanqi is thick and solid in appearance, with a long head with a straight profile; large eyes; long ears; thick neck; broad chest; a long back; a short, wide, sloping croup; and hard hooves. There is a mountain type and a plains type.

**Distribution**: Mainly Hejing and Hoxud counties, also the Yanqi Hui Autonomous County and Bohu County, in northern Bayingolin Mongol Autonomous Prefecture, Xinjiang Autonomous Region, China.

**Origins and history**: The Yanqi was developed over the centuries by crossing several ancient Central Asian breeds, Orlov and Don stallions, with Mongolian mares. The breed was forged in a habitat of the steppes in the high mountains.

**Character and attributes**: Undemanding, it is very well adapted to extremely cold temperatures. The plains type is a good ambler.

**Uses**: Used as a saddle horse, it is also raised for its milk and meat.

**Current status**: In 1980 there were 98,000 horses; the population fell to 20,160 by the end of 2006.

Neck carried
horizontally

Rather large head

Close-set hocks

Wide hooves

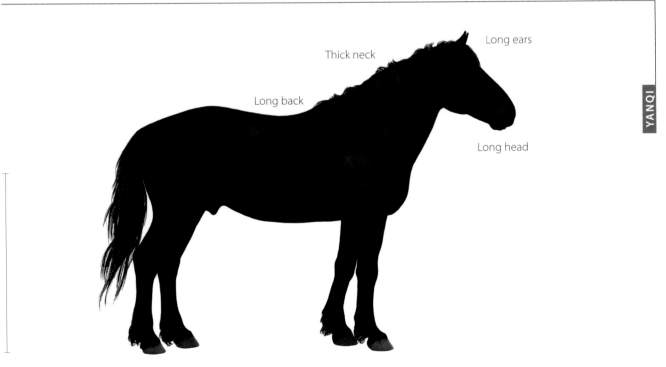

Long ears

Thick neck

Long back

Long head

# HEQU

Chinese: *Hequ*

Also called *Nanfan* and *He qu*

Ⓗ 1.38 m for mares; 1.41 m for males.

Ⓒ Bay, gray, black, sometimes chestnut.

**Description**: The rustic Hequ has a large head with a straight or slightly convex profile; large eyes; small ears; large nostrils; a fairly thin neck; an enormous chest, an adaptation to the lack of oxygen in its habitat (the heart and liver are also very developed for the same reason); and rather straight shoulders.

The rustic Hequ is found on the high Tibetan plateaus.

**Distribution**: Northeast of the Tibetan plateau, principally at the junction of the Yellow River with the Gansu (Gānnán Tibetan Autonomous Prefecture), Sechuan (Aba Tibetan-Qiang Autonomous Prefecture), and Qinghai (Henan Mongol Autonomous County) provinces, China.

**Origins and history**: This is an ancient native breed, which lives in Tibet at altitudes of 3,000–5,000 m. It is rather large for an Asian mountain horse, due to the rich pastureland where it is raised. It was the mount for Tibetan preachers and for the Han.

**Character and attributes**: This is a good mountain horse, very resilient to high altitudes and a good climber; it has good endurance, recovers well from effort, and is undemanding.

**Uses**: Traditionally a horse used for transportation and as a pack horse, it is a good draft horse for farm work.

**Current status**: The Hequ is doing very well in China, with 130,000 horses at the end of 2005.

# SANHE

Chinese: *sanhe*

Once called Hailar, Hai-La-Erh, haila'er, also Sanho, it was given the name Sanhe in 1955.

Ⓗ 1.46 m on average for mares; 1.48 m for males.

Ⓒ Mainly bay and chestnut, gray, bay dun.

**Description**: It has a head with a straight or slightly convex profile, large eyes, long ears, a long neck, prominent withers, broad chest, long back, robust legs, and hard hooves. The hair of the mane and tail is fine.

**Distribution**: Northeastern Inner Mongolia, China.

**Origins and history**: This recent breed was developed from native Chinese breeds and several breeds from the former Soviet Union—notably Mongolian, Orlov, Anglo-Norman, Anglo-Arab, and Percheron—for both saddle and harness. Resilient, it is raised outdoors all year long.

**Character and attributes**: This is a bold and docile horse, fast, strong, undemanding, resilient in cold temperatures (−40°C), and resistant to illness.

**Uses**: It is used as a saddle horse and for light driving.

**Current status**: At the end of 2005, there were only 720 horses. Protection for this breed should be a priority.

A Sanhe, adorned with Chinese decorations.

Somewhat thin neck

Enormous chest from adaptation to the rarefied air of the high Tibetan plateaus

Long ears

Fine mane and tail hair

Long back

Broad chest

## CHINA

# BUOHAI

Chinese: *bohai*

**Ⓗ** 1.48 m on average for mares; 1.49 m for males.

**Ⓒ** Mainly bay and chestnut, sometimes black and gray.

**Description**: This is a solid animal with a well-proportioned body, a head with a straight profile; large eyes; a long neck; prominent withers; a broad chest; long back; well-developed, sometimes long, sloping croup; robust legs; and hard hooves. There are two types, a light and a heavy type.

**Distribution**: Mainly in Guangrao and Kenli counties, and in the county-level city of Shouguang in northeastern Shandong Province, eastern China.

**Origins and history**: The Buohai certainly has Mongolian origins, and has been crossed with foreign draft horses, notably Ardennais and Soviet Draft.

**Character and attributes**: Of docile temperament, it grows quickly.

**Uses**: It is suitable both for riding and for farm work.

**Current status**: The Buohai is becoming extremely rare; there were only 112 horses in 2006. The breed should be protected.

## CHINA

# YILI

Chinese: *yili, iyi, ili*

**Ⓗ** 1.47 m on average for mares; 1.54 m for males, some are over 1.60 m.

**Ⓒ** Generally bay, chestnut, or black.

**Description**: The Yili is one of the tallest of Chinese breeds. It has a head with a straight profile; a wide forehead; large eyes; small ears; a thick, muscular neck; prominent withers; a broad chest; short, slightly sloping croup; robust legs; and hard hooves.

**Distribution**: Ili Kazakh Autonomous Prefecture, Xinjiang Autonomous Region, China.

**Origins and history**: The breed has been developed for more than a century through successive crossings among Kazakh mares and Don, Anglo-Don, and Orlov stallions.

**Character and attributes**: Easygoing, robust, and resilient, it is well adapted to a sometimes harsh environment.

**Uses**: It is suitable for riding and in harness, for recreation and sport, but it is also raised for its milk and meat.

**Current status**: The population is doing well, with 120,000 recorded in 2007.

## CHINA

### THE CHINESE KAZAKH

The Kazakh (see Kazakhstan, *p. 310*) is very widespread in China, where it is known as the Chinese Kazakh. It is most often bay, chestnut, and black, sometimes gray, measuring in Kazakhstan around 1.40 m. It is popular for its resistance to cold, its qualities as a saddle horse, and its production of milk and meat. In the past it was called *wusun*. At the end of 2007 the population of Chinese Kazakhs was 400,000 horses.

Long neck

Prominent
withers

Long back

Draft type

Thick, muscular
neck

Prominent withers

Robust legs

# Jilin

Also called: Jilin Harness Horse

Chinese: *jilin*

Ⓗ 1.44 m for mares; 1.51 m for males.

Ⓒ Generally bay, sometimes chestnut, rarely black.

**Description**: This is a strong, massive horse with a straight, wide back; a sloping croup; robust legs with sometimes close-set hocks; and hard hooves.

**Distribution**: Jilin Province, northeastern China.

**Origins and history**: This rather recent breed was developed in the mid-twentieth century, as the native horses were too small, both for riding and for draft work, from horses of the Mongolian type crossed with Ardennais, Don, Soviet Draft, Vladimir, Kabarda, and others.

**Character and attributes**: It is docile, has endurance, and is undemanding and an easy keeper. It is strong, fast, and good at pulling.

**Uses**: It is mainly raised as a draft horse for farm work, or for its meat.

**Current status**: The number of these horses isn't known, but we do know that the numbers have significantly decreased since the 1980s.

# Guanzhong

Chinese: *guanzhong*

Note: Not to be confused with the Chinese donkey of the same name. It was once called Guanzhong Harness Horse.

Ⓗ 1.52 m for mares; 1.53 m for males on average.

Ⓒ Mainly chestnut, sometimes bay.

**Description**: This solid harness horse has a head with a straight profile; long, sloping shoulders; a round croup; robust legs; and hard hooves.

**Distribution**: Guanzhong Zone, Shaanxi Province, but also the Shanxi and Hebei provinces and Xinjiang Region, China.

**Origins and history**: The breed was developed in the 1950s from Soviet breeds (Boudonny, Karabair) and Ardennais, crossed with native mares, both for riding and for draft work, in order to meet the needs of agriculture in its native region.

**Character and attributes**: This is a docile and powerful horse, with good pulling abilities and endurance. It is resistant to illness and is fertile.

**Uses**: It can be used for riding or for recreational harness.

**Current status**: The breed has suffered from mechanization and has become rare, with only 3,455 horses at the end of 2006.

Sloping croup

Robust legs

Hocks sometimes
close-set

Straight profile

Round croup

Robust legs

# NINGQIANG

Chinese: *ningqiang, mingling*

**H** 1.12 m on average.

**C** Bay, chestnut, black, roan, palomino, black/brown dun.

**Description**: Small and compact, it has a slender head with a straight profile, wide forehead, large eyes, small ears, unobtrusive withers, a short neck, an average-sized chest, quite muscular hindquarters, a sloping croup, robust legs, and solid hooves.

**Distribution**: Mainly Ningqiang County, also Nanzheng County, southwestern Shaanxi Province, China.

**Origins and history**: This is an ancient breed from central China.

**Character and attributes**: The Ningqiang is gentle, bold, and has good endurance.

**Uses**: It is a pack horse useful in the distant mountains.

**Current status**: Rare for a long time, there were only 3,301 horses in 1981, and its numbers had fallen to 360 individuals by the end of 2006, which makes it one of the rarest breeds in China.

# WENSHAN

Chinese: *wenshan*

**H** 1.08 m–1.12 m on average for mares; 1.12 m–1.18 m for males.

**C** Mainly bay, chestnut, gray.

**Description**: Very small and compact, the Wenshan has a rather large head with a straight profile, small ears, a short neck, straight shoulders, a slightly sloping croup, robust legs, and hard hooves. The tail is set high, and the hair of the mane and tail is thick.

**Distribution**: Guangnan, Funing, and Maguan counties, Wenshan Zhuang and Miao Autonomous Prefecture, Yunnan Province, China.

**Origins and history**: This is a local breed from the tropical and subtropical regions of Yunnan Province.

**Character and attributes**: It is very well adapted to the extremely hot temperatures and humidity of the climate; it is resistant to illness and has good endurance.

**Uses**: This is a pack horse, a saddle horse, and a light carriage horse that was used for farm work.

**Current status**: The breed is doing well and is widespread. There were 144,000 horses in 1980, and still 67,600 at the end of 2005.

# LICHUAN

Chinese: *lichuan*

**H** 1.18 m for mares; 1.25 m for males.

**C** Most often gray, bay, chestnut, or black.

**Description**: Rustic, with short legs.

**Distribution**: Lichuan, Hubei Province, China.

**Origins and history**: The Lichuan is a local horse from the east-central part of China, traditionally used for transporting goods.

**Character and attributes**: It is strong despite its small size.

**Uses**: It is primarily a pack horse.

**Current status**: Once common (130,000 horses in 1979), its numbers today are not known, but are probably declining due to mechanization.

## YONGNING

CHINA

Also called: Yongning Tibetan Horse

Chinese: *yongning*

**H** 1.22 m on average.

**C** Bay, chestnut, black, gray.

**Description**: A small horse, quite muscular, the Yongning has a short and slightly heavy head, with a somewhat convex profile; large eyes; small ears; a thick, muscular, short neck; prominent withers; a short back; sloping croup; short legs; and hard hooves.

**Distribution**: North of Lijiang, Shangri-La County, Diqing Tibetan Autonomous Prefecture, northwestern Yunnan Province, China.

**Origins and history**: It is one of the ancient breeds of mountain horses from the Tibetan plateau.

**Character and attributes**: It lives outdoors throughout the year, and also has great endurance.

**Uses**: It is essentially used as a saddle horse and a pack horse. The development of tourism in the region could make it a good trekking horse.

**Current status**: There were 4,520 horses at the end of 2005.

## ZHONGDIAN

CHINA

Chinese: *zhongdian*

**H** 1.20 m on average for mares; 1.28 m for males.

**C** Mainly bay and chestnut, more rarely black.

**Description**: This is a type of Tibetan horse (see Tibetan, *p. 342*). Small in size, it has a small head with a straight profile; a narrow forehead; large eyes; small ears; a short, quite muscular neck; a short, round croup; robust legs; and hard hooves.

**Distribution**: Shangri-La County (once called Zhongdian), Diqing Tibetan Autonomous Prefecture, northwestern Yunnan Province, China.

**Origins and history**: The breed belongs to the group of Tibetan Horses.

**Character and attributes**: It is simple and well adapted to the mountain regions at more than 3,200 m in altitude, resistant to cold and a lack of oxygen.

**Uses**: Ridden or as a pack horse, it is suitable for equestrian trekking.

**Current status**: This native breed had 7,100 horses in 1980 and 6,770 at the end of 2005.

## JINJIANG

CHINA

Chinese: *jinjiang, jinhong*

Note: Not to be confused with the Jianchang, a different breed.

**H** 1.24 m for mares; 1.25 m for males.

**C** Mainly bay, chestnut.

**Description**: This is a small horse with a head with a straight profile; muscular neck; slightly sloping croup; and short, strong legs.

**Distribution**: Jinjiang, Nan'an, Shishi, Fujian Province, southeast China.

**Origins and history**: This very ancient local breed has been raised for a long time separate from others.

**Character and attributes**: It has good pulling abilities, but is not very fast. It is well adapted to the subtropical climate and is resistant to illness.

**Uses**: It is used as a saddle horse, a pack horse, and in harness. It is also used for farm work such as rice-growing.

**Current status**: This breed is very rare and its numbers are very small, with probably fewer than a thousand horses. It is considered endangered.

# LIJIANG

Also called: New Lijiang

Chinese: *lijiang*

**Ⓗ** 1.25 m on average.

**Ⓒ** Bay, black, gray.

**Description:** This is a compact horse, with large eyes, a wide forehead, short neck, sloping shoulders, pronounced withers, short legs, and a slightly sloping croup.

**Distribution:** Lijiang Prefecture, Yunnan Province, southwest China.

**Origins and history:** This is a recent breed, which began to be developed in the middle of the twentieth century from Arabian, Yili, Hequ, Kabarda, and Ardennais blood. A study has shown that Lijiang mares that live in the mountains at more than 2,800 m in cold regions go into heat around one month later than Lijiangs living in the plains.

**Character and attributes:** It is robust and has good endurance.

**Uses:** This is a good pack horse.

**Current status:** This recent native breed is still being developed.

# GANZI

Also called: Tibetan-Sikang Pony

Chinese: *ganzi, ganzhi, sihang, xikang, kang, sikangihsi-k'ang, hsiangcheng*

**Ⓗ** 1.26 m for mares; 1.29 m for males.

**Ⓒ** Bay, chestnut, black.

**Description:** This is a Tibetan-type horse (see Tibetan, *p. 342*). The Ganzi has a compact body; a head with a straight profile; a rather long neck; broad chest; straight back; slightly sloping croup; long, robust legs; and hard hooves. The tail is set high, and the hair is long and thick. The Maiwa is a type of Ganzi that is found in Hongyuan County, Aba Tibetan-Qiang Autonomous Prefecture.

**Distribution:** Serxu, Sertar, Baiyu, Dege, Litang, Garze (Ganzi) counties, Garze Tibetan Autonomous Prefecture, and Hongyuan County, Aba Tibetan-Qiang Autonomous Prefecture, northwestern and northern Sichuan Province, China.

**Origins and history:** It belongs to the group of Tibetan horses.

**Character and attributes:** It has good endurance, is able to carry heavy loads, and is good at pulling. It does well at high altitudes.

**Uses:** Traditionally used as a pack horse, it can also be ridden for recreation or used for producing milk.

**Current status:** Unknown outside China, it is nevertheless doing well. From 170,000 horses in 1980, the population has increased to 402,409 at the end of 2005.

# YUSHU

Chinese: *yushu, gaoyuan, geji, gejihua*

**Ⓗ** 1.30 m for mares; 1.31 m for males.

**Ⓒ** Usually gray or bay (often mealy), more rarely black, chestnut, buckskin, bay dun, palomino.

**Description:** The Yushu is a Tibetan-type horse (see Tibetan, *p. 342*). A small horse, it has a somewhat wide head with a straight profile; large eyes; small ears; a rather horizontally set neck; broad chest; short, slightly sloping croup; robust legs; and hard hooves. The hair of the mane and tail is thick.

**Distribution:** Yushu Tibetan Autonomous Prefecture, Qinghai Province, China.

**Origins and history:** The Yushu is one of the group of Tibetan horses.

**Character and attributes:** Gentle, with great endurance, it is very resilient at altitudes of more than 4,500 m on the Tibetan plateau. It is a good mountain horse.

**Uses:** It is a good pack horse and is used for transportation.

**Current status:** There were 60,000 horses in 1980, and 35,100 at the end of 2005.

## CHINA

# CADAMU

Chinese: *chaidamu, cadamu*

🐴 1.29 m–1.36 m for mares; 1.31 m–1.40 m for males.

🎨 Mainly gray and bay, sometimes black, chestnut.

**Description**: This solid horse has a strong, round body; a small, short, but wide head with a straight profile; small, thick ears; a thin, short neck; broad chest; and short, robust legs.

**Distribution**: Qaidam (Chaidamu) Basin, salt swamps region, Dulan, Goldmut, Wulan counties, northern Tibetan plateau, Qinghai Province, China.

**Origins and history**: This is a horse of Mongolian type, originally from the Qaidam Basin, which accompanied regional nomads of Tibetan or Mongolian origin.

**Character and attributes**: This horse is well suited to work in swampy zones and the aridity of the Qaidam basin. It has good endurance.

**Uses**: It is used for riding or for producing meat and milk.

**Current status**: Once widespread (50,000 horses in 1978), there were only 13,043 of this local horse at the end of 2005.

---

## CHINA

# AGABA DARK HORSE

Also called: Sengseng Dark Horse

Chinese: *agaba*

🐴 On average 1.36 m for mares; 1.40 m for males.

🎨 Mainly black, sometimes dark bay.

**Description**: Of Mongolian type, the Agaba Dark Horse is distinguished by its always dark coat. It has a head with a straight or slightly convex profile; large eyes; small ears; a wide forehead; long neck; unobtrusive withers; a broad chest; muscular shoulders; a long back; short, slightly sloping croup; and small, hard hooves. The hide is very shiny.

**Distribution**: North of the Abag Banner, Inner Mongolia Autonomous Region, Xilingol League, northern China.

**Origins and history**: Although these types of Mongolian horses are ancient, this breed was only confirmed in 2009.

**Character and attributes**: It has a good temperament and endurance and is agile, fast, and strong. It can endure extremely cold temperatures and can live outdoors. It is resistant to illness.

**Uses**: This horse is well suited to recreational riding. The mares are used for milk production, and the Agaba Dark Horse is also raised for its meat.

**Current status**: The breed is rare, with 3,758 horses recorded in 2008.

---

## CHINA

### THE NANGCHEN, A TYPE OF YUSHU

The Nangchen horse, or Yushu-Nangchen, was described in 1994 by a French explorer, Michel Peissel, who considered it a particularly pure type of Yushu. But the Chinese do not differentiate within the Yushu breed. It is found in the Kham region, in Tibet. Measuring around 1.33 m, of various colors but mainly gray, chestnut, black, or dark bay, a few black/brown or bay dun, it is more slender than other Tibetan horses. It has a rather small head with a straight or slightly concave profile; large, protruding eyes; small ears; a rather long, slender neck; slender legs; a rounded croup; and small hooves. The mane and tail are thick. This horse cannot survive without the care it is given by its breeders: foals are covered with a felt blanket in the winter, and receive additional feed and sometimes, in the winter, a supplement of dry goat cheese. In the past, the Nangchen region was known for producing excellent horses. It is docile and sure-footed, has good endurance, is adapted to very high altitudes (up to 5,400 m), has a very good respiratory system, and it can amble.

The rdo-chu-rta of the Chamdo region is identical to the Nangchen.

## CHINA

# XIANGFEN

Chinese: *xiangfen*

**H** Around 1.38 m.

**C** Bay, chestnut.

**Description**: The Xiangfen resembles the Mongolian, but is heavier. It has a rather large head; a short, thick neck; broad chest; straight shoulders; a wide, slightly sloping croup; hard hooves; and a long, thick mane and tail.

**Distribution**: Xiangfen County, Shanxi Province, northeast China.

**Origins and history**: This recent breed has been developed since 1951. It is a local horse of Mongolian type, improved notably with Ardennais blood.

**Character and attributes**: It is bold and docile.

**Uses**: It is suited for riding and for light farm work.

**Current status**: The Xiangfen is a local breed, fairly unknown.

---

## CHINA

# YIWU

Also called: New Barkol

Chinese: *yiwu*

**H** On average 1.37 m for mares; 1.40 m for males.

**C** Mainly bay, sometimes black and chestnut.

**Description**: It has a stocky body and a head with a straight profile; large eyes; small ears; a long neck; wide withers; a broad chest; long back; slightly sloping croup; and robust legs with close-set hocks.

**Distribution**: Barkol Kazakh Autonomous County, Hami Prefecture, Xinjiang Autonomous Region, China.

**Origins and history**: The Yiwu was created by crossing Kazakh mares with Yili stallions. It is basically a military horse.

**Character and attributes**: The Yiwu has a docile temperament and is very resilient in the cold. It is a good mountain horse.

**Uses**: It is mainly used as a pack horse, but is also suitable for riding and for pulling.

**Current status**: This local breed is endangered, with only 326 horses at the end of 2007.

---

## CHINA

# XINI

Chinese: *xini, sini*

**H** On average 1.34 m for mares; 1.47 m for males.

**C** Most often bay, chestnut, black.

**Description**: This is a very muscular horse, with a slender head.

**Distribution**: Evenk Autonomous Banner, Hulunbuir Prefecture, northeastern Inner Mongolia, China.

**Origins and history**: This is a typical farm horse of this region of Inner Mongolia.

**Character and attributes**: It is strong. Very adaptable, it survives in the snow and can tolerate a range of climates.

**Uses**: It is a good harness horse and is used for farm work.

**Current status**: This is a local breed. There were 10,000 horses in 1982, but the current status is not known.

# SANDAN

Chinese: *Sandan*

**H** On average 1.38 m for mares; 1.45 m for males.

**C** Most often bay, sometimes chestnut and black.

**Description**: The boxy, solid Sandan has a delicate head with a straight profile; large eyes; small ears; a wide forehead; broad chest; long, sloping shoulders; a long back; wide, sloping croup; and robust legs.

**Distribution**: Sandan Horse Farm, town of Zhangye, Gansu Province, China.

**Origins and history**: This is basically a military horse, raised for the needs of the Chinese army. It was developed in 1953–1962 by crossing local mares with Don stallions, and has only a quarter Don blood.

**Character and attributes**: Sensitive and docile, the Sandan is fast, has good endurance, is at ease on mountain paths, and is well adapted to altitude. It is resistant to illness.

**Uses**: It is suitable for riding as well as in harness. No longer a military horse, it is now used for recreation and sport.

**Current status**: This local breed had only 3,026 individuals at the end of 2006.

---

# XILINGOL

Chinese: *xilingol, xilinguole*

**H** On average 1.41 m for mares; 1.46 m for males.

**C** Usually bay, chestnut, black, sometimes gray.

**Description**: The Xilingol is a light horse whose head has a straight or slightly convex profile; it has large eyes; small ears; a long, muscular neck; broad chest; long back; slightly sloping croup; robust legs; and a high-set tail.

**Distribution**: Southeastern Xilingol League, Inner Mongolia, China.

**Origins and history**: This recent breed was created in the 1960s by crossing Mongolian mares with Don, Thoroughbred, and Kabarda stallions. It is raised on the steppes of Xilingol. These crossings recall the attempts in neighboring Mongolia to create the New Mongolian.

**Character and attributes**: The Xilingol is docile and resilient.

**Uses**: This is a riding horse, which is also used for milk production.

**Current status**: This horse is very rare. There were only 364 of them at the end of 2005, but the breed is being developed.

---

# ZHANGBEI

Chinese: *zhangbei*

**H** On average 1.42 m for mares; 1.49 m for males.

**C** Mainly bay, chestnut, sometimes black.

**Description**: This solid horse has a powerful look. It has a wide forehead; small ears; a slender, muscular neck; broad chest; long back; short, sloping croup; and short, robust legs.

**Distribution**: Zhangbei, Kangbao, Shangyi counties, Hebei Province, China.

**Origins and history**: The breed was created by crossing Mongolian mares with Thoroughbred, Russian Draft, and Soviet Draft stallions.

**Character and attributes**: The Zhangbei is powerful and has excellent endurance.

**Uses**: It can be used for transportation, either under saddle or in harness.

**Current status**: The breed is on the brink of extinction, with only sixty-eight horses left at the end of 2006.

## CHINA

# KEERQIN

Chinese: *kerqin, ke-er-qin*

- 1.44 m for mares; 1.48 m for males.
- Bay, black, chestnut.

**Description**: The Keerqin has a head with a straight or slightly convex profile; wide forehead; large eyes; muscular neck; prominent withers; broad chest; long back; wide, slightly sloping croup; robust legs; and hard hooves.

**Distribution**: Ar Horqin Banner, Inner Mongolia, China.
**Origins and history**: The breed was created by crossings between local mares and Sanhe, Don, and Thoroughbred stallions with the goal of creating a saddle and harness horse.
**Character and attributes**: It is docile, resilient, fast, and powerful.
**Uses**: Its breeding focuses primarily on riding.
**Current status**: The breed is doing well; at the end of 2008 there were 63,313 horses.

---

## CHINA

# JINZHOU

Chinese: *jinzhou*

Note: Not to be confused with the Guizhou

- 1.49 m for mares.
- Mainly bay, sometimes chestnut or black.

**Description**: It has a head with a straight or slightly convex profile, wide forehead, large eyes, prominent withers, a broad chest, long back, and robust legs.
**Distribution**: Jinzhou district, Liaoning Province, northeastern China.

**Origins and history**: This breed was developed by crossing Mongolian horses with Arabian and Hackney horses, then in 1939 with Anglo-Norman, Anglo-Arab, Orlov, and half-blood Percheron, and then with Kabarda in 1949, but without much success with the latter. The Jinzhou has been developed in the farming region south of Liaoning Province, both for riding and for draft use.
**Character and attributes**: The Jinzhou has a good temperament, and is resistant to illness.
**Uses**: This is a good riding and harness horse.
**Current status**: This breed is on the brink of extinction, with only 93 horses at the end of 2006. There are no stallions to ensure the survival of the breed.

---

## CHINA

# HEILONGKIANG

Chinese: *heilongjiang*

- On average 1.50 m for mares; 1.54 m for males.
- Mainly bay, chestnut.

**Description**: It has a head with a straight profile; rather long ears; a broad chest; wide, slightly sloping croup; and a thick mane and tail.
**Distribution**: Heilongjiang Province, northeastern China.

**Origins and history**: This recent breed was created by mixing Mongolian with Don, Orlov, Soviet Draft, Ardennais, and other blood, with the goal of combining the robustness of Mongolian horses and the attributes of the other breeds.
**Character and attributes**: The Heilongjiang has a gentle nature; it is powerful, undemanding, and resistant to illness.
**Uses**: It is used for riding and for pulling.
**Current status**: This local breed is now considered endangered.

## HEIHE

Chinese: *heihe*

**H** On average 1.52 m for mares; 1.55 m for males.

**C** Bay or chestnut, a few black and gray.

**Description**: Rather compact and strong, the Heihe has a head with a straight profile, large eyes, long ears, a broad chest, and a rather short croup. There is also a lighter type.

**Distribution**: Heilongjiang Province, north of Manchuria, northeastern China.

**Origins and history**: This horse, which gets its name from the city of Heihe, in Heilongjiang, was developed from local and Mongolian horses. At the beginning of the twentieth century, it received contributions of Russian (Orlov) blood, then in the 1940s, French blood from the Percheron, Anglo-Arab, and Anglo-Norman.

**Character and attributes**: It has a gentle nature and good endurance; it is powerful and resilient in a cold climate.

**Uses**: It is a saddle and harness horse.

**Current status**: There were 11,000 horses in the 1980s, but this local breed is now considered endangered in China.

## TIELING DRAFT

Also called: Tieling Harness Horse

Chinese: *tieling*

**H** 1.43 m for mares.

**C** Mainly bay and black, rarely chestnut.

**Description**: It has a head with a straight profile; large eyes; a rather long neck; broad chest; long back; a well-rounded croup; and short, robust legs.

**Distribution**: Tieling County, Liaoning Province, China.

**Origins and history**: Bred on the Tieling Farm since 1949, this horse is the result of crossings among a herd of 44 draft mares, hybrids of Anglo-Norman, Anglo-Arab, and Percheron, with Ardennais, Soviet Draft, and Russian Draft, then with Orlov and Jinzhou horses. It was one of the best Chinese draft horses, but its population has declined due to mechanization.

**Character and attributes**: Docile and easy, it is a powerful, fast horse with good endurance.

**Uses**: It is basically a draft horse used for farm work and in harness.

**Current status**: Extremely rare, on the brink of extinction, there were only 30 individuals at the end of 2006—only mares, and no stallions.

## HENAN LIGHT DRAFT

Chinese: *henan*

**H** 1.50 m on average.

**C** Bay, chestnut.

**Description**: The Henan Light Draft has a rather large head; a fairly short neck; broad chest; wide, slightly sloping croup; and solid hooves.

**Distribution**: Henan Province, eastern China.

**Origins and history**: Raised in the agricultural plains of Henan Province, it is a heavy horse created both for riding and for pulling.

**Character and attributes**: It is strong.

**Uses**: This is a horse suitable for farm work and as a harness horse.

**Current status**: The breed is local and little known.

## MONGOLIAN OF INNER MONGOLIA

Mongolian horses (see Mongolian, *p. 314*) are very well represented in China, notably throughout Inner Mongolia, but also more widely in north, northeast, and northwestern China. The population was estimated at 86,700 horses at the end of 2005 (there were 1,700,000 horses in 1982). Sometimes called the Chinese Mongolian, this breed is popular for its ability to tolerate harsh living conditions. A more refined variety of the Mongolian, the Wuchumutsin, or Mongolian-Ujumqin, is found more specifically in the Xilinguole region and is popular among the Chinese. It measures on average 1.26 m for mares; 1.29 m for males.

## THE STATUS OF THE KYRGYZ HORSE IN CHINA

Of note in China is a large population of Kyrgyz horses, sometimes called the Chinese Kyrgyz. There were 27,000 at the end of 2008. They are primarily located in the Kizilsu Kirghiz Autonomous Prefecture, in the Xinjiang Uyghur Autonomous Region, western China.

# Myanmar

Once called Burma, this country is witnessing a decline in its horse population, except in some regions where the use of horses to pull carts or carry packs is still prevalent. Leisure riding is, however, developing steadily, as is equestrian tourism. Burmese horses are small, simple, and resilient.

MYANMAR

# SHAN

Also called: Burmese

Burmese: *shan myin*

Note: *Myin* means "horse" in Burmese.

**H** 1.32 m on average.

**C** Bay, dark bay, chestnut, gray, black.

**Description**: The Shan looks like the Manipur but is taller. It has a delicate head with a straight profile, unobtrusive withers, a broad chest, rather straight shoulders, a sometimes long back, slender legs, and small hooves.

**Distribution**: Shan state of eastern Myanmar (near China, Laos, and Thailand).

**Origins and history**: This ancient breed likely has Mongolian origins, to which other breeds have been added.

**Character and attributes**: The Shan is always docile, but sometimes unpredictable. It has good endurance and is robust, adapted to the mountains; however, it is not very fast, and its gaits are not among the most comfortable.

**Uses**: This is a small, versatile horse, especially good for riding and as a pack and harness horse. It was once used as a polo pony, primarily by colonists. Because of its size, it can make a good mount for children.

**Current status**: This local breed is doing fine.

MYANMAR

# MYANMAR

Burma has another type of small horse, the Myanmar (*Myanmar myin* in Burmese, or "Burmese Horse"), also called *bama myin* in the Magway region, in central Myanmar. Its origins are not known. Taller than the Shan, it measures around 1.45 m. It is resilient to heat and the monsoon. It is often used in harness.

## THE CONTROVERSIAL RIWOCHE HORSE

In 1995 an explorer, Michel Peissel, reported the discovery in Riwoche (Kham Region, Tibet, China) of a small horse living in the wild under a ledge at an altitude of 5,050 m. He described it as measuring 1.20 m, dark/brown dun, bay, black, with sometimes dorsal striping and striping on the upper posterior legs. Of primitive type, it has a rather triangular head, small eyes, thin nostrils; sloping croup, and thick hair.

The Chinese don't recognize it as a new breed. In the photos brought back from the expedition, this is a young animal, and these horses are probably a variant of Tibetan types, which are also very rustic, small, and have primitive coats. It also resembles the Tibetan Yongning, being of equivalent height and similar morphology, which today is found more to the south, but whose range of distribution in the past was perhaps different.

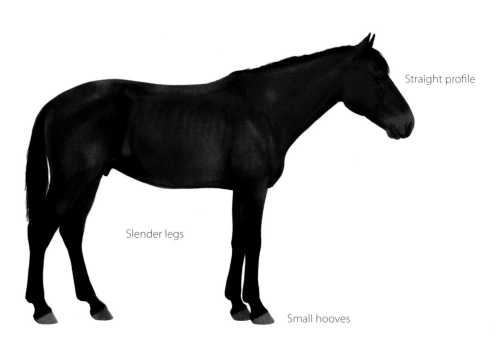

Straight profile

SHAN

Slender legs

Small hooves

# Thailand

In addition to foreign breeds, Thailand has a small native breed, well adapted to the hot and humid climate, but it is now suffering from competition with imported breeds, which are more in fashion. The development of equestrian tourism, combined with the breed's sure-footedness in the mountains, might, however, be of benefit to it in the coming years.

---

## THAILAND

# THAI

Also called: Siamese Pony

Thai: *mah klab, maah glab*

(H) 1.20 m–1.23 m.

(C) Bay, dark bay, some mealy, some with a dorsal stripe.

**Description**: A small horse, it resembles other breeds from the Indochinese peninsula, notably the Burmese Shan, with powerful legs and mane and tail hair that is quite thick.

**Distribution**: Thailand.

**Origins and history**: The very ancient Thai likely descends from the Mongolian or the Shan, but its origins are not known. Recently, some individuals have received foreign blood and are taller.

**Character and attributes**: Of calm nature, robust, with great endurance, it is sure-footed in mountainous terrain.

**Uses**: Small and versatile, it was a military horse, and it is still used as a pack animal, notably in the north of the country. It is often harnessed to carts and used to pull taxis. It is also used in equestrian tourism.

**Current status**: The breeding of Thai horses is not yet organized; there is no studbook and the original breed is becoming increasingly rare (there were probably a few thousand individuals in 2009), subject to crossings with Thoroughbreds or Quarter Horses. Associations have been established to come to the aid of this very ancient breed.

## THAILAND

### TOWARD A NEW THAI?

For the past fifteen years or so, crossings have taken place between Thai mares and Thoroughbred, then Quarter Horse stallions, resulting in mares measuring on average 1.35 m–1.45 m and stallions measuring 1.50 m, of all colors, often pinto, but not black. These are good quality animals, hardier, larger, more muscular, and with a broader chest than the original Thai. Arabian blood will also be used in the breeding. Crossings with the American Paint are also frequent. Tourists tend to seek out these bigger horses, which appear better suited for pulling carts or carrying riders, without realizing that this contributes to the disappearance of the small, original Thai, which is, however, robust and can carry heavy loads.

In Thailand one often comes across "taxis" that consist of a horse harnessed to some kind of cart.

Thick mane
and tail

Often mealy coat,
with a lighter
contour around
the eyes

Powerful legs

## Laos

Horse breeding is not of great importance in Laos. One does, however, encounter small animals that serve as pack horses and which are similar to other horses of Southeast Asia. The country's opening to tourism will perhaps gradually change the situation.

### LAOS

# LAOTIAN

Laotian: *ma* (which means "horse")

Ⓗ On average 1.10 m for mares; 1.20 m for males.

Ⓒ Bay, dark bay, also chestnut, sometimes gray, bay dun.

**Description**: The Laotian is very similar to the Vietnamese and other types from Southeast Asia. It has a straight profile, slender legs, a low-set tail, and a thick mane and tail.

**Distribution**: Laos.
**Origins and history**: This is the native horse of Laos, where it has been present for a long time. It is sometimes considered a sub-breed of the Vietnamese.
**Character and attributes**: It is resilient and has good endurance.
**Uses**: This is a versatile horse, mainly used as a pack horse. It is also ridden and driven. Its small size can make it a good mount for children.
**Current status**: The population of Laotian horses is declining.

There are around 132,000 horses in Vietnam, a stable population that is found mainly in the northern mountains and in the center of the country. Most are small native horses. The Kabarda is also present in

# ANNAMESE PONY

Also called: Vietnamese Horse, Color Horse

Vietnamese: *ngu'a nôi*

Ⓗ 1 m–1.25 m; on average 1.02 m for mares; 1.10 m for males.

Ⓒ Mainly dark bay, also light bay, gray.

**Description**: Very small, it has a rather large head with a straight profile; a short neck; thin, short legs; a sloping croup; and a low-set tail. The mane and tail are thick.
**Distribution**: Mainly Cao Bang, Lang Son, and Bac Giang provinces, mountain regions in northern Vietnam, but also elsewhere.
**Origins and history**: This is an ancient breed, present for a long time in Vietnam.

**Character and attributes**: It is rustic, resistant to illness, and hardy, well adapted to both heat and cold.
**Uses**: It is essentially used as a pack and draft horse, and is also raised for its meat.
**Current status**: It is doing well and its numbers are stable.

### THE WHITE VARIETY: THE NGU'A TRANG

The *ngu'a trang*, whose name in Vietnamese means "white horse," is a white variety used for medicine (bones, blood of pregnant mares: the equine chorionic gonadotropin hormone) and considered to be a type of Annamese Pony. Its numbers are small and decreasing. It is found in the mountains of the north.

# VIETNAMESE HMONG HORSE

Vietnamese: *ngu'a H'mông*

Ⓗ 1 m–1.12 m.

Ⓒ Bay, chestnut, bay dun, buckskin, black/brown dun, palomino, gray.

**Description**: The Hmong has a head with broad forehead and a slightly convex profile. The hair of the mane and tail are thick, and the mane is bushy.
**Distribution**: It is found mainly in Ha Giang Province, in the mountains of northern Vietnam.

**Origins and history**: This ancient breed, which developed in isolation from others, has only been recognized recently. Its origins are unknown, but it probably comes from Mongolian horses or other Asian breeds, from Timor or Sichuan. It may have received Arabian blood during French colonization in the nineteenth century.
**Character and attributes**: The Hmong is a docile and sure-footed animal.
**Uses**: It is used for riding and as a pack horse. Its meat is also consumed.
**Current status**: Although the breed is rare, the Hmongs remain attached to their horses, which are very useful, even today, for transportation in the mountains.

Vietnam, having been imported in the 1960s. It has been crossed a lot with native horses with a view to improving them and increasing their height. Horses are used for transportation and pulling, but also to produce meat and medicine. They are also used in tourism.

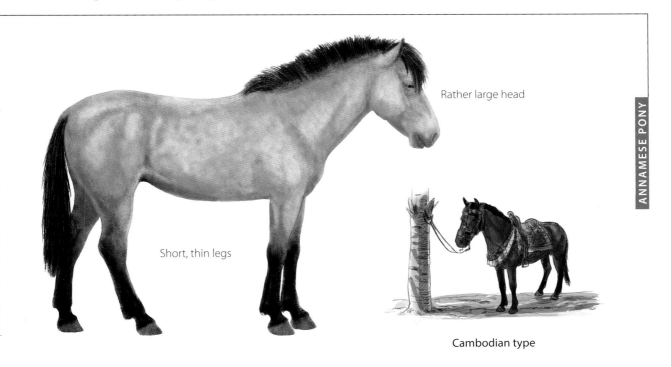

Rather large head

Short, thin legs

Cambodian type

# Cambodia

Equestrian activities were forbidden by the Khmer Rouge in the 1970s. Thus the entire horse industry needs to be developed from scratch in this country. Although the number of horses has sharply declined, small Cambodian horses are still very present in everyday life, but primarily as work animals, notably harnessed to carts. The development of equestrian tourism might open more avenues to them.

## CAMBODIA

# CAMBODIAN

Khmer: *sèèh Kâmpŭchea*

Ⓗ 1.25 m–1.30 m on average.

Ⓒ Mainly bay, dark bay, also chestnut.

**Description**: The Cambodian greatly resembles Thai and Vietnamese breeds. These are small, stocky, squarely built horses, with a head with a straight profile, short neck, unobtrusive withers, straight shoulders, thin legs, a sloping croup, low-set tail, and small hooves. The hair is thick, with the mane often cut short.
**Distribution**: Cambodia.

**Origins and history**: Although its origins are not well known, the breed has been in Cambodia for a long time.
**Character and attributes**: This is a small, rustic horse, undemanding and easy to keep.
**Uses**: It is used locally for transporting people and goods, notably for the markets, and transporting people in areas that are difficult to access by motorized vehicles, or for light farm work.
**Current status**: This local breed is widespread, but it is worth mentioning that in a few regions breeders are importing larger stallions from Vietnam and crossing them with Cambodian mares, and this new population of crossbred horses is growing.

South Korea recorded 27,000–28,000 horses in 2013, 90 percent of which are on the island of Jeju. In addition to its ancient native breed, the Jeju, which is today endangered, South Korea has around eight imported breeds present in small numbers, mainly

# JEJU

Korean: *jeju, cheju, tchedchu, jejuma, gwahama, toma*

Ⓗ 1.10 m–1.30 m.

Ⓒ Mainly chestnut, mealy bay, dark bay, black, occasionally gray, white, cream, pinto.

**Description**: The Jeju is a small, massive horse with a rather large head with straight profile; large, almond-shaped eyes; small ears; a short, rather thick neck; a slightly sloping croup; and a rather high-set tail. The mane and tail are thick and abundant, and the winter coat is dense.

**Distribution**: The island of Jeju-do, South Korea.

**Origins and history**: The Jeju likely has Chinese origins and probably received Mongolian blood in the thirteenth century. It has existed on its island for several centuries. The island of Jeju-do was considered in past centuries to be one of the best places in Korea to breed horses.

### CROSSED WITH THE THOROUGHBRED, THE HALLA

The Jeju is sometimes crossed with the English Thoroughbred and other Western horses to create an intermediate type called Halla. Taller than the traditional Jeju, it measures between 1.30 m and 1.45 m. Of variable appearance, from rather slender to actually massive, with rather almond-shaped eyes and a variety of colors, its mane and tail are thinner than those of the Jeju. In fact, it is now the most common type in South Korea. There are more than 16,000 hybrid horses of Halla type, essentially on the island of Jeju-do, where many are raised for meat. They are also found on the northern coast of Korea, in Naksan, for example, pulling small carts that play music for tourists.

**Character and attributes**: The Jeju is gentle, very resilient, very simple, and well adapted to the climate of Korea, which is both hot in the summer and harsh in the winter. It lives a long time.

**Uses**: It is suitable for riding and draft work and as a pack horse. The small Jejus make good mounts for children. Its meat is also consumed locally, and the horse has become a tourist attraction.

**Current status**: Once quite numerous (12,000 individuals in 1960), the Jeju is no longer used for farming and transportation, and its numbers have decreased significantly (around 1,392 horses, with 200 purebred Jejus registered). Although it has been classified a national treasure, and its numbers are slowly rising, it remains rare; there are very few purebred individuals remaining.

The Halla type, taller, more slender, and less rustic than the original Jeju from which it has been developed, is today much more widespread in South Korea than the Jeju.

Thoroughbreds for racing. The traditional uses, such as for the military and for transportation, have disappeared, but leisure activities have not completely taken over. As for its neighbor, North Korea, we haven't been able to obtain any information. But, given the history of these two countries, it would seem reasonable that animals there would be similar to the South Korean horses.

Short neck

Thick mane and tail

Almond-shaped eyes

Straight profile

To endure the cold Korean winters the rustic Jeju grows a dense and velvety coat.

Japan has twelve horse breeds, eight of which are native. Although those are now very popular, their numbers have fallen since World War II, due to mechanization. All are now protected, and their numbers are increasing (the indigenous population

---

JAPAN

# NOMA

Japanese: *noma, noma uma*

**⊕** 1.10 m–1.20 m, but often under 1.07 m.

**⊙** Bay, dark bay, chestnut, light gray, black. It also regularly has a particular color pattern, a yellowish tinge with a head that looks like that of some breeds of cows, with a face entirely lighter or darker leaving the appearance of "glasses" around the eyes, though this is not considered a true white marking.

**Description**: This is the smallest Japanese breed. Some individuals can be confused with Shetland ponies, but they aren't the same, as the Noma is less massive. It has a head that is rather large in proportion to its body, small ears, slender legs, and very small hooves. The hair of the mane and tail is long and very thick. It develops a beard in the winter.

**Distribution**: Ehime Prefecture, Japan.

**Origins and history**: The breed probably descends from Mongolian horses and was developed in the seventeenth century.

**Character and attributes**: Very gentle and calm, it is strong and can carry heavy loads.

**Uses**: Traditionally used as a pack horse and for transportation, it can be driven. Because of its small size and its good nature, it is an excellent mount for children. It is also good for equitherapy.

**Current status**: Once on the brink of extinction, the breed is now carefully protected. From only 27 individuals in 1988, its numbers have gradually increased to 84 in 2008. The Noma has been considered a cultural treasure of the city of Imabari since 1988. With its small size and its very thick mane and tail, one would think it came right out of a Japanese manga, and it is surprising that the breed is not more widespread and more popular.

---

JAPAN

# TOKARA

Japanese: *tokara, taokara, tokara uma, kagoshima*

**⊕** 1 m–1.22 m; 1.15 m on average.

**⊙** Mainly bay, dark bay, mealy black, with reddish highlights, without white markings.

**Description**: The Tokara is small, with large eyes, thin legs, and a slightly sloping croup. The hair of the mane and tail is thick and rather bushy.

**Distribution**: Tokara Islands, Kogoshima Prefecture, Japan.

**Origins and history**: Present for centuries on these islands, it probably has Mongolian origins. It lives in semi-freedom and was rediscovered in 1952 when only 40 or so individuals remained.

**Character and attributes**: It is simple and rustic.

**Uses**: It was once used for farm work (sugar cane) and as a pack horse, but today the breed lacks a clear niche, which poses a problem for its conservation, even if its size makes it a good mount for young riders.

**Current status**: The Tokara is recognized as a national treasure of Kagoshima Prefecture, but in 2008 there were only 115 individuals of this very rare breed.

of horses went from 1,500 in 1975 to 3,000 in 1991). The Japanese breed horses essentially for *ban-ei keiba* races—a distinctively Japanese discipline in which draft horses race while pulling a weight of 500 kg to a ton—for riding, and for meat production. In addition to the indigenous breeds, one finds mainly Arabian, Thoroughbred, Percheron, Breton, and other breeds. About 25,000 horses are raised annually.

Long, very thick tail

Small ears

The Noma's head often has a distinctive coloration, with a face that is darker or lighter than the hair surrounding the eyes and the cheeks.

Very small hooves

Thick and tousled mane

Thin legs

# YONAGUNI

Japanese: *yonaguni, yonaguni uma*

**H** 1.09 m–1.23 m; on average 1.15 m.

**C** Mainly bay, sometimes chestnut.

**Description**: This small Japanese breed has a broad head with rather small ears, a short neck, straight shoulders, and hard hooves. The mane and tail are quite thick.

**Distribution**: Yonaguni Island, the Ryukyu Islands, Okinawa Prefecture, Japan.

**Origins and history**: This ancient breed is perhaps linked to the Korean Jeju, but its origins are obscure. This horse has lived for a long time on its island isolated from other breeds.

**Character and attributes**: Docile and friendly, it is strong and has good endurance.

**Uses**: Once used for transportation, farm work, and in harness, the Yonaguni is now used for equestrian tourism. Its good nature makes it a useful horse for equitherapy.

**Current status**: The numbers of this very rare breed have fallen dramatically due to mechanization, and it now counts only around 120 individuals. It is well protected, but it is still not used enough to increase its popularity.

# MIYAKO

Japanese: *miyako, miyako uma, sumanuma, myakunuma*

**H** 1.17 m for mares; 1.20 m for males.

**C** Bay, bay dun, black/brown dun, chestnut.

**Description**: The Miyako resembles a Mongolian horse. It has a head with a straight profile, a horizontally set neck, slender legs, and a thick mane and tail.

**Distribution**: Miyako-jima Island, Okinawa Prefecture, Japan.

**Origins and history**: Present for a long time on the island, it is perhaps the issue of Chinese horses from Sichuan or even Korean horses. After World War II, crossings with taller imported stallions gave it its height.

**Character and attributes**: The Miyako is calm, undemanding, rustic, and resistant to illness.

**Uses**: It was once a versatile horse, notably a pack horse and used for farm work.

**Current status**: Once widespread, the breed has suffered from the mechanization of agriculture and had practically disappeared, with nineteen individuals in 2001. But thanks to conservation activity, it has increased slowly to forty individuals in 2012. The Miyako is considered a natural treasure of Okinawa Prefecture.

Short neck

Thick mane
and tail

Broad head

Hard hooves

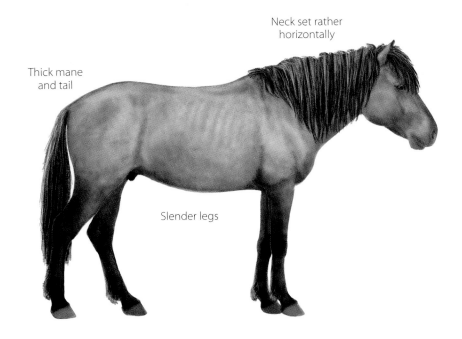

Neck set rather
horizontally

Thick mane
and tail

Slender legs

# MISAKI

Japanese: *misaki, misaki uma*

Ⓗ 1.24 m–1.38 m; on average, 1.32 m.

Ⓒ Mainly mealy bay in various shades, with a dorsal stripe, dark bay, rarely black or chestnut.

**Description**: Small, of rustic appearance but rather slender, the Misaki has a rather large head with a straight profile, with often unobtrusive nostrils; almond-shaped eyes; a short neck; small barrel; short, thin, solid legs; a short croup; and small hooves. The mane is bushy and the tail is not very long.

**Distribution**: Cape Toi, Kyushu Island, Miyazaki Prefecture, Japan.

**Origins and history**: The Misaki lives in the wild, grazing on the hills, and found freedom around three hundred years ago. It is likely that it has ancient Mongolian or Chinese origins.

**Character and attributes**: The Misaki is resilient and adapted to life in the open throughout the year in its natural environment. It is extremely simple and is content with very little.

**Uses**: This small horse left in the wild has become an extraordinary tourist attraction. Japanese tourists enthusiastically come all year long to take its picture, and, being used to the presence of people, it tolerates the admiring crowds.

**Current status**: The Misaki population is stable but has declined significantly. In 2011 the breed suffered from equine infectious anemia and fell from 115 individuals in 2008 to 82 in 2012, but it climbed back to 91 in 2013. The horses are encountering a few problems of overgrazing in the grassy zones and are tending to go into the forests to find food. This horse is recognized as a national natural treasure in Japan.

In Japan, Misakis grazing in their natural habitat are a true tourist attraction.

# DOSANKO

Japanese: *dosanko, hokkaido washu, hokkaido.*

Ⓗ 1.25 m–1.40 m.

Ⓒ Roan, bay, chestnut, buckskin, with dorsal stripe and dark extremities.

**Description**: This is the largest native horse breed in Japan. It is rather compact, resembling the Mongolian, but is more massive. It has a head with a straight profile; a broad forehead; short, thick neck; and rather short, strong legs. Its winter coat is very thick.

**Distribution**: Islands of Hokkaido, Honshu, and Kyushu, Japan.

**Origins and history**: This breed has origins in the Mongolian horse. One hypothesis proposes that it was brought to Hokkaido in the eighteenth and nineteenth centuries.

**Character and attributes**: The Dosanko is calm, hardy, strong, very resilient, with good endurance, well adapted to the harsh climate; it is able to survive in snow. It is also a comfortable ambler.

**Uses**: Today used for recreation and trekking, it was used a lot in the past as a pack horse. It is also enjoyed as a horse for *yabusame,* the Japanese practice of archery on horseback. Crossed with draft horses imported from Europe, it makes a good horse for *ban-ei keiba,* pulling races.

**Current status**: The breed has seen its numbers decline in the past few years, with only 1,254 individuals in 2008.

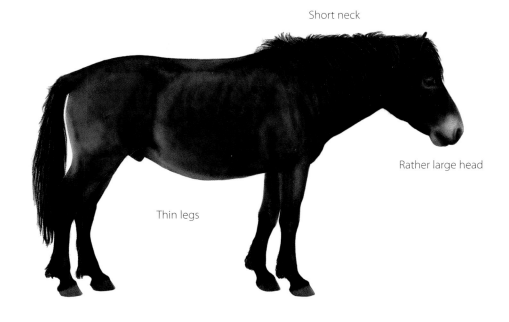

Short neck

Rather large head

Thin legs

Thick neck

Straight profile

Strong legs

# Kiso

Japanese: *kiso, kiso uma*

**Ⓗ** 1.24 m–1.42 m; on average 1.33 m for mares; 1.36 m for males.

**Ⓒ** Mainly bay, sometimes mealy bay, also chestnut or gray.

**Description**: The Kiso is rather compact, with a fairly large head; a short, thick neck; a broad chest; short, solid legs; and hard hooves. The mane and tail are thick.

**Distribution**: Nagano Prefecture, Japan.

**Origins and history**: It is possible that the Kiso has Mongolian origins, but its history remains little known. It is said to be the oldest Japanese breed.

**Character and attributes**: It is docile, robust, and easy to keep.

**Uses**: The Kiso is suited for riding or light draft work; it was once used for farm work and as a military horse. It is used today for equestrian tourism.

**Current status**: It was on the brink of extinction, but thanks to conservation work the breed's numbers have gradually climbed, and 149 individuals were recorded in 2008.

Archery on horseback, which requires much talent and cooperation between horse and rider, is one of the equestrian martial arts (*bajutsu*) inherited from the samurais.

# Ban'ei

Japanese: *ban'ei*

**Ⓗ** 1.45 m–1.64 m on average.

**Ⓒ** Bay, chestnut, gray.

**Description**: This is one of the most massive of draft horses. It weighs over a ton and has a very broad chest and very muscular croup.

**Distribution**: Japan.

**Origins and history**: This draft horse, the result of crossings among Percheron, Breton, and Belgian horses, is bred primarily to participate in *ban-ei keiba* races, pulling races that are very popular in Japan. It is not yet a truly separate breed. Some have a bit of Japanese Dosanko blood.

**Character and attributes**: Docile, the Ban'ei-type horse is extremely strong and powerful, selected for its ability to pull.

**Uses**: It is bred for the amazing draft races, the *ban-ei keiba* or *draft race*, true horse-pulling races invented by the Japanese. They are over 200 meters long and include a climb and a descent.

**Current status**: The Japanese love heavy horses, and the Ban'ei is popular and doing well.

Pulling races are hugely popular in Japan.

Heavy head

Broad chest

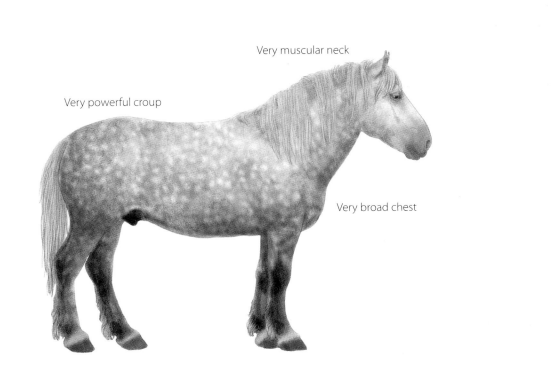

Very muscular neck

Very powerful croup

Very broad chest

# TAISHUH

Japanese: *taisho, taishu uma, taisu, tsushima*

**H** 1.07 m–1.36 m; on average 1.25 m for mares; 1.27 m for males.

**C** Black, bay, dark bay, sometimes chestnut, roan, with a dorsal stripe.

**Description**: The Taishuh resembles the Mongolian, with a rather large head, narrow chest, and a thick mane and tail.

**Distribution**: Tsushima Island, Nagasaki Prefecture, Japan.

**Origins and history**: This ancient breed has been raised since the eighth century.

**Character and attributes**: The Taishuh is very docile, strong, and simple. It has good endurance and is inclined to amble.

**Uses**: It was once used for transportation, agriculture, and as a pack horse.

**Current status**: This native breed is on the brink of extinction: there has been a sharp decline in its population. Only twenty-six individuals were recorded in 2006.

# Philippines

In the Philippines one finds astonishing white horses with pink manes, sometimes decorated with paper flowers, which appear to come out of a cartoon. The mane is, of course, dyed, and the goal is to attract tourists. In the past few years horses have become increasingly popular. One also finds the Quarter Horse, Arabian, and Thoroughbred. Although forbidden, regrettable stallion fights are still held in the Philippines.

# BAGUIO

Also called: Tagaytay

Philippino: *baguio, tagaytay*

**H** Around 1.34 m.

**C** Bay, dark bay, gray, roan.

**Description**: The robust little Philippine horses resemble other breeds from Southeast Asia. They have a head with a straight profile, rather short neck, and slender legs. There are several types, all more or less heavy.

**Distribution**: Philippines.

**Origins and history**: Philippine horses, the two main types being the Baguio and the Tagaytay, are the result of crossings among various horses imported to the islands, notably Chinese breeds. They received Arabian and Andalusian blood during Spanish colonization.

**Character and attributes**: They are known to be patient, affectionate, robust, and sure-footed.

**Uses**: Essentially recreational animals, notably for tourism, they are still used for transportation in mountain zones. They are also used in harness and for farm work.

**Current status**: These local horses remain popular in the Philippines, but their exact status is not known.

Filipinos sometimes dye the mane and forelock of their little horses pink to attract tourists.

Taishuhs grazing on Tsushima Island, Japan. This extremely rare breed has been on the island for centuries.

Rather short neck

Straight profile

Slender legs

Malaysia is not traditionally a country of horse breeders; there aren't many, and yet one does find two native breeds. In Malaysia, horses are essentially used for recreational riding. In addition to native horses, Malaysian riders also breed international breeds: Arabian, Thoroughbred, Shetland, Quarter Horse, and American Saddlebred, among others.

---

### MALAYSIA

# BAJAU

Malay: *bajau*

**H** Around 1.30 m.

**C** Dark bay, sometimes with white markings on the head and legs.

**Description**: Always of Southeast Asian type, the Bajau is a slender and light animal, with a head with straight profile; slender legs; and small hooves.

**Distribution**: Sabah state, notably the city of Kota Belud, eastern Malaysia.

**Origins and history**: These horses are connected to the Bajau, an ethnic group from Kota Belud, breeders and riders who are passionate about horses.

**Character and attributes**: The Bajau is simple, rustic, and both resistant to illness and very well adapted to the humid tropical climate.

**Uses**: An animal for work and recreation, it is ornately decorated during parades of Bajau riders, which are very popular locally.

**Current status**: The population is probably stable, but its status is not well known.

Ornately decorated Bajau riders.

---

### MALAYSIA

# KUDA PADI

Also called: Paddy Horse

Malay: *kuda padi*

**H** 1.40 m for mares; 1.45 m for males.

**C** Chestnut, bay, sometimes with white markings.

**Description**: The Kuda Padi resembles the other small horses of this region of the world: head with straight profile, short back, thin legs, and a rather thick mane and tail.

**Distribution**: Kelantan and Terengganu states, Malaysia.

**Origins and history**: The origins of this small "rice horse" (literal translation of *kuda padi*) remain obscure, but its name suggests a past of farm work in rice paddies.

**Character and attributes**: The Kuda Padi is rustic and simple, very prolific, and resistant to illness.

**Uses**: It is a versatile horse.

**Current status**: It is not noted as endangered, but its status is not really known.

Straight
profile

Slender legs

Small hooves

### MALAYSIA

## BIMO SIAM

Bimo Siam is what Malaysians call the result of crossings between different breeds of horses that are found in western Malaysia. It is more of a type than a true breed, although in time it could become one.

Indonesia has a surprisingly flourishing population of horses (446,000 in 2002) on its many islands, and it has many native breeds. The latter are sometimes crossed with Thoroughbreds to obtain taller horses. In addition to recreation and racing, horses are used a lot in harness and for transportation in mountain zones.

---

### INDONESIA

## TIMOR

Indonesian: *kuda timor*

**H** 0.92 m–1.10 m.

**C** Bay, dark bay, black, pinto.

**Description**: The Timor is the smallest Indonesian breed. It is slender, has a head with a straight profile, small ears, a short neck, rather straight shoulders, fairly prominent withers, a short back, strong legs, and small hooves.

**Distribution**: Small islands of the Sonde (Nusa Tenggara), Timor, Flores, Indonesia; it is also found in New Zealand.

**Origins and history**: It is probably the result of imported Indian breeds. It was itself exported to Australia, and has influenced the Australian Pony.

**Character and attributes**: The Timor is confident, very docile, and known to be cooperative. It has endurance, is fast and agile, and can carry heavy loads.

**Uses**: A versatile horse, it is driven and ridden by children and adults despite its small size; it is used for farm work and livestock herding (it is probably the smallest horse in the world used for herding livestock). It makes an excellent mount for children.

**Current status**: 20,000 animals were recorded in 2003.

---

### INDONESIA

## SUMBA AND SUMBAWA

Indonesian: *kuda sumba, kuda sumbawa*

**H** Around 1.22 m.

**C** Generally bay dun, black/brown dun, with a dorsal stripe, or bay.

**Description**: The Sumba and the Sumbawa are very closely related; the Sumbawa is slightly smaller. They are also similar to the Sandalwood. They have a rather large head; almond-shaped eyes; a short, muscular neck; unobtrusive withers; straight shoulders; a long back; sloping croup; slender legs; and hard hooves.

**Distribution**: Sumba Island for the Sumba, and Sumbawa Island for the Sumbawa.

**Origins and history**: The Sumba and the Sumbawa have origins in Mongolian and Chinese breeds.

### INDONESIA

#### THE BIMA VARIETY

A variety of Sumbawa is called Bimanese. It is a bit smaller (mares: 1.14 m; males: 1.18 m) and often dark bay. It is found in eastern Timor and eastern Nusa Tenggara. It is doing well.

**Character and attributes**: The Sumba and the Sumbawa are docile, agile, intelligent, confident, and fast, and they have good endurance. They are also very strong and can carry heavy loads despite their small size.

**Uses**: They are used for riding, as pack horses, and for light harness work. As in India, Sumbas are traditionally trained to dance in festivals, decorated for the occasion with small bells that ring with every movement.

**Current status**: These small local horses remain rather widespread, with around 50,000 horses in 2003.

The Sumba can be a dancing horse. Traditional dances are also very popular on Java.

Short neck

Small ears

Small hooves

Unobtrusive
withers

Rather large head

Slender legs

# BATAK

Indonesian: *kuda batak, deli*

**Ⓗ** 1.21 m–1.35 m.

**Ⓒ** Quite variable; all coat colors are possible, often dark bay, chestnut, black, or light gray.

**Description**: The Batak resembles the Manipur. It is slender, with a delicate head with straight profile; a short, thin neck; rather prominent withers; narrow chest; sloping shoulders; slightly sloping croup; and muscular legs. The Gayoe (or Gayo) variety, less elegant, is often dark bay and around 1.14 m; it is also bred in the north of the island of Sumatra.

**Distribution**: Island of Sumatra and other islands in the surrounding area, Indonesia.

**Origins and history**: The breed is the result of crossings between native mares and Arabian stallions. The Batak is sometimes used to improve other Indonesian horses. It was once used during ritual sacrifices.

**Character and attributes**: The Batak is very calm, fast, agile, hardy, and easy to keep.

**Uses**: It is used as a riding horse, notably for equestrian tourism, but it is also raised for its meat.

**Current status**: In 2003 the Batak population was estimated at 12,000.

The Batak is still used for simple transportation.

# SANDALWOOD

Indonesian: *kuda sandel*

**Ⓗ** 1.21 m–1.42 m.

**Ⓒ** Variable; black, light gray, chestnut, dark bay, bay, bay dun, sometimes pinto.

**Description**: The Sandalwood is slender; it has a small head with a straight profile, small ears, a rather long neck, sloping shoulders, a well-developed chest, long back, hard hooves, a thick mane and tail, and a fine coat.

**Distribution**: Java, Madura and, in the small Sonde islands (Nusa Tenggara), Sumba, Bali, Sumbawa, Indonesia, but also in Australia.

**Origins and history**: The breed is associated with the exporting of sandalwood. In the past it received Arabian blood.

**Character and attributes**: The Sandalwood is easy, docile, resilient, and fast, and it has good endurance.

**Uses**: It is versatile. It is also ridden in local races. It is a good mount for children.

**Current status**: Popular in Indonesia, the breed is doing well, with around 45,000 horses in 2003, and is the object of some attention.

A horse doesn't have to be a Thoroughbred to run fast! Indonesians love to test their Sandalwoods in gallop races.

Short, thin neck

Narrow chest

Small ears

Long back

Fine coat

## INDONESIA

# LOMBOK

Indonesian: *kuda lombok*

🅗 1.11 m for mares; 1.15 m for males.

🅒 Dark bay.

**Description**: It is small and light.
**Distribution**: Lombok, western Nusa Tenggara, Indonesia.

**Origins and history**: It is very similar to the Sulawesi, of which it is sometimes considered a type.
**Character and attributes**: It is rustic and easy to keep.
**Uses**: It is mainly a harness and pack horse.
**Current status**: This native breed is not the most widespread in Indonesia, with around 5,000 individuals in 2003.

## INDONESIA

# SULAWESI

Also called: Macassar

Indonesian: *kuda makasar, makasar, sulawesi*

🅗 1.17 m for mares; 1.21 m for males.

🅒 Mainly dark bay.

**Description**: It is small but strong, with solid hooves.
**Distribution**: Sulawesi, Indonesia.

**Origins and history**: Present on one of the largest islands of Indonesia, the Sulawesi resembles other Southeast Asian horses.
**Character and attributes**: It has good endurance and is powerful for its size.
**Uses**: It is often used in harness.
**Current status**: It is the most common breed in Indonesia, with around 190,000 horses in 2003.

## INDONESIA

# FLORES

Indonesian: *Flores*

🅗 Around 1.22 m.

🅒 Mainly dark bay, also bay, chestnut.

**Description**: It is related to the Timor, which it resembles.
**Distribution**: Flores Island, eastern Nusa Tenggara, Indonesia.

**Origins and history**: Like the Timor, it probably descends from Indian breeds.
**Character and attributes**: The Flores is rather robust.
**Uses**: It is used as a pack horse or saddle horse, and for working livestock.
**Current status**: In 2003 the population was estimated at 20,000 animals.

# JAVA

Indonesian: *java, jawa*

🅗 1.23 m–1.30 m.

🅒 Quite variable; all colors are possible.

**Description**: The Java is slender, light, with a head with a straight profile; long ears; a rather short, muscular neck; fairly sloping shoulders; prominent withers; a deep chest; long back; slightly sloping croup; and a rather high-set tail. The hair of the mane and tail is abundant.

**Distribution**: Island of Java, Indonesia.

**Origins and history**: Very ancient, probably a descendant of ancient Mongolian horses, it has received Arabian and Barb blood. The Priangan (also spelled Periangan or Perinagan) is a cross between Java and Arabian horses.

**Character and attributes**: The Java is docile, calm, amazingly resilient, strong, and hardy. It has good endurance and is well adapted to the tropical climate and the heat.

**Uses**: This is a versatile horse, often driven but also ridden, used as a pack horse, and so forth.

**Current status**: There were around 30,000 Javas in 2003.

## THE CLOSELY RELATED KUNINGAN

The Kuningan Pony (*kuda kuningan* in Indonesian), a very ancient breed similar to the Java, is present in Jawa Barat (7,500 horses in 2003). It is the issue of Mongolian, Chinese, and Southeast Asian breeds. It is most often bay-colored. Mares measure around 1.15 m, and males 1.20 m. It is often used in harness.

# BALI

Indonesian: *bali*

🅗 1.20 m–1.30 m.

🅒 Generally bay dun with dorsal stripe and dark extremities, or with zebra striping.

**Description**: The Bali is a primitive-type breed, with a rather large head and straight profile, almond-shaped eyes, small ears, straight shoulders, unobtrusive withers, a narrow chest, short back, slightly sloping croup, and very hard hooves. Its mane is bushy, and stands up.

**Distribution**: Island of Bali, Indonesia.

**Origins and history**: Its ancient origins remain obscure. It probably descends from Mongolian and Chinese breeds crossed with different Indian breeds after being imported.

**Character and attributes**: Very docile, it is robust and very strong for its small size. Rustic and hardy, it requires very little care.

**Uses**: Traditionally used as a saddle and pack horse, it is also a pleasant horse for equestrian tourism.

**Current status**: Once common, this small local breed has become rare. In 2003 there were only 1,250 individuals.

## SUMBAR

The little Sumbar (or more exactly Sumbar-Sandalwood-Arab) is a crossbred dating from the beginning of the twentieth century between the Sandalwood, Thoroughbred, and Arabian with the goal of creating a racehorse. It is found in western Sumatra. It is mainly dark bay. Mares measure around 1.32 m, males 1.40 m.

## MINAHASA

INDONESIA

The Minahasa (*kuda minahasa* in Indonesian) is the result of crossings between Sandalwoods and Thoroughbreds that have been going on since the end of the 1960s. It is found in northern Sulawesi. It is also used for racing. Mainly dark bay, it is of average size, with mares around 1.34 m and males 1.44 m. The breed is rare.

## INDONESIAN RACING HORSE

INDONESIA

Indonesian: *kuda pacu*

Acronym: KPI

H 1.55 m for mares; 1.65 m for males.

C Mainly dark bay, also bay dun.

**Description**: This Indonesian halfblood, light and solid, is the tallest breed in the country.

**Distribution**: Jakarta, Java, Yogyakarta, western Sumatra, Sulawesi, eastern and western Nusa Tenggara, Indonesia.

**Origins and history**: This recent breed (from the 1970s) was created by crossing Sandalwoods and Sumbas with English Thoroughbreds, with the goal of creating a faster and more powerful racehorse. It is bred carefully.

**Character and attributes**: It is fast and athletic.

**Uses**: This horse is bred for racing.

**Current status**: Although less widespread than other Indonesian breeds, there are more than 5,000 individuals. It is still being developed.

Opposite: Jeju mare in her winter coat, at the Jeju Horse Park, island of Jeju, South Korea. This small rustic breed has become extremely rare.

# Horses of North Africa

*Horses are everywhere in North Africa. Being driven or ridden, or ruling over fantasias, there are many opportunities to encounter horses in this region. Horses are kept whole, and this works out very well. Mares are raised separately for reproduction. Even horses for tourism are whole, as that is the norm. It is not customary to castrate horses. One breed is completely dominant in North Africa: the Barb-Arab, an energetic animal with multiple assets, which is found throughout the land. The original horse of this region of the world, the famous Barb, has become rare, and there are very few purebred animals left.*

Fantasia on the beach of Essaouira, Morocco.

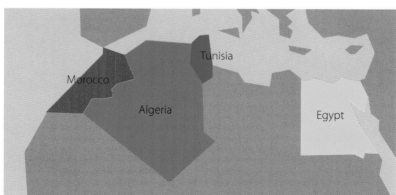

**Morocco and Algeria**
Barb
Barb-Arab
**Tunisia**
Mogod Pony
**Egypt**
Baladi

Opposite: For fantasias, horses are richly decked out with traditional trappings. These occasions are popular in North Africa both with inhabitants and with tourists.

# Morocco and Algeria

Morocco, a traditionally equestrian land, had 160,000 horses in 2005. Recreational riding is being developed, notably with the rise in equestrian tourism. Once a work animal, the horse is gradually evolving toward leisure and sport. The two main breeds in Morocco are the Barb and the Barb-Arab. These

## MOROCCO AND ALGERIA

# BARB

Arabic: *barb*

**H** 1.40 m–1.55 m.

**C** Bay, dark bay, chestnut, black, gray.

**Description**: The Barb can have a rather long, slender head; a straight or convex profile with an often bulging forehead; average-sized ears; a very muscular neck; prominent withers; long, generally sloping shoulders; a short back (often with only five lumbar vertebrae); a dished croup; low-set tail; long legs; and small, slender, resilient, and hard hooves. The hair of the mane and tail is thick, very abundant. Depending on the country, there can be a few variants; thus there are the Libyan, Algerian, and Moroccan Barbs, or even the Plains and Mountain Barbs.

**Distribution**: Mauritania, Morocco, Algeria, Tunisia, Libya, Spain, Italy, France.

**Origins and history**: A very ancient breed, raised by nomads, the Barb was a fearsome and sought-after war horse. In the past it had an important role as improver for other breeds, notably in Spain (Spanish Jennet), in Great Britain (English Thoroughbred), for many American breeds (such as the Mustang, Paso, and Criollo), and almost all African breeds.

**Character and attributes**: With a very calm but responsive nature, the Barb is an intelligent, energetic, and bold but docile horse. It is fast, can carry heavy loads, has great endurance, and is also rustic, undemanding, and resilient.

**Uses**: This is an excellent recreational horse, for trekking and endurance riding, whose nature is suited to giving riding lessons. Dressage, driving, starring in exhibitions—this very versatile horse can do it all.

**Current status**: The breed was on the brink of extinction, but has rebounded due to the rise in recreational riding, where its many assets make it quite popular. It still has low numbers for a breed of this importance, and it has suffered stiff competition from the Barb-Arab.

A fantasia saddle.

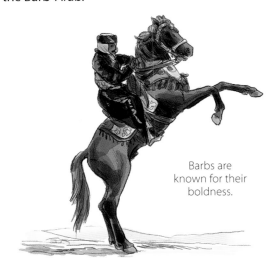

Barbs are known for their boldness.

## MOROCCO

### THE MOROCCAN SPORT HORSES OF SIDI BERNI

We must point out that in Morocco there is a fairly new breeding farm for sport horses, dating from 1985, in the area around Sidi Berni, near Rabat, which produces high-quality, tall sport horses from Moroccan mares and stallions known for their abilities in equestrian sports. This breeding program, certified by the Royal Moroccan Federation for Equestrian Sports, is producing a Moroccan sport horse breed, some of whom excel in show jumping competitions.

horses can be seen during traditional fantasias or in riding schools throughout the country. Moroccans also breed the Arabian, the Anglo-Arab, and the English Thoroughbred. A lot of mules are also bred in Morocco, where draft animals are still quite widespread. In neighboring Algeria (43,579 horses in 2003), the Barb, Barb-Arab, and the Arabian are also bred.

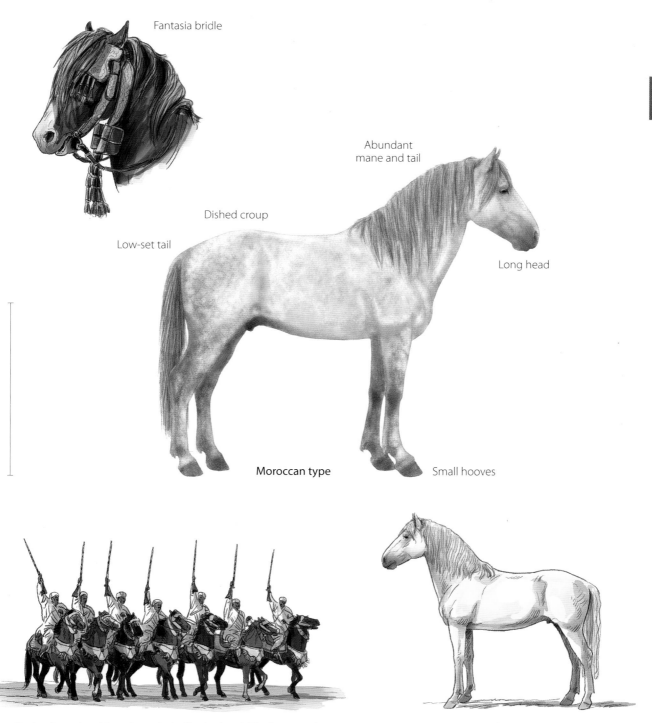

Fantasia bridle

Abundant mane and tail

Dished croup

Low-set tail

Long head

**Moroccan type**

Small hooves

During fantasias, riders shoot their rifles in the air. The horses, who are used to it, aren't afraid.

**Algerian type**

# BARB-ARAB

Arabic: *barb-arab*

ⓗ 1.40 m–1.55 m.

ⓒ Bay, chestnut, chestnut with light mane and tail, black, gray, with white markings on the head and legs.

**Description**: The morphology of the Barb-Arab is variable depending on the proportion of Arabian and Barb blood it has. It is considered better proportioned than the Barb; it is also taller and more massive than the Arabian. Its head is less chiseled than the Arabian's, but more slender than that of the Barb, with a rather straight profile, a muscular neck, a short back, and a slightly sloping croup. The mane and tail are long and silky. There are African variations of the Barb-Arab: the Beledougou (or Banamba), the Hodh in Mali, and the Sulebawa in Nigeria.

**Distribution**: Morocco, Tunisia, Algeria, Chad, Spain, France.

**Origins and history**: It was logical that the two important breeds of North Africa, the Arabian and the Barb, would be crossed to create an excellent horse. In fact, this cross has become a breed, one of the most common in North Africa.

**Character and attributes**: The Barb-Arab, a horse full of flair, is more athletic than the Barb, very energetic, but with a good character.

**Uses**: This very good saddle horse is very popular in fantasias. It is also encountered in equestrian tourism, or harnessed to carts.

**Current status**: The Barb-Arab remains very popular throughout North Africa and is doing well.

In North Africa, whether pampered in the stables or pulling heavy carts, the Barb-Arab is the most common breed.

# Tunisia

In addition to the Barb, Barb-Arab (in the majority), Arabian, and English Thoroughbred (in the minority), Tunisia has a native breed that has become rare, the Mogod Pony. The total number of equines (including donkeys and mules) in 2001 was estimated overall at 37,000 individuals.

# MOGOD PONY

Arabic: *mogod*

ⓗ 1.20 m–1.45 m at the tallest.

ⓒ Dark bay, gray, chestnut.

**Description**: The Mogod Pony resembles the Barb. It has a head with a straight profile, a broad forehead, large eyebrow arch, strong neck, short back, and powerful legs.

**Distribution**: Regions of Amdoun, Hellil Mogod, Nefza, mountains of northwestern Tunisia.

**Origins and history**: Connected to the rural breeders of the mountainous zones of northwestern Tunisia, the Mogod Pony was probably a former war horse of the Numidian cavalry.

**Character and attributes**: The Mogod Pony is calm and energetic, intelligent, agile, solid, strong, and very sure-footed. It has excellent endurance.

**Uses**: Traditionally a pack horse, it is also suited for riding and driving and makes a good polo pony.

**Current status**: Its numbers, very low, are not exactly known; there might be around a thousand animals. The breed needs to be counted and a conservation program is being put into place to prevent its extinction.

Muscular neck

Long, silky
mane and tail

Rather straight
profile

Short back

Broad forehead

Straight profile

# Egypt

Egypt, a North African country, door to the Middle East, is mainly known for its great lineages of the purebred Arabian, which is renowned throughout the world. It had 53,000 horses in 2002.

# BALADI

Arabic: *balali*

🄗 Around 1.40 m–1.50 m.

🄒 Often bay, chestnut, gray.

**Description**: This light horse resembles the Arabian.
**Distribution**: Egypt.

**Origins and history**: The Baladi is the native Egyptian horse; it is of Arabian type. It is sometimes crossed with the English Thoroughbred to produce a more athletic horse.
**Character and attributes**: It is fast with good endurance, though not as good as the Arabian.
**Uses**: This is a native, very versatile horse, used primarily to pull carts or for equestrian tourism.
**Current status**: Baladis are widespread in Egypt.

Opposite: Barb, Morocco.
The thick stone walls of Moroccan stables provide cool shade that is very welcome in extremely hot weather.

# Horses of West Africa

*West Africa is not traditionally a region of the world that raises or selectively breeds horses, mainly due to the presence of the tsetse fly, carrier of trypanosomiasis, an illness that affects horses and can decimate livestock. The African horse sickness is another illness that has impeded the development of horse breeding in this region. This doesn't mean that there are no horses in West Africa, especially since campaigns to eradicate the tsetse fly have helped increase the number of horses. There are in fact a few native breeds, completely unknown outside their country, often crossed among themselves, but generally well rooted, that can be easily observed when one travels through this region. And the value of the horse, the traditions linked to it, are very well anchored here. The breeds of West Africa are very strongly influenced by the North African Barb. The equestrian sector here is gradually being developed.*

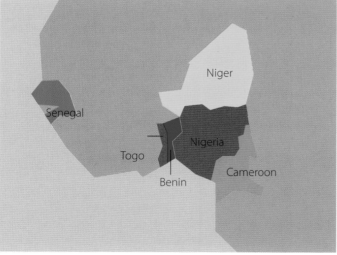

**Senegal**
Fleuve
M'par
M'bayar
Fouta
**Niger**
Manga
**Togo and Benin**
Koto-Koli Pony (also
   Togo Pony)
**Nigeria**
Nigerian Horse
**Cameroon**
Mousseye
Dongola (also West
   African Dongola)

In Senegal the horse is still a very useful means of transportation, usually in harness.

Opposite: Senegalese horses are very resilient animals, enduring a very hot climate and sometimes hard work.

One sees many horses in Senegal, often a bit skinny, harnessed to various carts. The different Senegalese breeds—Fleuve, Foutanke, M'par, and M'bayar—have been crossbred a lot, which means that the purity of the breeds is not clear. The horse

---

# FLEUVE

Also called *narugor* by the Wolof

🅗 Often over 1.40 m, up to 1.50 m.

🅒 Usually different shades of gray: speckled gray, dark gray, light gray.

**Description**: This is a light horse, the tallest of the Senegalese breeds, with a slender head; a rather narrow chest; slender, long legs; and a dished croup.
**Distribution**: Senegal.
**Origins and history**: The Fleuve is the result of crossings between Barbs and small horses native to Senegal. It was once the horse of the elite.
**Character and attributes**: The Fleuve is energetic and fast, and the Senegalese say that it has wonderful gaits. It is well adapted to the Sudano-Sahelian environment.

**Uses**: It is above all a saddle horse, but can also be driven.
**Current status**: This native breed is considered to be one of the best in Senegal. Its exact numbers are not known.

Ridden bareback in the bush or driven in town, there are still many horses in Senegal.

---

# M'PAR

🅗 1.25 m–1.35 m.

🅒 Variable; often bay, dark bay.

**Description**: The M'par resembles the M'bayar, but is smaller. It has a long back and slender legs. It often suffers from its breeding conditions; the animals that are well fed and cared for show better physical development.

**Distribution**: Louga and Thies (former Cayor) regions, Senegal.
**Origins and history**: Originally from Cayor, the M'par is the result of crossings of M'bayar mares and Fleuve stallions.
**Character and attributes**: The M'par has good endurance and is very rustic, well adapted to the hot climate.
**Uses**: It is often used for farm work, harnessed, and can also be used to teach young riders.
**Current status**: The breed remains local, and its exact numbers are not known.

---

# M'BAYAR

🅗 1.37 m–1.45 m.

🅒 Generally dark bay, also chestnut, gray.

**Description**: This is a stocky animal, well-built, with a large head, short neck, broad chest, and muscular legs.
**Distribution**: Diourbel (former Baol) region, Senegal.

**Origins and history**: The existence of very small horses in West Africa has been recorded since the Middle Ages. This horse originated in M'bayar, Senegal. It is a former military horse, connected to the Wolof.
**Character and attributes**: It is docile, undemanding, and rustic. It has good endurance and is very resilient to heat.
**Uses**: It is well suited to farm work, and it is often harnessed.
**Current status**: This native breed has not been counted.

population is growing slowly. One also finds English Thoroughbreds, Arabians, Barbs, and Barb-Arabs, as well as some French Warmbloods. These horses are used to improve the local breeds, which have a tendency to increase in size, notably at the national stud farm at Dahra. There are around 500,000 horses in Senegal. Essentially, horses are used in harness, for transportation, farm work, and recreation. The equestrian industry is being developed.

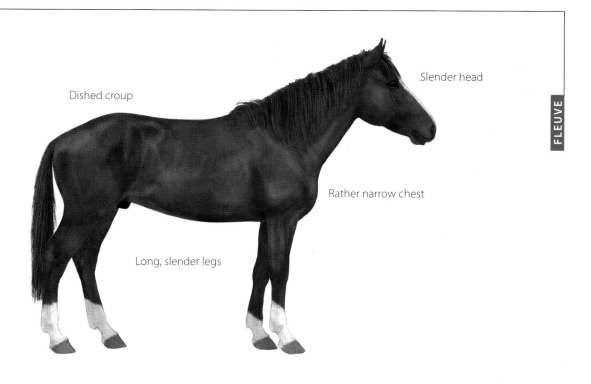

Dished croup

Slender head

Rather narrow chest

Long, slender legs

FLEUVE

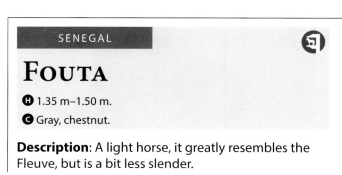

SENEGAL

# FOUTA

**H** 1.35 m–1.50 m.
**C** Gray, chestnut.

**Description**: A light horse, it greatly resembles the Fleuve, but is a bit less slender.

**Distribution**: Senegal.
**Origins and history**: The Fouta is the result of crossings between M'bayar mares and Fleuve stallions.
**Character and attributes**: It is rustic and resilient.
**Uses**: It is a horse used for riding, driving, or farm work.
**Current status**: The exact status of this local breed is not really known.

# Niger

The number of horses in Niger is increasing. In 2009, the population was estimated at 235,965. The horses are work animals, essentially used in harness for transportation. In the realm of recreation, horse racing and fantasias are enjoyed by Nigeriens. In addition to native horses, one also finds the Barb-Arab, which is becoming quite popular again in Africa. One can also find a horse called the Djerma, which is another name for the Dongola (see Cameroon, *p. 404*). In general, the horse remains a very popular and prestigious animal. The breeds of Niger need to be registered, and a great deal of research into the horses of Niger remains to be done.

---

(see Cameroon, *p. 404*)

## NIGER

# MANGA

 Around 1.40 m.

ⓒ Black, gray, often with large white markings.

**Description**: This is a slender horse that resembles the Barb and the Arab. Its head has a rather straight profile, prominent withers, thin legs, a slightly sloping croup, low-set tail, and small hooves. The hair of the mane and tail is fine, smooth, not very thick.
**Distribution**: Zinder region, southern Niger.
**Origins and history**: The Manga is a type of horse that can be seen in Niger. The horses of Niger are always more or less hybrids of the Arab, and they are considered to be more types than distinct breeds.

**Character and attributes**: The horses of Niger are hardy, resilient, and adapted to the heat.
**Uses**: Like the other types of horses in Niger, the Manga is a versatile horse, which can be ridden, harnessed, and used for daily work, recreation, and sport.
**Current status**: Its status is unknown.

## NIGER

### OTHER TYPES IN NIGER

In addition to the Manga, there is also mention of the Aïr Horse (also called *dan baguézan*) and the Gobir Horse (also called Haoussa, Hausa in English), a variety of the Dongola, which is also present in northern Nigeria. A Todori Pony is sometimes also mentioned.

---

# Togo and Benin

In Benin the horse population is very small, with around 6,000 animals counted. In Togo, the horse is essentially a show animal, and there are only around 2,000 there. Horse breeding is almost nonexistent in these two countries, and many animals (mainly males) are imported from Sahelian countries. In Lome (Togo), however, small landowners are beginning to raise horses. The animal remains prestigious.

---

## TOGO AND BENIN

# KOTO-KOLI PONY

Also called: Togo Pony

ⓗ 1.10 m–1.30 m.

ⓒ Bay, chestnut, sometimes with a dorsal stripe.

**Description**: It resembles the Barb, but is much smaller, with slender legs.
**Distribution**: North of Togo and north of Benin, but also Burkina Faso.
**Origins and history**: The Kotokolis (or Tem), of Togolese ethnicity, were riders, and the horse was used in their military. Now less useful in that capacity, the horse has become a parade animal. During the Festival of Knives—Adossa—in Sodoké, horse racing and dancing horses, decorated with their most beautiful adornments, are featured.

**Character and attributes**: It is simple and resilient.
**Uses**: This is a show and racehorse.
**Current status**: Having lost their use as war horses, their numbers are now very low. We don't know a great deal about them.

A Koto-Koli Pony and its rider during the Feast of Knives, Togo.

# Nigeria

In Nigeria the very active livestock breeding industry is mainly handled by the Fula, and involves primarily cows, sheep, and goats. The breeding of horses, prestigious animals, is not well established, and the number of horses is declining. One does, however, find small horses of Barb type, well adapted to the climate and native use, that is, mainly for transportation (ridden or driven) and as pack animals.

## Nigerian Horse

⊕ 1.42 m–1.44 m.

ⓒ Mainly light gray, but all colors are possible.

**Description**: Compact, it resembles both the Barb and the Dongola. It has a long head with a straight profile, large eyes, small ears, a rather short neck, sloping shoulders, a sloping croup, and a low-set tail. Its size could increase with more favorable breeding conditions.

**Distribution**: Niger, Nigeria, Mali.

**Origins and history**: The Nigerian Horse, with its Barb origins, is the most common horse in Nigeria.

**Character and attributes**: Docile and reliable, the Nigerian Horse has great endurance. It is fast, robust, and resilient in the heat.

**Uses**: A versatile horse, it is used as a saddle horse, for pulling, and as a pack animal.

**Current status**: The breed's numbers are probably low and decreasing. We have little information about its status.

### NIGERIA

### Other Types in Nigeria

Among the other types of Nigerian horses, one sometimes finds mention of the Bhirum or Pagan in the northeast, small, similar to the Mousseye; the Bornu, a variety of Dongola, also in the northeast; and the Sulebawa, a Barb-Arab type.

Low-set tail

Long head

Rather short neck

NIGERIAN HORSE

The horse population in Cameroon is estimated at more than 16,000. Horses are raised primarily in the north (the Adamawa and far northern provinces). There is increasing interest in the horse for leisure activities and for display in fantasias, but also for work. However, breeding is encountering difficulties related to pastureland, lack of water, and the tsetse fly.

---

CAMEROON

# MOUSSEYE

It is also known by various other names.

**H** 1.25 m on average.

**C** Mainly bay, then chestnut, chestnut roan, roan.

**Description**: Small and solid, the Mousseye has an average-sized head with concave profile; an unobtrusive brow line; small ears; a short, thick neck; a small, pronounced barrel; short legs; and small hooves. The mane is rather bushy and the tail low-set.

**Distribution**: Banks of the Logone River, southwest Chad, northern Cameroon.

**Origins and history**: The origins of the Mousseye are not known. It is possible that it is the issue of the Barb and that it received blood from the Nigerian Horse; it has been forged by its environment. It was used for war and hunting, is still used in many rituals and customs, and is still of great importance to the Mousseys. Highly regarded animals, they are mourned when one of them dies. The Mousseys would never eat horse meat.

**Character and attributes**: Docile, easy, and undemanding, the Mousseye has light gaits. It is also extremely rustic and robust, and can carry a lot. It is resistant to the tsetse fly, a quality that allows it to survive in humid zones where no other horse can live.

**Uses**: It is traditionally ridden. It is also suitable for young riders.

**Current status**: Now very rare, threatened with extinction, this horse is protected by the Cameroon authorities. Because it is resistant to the tsetse fly, its breeding could be developed elsewhere in Africa.

---

CAMEROON

# DONGOLA

Also called: West African Dongola

**H** 1.48 m–1.52 m.

**C** Black, bay, chestnut, with large white markings on the legs and head, and often under the barrel. It often has eyes of different colors.

**Description**: A light horse, it resembles a small Barb, with a head with a very convex profile, sometimes a bit large, prominent withers, and a sloping, muscular croup. It is one of the most characteristic of African horses.

**Distribution**: Cameroon, Sudan, Ethiopia, Somalia, Chad, Mali, Eritrea.

**Origins and history**: The Dongola's origins are not known. It probably has Barb blood, then was later crossed with the Arabian and the Barb-Arab.

**Character and attributes**: The Dongola is fast and undemanding. It has great endurance.

**Uses**: It is mainly a saddle horse, but is also used for racing.

**Current status**: It is widespread throughout Africa. There were some purebreds in the Bahr el-Ghazal region in Sudan. Some Dongola populations are resistant to the tsetse fly (trypanotolerant).

---

CAMEROON

## TYPES AND NAMES OF THE DONGOLA IN AFRICA

- Yagha, Mossi in Burkina Faso; also called Burkinabe Horse
- Bahr el-Ghazal (or Ganaston, or Kreda) in Chad
- Djerma, Bandiagara (or Gondo), Haoussa (or Hausa) in Niger
- Bornu in Nigeria
- Songhoi in Mali

Short, thick neck

Small ears

Short legs

Small hooves

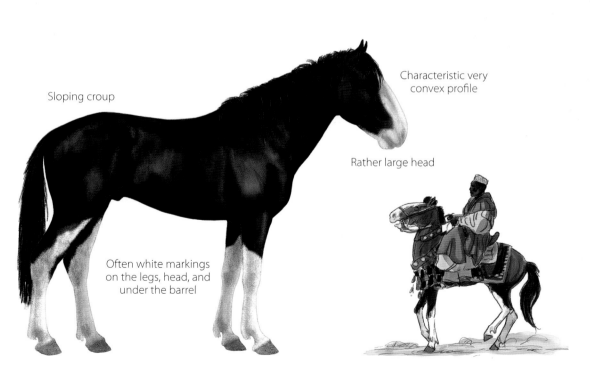

Sloping croup

Characteristic very convex profile

Rather large head

Often white markings on the legs, head, and under the barrel

The Dongola is one of the most identifiable breeds in Africa.

# Horses of East Africa

*Like West Africa, East Africa is not really known for its horse breeds, again, because of the presence of the tsetse fly and African horse sickness, which greatly complicates their breeding. Let's remember that the natural equine of sub-Saharan Africa is the zebra, which is protected from the tsetse fly by its stripes and is resistant to the African horse sickness, whereas the horse is originally from Eurasia. However, in Ethiopia, a country where the altitude of some of its high plateaus in part protects from the tsetse fly, one finds the largest number of African horses, and one of the largest densities of horses in the world. And so the horse is quite present in East Africa.*

▶

**Sudan**
Western Sudan Pony
Sudan Country-Bred
**Ethiopia**
Abyssinian
**Somalia**
Somali Pony

Top left: Ethiopian rider.

Bottom: A group of Ethiopian riders from the equestrian Oromo tribe, their horses decorated for a festival.

Opposite: Abyssinian horses are extremely common in Ethiopia.

A country of both North and East Africa, Sudan probably has more than 20,000 horses, which are used mainly as draft animals, for transportation, and for recreation. In the twentieth century this country

---

SUDAN

# WESTERN SUDAN PONY

Arabic: *gharbaui*

🅗 1.40 m–1.45 m.

🅒 Often light gray, bay, chestnut, with white markings on the legs and head.

**Description**: It is slender and resembles the Barb, with a head with a convex profile; a short, muscular neck; and slender legs.

**Distribution**: Southwestern Kodofan, south of Darfur, Sudan; southern Chad.

**Origins and history**: This is another breed that has descended directly from the Barb, but it was targeted for improvement in the twentieth century, with contributions of Thoroughbred and Arabian blood.

**Character and attributes**: The Western Sudan Pony has excellent endurance.

**Uses**: Used as a saddle and draft horse, it is well suited to sport.

**Current status**: Not much is known about this native breed.

---

SUDAN

# SUDAN COUNTRY-BRED

Acronym: SCB

🅗 Around 1.50 m.

🅒 Bay, dark bay, chestnut, roan, gray, black.

**Description**: It might be described as a sort of Sudanese halfblood.

**Distribution**: Sudan.

**Origins and history**: Of recent origin, this breed was created by crossing Arabian horses with Thoroughbreds and native breeds (notably the Dongola and the Western Sudan Pony). The Tawleed is a variety of the breed that is found in Khartoum, again improved with Thoroughbred blood, and is thus less robust.

**Character and attributes**: It is more athletic than other native breeds, but less resilient.

**Uses**: It is bred for riding.

**Current status**: The breed is doing well.

established a policy for breeding and improving their native breeds, with contributions of Arabian and Thoroughbred blood. There are two native breeds: the Western Sudan Pony and the Sudan Country-Bred. It is hoped that horse breeding and recreational riding will develop in this country, where many improvements still need to be made.

Short neck

Convex profile

Slender legs

Whereas horses are fairly rare in many African countries, they are found just about everywhere in Ethiopia, traditionally a nation of riders (notably the Oromo tribe). In addition, motorized vehicles are subjected to very high taxes, and so the horse

### ETHIOPIA

# ABYSSINIAN

Oromo: *oromo*

Some people call it Gala or Galla, terms to be avoided, because they are very insulting for the Oromo.

**H** 1.38 m–1.45 m.

**C** Black, bay, dark bay, gray, light gray, less often chestnut, bay dun, palomino, sometimes with blue eyes.

**Description**: It looks like a small Barb-Arab. It has a slender head, thin neck, slender legs, and a sloping croup. There are two types: the Bari (literally "eastern type") in eastern Ethiopia and the Galbed ("western type") in western Ethiopia.

**Distribution**: Abyssinia.

**Origins and history**: It probably originates in the Barb and the Persian Arabian, and might have been crossed with the Dongola, Somalian, then with the Arabian. This is the horse of the Oromo, an equestrian people, who take very good care of their animals.

**Character and attributes**: Bold, active, easy to handle, calm, fast, with good endurance, it is also very rustic and sure-footed. It probably also is resistant to the tsetse fly.

**Uses**: It is above all a work horse, still very useful as a pack horse, for transportation, harnessed, and farm work. The Oromo, one of the last equestrian peoples, like to decorate their horses with beautiful adornments (red pompoms) on various occasions (weddings, feast days, among others). They play an equestrian game called *guugsii* or *garnaamaa*, in which two teams chase each other while throwing long sticks at each other, which is similar to the Turkish *cirit*.

**Current status**: A native breed, it is very widespread and is doing quite well, and benefits from the taxes that are imposed on motorized vehicles, and from a still very rural way of life in Ethiopia. Ethiopian horses have been the object of recent studies, which should enable us to know more about them soon.

In Somalia, one of the poorest countries in the world, with a difficult political situation, breeding also suffers regularly from the terrible drought. Horses are therefore not a priority, and the ancient Somali breed has become rare.

### SOMALIA

# SOMALI PONY

Arabic: *somali*

**H** 1.40 m.

**C** Gray, chestnut.

**Description**: It resembles the Abyssinian, but is smaller.

**Distribution**: Somalia.

**Origins and history**: Under the name of Somali Pony, one finds different types that descend from Arabian horses and are often again crossed with Arabians (Arab-Somali). One also finds horses that have been returned to the wild in the Sanaag region, on the border of Somaliland.

**Character and attributes**: The Somali Pony is powerful, simple, and easy to raise, and it is fairly resistant to attacks by the tsetse fly.

**Uses**: It is used as a riding horse.

**Current status**: It has become quite rare, having suffered from years of drought and the expansion of motorized vehicles, and its bloodline has become diluted due to much crossing.

continues to be an attractive option. There are a great number of them; the population was estimated in 2011 to be 2 million, which makes it one of the countries with the largest equine population. The common breeds in Ethiopia are the Oromo and the Dongola. Horses are used for work, and are still very useful in the mountain regions. There is also a very old tradition of importing horses in Ethiopia.

Thin neck

Slender head

Slender legs

The traditional Ethiopian equestrian game is *guugsii*, during which riders chase and throw long sticks at each other, recalling how warriors were trained in the past.

# Horses of Southern Africa

*Southern Africa, which includes countries in the south of Africa, is a region that up to now has been relatively spared from the tsetse fly, although climate change suggests there may be reason to fear problems in the future. There is equine plague, but a country like South Africa can rely on vaccination. Because of these difficulties, horse breeding has historically not reached that far, and the breeds here are all developed from horses imported in the seventeenth and eighteenth centuries by colonists, especially in South Africa. Regularly the subjects of documentaries, the horses of Namibia, returned to the wild in the desert, are perhaps the most famous in this part of Africa.*

Rider in South Africa during a workout.

Below: South Africa, Transvaal region.

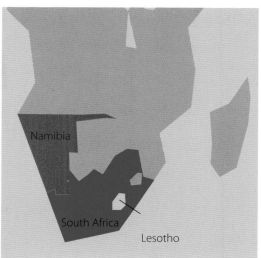

Namibia

South Africa

Lesotho

**Namibia**
Namib Desert Horse
**South Africa**
Nooitgedacht Pony
South African Boer
Cape Boer Horse
South African
   Vlaamperd
South African
   Miniature
South African
   Warmblood
**Lesotho**
Basuto

Opposite: The Nooitgedact is a very beautiful South African breed.

## Namibia

A country that is among the driest in the world, Namibia mainly breeds donkeys and does not have a tradition of horse breeding. However, thanks to the desert of Namib there is the Namib Desert Horse, famous for its resilience in hostile living conditions; it is one of the rare large mammals that can survive in this region.

NAMIBIA

# NAMIB DESERT HORSE

**H** 1.45 m–1.60 m.
**C** Always bay, dark bay, or chestnut.

**Description**: Although now living in the wild, its appearance still recalls the saddle horse that it was not long ago. It is notably rather tall for a wild horse. It has a head with a straight or convex profile, large ears, a slender neck, prominent withers, rather sloping shoulders, a narrow chest, a dished croup, long legs, and hard hooves.
**Distribution**: Namib Desert, Namibia.

**Origins and history**: Although the origins of this small population of wild horses is uncertain, they probably descend from German military horses abandoned during World War I that adapted to life in the desert, to escape the threat of predators such as the spotted hyena.
**Character and attributes**: Very resilient, extremely simple, it has adapted to life in the wild in extremely difficult desert conditions.
**Uses**: The horses of the Namib Desert are primarily a tourist attraction.
**Current status**: This wild horse is still rare, with around 150 horses. To preserve the wild fauna, it is not, however, desirable that this population grow.

## South Africa

South Africa, the most economically powerful African country, has one of the most beautiful horse populations on the continent. There are slightly fewer than thirty breeds of horses bred in this country, and most are exotic. South Africa didn't have a traditional native breed of horse, but the Dutch and British colonists developed several from Western breeds.

SOUTH AFRICA

# NOOITGEDACHT PONY

Afrikaans: *Nooitgedachtperd, Nooitgedachter*
**H** 1.38 m–1.53 m.
**C** Often bay, gray, also chestnut, roan.

**Description**: It is compact, with a slender head; a wide forehead; large eyes; long, sloping shoulders; a short back; muscular croup; and very hard hooves.
**Distribution**: South Africa, Botswana.
**Origins and history**: The Nooitgedacht Pony descends from the Basuto and thus from the Cape Horse (now extinct), crossed with Boer and Arabian. Its breeding began recently, in 1951.

**Character and attributes**: Considered very intelligent, it is gentle, bold, and robust, has good endurance, and can carry a lot. It is very sure-footed and a good mountain horse. Some horses—fewer and fewer—are predisposed for the amble and the tölt (such a horse is called a *tripler* locally), gaits inherited from the Basuto.
**Uses**: It makes a good versatile mount for adults and children, for teaching and competition. It is also a good polo pony and trekking horse.
**Current status**: The Nooitgedacht Pony is rare. In 2013 there were 876 mares, 89 geldings, and 430 stallions registered.

Dished croup

Prominent withers

Slender neck

Narrow chest

Long legs

Herd of Namib Desert Horses going to a water source in the desert.

Muscular croup

Short back

Slender head with wide forehead

# SOUTH AFRICAN BOER

Afrikans: *suid-afrikaanse Boerperd*

Note: Not to be confused with the Cape Boer Horse or *kaapse Boerperd*.

**H** 1.42 m–1.55 m for mares; 1.44 m–1.62 m for males.

**C** Bay, chestnut, black, gray, roan, palomino, buckskin.

**Description**: The South African Boer has a head with a straight or slightly convex profile; a broad forehead; a rather high-set neck; solid legs; a muscular, rather horizontal croup; high-set tail; and hard hooves. It has a thick, wavy mane and tail.

**Distribution**: South Africa, Botswana.

**Origins and history**: The South African Boer is the descendant of the now extinct Cape Horse. The first breed developed in South Africa, the Cape Horse was the fruit of crossings among Arab, Barb, and Andalusian horses imported in the seventeenth and eighteenth centuries. The South African Boer has also been influenced by Flemish, Hackney, and Cleveland Bay blood.

**Character and attributes**: Calm and intelligent, it has good endurance. This rustic horse is comfortable to ride, and some have five gaits (including the slow gait and rack).

**Uses**: This is a sport horse, used for recreation and trekking. Its average size and its nature makes it suitable for children and adults.

**Current status**: There are around 2,500 horses.

In southern Africa, some safaris use a horse to approach the wild fauna. Here horse and rider come close to a herd of zebra.

# CAPE BOER HORSE

Afrikans: *kaapse Boerperd*

**H** 1.42 m–1.62 m.

**C** Often dark bay.

**Description**: Its Hackney and American Saddlebred origins are quite evident, as it has a proud bearing. It has a rather long head with a straight profile, a wide forehead, large eyes, rather long ears, a high-set neck, broad chest, short back, and a high-set tail.

**Distribution**: South Africa.

**Origins and history**: The origins of the Cape Boer Horse go back to horses imported to Southern Africa from Java in 1653.

**Character and attributes**: The Cape Boer has an alert but poised and cool temperament; it is still undemanding and rustic. It is agile and comfortable to ride, and some have five gaits.

**Uses**: It is a very versatile saddle horse, suitable for dressage, show jumping, and recreational riding of all kinds.

**Current status**: The breed is being developed, and outcrosses haven't been authorized since 1999. In 2013 there were 1,924 horses registered.

Thick, often wavy
mane and tail

Wide forehead

Muscular and rather
horizontal croup

Rather long ears

High-set neck

High-set tail

Short back

# SOUTH AFRICAN VLAAMPERD

Afrikaans: *suid-afrikaanse Vlaamperd*

The name means "Flemish horse," but it should not be confused with the European Flemish Horse (*Vlaams Paard* in Dutch).

🔵 1.54 m on average.

🔵 Mainly black; dark bay is authorized for mares.

**Description**: It looks a lot like the Friesian, from which it did in part descend, but is more slender. It has a rather long head with a straight profile; a high-set, arched neck; long legs; and a round croup. The mane and tail are thick.

**Distribution**: South Africa, especially in Western Cape Province.

**Origins and history**: This draft breed was developed from the Friesian (imported into South Africa at the beginning of the twentieth century), the ancient Cape Horse (extinct), the Hackney, and the Thoroughbred, then from Oldenburg and Cleveland Bay blood.

**Character and attributes**: Docile and powerful, it has high-stepping gaits.

**Uses**: This is an excellent carriage horse that can also be ridden.

**Current status**: The breed is small in numbers, with around 200 horses in 2013, but a few enthusiasts are supporting it.

# SOUTH AFRICAN MINIATURE

Afrikaans: *suid-afrikaanse Miniatuur Perd*

🔵 0.95 m–1 m for mares; not taller than 0.09 m for stallions; not taller than 1 m for geldings.

🔵 All colors are possible.

**Description**: It looks like a miniature saddle horse, with a slender head and large eyes, a wide forehead, slender nose, broad chest, short back, and hard hooves.

**Distribution**: South Africa.

**Origins and history**: Since 1945 the South African Miniature has been developed from Shetlands and small Arabian stallions. The breed was recognized in 1989. In recent years, American Miniature Horses have been imported.

**Character and attributes**: It is gentle, agile, easy to handle, and undemanding.

**Uses**: These are essentially pets that can pull a small, light cart.

**Current status**: The breed is being developed, with only 700 animals registered.

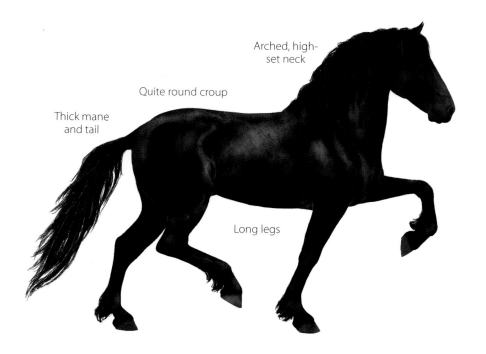

Arched, high-set neck

Quite round croup

Thick mane and tail

Long legs

SOUTH AFRICA

# SOUTH AFRICAN WARMBLOOD

Afrikans: *suid-afrikaanse Warmblood*

🇭 1.55 m for mares; 1.60 m for males.

🇨 Often bay, chestnut.

**Description**: This is an athletic horse, with a head with a straight profile, large eyes, prominent withers, sloping shoulders, and a long, sloping croup.
**Distribution**: South Africa.

**Origins and history**: The European sport horses (Hanoverian type) were crossed with native horses and Thoroughbreds, creating a type of South African halfblood. For now, it is more a sport horse registry than a completely separate breed.
**Character and attributes**: It is a calm and powerful horse, with lovely gaits.
**Uses**: It is essentially bred for competition in show jumping, dressage, and eventing.
**Current status**: The breed is being developed; the South African Warmblood Horse Society counted 7,000 registered horses in 2013.

A mountainous, landlocked country next to South Africa, the kingdom of Lesotho had 109,000 horses in 1999. One finds primarily the Basuto there, a small native horse that almost disappeared in the past. It is, however, well adapted to mountain zones and to altitude, and thus is increasingly popular with recreational riders. The Lesothans also breed a few English Thoroughbreds for riding and racing.

---

LESOTHO

# BASUTO

**(H)** Around 1.42 m.
**(C)** Simple coats, often light gray, bay, chestnut.

**Description**: This little horse has a large head with a straight profile; a long, thin, swan-like neck; prominent withers; straight shoulders; a long back; dished croup; low-set tail; short, slender legs; and very hard hooves. The mane and tail are not particularly thick.

**Distribution**: Lesotho, South Africa (notably the region of Transvaal, in the northeast).

**Origins and history**: The Basuto, developed in the mountain regions of Lesotho beginning in the late nineteenth century, descends from Cape Horses, which themselves came from Arabian and Barb stock, and horses from Java that were brought to South Africa by the Dutch. It then again received Arabian blood.

**Character and attributes**: The Basuto is reliable, bold, rustic, extremely resilient, and undemanding. It has endurance and is sure-footed on mountain terrain. It has a form of amble called *tripling*.

**Uses**: Mainly used for transportation and as a pack horse, it is also well suited to polo. It is a good trekking horse and can excel in endurance races.

**Current status**: This breed has encountered some difficulties: a decline in its usefulness, epidemics, exporting, and too much crossbreeding with other breeds. It was on the brink of extinction in the 1950s, but has been doing fairly well since then.

Large head

Prominent
withers

Long back

Thin mane
and tail

Long, thin neck

Short, slender legs

# Horses of North America

*Although there are millions of horses in Asia, and even though Europe is home to half the horse breeds in the world, in the collective imagination the land of horses is America, with its wide open spaces, its ranches, and its cowboys. But this is to forget rather quickly that the horse had disappeared from the entire American continent by the end of the Pleistocene, around 12,000 years ago, and that in the sixteenth century the conquistadors brought them back, greatly impressing the native peoples, who had never seen such an animal.*

*What is striking in North America is of course the large number of very distinct breeds, all selected for their good nature, but also the diversity of those breeds. All special characteristics are appreciated: colorful coats, special gaits. … Unlike European horses that have come out of military traditions, without the broken amble or a great variety of coat colors, North America cultivates its original horses.*

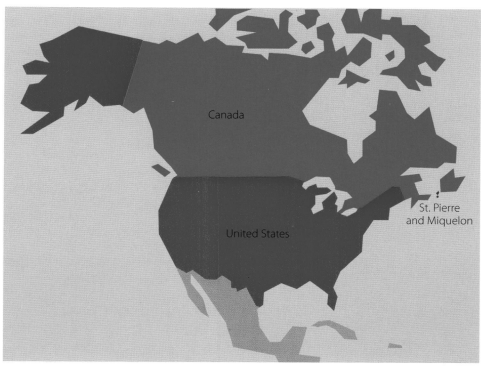

**Canada**
Newfoundland Pony
Lac La Croix Indian Pony
Sable Island Horse
Canadian
Canadian Cutting Horse
Canadian Rustic Pony
Canadian Sport Horse
Royal Canadian Mounted
  Police Horse

**St. Pierre and Miquelon**
Miquelon Horse

**United States**
American Miniature Horse
American Shetland
Pony of the Americas
American Walking Pony
Assateague and Chincoteague
Welara Pony
Spanish Barb
Banker
Choctaw

Blazer
Mustang (also American Feral
  Horse, Wild Mustang)
Spanish Mustang
Florida Cracker Horse (also
  Florida Cow Pony, Grass Cut)
Marsh Tacky (also Carolina
  Marsh Tacky)
Nokota
Morgan
Morab
Pintabian
Tiger Horse (also Soulon Tiger

Horse)
North American Curly Horse
Kentucky Mountain Saddle
  Horse
Rocky Mountain Horse
Missouri Fox Trotter
Appaloosa
Quarter Horse
American Paint Horse
Moyle Horse
Tennessee Walking Horse (also
  Tennessee Pacer, Walker)
Spotted Saddle Horse (also
  National Spotted Saddle
  Horse)
Colorado Ranger (also
  Rangerbred Horse)
Racking Horse
National Show Horse
Standardbred (also
  American Standardbred)
American Cream and White
  Horse (also Cremello)
Camarillo White
American Saddlebred (also
  Saddle Horse)
American Warmblood
American Cream Draft
North American Spotted Draft
  Horse
Palomino
Pinto
Virginia Highlander
Quarab
AraAppaloosa (also Araloosa)
Walkaloosa (also Gaited
  Appaloosa)
Morocco Spotted Horse (also
  Moroccan Spotted Horse)
Montana Travler

Opposite: The Appaloosa, originally bred by the Nez
Perce Indians, is the best known of all spotted breeds.

Horse breeding is doing very well in Canada, which had 963,500 horses in 2010. Horses there are essentially recreational animals (notably used in Olympic disciplines), and are also used in Western riding and livestock herding. Racing is also popular. In addition to its own breeds, there are various other breeds from the United States. In Canada the horse is often considered to be an affectionate animal, a pet, to which the owner is very close.

## CANADA

# NEWFOUNDLAND PONY

**Ⓗ** 1.15 m–1.45 m.

**Ⓒ** Black, bay, dark bay, light gray, a few roans.

**Description**: Powerful, it has a small head with large eyes and small ears, a muscular neck, rather straight shoulders, unobtrusive withers, and a sloping croup. It has thick mane and tail and a thick winter coat. Some types are more slender, others more stocky.

**Distribution**: Newfoundland, Labrador, Canada.

**Origins and history**: An old native breed of the Newfoundland islands, the Newfoundland Pony descends from British horses imported in the seventeenth century (probably Exmoor, Dartmoor, New Forest, Connemara, Welsh Mountain, Highland, and Galloway, an extinct breed). It has been forged by a hostile environment and lives outdoors.

**Character and attributes**: It is intelligent and docile, has good endurance, and is very rustic and sure-footed.

**Uses**: It is used as a saddle horse and carriage horse, in the past as a pack horse, and for work in the fields.

**Current status**: Once relatively widespread, it has become very rare, losing its usefulness to mechanization, and was on the brink of extinction (going from 12,000 individuals in the 1970s to fewer than one hundred). It is today carefully preserved and the population is now stabilized, even though its numbers are still low with fewer than 400 animals in 2013.

## CANADA

# LAC LA CROIX INDIAN PONY

Acronym: LLCIP

**Ⓗ** 1.21 m–1.34 m for mares; 1.32 m–1.44 m for males.

**Ⓒ** Black/bay dun, bay, black, often with primitive markings (dorsal stripe, zebra striping on the legs), sometimes with rather discreet white markings on the legs and head.

**Description**: It has a head with a wide forehead; small ears; a strong, slightly arched neck; unobtrusive withers; sloping shoulders; a sloping croup; and small, very hard hooves. The long mane is sometimes double. The hair can be slightly wavy.

**Distribution**: Northern Ontario, Canada.

**Origins and history**: It is probably the result of crossing carried out by the Indians of Lac La Croix in the nineteenth century, between the Canadian horse and Spanish-type Mustangs. Natural selection made it robust.

**Character and attributes**: Very intelligent, sensitive, and energetic, it is very rustic, easy to keep, and sure-footed.

**Uses**: It is suited to the saddle, and makes a good horse for the family or for young riders.

**Current status**: The breed was on the brink of extinction in the 1970s, then through conservation efforts had increased to around one hundred animals by 2013.

Small ears

Large eyes

Sloping croup

Thick mane
and tail

Muscular neck

Wide forehead

Thick mane and tail,
sometimes slightly wavy

Small hooves

# Sable Island Horse

**H** Around 1.40 m.

**C** Mainly bay, dark bay, chestnut, liver chestnut, more rarely gray, black.

**Description**: The Sable Island Horse is compact and stocky, with a large head with a straight, sometimes convex profile; wide forehead; short, wide neck; rather straight shoulders; a short back; sloping croup; short and strong legs; and a good, small barrel. The hair of the mane and tail is thick.

**Distribution**: Sable Island, Canada.

**Origins and history**: These are descendants of French horses (probably from northern France), imported at the beginning of the eighteenth century, which were returned to the wild on the small island off the coast of Nova Scotia, which is more exactly a sandbar without trees, with poor vegetation.

**Character and attributes**: It is rather docile if it is captured young. Rustic and very resilient, it is simple and adapted to the difficult conditions on Sable Island.

**Uses**: It lives in a feral state without interference from humans except when necessary to regulate the population (for ecological reasons). Then it is captured and sold on the continent; they can be broken to ride (for recreational use) or to drive.

**Current status**: The breed is very rare (around 300 horses) and is now protected.

On little Sable Island, lost in the Atlantic Ocean and battered by sometimes violent winds, the living conditions are harsh for the Sable Island Horses.

# Canadian

**H** 1.42 m–1.63 m.

**C** Mainly black, also bay, sometimes chestnut, a few grays, palomino and cream.

**Description**: The Canadian is a powerful horse, with a short, boxy head with a wide forehead and straight profile; large eyes; rather short ears; a powerful, high-set neck; broad chest; slightly prominent withers; long, sloping, and muscular shoulders; a short back; muscular and slightly sloping croup; high-set tail; and large hooves. The hair of the mane and tail is abundant, fine, long, and wavy.

**Distribution**: Quebec, Canada.

**Origins and history**: This is an ancient carriage horse converted for riding, the issue of French horses of unknown breed, imported beginning in 1665. In the past there were three types of Canadian horse, which have since disappeared and blended: a heavy type, a trotter type, and the famous Canadian Pacer, an ambler that probably resulted from crossings between Canadians and Narragansett Pacers (a now extinct breed). The Canadian Pacer has had an important role in North America, notably in the creation of the Standardbred, the American Saddlebred, and the Tennessee Walking Horse.

**Character and attributes**: The Canadian is docile, vigorous, rustic, and undemanding; it has good endurance. It has a long lifespan.

**Uses**: It is a good saddle horse and still perfect for harness, including in competition.

**Current status**: Once widespread, the breed has been strongly threatened with extinction (there were only 222 remaining in 1995, and 423 in 2001), but its numbers have improved greatly through the efforts of a few enthusiasts, and there are now 7,000 horses.

Sloping croup

Short, wide neck

Wide forehead

Rounded barrel

High-set neck

Fine, wavy
mane and tail

Short back

Short head

# CANADIAN CUTTING HORSE

**H** Around 1.50 m–1.60 m.

**C** Liver chestnut, gray, palomino—all colors are possible.

**Description**: It is generally taller, longer, and lighter than the Quarter Horse, which it greatly resembles. It has a small head with a slightly convex profile; a straight neck; sloping, powerful shoulders; a broad chest; a very powerful, muscular, dished croup; short, solid legs; and small hooves.

**Distribution**: Canada.

**Origins and history**: This is not truly a breed, but a popular type of ranch horse from Canada, created from Quarter Horse and European horses, notably Spanish.

**Character and attributes**: Intelligent, bold, with a very balanced nature, reliable, and easy, the Canadian Cutting Horse is agile, fast, and very responsive, with good cow sense.

**Uses**: This is above all a herding horse, which of course excels in Western disciplines. It is a good recreational horse, both for trekking and in harness.

**Current status**: This type of horse, popular in Canada, is doing well.

The Canadian Cutting Horse was initially bred to herd livestock and work on ranches.

# CANADIAN RUSTIC PONY

**H** 1.27 m–1.37 m.

**C** Gray, bay, bay dun, buckskin, black/brown dun, generally with a dorsal stripe and zebra striping on the legs.

**Description**: With a primitive appearance, it has a convex or straight profile; large, prominent eyes; small ears; a thick neck; a slightly inclined croup; and strong legs. The mane tends to stand straight up.

**Distribution**: Canada.

**Origins and history**: This breed was developed recently, at the end of the 1980s, from Arabian, Welsh Mountain, and, more unusually, a Tarpan from the Munich Zoo.

**Character and attributes**: It is gentle, rustic, and good at jumping.

**Uses**: It is a family breed that is suitable for riding or driving.

**Current status**: The status of this recent breed (whose numbers are small) is not known.

Powerful croup

Small head with slightly convex profile

Broad chest

# CANADIAN SPORT HORSE

Formerly also called: Canadian Hunter, renamed Canadian Sport Horse in 1984

**H** Around 1.62 m.

**C** Bay, dark bay, chestnut, gray.

**Description**: This athletic sport horse resembles English and Irish Hunters.

**Distribution**: Canada.

**Origins and history**: This is not a breed, strictly speaking, but horses inscribed in the Canadian sport horse registry. Many of them are the result of crossings between Canadian horses and Thoroughbreds.

**Character and attributes**: It is powerful and a good jumper.

**Uses**: It is intended for show jumping competitions, dressage, and eventing.

**Current status**: Because of the great popularity of equestrian sports in Canada, this type of horse is doing very well, and its numbers continue to grow.

# ROYAL CANADIAN MOUNTED POLICE HORSE

**H** 1.62 m–1.74 m.

**C** Always black.

**Description**: This is a tall saddle horse, very athletic.

**Distribution**: Canada.

**Origins and history:** This is not a specific breed, but a type of horse used by the Canadian Mounted Police, the result of crossings between English Thoroughbreds and black mares, notably Hanoverians. The Canadian Mounted Police have been breeding their own horses since 1939.

**Character and attributes**: They are extremely calm and brave.

**Uses:** Bred essentially to be horses for the Canadian Mounted Police, they are sometimes sold and make good saddle horses.

**Current status**: Raised for a very specific use, there are not very many of these horses.

# St. Pierre and Miquelon

On St. Pierre and Miquelon, the French archipelago in North America, there is a population of horses living outdoors. They are not really wild, because they are owned, but they raise environmental issues by overgrazing certain areas, while elsewhere encouraging the maintenance of open areas favorable to some wild species.

# MIQUELON HORSE

**H** 1.40 m.

**C** Bay, dark bay, chestnut, gray.

**Description**: It resembles a smaller Canadian horse.

**Distribution**: St. Pierre and Miquelon.

**Origins and history**: It is not yet truly a breed, even if things seem to be moving in that direction, but a small population that has developed over time on the archipelago. Their origin isn't known; it is perhaps the result, like the Canadian horse, of French, Norman, and Breton horses. It seems that it might have received Clydesdale, Quarter Horse, and Appaloosa blood. Due to the proximity of St. Pierre and Miquelon to Newfoundland, one might wonder what its connection with the rare Newfoundland Pony might be.

**Character and attributes**: They are particularly robust.

**Uses:** They are used mainly for trekking, less for light farm work or meat consumption.

**Current status**: A census taken in 2007 counted 168 horses on the archipelago. An association has been formed to protect the breed.

Opposite: The Quarter Horse, native to the United States, is very popular and widespread throughout the world, in particular throughout North America.

A great equestrian nation, the United States has a large number of breeds, among the most famous and admired. It also has the greatest number of horses of any country in the world; in 2011 around 10,150,000 horses were counted (with Texas in the

# AMERICAN MINIATURE HORSE

**H** Maximum of 0.86 m.

**C** All colors are possible; unique colors are sought after.

**Description**: This is undoubtedly the most characteristic of all miniatures. It resembles a mini saddle horse, and often resembles a small Arabian. It has a head with a straight profile; a wide forehead; large, prominent eyes; a straight or slightly concave profile; a long neck; long and sloping shoulders; and a short back. The hair of the mane and tail is shiny and silky.

**Distribution**: United States, Canada, Europe.

**Origins and history**: Mainly developed in the twentieth century, its origins are varied. One finds Shetland crossed with Hackney, Arabian, Thoroughbred, and Welsh, as well as Falabella. The studbook is now closed.

**Character and attributes**: It is intelligent, agile, and gentle.

**Uses**: This is essentially a popular pet, which is also used in equitherapy. Its small size should not detract from its basic needs as an equine (space, trimming the hooves, and so forth).

**Current status**: The breed is doing extremely well, with around 160,000 American Miniatures registered.

American Miniature foals are tiny.

# AMERICAN SHETLAND

**H** Maximum of 1.12 m.

**C** Bay, chestnut, roan, cream, buckskin; all colors are possible.

**Description**: Taller and much more slender than a Shetland, it is clearly distinguished from its ancestor and, despite their common name, they should not be confused. It looks more like the Hackney Pony. It has a long head with a straight profile; rather long ears; a rather long and slender neck; sloping shoulders; and fairly long legs. The hair of the mane and tail is rather thick. It sometimes has the posture of a Hackney, with the hind legs held well behind.

**Distribution**: United States, Canada.

**Origins and history**: Developed from the Shetland Pony, whose name it retained, the American Shetland (divided in the studbook into divisions A and B, the A registering traditional Shetlands) was later crossed with small Welsh, Hackney, Arabian, and Thoroughbred horses.

**Character and attributes**: The American Shetland is intelligent, usually calm and docile, but sometimes lively, robust, and endowed with high-stepping gaits.

**Uses**: This is an excellent horse for children, both for riding and for driving. It even participates in sulky trotting races.

**Current status**: The breed is doing well.

lead, followed by California, Florida, and Oklahoma). The equestrian industry is an important part of the economy, both for sports and for leisure. The United States has favored the breeding of horses with excellent character, with a great diversity of coat colors, and with supplemental gaits that are encouraged or developed in many breeds. American breeds, easily recognizable, have many assets, and are hugely successful throughout the world.

Long neck

Large, prominent eyes

Silky mane and tail

AMERICAN MINIATURE HORSE

Slender neck

Long head

Rather long legs

AMERICAN SHETLAND

## UNITED STATES

# PONY OF THE AMERICAS

**Acronym:** POA

**Ⓗ** 1.12 m–1.33 m, a maximum of 1.40 m.

**Ⓒ** Always spotted, with the same types of coats as the Appaloosa, and similar characteristics (visible white sclera, striated hooves, and marbling around the eyes, on the nose, and on the genitals).

**Description:** The head resembles that of the Arabian, with a slightly concave profile; large, prominent eyes; and a wide forehead. It has a broad chest; sloping shoulders; prominent withers; a short back; a long, rather horizontal croup; a high-set tail; and wide hooves.

**Distribution:** United States, Canada.

**Origins and history:** This recent breed, founded in 1954, is the result of crossings among Shetland, Arab, Appaloosa, then Quarter Horse and Welsh, with the goal of creating a good children's mount with an attractive coat.

**Character and attributes:** Docile, easy, and intelligent, it is fast, robust, and good at jumping, with high-stepping gaits.

**Uses:** Versatile, it is a very good mount for the youngest riders and for smallish adults; for this reason, it is often used for teaching.

**Current status:** Quite popular in North America, the breed is doing very well, with more than 50,000 individuals.

A characteristic of spotted breeds is the very visible white sclera of the eyes.

## UNITED STATES

# AMERICAN WALKING PONY

**Ⓗ** 1.20 m–1.42 m.

**Ⓒ** All colors are possible.

**Description:** It has a rather small head with a straight profile; long, arched neck; broad chest; long, sloping shoulders; muscular hindquarters; and a high-set tail.

**Distribution:** United States (notably in Georgia).

**Origins and history:** A recent breed, the American Walking Pony was created in 1968 from crossings between the Tennessee Walker and the Welsh, with the goal of creating a good gaited pony.

**Character and attributes:** It is a good jumper. It has a variety of supplemental gaits, called the *pleasure walk, merry walk, slow gait*, and *rack*.

**Uses:** It is popular as a comfortable mount for young riders or adults, in English-style riding (show jumping, dressage) or Western riding. Its soft gaits naturally make it well adapted for recreational riding.

**Current status:** We lack information on its status.

As its name indicates, this American Walking Pony has supplemental gaits. Shown here is the pleasure walk.

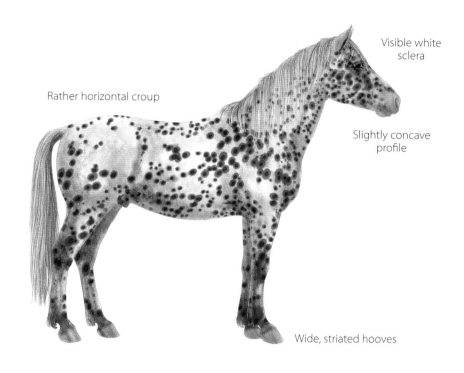

Visible white
sclera

Rather horizontal croup

Slightly concave
profile

Wide, striated hooves

Long, arched
neck

High-set tail

Broad chest

# ASSATEAGUE AND CHINCOTEAGUE

It is called the Chincoteague pony on the island of Chincoteague, and the Assateague pony on the island of Assateague

**H** 1.22 m–1.47 m.

**C** Often black pinto or chestnut pinto, but all colors are possible.

**Description**: It has a long head with a straight, sometimes concave profile; small ears; a short neck; slender legs; a rather sloping, round croup; and a low-set tail. The hair of the mane and tail is thick.

**Distribution**: The islands of Assateague and Chincoteague, off the coast of Virginia, United States, as well as a few breeding farms elsewhere in the United States.

**Origins and history**: The presence of horse populations on the islands of Assateague and Chincoteague has been the object of much speculation. It was long thought that they were the result of horses that escaped from a shipwrecked boat, and some believe they descended from the Pottok. In reality, the horses were transported there in the seventeenth century by colonists to avoid paying taxes. Since the eighteenth century, during an annual festival, farmers have gathered the horses to capture them. This festival is still popular; the culmination of the spectacle is the moment when the ponies, pushed by cowboys, swim from Assateague to Chincoteague through the narrowest part of the channel, before being sold at auction. In 1939, twenty Mustangs and a bit later, some Arabians, were introduced to avoid too much inbreeding.

**Character and attributes**: They are independent, intelligent, but docile once they are broken, resilient and rustic, undemanding and capable of eating algae to survive.

**Uses**: Once captured, they are suitable as mounts for young or small adult riders.

**Current status**: There are around 300 on the islands and a thousand on the mainland. A children's book, *Misty of Chincoteague* by Marguerite Henry, published in 1947, made these wild horses famous, which ensures them a promising future.

Each year cowboys make Chincoteague ponies swim across the channel to sell them at auction.

# WELARA PONY

**H** 1.17 m–1.52 m.

**C** Often gray, all colors, except spotted, are possible.

**Description**: It has a small head with a slightly concave profile; small ears; a long, muscular, arched neck (always resembling the neck of a stallion); sloping shoulders; a short back; a long and rather horizontal croup; and a high-set tail.

**Distribution**: United States, United Kingdom.

**Origins and history**: This breed is the result of crosses between an Arabian and a Welsh, and the name Welara is the contraction of the names of those two breeds. The Welara is of both British and American origin. The first crosses were made in the United Kingdom at the beginning of the twentieth century, but in 1981 the breeding register was opened in the United States, and the Americans are very fond of this breed. It is sometimes crossed with the English Thoroughbred to produce a taller animal.

**Character and attributes**: It is intelligent and gentle, and is a good jumper.

**Uses**: It is suited to show jumping and dressage, but also for Western riding and for driving.

**Current status**: Although popular, this recent breed is rather limited, with only around 1,500 individuals.

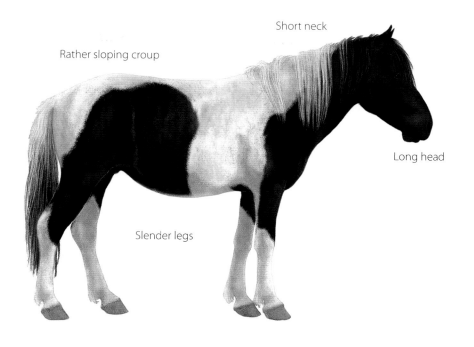

Rather sloping croup

Short neck

Long head

Slender legs

Arched neck

Slightly concave profile

Long and rather horizontal croup

Small head

# SPANISH BARB

**H** 1.35 m–1.45 m.

**C** Chestnut, black, roan, bay dun, black/brown dun, gray, pinto.

**Description**: The Spanish Barb has a head with the straight or slightly convex profile characteristic of Spanish horses, a wide forehead, sloping shoulders, and a round croup. The hair of the mane and tail is long and thick; it sometimes has a double mane.

**Distribution**: United States.

**Origins and history**: The Spanish Barb is the result of a project of reconstitution and selection from some thirty horses. Although it greatly resembles the Spanish Mustang, with which it shares the same ancestors, the Spanish Barb is being reconstituted to recover the breed as it was upon its arrival in America, and not as it has become over time through the Spanish Mustang.

**Character and attributes**: The Spanish Barb is intelligent, bold, and agile. It has endurance and good cow sense.

**Uses**: This is a good recreational horse, used for trekking and Western riding.

**Current status**: It is rare, with fewer than 2,000 horses.

---

# BANKER

**H** 1.32 m–1.50 m.

**C** Buckskin, bay dun, bay, dark bay, chestnut, cream, a few pinto.

**Description**: Compact, the Banker has a head with a straight or slightly convex profile, a wide forehead, high-set neck, narrow chest, long shoulders, a short back, solid legs, a sloping croup, and a low-set tail. The hair of the mane and tail is long and thick.

**Distribution**: Outer Banks of North Carolina, notably the Shackleford Islands, Ocracoke, United States.

**Origins and history**: Of Spanish origin, abandoned by the conquistadors, Bankers live, or rather survive, on the Outer Banks, on sandy islands, banks of sand with poor grass and very hot summers. Because they are isolated they have ultimately formed a homogeneous population.

**Character and attributes**: Docile once tamed, the Banker has endurance and is rustic. It has natural supplemental gaits, the amble and tölt.

**Uses**: Once tamed and broken, it can make a good saddle horse.

**Current status**: Although the population was once at several thousand animals, they became troublesome for construction projects and were in part destroyed. Its history and genetic importance are now recognized, and the Banker is being watched and protected.

A herd of Bankers on the beach.

Long, thick mane
and tail

Round croup

Spanish-type head

High-set neck

Short back

Narrow chest

# CHOCTAW

**❶** 1.37 m–1.47 m.

**❸** Often pinto, but all colors are possible; it has the dun gene and its corresponding primitive markings.

**Description**: The Choctaw resembles the Mustang. It has a head with a straight or slightly convex profile, wide forehead, lightly arched neck, long back, long legs, a sloping croup, low-set tail, and hard hooves. The mane and tail are thick.

**Distribution**: Mississippi, United States.

**Origins and history**: Like those of the Florida Cracker Horse, its bloodlines are from the horses of the first colonists. It was raised by the Choctaw tribe. It almost disappeared, first suffering in the nineteenth century when the Choctaws were placed on a reservation and their horses were slaughtered, then in the twentieth century when they were no longer of great use.

**Character and attributes**: Intelligent, resilient, agile, and with good endurance, the Choctaw has good cow sense. Some animals amble.

**Uses**: This is a good work horse and suited for Western riding.

**Current status**: Having fallen to only around a hundred individuals, the breed is still endangered, although it is slowly growing, with probably fewer than 300 horses in 2013.

# BLAZER

**❶** 1.35 m–1.50 m.

**❸** Often black, bay, dark bay, chestnut, palomino, bay dun, black/brown dun, never pinto or spotted, sometimes with white markings on the head and legs.

**Description**: The Blazer has a slender head; long, very sloping shoulders; prominent withers; a short back; round croup; and robust legs.

**Distribution**: Northwestern United States.

**Origins and history**: This recent breed was developed in the 1950s by an enthusiastic breeder from a founding stallion, Little Blaze. It is a mixture of Quarter Horse, Morgan, American Saddlebred, and Thoroughbred. The breed's association was created in 2006.

**Character and attributes**: One of the essential criteria for its breeding is a good character, and the breed has been developed around that. The Blazer is thus particularly docile, reliable, and easy to ride. It is also intelligent, robust, and easy to keep.

**Uses**: Basically a ranch horse, it is versatile, well-suited to Western riding and trekking, but also for more English-style disciplines. It adapts well to different types of riders and makes a good lesson and family horse, as well as a horse for equitherapy, because it is not too tall and has an easygoing nature. It can make a good mount for young riders.

**Current status**: This American breed is not very well known, but its gentleness and versatility are popular among connoisseurs.

Slightly arched neck

Wide forehead

Long back

Low-set tail

Hard hooves

Prominent withers

Round croup

Robust legs

# MUSTANG

Also called: American Feral Horse, Wild Mustang

**Ⓗ** 1.35 m–1.52 m.

**Ⓒ** All colors are possible, including pinto, bay dun, black/brown dun.

**Description**: The Mustang has a variable morphology, with a rather large head with a straight or convex profile; strong neck; straight shoulders; unobtrusive withers; short back; dished croup; rather short, solid legs; and very hard hooves.

**Distribution**: Nevada, Wyoming, Washington, Oregon, Idaho, Utah, Colorado, Montana, California, Arizona, New Mexico, United States. They are also found in Canada, in Alberta and British Columbia.

**Origins and history**: The famous Mustang is basically the issue of the conquistadors' horses, Iberians and Barbs, which returned to the wild in the sixteenth century, and to which all sorts of horses also returned to the wild were added. Natural selection forged this horse.

**Character and attributes**: From its life in the wild it maintains an assertive, spirited, bold character, but once broken it can become a pleasant horse. It has endurance, is fast, robust, rustic, undemanding, and sure-footed.

**Uses**: When caught and broken at a young age, it makes a good mount. It is a good endurance horse. It is also often used in rodeos.

**Current status**: Once very widespread (up to two million horses estimated at the beginning of the twentieth century), it almost disappeared in the mid-twentieth century: it was targeted for eating the grass of other livestock, and it was slaughtered in the hundreds of thousands in sadly famous massacres, often carried out from planes, which caused a great deal of outcry among horse lovers. A true American symbol, it is now protected, and many of the horses have been adopted. Their population is estimated at between 26,000 and 37,000 horses.

## A FEW MUSTANG POPULATIONS

The most common Mustangs, called Comstocks, live in Nevada; then there are the Pryor Mountain Mustangs of Wyoming. Of note, too, are the Sulphur Springs Mustangs of Utah, the Coyote Canyon Mustangs of California, and the rare Spanish Mustang (see *p. 444*).

Comstocks are in a somewhat separate category: living on private properties they are not really considered to be wild, and do not benefit from official protection measures like other Mustangs. Associations work to protect them. They are often bay or chestnut.

Mustangs of Wyoming, which have Spanish blood, are called Pryor Mountain Mustangs; they are mountain horses and thus stockier than the others. There are fewer than 200 of them. Compact, they measure around 1.42 m–1.47 m. They have a straight, sometimes convex profile, which becomes more slender toward the muzzle; a slightly arched neck; slightly sloping shoulders; slightly sloping croup; low-set tail; hard hooves; and a very thick mane and tail. They are often black/brown dun,

bay dun, with a dorsal stripe and zebra striping on the legs, but also bay, black, chestnut, roan. They are reputed to be very intelligent and brave, and to make very good endurance or trekking horses. Some have supplemental gaits.

The horses of Coyote Canyon are the last Mustangs in Southern California. They measure under 1.50 m, and have large eyes; large ears; a short, high-set neck; rather sloping shoulders; fairly short legs; and very hard hooves. They are related to Spanish horses. Some thirty horses still lived in the Anza-Borrego Desert of California until 2003, the date when they were moved.

## THE ABSTANG: A CROSSING DESTINED TO BECOME A BREED?

In Utah, beginning in the 1990s, crossings have taken place between Mustangs and Arabians. Measuring around 1.50 m–1.55 m, of various colors, the horses resulting from these crossings, nicknamed Abstangs, are reputed to be very energetic and sure-footed and to have excellent endurance, which makes them popular for endurance races and trekking.

Dished croup

Unobtrusive withers

Rather large head

Solid legs

Hard hooves

Mustangs, persecuted for a long time, ended up becoming one of the symbols—of freedom and wildness—of the United States.

# SPANISH MUSTANG

**⊖** 1.30 m–1.52 m; an average of 1.47 m.

**☉** Often pinto, bay dun, buckskin, black/brown dun.

**Description**: Of Iberian type, it has a rather large head with a straight or convex profile, rather long ears, a narrow chest, short back, strong legs, round croup, and a low-set tail.

**Distribution**: United States.

**Origins and history**: The Spanish Mustang is the type of Mustang directly descended from Spanish and Barb horses, so they are old-type Mustangs, the most original, later forged by life in the wild. Other Mustangs have in fact received a lot of blood from other breeds. Many Spanish Mustangs have been domesticated and raised in traditional ways.

**Character and attributes**: Spanish Mustangs are known to be very intelligent and have great endurance. Some are amblers.

**Uses**: It can make a good saddle horse, notably for endurance races.

**Current status**: Spanish Mustangs are rare, with around 1,500 horses, and are the objects of conservation measures. They are extremely popular among enthusiasts seeking an original type of American horse. They are also registered in the American Indian Horse Registry (AIHR).

The Mustangs of Sulphur Springs have especially visible primitive markings, including a sometimes very wide dorsal stripe.

### KIGER, CERBAT, SULPHUR SPRINGS, AND COLONIAL SPANISH HORSE: FOUR TYPES OF SPANISH MUSTANG

It has been said that the Kiger, discovered in the 1970s, is the purest strain of Spanish Mustang. It is found in Oregon. It is of very uniform type, a carrier of the dun gene, often a beautiful bay dun color with primitive markings, black legs, and a dorsal stripe. It is a muscular horse measuring between 1.37 m and 1.57 m, with a head with an often slightly convex profile; small ears; sloping, muscular shoulders; a slightly sloping croup; low-set tail; and hard hooves. The mane and tail are thick, sometimes bi-colored. Kigers have been enormously successful when they are offered for adoption, and they have been bred under the name of Steens Mountain Kiger.

The Cerbat Mountain Spanish Mustang is found in Arizona. It is bay, chestnut, or roan, with a convex profile and often a double mane.

The Sulphur Springs Mustang, or Spanish Sulphur, in Utah, is very interesting genetically speaking. Sometimes called the "zebra horse of Utah," it can be bay dun, black/brown dun, sometimes bay, black, chestnut, palomino, or roan, with a sometimes very large dorsal stripe (sometimes called a triple dorsal stripe); zebra striping on the legs, very prominent on the front legs; bars on the chest, and a bi-color mane and tail. It measures 1.47 m and resembles the Sorraia (see *p. 82*). Foals are born with the same type of striping as Sorraia foals, which suggests a kinship. It has a wide forehead, convex profile, narrow chest, sloping croup, and a low-set tail. It is very rustic, very simple, and agile, with excellent endurance. Protected, there are now between 135 and 180 horses.

As for the Wilbur-Cruce Colonial Spanish Mission Horse, which descends directly from horses imported from Spain at the end of the seventeenth century, it is located in Arizona, near Mexico, on the Wilbur-Cruce ranch, where it has been raised in semi-freedom; some horses are taken out regularly to work livestock. It is mainly chestnut, with all the shades of that coat color; a few are bay or, more rarely, pinto, black, or gray.

All these horses are rare. They are the descendants of the Colonial Spanish Horse, a name given to the first Iberian and Barb animals that arrived with the colonists.

Rather long ears

Round croup

Low-set tail

Narrow chest

Resilient legs

# FLORIDA CRACKER HORSE

Also called: Florida Cow Pony, Grass Cut

**H** 1.37 m–1.52 m.

**C** Liver chestnut, bay, gray, black/brown dun, frequently with white markings on the head and legs.

**Description**: It is very similar to the Choctaw. It has a head with straight or slightly concave profile; wide forehead; refined nose; slender neck; sloping shoulders; slightly prominent withers; a short back; short, sloping croup; slender legs; and a low-set tail.

**Distribution**: Florida, United States.

**Origins and history**: These horses are descended from the first Barbs and Iberian horses (such as the Spanish Jennet and Sorraia) imported by the colonists in the sixteenth century, some of which returned to the wild. The Seminole Indians captured and trained them, as did cowboys.

**Character and attributes**: The Florida Cracker is fast and agile. It has wonderful endurance and comfortable supplemental gaits, the amble and the broken amble, called "coon rack" for this breed.

**Uses**: It can make a good ranch horse, and is always suitable as a Western riding horse, or for recreation.

**Current status**: Its numbers have fallen, as the Cracker has suffered from strong competition with the Quarter Horse, which is more powerful. But enthusiasts are protecting the breed; there are around 1,000 horses.

---

UNITED STATES

# MARSH TACKY

Also called: Carolina Marsh Tacky

**H** 1.42 m–1.47 m on average.

**C** Bay dun, black/brown dun, bay, roan, mealy black, chestnut, sometimes with white markings on the head and legs, with primitive markings on coats diluted by the dun gene (dorsal stripe, light striping on the legs, but also a black marking above the eye).

**Description**: This small horse has a head with a straight or slightly concave profile that becomes slightly convex at the nose, large eyes, a wide forehead, slightly arched neck, prominent withers, narrow chest, sloping shoulders, short back, very sloping croup, low-set tail, and hard hooves. The hair of the mane and tail is thick and long.

**Distribution**: South Carolina, United States.

**Origins and history**: Similar to the Florida Cracker and the Banker, it is the descendant of Iberian horses imported by the conquistadors. Many lived in the wild in the marshes of South Carolina.

**Character and attributes**: The Marsh Tacky is intelligent, gentle, calm, and bold; it has good endurance and is sure-footed, even on loose soil. It is indeed well adapted to a swampy environment. Easy to keep, it is undemanding. Some walk in a broken amble.

**Uses**: This is a good recreational horse, also used for working livestock and for endurance races.

**Current status**: Very rare and on the brink of extinction, the breed counts fewer than 300 individuals. Enthusiasts are trying to encourage its development. Given its Iberian look, its colors and attributes, they should be successful.

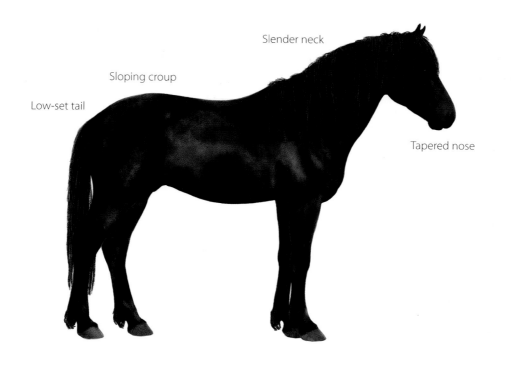

Slender neck

Sloping croup

Low-set tail

Tapered nose

Thick mane and tail

Wide forehead

Low-set tail

Narrow chest

## UNITED STATES

# NOKOTA

**H** 1.47 m–1.52 m.

**C** Varied; often roan, black, light gray, bay, sometimes pinto, often with the dun gene that gives primitive markings, often with white markings.

**Description**: The Nokota has a head with a straight or slightly concave profile, wide forehead, large eyes, slightly prominent withers, sloping shoulders, a short back, very sloping croup, solid legs, a low-set tail, and hard hooves. The hair of the mane and tail is long and thick. There is a smaller traditional type and a taller ranch type, which has been crossed with other breeds (Thoroughbred, Spanish, draft).

**Distribution**: United States (notably, North Dakota), Canada; a few in Sweden and France.

**Origins and history**: This horse population has a surprising history: it was accidentally enclosed in the Theodore Roosevelt National Park in the 1950s when the park was being created. It descends from the last Mustangs present in the region. At first the park didn't want the horses and tried to get rid of them, then later it attempted to cross them to increase their commercial value. Some enthusiastic ranchers saved the horse, buying as many as they could and then breeding them. They called them Nokota and launched a new breed.

**Character and attributes**: The Nokota is very intelligent, energetic, agile, and rustic. Some individuals have the amble.

**Uses**: It is a good recreational horse, very well suited to Western riding and trekking, but which can also excel in English-style disciplines such as dressage or show jumping.

**Current status**: The breed is still very rare, with probably fewer than 500 purebred animals in 2013.

## UNITED STATES

# MORGAN

**H** 1.43 m–1.53 m.

**C** Mainly bay, dark bay, chestnut, black; moderate white markings are authorized.

**Description**: Rather small, the Morgan has a small and slender head; a straight or slightly concave profile; large eyes; small ears; a wide forehead; high-set neck; powerful, sloping shoulders; a short back; wide, horizontal croup; and slender, solid legs. Its posture, with the hind legs stretched back from the vertical, is characteristic of the breed.

**Distribution**: Vermont, Massachusetts, Connecticut, elsewhere in the United States; Canada; United Kingdom.

**Origins and history**: The breed descends from an exceptional stallion born in 1789, Justin Morgan, of unknown origins, that transferred its type to the local mares with which he was crossed.

**Character and attributes**: The Morgan is very intelligent, docile, and bold. It is powerful and fast, and has high-stepping gaits. It is resilient and hardy.

**Uses**: Very versatile, it is a good family horse, for recreation, but also for competition; it is suited to all disciplines, both ridden and driven.

**Current status**: Very popular in the United States (close to 180,000 horses), they are also bred abroad, although the breed is not as well known internationally.

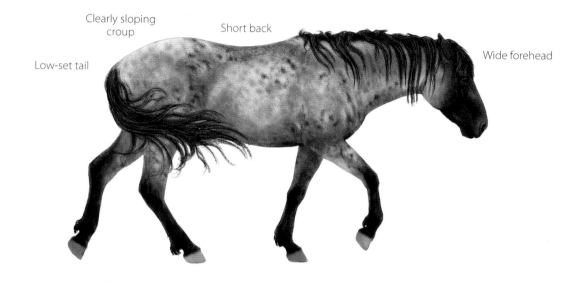

Clearly sloping croup

Short back

Wide forehead

Low-set tail

High-set neck

Horizontal croup

Small, slender head

Characteristic backward-pointing posture

# MORAB

**H** 1.47 m–1.57 m on average, but can reach 1.63 m.

**C** Mainly bay, chestnut, gray, also bay dun, palomino.

**Description**: This is a compact horse with a slender head and slightly concave profile; wide forehead; large, prominent eyes; small ears; a long, arched neck; broad chest; sloping shoulders; prominent withers; a short back; a horizontal, muscular croup; long, strong legs; and a high-set tail which can be held aloft. The hair of the mane and tail is thick, silky, and often wavy.

**Distribution**: United States.

**Origins and history**: Breeding of the Morab began at the end of the nineteenth century, through crossings between Arabians and Morgans, with the goal of combining the attributes of both breeds.

**Character and attributes**: It is calm and intelligent, adaptable and vigorous, and lives a long time.

**Uses**: This is a good recreational horse for the entire family, for English or Western riding.

**Current status**: The breed is not very known outside its country, but its attributes are appreciated.

# PINTABIAN

**H** 1.47 m–1.57 m.

**C** Pinto (mainly tobiano).

**Description**: This is an Arabian with color. It has a slender head with a concave profile; wide forehead; large eyes; small ears; an arched neck; sloping shoulders; a short back; horizontal croup; slender legs; high-set tail; and small, hard hooves. The skin is fine.

**Distribution**: United States (mainly Minnesota); Canada; a few in Europe (United Kingdom, France, Belgium, Germany, Austria).

**Origins and history**: This recent breed was created in the 1980s with the Arabian, whose standards reject pinto animals. By crossing with pinto horses, breeders were able to introduce the pinto gene, and now seek to obtain a horse that is 99 percent Arabian. It is a rather long selection process.

**Character and attributes**: It is intelligent, easy to handle, and energetic, with lovely gaits.

**Uses**: This recreational horse is also a good endurance competitor.

**Current status**: The breed is still being developed, with a thousand individuals in 2013, and is becoming increasingly popular.

Often wavy
mane and tail

Horizontal croup

High-set tail

Broad chest

Horizontal croup

High-set tail

Arabian-type head

Small hooves

# Tiger Horse

Also called: Soulon Tiger Horse

**H** 1.52 m on average.

**C** Spotted, often like a leopard; the hooves are often striated and the sclera of the eye is visible.

**Description**: The Tiger Horse has a convex profile, large eyes, a wide forehead, and a highly arched neck. There are two types: the "heavenly type," which is a bit stockier, and the thinner "royalty type," which has straighter shoulders and whose natural gaits are more pronounced. Depending on the individual, the mane and tail can be fine or thicker.

**Distribution**: United States; a few in Canada; Germany; New Zealand.

**Origins and history**: This is a recent breed, developed since 1992 with the goal of creating a good, athletic horse with soft gaits and an attractive coat, especially from Appaloosas and gaited breeds all with similar characteristics. Another goal is to create a horse that resembles the ancient Chinese breed from the Tang Dynasty, the Soulon.

**Character and attributes**: Intelligent, gentle, easy with humans, it has supplemental natural gaits (fox trot, running walk, stepping pace, and others).

**Uses**: This recreational horse, well suited for equestrian trekking, is also a good ranch horse.

**Current status**: This new breed is being developed: in 2013 there were around 115 animals registered, 20 of which were of Soulon type. It is beginning to be known in the United States and to be exported abroad.

---

UNITED STATES

# North American Curly Horse

Once called the American Bashkir Curly, through analogy with the curly Russian breed, but the name was abandoned since their origins are different.

**H** 1.42 m–1.63 m.

**C** Variable; pinto, spotted.

**Description**: As its name indicates, this horse has the unusual characteristic of having a hide, mane, and tail that are curly, to varying degrees depending on the individual. It has a head with a straight profile, wide forehead, muscular neck, unobtrusive withers, short back, and muscular croup. The mane and tail, fine and silky, are thin and are almost nonexistent in the summer: they grow back in the winter, which is when the coat becomes long and curly.

**Distribution**: United States, notably Nevada; Canada; a few in Europe (France, Germany).

**Origins and history**: The breed was developed from a herd of curly Mustangs discovered in 1898 in Nevada, of mysterious origin. The Curly doesn't seem to have ties with the often curly Russian breeds of Bashkir or Lokai.

**Character and attributes**: It is particularly gentle and robust, with good endurance; it is very resilient in the cold because of its hide. It is hypoallergenic, which makes it a good breed for people who are allergic to horses.

**Uses**: Versatile, it is suitable for many disciplines, including both Western riding and show jumping, and it is a pleasant recreational horse.

**Current status**: This very original breed is still fairly rare, but is being actively developed.

The surprising Curly also has a curly forelock and curly hair inside its ears.

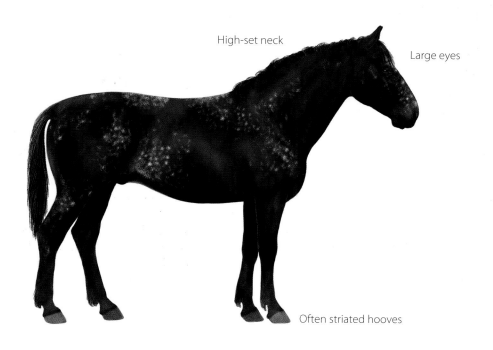

High-set neck

Large eyes

Often striated hooves

Fine, silky, curly
mane and tail

Straight profile

Short back

The hair grows in curly

# KENTUCKY MOUNTAIN SADDLE HORSE

**H** Two categories of height: A: over 1.47 m; B: from 1.12 m to 1.47 m.

**C** Often chocolate, bay, gray, cream; white markings on the head, legs, and barrel are possible. Pinto and spotted horses of this breed are registered separately in the Spotted Mountain Horse Association.

**Description**: The Kentucky Mountain Saddle Horse is generally an average-sized horse. It has a head with a straight profile; wide forehead; an arched, fairly high-set neck; broad chest; unobtrusive withers; sloping shoulders; a short back; and a round croup.

**Distribution**: United States; Canada; a few in Europe.

**Origins and history**: Their exact origin is unknown, but they are related to the Tennessee Walker.

**Character and attributes**: It is intelligent, gentle, calm, rustic, and easy to keep. It has comfortable supplemental gaits (including the rack).

**Uses**: This is a pleasant recreational horse, versatile, suited for English or Western riding, and its comfortable gaits make it an excellent trekking horse.

**Current status**: The breed is doing well.

# ROCKY MOUNTAIN HORSE

**H** 1.43 m–1.63 m.

**C** It has a characteristic coat, mainly chocolate brown with very light flaxen mane and tail and beautiful golden highlights, but there can also be other colors, as well.

**Description**: The Rocky Mountain Horse has a slender head, slightly arched neck, broad chest, prominent withers, sloping shoulders, long back, slender legs, and very hard hooves.

**Distribution**: Kentucky, United States; a hundred or so in Europe.

**Origins and history**: It has Iberian origins in common with the American Saddlebred and the Tennessee Walker.

**Character and attributes**: Very gentle, calm and reliable, intelligent, agile, and sure-footed, it can carry a lot, has endurance, and is very comfortable to ride thanks to its natural amble and its natural supplemental gaits. It lives a long time.

**Uses**: This utility horse, popular for traveling easily over long distances thanks to its comfortable gait, is becoming a popular recreational horse, suitable for the entire family. It is also a good endurance race competitor.

**Current status**: Though its numbers have been small for a long time, this original breed is becoming popular thanks to its recreational qualities, its very attractive coat, and its comfortable amble. It is becoming known in Europe.

The Rocky Mountain Horse excels at the tölt, one of the most comfortable gaits for a rider.

Arched neck

Unobtrusive
withers

Round croup

Broad chest

Slightly arched neck

Slender head

Slender legs

# MISSOURI FOX TROTTER

**❶** 1.42 m–1.63 m.

**❸** Often chestnut, also bay, dark bay, black, roan, gray and pinto, with white markings on the head and legs.

**Description**: The Missouri Fox Trotter has a small, slender head with a straight profile, large eyes, broad chest, sloping shoulders, short back, and muscular croup. The hair of the mane and tail is thin and not very thick.

**Distribution**: United States (mainly Missouri); Canada; Europe (notably Germany).

**Origins and history**: Developed at the beginning of the nineteenth century, this breed is the fruit of a lot of mixing. The goal was to create a comfortable and fast horse by crossing the Morgan, Thoroughbred, Arabian, and Barb, then the American Saddlebred and Tennessee Walker.

**Character and attributes**: It is very docile, has good endurance, and is very comfortable due to its four-beat special gait, the fox trot, when the horse seems to walk with the front legs and trot with the back.

**Uses**: The Missouri Fox Trotter is now a recreational horse, for Western riding. Its easy nature and smooth gaits make it a good mount for learning to ride and for equitherapy.

**Current status**: Very popular in the United States, the breed is doing well, but it is still not well known abroad.

*The Missouri Fox Trotter also does the fox trot when at liberty.*

# APPALOOSA

**❶** 1.47 m–1.65 m.

**❸** Characteristic spotted pattern with various distribution of the spots: "leopard" (most common, with spots on a white foundation); "snow-flake" (more rare, white spots on a dark coat); "spotted blanket" (with a spotted white croup); "white blanket" (with a solid white croup); "frosted" (light spots on a dark croup); and "marble" (white marbling on a dark coat). The base color is variable. Hooves are often striated, and the sclera of the eye is white, the skin marbled. There can also be Appaloosas with a "solid" coat, without spotting. The color isn't set until a horse is two years old.

**Description**: It has a small head with a straight profile, muscular neck, sloping shoulders, unobtrusive withers, short back, very powerful croup, and small hooves. The hair of the mane and tail is short and not very thick.

**Distribution**: United States, mainly in the West; a few throughout Europe and Australia.

**Origins and history**: This is the horse of the Nez Perce Indians, created from horses imported by the conquistadors (horses with spotted coats were once popular in Europe, before they disappeared), and it derives its name from the Palouse River, on the banks of which it was raised. It was later crossed with Quarter Horse, Arabian, and Thoroughbred, sometimes too much so, which means that some animals look very much like Quarter Horses.

**Character and attributes**: The Appaloosa is docile, gentle, and easygoing. It has endurance, is an easy keeper, and like the Quarter Horse is capable of impressive speed.

**Uses**: This is a family horse for recreation, versatile, very good for Western riding, also popular in shows and circuses, and for trekking.

**Current status**: After almost becoming extinct, it is one of the most famous of American breeds, due to its astonishing colors and its alluring Indian origins, and the breed, known by all riders, is doing very well.

### THE NEZ PERCE HORSE: IN SEARCH OF THE ORIGINAL APPALOOSA

The Nez Perce Indian breeders have been trying since 1995 to recreate the original type of Appaloosa (Nez Perce Horse), and after serious reflection crossed the current breed with the Akhal-Teke, which is rather surprising because the origins of the Appaloosa are Iberian and not Turkoman. But the crossing proved to be very interesting, producing a horse with great endurance, intelligent, sensitive, very close to its rider, and distinguishable from the Quarter Horse. Thus the Nez Perce Indians again showed their intelligence as breeders: to introduce metallic reflections into the spotted coat, thereby enhancing the breed's original look, was genius.

Thin mane and tail

Muscular croup

Small, slender head

Short, thin
mane and tail

Visible white sclera

Small head

Marbling on the
mouth, around the
eyes, and genitals

Small, striated hooves

The Nez Perce type, crossed with the Akhal-Teke, is more
slender, with a more golden-hued coat.

# QUARTER HORSE

**H** Around 1.45 m–1.62 m.

**C** Often chestnut, dark chestnut, bay, sometimes bay dun, chestnut roan, black, palomino: coats are quite varied and colored, because all solid coats are accepted, except white.

**Description**: This average-sized horse has a particularly muscular and robust appearance: the neck, back, and hindquarters are very powerful. The head is rather small and wide. The most striking criterion of identification is probably the particularly developed croup, which is also noted in the foals of this breed.

**Distribution**: Native to the United States, it is the most widespread breed in the world.

**Origins and history**: The Quarter Horse, one of the oldest of American breeds, descends from Iberian and Eastern horses, crossed with the ancestors of English Thoroughbreds. This incredible sprinter is the fastest in the world over quarter-mile courses, 440 yards (around 402 m), from which it derives its name (it was first called the Quarter Running Horse). These races were first organized in the streets, in Virginia and the Carolinas. For Americans, it is the best horse in the world, given its many attributes.

**Character and attributes**: The Quarter Horse has a particularly docile nature, is cooperative, adaptable, calm, and reliable following many years of selection for good character. It has agility, speed, suppleness, energy, intelligence, and endurance; it is brave and has a natural "cow sense," which is especially developed in some lineages. Fast and responsive, it has incredible speed at take-off. Its movements are smooth. Although an athlete, it is a rather easy horse to keep.

**Uses**: The Quarter Horse excels in Western riding (reining, trail, cutting, and others), its specialty, but it also makes a good carriage horse and is used for trekking, racing, polo, and so forth. Its excellent, reassuring character makes it good for beginning riders. The quintessential horse of cowboys and Western riding, it is very versatile and succeeds in many other disciplines as well.

**Current status**: The breed is the most popular in the world, and it is very widespread with around 5 million horses registered with the American Quarter Horse Association—it could not do better.

The head is characteristic: rather small, with a wide forehead; large, wide-spaced eyes; narrow muzzle; and large nostrils.

Basically a versatile ranch horse, the Quarter Horse is incontestably one of the best horses for herding livestock.

For children, there is a smaller type of Quarter Horse, the American Quarter Pony. Combining the excellent temperament of the Quarter Horse and a more accessible size for a young rider, it makes a perfect lesson horse.

A typical Western saddle, made of leather, decorated with elaborate motifs.

In Western riding the Quarter Horse is the champion of fast sliding stops.

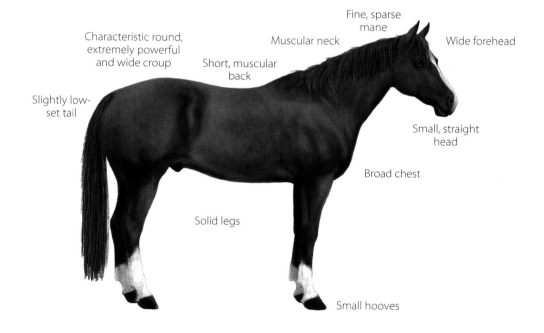

Fine, sparse mane

Muscular neck

Wide forehead

Characteristic round, extremely powerful and wide croup

Short, muscular back

Slightly low-set tail

Small, straight head

Broad chest

Solid legs

Small hooves

Due to their incredibly fast starts and bursts of speed, Quarter Horses are also used in racing, often practiced today on straight, 300-meter courses.

# AMERICAN PAINT HORSE

**H** 1.45 m–1.60 m.

**C** Overo pinto (pinto with irregular spots, the white does not go beyond the line of the back and reach the head, mane and tail flecked with white, often dark legs, incomplete stockings); tobiano (pinto with very round spots, the white goes over the back and generally doesn't reach the head, often with four stockings); tovero (white head with dark spots possible on the ears, mouth, around the eyes, single-color mane and tail, white that goes over the back, stockings). Sometimes foals are born solid, with a solid coat color. They sometimes have blue eyes.

**Description**: The American Paint Horse has the characteristic morphology of the Quarter Horse, with a small head; a powerful, muscular croup; muscular legs; and small hooves. The mane and tail are fine.

**Distribution**: United States, Canada, Europe (France, Germany, Italy, Great Britain).

**Origins and history**: It is the result of the same mixtures as the Quarter Horse, and it is the Quarter Horse type that differentiates the Paint from the Pinto. The only crossings possible are with the Thoroughbred and the Quarter Horse. Pinto horses, often used by the Indians, were excluded from the Quarter Horse registry.

**Character and attributes**: Intelligent, docile, and calm, with the renowned cool temperament of American horses, it is also fast and agile.

**Uses**: This is a versatile horse for Western riding, recreation, trekking, but one that can be used in other disciplines.

**Current status**: Popular especially because of its unique colors, the Paint is doing well: it is the second most widespread breed in the United States.

An overo stallion and a tobiano mare.

# MOYLE HORSE

**H** Around 1.55 m.

**C** Bay, dark bay.

**Description**: Some Moyles have the astonishing peculiarity of two small horny growths on their forehead, like some Chinese Datongs. It has a straight profile, arched neck, sloping shoulders, short back, sloping croup, and wide hooves. It has two fewer vertebrae than other horses, and the Moyle family think that it also has a heart and lungs that are particularly well developed, explaining its exceptional endurance.

**Distribution**: Idaho, United States.

**Origins and history**: It descends from the Mustang, Spanish Barb, Cleveland Bay, and old Morgan lineages, with a small amount of Thoroughbred blood. It is always bred on the ranch of the Moyle family.

**Character and attributes**: The Moyle is intelligent and calm; it stands out for its great endurance. It is robust and fast. It is also very comfortable due to particularly well constructed shoulders.

**Uses**: This is a saddle horse that excels in endurance races.

**Current status**: This astonishing breed, very rare, is little known, with a hundred or so horses in existence. With its qualities and its unique characteristics it deserves to be better known.

### BREEDS WITH BUMPS ON THEIR FOREHEAD

Horses of other breeds can sometimes, though rarely, be born with two small bumps on their forehead, sorts of bony protuberances. These are even sometimes called "horns," though that is misleading. The only breed in which this happens fairly frequently is the Chinese Datong, though they are found on some Spanish Chartreux (an ancient lineage of Andalusian) and Moyles in the United States. It is possible that the Moyle inherited this characteristic from its ancient Iberian ancestors.

Fine mane and tail

Powerful croup

Small head

Tovero pinto

Small hooves

Short back

Two small bumps appear on
the forehead of some Moyles

Straight profile

Wide hooves

The two bumps are quite visible
from the front.

# TENNESSEE WALKING HORSE

Also called: Tennessee Pacer, Walker (once Plantation Walker)

**H** 1.50 m–1.60 m.

**C** Often black, also bay, dark bay, chestnut, gray, roan, sometimes with white markings on the head and legs.

**Description**: This very characteristic light horse has a rather large head with a straight profile; a long, curved, high-set neck; broad chest; strong, sloping shoulders; a muscular, rather horizontal croup; and a high-set tail. The mane and tail are long and abundant. It is trained to stand in a characteristic posture, the back legs stretched out behind. Traditionally, the tail was clipped (the lowering muscles were cut to make the tail stand up). Hooves are sometimes left long and are shod with special shoes to accentuate the unique gaits, a very controversial practice. Tail clipping and gait enhancement, potentially harmful to the animals, will most probably eventually be discontinued.

**Distribution**: United States, especially in the South, and breeding farms throughout the world.

**Origins and history**: The breed was first developed in the late eighteenth century on cotton plantations, and was later established with the birth of a foundation sire, Black Allan (born in 1886), the offspring of an American trotter and a Morgan mare, who had a very particular gait. There were then crossings to the Thoroughbred, American Saddlebred, Narragansett Pacer (extinct), and Canadian Pacer (extinct).

**Character and attributes**: It is docile, calm, easy to keep, and extremely comfortable due to its four-beat gaits, its "running walk," a spectacular fast gliding step, and its "flat walk," a slow gliding step, with the head bobbing along in time, as well as its "rocking chair canter," a slow gallop with a rolling motion.

**Uses**: A versatile, and excellent recreational horse, used in harness and in the show ring. With its pleasant gaits it is an ideal lesson horse for beginners.

**Current status**: The breed, very popular and growing, is one of the most widespread in the United States.

The running walk of the Tennessee Walker is a very comfortable gait.

# SPOTTED SADDLE HORSE

Also called: National Spotted Saddle Horse

**H** 1.50 m–1.63 m.

**C** Always pinto, the hooves are always light, sometimes with black stripes.

**Description**: It looks like the Tennessee Walker, but is smaller and stockier. It has a slender head with a straight or slightly convex profile; large eyes; small ears; a high-set, muscular, very slightly arched neck; sloping shoulders; a short back; and a slightly sloping, rounded croup. The tail is set high, and the hair is rather thick.

**Distribution**: Tennessee, United States.

**Origins and history**: This recent breed, developed since 1979, was created by crossing horses of pinto type with Iberian ancestry with the Morgan, Standardbred, and Tennessee Walker, but also with Mustang, Paso Fino, and Peruvian horses. There are several registries for them, and the animals must present the right type, the right color, and supplemental gaits.

**Character and attributes**: This is a docile, sure-footed horse endowed with supplemental gaits (such as the rack or running walk); it has the amble instead of the trot.

**Uses**: This saddle horse is suitable for show jumping competitions, dressage, trekking, and recreational riding in general.

**Current status**: The breed is doing well.

Long, high-set neck

Rather horizontal croup

Rather large head

Broad chest

Characteristic posture
when standing

High-set neck

Slightly sloping
croup

Short back

Thick mane
and tail

Head with
straight profile

Characteristic posture when standing

# Colorado Ranger

Also called: Rangerbred Horse

**H** 1.57 m on average.

**C** Often spotted, never pinto.

**Description**: Although its coat might be confused with the Appaloosa, which it resembles, it is not an Appaloosa. It is compact, with a head with an often straight profile; wide forehead; slender nose; large eyes; sloping shoulders, unobtrusive withers; a short back; and a muscular, rather short, sloping croup. Its mane and tail are generally thicker and longer than those of the Appaloosa.

**Distribution**: Colorado, United States.

**Origins and history**: The breed began at the end of the nineteenth century, and it is the result of two Arabian and Barb foundation stallions. It received Thoroughbred, Quarter Horse, Appaloosa, AraApaloosa, and more Arabian blood. At the beginning of the 1980s it even received Lusitano blood.

**Character and attributes**: The Colorado Ranger has endurance, sure-footedness, and smooth gaits. It has good cow sense.

**Uses**: Basically a ranch horse, it makes a perfect recreational horse for Western riding and trekking.

**Current status**: Less well known than other American breeds, it is popular locally.

# Racking Horse

**H** 1.57 m on average.

**C** All colors are possible.

**Description**: Similar to the Tennessee Walker, it has a slender head; a long neck; sloping shoulders; a long back; long, slender legs; and a round, sloping croup. The tail is set high.

**Distribution**: Alabama, United States.

**Origins and history**: The breed has been recognized since 1971. It was a plantation horse in the southern United States. It is descended from the Tennessee Walker, of which it was once considered a type.

**Character and attributes**: This is an intelligent, calm, gentle, and agile horse. It is quite comfortable thanks to its particular gait, the rack, which it performs while keeping its head immobile. Because of this gait and its endurance, its rider can go for a long time without tiring.

**Uses**: Versatile, it is suited to both saddle and harness. Serene and comfortable, it is also a good horse for teaching new riders.

**Current status**: This popular breed is doing very well.

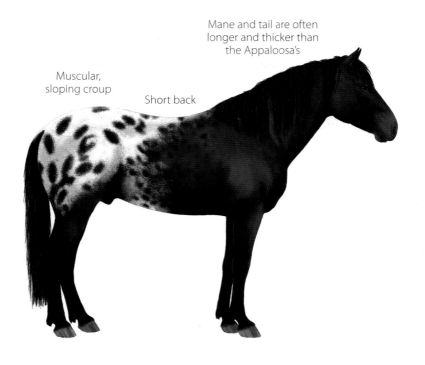

Mane and tail are often longer and thicker than the Appaloosa's

Muscular, sloping croup

Short back

High-set tail

Long back

Long, slender legs

# NATIONAL SHOW HORSE

**H** 1.52 m–1.62 m.

**C** Various, often bay, chestnut, black, gray, pinto.

**Description**: The National Show Horse has a rather small, refined, short head with a straight or concave profile; large eyes; small ears; a slender, very long, high-set neck; prominent withers; sloping shoulders; a short back; rather horizontal croup; and high-set, often long tail.

**Distribution**: United States.

**Origins and history**: This is a very recent breed, whose registry was established in 1981 and which is the result of crossings between Arabian and American Saddlebred horses. The goal was to produce a refined sport horse.

**Character and attributes**: It has good endurance and is strong, with naturally high-stepping gaits, as well as supplemental gaits (rack).

**Uses**: This is a versatile sport horse, also used for recreation (show jumping, dressage, Western riding, endurance), and, as its name indicates, it is a show horse.

**Current status**: This new breed is growing quickly.

# STANDARDBRED

Also called: American Standardbred

**H** 1.42 m–1.72 m.

**C** Often bay, dark bay, also black, chestnut, liver chestnut, sometimes gray and roan, a few pintos.

**Description**: Since it is selected above all for speed, its morphology can be variable, but it resembles the Thoroughbred, from which it has descended, though it is smaller and stockier. It has a rather large head with a straight profile; broad chest; powerful shoulders; slightly prominent withers; long back; very powerful croup; and solid legs. Its unique quality is having a croup that is always slightly higher than the withers.

**Distribution**: United States; Canada; Europe; Australia; New Zealand, and elsewhere in the world.

**Origins and history**: This famous American trotter is at the top of the list in trotting races, which makes it the most renowned trotter in the world. It can also be a pacer, pacing races being popular in the United States. The breed is the result of crossings between a foundation of English Thoroughbred and Canadian, Norfolk Trotter (extinct), Hackney, Arab-Barb, and Morgan. The foundation stud was named Hambletonian 10. Good horses can be sold for astronomical sums.

**Character and attributes**: Bold, confident, energetic, and docile, it has a powerful spring.

**Uses**: It is essentially raised for trotting and pacing races, although it can be used as a saddle horse.

**Current status**: The breed is very popular in the United States and throughout the world, wherever there are trotting races.

Pacing races in harness are one of the specialties of the Standardbred.

Very long, high-set neck

High-set tail

Short, refined head

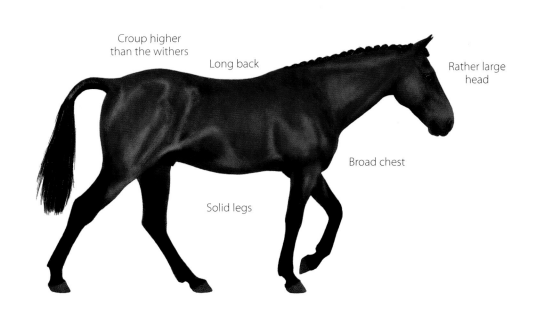

Croup higher than the withers

Long back

Rather large head

Broad chest

Solid legs

# AMERICAN CREAM AND WHITE HORSE

Also called: Cremello (once erroneously called Albino)

**H** 1.55 m–1.60 m on average.

**C** White or cream, pink or pale brown skin, blue, brown, or light brown eyes. These are true whites with light skin, not to be confused with all the horses that appear white but are in fact very light gray, with darker skin. The hooves are light. The mane and tail are thin.

**Description**: The type is not yet homogeneous. It tends to have large eyes; a long, refined neck; sloping shoulders; a short back; and a round, muscular croup.
**Distribution**: United States; Europe (notably France, Belgium, United Kingdom).
**Origins and history**: White horses have always been a symbol of prestige, and Americans have turned this type of horse into a breed. Initially a color registry like the Pinto or the Palomino, in 2002 the Cream and White registry closed enrollment in its studbook and thus took the first steps toward creating an entirely different breed. The founding stud was probably a cross between Arab and Morgan, but many breeds were registered (Lusitano, Spanish, Barb, Quarter Horse, Arabian, and others). The French national stud farm recognized the breed in 2005.
**Character and attributes**: Docile and confident, it is reputed to be easy to train. Because of its pink skin, it requires shelter from the sun, but is no more fragile than any other breed.
**Uses**: This is a recreational horse, for English or Western riding. It is also popular in the circus or for equestrian exhibitions because of its singular color.
**Current status**: American Cream and White horses are increasing in number.

With blue eyes and pink skin that is very visible at the nose, the American Cream and White is distinguished by its unique appearance.

# CAMARILLO WHITE

It is sometimes erroneously called albino, and sometimes confused with the American Cream and White.

**H** 1.55 m–1.65 m.

**C** Always white with pink skin: it carries a special gene (W4 allele) causing the white color.

**Description**: This compact horse has large eyes, prominent withers, and solid legs.
**Distribution**: United States.
**Origins and history**: The breed descends from a Spanish Mustang, a white stallion called Sultan, and dates to the beginning of the twentieth century. After being on the brink of extinction in 1991, when there were no more than 11 horses, the breed was saved thanks to crossings mainly with Andalusians and Standardbreds.
**Character and attributes**: It is calm and docile.
**Uses**: This is a saddle horse, and is enjoyed in circuses and parades.
**Current status**: The breed remains rare, with very small numbers and only a few births a year. With its original, immaculate white coat, it should attract an increasing number of enthusiasts.

Round croup

Long, slender neck

Large, often blue eyes

Pink skin

Light hooves

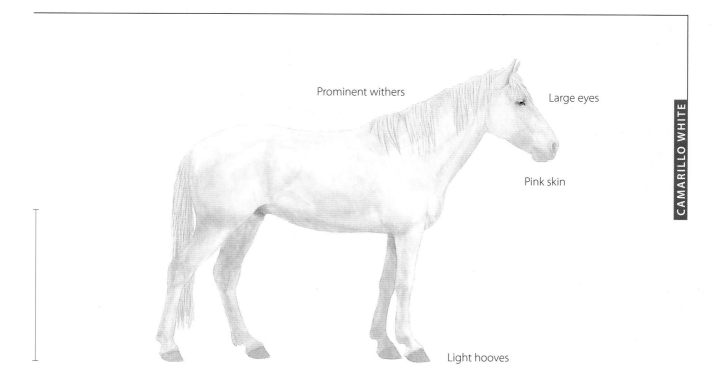

Prominent withers

Large eyes

Pink skin

Light hooves

# AMERICAN SADDLEBRED

Also called: Saddle Horse (once called Kentucky Saddler)

**Ⓗ** 1.52 m–1.75 m.

**Ⓒ** Bay, chestnut, black, gray, palomino, a few roans, often with moderate white markings on the head and tail.

**Description**: With a very characteristic look, it has a small, refined head with straight profile; large eyes; small ears; a long, curved neck set very high; a broad chest; prominent withers; long, slightly sloping shoulders; a long back; short, horizontal croup; long, slender legs; and a high-set tail. The hair of the mane and tail is fine and silky. The hooves are sometimes left long and shod with special shoes to accentuate the gaits, and the tail is sometimes clipped, both controversial practices. When standing its legs are extended behind.

**Distribution**: United States; Canada; but also Europe and South Africa.

**Origins and history**: Originally from Kentucky, it is the result of crossings between trotters and pacers imported from Europe in the seventeenth century and English Thoroughbred, Morgan, Galloway (extinct), Narragansett Pacer (extinct), and Hackney horses.

**Character and attributes**: It is very docile, energetic, affectionate, and intelligent. It is very comfortable and can have up to five gaits, with the stepping pace or slow gait, and the rack.

**Uses**: Versatile, it is suitable for the saddle as well as for light harness and is a popular show horse. Although energetic, its good nature makes it an appropriate horse for young riders.

**Current status**: Americans adore this breed, which is doing very well.

Half Saddlebred

## THE HALF SADDLEBRED

Created in 1971, the Half Saddlebred Registry takes into account halfblood American Saddlebred horses, one of whose parents is of another breed. The type can be variable in function of the non-Saddlebred parent, but they are always elegant animals with endurance.

# AMERICAN WARMBLOOD

**Ⓗ** 1.62 m–1.72 m.

**Ⓒ** All colors are possible, including pinto. This enables the creation of a sport horse that is sometimes multi-colored, which more easily indicates its American origin.

**Description**: This is a type of halfblood, physically similar to European sport horses, with a head with generally straight profile; a long, powerful neck; a short back; and long, muscular legs.

**Distribution**: United States.

**Origins and history**: This is not a breed in itself, but a type of American sport horse, which can be entered in two registries: the American Warmblood Registry and the American Warmblood Society. It has received blood from European sport horse lineages, the Thoroughbred, and the Arabian. It is essentially selected for sport results.

**Character and attributes**: It is a powerful horse, and a good jumper.

**Uses**: It is bred principally for dressage, show jumping, eventing, and hunting, and excels in these competitions.

**Current status**: The breed is doing well.

Fine, silky mane and tail

Straight profile

Rather horizontal croup

High-set head

High-set tail, sometimes clipped

Long legs

Characteristic posture when standing

Muscular croup

Head with straight profile

Long legs

# AMERICAN CREAM DRAFT

**H** 1.50 m–1.75 m.

**C** Cream, often pink skin, light brown or amber-colored eyes, with frequent white markings on the legs and head.

**Description**: This heavy and massive draft horse weighs between 750 kg and 950 kg. It has a long head with a straight profile; a very muscular neck; unobtrusive withers; very powerful shoulders; a broad chest; muscular, dished croup; and wide hooves. The hair of the mane and tail is thick and often wavy.

**Distribution**: United States.

**Origins and history**: An American draft could only be a color horse! This astonishing Cream Draft began with a heavy mare of that color, Old Granny, who lived at the beginning of the twentieth century and was crossed with other draft horses (Percheron, Belgian, Shire, and others).

**Character and attributes**: The American Cream Draft has a good nature; it is calm, strong, and powerful.

**Uses**: It is above all a harness horse, built for pulling.

**Current status**: This draft horse with an original coat is still very rare (350 horses in 204).

Amber eyes are a possible trait of horses with a cream coat.

# NORTH AMERICAN SPOTTED DRAFT HORSE

**H** 1.62 m–1.72 m.

**C** Pinto.

**Description**: This large, massive draft horse has a large head with a rather straight, sometimes slightly convex profile; an arched neck; rather straight shoulders; a short, strong back; strong legs; a powerful croup; a rather high-set tail; and wide hooves. The hair of the mane and tail is thick and sometimes slightly wavy.

**Distribution**: Minnesota, United States.

**Origins and history**: The breed began in the 1970s, from a cross between a Spotted Moroccan stallion and a Percheron mare, and the North American Spotted Draft Horse Association was established in 1995. The goal is to obtain a pinto draft horse from draft breeds such as the Percheron, Belgian, Clydesdale, Suffolk, or Shire. The breed would become the second color draft created in the United States, along with the American Cream Draft.

**Character and attributes**: It is gentle, easy, sensitive, intelligent, confident, and robust and has good endurance.

**Uses**: It is essentially a harness and recreational horse. It is also used in vaulting.

**Current status**: The breed is still being developed, but this rare joining of power and pinto coat should prove to be popular.

### AMERICAN DRAFT HORSES

Although the United States doesn't have a lot of native draft breeds, that doesn't prevent Americans from breeding them, notably the Percheron, the most numerous draft breed in this country, as well as the Belgian. American breeders have goals that are a bit different from those of European breeders, so American draft horses can end up exhibiting slightly different characteristics. This presence of European breeds in the United States has proven very useful: thus in the 1990s French breeders sought out the American Percheron, larger but of a lighter build, to lighten their model, which had become too fat due to its selection for meat. And it is also thanks to the Americans that the Flemish Draft, which had disappeared from Europe, was saved: it has been found in Amish communities.

Very muscular neck

Powerful croup

Often wavy mane
and tail

Broad chest

Wide hooves

Arched neck

Powerful croup

Often slightly wavy
mane and tail

Strong legs

# COLOR REGISTRIES: THE FAMOUS PALOMINOS, PINTOS, AND OTHERS

Americans are very big fans of horses with unusual coloring. If the Palomino and Pinto are the most famous of American color registries (see below), there are other American registries connected to coat color, like the Dun and Buckskin Registry, which includes horses that carry the dun gene (producing bay dun,

## PALOMINO

**Ⓗ** 1.42 m–1.73 m.

**Ⓒ** Palomino, shiny, very golden, white markings possible on the head or legs. The eyes are often dark or of a beautiful light brown color. The hooves are often light.

**Description**: The American Palomino must have the appearance of a saddle horse. In fact, it is often an American Saddlebred type, with a small head with straight profile, small ears, rather slender legs, and a fine mane and tail.

**Distribution**: United States.

**Origins and history**: From a coat color that is found in other horse breeds, Americans have created a registry tied to that color, and horses that are registered must also correspond to certain morphological criteria (size, type). The recessiveness of the "palomino" gene does not allow the creation of a separate breed. This golden coat has always been popular among Americans.

**Character and attributes**: This is a typical American saddle horse, docile and calm.

**Uses**: It is used for exhibitions, the circus, and in parades.

The Palomino is a popular circus horse due to its golden color. Here, a lasso exhibition, popular at rodeos.

## PINTO

**Ⓗ** Variable, with a "miniature" category.

**Ⓒ** Pinto; the eyes can be blue.

**Description**: There are different types of Pinto: pony (1.18 m–1.48 m), Stock Horse (which resembles a Quarter Horse), Hunter (a powerful saddle horse), Pleasure (Arabian type), and Saddle (which resembles a Saddlebred).

**Distribution**: United States; Canada; Europe.

**Origins and history**: The Pinto is another American registry created from a coat color; it is not a true breed. The Pinto has been recognized in the United States since 1963. The registry is open to many breeds. A Paint, with which the Pinto is sometimes confused, can belong to the Pinto registry, but a Pinto is not necessarily a Paint. Horses of pinto coloring, originally Iberian and Barb, were very popular with the Indians. There are of course pinto horses throughout the world, but only Americans have really formally recognized them.

**Character and attributes**: It has the nature of the breeds from which it comes, and thus, in the United States, it often has the good nature, docile and reliable, of American horses.

**Uses**: This is a good recreational horse that can also excel in competition.

**Current status**: Color horses being popular, Pintos are doing very well.

Blue eyes appear regularly with pinto coats.

buckskin, and black/brown dun coats, and primitive markings: dorsal stripe, zebra striping on the legs, and others). There is also the Brindle and Striped Equine International, which lists the very rare "striped" horses, including brindled horses, the coat one encounters regularly in cows or dogs but that is very rare in horses.

The Palomino's coat varies depending on the season, lighter in the winter, darker in the summer. Although Americans have established a color registry for it, this color is encountered in many breeds throughout the world.

Indians particularly like pinto horses. In Europe the pinto coat has, on the contrary, often been eliminated from breed standards. This coat is present almost everywhere throughout the world.

# Virginia Highlander

**H** 1.32 m–1.42 m.

**C** Often roan, also chestnut, black, gray.

**Description**: This is a small, light horse, with a head with straight profile and large eyes.

**Distribution**: Virginia, United States.

**Origins and history**: This recent breed descends from a founding stallion, Pogo, a cross of Welsh, Arabian, and Tennessee Walker, born in 1960, which was then crossed with Arabian, Welsh, Tennessee Walker, Morgan, Saddlebred and Hackney. The goal was to create a small gaited horse, easygoing and pleasant to ride.

**Character and attributes**: The Virginia Highlander is gentle, easy to handle, and sensitive, and has the special quality of having a supplemental gait, a broken amble, which makes it comfortable to ride.

**Uses**: It is suitable as a mount for young riders and beginners.

**Current status**: The promotion of this breed is no longer assured, as its association seems to have dissolved in 2002. It was already very rare, with only around fifty horses, and there is no recent information about its status.

# Quarab

**H** 1.44 m–1.62 m.

**C** All colors are possible, notably pinto, except Appaloosa-type spotted coats.

**Description**: Depending on the individual, it looks more like a Quarter Horse or an Arabian. It has a slender head, large eyes, a wide forehead, long neck, sloping shoulders, and powerful hindquarters, but it is less powerful than the Quarter Horse.

**Distribution**: United States; Europe (Germany, Italy).

**Origins and history**: As its name suggests, this recent breed (1989) is a cross between Arabian and Quarter Horse, or between Arabian and Paint Horse.

**Character and attributes**: It is intelligent, and combines the power of the Quarter Horse and the endurance of the Arabian. It is a bit livelier than a Quarter Horse.

**Uses**: It is suited for Western or English riding, and excels in endurance racing. It is a good trekking horse.

**Current status**: The breed is doing well.

# AraAppaloosa

Also called: Araloosa

**H** 1.50 m–1.60 m.

**C** Spotted.

**Description**: This is a sort of Appaloosa halfblood. It is more refined than an Appaloosa. It has a slender head, a long neck, and a high-set tail.

**Distribution**: United States.

**Origins and history**: To create the AraAppaloosa, Arabian blood was introduced. In this endeavor there has been the desire to recover the "original" Appaloosas of the Nez Perce Indians, which were massacred along with most of their other horses, but also to produce an animal that would combine the qualities of the Arabian and the Appaloosa.

**Character and attributes**: It is intelligent and sure-footed and has good endurance.

**Uses**: This is a good recreational horse, for Western riding and endurance racing.

**Current status**: The breed is popular in the United States.

## UNITED STATES

# WALKALOOSA

Also called: Gaited Appaloosa

**H** 1.42 m–1.54 m on average.

**C** Spotted, with visible white sclera of the eye; marbling is possible around the eyes and on the nose, and the hooves are striated.

**Description**: This is an Appaloosa-type horse. It has a head with straight profile, a sometimes arched neck, sloping shoulders, and a slightly sloping croup.

**Distribution**: United States.
**Origins and history**: This is not presently a breed but a registry with precise criteria, which since 1983 has enabled the registration of horses of Appaloosa type that have supplemental gaits, gaits that the current Appaloosa has lost due to too much crossing with the Quarter Horse, Arabian, or Thoroughbred.
**Character and attributes**: Gentle, it has supplemental gaits, including an amble called "Indian shuffle," which makes it very comfortable to ride.
**Uses**: This is a good horse for recreation, herding livestock, and trekking.
**Current status**: The Walkaloosa is being developed.

## UNITED STATES

# MOROCCO SPOTTED HORSE

Also called: Moroccan Spotted Horse

**H** 1.54 m–1.62 m.

**C** Always pinto, often tobiano, often black and white.

**Description**: This horse is a light harness type. It has a head with a straight profile; a long, slender neck; a rather long back; long, thin legs; and rather large hooves.
**Distribution**: Midwest region, notably Iowa, United States.
**Origins and history**: The breed was considered to be extinct until 2007, when an abandoned herd of these horses was discovered in Missouri. It was developed at the beginning of the twentieth century from colored types of Barb, Hackney, American Saddlebred, and French horses (probably Anglo-Norman), and was popular in the 1930s before declining after 1970.
**Character and attributes**: It is active, has endurance, lives a long time, and has lovely gaits. Some have supplemental gaits.
**Uses**: This saddle horse was once enjoyed as a parade horse.
**Current status**: The breed has practically disappeared, mainly due to bad management; it suffers notably from problems of inbreeding and from a lot of disagreement among the breeders. There is great concern for this breed, whose reproductive stock has dispersed. If nothing is done to save the few remaining animals, the breed will very soon disappear.

## UNITED STATES

# MONTANA TRAVLER

**H** Around 1.60 m.

**C** Often chestnut, bay, black.

**Description**: It has a head with a straight profile; a long, rather thin neck; a narrow but deep chest; prominent withers; and solid feet.
**Distribution**: Montana, United States.
**Origins and history**: This breed, whose association was created in 1983, emerged at the beginning of the 1930s, from Hambletonian horses (extinct), American Saddlebred, Morgan, Tennessee Walker, and Thoroughbred. The breed's founding stallion was called Montana Travler.
**Character and attributes**: The Montana Travler is confident, bold, and gentle, and has endurance. Well adapted to the mountains, it is sure-footed. It is comfortable, and some have a supplemental gait. It has good cow sense.
**Uses**: This is a versatile saddle horse, mainly used as a ranch horse.
**Current status**: It is still very rare, with around 300 horses. The breed doesn't seem to have taken off, and its promotion no longer seems certain, even if these horses can still be occasionally found. The breed suffered from the economic crisis of 2008.

# Horses of Central America and the Caribbean

*Located between North and South America, this region of the world is filled with Iberian-type horses and Quarter Horses. There is a very large equine population here (especially in Mexico). These are traditionally lands where Criollos and Pasos, the two major types of horses in Latin America, are bred. The Paso Fino of Puerto Rico has acquired an international reputation for its beauty and the liveliness of its gaits, while in the Bahamas there is the Abaco Spanish Colonial Horse, a breed that has been on the brink of extinction (which has been known for years) due to a combination of bad luck and a lack of means to sustain it. Alongside those, the recent Mexican Azteca breed, a perfect synthesis of North and South American influences through its crossing with Quarter Horses and Iberians, is thriving, and can only continue to thrive in the coming years.*

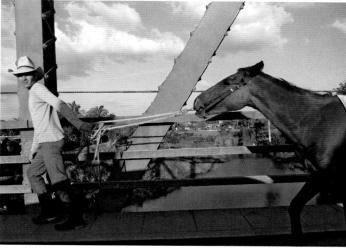

Top left: Tethered livestock herding horse, Costa Rica.

Top right: In Cuba, horses are regularly used as a means of transportation, even in towns (this is in Santa Clara).

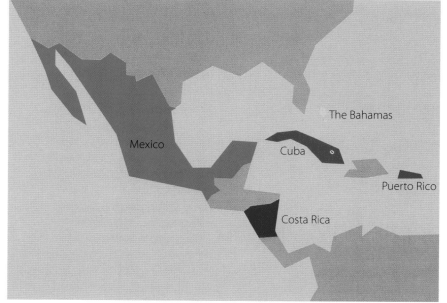

**The Bahamas**
Abaco Spanish
  Colonial Horse
**Cuba**
Cuban Paso (also
  Cuban Gaited
  Horse)
Patibarcina
Cuban Pinto
Cuban Trotter
**Puerto Rico**
Paso Fino
**Mexico**
Galiceño
Azteca (also National
  Horse of Mexico)
Criollo Militar
**Costa Rica**
Costa Rican Saddle
  Horse

Opposite: Azteca stallion. This recent breed has attractive qualities that make it an increasingly sought-after horse.

We know of horses in the Bahamas because of the extremely rare Abaco Spanish Colonial Horses, which live on Great Abaco Island, the largest of the Abaco

---

THE BAHAMAS

# Abaco Spanish Colonial Horse

Also called: Abaco Barb

**H** 1.32 m–1.47 m.

**C** Bay, pinto, roan, chestnut, black, with many white markings.

**Description**: Compact, this is a Spanish-type horse with thick mane and tail hair.

**Distribution**: Great Abaco Island, Bahamas.

**Origins and history**: Legend has it that, following a shipwreck, these Iberian horses reached the islands by swimming and managed to survive on them. They might also have been unloaded there and abandoned by the conquistadors. When people settled on Great Abaco in the twentieth century, cohabitation was rather difficult; then, in the 1960s, a child was killed while trying to ride a wild horse, and to avenge his death the inhabitants slaughtered almost all the animals (there were around 200); only three survived. They began to reproduce and the population grew to about 35 animals. Unfortunately, in 1999, Hurricane Floyd dispersed chemical products into the environment, herbicides and pesticides that the horses ingested, and they were forced to move from their traditional lands to overly rich pastureland that had been planted for cows. They then became fat, which caused many to founder.

**Character and attributes**: The Abaco Spanish Colonial Horse has good endurance and is resilient.

**Uses**: It lives only in the wild.

**Current status**: Although it is protected, the Abaco Spanish Colonial Horse is currently on the brink of extinction: there were only 6 horses remaining in 2010, and in 2013 only one seventeen-year-old mare, Nunki, survived. A pinto stallion of around 15 might still be alive in the wild, but he hasn't been seen in some time. This extinction illustrates the extreme vulnerability of all small populations living in the wild. Enthusiasts are desperately trying to save the breed by collecting donations to have the ova of Nunki harvested.

---

# Cuba

In Cuba, the famous archipelago of the Caribbean, one finds horses almost everywhere, mainly pulling carts, but also being ridden: they are still a regular means of transportation. In addition to their traditional breeds, the Cubans breed the Arabian, Appaloosa, Percheron, Morgan, Belgian, Shetland, Welsh Pony, Thoroughbred, Quarter Horse, and Andalusian.

---

CUBA

# Cuban Paso

Also called: Cuban Gaited Horse

Spanish: *cubano de paso*

**H** 1.45 m–1.51 m.

**C** Mainly bay, dark bay.

**Description**: The Cuban Paso resembles other Paso-type horses. It has a small, slender head with a usually straight profile, large eyes, a wide forehead, strong neck, muscular and slightly sloping croup, and strong legs. The hair of the mane and tail is thick.

**Distribution**: Cuba.

**Origins and history**: The Cuban Paso descends from horses brought by the conquistadors and has been popular due to its comfortable gaits.

**Character and attributes**: Energetic, spirited, and docile like other Pasos, it has a supplemental gait locally called *marcha fina y gualdrapeada*, which makes it very comfortable to ride.

**Uses**: It is above all a saddle horse, also used for transportation, and women especially like its comfortable gaits. It can also make a pleasant trekking horse for equestrian tourism.

**Current status**: Native, with small numbers, it is currently the object of conservation measures.

Islands, a place with few inhabitants. The breed is on the brink of extinction. Following successive catastrophes, some horses have died; others have not been able to reproduce. Thus the Bahamas will lose its only native breed, and an interesting lineage of horses will die out with the Abaco Spanish Colonial Horse.

Large eyes

Thick mane and tail

Solid legs

ABACO SPANISH COLONIAL HORSE

Strong neck

Small, slender head

Thick mane and tail

CUBAN PASO

# PATIBARCINA

Spanish: *patibarcino*

**H** 1.48 m–1.52 m.

**C** Chestnut, bay; carries the dun gene, it often has a dorsal stripe and zebra markings on the legs.

**Description**: This is a smallish, Iberian-type horse. It has a head with a straight or slightly convex profile, rather large ears, a broad chest, sloping shoulders, a rather long back, and a sloping croup.

**Distribution**: Cuba, notably in the mountain region of Escambray.

**Origins and history**: The breed originated with a stallion called Lobo, carrier of the dun gene. It is of Iberian and Barb origin, crossed with the Cuban Trotter.

**Character and attributes**: The Patibarcina is known to be intelligent, very lively, resilient, strong, and fast.

**Uses**: It is popular as a saddle horse and for working livestock.

**Current status**: This native horse is common.

In Cuba, horses are still often used harnessed to various carts.

# CUBAN PINTO

Spanish: *pinto cubano*

**H** 1.44 m–1.52 m.

**C** Pinto.

**Description**: This is a compact, muscular horse of Criollo type, with a head with a straight or slightly convex profile, a wide forehead, rather long neck, and sloping croup. The hair of the mane and tail is thick.

**Distribution**: Cuba.

**Origins and history**: Since the 1960s–1970s this recent breed has been developed from Criollo mares crossed with Quarter Horse and Thoroughbred stallions, on the foundation of a pinto coat. Its crossings evoke the American Paint Horse, which it resembles, but the Cuban Pinto is more typically Iberian, with less powerful hindquarters.

**Character and attributes**: It is docile and agile.

**Uses**: This is a saddle horse, popular for working livestock; it can also be used as a recreational horse for trekking.

**Current status**: Popular locally, the breed is fairly common.

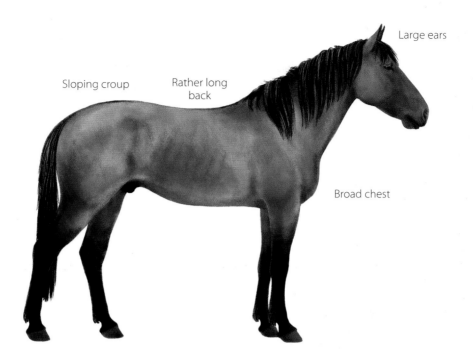

Sloping croup

Rather long back

Large ears

Broad chest

# CUBAN TROTTER

Spanish: *criollo de trote, cubano de trote*

**H** 1.48 m–1.50 m on average.

**C** Bay, dark bay, black.

**Description**: Despite its name it doesn't have the morphology of a racing trotter, rather that of a Criollo-type horse. It has a head with a straight or slightly convex profile; small ears; a wide, strong neck; a rather sloping croup; and strong legs.

**Distribution**: Cuba.

**Origins and history**: A descendant of the Iberian horses of the conquistadors, it has been improved with Morgan blood.

**Character and attributes**: The Cuban Trotter is intelligent, calm, but energetic and vigorous, resilient, and agile, with good endurance. It gets its name from its energetic trot.

**Uses**: This saddle horse is popular in Cuba for working livestock.

**Current status**: This local breed is rather common.

# Puerto Rico

An island located in the Caribbean, Puerto Rico is an unincorporated United States territory, a small country that nevertheless has a very famous breed, the Paso Fino, a spectacular gaited horse extremely popular outside its borders, in South America, North America, and as far as Europe. Colombia breeds a similar breed and the two lineages are often mixed.

## PUERTO RICO

# PASO FINO

Spanish: *paso fino*

Ⓗ 1.30 m–1.55 m.

Ⓒ Variable.

**Description**: The Paso Fino is an Iberian-type horse. It has a slender head with a straight or slightly convex profile, large eyes, small ears, a muscular and arched neck, sloping shoulders, a short back, a slightly sloping and muscular croup, and hard hooves. The mane and tail are long and abundant. The skin is fine and the coat silky.

**Distribution**: Puerto Rico, Dominican Republic, Colombia, United States, Europe.

**Origins and history**: The Paso Fino, very well-known in Latin America, descends from the ancient Spanish Jennet and the Barb.

**Character and attributes**: The Paso Fino is particularly docile, calm, easygoing, sensitive, and intelligent. It is agile and sure-footed and is well-known for its broken amble. Its very lovely natural gaits, *paso fino, paso corto,* and *paso largo,* but also *sobre paso* and *andadura,* are extremely comfortable and reassuring. It is also rustic and easy to keep.

**Uses**: This saddle horse is used for recreation, notably trekking, for parades, gaited competitions, or even dressage. It is also popular in the United States for Western riding.

**Current status**: The breed, popular for its excellent attributes, is doing well, both in its country and throughout the world, notably in North and South America, where there are many of them.

# Mexico

Horses are still very important in Mexico, notably in the underserved hinterlands where they are still used as work animals. The number of horses here was estimated at 6.35 million in 2011, which makes it a country with one of the largest equine populations. In addition to Mexican breeds, the Quarter Horse is very widespread and popular in Mexico.

## MEXICO

# GALICEÑO

Spanish: *galiceño*

Ⓗ 1.22 m–1.37 m.

Ⓒ Bay, chestnut, black, roan, bay dun, black/brown dun, palomino.

**Description**: Small, of Iberian type, the Galiceño has a head with straight or slightly convex profile; large eyes; a rather short, muscular, but rather slender neck; a narrow chest; rather straight shoulders; a short back; sloping croup; solid legs; and small hooves.

**Distribution**: Mexico, United States.

**Origins and history**: It descends from the Spanish Galiceño and the Portuguese Garrano, imported in the sixteenth century by the conquistadors.

**Character and attributes**: It is intelligent, docile, agile, and fast, has endurance and can carry heavy loads, is robust and has cow sense. It is also comfortable, thanks to a supplemental gait, the "running walk."

**Uses**: Traditionally a versatile horse, it has become a good family horse, popular for children, but also suitable for adults. It is also a good sport horse, notably for show jumping or Western riding.

**Current status**: The breed, which has been exported to the United States, is doing rather well.

Muscular neck

Fine skin

Abundant, long and
silky mane and tail

In the *paso*, a very comfortable gait, the end of
the tail is somewhat raised.

Rather short neck

Sloping croup

Narrow chest

# AZTECA

Also called: National Horse of Mexico

Spanish: *azteca*

**H** 1.50 m–1.55 m.

**C** Often bay, also bay dun; all coats are possible, except pinto and spotted.

**Description**: Compact and muscular, it has a head with a straight or slightly convex profile; small ears; a slightly arched, muscular neck; broad chest; sloping shoulders; short back; long, round, slightly sloping croup; slender, resilient legs; and small, hard hooves. The mane and tail are abundant.

**Distribution**: Mexico, El Salvador, United States, a few in Europe.

**Origins and history**: A relatively recent breed, the Azteca was established in 1972 from crossings between Andalusian or Lusitano stallions and Criollo and Quarter Horse mares, with the goal of creating through the combination of Iberian and American qualities an excellent recreational horse that could also work livestock. Now the breed is essentially crosses between Andalusians and Quarter Horses.

**Character and attributes**: The Azteca is docile, cool and energetic, bold, fast, and agile. It inherited good cow sense from its various ancestors. It also inherited the energetic Iberian gaits.

**Uses**: A pleasant, versatile recreational horse, it excels as a work horse, and thus in Western riding.

**Current status**: The breed is developing rapidly, and its qualities are attracting an increasing number of riders. Americans are developing their own lineage, which they call the American Azteca and which is sometimes pinto due to some Paint Horse crosses.

A Mexican rider. The Azteca is as responsive as it is agile.

# CRIOLLO MILITAR

Spanish: *criollo militar*

The result of crossings of Spanish, Arabian, Barb, Quarter Horse, and Thoroughbred, with many herds raised outdoors, notably in the north of the country, the Criollo Militar is a small, rustic horse. Since 1927 it has been bred by the Mexican Secretariat of National Defense in Chihuahua State, which explains its name. A 2006 report by the FAO estimated its population at 2,000 horses and noted the lack of information about it.

Mexican saddle

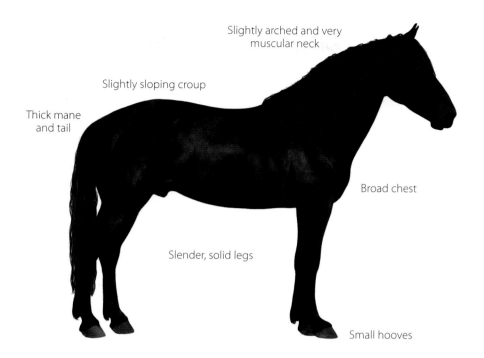

Slightly arched and very
muscular neck

Slightly sloping croup

Thick mane
and tail

Broad chest

Slender, solid legs

Small hooves

Located in the middle of the isthmus separating North and South America, this small Central American country breeds a single native breed, primarily for recreation, a Paso that is becoming increasingly popular. It seems logical that this breed will grow in importance.

# COSTA RICAN SADDLE HORSE

Spanish: *caballo costarricense de paso*

🄷 1.46 m–1.52 m for mares; 1.48 m–1.56 m for males.

🄲 Often bay, dark bay, gray, white, all colors except pinto.

**Description**: The Costa Rican Saddle Horse has a head with a straight or slightly convex profile; wide forehead; rather long, arched neck; short back; muscular legs; and a muscular and rounded croup. It has fine skin and hair.

**Distribution**: Costa Rica, United States.

**Origins and history**: With origins in the Barb and the Andalusian, and of course in the Peruvian Paso, the Costa Rican Saddle Horse has been actively selected since around 1850, with a breeding registry created in 1974.

**Character and attributes**: Intelligent, sensitive, energetic, and agile, this saddle horse is also sure-footed. Like all good saddle horses it has supplemental gaits, and its gaits are lovely and high-stepping.

**Uses**: Essentially a saddle horse, it is popular as a comfortable horse for recreation or trekking.

**Current status**: The breed is known in its country for its many attributes, and 9,000 horses were registered in 2013. Increasingly sought after, it is doing well and its population is expanding, notably toward the United States.

Arched neck

Muscular croup

Fine mane
and tail

Fine hide

# Horses of South America

*South America, with its pampas, its gauchos, its Criollos, its Pasos, is most certainly an equestrian land with a strong Iberian influence. Horses did not exist on the continent before the conquistadors imported them in the sixteenth century. The breeds that have developed there are thus all the result of Iberian and Barb horses, and that common origin explains their resemblance to each other. Nevertheless, local natural environments and breeding by humans have gradually differentiated the various types. Less known throughout the world than the North American cowboys, the gauchos and their efficient work horses demonstrate unique and strong equestrian traditions.*

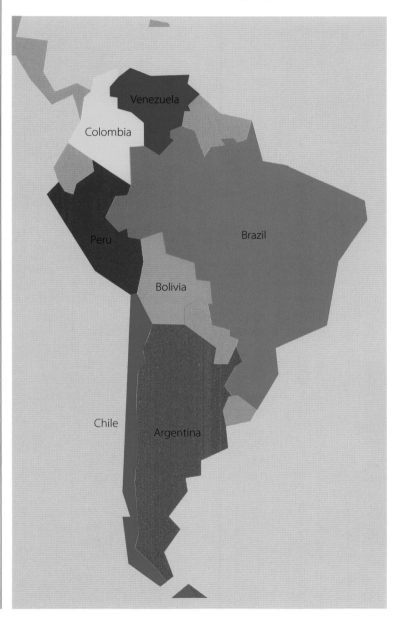

**Colombia**
Colombian Paso Fino
   (also Colombian Criollo,
   Colombian Walking
   Horse)
Trochador (also Trocha
   Horse)
Trote y Galope
**Venezuela**
Venezuelan Criollo
**Brazil**
Piquira Pony
Pantaneiro
Marajoara
Campolina
Mangalarga Marchador
Brazilian Pony
Puruca Pony (also Puruca
   Mini Horse)
Lavradeiro
Baixadeiro
Crioulo (also
   Northeastern)
Pampa

Campeiro
Brazilian Sport Horse
   (also Brazilian)
**Peru**
Andean (also Peruvian
   Criollo)
Peruvian Paso (also
   Peruvian Stepping
   Horse, Peruvian
   National Horse)
**Bolivia**
Sunicho (also Bolivian
   Pony)
**Chile**
Chilote (also Chilote
   Pony)
Chilean
**Argentina**
Falabella
Argentine Criollo
Petiso Argentino
Argentine Polo Pony
Argentine Warmblood
Argentine Draft Horse

Brazilian Crioulo–type horse, in the state of Rio de Janeiro, Brazil.

Opposite: Criollos often have white markings on their head and legs.

Located in northwestern South America, Colombia had 2,750,000 horses in 2005. Alongside breeds imported from abroad, the pragmatic Colombians developed only gaited breeds, extremely comfortable and therefore increasingly popular horses. Docile and of average height, these animals make excellent recreational horses.

---

COLOMBIA

# COLOMBIAN PASO FINO

Also called: Colombian Criollo, Colombian Walking Horse

Spanish: *paso fino colombiano*

**H** 1.39 m for mares; 1.40 m for males.

**C** Bay dun, bay, black, gray, but also chestnut.

**Description**: The Colombian Paso Fino has a head with a straight profile and wide forehead; large eyes; a muscular, strong, high-set neck; rather broad chest; and muscular, sloping croup. The hair of the mane and tail is abundant, silky, and smooth.

**Distribution**: Colombia, United States, Europe.

**Origins and history**: Although often confused and crossed (notably in Europe and the United States) with the Puerto Rican Paso Fino, which it greatly resembles, the Colombian Paso Fino is a different lineage, the issue in large part of Barb horses imported by the conquistadors.

**Character and attributes**: The Colombian Paso Fino is gentle, sweet, and full of verve. It is known for its particularly comfortable gaits.

**Uses**: This is a versatile horse, pleasant as a recreational or work horse, popular for dressage or in parades.

**Current status**: The Colombian Paso Fino is very popular in its country, and Colombians consider it the best saddle horse in the world.

---

COLOMBIA

# TROCHADOR

Also called: Trocha Horse

Spanish: *trochador, trocha pura colombiana, trocha colombiana*

**H** 1.37 m on average for mares; 1.41 m for males.

**C** Often chestnut, also bay, but other basic colors are possible.

**Description**: It greatly resembles the Colombian Paso Fino, to which it is related. It has a head with a straight profile; a wide forehead; a muscular, high-set neck; and small hooves. The mane and tail are abundant.

**Distribution**: Colombia.

**Origins and history**: Of both Andalusian and Barb origin, the Trochador is a variety of the Colombian Paso Fino that has been specifically bred since the 1960s. Now the two lineages are quite differentiated.

**Character and attributes**: The Trochador is energetic but docile. It is agile, has good endurance, and stands out for its characteristic, very comfortable, very fluid gait, the *trocha* (a diagonal four-beat gait, a sort of very fast and smooth trot, similar to the American "fox trot").

**Uses**: This is a pleasant, versatile saddle horse that is well suited for recreational riding.

**Current status**: The breed is doing well.

Muscular neck

Wide forehead

Thick, silky
mane and tail

Straight profile

High-set,
muscular neck

Straight profile

Abundant mane
and tail

Small hooves

# TROTE Y GALOPE

Spanish: *trote y galope, troton, trote y galope reunido colombiano, trochau y galope reunido colombiano*

**H** 1.44 m–1.52 m.

**C** Often chestnut; all colors are possible, except pinto.

**Description**: An elegant horse, it is a variety of the Colombian Paso Fino, with an arched, very high-set muscular neck. The hair of the mane is usually cut.
**Distribution**: Colombia, a few in the United States.
**Origins and history**: This recent breed, a variety of the Colombian Paso bred since 1930, is the result of crossings between Andalusian or Lusitano and Colombian Paso, which gives it an influence more strongly Iberian than Barb.

**Character and attributes**: It is known to be very intelligent, energetic, docile, and full of energy. Its gaits are very comfortable, with a *trote* similar to the trot but without a moment of suspension, and a very collected gallop.
**Uses**: Versatile, it is well suited to equestrian trekking and dressage, and it is also a good work horse.
**Current status**: The breed is popular in Colombia.

# Venezuela

In addition to its native breed, in Venezuela one finds the Thoroughbred, Arabian, Quarter Horse, Shagya Arab, Andalusian, Appaloosa, and others. Horses are used for farm work, transportation, and racing, but their numbers are decreasing. Sport and recreational horses are above all bred in the center of the country (district capital of Caracas, Miranda, Aragua, Carabobo), while the Criollo-type horses are more prevalent in Los Llanos.

# VENEZUELAN CRIOLLO

Spanish: *criollo venezolano, llañero*

**H** 1.42 m on average.

**C** Various: bay, dark bay, chestnut, black, palomino, pinto, gray, roan, chestnut roan, black/brown dun, bay dun, often with a dorsal stripe.

**Description**: It resembles the Argentine Criollo, but is lighter, with a head with a straight or sometimes slightly convex profile; a rather narrow chest; a short, dished croup; slender legs; and small, hard hooves. The hair of the mane and tail is thick and abundant.
**Distribution**: Venezuela.

**Origins and history**: Of Spanish origin, similar to the Argentine Criollo, the Venezuelan Criollos descend from horses brought in the sixteenth century by the conquistadors, and the breed was forged in Los Llanos, the vast plains in northwestern Venezuela.
**Character and attributes**: It is calm, but very responsive and lively if required. It also has good endurance and is undemanding, and easy to keep, with good cow sense.
**Uses**: Mainly used as a riding horse, it is good for working livestock. It is also used in equestrian tourism.
**Current status**: The breed has suffered from too much crossbreeding and requires a lot of vigilance, but this has only been noticed recently.

Mane often cut

Muscular croup

Neck set very high,
very muscular

Short, dished croup

Straight profile

Rather narrow chest

Small, hard hooves

With 5.5 million horses in 2011 (as opposed to 5.9 million in 2003), the horse population in Brazil, although decreasing, is one of the largest in the world.

# Piquira Pony

Portuguese: *piquira, piquira marchador*

**H** Not over 1.28 m (on average 1.20 m) for mares; 1.30 m (on average 1.22 m) for males.

**C** All colors are possible, except white (albino).

**Description:** The breed is still rather variable. It has a head with a straight profile, large forehead, small ears, very prominent withers, sloping shoulders, and a slightly sloping croup. Its hide and mane and tail are thin and silky.

**Distribution:** Brazil, notably the state of Bahia.

**Origins and history:** The breed is the result of crossings among Shetlands and small gaited Brazilian horses, with the goal of creating a small mount for children with the comfortable gaits of larger horses.

**Character and attributes**: The Piquira is very docile and calm, has endurance, and has inherited the energy of the gaited breeds.

**Uses:** These are ideal, versatile mounts for children, and perfect for beginning riders because of their temperament and the comfort of their gaits.

**Current status:** The breed is still being developed.

Docile and small, the Piquira Pony is popular with the youngest of riders.

# Pantaneiro

Portuguese: *pantaneiro, bahiano, baiano, mimoseano, pantaneiro criollo, poconeano*

**H** 1.35 m on average for mares; 1.40 m on average for males.

**C** Gray, also bay, dark bay, pinto.

**Description**: It has a head with a straight profile, a muscular neck, broad chest, short back, slightly sloping croup, and hooves that are resilient in wet environments.

**Distribution:** West-central Brazil, in the Pantanal, state of Mato Grosso.

**Origins and history**: Horses—certainly Iberians and Barbs, but also later Criollos—were imported during the colonization of the Pantanal, a vast, humid zone, and only the most resilient survived. Natural selection thus has played a role in shaping the breed.

**Character and attributes**: Intelligent, docile, and lively, it has good cow sense. Very resistant to illness (in particular to equine infectious anemia) and well adapted to the hot and humid climate of the Pantanal, the Pantaneiro is one of the rare breeds that is able to survive there, which makes it essential in this region.

**Uses:** It is basically a good horse for working with livestock, and is also a good trekking horse and recreational companion.

**Current status:** The breed is greatly endangered, mainly due to too much outcrossing. It is vulnerable and needs to be watched, even though conservation measures have been put in place.

Pantanal rancher herding his livestock.

Horses are primarily used for sport and recreational activities, but also for farm work. Brazilians do not eat horse meat. Breeding is very active, with high-quality Brazilian breeds. Brazil also breeds many foreign horses (Thoroughbred, Breton, Percheron, Arabian, Morgan, Lusitano, Quarter Horse, and others).

Small ears

Prominent withers

Slightly sloping croup

Fine, silky mane and tail

**PIQUIRA PONY**

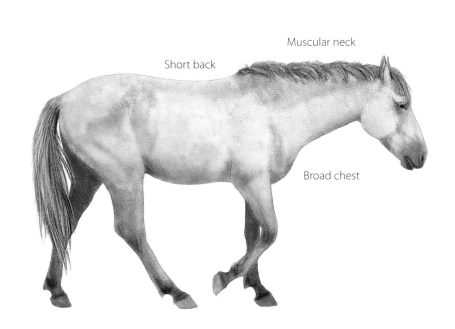

Muscular neck

Short back

Broad chest

**PANTANEIRO**

# MARAJOARA

Portuguese: *marajoara*

**Ⓗ** 1.30 m–1.50 m for mares; 1.35 m–1.56 m for males.

**Ⓒ** All colors are possible, except pinto and white (albino).

**Description**: It has a head with a slightly convex or straight profile, a broad chest, prominent withers, sloping shoulders, and a slightly sloping croup.

**Distribution**: Marajo Island, Pará state, northern Brazil.

**Origins and history**: It is descended from Portuguese horses, Lusitanos, and has adapted to the local environment. Crossed with Shetlands, it created the Puruca breed.

**Character and attributes**: It is active and energetic, docile and strong, and has good endurance. Rustic, the breed is very well adapted to the heat and swampland, where other horses couldn't survive.

**Uses**: This is a very good work horse, used for transportation and farm work, and one that is also suitable for recreational riding.

**Current status**: The breed flourished up to the middle of the nineteenth century, then the population grew too large and it had to be regulated. The island still has a lot of horses, but most have been crossbred and purebred individuals are no longer as common.

Brazilian saddle, with its thick blanket of colored sheep's wool

# CAMPOLINA

Portuguese: *campolina*

**Ⓗ** 1.45 m–1.52 m.

**Ⓒ** Often gray, also bay, roan, chestnut, pinto, often with the dun gene that gives them primitive markings (zebra striping, dorsal stripe).

**Description**: It resembles the Mangalarga, but is heavier. The profile of the head is extremely, sometimes excessively convex, which is one of the unique characteristics of this breed, and it makes it highly identifiable. It has an arched neck; long, sloping shoulders; rather prominent withers; a fairly long back; and a wide croup. The mane and tail are silky.

**Distribution**: Brazil, notably in Minas Gerais state.

**Origins and history**: Even though the breed is not very old, its origins are rather unclear. It was developed in the 1870s from Clydesdale, Holstein, Anglo-Norman, American Saddle Horse, Barb, Mangalarga, and other horses.

**Character and attributes**: The Campolina is docile and energetic, and has comfortable supplemental gaits (*picada* and *batida*).

**Uses**: This horse is suitable for the saddle and as a light draft horse; it is popular for dressage and for all recreational riding, notably trekking.

**Current status**: This breed, one of the most widespread in Brazil, is doing very well and is becoming increasingly popular.

Campolina mare and foal with their characteristic profile

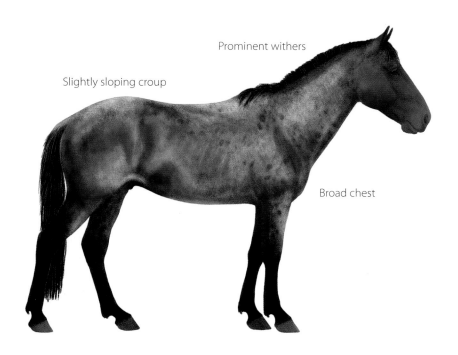

Slightly sloping croup

Prominent withers

Broad chest

Silky mane
and tail

Very convex profile,
typical of the breed

Rather prominent
withers

The Campolina is popular for its comfortable gaits.

# Mangalarga Marchador

Portuguese: *mangalarga marchador, mangalarga, mineiro*

**H** 1.46 m on average for mares; 1.52 m on average for males.

**C** Often bay, chestnut, roan, gray.

**Description**: This Iberian-type horse has a rather long, triangular head, with a wide forehead and tapered muzzle, and straight profile; large eyes; a muscular, rather high set neck; prominent withers; long legs; a sloping, muscular croup; a high-set tail; and hard hooves. It has fine skin; the hair and the mane and tail are silky, smooth.

**Distribution**: Brazil, notably the states of Minas Gerais and Sao Paulo; Uruguay; a few have been exported to the United States; a few in Canada and Europe (Italy, Spain, Germany).

### Mangalarga Paulista

Sometimes called the Brazilian Saddle Horse (*sela brasileiro*), the Mangalarda Paulista resembles the Mangalarga Marchador, but is more slender and more athletic. It is also taller (around 1.52 m). The Mangalarga Paulista and the Mangalarga Marchador were once the same single breed, the Mangalarga, then they were divided. The Mangalarga Paulista received blood from Thoroughbred, Anglo-Arab, Lusitano, and American Saddlebred horses, making it more refined, and more athletic, but it has less comfortable gaits than the Marchador. Resilient and with endurance, it is well suited to sport riding. The Mangalarga Paulista is doing very well.

**Origins and history**: Developed since 1740 from a Lusitano Alter Real stallion called Sublime and Criollo mares and Spanish Jennets, an extinct breed from which it has inherited magnificent gaits, the Mangalarga Marchador has been dissociated from the Mangalarga Paulista to preserve the latter breed. It is sometimes mated with the Campolina to create a "Mangolina," a crossing that will perhaps end up as a breed.

**Character and attributes**: It is particularly docile, but active, confident, and intelligent. It is also vigorous and has endurance, is rustic and sure-footed, and has cow sense. It doesn't trot, but has very comfortable gaits, *marcha batida* and *marcha picada*.

**Uses**: A versatile mount suitable for dressage but also show jumping, it is an excellent horse for herding livestock. Its easygoing nature makes it a good mount for inexperienced riders. It is popular for parades.

**Current status**: The breed is very popular in Brazil and is doing extremely well. It is one of the most widespread in the country. It is also increasingly exported abroad.

Mangalarga Paulista

# Brazilian Pony

Portuguese: *pônei brasileiro*

**H** 0.90 m–1.10 m.

**C** Quite variable, including pinto and Appaloosa spotting.

**Description**: It is very small, with a head with straight or concave profile, large eyes, small ears, a long neck, prominent withers, sloping shoulders, a broad chest, short back, round croup, and silky and abundant mane and tail.

**Distribution**: Brazil.

**Origins and history**: The breed descends from crossings among Shetlands and Falabellas, and other small South American horses.

**Character and attributes**: It has a very docile temperament and is very robust and strong.

**Uses**: This is an ideal mount for young children, and for riding instruction.

**Current status**: The breed is popular for teaching beginners.

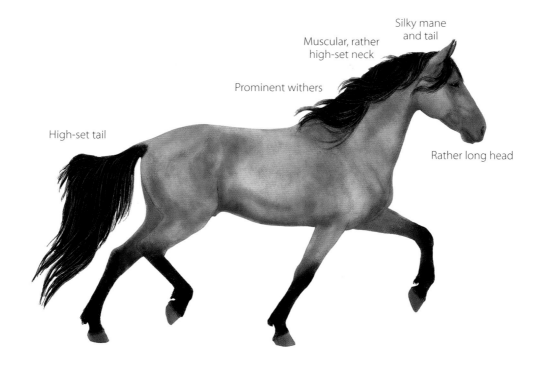

High-set tail

Prominent withers

Muscular, rather high-set neck

Silky mane and tail

Rather long head

# PURUCA PONY

Also called: Puruca Mini Horse

Portuguese: *puruca*—not to be confused with the Piquira, a recent gaited pony.

 1 m–1.16 m for mares; 1.10 m–1.18 m for males.

 Quite variable.

**Description**: It has a head with a straight or convex profile; large eyes; small ears; unobtrusive withers; a broad chest; sloping shoulders; a short back; long, muscular, slightly sloping croup; short, muscular legs; and small, hard hooves. Its mane and tail are silky and thick.

**Distribution**: Marajo Island, Pará state, Brazil.

**Origins and history**: Of rather recent origin, the breed descends from three Shetland stallions imported from France onto Marajo Island at the end of the nineteenth century, which were crossed with native Marajora horses. The breed was very popular with local farmers as a herding horse.

**Character and attributes**: Particularly docile and calm, but energetic, with comfortable gaits, it is strong, resilient, and rustic.

**Uses**: It is an excellent, comfortable saddle horse, suitable for children.

**Current status**: With fewer than 1,000 animals, the Puruca Pony is in great danger of extinction. It has suffered from too much crossbreeding.

# LAVRADEIRO

Portuguese: *lavradeiro, lavradeiro criollo*

ⓗ Around 1.40 m.

ⓒ Often chestnut, bay, dark gray, roan.

**Description**: The Lavradeiro has small ears, a short back, and a sloping croup. The hair of the mane and tail is thick and abundant.

**Distribution**: Roraima, northern Brazil.

**Origins and history**: The Lavradeiro is the result of mainly Spanish and Portuguese horses introduced during the colonization of Roraima as mounts to keep and herd livestock. Raised in semi-freedom, some became completely feral, and the Lavradeiro was thus forged in part by natural selection.

**Character and attributes**: It is intelligent, has endurance, and is simple and rustic, well adapted to sometimes difficult climate conditions. The breed is very fertile and resistant to illness.

**Uses**: Once they are tamed and broken, these wild horses prove to be very docile.

**Current status**: In 2010 there was a small number of Lavradeiro horses, between 1,260 and 1,680.

---

# BAIXADEIRO

Portuguese: *baixadeiro*

ⓗ Around 1.40 m.

ⓒ Often bay, dark gray.

**Description**: This is a small, light, rustic horse, with a head with straight profile.

**Distribution**: Maranhão state, Baixadas, Brazil.

**Origins and history**: Sometimes confused with the Marajoara, with which it likely shares origins, it is different, however, and is not found in the same place. It is the issue of Iberian horses (notably Garraños) and Barbs.

**Character and attributes**: Rustic, resistant to illness, it is well adapted to difficult environmental conditions, including periods of flooding.

**Uses**: It is used for riding and for working livestock.

**Current status**: The breed is endangered, but protected by a conservation program.

---

# CRIOULO

Also called: Northeastern

Portuguese: *crioulo brasileiro, sertanejo*

ⓗ 1.42 m on average for mares; 1.43 m on average for males.

ⓒ Often dark bay; frequent dorsal stripe and striping on the legs.

**Description**: This is the brother of the Argentine Criollo (see *p. 510*), although the Brazilian Crioulo is considered to be lighter, resembling the Barb. It has a short head with a more or less convex profile; and a fairly level croup.

**Distribution**: Mainly Rio Grande do Sul, Sao Paulo, southern Brazil.

**Origins and history**: *Crioulo* is the Portuguese term for *criollo*, and it is, in fact, the Brazilian variety of Criollo, which has its origins in the Portuguese and Spanish horses that were imported by the conquistadors.

**Character and attributes**: It is intelligent, energetic, bold, responsive, and agile.

**Uses**: An excellent horse for recreation, as well as for working livestock, it also excels in Western riding.

**Current status**: The breed is doing very well in Brazil, where it is the most widespread.

## BRAZIL

# PAMPA

Portuguese: *pampa*

**Ⓗ** Minimum of 1.40 m for mares; minimum of 1.45 m for males.

**Ⓒ** Always pinto.

**Description**: The quite muscular Pampa has the look of a saddle horse. It has a head with a rather straight profile; large eyes; a long neck; prominent withers; a broad chest; sloping shoulders; and a long, wide, muscular, slightly sloping croup. The skin, hide, and mane and tail are fine.

**Distribution**: Rio Grande do Sul, Brazil.

**Origins and history**: *Pampa* is the Portuguese term to describe the pinto horse, and Pampa horses are indeed a sort of equivalent of the North American Pinto: horses are selected for their coat, except that Pampas are issued from Brazilian breeds: Crioulo, Mangalarga Paulista, Mangalarga Marchador, Campolina, and Campeiro, but also Anglo-Arab. This gives them Brazilian morphology, and not at all the look of a North American horse.

**Character and attributes**: It is spirited, energetic but docile, often with lovely supplementary gaits.

**Uses**: This is a good saddle horse, popular for recreational riding.

**Current status**: Popular because of its color, the Pampa is doing rather well.

## BRAZIL

# CAMPEIRO

Portuguese: *campeiro, marchador das araucárias*

**Ⓗ** 1.40 m–1.52 m for mares; 1.42 m–1.54 m for males.

**Ⓒ** Often dark bay, dappled bay, dark gray.

**Description**: The Campeiro has a head with a straight or slightly convex profile; light neck; wide, slightly sloping croup; and slender but solid legs.

**Distribution**: Santa Catarina state, Rio Grande do Sul, southern Brazil.

**Origins and history**: Horses of Spanish and Portuguese origin were imported by the Spanish Jesuits in 1546 into the mountains of the state of Santa Catarina, where they became feral. In 1912, a Belgian breeder decided to improve these horses by crossing them with Arabian and French stallions, which resulted in the Campeiro.

**Character and attributes**: It is known to be very intelligent and docile. It has a comfortable supplementary gait.

**Uses**: It is well suited for trekking, recreational riding, and driving.

**Current status**: The breed is very small in number.

## BRAZIL

# BRAZILIAN SPORT HORSE

Also called: Brazilian

Portuguese: *brasiliero de hipismo*

**Ⓗ** 1.70 m–1.75 m.

**Ⓒ** Mainly bay, dark bay, chestnut.

**Description**: This is a tall saddle horse, athletic, muscular.

**Distribution**: Mainly Sao Paulo, Brazil.

**Origins and history**: This recent sport breed has been developed since 1970 from stallions of different saddle breeds (Thoroughbred, Andalusian, Hanoverian, Trakhener, Holstein, Selle Français, Irish Hunter, and others) crossed with Crioulo mares. The idea is to create a jumper unique to Brazil.

**Character and attributes**: It is docile and energetic.

**Uses**: It is bred for Olympic equestrian sports: show jumping, dressage, eventing.

**Current status**: Still being developed, the breed is doing fine.

Peruvians breed horses that are greatly respected throughout South America. In the 2000s there were 1,062,000 horses. Horses continue to be useful in

# ANDEAN

Also called: Peruvian Criollo

Spanish: *andino, criollo peruano*

**H** 1.21 m–1.35 m.

**C** Often black, dark bay, chestnut.

**Description**: The Andean is more angular than the Peruvian Paso. It has a rather large head with a convex profile; short, muscular neck; rather narrow chest; and small, hard hooves. The hair of its hide is dense.

**Distribution**: Peru.

**Origins and history**: This is the type of Criollo that is found in Peru. Like most of the other Latin American breeds, it is the issue of the Spanish horses of the conquistadors, and has adapted to the environment and climate of the Andes and to life in the mountains.

**Character and attributes**: It is calm, docile, and strong, with great endurance. It is an extremely resilient and sure-footed mountain horse. It can amble.

**Uses**: It is primarily a horse for transportation and carrying loads. It makes an excellent trekking horse.

**Current status**: The breed is considered vulnerable.

## DIFFERENT TYPES OF PERUVIAN CRIOLLOS

In addition to the Andean there are several other types of Peruvian Criollos:

- The Morochuco is a more powerful variety, raised in the mountains (notably in the region of Ayacucho) with a very convex head and a short neck. It resembles the Peruvian Paso, but is smaller and more angular. It measures 1.23 m–1.43 m. It is believed that the breed was started by the Jesuits. With good endurance and the amble, these horses are popular in Peru.
- The Chumbivilcas is a type of Andean measuring around 1.43 m, often of bay or gray color, bred notably in the province of Cuzco and the region of Apurimac, in southern Peru. It is more developed than the Morocucho; it is agile and endowed with great endurance.
- The Cholal, or Chola, sometimes called Serrana, is a variety of the Andean considered to be rather ordinary, robust, and easy to keep.

# PERUVIAN PASO

Also called: Peruvian Stepping Horse, Peruvian National Horse

Spanish: *peruano de paso, paso peruano, costeño, costeño de paso, el caballo costeño de paso aclimatado a la altura*

**H** 1.42 m–1.54 m.

**C** Mainly chestnut and bay, also dark bay, black, gray, palomino, roan, with white markings possible on the legs and head, and often the dun gene and its primitive markings (dorsal stripe, zebra striping on the legs).

**Description**: This is a compact horse, with a head that resembles that of the Barb, small with a straight or slightly convex profile; large eyes; a muscular, high-set neck; sloping shoulders; round, sloping croup; and slender legs.

**Distribution**: Mainly in northern Peru, also El Salvador, Uruguay, United States.

**Origins and history**: It is the issue of Barb and Spanish horses (among others, the Spanish Jennet) brought by the conquistadors. Raised in isolation, a particular type has been forged over the centuries.

**Character and attributes**: The Peruvian Paso is calm and spirited at the same time, hardy and resilient; it has good endurance and very good lung capacity due to its adaptation to the mountains. It is very sure-footed and has a good sense of direction in this type of terrain. It is endowed with a natural supplemental gait, the *paso llano*, which is exceptionally comfortable. It also has good cow sense.

**Uses**: This saddle horse makes an excellent trekking and popular recreational horse.

**Current status**: Now less vulnerable than it has been, with a consolidation of its numbers, this breed has been recognized internationally and is considered a national symbol. It has been protected since 1992.

rural areas, both for draft work and for transportation. Given the Andes mountain range, Peru has breeds that are comfortable in the mountains.

Short, muscular neck

Chagras rider (equatorial Andes) with the famous clog-shaped stirrups.

Small, hard hooves

Muscular neck set high

Round croup

The *paso llano* is one of the breed's natural gaits.

Slender legs

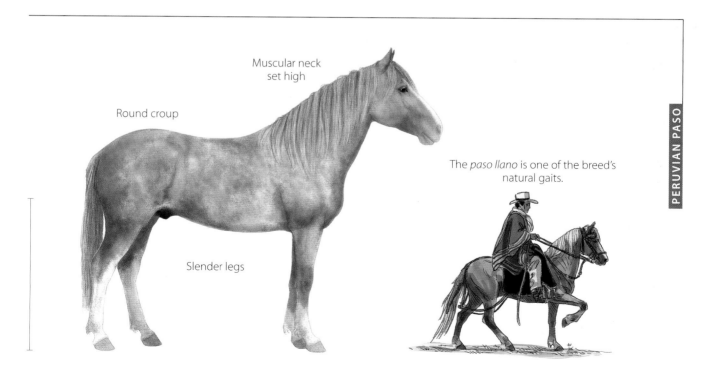

# Bolivia

In Bolivia, a country of mountains and high plateaus, where many cows are raised, horses are mainly used for working livestock. There were around 320,000 in 2003, notably of Criollo type. The little Bolivian Sunicho, unfortunately, is becoming increasingly rare.

---

### BOLIVIA

# SUNICHO

Also called: Bolivian Pony

Spanish: *sunicho*

**H** 1.20 m–1.30 m.

**C** Often bay, dark bay.

**Description**: This is a small, light, rustic horse, which resembles a small Criollo.

**Distribution**: Mainly in Altiplano, a very high plateau of the Andes range in Bolivia.

**Origins and history**: The Sunicho is a descendant of Iberian horses imported by the conquistadors, forged by a high-altitude environment.

**Character and attributes**: Rustic and resilient, it is well acclimated to a sometimes difficult climate and life at high altitudes.

**Uses**: It is a versatile animal: a pack horse and carriage horse that can be used for farm work or for working livestock when under saddle.

**Current status**: It is rare today, having endured strong competition from donkeys.

---

# Chile

The last count of the horse population in Chile was done in 1997, with more than 400,000 animals recorded. In addition to two-well established native breeds that are unknown outside the country, Chile breeds various foreign horses, including the Quarter Horse, Hanoverian, Percheron, Hackney, and Belgian.

---

### CHILE

# CHILOTE

Also called: Chilote Pony

Spanish: *chilote, mampato*

**H** 1.13 m–1.21 m; maximum of 1.25 m.

**C** Often black, also bay, gray, black/brown dun.

**Description**: Small and compact, the Chilote has a head with a straight or convex profile, large eyes, small ears, an arched neck, short back, and dished croup.

**Distribution**: Chiloe Island, Chile.

**Origins and history**: These are descendants of perhaps Asturcóns or Galicians that were brought to the island in the sixteenth century by the conquistadors; they have remained very pure due to their isolation. They seem to have decreased in size, adapting to the island conditions. Some live in the wild. The breed has been recognized since 1999.

**Character and attributes**: It is docile, strong, and sure-footed and can carry heavy loads.

**Uses**: It can be used for riding or for driving. Because of its size, it can make a good mount for young riders and for teaching beginners.

**Current status**: The breed is rare, but is now watched: there are slightly more than 450 individuals.

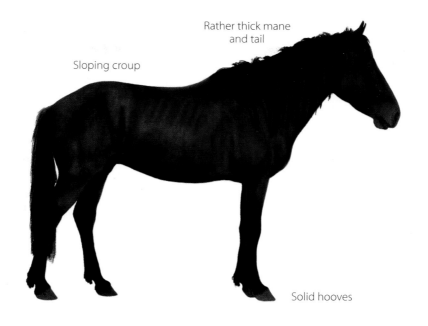

Rather thick mane
and tail

Sloping croup

Solid hooves

Arched neck

Small ears

Dished croup

# CHILEAN

Spanish: *chileño, corralero*

ⓗ 1.40 m–1.50 m.

ⓒ Often bay dun, bay, chestnut, gray.

**Description**: Of Criollo type, stocky, compact, and muscular, it resembles the Argentine Criollo. It has a head with a slightly convex profile; small ears; a short, thick neck; a long croup; and short legs. It has thick skin and a dense coat. The hair of the mane and tail is thick and usually wavy.

**Distribution**: Chile.

**Origins and history**: It is also a descendant of Iberian and Barb horses brought by the conquistadors, selected for its abilities in working livestock.

**Character and attributes**: The Chilean is intelligent, very docile, bold, agile, fast, and sure-footed. Very robust and resistant to illness and climate variations, it also has cow sense.

**Uses**: This is a good saddle horse, for trekking and working livestock (for example, for the Chilean rodeo, a very popular sport in Chile, which consists of stopping a bull on horseback). It can thus also be a good horse for Western riding.

**Current status**: The breed is very respected in Chile, but not well known outside the country.

Huaso horseman

## Argentina

Argentina, a country of gauchos and Criollos, but also of the game of polo, is, in the collective imagination, one of the most remarkable equestrian lands in the world. In this country of breeding and tradition, horses have always played an essential role, whether for working livestock, recreation, or sport. There were around 3.59 million horses in 2011.

# FALABELLA

Spanish: *falabella*

ⓗ Always under 0.76 m.

ⓒ Often spotted, but all colors are possible.

**Description**: Tiny and slender, the Falabella has a refined head with straight or slightly convex profile, large eyes, very small ears, and slender legs. The coat is silky and the mane and tail abundant.

**Distribution**: Argentina, United States, Canada, Europe.

**Origins and history**: This tiny breed was developed by the Falabella family in the middle of the nineteenth century, from small horses found among the Pampas Indians, to which was added the blood of small Thoroughbreds, Criollos, Arabians, and Shetlands.

**Character and attributes**: The Falabella is calm, friendly, intelligent, and adaptable, with exceptional longevity; it can live to the age of 40. It requires attentive care, with space and the attention required by equines.

**Uses**: This is exclusively a pet.

**Current status**: Although the Falabella is probably the most famous miniature breed, it is still not very common, but it does have fans.

A Falabella playing with a special equine ball

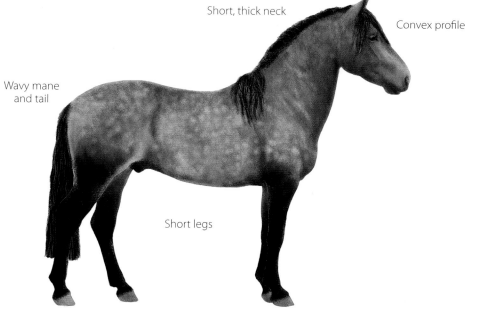

Short, thick neck

Convex profile

Wavy mane
and tail

Short legs

Silky mane
and tail

Very small ears

Slender legs

# ARGENTINE CRIOLLO

Spanish: *criollo argentino*

**Ⓗ** 1.45 m on average.

**Ⓒ** Quite variable colors, with rather obvious white markings on the legs and head, often with very particular and typical speckling; roan, bay dun, black/brown dun, frequently with primitive markings, dorsal stripe and zebra striping on the legs.

**Description**: Compact, the Argentine Criollo has a short head, with a straight or slightly convex profile; wide forehead; rather long ears; arched neck; sloping shoulders; rather short back; short, strong legs; muscular croup; and hard hooves. Its mane is often cut short.

**Distribution**: Argentina, South America; a few in North America and Europe.

**Origins and history**: Probably the most famous of all the Criollos of Latin America, the Argentine Criollo is, like its cousins, the issue of a Barb and Iberian-type horse brought by the conquistadors in the sixteenth century who escaped into the pampas, adapting perfectly to that environment over the centuries.

The Criollo is thus in part the result of natural selection. It is the horse of gauchos.

**Character and attributes**: It is confident and fast. It also has incredible endurance, is resilient and hardy, and lives a long time. It has cow sense, and some can amble.

**Uses**: This is above all an excellent horse for working livestock (and thus for Western riding). It is popular also for endurance competitions, polo, and as a trekking horse. But it can be a good horse in other disciplines, as well.

**Current status**: The breed is doing fine.

Gaucho watching his sheep

# PETISO ARGENTINO

Spanish: *petiso argentino*

**Ⓗ** 1 m–1.22 m.

**Ⓒ** Quite variable.

**Description**: It has a small head with small ears; a wide, muscular neck; and short, strong legs.

**Distribution**: Argentina.

**Origins and history**: This recent breed was developed in the first half of the twentieth century from crossings among Shetland and Welsh horses, with a bit of Criollo blood.

**Character and attributes**: It is intelligent, gentle, energetic, bold, and agile. It is robust and easy to keep.

**Uses**: This is a good horse for children, ideal for teaching beginning riders.

**Current status**: The breed seems to be doing fine.

Richly decorated Argentine stirrups

Rather long ears

Wide forehead

Short, strong legs

Traditional bridle with straps on the face. Criollos often have shaved manes.

# ARGENTINE POLO PONY

Spanish: *caballo de polo*

🅗 1.56 m on average.

🅒 Often bay, dark bay.

**Description**: Athletic, the Argentine Polo Pony has a head with a straight profile; large eyes; a long neck; long, sloping, muscular shoulders; a short, muscular back; and a muscular croup.

**Distribution**: Argentina; England.

**Origins and history**: This horse, the result of crossings among Thoroughbreds and Argentine Criollos, is meant to make an excellent polo pony, as that very ancient equestrian game is quite popular in Argentina. It has been bred since the beginning of the twentieth century.

**Character and attributes**: It is intelligent, bold, confident, energetic, calm, easy to handle, resilient, supple, very agile and fast, good at starting and stopping. Its gaits are elastic and comfortable.

**Uses**: Although its primary use is for polo, it is also suitable as a saddle horse in many other disciplines.

**Current status**: Thanks to its many assets, the breed is doing well.

The Argentine Polo Pony is bred above all for the game of polo, at which it excels.

# ARGENTINE WARMBLOOD

Spanish: *silla argentino*

🅗 Around 1.70 m.

🅒 Often bay, chestnut, roan.

**Description**: This is a sport saddle horse type, with a silky hide.

**Distribution**: Argentina.

**Origins and history**: This recent breed is the issue of the same crossings as the Argentine Polo Pony—Criollo and Thoroughbred—but it has also received Irish Hunter, Irish Draft, Hanoverian, Holstein, and Selle Français blood.

**Character and attributes**: It is energetic, lively, and has good endurance.

**Uses**: This horse principally bred for show jumping and eventing.

**Current status**: The breed is popular for equestrian sports.

# BAGUAL

Like the Mustangs of North America, the Bagual is a horse of the conquistadors that returned to the wild. It is not really a breed, but a population living in the wild. They are of Criollo type, and are found in Argentina (province of Santa Cruz, Los Glaciares National Park) and in Chile.

Long neck

Muscular croup

Short back

Straight profile

# ARGENTINE DRAFT HORSE

Spanish: *tiro argentino*

**H** Usually over 1.50 m.

**C** Dappled gray, black.

**Description**: It resembles a Percheron, but is lighter, with a muscular neck and strong legs.
**Distribution**: Argentina.

**Origins and history**: It is a crossbreed with a foundation of Percheron blood.
**Character and attributes**: It is docile, energetic, robust, powerful, and long-lived.
**Uses**: In addition to the breed's pulling abilities, the mares are also used to produce mules.
**Current status**: The breed is in decline.

# Horses of Oceania

*The horses of Oceania are mostly located in Australia and New Zealand, but they are also found on other islands. As in America, there weren't any horses in Australia or anywhere else in Oceania. Those that are found there today all originate in horses imported by European colonists, in particular in the nineteenth century, which explains why there are few original breeds in this region of the world. Those that exist are essentially the result of British or Indonesian horses. Paradoxically, the most famous, internationally known horse of Oceania, the Brumby, is not always the most popular breed locally. Including the Brumby, Australia has the largest population of wild horses in the world.*

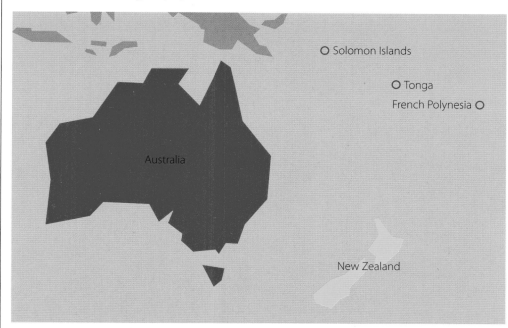

**Australia**
Australian Pony
Brumby
Waler
Australian Stockhorse
Australian Draught Horse
Coffin Bay Brumby
**New Zealand**
Kaimanawa
**Solomon Islands**
**Tonga**
**French Polynesia**
Marquises

Left: Herd of Kaimanawas, a wild horse of New Zealand.

Opposite: Kaimanawa mare and foal in the snow.

Although horses played an important role in the history of Australia, here as elsewhere their use has shifted to recreation and sport, with a large decline in the number of draft horses. Importing foreign breeds

---

AUSTRALIA

# AUSTRALIAN PONY

**H** 1.21 m–1.42 m.

**C** Often gray; all coat colors, except pinto, are possible.

**Description**: This is a slender animal, with a head with straight profile; wide forehead; large eyes; small ears; arched neck; long, sloping shoulders; short back; slightly sloping croup; and short legs. The hair of the mane and tail is thick.

**Distribution**: Australia, New Zealand.

**Origins and history**: The breed is the result of many crossings among Timor, Exmoor, Shetland, Welsh Mountain, Welsh Cob, Hackney, Arabian, and Thoroughbred horses imported to Australia at the beginning of the 1800s. Its breeding developed in the 1920s. The studbook has been completely closed to outside blood since 2005.

**Character and attributes**: The Australian Pony is sensitive and robust, and is a good jumper.

**Uses**: A saddle pony, it is a good mount for teaching children, or for youth competition, whether in show jumping, driving, or endurance riding.

**Current status**: This native breed is popular and is doing well.

---

AUSTRALIA

# BRUMBY

**H** 1.35 m–1.50 m.

**C** Often bay, dark bay, black, but all coat colors are possible.

**Description**: With the typical appearance of a wild horse, the Brumby has a large head, short neck, straight shoulders, short legs, and hard hooves. The hair of the mane and tail is long. In addition to the traditional Brumby (Australian Brumby), there are several types: the Brumby of the Namadgi National Park, the Brumby of the Kosciuszko National Park, and the Brumby of the Guy Fawkes River National Park. The mealy Brumby is found on the southern coast of Geraldton, in the west.

**Distribution**: Mainly in the southwest, notably the Australian Alps, and the northeast, Queensland, Australia.

**Origins and history**: Returned to the wild, the Brumby is the result of crossings among various horses imported to Australia by the British beginning in 1790 (Cape Horses, Timor, Arabian, Thoroughbred, and others), who escaped and adapted to life in the bush. They proliferated there, to the consternation of ranchers, who slaughtered them by the thousands, generating international protest. They do cause environmental damage (soil erosion, trampled vegetation) that cannot be ignored.

**Character and attributes**: The Brumby is intelligent, independent, resilient, fast, and sure-footed. It has a fierce nature, and has become fearful after years of being hunted.

**Uses**: Once tamed and broken, the Brumby can make a recreational horse. A certain number are adopted every year. These horses are hunted and sold for their meat.

**Current status**: The Brumby population, estimated at more than 300,000 animals, is still considered excessive by the Australian authorities. There have been attempts to sterilize them to control the population, but this has proven a lengthy and costly process. The Brumby's image remains ambiguous, going from that of a competitor with livestock and a ravager of natural environments, to that of a living symbol of Australia. It is a complex situation that has not yet been resolved.

remains expensive and thus involves only breeds with commercial value (Thoroughbreds, sport horses). This doesn't prevent Australians from breeding many horses, including the Saddlebred, Arabian, Appaloosa, Hanoverian, Oldenburg, Lusitano, and Shetland. The number of horses in Australia is estimated at 1.2 million, and, with the Brumby, this country has the largest population of wild horses in the world.

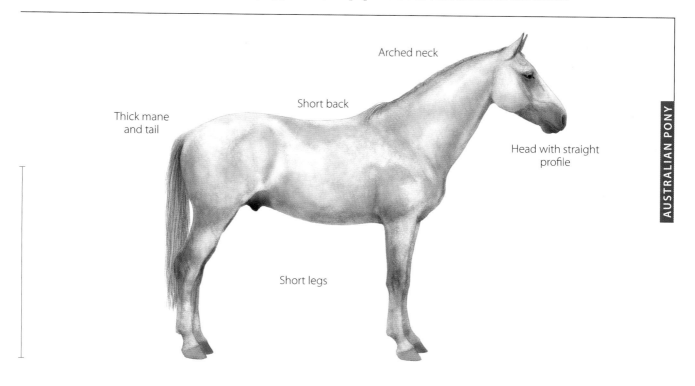

**AUSTRALIAN PONY**

Arched neck

Short back

Thick mane and tail

Head with straight profile

Short legs

**BRUMBY**

Short neck

Large head

Hard hooves

Herds of wild horses are not always seen in a positive light in Australia.

# WALER

Once called New South Waler.

🅗 1.32 m–1.73 m; on average 1.47 m–1.63 m.

🅒 Bay, dark bay, chestnut, gray, sometimes palomino, roan, bay dun.

**Description**: It has a head with a straight profile, large eyes, sloping shoulders, sloping croup, solid legs, and hard hooves. There are several types (heavy, average, light, pony).

**Distribution**: Australia.

**Origins and history**: The Waler is the result of crossings among horses imported by the colonists: Thoroughbred, Arabian, Barb, Anglo-Arab, Timor, Clydesdale, Percheron, Cleveland Bay, and others. The majority of individuals blended with the Australian Stockhorse. At first more a type than a breed, it is now becoming a distinct breed under the efforts of the Waler Horse Society of Australia.

**Character and attributes**: It is intelligent, docile, and bold, fast, undemanding, and robust, with good endurance.

**Uses**: It is a versatile saddle horse, suitable for recreation as well as for more advanced sport activities (dressage, show jumping, eventing, and endurance).

**Current status**: The Waler, sometimes classified as an extinct breed, did almost disappear, absorbed by the Australian Stockhorse, but it is recovering. There were around 700 horses in 2012.

Australian saddle.

# AUSTRALIAN STOCKHORSE

🅗 1.45 m–1.65 m.

🅒 Often bay, also chestnut.

**Description**: This is a muscular horse. It has a rather small head with straight profile; wide forehead; large eyes; rather long, slightly arched neck; prominent withers; powerful, but not overly muscular hindquarters; and solid legs.

**Distribution**: Australia.

**Origins and history**: The Australian Stockhorse is the result of much crossbreeding among horses brought by the colonists with a main foundation of local Walers, Thoroughbreds, and, more recently, Quarter Horses. It has been officially recognized since 1971.

**Character and attributes**: The Australian Stockhorse is intelligent, docile, calm, bold, confident, agile, resilient, and fast, with good endurance. It is a good jumper.

**Uses**: This versatile saddle horse is particularly suited to working with livestock and for Western riding. But it is also popular for dressage and show jumping competitions, and for polo, as well as for recreation and trekking.

**Current status**: The breed is doing very well. It is one of the most widespread in Australia, very popular for its many assets.

A stockman (Australian cowboy) and his horse at work.

Sloping croup

Large eyes

Straight profile

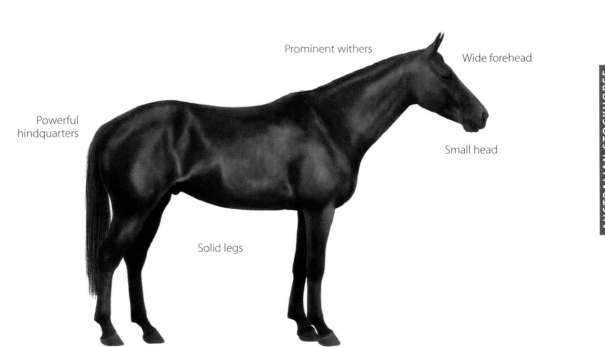

Prominent withers

Wide forehead

Powerful
hindquarters

Small head

Solid legs

# AUSTRALIAN DRAUGHT HORSE

**H** 1.62 m–1.80 m.

**C** All solid coat colors are possible; roan, often with white markings on the legs and head.

**Description**: The Australian Draught Horse weighs between 600 kg and 900 kg. It resembles the Shire and the Clydesdale, from which it has partly descended. It has a head with a wide forehead; large eyes; long, muscular neck; broad chest; slightly prominent withers; wide, powerful, slightly rounded croup; and wide hooves. The hair of the mane and tail is long, thick, and sometimes slightly wavy; it has feathering on the legs.
**Distribution**: Australia.
**Origins and history**: This draft horse is the result of heavy breeds imported by the colonists in the nineteenth century, notably Shire, Clydesdale, Suffolk Punch, Percheron, and a few Belgians.
**Character and attributes**: Intelligent and calm, it is a strong and powerful horse.
**Uses**: This draft and carriage horse is sometimes also ridden.
**Current status**: A native horse, it is no longer useful due to the rise of mechanization, and its numbers are now low.

A young Australian Draught Horse is worked in long lines to prepare it for being harnessed.

# COFFIN BAY BRUMBY

Not long ago the Australian name was Coffin Bay Pony, but "Pony" was changed to "Brumby" in 2008.

**H** No taller than 1.47 m.

**C** Often bay, dark bay, less often chestnut, gray, roan, bay dun, never pinto. It sometimes has small, rather discreet white markings on the head or legs.

**Description**: It resembles the Timor.
**Distribution**: Eyre Peninsula, Coffin Bay, South Australia.
**Origins and history**: This population, which lives in semi-freedom, is the result of some sixty Timors imported from Indonesia in the middle of the nineteenth century, that were then crossed with Arabian, Clydesdale, and Hackney horses. Often confused with the traditional Brumby, the Coffin Bay lives in stables.
**Character and attributes**: Intelligent and rather friendly even in the wild, it is robust.
**Uses**: Once used for polo and in harness, it is now used more in recreational riding.
**Current status**: The herd has around forty horses. Animals are sold at auction once a year.

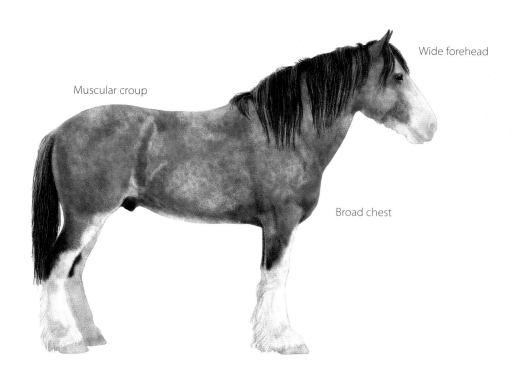

Wide forehead

Muscular croup

Broad chest

# New Zealand

In 2011 the number of horses in New Zealand was dropping, with a population estimated at 56,500 animals. Horses there are essentially used for recreation, but there is also harness and Thoroughbred racing. The New Zealanders breed many breeds, many of British origin. There are fewer wild horses than in Australia.

# KAIMANAWA

**H** 1.27 m–1.52 m.
**C** Often bay.

**Description**: There is a lot of variation within this breed. It is generally quite muscular, with a refined head; wide forehead; large eyes; short neck; usually straight shoulders; and small, hard hooves.
**Distribution**: North Island, Kaimanawa Mountains, around Waiouru, New Zealand.
**Origins and history**: The Kaimanawa is an ancient domestic horse that was returned to the wild, the New Zealand equivalent of the Brumby—wild horses are mentioned beginning in 1876. Its origins are in the Exmoor, Welsh, and military horses released into nature. It raises problems of soil trampling in certain places, to the detriment of the local flora. Many are sent to the slaughterhouse during population culling. An association works to have them adopted, since they can very easily be turned into saddle horses.

**Character and attributes**: It is intelligent, with excellent endurance, hardy, resilient, and sure-footed, and is a good jumper.
**Uses**: Tamed and broken, it makes a pleasant saddle horse.
**Current status**: The Kaimanawa is still rare, with around 300 horses in the wild (and more now living in a domestic setting).

A fight between wild stallions.

# Solomon Islands

A herd of wild horses was identified in Yandina, in the Russell Islands, around ten years ago. We don't know how many (maybe a hundred) nor where they came from, unless they are ranch horses imported then returned to the wild, the result of crossings among many breeds.

# Tonga

The Tonga Islands, a sovereign state of Polynesia, are formed by an archipelago of islands, on which a population of small horses of light type, some of which live in the wild, has been noted. There were 10,555 animals in 1985, and more than 3,255 in 2001. Like almost everywhere else, this decrease is connected primarily to changes in lifestyles.

Short neck

Wide forehead

Large eyes

Small, hard hooves

The archipelagos of French Polynesia are found in the Southern Pacific Ocean, very far to the east of Australia. There is a small population of horses on the Marquesas Islands.

## FRENCH POLYNESIA

# MARQUISES

**Ⓗ** Around 1.40 m–1.45 m.

**Ⓒ** Chestnut, bay, dark bay, bay dun, often with dorsal stripe; a few gray, white markings are frequent.

**Description**: These light horses are of homogeneous type: a head with a straight profile; a rather long, slender, high-set, sometimes "stag-like" neck; narrow chest; prominent withers; slender legs; and very sloping croup. The tail is often held high. The hair of the mane and tail is rather thin, not always very long.

**Distribution**: French Polynesia, Marquesas Islands, notably Ua Huka, nicknamed "Island of Horses."

**Origins and history**: Considered to be a horse population and not really a breed, the Marquesas horses have, however, lived on these islands for a long time, and Paul Gauguin even painted them. They are believed to have descended from horses imported from Chile in the 1840s, and they probably have Spanish origins. These horses live for the most part in the wild and are regularly captured to be broken for riding.

**Character and attributes**: Although living in the wild, the Marquesas horse is not really fearful, but is rather curious. It is a gentle, robust, and strong horse. It is sure-footed enough to walk around the rocky slopes of the island.

**Uses**: This is a horse used mainly for transportation, as a hunting horse, and for equestrian tourism, but also as a pack horse.

**Current status**: There are around 3,000 horses on Marquesas Island, and they are a true local treasure. All the inhabitants have a horse, and they are popular among children, and so the breed is not endangered.

Polynesian rider on the beach, riding peacefully along the Pacific coast.

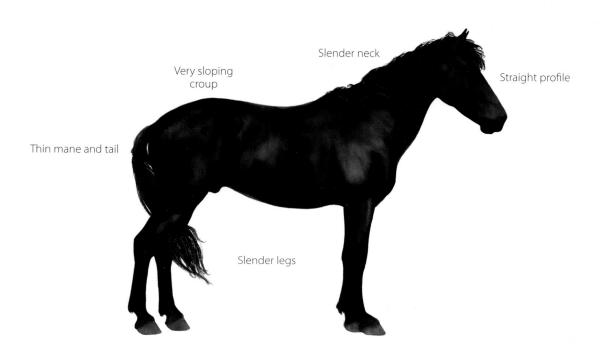

Slender neck

Very sloping
croup

Straight profile

Thin mane and tail

Slender legs

# Conclusion

## Changing How We Think of Horses

This guide is the culmination of several years of reflection, research, and work; it has consumed my entire life, both day and night.

What is most obvious is that it has definitively changed the way I look at horses.

In learning about their fragility, the rarity of most breeds, and their close, unbreakable, ties with humans, I came to respect them even more than I did before.

As I got to know them, discovering the least known among them, the small, the common, the forsaken, I became convinced that no breed is superior to any other. That, beyond economic considerations, a Quarter Horse of good lineage has no more value than a horse from Sable Island. That a priceless Thoroughbred is no more important than one of the last horses on the Faroe Islands. And that the anonymous enthusiasts who are trying to save the Losina, the horse of Auvergne, or the Marwari; or Tatiana, who in the heart of Siberia breeds Transbaikals, with their curly hair, their primitive marking on their shoulder—those people from the four corners of the globe who, over the years, have spoken to me about their horses with such passion and humility, are all as important as the equestrian stars who enthrall their audiences.

After completing this guide I believe even less than before in equestrian norms. Equine diversity—and the diversity among riders, as well—is essential and precious.

The drawings of Yann Le Bris found in these pages, his amber-hued horses, his iridescent grays, the wind he creates off the shores of Iceland or elsewhere, have also definitively changed my view of horses. It is impossible to look at them now without seeing the new details that he has brought to light.

To increase our knowledge of horses, to focus the reader's attention on the breeds, is indeed one of the goals of this work.

But if the book can go even further and contribute to making a small change, to focus the attention that is paid to horse breeds around the world, to increase awareness of the urgency of protecting the endangered breeds, then it will have succeeded in another of its goals.

Do we still need the horses that are disappearing?

I worked for several years in the challenging realm of the conservation of birds of prey. Conway McMillan, a condor specialist, said: "What really matters in saving condors and their like is not so much that we need condors, as that we need to develop the human qualities that are necessary to save them. Because those are the very qualities we will need to save ourselves."

Whether condors or horses, all the conservation efforts in the world have this in common: the path that we take is as essential as the goal. It reveals to us that which we are not ready to give up, but also that which we are disposed to discover.

As for me, I will never be prepared to give up the Cleveland Bay, nor any of its fellow bearers of manes.

This guide is not just a technical encyclopedia of the various breeds throughout the world; it is also a section of that path on the way to those discoveries.

Our section of the path is very long; on it we encounter the Navarre Burguete, as well as in the distance the resounding gallop of the ancient Spanish Jennet.

## A call for contributions

Despite the years of research devoted to this work, there is still a lot of information and details missing for many breeds, and it is possible that there are lapses. Some breeds haven't been illustrated due to a lack of documentation. Some have been with the small amount of documentation we had available. A huge thank you in advance to anyone who might be able to provide any missing information and thus contribute to a knowledge of the horses of the world. Please write or send photos to this email address: allhorsesoftheworld@gmail.com.

This mare is a Camargue, a very ancient breed from the South of France.

# Acknowledgments

My thanks go out to all my contacts throughout the world who generously agreed to answer questions about their horses in distant lands. Each of their answers brought dreams, journeys, escape, and a great deal of knowledge: Dc Jigjidpurev Sukhbaatar (Programme Officer at FAO in Mongolia); Dc Khayankhyarvaa Terbish (Department of Biology, Ecology, Amphibians and Reptiles, Conservation Biology, National University of Mongolia); Nandintsetseg D. (National University of Mongolia); Arthur Mariante (Brazil); Ava Hunt (secretary general of the Rare Breeds Conservation Society of New Zealand); Marilyn Jenks and Kerry Wilson (of the Kaimanawa Heritage Horses Association, New Zealand, http://kaimanawaheritagehorses.org); Dc Carlos Mezzadra (national coordinator for biogenetics research, Instituto Nacional de Tecnología Agropecuaria [INTA], Argentina); Argerie Cruz Méndez (Costa Rica); Tlou Caswell Chokoe (South Africa); Mamadou Diop, PhD (national coordinator of PROGEBE- Senegal); Dr Thi Thuy Le (National Institute of Breeding, Ministry of Agriculture and Rural Development, Viet Nam); Dr Kalaya Boonyanuwat (Thailand); Adrien Kumar Raymond (Malaysia); Piseth Hang (Cambodia Pony Welfare Organization [CPWO], Cambodia); SAR Chetra, PhD (assistant director of the department of production and animal health, ministry of Agriculture, Forest and Fishing, Cambodia); Yang Hongjie and Chen Weisheng (China); Dr Tashi Yangzome Dorji (Bhutan); Jigme Dorji (National Center of Biodiversity, ministry of Agriculture and Forest, Bhutan); Dc Malam Gadjimi Adam Kade (program head, Executive Secretary of the Association of the Redynamism of Breeding in Niger [AREN]); Dr Yan Naing Soe (Burma); Anna Louisa Joensen (of faroehorse.org); Francesco Russo (President of the ARACSI Association, Sicily); the Syndicat hippique du Haut-Faucigny (for the Megève Horse); Aline Plancherel (of the Fédération d'élevage du cheval de sport suisse, for the Einsiedler studbook); Pierre-André Poncet (of HIPPOP, Switzerland); Tamara Kartvelishvili (Georgia); Tamás Szobolevszki (Hungary); Patrick Reisdorff and André Nepper (Luxembourg); Fakhrat Eminov (Azerbaïdjan); Dr Ashok Gupta (India); Kittipong Poomsang (Thailand); Dr Dinesh Prasad Parajuli (Nepal); Tatiana Pankova (breeder of Transbaïkal Horses); Marilynn Moyle (for the breeding of Moyles, United States); Driaan Fourie and Christiane Slawik (Nooitgedachter Breeding Society, South Africa); Marina Van Blerk (for the Vlaamperd, Welgegund Boerdery, South Africa); Cristine Holt (for the Moroccan Spotted Horse, United States); Victoria Varley (for the Tiger Horse, United States); Sara Tharp (for the Montana Travler, United States); Jorge A. Gutierrez (for the Costa Rican Paso); Jose Luis Canelon Perez (for the Venezuelan Criollo); and finally, the Jeju Horse Park Museum (Korea), especially Jong Hye-Young. Thanks, too, to Julien Massip, the geopolitician, for his very useful advice; Philippe J. Dubois for his help with Asian horses and bibliographic sources; and François Moutou for his help with various questions.

Thanks also to the anthropologist Robert D. Martin for the phylogenetic data he provided.

Thanks go to the following people for their help with photographic research: Julien Birard; Jean-Luc Bourrioux; Pierre and Anne Crouzier; Sandrine Dhondt; Jeremy Dubois; Valentin and Jan Dubois; Yves Dubois; Marc Duquet; Sarah and Magali Goliard; Audrey Gory; Alain Laurioux; Margaux Mégnin; Georges Olioso; Tatiana Pankova; Thierry Quélennec; Julie Riegel and Amadou Sène; Hélène Roche; Jean-Pierre and Sylvie Rousseau; Thierry Ségard; Jean-François Terrasse; Matthieu Vaslin; Jan Maree Vodanovich; Kelly Wilson; Maxime Zucca; and all the naturalists and riders who pointed me in the right direction or let me delve into their photo collections!

Thanks to Guy Flohart who sometimes let me work at his home, in Audresselles, with the gray sea at the other end of the square.

Many thanks to Laurence Le Bras, conservator in the department of manuscripts at the Bibliothèque nationale de France, for her enormous help.

… and to Jean-Louis Gouraud for his encouragement and, with his adventures and stories about Kabardas and other Barbs, for having contributed a long time ago to my dreams of the horses of the world.

… and to Martine Desbureaux for her careful review of the manuscript, and Jean-Yves Grall for his patience.

Thanks to my family for all their help and for putting up with my equine obsessions for so long!

Special thoughts go out to my friend Bertrand Eliotout, who passed away in Zimbabwe, and who taught me the importance of following one's dreams.

This book owes a great deal to the attentive work carried out by the FAO and its various experts throughout the world as they watch threatened domestic breeds. The gathering of information by this organization, its commitment to the preservation of domesticated biodiversity, its communications on the subject to the public at large, and its sharing of knowledge, have been absolutely essential. One can only hope that they will continue this work with strength and determination, and that they will have the means to do so.

Above all, thank you to Charlotte Jacobsen, the Akhal-Teke of editors, for her energy, her perspicacity, her support, and her great rigor.

## Photo Credits

The publisher sincerely thanks the photographers who have granted gratis permission to use the photographs in this book: Julien Birard, p. 491; Jean-Luc Bourrioux, p. 399; Pierre Crouzier, p. 30; Sandrine Dhondt, pp. 22,78,79 (left); Marc Duquet, p. 208; Sarah Goliard, p. 279; Alain Laurioux, pp. 318, 319, 406, 407; François Moutou, p. 479 (left); Élise Rousseau, pp. 24 ,25 ,31 , 75, 136, 245, 278, 300, 301, 336, 389, 397, 398, 413, 478, 490, 526; Sylvie Rousseau, pp. 390, 391; Thierry Ségard, pp. 79 (right), 137, 277 ; Christiane Slawik, p. 412; Matthieu Vaslin, pp. 10, 317; Jan Maree Vodanovich, p. 515; Kelly Wilson, p. 514; Maxime Zucca, p. 479 (right).

Thanks, too, to Élise Rousseau for her work in collecting and preparing the photos.

# Bibliographic Sources

It is impossible to provide a complete bibliography of the enormous number of documents and websites that have been used to document this work, but the following are the most important.

## General Works

Blanc, H. L., *Guide du cheval et du poney*, Delachaux et Niestlé, 1983.

Bongianni, M., *Les Chevaux*, Solar, 1987.

Haller, M., *L'Encyclopédie des races de chevaux*, Chantecler, 2003.

Harris, M. C., *Chevaux sauvages du monde*, Delachaux et Niestlé, 2010.

Harris, M. C., Swinney N. J., *Chevaux, 100 races exceptionnelles à travers le monde*, GEO/Prisma Presse, 2010.

Hendricks, B., *International Encyclopedia of Horse Breeds*, University of Oklahoma Press, 2007.

McBane, S., *Chevaux du monde*, Nathan, 1998.

Porter, V., *Mason's World Dictionary of Livestock Breeds, Types and Varieties*, 5th ed., Cabi Publishing, 2002.

Ravazzi, G., edited by V. Simeon, *L'Encyclopédie mondiale du cheval. Plus de 150 races de chevaux de selle et de poneys de tous pays*, De Vecchi, 2010.

Ripart J., *Chevaux du monde*, La Martinière, 2001.

Silver, C., *Guide of the Horses of the World*, Elsevier, 1976.

Swinney, N. J., *Horse Breeds of the World*, Hamlyn, 2006.

## Specialized Works

Baradat, M., "Le Cheval cambodgien," *Revue d'élevage et médecine vétérinaire des pays tropicaux*, 1, 1948.

Bayarsaikhan, B., *Travelling by Mongolian Horse*, Interpress Co, Ulaanbaatar (Mongolia), 2006.

Bianquis, I., "Les produits laitiers et alcools de lait en Mongolie. Rites, croyance et lien social," http://www.lemangeur-ocha.com/texte/les-produits-laitiers-et-alcools-de-lait-en-mongolie/, 2004.

Bokagne, F., Bouba M., "Évolution et situation actuelle de l'élevage au Cameroun," report of the DVM, Ahmadu Bello University, MINEPIA, Cameroon, 2005.

Capková, Z., Majzlík, L., Vostrý, L., Andrejsová L., *Analysis of Inbreeding and Generation Interval of Silesian Noriker and Czech-Moravian Belgian Horse*, Czech University of Life Sciences, Prague, 2009.

Cardinale, E. (Cirad), Seignobos, C. (IRD), "Le poney musey et les pratiques vétérinaires (région de Gobo, Nord-Cameroun)," *Anthropozooligica*, 39 (1), 2004.

Chabchoub, A., Mbarki, Z., Lasfar, F., Landolsi, F., Turki, I., Ouragh, L., "Polymorphisme protéique sanguin chez le poney de Mogod de Tunisie," *Revue d'élevage et de médecine vétérinaire des pays tropicaux*, 59, 2006.

Danvy, S., Dubois, C., Guérin, G. (INRA), Grison, A. C., *Génétique des robes de base*, Les Haras nationaux, Institut français du cheval et de l'équitation, August 2011.

Dubois, P. J., Perriquet, J.-C., Rousseau, É., *Nos animaux domestiques. Le tour de France d'un patrimoine menacé*, Delachaux et Niestlé, 2013.

Ewers, J. C, *The Horse in Blackfoot Indian Culture, with Comparative Material from Other Western Tribes*, US Government Printing Office, 1955.

Ferret, C., "À chacun son cheval! Identités nationales et races équines en ex-URSS (à partir des exemples turkmène, kirghize et iakoute)," *Cahiers d'Asie centrale*, 19–20, 2011.

Ferret, C., *Une civilisation du cheval. Les usages de l'équidé de la steppe à la taïga*, Belin, 2009.

Gupta, A. K, Tandon, S. N., Pal, T., Bhaedwaj, A., Chauhan, M., *Phenotypic Characterization of Indian Equine Breeds: A Comparative Study*, National Research Centre on Equines (ICAR), India, 2012.

Habe, F., Rus, J., *Horse Breeding in Slovenia*, Taiex Seminar Equus, University of Ljubljana, Veterinary Faculty, National Horse Breeding Service and Biotechnical Faculty, Horse Center Krumprk, Slovenia, 2005.

Harmsted, Chubb S., *Frontal Protuberances in Horses: An Explanation of the So-Called "Horned Horse,"* American Museum Novitates, 740, American Museum of Natural History, New York City, 1934.

Hund, A., *The Stallion's Mane: The Next Generation of Horses in Mongolia*, World Learning-S.I.T. SA, Mongolia, 2008.

Kluger, W., *Rare Breeds and Varieties of Greece, Atlas 2010. Synonyms, Occurence, Description of Rare Breeds and Variety in Greece*, Monitoring Institute of Rare Breeds and Seeds in Europe/SAVE Foundation, 2009.

Langlois B., "Histoire, ethnologie et importance sociale de la traite des juments en Asie centrale," *Revue d'ethnozootechnie*, 94, varia no. 11, 2013.

Luque, M., Rodero, E., Peña, F., Molina, A., Goyache, F., Herrera, M., "The Raising System for Marismeña Equine Breed in the Natural Park of Doñana (Spain)," in *Book of Abstracts of the 56th Annual Meeting of the European Association of Animal Production*, no. 11, 2005.

Masuda, M., Tsunoda, J., Nomura, H., Kimura, N., Altangerel, G., Namkhai, B., Dolj, U., Yokohama, M., "New Primitive Marking (Bider) in Mongolian Native Horse and *Equus przewalskii*," *Journal of Equine Science*, 18 (4), 2007.

Menegatos, J., *The Rare Horse and Pony Breeds in Greece*, http://www.agrobiodiversity.net/greece/pdf/Heavy_Animal/Greek_Horses.pdf.

Ndiaye, M., *Contribution à l'étude de l'élevage du cheval au Sénégal*, thesis, École inter-États des sciences et médecine vétérinaire, n° 15, 1978.

Raveneau, A., *Inventaire des animaux domestiques en France*, Nathan, 2004.

Rousseau, É., "Le cheval mongol en 2012–2013: un patrimoine équestre préservé," *Revue d'ethnozootechnie*, 94, varia no. 11, 2014.

Rousseau, É., "La marque primitive sur l'épaule: liens entre chevaux domestiques de race mongole, yakoute, transbaïkale et cheval de Przewalski," *Revue d'ethnozootechnie*, 94, varia no. 11, 2014.

Rousseau, É., *Le Baudet du Poitou, le Trait poitevin mulassier et la Mule poitevine*, Geste Éditions, 2001.

Seignobos, C., *Les Poneys du Logone à l'Adamawa, du XVIIe siècle à nos jours*, Cavalieri Dell'Africa, Centro Studi Archeologia Africana, Milan, 1995.

Seignobos, C., "Élevage social du poney musey, region de Gobo, Nord-Cameroun," *in* C. Baroin (ed.), J. Boutrais (ed.), *L'Homme et l'animal dans le bassin du lac Tchad*, IRD, 1999.

Yoo-Kyung, K., "In Search of the Jeju Horse," *Koreana*, vol. 25, no. 162, The Korea Foundation, 2013.

Žaparov, A., trans. C. Ferret, "L'élevage du cheval au Kirghizistan," *Études mongoles et sibériennes, centrasiatiques et tibétaines*, 41, 2010.

[Collective], HN Conseil Ingénierie, *Étude de la filière cheval à Saint-Pierre-et-Miquelon*, Les Haras nationaux, 2008.

**Two expedition reports written by Michel Peissel for the Loel Guinness Foundation can be found in the archives of the Bibliothèque nationale de France:**

Peissel, M., *Expedition for the Study of Tibetan Horses and Veterinary Care*, 1992–1993.

Peissel, M., *The Nangchen Horse of Tibet, a Report on the Horse Breeds of Tibet*, 1993.

## FAO Reports

The reports of the FAO on animal genetic resources have been of enormous help. The reports focus by country on the state of farm animals and their breeding, and therefore they often discuss local breeds of horses. There is almost one report per country, more than 167. And so it is impossible to cite all the reports, but they have all served as bibliographic resources. They date at the earliest from 2002, often from 2003, also from 2004 and 2005, are in English, Spanish, Portuguese, and French, and have generally been produced by the ministries of agriculture of the countries under study. Among the various FAO publications we can cite:

Adamovich, A., *Country Pasture/Forage Resource Profiles Latvia*, 2005.

Sukhbaatar, J., *Development of the Mongolian Industrial Livestock Production Sector and Its Impact on Animal Genetic Resources*, 2012.

Tamolo, A. Lekota, *The State of the Basotho Pony in Lesotho*, 2003.

A treasure trove of information can be found on the FAO website: http://dad.fao.org.

## Websites

The websites listed below can be accessed in different languages. They represent only a few sites among many others; it is impossible to list them all here.

### General sites

The Equinest, an English-language site providing general information on horses, as well as specific information on individual breeds: http://www.theequinest.com.

FAO website: http://dad.fao.org.

The French national stud-farm site, where there is information on breeds recognized in France: http://www.haras-nationaux.fr.

Site of a French park project to gather breeds of horses: http://www.parcchevauxdumonde.com.

An Italian agricultural education site: http://www.agraria.org.

An Italian site on horse populations: http://www.anagrafeequidi.it.

The Italian Association of native breeds threatened with extinction: http://www.associazionerare.it.

The Spanish Association of Farm Breeds: http://www.feagas.com.

A site for rare breeds in Canada: http://rarebreeds-canadaeasternontariochapter.com/horses-ponies.

The Society of Native Indian Horses: http://www.horseindian.com.

Domestic resources of Turkey: http://turkey.finidhyn.info/photos/index.html.

The Swiss Federation of Ponies and Small Horses: http://www.svpk.ch.

The German Equestrian Federation: http://www.pferd-aktuell.de/pferdesport-pferdezucht/deutsche-reiterliche-vereinigung.

An interesting site for wild horses, the Large Herbivore Network: http://www.ecnc.org/projects/ecosystem-and-species-management/lhnet/.

Wikipedia, in different languages, also offers a lot of photos and information on many breeds.

## A few sites on specific breeds or types

Abaco Spanish Colonial Horse: http://arkwild.org/blog.

Andalusian: http://www.ancce.es.

Argentine Petiso: http://www.petisoargentino.com.ar.

Argentine Polo Pony: http://www.poloargentino.com.

Australian Draught Horse: http://www.australiandraughthorse.com.

Australian Stockhorse: http://www.ashs.com.au.

Auvergne: http://www.chevalauvergne.fr.

Auxois: http://www.traitauxois.com.

Belgian Draft: http://www.chevaldetrait.be/fr/trait-belge.

Belgian Sport Horse: http://www.sbsnet.be.

Boulonnais: http://www.boulonnais.fr.

Breton: http://www2.cheval-breton.fr.

Camargue: http://www.aecrc.com.

Campeiro: http://cavalocampeiro.com.

Carolina Marsh Tacky: http://www.marshtacky.org.

Caspian: http://www.caspianhorsesociety.org.uk.

Castillonnais: http://www.chevaldecastillon.com.

Catalan Pyrenees Horse: http://www.rac.uab.es/descripcio/AHPDESCcas.htm.

Catria: http://www.cavallodelcatria.it.

Chincoteague: http://www.pony-chincoteague.com.

Comtois: http://www.chevalcomtois.com.

Eriskay: http://eriksaypony.com.

Falabella: http://www.minifalabella.com.ar.

Faroe: http://faroehorse.org.

Flemish: http://www.vlaamspaard.be/fr.

Frederiksborg: http://frederiksborg.com.

Freiberg: http://www.cheval-franchesmontagnes.ch/french/chevalfm.php.

French Saddle Pony: http://www.anpfs.com.

Galician: http://www.cabalogalego.com.

Garrano: http://garrano.ipvc.pt.

Hanoverian: http://www.hannoveraner.com.

Holstein: http://holsteiner-verband.de.

Kaimanawa: http://kaimanawaheritagehorses.org.

Kinsky: http://www.equus-kinsky.cz.

Kirghiz: http://www.atchabysh.org.

Kladruby: http://www.nhkladruby.cz.

Landais: http://www.poneylandais.com.

Luxembourg Saddle Horse: http://www.studbook.lu.

Menorquin: http://www.cavalls-menorca.com.

Morab: http://www.puremorab.com and http://morab-imba.com.

Morgan: http://www.morganhorse.com.

Nooitgedacht: http://www.marmari.co.za.

North American Spotted Draft: https://sites.google.com/site/naspotteddrafthorseassn.

Percheron: http://www.percheron-France.org/fr.

Przewalski's Horse: http://www.takh.org.

Sicilian: http://www.sicilia-aracsi.it.

Sorraïa: http://www.sorraia.org.

South African Boer: http://www.saboerperd.com.

South African Saddle Horse: http://www.sawarmbloodhorses.com/about.html.

Thai: http://www.thaipony.net/, http://thaihorsefarm.com/, http://www.lampangponywelfare.org.

Tiger Horse: http://www.tigrehorse.com.

Tolfetano: http://www.cavallotolfetano.it.

Trakehner: http://www.trakehner-verband.de.

Venezuelan Criollo: http://jineteycaballo.blogspot.fr.

Ventasso: http://www.cavallodelventasso.it.

Waler: http://www.walerhorse.com.

Walkaloosa: http://www.walkaloosaregistry.com/registration.html.

Zangersheide: http://www./zangersheide.com.

Žemaitukas: http://www.zemaitukas.lt.

# Index of Horse Names

# Some Extinct Breeds

**United Kingdom**

- Barra Pony (Scotland)
- Cushendale (Northern Ireland)
- Devon Pack Horse (England)
- Galloway Pony (Scotland)
- Gocan (Scotland)
- Goonhilly (England)
- Great Horse or Old English Black Long Mynd (England)
- Hebridean Pony (Scotland)
- Manx
- Norfolk Trotter (blended with the Yorkshire Coach Horse and the Hackney)
- Pennine Pony (England)
- Tiree (Scotland)
- Vardy (England)
- Yorkshire Coach Horse (England; blended with the Hackney)

**Norway**

- Lofoten Pony
- Lyngen Pony

**Spain**

- Aragonesa
- Catalan
- Spanish Jennet (blended with the Andalusian)

**Italy**

- Cremonese
- Neapolitan (being reconstituted; see p. 110)
- Pugliese

**Croatia**

- Krk Island Pony, or Krcki konj

**Bosnia and Herzegovina**

- Busa Pony

**France**

- Angevin (blended with the Selle Français)
- Augeron (absorbed by the Percheron)
- Berrichon (absorbed by the Percheron)
- Bidet Breton (absorbed by the Breton Draft)
- Brennou
- Burgundy Horse (absorbed by the Auxois)
- Charentais (blended with the Selle Français)
- Charolais
- Corlay (integrated into the French Chaser)
- Limousin
- Morvan Bidet
- Nivernais
- Normandy Coach Horse
- Ouessant Pony
- Saône-et-Loire
- Tarbais or Navarrin
- Trait de la Loire (absorbed by the Percheron)
- Trait du Maine (absorbed by the Percheron)
- Vendéen

**Germany**

- Emscherbrücher

**Switzerland**

- Burgdorfer
- Erlenbach

**Latvia**

- Baltic Ardennes
- Baltic Trotter
- Latgale Trotter

**Poland**

- Mazury
- Poznan

**Hungary**

- Hungarian

**Romania**

- Banat
- Dobrogeana Lalomita
- Romanian Mountain horse
- Transylvanian

**Bulgaria**

- Bessarabian
- Bulgarian Native, or Deliorman
- Dolny-iskar
- Rila Mountain
- Stara Planina

**Ukraine**

- German Bessarabian
- Nogai
- Strelet Arabian

**Georgia**

- Kolkhuri

**Russia**

- Amurskaya
- Bityug Chilkovskaya
- Chuvashskaya
- Cossack
- Karel'skaya or Karelian
- Kuban
- Lovetskaya
- Obva
- Onega
- Orlov-Rostopchin (being reconstituted, see p. 266)
- Tomskaya

**Turkey**

- Karacabey
- Karacabey/Nonius
- Rumelian Pony

**Uzbekistan**

- Argamak

**India**

- Dhanni
- Jumla Pony

**China**

- Soulun

**Japan**

- Nanbu

**Tunisia**

- Nefza Pony

**South Africa**

- Calvinia
- Cape Draft Horse
- Le Cap Horse
- Namaqua Pony

**Canada**

- Canadian Pacer
- Frencher
- St. Lawrence

**United States**

- Conestoga
- French Coach
- German Coach
- Narragansett Pacer

# Parts of the Horse

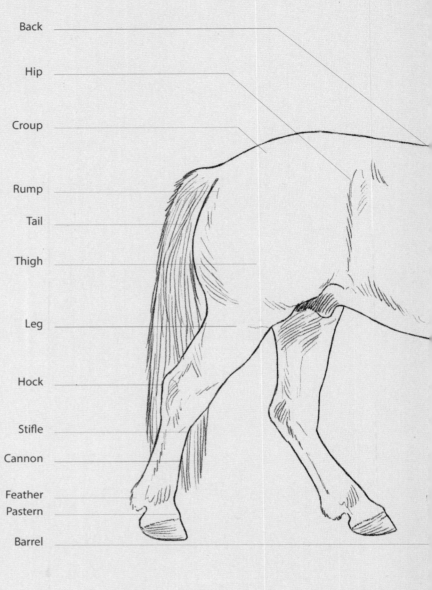

Back

Hip

Croup

Rump

Tail

Thigh

Leg

Hock

Stifle

Cannon

Feather
Pastern

Barrel

**Mare**
*(barrel often a bit rounder;
neck is more slender)*